清华大学艺术博物馆
展览丛书
COLLECTION OF EXHIBITION CATALOGUES
TSINGHUA UNIVERSITY ART MUSEUM

理想之境

马里奥·博塔的建筑与设计

1960-2017

THE REALM OF IDEALISM

MARIO BOTTA

ARCHITECTURE AND DESIGN

清华大学艺术博物馆　马里奥·博塔建筑事务所　编著

中国建筑工业出版社

图书在版编目（CIP）数据

理想之境：马里奥·博塔的建筑与设计：1960–2017 / 清华大学艺术博物馆，马里奥·博塔建筑事务所编著. — 北京：中国建筑工业出版社，2017.9
（清华大学艺术博物馆展览丛书）
ISBN 978-7-112-21216-3

Ⅰ. ①理… Ⅱ. ①清… ②马… Ⅲ. ①建筑设计—作品集—瑞士—现代 Ⅳ. ①TU206

中国版本图书馆CIP数据核字(2017)第218617号

本书包含瑞士建筑师马里奥·博塔1960年至今的重要建筑项目及设计作品，分为10个单元进行了图文并茂的介绍，同时结合相关领域学者的评论文章，从不同角度剖析了博塔的建筑设计艺术，且系统完整地梳理了博塔的个人生平和所获成就。

本书可供相关专业工作者和大专院校建筑学、环境艺术设计等专业的师生参考，也可为广大文化工作者和艺术爱好者保存。

责任编辑：吴　绫　吴　佳　李东禧
责任校对：王雪竹

理想之境
马里奥·博塔的建筑与设计 1960–2017
清华大学艺术博物馆　马里奥·博塔建筑事务所 编著
*
中国建筑工业出版社出版、发行（北京海淀三里河路9号）
各地新华书店、建筑书店经销
北京图文天地制版印刷有限公司制版
北京方嘉彩色印刷有限责任公司印刷
*
开本：965×1270毫米　1/16　印张：31¼　字数：762千字
2017年9月第一版　2017年9月第一次印刷
定价：298.00元
ISBN 978-7-112-21216-3
（30829）

清华大学艺术博物馆
展览丛书

COLLECTION OF EXHIBITION CATALOGUES
TSINGHUA UNIVERSITY ART MUSEUM

主办单位：清华大学艺术博物馆
协办单位：马里奥·博塔建筑事务所
支持单位：瑞士驻华大使馆
展览总策划：冯　远
展览负责人：杨冬江

展览统筹：王晨雅　弗朗切斯科·梅洛尼　王　鹏
展览设计：弗朗切斯科·梅洛尼　保拉·佩兰蒂尼　马尔科·莫纳塔　刘雅羲
视觉设计：王　鹏
展览执行：王晨雅　钟子澂　许　诺　刘雅羲　兰　钰　张　明　王　兆

图录统筹：王晨雅　艾莉希亚娜·迪贝纳尔多　弗朗切斯科·梅洛尼
图录设计：艾莉希亚娜·迪贝纳尔多　王　鹏
图录编辑：王晨雅　张　明　钟子澂　许　诺　郑恬辛　艾莉希亚娜·迪贝纳尔多　弗朗切斯科·梅洛尼　保拉·佩兰蒂尼
图录翻译：钟子澂　艾莉希亚娜·迪贝纳尔多　凯伦·里耶斯

Host: Tsinghua University Art Museum
Co-organizer: Mario Botta Architetti
Supporting organization: Embassy of Switzerland
Chief Curator: Feng Yuan
Project Manager: Yang Dongjiang

Exhibition Coordinator: Wang Chenya Francesco Meroni Wang Peng
Exhibition Design: Francesco Meroni Paola Pellandini Marco Mornata Liu Yaxi
Visual Design: Wang Peng
Exhibition Team: Wang Chenya Zhong Ziwei Xu Nuo Liu Yaxi Lan Yu Zhang Ming Wang Zhao

Catalogue Coordinator: Wang Chenya Elisiana Di Bernardo Francesco Meroni
Catalogue Design: Elisiana Di Bernardo Wang Peng
Catalogue Edit: Wang Chenya Zhang Ming Zhong Ziwei Xu Nuo Zheng Tianxin Elisiana Di Bernardo Francesco Meroni Paola Pellandini
Catalogue Translation: Zhong Ziwei Elisiana Di Bernardo Karen Ries

序一

冯 远
清华大学艺术博物馆馆长

英国前首相丘吉尔说过：“我们塑造了自己的建筑，而建筑反过来也塑造了我们”。建筑与人类密切联系，我们每天的生活起居、遮风避雨、有诗意品味的生活质量，都与建筑难以分开，建筑成为我们生命、生活、生存的一部分。然而，建筑与人的关系又是一个深奥的问题，如何解答这个难题？马里奥·博塔的建筑实践给我们提供了一个个性化十足的解答路径。

作为国际级建筑大师，马里奥·博塔的建筑理念充满人文性和理想性。他融合了严谨的理性主义传统和深厚的历史文化底蕴，用富有时代特色的当代建筑语言回应久远的历史记忆。他虔信一座建筑承载着一个地区的“根源和记忆”，在“记忆”的土地上，务必保留日渐丧失的地域特征和历史特色。博塔以在提契诺州设计的独栋住宅而闻名，他设计的建筑涉及学校、银行、行政大楼、图书馆、博物馆、宗教建筑等多种类型，已完成的建筑设计项目数量令人惊讶。此次展览集中展示马里奥·博塔1960年至2017年间的部分建筑和设计作品。其中，无论是生活空间或工作空间，公共建筑或宗教建筑，无不展示出博塔简明有力而内涵丰富的风格特色。他强调建筑要发挥其促进社会转型的潜在功能，发挥先导性作用。他善于使用抽象几何的线条，以精致的细部造成光与影的对话，进而营造出丰富多彩的空间形态。他对建筑与环境的关系异常重视，追求建筑与其周边景观的协调，努力探寻一种诗意的空间秩序感。显然，博塔的建筑风格和手法也影响到他涉及其他专业领域的设计理念，我们从他设计的座椅、家具、灯具、手表等物件可以瞥见其建筑的影子。此次展览举办地清华大学艺术博物馆就是博塔设计的典范，缓缓上升的步行阶梯和顶层天花板的自然采光，博物馆与大学主楼以及整个校园之间的关系，无不印证着博塔独特的建筑理念。

清华大学有着悠久的建筑与设计的历史和传统，其建筑学院的前身建筑系就是由著名建筑学家梁思成先生于1946年创办，其美术学院更是承续了原中央工艺美术学院的优良传统。我想，此次清华大学艺术博物馆举办的博塔建筑与设计展，不仅为清华的师生们展示国外知名建筑师的精彩作品，更将促进国内外建筑设计领域的相互借鉴和学习，共同铸造人类赖以栖居的“理想之境”。

2017 年 8 月

PREFACE I

Feng Yuan

Director of Tsinghua University Art Museum

Former UK Prime Minister Winston Churchill once commented, "We shape our buildings; thereafter they shape us." The buildings are closely related to human beings. We have to live in, use and appreciate buildings every day with the poetic quality of life, so that they become part of us. However, the relationship between buildings and the human being is another profound question to tackle. The architectural practices of Mario Botta provide us with a personalized solution.

As a world-class architect, the architectural idea of Mario Botta features humanity and ideality. He integrates the strictness of rationalism with historical and cultural profundity, echoing with the remote memory of history by contemporary architectural language of epoch characteristics. He holds the pious belief that a building bears the "origin and memory" of a place, and it's necessary to retain the fading regional features and historical characteristics on the land of memory. Botta has been known for the detached houses he designed in Ticino. The buildings he designed involve the types of school, bank, administrative building, library, museum and religious building, and the number of his architectural design projects is marvelous. This exhibition focuses on part of the architectural and design works of Mario Botta between 1960 and 2017, of which, both living space and working space, public buildings and religious buildings, all well show the simple, powerful and inspiring style of Botta. He stresses that architecture should exert its potential function of boosting social transformation and playing a guiding function. Adroit in using abstract and geometrical lines and creating the dialogue between light and shadow by refined details, he managed to launch diversified spatial forms. He also values the relationship between architecture and environment very much, seeking the coordination between the architecture and neighboring landscapes for a poetic sense of spatial order. Clearly, the architectural style and techniques of Botta have effect on his idea of article designs in other fields; we can find a trace of his architectures from the armchairs, furniture, lamps and watches from his design works. Tsinghua University Art Museum, the venue of this exhibition, is an outstanding example of Botta's architecture: the ascending stairs and the natural lighting through the top ceiling, and the relationship between the museum and the university's main building as well as the whole campus are the best proof of the unique architectural idea of Botta.

Tsinghua University has a long-standing history and tradition in architecture and design. The Department of Architecture, the predecessor of its School of Architecture, Tsinghua University, was founded by the famous architect Liang Sicheng in 1946, and its Academy of Arts & Design continues the good tradition of the former Central Academy of Arts and Design. I believe the recent exhibition of Botta's architectures and designs held by Tsinghua University Art Museum will not only present the works of renowned architect abroad but also promote mutual learning between domestic and overseas architectural design domains, thus jointly creating a "realm of idealism" for human living.

August, 2017

序二

戴尚贤
瑞士驻华大使

毋庸置疑，在过去的25~30年间，中国显现出全世界最壮观的发展速度。新兴城市不断涌现，成千上万样式各异的住房和建筑物以惊人的速度拔地而起、创下新高。在住房与基础设施建设、建筑学与城市规划方面，弥补落后的时间是一个重要的问题。当下面临的挑战是如何超越时间并满足经济高速发展与人口急剧扩张所带来的巨大需求。

在这座用吊车、砖头、混凝土、玻璃以及钢筋制造的物质丛林里，一些建筑因其无畏、新颖的气质，与其他重复而沉闷的同类建筑物形成鲜明对比。为了回应中国建设者的召唤，同时也被这个复兴中的古老国度正在经历的前所未有的经济繁荣和开放所吸引，时下著名的建筑师们纷纷来华开设工作室并展开他们的图板。得益于独有的资源，这些建筑师们跨越边界、开拓未知领域，把一座座城市改造成为融入当代建筑理念的生活博物馆。

瑞士，作为创新、新兴科技和可持续发展领域的领军角色，同样以其在建筑领域的先锋地位而感到自豪。因此毫不意外地，一些顶尖的瑞士建筑大师在中国已经脱颖而出，诸如赫尔佐格和德·梅隆事务所设计了蔚为壮观的北京鸟巢奥林匹克体育场，马里奥·博塔则设计了著名的上海衡山路12号精品酒店和多座卓越的建筑。

正是如此，作为中国排名第一的大学和中国建筑学的领军学府，清华大学也选择在马里奥·博塔的最新建筑作品——清华大学艺术博物馆的开馆仪式上，向这位建筑师致以了敬意。现在，这位来自瑞士提契诺州的著名建筑师，将在他自己的建筑创作中举办个人作品回顾展。此次展览恰逢时机，突出了建筑师30多年来长期频繁来华所建立的稳固关系。几年前，在提契诺州与我相见时曾称呼我为“我的”大使的建筑师，其自身为中瑞两国的友谊做出了卓越的贡献！在这些精心设计的墙面上，将呈现80余项他的设计作品，制作时间跨越了紧张却从未间断的50年职业生涯。马里奥·博塔曾这样描述自己：“我总是对工作痴狂，首要的热忱就是我的工作。解决一个问题、发展一个概念，这对我来说就是涅槃。”

马里奥·博塔传承了一份伟大的遗产。20世纪60年代，博塔在职业生涯初期便与瑞士著名建筑师、拥有远见卓识的业界标杆人物勒·柯布西耶一起工作。从设计家庭住宅开始，马里奥·博塔迅速扩大了他的活动领域，创造了一系列具有象征性的作品：教堂（包括巴黎地区的大教堂）、图书馆、银行、博物馆等。其中包括美国旧金山的现代艺术博物馆、瑞士巴塞尔的丁格利博物馆和韩国首尔的三星艺术博物馆等，此处仅举几例。

马里奥·博塔的作品因其对天然材料、玻璃、砖块和石料等的运用而与众不同。除水平横向条纹外，其风格的独特之处还体现在对圆形、直角与线条、连续性与断裂的交替应用。博塔一贯怀着对建筑使用者的敬意，和谐的平衡贯穿始终、无处不在，保持形式的纯粹。他手法娴熟低调，凭借对几何形式的美学敏锐度，创造出一种鲜明的建筑构图，让人联想起西文字体Helvetica的印刷物。从威尼斯到莫斯科，瑞士提契诺的知名建筑师们在欧洲留下了属于他们的印记，现在马里奥·博塔转而在这个探索城市化的新黄金国度建立自己的声望。博塔永远不让自己困于束缚之中，哪怕是自己所创造的束缚，因为他拥有不可思议的创新性与创造力：“有时我尝试用不同的方式处理问题，但只有回归自我时才能得到平静。建筑学是人与自然之间永恒的斗争。”

为了马里奥·博塔所代表的一切，为了他曾带给我们、并将持续展现给新一代建筑师的作品，我要感谢清华大学艺术博物馆邀请马里奥·博塔走进他亲自设计的建筑中。这个展览是一次可贵的机会，让中国学生和普通公众能够探索建筑大师马里奥·博塔在欧洲、美洲和亚洲所创造的杰出成就。这场重要的展览也进一步加深了中瑞两国的文化交流。总而言之，这也是分享建筑设计理念的一种方式，用当代的语言将过去与现在连接在一起，超越功能性地表达了核心的关键，也就是情感。

2017 年 7 月

PREFACE II

Jean-Jacques de Dardel

Swiss Ambassador to China

Over the past 25 to 30 years, China has indisputably witnessed the most spectacular development of any country in the world. Virtually everywhere, cities have emerged from the earth and hundreds of thousands of housing facilities and buildings of all kinds have sprung up in record time. In terms of housing and infrastructure, architecture as well as urbanism, it was a question of making up for lost time. The challenge was to beat the clock and meet the colossal needs of an economy and a population in a period of mind-boggling expansion.

In the midst of this inert jungle made up of cranes, bricks, cement, glass and steel, certain buildings stand out in sharp contrast to the repetitive dreariness by dint of their daring and originality. Answering the call of the new Chinese architects and lured by the unprecedented economic boom and openness of the resurgent Middle Kingdom, the most renowned architects of the time came to set up shop and install their drawing boards. Availing themselves of resources simply unimaginable elsewhere, they were able to cross boundaries and pioneer into unexplored territory, transforming numerous cities into living museums of contemporary architecture.

Switzerland - a reputed champion in the field of innovation, new technologies and sustainable development - also prides itself on its vanguard position in the domain of architecture. And so, not surprisingly, some of our finest architects have left their mark in China: Herzog and de Meuron designed the spectacular Bird's Nest Olympic Stadium in Beijing, while Mario Botta created the famous Twelve at Hengshan Hotel in Shanghai as well as numerous other remarkable edifices.

Quite appropriately, Tsinghua University, the top-ranking Chinese university and China's leading school of architecture, has chosen to pay resounding tribute to Mario Botta on the occasion of the inauguration of his latest major creation: the Tsinghua Art Museum. A vast retrospective on the work of the architect from Ticino, within the very walls of the museum which he created: a fitting conjunction highlighting the strong and already long-standing bonds formed with a person who has carried out more than three dozen extended stays in China. The same person who addressed me as *"My" Ambassador* upon our meeting a few years ago in Ticino, affectionately referring to the Chinese-Swiss links to which he himself so greatly contributed! Within these walls, which are his walls, some 80 projects spanning 50 years of intense and uninterrupted professional activity are on display for the visitor. In the words of Mario Botta: *"I have always been a frenetic worker; my primary passion is my work. To resol ve a problem, to develop a concept: for me, this is nirvana."*

Mario Botta comes from a great heritage, continuing in the tradition of Le Corbusier, another major Swiss architect, a visionary who has become a universal reference, with whom it was his privilege to work early on in his career in the late 1960s. Beginning with the design of family houses, Mario Botta rapidly enlarged his field of activity to create works that have become emblematic: churches, a cathedral in the region of Paris, libraries, banks and museums, among which we find the MOMA in San Francisco, the Musée Tinguely in Basel, and the Samsung Art Museum in Seoul, to name only a few.

Buildings designed by Mario Botta stand out from all others by his use of natural materials, glass, brick, and stone. Composed of horizontal, zebra-like stripes, his trademark style consists of an alternation of rounded forms and right angles, straight lines, continuity and breaks. Always and everywhere, there reigns a harmonious equilibrium, the form remaining pure, with an omnipresent respect for those destined to utilise the building. Adept at the use of understatement while sensitive to the perfect aesthetics of simple forms, he creates what is self-evident, a kind of architectural typography reminiscent of the Helvetica font of print. Raising high the banner of renown of the Ticino architects who, from Venice to Moscow, have left their mark on Europe, he has at present established his reputation in China, the new Eldorado of urban experimentation. Never allowing himself to be locked into a straitjacket, be it even one of his own making, for he is incorrigibly innovative and creative: *"At times, I try to do things differently, but I am at peace with myself only when I return to my trademark style. Architecture is an ongoing combat between man and nature."*

For all that he represents, and for the example he has given us and will continue to provide for new generations of architects well into the future, I thank the Tsinghua Art Museum for having invited Mario Botta into the walls that he himself designed. What a splendid opportunity for Chinese students and the general public to discover the most significant achievements bearing the mark of the masterful architect Mario Botta in Europe, America and Asia! This major exhibition further enhances the cultural exchanges between our two countries. All told, it is also a way of sharing a vision of architecture that links the past to the present in a contemporary language going beyond the functional to express the essential, that is to say, the emotional.

July, 2017

前言

杨冬江
清华大学艺术博物馆副馆长

在当今建筑界先锋性、实验性和颠覆性创新成为主体基调的氛围中，马里奥·博塔的作品饱含一种穿透时空的秩序之美与沉静力量，连接着历史经典、传承着人文记忆、构建着当下生活日常。一个建筑作品的形式本身是其设计哲学的物化，马里奥·博塔是设计逻辑与图纸表达皆清晰的建筑师代表，建筑的形态以及细部的生成都能在其最终作品中找到缘由，早期作品的连续墙面与砌筑细节让同时代的很多建筑师都望其项背。

在马里奥·博塔的建筑哲学里，场所永远是放在第一位的，场域的重要性、城市文脉的层次是他作品构思的出发点；自然光、重力这两种自然因素同构在他的作品中，光线与空间、重力与构造的关系传递着一种自然、平衡的美感；几何性、对称性、秩序与自然材质是他对建筑形态与建筑材质的审慎选择，对称的空间与对简洁形态的偏好让他的建筑更容易被理解和在使用中辨识，自然材质的坚固与耐久性让空间历久弥新、不易被时光溶蚀了空间的品质，为空间的功能更迭提供了更多的可能性；场所记忆、对历史的尊重与建筑伦理是博塔以建筑回映历史、回应日常生活的方式与方法，在他的建筑哲学里建筑不是没有历史脉络的创作，也不是一纸图画，而是基于场所记忆、当下生活的容器。概括而言，场所要素、自然因素、秩序构造与建筑伦理是马里奥·博塔建筑设计哲学的四个维度，超越视觉单一维度的丰富性为其作品赢得了国际认可，屡获殊荣，如：1986年的美国芝加哥建筑奖、1995年的欧洲文化奖、1999年的法国荣誉军团骑士团勋章、2003年在的瑞士文化大奖、2006年的欧盟文化遗产奖、2010年的建筑与设计基金会“全球建筑贡献金奖”。

马里奥·博塔的建筑哲学并不是一朝一夕形成的，追溯其学术渊源，他在威尼斯大学建筑学院所师从的意大利建筑大师卡洛·斯卡帕和艺术史教授朱塞佩·马萨里奥尔在学术上都对他的设计产生了重要的影响。斯卡帕对细部近乎痴迷的关注、在图纸上对空间使用进行反复推敲、如艺术家塑形般进行施工建造让他深受影响；而马萨里奥尔则为马里奥·博塔打开了历史的一扇窗，让年轻的他去理解建筑与城市文脉、城市演进中建筑适应性的问题。

离开学院学习后的职业生涯初始，马里奥·博塔在两大现代主义巨匠勒·柯布西耶和路易斯·康的指引下进行项目设计，这段经历为他的建筑职业生涯带来了决定性的影响。柯布西耶对现实的把控、对自然的态度，以及强调建筑作为城市空间连续体的观念让博塔越来越正视场地场所以及城市文脉的思考，柯布西耶用系统科学的方法反思建筑功能之间的组织关系，也对他的创作有着重要的影响，博塔曾多次评价柯布西耶："他就像建筑界的爱因斯坦。他将20世纪建筑的问题明确地提出来，他有一种通过建筑空间救赎社会问题的强烈信仰"；路易斯·康对博塔的影响则是显性的，众多评论家都对此给予了论述，也非常喜欢将路易斯·康与博塔的建筑形体、自然光借用和材质运用进行比较。逐步明晰的建筑哲学、设计方法与项目建造实践让博塔快速成长并建立起自己的风格。1970年，马里奥·博塔回到瑞士卢加诺开设了自己的设计事务所并开启了属于自己的建筑事业。在长达50余年的创作生涯中，马里奥·博塔与团队共完成了近600个设计项目，其涉猎建筑类型之广、功能设置之精巧和设计完成度之高，以及手稿对于设计逻辑与形式逻辑的清晰表达成为世界各地建筑师和青年学生研习的范本。

本次在清华大学艺术博物馆展出的"理想之境——马里奥·博塔建筑与设计1960-2017"，是马里奥·博塔在中国大陆首次举办的个人建筑艺术回顾展。本次展览共分为10个展览单元。其中，建筑设计按9个类别进行展示：居住空间、办公空间、学校及休闲空间、酒庄、城市空间、图书馆、博物馆、剧院、宗教建筑，展出的作品总数量达229件，其中建筑手稿157张、建筑模型13件；另外，展览还将展出他的14幅产品设计草图和45件产品实物。从丰富多元的建筑作品和产品设计当中，可以窥见马里奥·博塔已将设计完全作为他日常生活的全部。希望在博塔先生自己设计的博物馆中举行的此次回顾展，能够让他的哲学、建筑、生活有一次最为完整地呈现。

2017年7月

FOREWORD

Yang Dongjiang

Vice Director of Tsinghua University Art Museum

Amid the present atmosphere of pioneering, experimental and disruptive innovations making the keynote, the works of Mario Botta are full of the beauty of order and the power of tranquility that penetrate through time and space, connect historical classics, inherit humanistic memories and build the existing life. The form of an architectural work is the materialization of a design philosophy; Mario Botta is a representative architect with clear design logic and drawing expressions, and the forms of architecture and generation of details can find their reasons in his works. Many other architects of his time are never able to compete in the details of continuing wall space and bricklaying found in his early works. According to the architectural philosophy of Mario Botta, the site is usually in the first place; the importance of the field and the levels of urban culture are both the starting point of his work's conception; the two natural factors of natural light and gravity are both reflected in his works, with the relationship between light and space and gravity and construction transmitting the beauty of nature and balance; geometry, symmetry, order and natural material show his cautious selection of architectural forms and materials; the symmetric space and preference for concise forms make his architectures better understood and recognized in use; the firmness and endurance of natural materials make the space unfading, having the quality of space not easily eroded by time and providing more possibilities for the functional change of the space; the memory of site, the respect for history and the architectural ethics are the ways and methods for Botta to review the history and respond to daily life through architecture, so that the architecture is not a creation without historical context or a drawing in his architectural philosophy, but a container of the immediate life on the basis of the memory of site. To sum up, the site, natural factors, order construction and architectural ethics are four dimensions in Mario Botta's philosophy of architectural design, so that the richness beyond the single dimension of vision wins his works int'l recognition and honors, such as Chicago Prize in 1986, European Literary Award in 1995, Legion of Honor in 1999, Swiss Award in 2003, EU Prize for Cultural Heritage in 2006 and UIA Gold Medal for Outstanding Architectural Achievement.

The architectural philosophy of Mario Botta was not formed easily. To trace his academic experience, we can find that his learning from Carlo Scarpa, an Italian master of architecture and from Giuseppe Mazzariol, a professor of the Art History, both in IUAV, has significant impact on his style. Scarpa had an obsessive attention to details, thought over space use on the drawing, and conducted construction like an artist's creating shapes, all having in-depth effect on Botta; while Mazzariol opened a window of history for Mario Botta to let the young man understand the architecture and urban culture, and the adaptability of architectures during urban evolution.

At the beginning of his career after leaving the school, Mario Botta started project designs under the guidance of Le Corbusier and Louis Kahn, both masters of modernism. The experience posed a decisive impact on his practice as an architect. Corbusier's management of the reality, his attitude toward nature and his emphasis on making the architecture a continuum of urban space drove Botta to think more and more about site, place and urban culture; and Corbusier's systematic and scientific way of reflecting on the structural relationship between architectural functions also has a significant impact on his creation. That's why Botta commented on Corbusier repeatedly, "He's like Einstein in the circle of architecture. He explicitly raised the problems of architectures in the 20th Century, and he has a strong belief in salvaging societal issues by architectural space". The impact of Louis Kahn on Botta is outward, on which many critics commented; they also love to compare Louis Kahn with Botta in architectural shape, use of natural light and application of materials. The gradually apparent architectural philosophy, the design method and the practice of project building made Botta grow fast and build up his own style. In 1970, Mario Botta returned to Lugano, Switzerland to open his own design firm and launched his career as an architect. During more than five decades of creation, Mr. Botta co-completed nearly 600 design projects with his team, with such a wide range of architectures involved, such delicate functions set, such a high level of design completion and such a clear expression of design logic and formal logic that he's become a good example for architects and young students to learn from.

The recent exhibition *THE REALM OF IDEALISM - Mario Botta Architecture and Design 1960-2017* in Tsinghua University Art Museum is the first personal architectural art retrospective show that Mario Botta gives in mainland China. The exhibition consists of 10 modules, among which the architectural designs are shown by 9 categories: living space, working space, school and leisure space, chateau, urban space, library, museum, theatre and religious building, amounting to 229 in total and including 157 architecture manuscripts and 13 models; besides, the exhibition will also show 14 sketch designs of products and 45 products in kind. From diversified architectural works and product designs, it's not hard to see Mario Botta has made design the whole of his life. We hope this retrospective show held in a museum designed by Mario Botta will have a complete presentation of his philosophy, architectures and life.

July, 2017

目录

CONTENTS

几点思索

马里奥·博塔

建筑与全球化

建筑最初存在的意义是作为物质世界独特而不可复制的一种改造行动，地域风格特色是建筑作品与环境之间的联系，不容忽视。将同一个项目在不同的地方进行复制，听起来是对建筑本质的亵渎。事实上，全球化文明在过去几年中不断扩张，以“改造的必要性”之名使得地区和城市在发展现代化的历程中逐渐丢失了地域特征和历史特色，也就是说，丢失了它们的文化身份。

在全球化进程中，无论欧洲、美洲还是远东地区，发达社区的需求几近相同。但是，将世界各地经济与社会的相互依存与人类生活环境模式的同质化相混淆，是非常严重的错误。

一个社区的文化身份往往揭示了地区之间的差异，即便在全球化时代也是如此。这一身份关乎地理、历史、文化形态，在某一件建筑作品中往往表现为构建与环境对话的契机。

作为一名建筑师，我力求确保建筑周边环境成为作品不可分割的一部分。

物质空间所具备的（地理、历史的或记忆）条件，可以作为特定因素供建筑师预先纳入考虑。

现代主义运动之后的当代建筑师

20世纪下半叶，建筑设计开始对地理和历史因素更加重视（这种关注始终存在，因为建筑是将自然环境转变为文化环境的过程）。这一批判性运动使得建筑在现代主义运动第一阶段即“国际风格”的基础上继续发展。20世纪上半叶，建筑大师们主要面对的问题是战后的现代化需求，然而随着后来涌现的各种需求不断增长，批判意识逐步增强，这使得建筑——尤其是那些带有历史印记城市中的建筑变得丰富起来。后者与物质环境、经历的变迁以及不同社区所独有的文化身份紧密关联。因此，如今我们可以断言：建筑实践领域便是（或者应当是）“记忆的领土”。

过去数年中，建筑文化得益于生态意识的发展而日益丰富，更注意使用当地材料，常常在资源稀缺问题上反省自身，有时也会使用传统的或本地的技艺，以提高环境可持续性的发展模式，努力探索促进与环境之间的对话。

在20世纪初现代主义运动的建筑作品中，这些态度已经小范围存在，在如今技术和文化的现状中，它们已经发展成为社会公则，必须纳入考虑之中并成为以全新方式处理建筑的前提条件。

20世纪建筑文化所取得的成就在生活环境品质方面创造了巨大益处，但现在需要依靠新一代人的力量，去恢复这些建筑专业必不可少的原生价值，赋予它们新的动力与视野。

文化还是美化

在全球化造成的所有破坏中，建筑与自然环境、环境的可持续性，以及建筑与历史记忆之间的调和几乎没有受到人们的关注。最主要的问题在于对审美化的执着和自以为是的形式主义，这一点可从随意又造作的建筑形态中看出来，这些建筑形态通常与地形结构毫无共鸣，所用材料越来越多地只追随时尚潮流，随意搬用，不顾建筑原则和地形条件。

现代建筑获得了审美化的外形，却失去了真正为艺术和公众而存在的能力。这样的建筑往往代表着向市场利益的彻底投降（从客户和建筑师的角度来说）。在今天的消费社会里，所有物品都可以商品化，建筑往往沦为一种形象，被忽视的建筑质量和材料寿命本应是建筑的内在价值。虚有其表的审美观所剥夺的，是建筑的基础，即一种抗衡地心引力且寻找结构平衡的艺术，一种根植于土地、怀揣记忆与希望的艺术。建造是一种集体行为，建筑则是人类制度体系的反映，正因如此，我们能够通过存留至今的建筑来解读历史文明。寺庙、教堂、剧院和宫殿已经成为城市肌理中的个性特征，并在过去的年月中成为城市的基础，它们见证了历史和文明的变迁，构成了我们文化身份的一部分。这些建筑使我们明白，石头是如何能够象征文化抱负和前人价值观的。这一观点呼吁人们将建筑看作一种文化手段（而不仅是技术和功能层面的解决方案）。不幸的是，过于矫饰、唯美化和拙劣的装饰性使得当代建筑的价值愈显贫乏。

建筑，最初的艺术

当一件建筑作品能够令使用者对某个场所的环境、地形和历史价值展开思考，它就恢复了建筑的原始意义——改变物质环境的工具。

在建筑师职业生涯中，我常常试图避开纯理论或抽象的项目，因为我坚信其中潜藏着唯美化的风险。相反，如果相信语境可以成为项目的一部分，环境状况就能为建筑师带来非常重要的依据与灵感。我对项目最初的价值观很感兴趣：新建筑缘何扎根于土地，甚至可以改变地壳的外观。建筑师优先考虑的事情应该有审视语境、寻求解决方案、将自然环境与周边因素纳入考虑，好比将新的建筑看作先前已有的自然存在（能做到这样就是杰出的建筑师了）。

建筑所承载起的理念，是人类改变其生活的土地的行为，建筑通过在这土地上扎根，同时也改变了天际线。

建筑作品通过万有引力定律与土地结合，通过光线塑造出建筑外形，通过影子投射勾勒出结构，它存在于太阳起落、四季更迭、季节变换的空间之内。

在这个建筑形态高度同质化的时代，我更乐于指出，建筑形象多年以来发生的变化可以说是一种事实的见证，它们是人类生活在地球上所留下的原始符号。

享受风景与光照、感受四季的变幻，可与环境对话的材质塑造，确保新形状能够重现历史形态——这些都是建筑师的目标，亦可理解为公民的生存权利。建筑师的语言不能局限在抽象形态、形式选择或预设形象中；建筑的力量在于重新定义其与周遭空间关系质量的能力，而不仅将自身局限于建筑体积之中。一件建筑作品的质量在于其空间组织的能力，在于能否通过新建筑与周围环境建立更好的关系。

每个项目都是一次公众行为

空间的用途自然是多种多样的，正如土地所有权的模式，但这与建筑的公众价值并不冲突。一座城市不能被视为一件私有财产，因为每一块土地、每一条街、每一个广场与每一座建筑，无论所有权和功能如何，都促成了集体空间的建构。因此，虽然私有空间随着时间推移不断增多，也同样是集体世界的一部分。

在这些项目中，建筑师通常要遵守程序和客户要求。但项目即便是为私人客户实施的，建筑师也不能忘记：建造本身仍是一种公众行为。在将城市作为一个整体观察时便能清楚地意识到这一点。城市肌理——尤其是在西方文化滋养下的欧洲城市——毫无疑问是最智慧、最先进，也是最具包容性的社会生活和集体生活的组织模式，这个模式形成于人类文明的长期发展过程之中。

现代英语单词“城市”源自古拉丁语的civitas，指的是公民、社会聚集等。城市，既意味着公民身份成形之地，也是建筑的公众使命反复验证之地。在当今的全球化时代，缺少公民共同价值的不成形的特大城市在世界各地萌发，我们应当批判性地审视自身，重温欧洲城市历史这堂文化课。

建筑，一项前瞻性艺术

一件建筑作品应当始终诠释着所处地点的空间与环境潜力，捕捉这一潜力并赋予其新的意义。如果剖析过去几个世纪中的城市层级发展，就会发现建筑往往如震荡测试仪一般，映射出某个群体的期待与抱负，并促进其发展。

正如项目的期望，建筑设计的开展必须以理解当下的社会、政治与文化进程为前提，这样才能提出新的解决方案。

好的建筑就如最佳的艺术实践，能够促进社会转型。建筑发挥着先导性作用，虽然同时也潜藏着错误解读的风险，但历史表明，通常都能够找到适合未来生活的状态。

为了能在当下的时代中扮演好这个角色，建筑师应当问自己：生存、工作、共同生活、教育、祈祷的意义是什么？换言之，他们必须能够代表生活在同一时代人们的人类文明。建筑语言应当构建的形态是：在特定的情况下，能够建立满足群体需求的，城市与城区的实体环境。

现代主义运动和20世纪艺术先锋派的大师们教会了我们：建筑思维是一种“整体方案”。赫尔曼·穆特修斯宣称：规划应当“从勺子做到城市”，他的箴言和判断力直到今天仍然正确。建筑师们试图将这一原则运用到设计实践的各个方面：建筑物、物品设计、景观设计以及其他各种在空间中具有形象的设计形式。所有这些不同的实践有助于达到一个共同的目标：持续发展我们居住其中的现实世界。

技术或艺术

技术知识在建筑中是必不可少的，但多数情况下它仅是一种先决条件。如果建筑仅局限于技术或功能，那么人们也许能够建造出具有全新功能的建筑、城区和城市，但却无法创造出符合文明价值、历史文化并具有美的场所。近年来，由马克·欧杰提出的“非场所”概念被广泛传播。这一概念指的是现代社会中无特定身份的空间，设计原因仅仅在于提供冷气环境、符合投机目的或市场逻辑，比如大型购物中心、机场、郊区和一些残留空间，它们是没有个性，不产生互动和生活场景的空间。“非场所”的现实正好证明了单纯依靠技术知识并不足以保证建筑品质：一切都运转良好，但空间不具备个性的定位，便无法促使人们参与其中。只有当空间具备自己的特征，能够促进互动关系，才能保证人们的参与。

正如技术一样，艺术也是一种知识形态，但不同之处在于艺术语言的极其丰富。这一丰富和复杂性可能引发质疑和各种解读，并往往与文化、符号和社会层面相互交织在一起。

我想谈谈几位当代建筑师的经验，比如约翰·伍重、阿尔瓦罗·西扎和安藤忠雄。这些伟大的建筑师们证明了建筑可作为一种文化表达而存在，能够满足某个群体的期望和抱负。在他们的作品中，能够听到一种得到认可、尊崇，成为历史组成部分的文化记忆回声。

在我年轻时，有幸遇见其他几位大师，同样证实了这一点。我想到了卡洛·斯卡帕，我在威尼斯建筑学院时的教授；勒·柯布西耶，在他位于威尼斯的工作室（与朱利安·德拉富恩特和何塞·奥布雷利艾合作的），我参与了城市医院这一新项目的开发；我还想到了路易斯·康，我曾协助他进行威尼斯双年展花园的会议建筑项目。这三位大师，每一位都富有诗意，同样都严厉地抵制全球文化所带来的同质化。

新事物的记忆

技术的现代化进程已经导致了与传统之间的破坏性断层，时常给我们生活空间的质量带来负面影响。鉴于持续发展的、强有力的全球化进程，建筑必须担负起这样的使命：将空间重塑为具有公民特性的场所，重新建立起有助于集体生活的环境。

在这一点上，我时常怀着敬意想起路易斯·康。他认为“过去如同朋友”，这并非暗示着对过去的留恋，而是指这样一种态度：利用来自历史的最佳经验去判断某种新建筑语言的合理性。这种呼吁在伟大的现代艺术家身上十分常见（克利、摩尔、毕加索、贾科梅蒂），他们都致力于寻找一种当代语言，来唤起伟大的历史价值。在建筑领域，提起古希腊对于勒·柯布西耶的意义、罗马建筑对于路易斯·康的意义，或是工匠知识对于卡洛·斯卡帕的意义，就已经足够了。所有这些艺术家都完成了充满古老记忆的当代图景。

重读过去并不意味着以任何方式效仿著名的案例，而是学习如何处理建筑学的历史和记忆、不同的建筑技巧以及特定的地理与历史环境。

这项挑战将令我们知道，我们是否有能力书写出值得文明史回溯的新篇章。

CONSIDERATIONS

Mario Botta

Architecture and globalization

The very first raison d'être of architecture lies in the unique and unrepeatable act of transforming the physical world; it cannot disregard the *genius loci*, the bond that exists between the work and its environment. The reproduction of the same project in different places sounds like an offence to the very nature of architecture. Conversely, the culture of globalization that has spread in the past few years, in the name of the necessary transformation of territories and cities, does not allow territories and cities to develop and modernize according to their *genius loci*, their history and, in other words, their identity.

In the modern process of globalization, the needs of developed communities appear to be all the same, whether they are in Europe, America or the Far East. However, it is a serious mistake to confuse the economic and social interdependence among the various parts of the world with a general homogenization of models of settlement and organization of the living environment of humankind.

The cultural identity of a community always reveals differences among the regions, even in the era of globalization. Identity is both a geographical, historical and cultural mold; and in a work of architecture it should always represent an opportunity to create a dialogue with the environment.

As an architect, I try to ensure that the surrounding environment becomes an integral part of the work of architecture.

The physical space owns a (geographical, historical or mnemonic) condition, which can be considered a privileged material that the architect is expected to take into consideration.

Architects today, in the wake of the Modern Movement

In the latter half of the 20th century, architecture started paying higher attention to the geographical and historical context (a kind of attention that has always existed as such, since architecture converts a natural condition into a cultural condition). This critical movement enabled architecture to move on from the first phase of the Modern Movement, a phase that has been approximately defined "International Style". In contrast with the call for postwar modernization that the Masters of the first half of the past century had to face, in the most recent past, a growing need has emerged, alongside an ever greater critical awareness, to enrich architecture, in particular the architecture of cities, with historical memory. The latter is related to the physical context, the transformations it has undergone and the very own identities of the different communities. This is why today we can assert that the field of action architecture works within is (or should be) the "territory of memory".

Over the past few years the culture of architecture has been enriched by ecological awareness, it has become more sensitive to the use of local materials, it has questioned itself with regards to the scarcity of resources, at times it has also resorted to traditional or vernacular techniques, and it has privileged the search for a dialogue with the environmental context, with the aim of developing models for an improved environmental sustainability...

These new attitudes, which obviously already existed to a lesser extent in the works of the Modern Movement in the early 20th century, are nowadays technical and cultural realities; they have become a social must, which has to be taken into consideration; they are the conditions of a new way of dealing with architecture.

The achievements attained by the culture of architecture in the 20th century have created great benefits with regard to the quality of the living environment; but now it is up to the new generation to recover those primordial values, which are essential for the discipline, and to give them new momentum and visibility.

Civilization or Aestheticism

Among the damage caused by globalization, there is not only a scarce attention of architecture to the natural context, to environmental sustainability and to a reconciliation with the historical memory. The main problem is the obsession with aestheticism and self-referential formalism, which we can recognize in the arbitrariness and the mannerism of its shapes, which very often have almost nothing in common with the tectonic structure; materials are tied more and more to fashion trends, images are cloned regardless of construction principles and topographical conditions.

Modern architecture acquires aestheticized configurations, thus losing its ability to be a true artistic and public presence. This kind of architecture often stands for a total surrender (on the part of the client and of the architect) to exclusive market interests. In today's consumer society, where everything is commodifiable, architecture is often reduced to an image, very much to the detriment of the structural quality and the lifespan of materials, which should be intrinsic values of the architectural work. The ostentation of aestheticism denies the very same foundations of architecture, i.e. an art that finds its reason of being in the gravity and the balance of the construction, an art that takes roots in the mother soil, that bears ancestral memories but also new expectations. The building of space remains a collective good, and architecture has always been a mirror of human institutions. This is why we can read the history of past civilizations through the buildings that have survived until today. Temples, churches, theaters and palaces, which have been a feature of the urban fabric and the production infrastructures over the years, are witnesses to history and civilization and have become part of our identity. These buildings allow us to understand how these stones represent the cultural ambitions and values of the people that came before us. From this point of view, architecture is called upon to be an instrument of culture (not only of technical and functional solutions). Unfortunately, the present scenario underlines the poverty of modern values with manneristic, aesthetic and badly decorative images.

Architecture, a primordial art

When a work of architecture manages to make the end-user wonder about the value of the context, the geography and the history that characterize a place, it recovers the meaning of primordial art, which recalls that it is an anthronization tool of a physical environment. In my career as an architect, I have always tried to avoid purely theoretical or abstract projects, in the firm belief that they conceal the risk of aestheticism. On the contrary, if you believe that the context can become part of the project, the environmental situation provides the designer with important arguments and stimuli. I am interested in the founding value of architecture, in the way the new building takes roots in the earth and can even change the profile of the earth's crust. Questioning the context and looking for solutions that consider the natural environment and the setting must be a priority for the designer, as if the new building were a pre-existing natural presence (that would be excellent for the architect).

Architecture bears the idea of an action whereby humankind transforms the soil he lives on and, by taking roots in the soil, the building also manages to change the skyline.

The work of architecture, which is bound to the earth by the law of gravity, is shaped by light and finds its own conformation through the shadows. It lives in the space of the solar cycle, of the changing seasons and climate changes.

In these times of homogenization of shapes, I like to point out the changes that architectural images undergo over the years, the way works of architecture can bear witness to the fact that they are primordial signs of humankind on earth.

Enjoying the landscape and the light, going along with the changing seasons, shaping materials that communicate with the surroundings, ensuring that the new shapes recall ancestral presences; these are some aims of the architect, which can also be considered living rights of the citizens. The architect's language cannot be limited to abstract shapes, formal choices or pre-established images; the power of architecture lies in its ability to re-define the quality of spatial relationships with the surroundings; and not to limit itself to mere built volumes. The quality of a work of architecture lies in its ability to provide for a better organization of space through the relationships that the new building creates with its surroundings.

Every single project is a public act

Of course there are many different uses of space as well as numerous land ownership models, but this does not contradict the public value of architecture. A city cannot be considered a private property, because every single parcel of land, every street and square, every building, irrespective of the ownership system and the different functions, contribute to the creation of a collective dimension. Thus, also the space of private properties, within a growth that takes place over the time, is part of a collective reality.

In their projects architects often have to comply with programs and client's requirements. But even when the project is carried out for a private person, the architect must not forget that the construction remains a public act. This becomes very clear if one observes a city as a whole. The urban fabric, especially in European cities, which are bound to Western culture, is without doubt the smartest, most advanced and welcoming organization model for social life and collective living that has ever been realized in the long-lasting process of the anthropization of the earth.

The modern English word *city* derives from the ancient Latin term *civitas*, i.e. citizenship, social aggregation. The city, meant as the place where citizenship materializes, reiterates the public mission of architecture. In the present age of globalization, with shapeless megalopolises without any more value of citizenship in cohabitation sprouting all over the planet, we must question ourselves critically and re-read the cultural lesson of the historical European city.

Architecture, a forward-looking art

A work of architecture should always interpret the spatial and environmental potential of a place, take possession of it and provide it with new meanings. If we interpret the stratification of our cities over the centuries, we can observe that architecture often acts as a seismograph, which is able to interpret the expectations and the ambitions of a community, thus promoting its development.

Just as a project anticipates the future work with the design, architecture must be able to understand the ongoing social, political and cultural processes in order to offer new solutions.

Good architecture, like the best artistic practices, promotes social transformation. It has a pioneering role, that at times can also conceal the risk of wrong interpretations, but history generally manages to find the conditions for future life.

In order to perform this role in modern times, architects have to ask themselves what it means to live, work, live side by side, teach, pray; in other words, they must represent humankind culturally as people who live their own time. The language of architecture must create shapes that, in the specific situation, are able to build physical, urban and territorial settings that meet the needs of the community.

The masters of the Modern Movement and of the 20th-century artistic avant-garde have taught us that architectural thinking is a "total project". Hermann Muthesius claimed that planning should be done "from the spoon to the city"; his motto and his intuition are still true today. Architects try to apply this principle in the various aspects of design practice: architectural building, object design, scenic design and all other forms that become images in space. All these different experiences contribute to reaching the common aim of constantly developing the physical world we live in.

Technique or art

Technical knowledge is essential for architecture, but in most cases it is a mere prerequisite. If architecture is limited to technique or functions, it may be able to build new functional buildings, districts and cities, but it is unlikely that it will build places that meet the values of civilization, historical culture and beauty. In recent years, the notion of "non-places", coined by Marc Augé, has become widespread. The term non-places indicates the anonymous spaces of modern society, which are merely designed to meet cold functional requirements or speculative interests or market logics: shopping malls, airports, suburbs, leftover spaces, with no character nor spaces for interaction and life...

"Non-places" are the evidence that technical knowledge alone is not enough to guarantee the quality of architecture: everything can work properly but there is no special identity of space, nothing stimulates participation. Only a space with its very own character, which promotes mutual relations, can guarantee participation.

Art is also a form of knowledge, like technical knowhow, but it differs due to the complexity of its language, the questions and the different interpretations it can arouse and that are constantly intertwined with the cultural, symbolic, social aspects, etc.

I like to recall the lessons of some contemporary architects like Jorn Utzon, Alvaro Siza, Tadao Ando; these great masters have proved that architecture exists as a cultural expression, which is able to meet the expectations and ambitions of a community. In their works one can hear the echo of a cultural memory, which we recognize and admire as part of our history.

The same is true for some other masters I had the privilege to meet in various moments of my youth: I am thinking of Carlo Scarpa, who was one of my professors at the Istituto Universitario di Architettura in Venice; Le Corbusier, in whose Venice studio (with Jullian de la Fuente and Josè Oubrerie) I participated in the development of the new project for the city hospital; last but not least I am also thinking of Louis Kahn and the time I assisted him in developing the project for the Conference building in the gardens of the Biennale in Venice. These three masters, each one of them according to their own poetry, have put up a critical resistance to the homogenization imposed by the global culture.

The memory of novelty

The process of technological modernization has imposed a traumatic break-up with traditions and very often creates negative conditions for the quality of our living space. In the light of the on-going strong globalization process, architecture has to take on the mission of re-establishing space as a place of civil identity that can recreate environments promoting collective living.

In this respect, I have often recalled Louis Kahn who refers to the "past as a friend". This does not imply nostalgic trips in the past. It rather refers to an attitude that aims to justify the new language by means of the best lessons that come from historical memory. This call is typical of the great modern artists (Klee, Moore, Picasso, Giacometti) who have committed themselves to the search of a contemporary language that can evoke the values of the great past. In the field of architecture, it would be enough to mention the significance that Ancient Greece had for Le Corbusier, Roman architecture for Louis Kahn or artisan knowledge for Carlo Scarpa... all these artists have achieved a contemporary composition, rich in ancestral memories.

Re-reading the past does not in any way consist in imitating well-known examples; it implies dealing with the discipline's history and memory, the different building skills as well as the specific geographical and historical context.

This challenge will tell us if we have been able to write a new chapter that is worth going down in the history of our civilization.

宗教建筑的几点说明

鲁道夫·阿恩海姆

有口皆碑的艺术作品都具有象征性，建筑作品也不例外。我所说的“象征性”是指这些建筑除了具有诸如遮蔽、保护和方便使用者日常活动的功能外，还能够通过视觉外观传递其功能的精神与哲学意义。如果一座市政厅、一家医院或是一处私人住宅是一件好的建筑作品，它便能通过形态所表达的内容来反映人类的需求。这种象征意义不是某些思想家从“外部”应用于建筑的一种附加诠释，而是设计自身的本质和精髓所在。

要做到这一点，建筑的象征性应当通过视觉形态的各个层面令观看者自发地感受到，比如大小、形状和空间关系。这种视觉语汇的要素是几何形状，一件作品正是通过几何形状向人们表达思想的。不过，区别“开放符号”和“闭合符号”是有必要的。“开放符号”是设计师在每次创作时新得到的，但无论在哪种文化背景中，解决方法一旦获得，往往会被固化为标准并替代了个人的创造力，也就形成“闭合符号”，逐渐演化为语义标签，最终沦为信息的工具。这种自发意义再也无法令人发觉建筑的内涵。观看者只会理解为“这是一家酒店”或“这是一间教堂”，并无其他。一旦走入这样的捷径，建筑本身就黯然失色了。

这些想法被收录于一本以意大利文和法文出版，设计精美的书籍——《一间教堂的设计》，由让·佩提为瑞士建筑师马里奥·博塔所编，并即将以德文和英文出版。该项目是在洛迦诺附近提契诺州的蒙哥诺山村设计一座新的教堂。1986年，位于蒙哥诺的一座17世纪教堂在一场雪崩中被毁。在新教堂的设计中，博塔避免了传统教堂建筑中“闭合符号”的僵化效应。他设计的教堂风格现代，与过去迥然不同，但并未刻意标新立异。相反，这座教堂致力于通过简洁、直观的几何形特征来满足祭祀场所的基本需求。

博塔设计的教堂高耸入云，满足了莱昂·巴蒂斯塔·阿尔贝蒂的要求：教堂应当独立于周围的日常生活，并高出日常生活。这是一个简洁的石制圆柱体建筑，与村民们早已熟知的建筑形象颇为不同。并非指简洁直观的形象与乡村生活格格不入——毕竟有人联想到了农场中的粮仓——而是指将这样一座圆柱体建筑作为当地的教堂是十分令人吃惊的。更确切地说，这座建筑的圆柱体截面是椭圆的，并在超过人体高度后开始倾斜。这种对完整形态的

摘自《设计语言》，1993年3月，第一卷，第247到252页。

切断处理也许会使村民回想起那片废墟，那片雪崩之后的废墟。不过，就建筑的本质属性来说，倾斜的屋顶平面使得圆柱体上部形成类似尖塔的形状，就如传统教堂一般直插云霄。同时，屋顶平面相对于高处向后倾斜，好似一名礼拜者；屋顶覆盖着玻璃，将教堂和教众引向太阳，正如所有传统教堂的做法一样。

此外，建筑师为倾斜的屋顶平面设计了一个完美的圆形。由于内部空间以矩形为基础，因此墙体应当逐渐适应屋顶的圆度，从而逐层改变形状。这一复杂变化并不容易实现，尤其在建筑椭圆柱体的较长轴线与屋顶中线成直角的情况下。然而，一旦理解了这个复杂的形状，在由地面生活空间上升至完美圆形窗口的过程中，教众的心灵便可以得到升华。当然，只在特定的角度才能发觉到倾斜的屋顶。通过圆殿中放置十字架的墙面上方，能够看到丝毫没有被减弱的风景，支撑结构与圆形屋顶的垂直轴线在此相汇。

这座建筑整体上看通过符号化引起了椭圆和圆形之间的相互作用。乔万尼·波奇在博塔书中写了一段文字，以充分的理由表明，自文艺复兴以来西方建筑和绘画的历史上就有描绘这种主题的庄严传统。事实上，帕诺夫斯基在一篇关于艺术评论家伽利略的随笔中提醒人们，伽利略拒绝采纳他的朋友开普勒的发现：我们的行星轨迹系统不是由同心圆构成的，而是由椭圆形构成的，太阳是这些椭圆形的焦点之一。哥白尼体系的完美对称秉持一种人文主义信念：球体或圆形的完美几何形态淋漓尽致地表现出上帝的完美，因此适合圣堂的几何形状应当是球形和圆形。在一本有关人文主义时期建筑原则的书籍中，维特考尔探讨了文艺复兴时期集中式教堂的哲学与神学偏好，并展示了达·芬奇所设计的此类教堂。当然，洗礼堂也遵循了这一完整的中央形制。但出于功能考虑，难以调和巴西利卡式传统布局与集中式平面布局之间的圣坛位置。

在向风格主义发展的过程中，椭圆形平面被引入建筑设计。帕诺夫斯基以米开朗基罗的第一个项目作为最早的案例——尤里乌斯二世的坟墓。在17世纪的巴洛克时期，椭圆形变成一种常见的形态。博洛米尼在他设计的四喷泉圣卡洛教堂中使用了较长的轴线，将入口置于一端，圣坛所在的后殿位于另一端。

博塔在设计蒙哥诺教堂时，用椭圆的短径作为建筑主轴线，与垂直于地面的屋顶对称轴线保持一致。他的构思实际上是通过一种对位关系实现圆形和椭圆形传统交替方式的现代演绎。从哲学和神学的角度而言，这是在充满神圣意味的圆形屋顶限定下，位于世间的椭圆形和矩形空间的对峙。

显然，当建筑超越与其传统功能相关的“闭合符号”，依靠视觉形象的表达形成“开放符号”时，它们的意义主要体现于人的视觉感受和所表达出的态度，并非它们的实际应用。就教堂建筑而言，这意味着设计师将更加关注特殊仪式所体现出的人类基本特性，至少对蒙哥诺的罗马天主教堂来说是如此。设计师本身可能是信徒，他便能够在教义中领悟更深层的、艺术家们所关注的人类特性；他也可能信仰其他宗教，甚至是无神论者。不是信徒并不意味着拒绝或忽视教义，反而可能是尊重教义，尊重其作为人们可以分享的基础价值的载体。

柯布西耶的朗香教堂，马蒂斯所装饰的旺斯教堂，以及威廉·鲁宾就其发表了大部专著的阿西教堂同样如此。乔治·鲁奥也是曾参与阿西教堂项目的艺术家，他是一名忠实的信徒。但博纳尔、吕尔萨、莱热、夏加尔、里希耶和利普希茨有所不同，他们当中有共产主义者、无神论者和东正教犹太人。最典型的案例是雅各布·利普希茨设计的圣母玛利亚圣坛雕像，是其最精美而深刻的作品之一。在作品背面刻有这样的字眼：雅各布·利普希茨，犹太人，忠于其祖先的信仰；创作这尊圣母像是为了促进俗世人类之间的谅解。圣灵的生命为上。

由于这些艺术家和设计师都是现代主义者，他们放弃了约定俗成的风格从而寻找全新的表现力。就宗教建筑而言，这意味着像马里奥·博塔这样一名优秀的建筑师放弃了大部分对传统的表面化应用，但他并不忽视传统，而是重新探索人类情感和思想的更深层内核。

鲁道夫·阿恩海姆

鲁道夫·阿恩海姆于1904年出生在柏林的一个犹太家庭。他进入柏林大学，在马克思·韦特默和沃尔夫冈·科勒的指导下学习格式塔心理学，后将其运用于艺术创作中。25岁左右，阿恩海姆开始撰写影评，为《世界舞台》Die Weltb ü hne的文化部门效力。纳粹掌握政权后，他于1933年迁往罗马，之后的6年都在罗马生活并撰写电影与广播评论。第二次世界大战爆发后，他前往伦敦成为英国广播公司的一名战时翻译。1940年，他迁往美国，1943年成为萨拉姆·劳伦斯学院的心理学教授，并在社会研究新学院担任客座讲师。在这段时间，他获得了两项重要的奖励：洛克菲勒基金会奖学金和古根海姆奖学金。1951年，阿恩海姆又一次获得了洛克菲勒基金会奖学金，之后他暂时离开教学岗位，撰写了他的代表性著作《艺术与视知觉：创造性人才的心理》（1954年）；这本书后来于1974年修订、扩充并再版，至今已被翻译成14种语言。他的其他主要著作还包括：《视觉思维》（1969年）、《中心的力量：视觉艺术构成研究》（1982年）以及《艺术与视知觉》。

阿恩海姆于1968年受聘成为哈佛大学艺术心理学教授，在那里工作了6年。他于1974年退休，与妻子迁往密歇根州的安阿伯市，其后担任密歇根大学的客座教授，在那里工作了10年。

阿恩海姆是美国美学协会的一员，并担任了两届主席；他曾担任三届美国心理学会的心理学和艺术分会的主席；1976年被推选为美国艺术与科学学院的一员。2007年，阿恩海姆于安阿伯市逝世。

NOTES ON RELIGIOUS ARCHITECTURE

Rudolf Arnheim

All works of art worth their name are symbolic, and works of architecture are no exception. By symbolism I mean that these works, in addition to their physical functions, such as that of sheltering, protecting, and facilitating the activities of their users convey through their visible appearance the spiritual and philosophical meaning of their functions. If a town hall or a hospital or a private home is a work of good architecture, it proclaims its human calling by what its shape expresses. This symbolic meaning is not simply an attribution applied to the building by some thinker "from the outside" as a kind of added interpretation, but it is of the very nature and essence of the design itself.

To do its job, the symbolism of a building has to be spontaneously apparent to the viewers' eyes through the various aspects of visual form, such as size, shape, and spatial relation. The elements of this visual vocabulary are the geometrical shapes, by which a work speaks to us. It is useful, however, to distinguish open symbols from closed symbols. Open symbols are freshly derived by designers. Every time they draw on their medium. In every culture, however, solutions once obtained tend to freeze into standards replacing individual invention. Such closed symbols become semantic labels; they are reduced to mere tools of information. Their spontaneous meaning no longer alerts the eye to evoke the building's meaning. The viewer understands, *this is a hotel or this is a church* and leaves it at that. But every time this convenience operates, architecture fades.

These thoughts were revived by the publication in Italian and French of an attractively designed book, *Project for a Church*, edited by Jean Petit for the Swiss architect Mario Botta and about to be published also in English and German. The project designs a new church for the mountain village of Mogno in the Ticino near Locarno. In 1986, the 17th century church of Mogno was destroyed by an avalanche. In designing a new church, Botta avoided the paralyzing effects of the closed symbols of traditional church architecture. His church is modern in style, shockingly different, but in no way struggling for sensational novelty. On the contrary, it aspires to meet the basic demands of a temple of worship by deriving them simply and directly from expressive traits of basic geometrical shapes.

Botta's church reaches for the sky and meets Leon Battista Alberti's demand that it be *isolated from, and raised above, the surrounding everyday life*. It is a simple stone cylinder, quite different from the shape to which the villagers had been accustomed. Not that starkly simple shapes are alien to rural living - one is reminded of the silos on our own farms–but to be presented with such a cylinder as the local church must be startling. More precisely, the cylinder of the building is elliptical in section, and somewhere above the height of the human body it begins to be cut off by an oblique plane. This harsh interruption of a perfect

Taken from *Languages of Design*, 1993, 3, vol. 1, pp. 247-252.

shape might remind villagers of the ruins, several of which they saw after the avalanche struck. More essentially, however, the oblique roof plane sharpens the upper part of the cylinder into a kind of steeple, poking into the sky in the manner of traditional churches. At the same time, the tilted plane of the roof offers itself by its backward leaning to the heights above like a worshipper, and since the roof is covered with glass it orients the building and its congregation to the sun, as churches have traditionally done.

Moreover, the tilted plane of the roof is given by the architect the shape of a perfect circle. Since the internal space has a rectangular base, its walls must adapt gradually to the circularity of the roof, changing shape from layer to layer. This sophisticated transformation is by no means easy to visualize, especially since the longer axis of the building's elliptical cylinder is oriented at right angles to the midline of the roof. Once this complex shape is understood, however, the minds of the congregation are presented with a sublimation of the terrestrial living space, rising to the perfection of the circular oculus. Of course, the roof, being tilted, is seen by the congregation only in perspective. Its undiminished view is reserved to the location of the crucifix on the wall above the apse. The place where the figure is attached meets the perpendicular axis of the roof's circle.

The building as a whole plays on the symbolically evocative interplay of ellipse and circle. In a short contribution to Botta's book, Giovanni Pozzi alludes with good reason to the venerable tradition of this theme in the history of Western architecture and painting since the Renaissance. In fact, Panofsky in his essay on Galileo as a critic of the arts has reminded us that Galileo refused to adopt his friend Kepler's discovery that our planetary system does not consist of a set of concentric circles but of elliptical trajectories with the sun placed in one of the foci of these ellipses. The perfect symmetry of the Copernican system was in keeping with the Humanistic belief that the perfection of God was best expressed in the perfect geometrical shape of the sphere or circle and that therefore the appropriate shape of the sanctuary was centric and circular. In his book on the architectural principles in the age of Humanism, Wittkower discusses the philosophical and theological preference for centralized churches in the Renaissance and illustrates Leonardo da Vinci's designs for such churches. Baptisteries, of course, were examples of such complete centric shape. For the purpose of churches, however, it was difficult to reconcile the location of the altar in the tradition of the basilica with a centralize ground plan.

It took the development toward Mannerism to introduce elliptical ground plans to architecture. As an earliest example, Panofsky cites Michelangelo's first project for the tomb of Julius II, and during the Baroque period of the 17th century the ellipse became a familiar shape. In his church of San Carlo alle Quattro Fontane, Borromini used the longer axis of the church, placing the entrance at one end and the apse with the altar at the other. Botta in designing his Mogno church, now under construction, used the shorter diameter of his ellipse as the building's main axis, in keeping with the dominant symmetry axis imposed by the roof at right angles to the ground plan. His composition amounts to a modern synthesis of the traditional alternative between circle and ellipse by confronting the two in a contrapuntal relation. Philosophically and theologically, this is a confrontation of the worldlier ellipse and the rectangular space it controls with the more sacred realm of the circular roof.

It will be evident that when buildings go beyond the closed symbols associated with their conventional function and rely instead on open symbols drawn from the spontaneous expression of visual shapes, their meaning also will be seen primarily in the human vision and attitude they express, rather than in their practical application. In the case of church architecture, this means that the designer has his or her mind on the basic human qualities emerging from the particular ritual – in the case of the Mogno church that of Roman Catholicism. The designer may be a believer, visualizing in the doctrine the deeper human qualities with which artists are concerned, or may adhere to a different religion or be an atheist. Not being a believer does not have to mean that one rejects or ignores a doctrine. It may mean respecting it as the carrier of underlying values one can indeed share.

This has been the case in Le Corbusier's chapel at Ronchamp, Matisse's decorations for the chapel in Vence, and the church of Assy, on which William Rubin has published an extensive monograph. One of the artists contributing to Assy, Georges Rouault, was indeed a faithful believer. Not so the others, Bonnard, Lurçat, Léger, Chagall, Richier, and Lipchitz, among whom there were communists, atheists, and orthodox Jews. The most significant example is Jacques Lipchitz's altar statue of the Virgin, one of his finest and most profound works, on whose back he put the inscription: *Jacob Lipchitz, Jew, faithful to the religion of his ancestors, has made this Virgin to foster understanding between men on earth that the life of the spirit may prevail.*

All these artists and designers were modernists, in the sense that they abandoned stylistic conventions to refresh the expressive eloquence of their media. In the case of religious architecture, this means that a good designer like Mario Botta gave up most of the literal applications of tradition, not to ignore them but to probe once again the deeper core of human feeling and thought.

Rudolf Arnheim

Rudolf Arnheim was born into a Jewish family in Berlin, in 1904. He attended the University of Berlin where he learned Gestalt psychology from studying under Max Wertheimer and Wolfgang Köhler and applied it to art. In the mid-20s, Arnheim started writing film criticism and worked on the cultural section of Die Weltbühne. After the Nazis came into power, in 1933, he moved to Rome where he lived and wrote about film and radio for the next six years. When World War II broke out, he moved to London, and he worked as a wartime translator for the British Broadcasting Corporation. He moved to the United States in 1940. In 1943 he became a psychology professor at Sarah Lawrence College and a visiting lecturer at the New School of Social Research. Around this time he received two major awards.: the Rockefeller Foundation Fellowship and the Guggenheim Fellowship. In 1951, Arnheim got another Rockefeller Foundation Fellowship so that he could take a leave from teaching and wrote his magnum opus, Art and Visual Perception: A Psychology of the Creative Eye (1954); the book was revised, enlarged and published as a new version in 1974, and it has been translated into fourteen languages. Other major books have included Visual Thinking (1969), and The Power of the Center: A Study of Composition in the Visual Arts (1982). Art and Visual Perception.

Arnheim was invited to join Harvard University as Professor of the Psychology of Art in 1968, and he stayed there for six years. He retired in 1974 to Ann Arbor, Michigan, with his wife and became a Visiting Professor at the University of Michigan where he taught for ten years.

He was a member of the American Society for Aesthetics and was their president for two terms, and was also the president for the Division on Psychology and the Arts of the American Psychological Association for three terms. In 1976 he was elected a Fellow of the American Academy of Arts and Sciences. He died in Ann Arbor in 2007.

事物的人文内涵

加布里埃尔·卡佩拉托

马里奥·博塔已将他的事业转化为使命。他是一位将作品深深扎根在社会语境中的建筑师，也是一位随时准备好展示个人风格的建筑师，他在故乡提契诺州的振兴中扮演了重要的角色。

博塔的作品的确令人印象深刻，不仅因为所包含的主题范围极广。他所接受的委托极其多样化，要求甚高；他完成了无数的设计项目，参与了许多设计竞赛，并完成了多种不同类型的建筑。这些作品中包括图书馆、博物馆、教堂和住宅，它们见证着这位建筑师的语言和设计过程的逐步发展。

博塔的多样性充满创造力，这源于他理想的滋养。他时常就现实情况拷问自己，更重要的是放眼未来，尽管身处于充满矛盾、复杂，有时甚至是绝望的时代之中。

在他的研究、思考和建筑设计中，总是致力于融合现存事物与新的创造，以此获得一种新的平衡。因此，在其已完成的作品中，博塔揭示出战胜过去的唯一方法即是回应当下，采取将过去所获得的有效经验结合自身表现力的方式。

马里奥·博塔向我们展示了一种宁静而谦逊的当代感，执着勇敢、紧随时代。这是因为其与生活的现实密切相关。在这种情况下，每件事情都需要经过讨论。这种进行建筑的方式比以往任何时候更加合理——正如生活自身一样持续推进和改变。石头就是石头，岩石就是岩石，土壤就是土壤，女士的脸就是女士的脸。但真正的意义是内在的，藏于事物深层的，由于和其他事物产生关联而获得新的意义：这就是生活的真谛。一种持续的使命感所带来的紧迫性成为他生存的基础，促使他致力于为社会服务。他不再是这个社会的天才发明家或创造者，而是成为了他所生活其中的团体的服务者。

建筑是一种用空间、体积、结构和材料等作为符号进行传播的行为，按照这种理解，建筑成为了一种回应，一种源于日常现实、人际交往的混凝土必需品，这种回应源于建筑师的解读，因此能够将理想、思想与行动融为一体。

博塔的建筑因而常常忠于某个场所，即使这一场所有时与建筑是对立的。建筑的形式粗犷又明确；建筑的特征与其诞生的土壤和开辟的空间同样重要，在密切的对话与相互依存的

摘自马里奥·博塔，《公共建筑》，米兰：史基拉出版公司，1998 年，第 205-211 页。

关系中产生共鸣。另外，博塔的建筑涉及几何学、调研、直线、角线、曲线和折线。在日常事件所产生的巨大力量中，想象之美指向结构、材质的自然面貌以及在环境的爆发力和张力下相互作用而成的空间质感。建筑的体块感强烈、稳定，平面、外观和墙体均被分解，光线被视为塑造空间的力量，进入由内到外、由外到内不断流淌的恒定状态。

随着博塔逐渐成长为一名建筑师，他越来越相信空间的创造源自建筑师的心灵，迫切想要追寻遥远过往中最深处的秘密。然而，博塔所追寻的过去不是陌生、空洞或肤浅的过去。其本质取决于他对自身所处环境的意识，取决于他与环境之间的持续对话。

没有这样的信念，我们就不能理解他的建筑方法中饱含的人文内涵。

构造几何学

传统的建造行为往往暗含一些神圣之意。对于博塔而言，“建造”意味着执行与开始某项技艺，使其成为自学习过程中必不可少的一部分。建造是建筑学中基本的、核心的活动。建造等同于生活，就像生活等同于为空间赋予形态。这似乎符合博塔的思维结构，他认为已完成的建筑可以看作是一种定义事物、联系事物、为事物赋予形态的独特手段。因此，所有建筑的建造过程都是对原则和原理的理性反思。

马里奥·博塔比其他任何建筑师都更加始终如一地坚持将自己的思维和创造性理念与自己的项目设计方法纳入统一的体系之中。

他的目标是在每次创作中严格地选择组成的要素和已有语义关系，通过秩序、几何学和类型学清晰地表达出来。因此，对于博塔而言，建造的试验性仍要比结构性来得重要，因为建筑作品一旦建成，其结构便会被忘却或破坏。作品的形象似乎源自其直观性以及美学及方法论的力量——这些要素在古典建筑类型中就已确立，例如各种关系、节奏、平衡与比例之间的和谐。

博塔在自己的项目中使用的方法反映出他的能力所在：“新”的建筑有机体如何被创造出来并在实践中发挥作用。出于自身的目的，博塔学习并参考了主要的形式语言、纯粹的体块和基础几何学研究。这种方式证明了在实际层面上，建造确实为结构工程，即建造是由挖掘土地、浇筑地基、垒砌砖块、建造墙体、重力法则、对光的研究和细节特性共同决定的。他的作品代表着一种全球化的建筑理念：建造是创造性行为必不可少的一部分，是生活最根本的、决定性的部分，是建筑学的原则。

建筑的易逝性

马里奥·博塔在自己的作品中展示了一种理念：建筑设计意味着从最深层次理解结构的最难之处。建筑在与环境对话的同时，也与其相对立，建筑会成为环境的一部分，同时也要呈现自己如何面对恒久时间的考验。

马里奥·博塔多年来一直在与当代建筑的弱点做斗争——这些弱点来自于肤浅的、前后矛盾的思维，而我们往往把这样的思维与时髦的、短暂的、装模作样的事物联系在一起。这些现象如闲言碎语，却从本质上向我们证实着当今建筑的早衰、不堪一击、脆弱的材质，易损的性质。博塔认为，建筑的魅力和力量源自其从计划转化为成品的能力，始终约束和改变周围事物的能力，关系到新的生活状态，生活从那一刻开始与建筑一同发展，同时与其自身的易逝性斗争。

真正的建筑能够通过其形式、构造、建造方法以及自身存在而延续下去。事实上，所有在建筑层面取得成功的建筑，在建造层面也是成功的。博塔充分地表达了这种思想，他用一种现代的敏感性诠释了建筑师——过去的工匠——不是那种怀旧的、被人忽视的工匠，而是在自己的时代尽情展露才华的工匠，他们知道建筑行业与一些简单的技艺相关，这些技艺往往被当作建筑传统而世代流传。博塔通过理解结构而设计建筑，他的能力在于能够将自己的创意和项目设计理念通过结构、通过极度重视的细节，淋漓尽致地表现出来。

规划的类型学

在所有项目的开发中，指引着马里奥·博塔，并确保项目能够呈现预期建筑形态的那些创意萌芽，是多种不同概念和技术的缩影，这些概念和技艺足够丰富，能够将某个特定的时刻转变为精心构造的对象。

在文艺复兴时期，人是宇宙的中心。“理念之美”是通过作品的完整性获得的，而作品的完整性基于各个部分的整合、各个维度的和谐以及精准无疑的形态，多一分则过度，少一分则不足。一种纯粹而普遍的几何学秩序将实体空间转化成放置建筑作品之地。对马里奥·博塔而言，他对技术的精通使其能够理解、唤起并运用属于过去的传统建筑的形态、符号和图形，构建出的基本形态完整而真实，是生活的一部分，也是社会文化的一部分。因此，他的建筑都是易于理解且清晰直率的，有时却也令人困惑——参观者可能惊讶于它们的简洁。这种基本形态并不那么容易复制。这段漫长的旅程中，缜密而复杂的意识使建筑师能够以他希望的方式来展现建筑。但是，观看者的注意力往往会被易识别的、直接而表面化的秩序所吸引。

博塔的建筑作品的面貌统一、紧凑——甚至几乎是一个单体——这一特性往往会被次要元素的构成所平衡，这使得建筑在各个方面都十分均衡。这形成了他的作品中最为显著的特质：摒弃附加的内容，凸显了建筑的精准、完美的和谐与平衡。正因如此，马里奥·博塔使自己成为了从概念过渡到形态的诠释者，通过结构去表达创作的精髓。

在博塔的设计语言中，几何学是具有驱动性的理念，支撑起计划与行动，从而带来具有自主性的建筑作品。通过调查和几何学研究，他得以明确每个项目的起源、概念和维度。在博塔的作品中，设计变成了“选择”：选择精确的形态，选择建造的结构原理，选择功能的分布。建筑师是创造者，提出自己的原则，将建筑作为一个学科来掌控。在各个要素相互融合，共同塑造一件完整作品的过程中，几何学清晰地反映出设计语言的连续性和间断性。

在《走向新建筑》一书中，勒·柯布西耶谈道：“建筑与风格没有任何关联。建筑呼吁更高的才能。”这句话在博塔身上得到了精确的诠释，因为他的建筑所扎根的土壤是真正的物理上的实体，他的作品产生于秩序、劳动和繁重的建筑行业，使某个地方变得神圣。几何学是建筑揭示自身的直接手段，几何学为各个体块设定恰当的空间关系和比例。建筑依据线条、图形和形态构成的形式法则发展而来，当这些元素放到一起时，便会构成多个符合几何学原理的单元，反映出极强的创造力和严谨的原则。从事一个项目需要有想法，确定理念，有条理地表达这些理念，使它们易于解读。需要自我剖析，需要制定一个确切的目标，为几何表面赋予形态并将其转化为空间。从事一个项目需要概括出大致计划，计划往往追随直觉。建筑中的对抗意味着以精确的几何学定位表皮和体块之间的矛盾。如果没有真实性或连贯性，可能不会产生这样的对抗，当然，也就不会有优秀的、耐久的建筑。博塔成功了，在于他的作品，也在于他的真实且始终如一。他知道建筑往往会打败时间、流言蜚语、潮流与批评家，于是他接受了这场挑战和竞争。

加布里埃尔·卡佩拉托

加布里埃尔·卡佩拉托于1949年生于帕多瓦。他于1978年从威尼斯建筑大学（IUAV）毕业，获得博士学位，随后他在本校研究理论与建筑设计。1979年，他在帕多瓦建立了自己的设计工作室，并与多个意大利和国际专业工作室合作。他在意大利和欧洲许多重要场地策划了多场展览。丰富的建筑研究经历深化了他对于现当代建筑的认识，并与多家顶尖杂志和期刊合作。门德里西奥成立建筑学院之后，他于1996年开始担任建筑师马里奥·博塔的助手，后者是建筑设计系一年级学生的教授及教导主任。

THE HUMAN MEANING OF THINGS

Gabriele Cappellato

Mario Botta has transformed his profession into a mission. Here is an architect whose work is deeply rooted in its social context, an architect prepared to make a personal stand, and to take a leading role in the redemption of the Ticino, his native land.

Botta's body of work is indeed impressive, not least because it has always embraced a vast range of subjects. The commitments he has taken on have been diverse and demanding, he has completed countless design projects, taken part in countless competitions, and completed buildings of many different kinds. These works, which include libraries, museums, churches, and houses, testify to the gradual development of the architect's language and design process.

Botta's restlessness is productive, because it is nourished by profound ideals. He constantly questions himself about the present, but above all looks to the future, despite living in an age marked by contradiction, complexities, and sometimes pure despair.

In all his research, his thinking, and his architecture, he seeks to establish a synthesis of that which already exists and the 'new' - a synthesis that will lead him towards a new equilibrium. So, in his completed works, he reveals that the only way to win the battle against the past is to respond to the present with a combination of valid references from the past and his own expressive energies.

Mario Botta gives us a limpid, modest sense of the contemporary that is unyielding, courageous, and right up-to date. This is because it is intimately bound up in the reality of life. Here everything is up for discussion. More than ever before, it is the right way to make architecture – constantly hanging and transforming, just like life itself. Stones are stones, rock is rock, the earth is the earth, the face of a woman is the face of a woman. But the meaning lies inside, within things, and things placed in relationship with others acquire new meanings: that is what life is all about. The urgency of a constant commitment, fundamental to his existence, places him at the service of society, where he is no longer the genius-inventor or creator, but the servant of the community in which he lives.

Architecture is an act transmitted across signals made of space, volume, structure and materials, and architecture understood in this way becomes a response to concrete necessities developed through everyday realities, through meeting with people, and through the interpretation of the architect, who thus can weave together the elements of ideal, thought and action.

Botta's architecture thus always adheres to the place even when it contrasts with it. Its forms are rugged and distinct; its features as essential as those of the earth from which it is born and to which it cleaves, in an intimate dialogue that resonates with relationships

Excerpted from *Mario Botta Public Buildings*, SkiraEditore, Milan 1998, pp. 205-211.

in which each part refers to the other. And again, here are geometry, study and research, straight, angular, curved and broken lines. Here again is the brute force engendered by everyday tasks in which the beauty of imagination refers to the natural aspect of the structure, the materials, and the spatial qualities that pursue each other with sudden explosions and tensions in the landscape. Here the massing is strong and secure, plans, surfaces, and walls are broken down, and light is selected as the generating, building force of the space that flows in a constant narration, expanding from within to without, and vice-versa.

As Botta has evolved as an architect, he has become increasingly convinced that the creation of space springs from the mind of the architect, and involves an imperative to search for the deepest secrets of the remote past. And yet the past that Botta seeks is not an alien, empty or superficial past. Its nature is determined by his awareness of his environment, by his constant dialogue with his surroundings.

Without this faith we cannot understand the human meaning of his approach to architecture.

Constructed Geometry

The action of building traditionally implies something sacred. For Botta, "building" means both acting and initiating a technique that becomes an integral part of his own learning process. Building is a primary, central activity of architecture. Building is equivalent to living, just as living is equivalent to giving form to space. This would seem to correspond to the structure of Botta's thinking, in which finished architecture may be considered as a specific means of defining, connecting and giving form to things. It follows from this that building is the rational reflection upon the principles and the principle of all architecture.

Mario Botta has been more coherent and consistent than any other architect in combining his thoughts and creative ideas with his own project methods into a unified system.

His goal is the rigorous selection of those compositional elements and of those syntactic relationships that are present in any created work and exhibited through order, geometry and typological clarity. Thus, the experimental aspects of building remain, for Botta, more important than the structural aspects. Consequently, once the work is built, it appears as if it had forgotten or destroyed its structure. Its image seems to stem from its immediacy and from its aesthetic and methodological force - elements that are founded on classic architectural categories such as the harmony of relationships, rhythm, balance and proportion.

His approach to his own projects always reflects his fascination with both how the "new" architectonic organism will be created and how it will function in practice. He sets, as his own point of departure and arrival, the study of, and reference to, primary forms, pure masses and elementary geometry. In this way, the building affirms, in practical terms, the work of construction, which is determined by the digging of the land, the filling in of the foundation, the laying of bricks, the building of the walls, the sense of gravity, the study of light, and the nature of the detail. His work is a global conception of architecture, in which to build means to be an integral part of the creative act, which is a fundamental and definitive part of life and of the discipline of architectonics.

The Ephemeral Nature of Buildings

Mario Botta demonstrates in his works that practising architecture means understanding, in its deepest sense, the difficult problem of construction. Architecture, while accepting the dialogue with its surroundings, also stands as a contrast to them, both becoming a part of them and simultaneously presenting its own challenge to the endurance of time.

For years Mario Botta has struggled against the weaknesses of contemporary architecture - weaknesses born out of the superficial and inconsistent thinking that we associate mainly with the fashionable, the ephemeral and the disguised - all phenomena that essentially confirm for us, in terms of idle gossip, the premature old age of today's architecture, its vulnerability, the fragile nature of its materials and the perishable nature of its elements. Botta maintains that the fascination and power of architecture stem from its capacity to transform itself from project to finished work, constraining and changing all around it in relation to the new state of life that from that moment on will develop with the new building which, in turn, will have to struggle with its own perishable nature.

Real architecture is able to pass on, with its form and its composition, its own method of constructing itself, and thus of existing. In fact, any building that succeeds at an architectonic level also succeeds at a constructive level. Botta gives full expression to this thought, in that he interprets with a modern sensibility the architect - artisan of the past - not the artisan of a nostalgic, neglected past, but one who lives fully in his own time, and in the knowledge and the awareness that the profession of building is linked to a few simple techniques that are continuously handed down in the tradition of making architecture. Botta builds by understanding construction, that is with the ability to give maximum expression to his creative and project design ideas right up to the construction itself, with extreme attention to detail.

The Typology of the Plan

The germ of the idea that guides Mario Botta in the development of all his projects and ensures that the project can assume the desired architectonic form, is a microcosm of many different concepts and techniques, which is rich enough to be capable of translating a particular moment into a constructed object.

In the age of the Renaissance, man stood at the centre of the universe. The "ideal beautiful" was provided by the totality of the work, which was created on the basis of the integration of the parts, the harmony of dimensions, and definite, precise forms to which nothing might be added and from which nothing might be taken away. It was a pure and universal geometrical order that embraced the physical space into which the architectural work had been placed. It is thus for Mario Botta, whose intimate knowledge of his craft allows him to understand, and to draw back into his memory, forms, signs and figures that belong to the past and to the tradition of architecture, to its elementary form, complete and real, and part of the life and culture of a society. His buildings are thus comprehensible and explicit, but also sometimes disconcerting in that they can leave the visitor almost surprised at their simplicity. This elemental form is not so easy to reproduce. It belies a long journey, an articulated and complex awareness that allows the architect to show architecture as he desires it to be. However, the attention of the onlooker is attracted to a recognizable and immediate order that is direct and apparently taken for granted.

The unifying and compact - almost monolithic - aspect of Botta's buildings is always balanced by a composition of "secondary" elements that are extremely well balanced in every respect. This makes his total absence of superfluity all the more apparent, and confirms the precise and perfect harmonic balance of his buildings. Thus does Mario Botta make himself the interpreter of the transition from idea to form, expressing through construction the essence of his creative journey.

In his language, geometry is the driving idea that sustains the act of planning itself, which leads to an architectonic construction that possesses its own autonomy. Through study and geometrical research he is able to confirm the origin, the concept and the dimensions of every project. In Botta's works, the design thus becomes the "choice" of precise forms, of rules that give structure to the construction, of schemes of functioning. The architect as creator draws upon his own principles, and architecture, as a discipline, is in control. Geometry is a clear reflection upon the continuity and discontinuity of language, on the duration of the elements that combine to form a finished work.

In *Versune Architecture*, Le Corbusier states that "architecture has nothing to do with styles. It solicits higher faculties". This phrase is accurately interpreted by Botta, because his architecture, rooting itself in the soil as a real, physical entity, is generated by order, work and the onerous business of building. It makes the place sacred. Geometry is the direct correspondence by which architecture reveals itself, assigning to the various masses the correct spatial relationships and the right proportions. Architecture develops according to a rule determined by lines, figures and forms, which, when brought together, constitute units of a geometric principle, and which represent intense creativity and a rigid discipline. To embark on a project is to have ideas and to fix them, ordering them so as to make them readable and communicable. It is to expose oneself; to demonstrate a precise goal; to give form to a geometric surface that transforms itself into spaces. To embark on a project is to outline a plan of confrontation, and confrontation always follows the moment of intuition. Confrontation in architecture is the acceptance of the contest fought between surfaces and masses, in a precise geographical location. If there is no sincerity or coherence, there can be no such confrontation, and consequently no good architecture that is able to endure. Botta succeeds, in his works, in being sincere and coherent, because he accepts the challenge and the contest in the full awareness that architecture can always defeat time, gossip, fashion and the critics.

GABRIELE CAPPELLATO

Gabriele Cappellato was born in Padua in 1949. In 1978 he graduated from the University of Venice Architecture (IUAV) with a doctorate and worked as a researcher in Theory and Architectural Design at the same university. In 1979 he establisned his own design studio in Padua and since then he has collaborated with several Italian and international professional studios. He has curated exhibitions in important venues in Italy and Europe. His intense architectural research led him to deepen his knowledge of modern and contemporary architecture and to collaborate with important magazines and journals. Since the establishment of the Academy of architecture in Mendrisio, in 1996, he has worked as assistant to architect Mario Botta, Professor of Architectural Design for first year students and Dean of students.

时机：光线与色彩的几何

利奥内洛·普皮

“我本来可能成为一名摄影师或画家。”马里奥·博塔曾在一场耗时很长的采访中对安东尼奥·诺力这样说道，这篇采访后来刊登在2009年11月23日的《共和报》上。“但最终我还是决定去规划和制图。我在15岁时发现建筑具有某种魔力，于是我建造了平生第一座房子。”这就是位于杰内斯特雷里奥的牧师住宅，现在看来是一个不可思议的奇迹。将这件任务委托给这位满怀抱负、还处于职业早期的建筑师的人，是“在工作室里带着他作为学徒工作”的蒂塔·卡尔洛尼。

“我每天都要前往建筑工地，检查工程进度如何以及是否按我的设想进行；我在那里也发现了许多之前并不了解的建筑技巧和工艺。此外，观察一个场所如何被改造时，我感受到了愉悦。”当然，“第一件作品的质朴生涩引发了许多语言上的质疑，由此我领悟到了创造力对一件建筑作品来说是何等重要”。的确，在他的职业生涯中，所谓的“科班学习”很大程度上是在各种类型的“建筑工地经验”中完成的。与传统从业路径相比，他的职业生涯似乎是“颠倒”的，同时又令人感到有点老式，至少是源于其故乡提契诺州历史悠久的石匠传统。这些石匠在离开故乡的山谷和湖泊之后，去往意大利以及欧洲的各大文化中心地，创造出无与伦比的辉煌成就，而他们唯一的行囊就是在锤炼基础建造技术的过程中所积累的专业工艺经验。

不要低估年轻的博塔在卡尔洛尼的工作室里所受到的熏陶，由于阿尔多·罗西的教导，工作室里充斥着新理性主义的气息，他倡导的是构成比功能更重要，提倡恢复类型学主题，并关注建筑与城市肌理之间的关系。这种风气使设计师们在建筑实践中并无顾虑，但在开始之前总是充分考量和重视场所的历史和自然遗产：乡间房屋和小型罗马式教堂一样，拥有引人注目的巨大空间；但丁·伊塞拉所言的“风景”之中有着“阿尔卑斯湖泊闪闪发光的美丽，同时也有引人入胜的悬崖峭壁”。因此，博塔早期作品中的“质朴”也就不难理解了。

说到这里，应该再谈谈博塔所接受的特殊训练：那条“颠倒之路”。他对此从不回避并相当看重，在工地上的勤勉工作使他对工作逐渐变得“贪心”。这是一种能给他带来快乐的

摘自马里奥·博塔，《建筑与记忆》，米兰：贝希特勒现代艺术博物馆，Silvana出版公司，奇尼塞洛巴尔萨莫，2013年，第86-95页。

日常习惯，还有一点好处，便是令他在开始进行学术课程之前积累了“广泛的经验”，之后形成了一种推动力、驱动力和自我需求：对于时机的控制和掌握，正是这名艺术家与众不同的能力。

在文首的那次采访中，安东尼奥·诺力颇有些挑衅地问博塔：机会对于他的成功有多大的重要性。马里奥给出了一个意味深长的回答：“机会总是扮演着很重要的角色。但我们每个人都要具有引导机会的能力，而不能只是服从于机会。也许会有一天，所有事情都可以预见的时候，你却遇到了一个预期之外的形象；此时你必须知道自己是想要使用它、发展它还是放弃它。”具备把握时机的能力是必要的，掌握这一能力需要经过训练，也需要经历尝试和失败，而这些“在学院教育体系中不可能实现，只有在技术领域中，或者在实践中才有可能实现”。只能先通过技术层面的基础学习来“塑造”艺术家，随后，他慢慢达到技术自如的境界，这时拥有了不断重复个人特色的自由，直到某些“事情”提醒他不能再进行任何改变，准确地说，他在这时候才真正地把握了时机。因此，这就是“工程师与建筑师之间的差异”（就如散文作家与诗人之间的差异、插图画家与画家之间的差异等）。工程师在“既定”时间内进行测量与计算，而建筑师则根据自己的时机进行“判断”，因此建筑师的工作并不是核实，而是创造。这一过程是“年少的博塔从自由的绘图桌奔向建筑工地的过程”，是“持续学习的领域”，是“艰难、回报丰盛、时而却十分严酷的尝试”，在建筑空间中留下了不可磨灭的印迹。其中，时机所能做到的无非是将所有“错误状态”排除在外，最终成就一种“正确状态”。

马里奥在米兰的学习使他获得了进入大学的必要学历，随后在选择到哪里进修大学课程时，他毫不犹豫地选择了威尼斯。在那里，他有幸遇到了一位重量级人物：朱塞佩·马扎里奥，并与其成为朋友。马扎里奥不仅教授艺术史，也管理着这座城市的一个文化机构：奎里尼·斯坦帕利亚基金会。他是那个引领博塔深入了解威尼斯的人，并向博塔解释道：“所有非同寻常的城市都是艺术作品：没有哪座城市像威尼斯这样具有开放性和无穷无尽的可读性”。正由于威尼斯不完整的城市形态结构，所以它并不适合呆板的沉思，而是适合即时的参与。因此，“在所有的城市中，它可能是最现代的一座，因为它从来也不像佛罗伦萨一样‘古典’，它始终保持开放的形态直至现在，如时代的诗篇，因色彩与节奏而显得独特。”“这座城市不能以传统思路去理解成封闭的形态”，它是“生机勃勃”的，其现代性的秘诀在于它在时代与自身形态之间进行身份定位的能力。

随着年轻的博塔对威尼斯越来越熟悉，他情不自禁地感受到“空间连续性的表达以及城市主体价值的表达”，从而确定了他不可撼动的信仰：建筑“不是在某个地方建造，而是建造这个地方。建筑需要以某个地方独有的方式来表达它的特点、身份和起源”，而这需要“致力于回忆领域”。

出于上述原因，博塔在全球化混乱初现征兆时便抵制了后现代主义的诱惑。他轻视后现代主义，因为它将风格与历史混为一谈，从而把历史变成了讽刺漫画，因为它对回忆的需求仅限于重现表象与体积；至于全球化，他抨击的是其否定场所概念，抨击其宣告历史的终结。在这种情况下，他开始认识到对于空间组织的需求中包含了人类的生存，也包含了永续的伦理和美学要素，这使他意识到建筑师清晰明确的社会责任，并因意识到这一责任由于自己身在历史之中而被证实。

为此，马扎里奥促成了这位来自提契诺的年轻天才与勒·柯布西耶的会面。马扎里奥强烈希望这位威尼斯的“巨擘”能够参与规划位于边境的一座新医院——这一定能激动人心，令世人震撼。最后的重点是，自马里奥初涉建筑界开始就指引着他的“对现实与自然的敏感”日渐成熟，使他在威尼斯再一次通过个人交往获得了更多的关注和建议。

首先是和路易斯·康的交往，当时，这位来自爱沙尼亚的大师前往威尼斯参与国会中心的规划，但没有成功。博塔夜以继日地伴随着他，逐渐发现“他的力量、直觉与智慧”，并坚信他扮演着“20世纪建筑文化的救世主”角色。

之后是与卡洛·斯卡帕的交往，他指导马里奥直至其毕业。他近乎偏执地关注细节，具有严格的工匠精神和贵族般的优雅，令马里奥折服。当然还有他围绕有机空间直觉所进行的持续而执着的实验，在他看来，这样的直觉并非源于深思熟虑，而是源于身处其中。

一方面，近20世纪60年代末时，如果博塔在所谓的学术训练阶段没有克制住参与独立设计的做法，另一方面他的作品不可能不受到学生时代经历的影响，这种影响虽然是持续的。但是，类似斯塔比奥住宅这样创作于1965年，并于两年后面世的作品，虽明显是在“向勒·柯布西耶致敬”，其中却仍然隐含有未来原创作品的基因（内部空间的多层结构；用灯光而非造型塑造空间关系；使用未经修饰的钢筋混凝土；强化几何构成的张力），这些种子都将在清朗碧绿的山丘和光线弥漫的提契诺萌发，繁荣于70~90年代他的一系列杰作之中。其中第一件作品是位于卡代纳佐的住宅，1970~1971年间创作并建造而成。

博塔的住宅作品随后接二连三地问世，仿佛创造力和想象力取之不竭。这些作品总是位于自然和历史景观的关联之中，从未有所偏差。建筑以一种真实的、新鲜的、开创性的、建筑诗学般的开放形式进行实体建造，创造出一种极富原创性的语言，以几何、色彩与光线之间的辩证逻辑为特点。因此，应当将位于普乐嘉桑那、马萨尼奥、维加内罗、莫尔比奥、瓦卡洛、达罗和贝尔纳雷焦的建筑，与诺瓦扎诺的公寓建筑、兰希拉建筑、格塔多银行和卢加诺的五大洲中心、巴塞尔的瑞银集团总部、卢加诺的嘉布遣会修道院图书馆、维勒班的视听图书馆、东京的和多利美术馆、尚贝里的剧院和安德烈马尔罗文化中心、蒙哥诺的圣乔瓦尼巴蒂斯教堂、波代诺内的奥德利柯小教堂和萨尔迪拉纳的圣彼得教堂相比较。

事实上，这些作品是他20余年以来所取得的建筑成果。在这期间，博塔要了解与解决最为复杂多样的类型学问题，将其凝结在具有明显原创性和建筑诗意的作品之中，同时逐渐确立了拥有多变形态的一种几何语言的基本结构，这一语言永远不可能固化在某个纯粹的、封闭的单体造型之中，它将在光线中经受考验，被险要的、戏剧化的、充满活力或是已有的时机所激发，基于自然和历史场景而建立。因此，正如先前所言，这样的一种语言无法用抽象化的存在逻辑进行表述，要证实某种理念的存在，首先需要自证其存在的可能性，随后在其存在过程之中不断地通过穷尽、图形化、建筑实验及误差来证明其存在的意愿。

因此，我们面临这样一个过程：当艺术创作的质量从不断调整的状态转化为不变的，可以说是新柏拉图式的标准，并与适当功能的道德需求联系在一起时（“一座房屋——也可能是一家酒店、一座办公楼、一家银行——构成它的不仅仅是那几平方米的面积”，这是博塔在采访中将与诺力探讨的内容），事实上，他除了追溯与重现以外，什么也做不了，重要的是这一场所的此时、此地，建筑不是在某个地方建造，而是建造这个地方（马里奥的这番表达值得反复强调），以此融入到历史的河流之中。

不过，这一态度显然在他建筑实践的前20年，从提契诺州走向整个欧洲，与富饶的历史和记忆交流的这一时期得到了更多应用。“当你参与锡耶纳、威尼斯和阿姆斯特丹的建造时，感觉仿佛置身天堂。这些城市是对历史最正式的表达。”当建筑师的活动变得日益全球化后，马里奥在90年代初期或多或少需要面临的情况是迷失方向（失去时间感或空间感），这可能是毁灭性的，可能导致妥协和逃避，沦为不负责任的后现代主义，即使以讽刺的态度来进行实践。但这“只在文学方面是有趣的，如果用在石头和水泥上，可能导致很严重的问题”，因为“建筑是无法逃避的”，是“不能像某个项目一样在人们不喜欢时被叫停，或是像一本令人失望的书一样被扔到一边”。

那又该如何？如何在建筑理念遭遇全球化挑战的时代，接受国际建筑师的身份，在全球范围内承接项目？比如想一想“在韩国，花费整整几个小时在一座建筑年龄不过30年的城市里穿行”，同时还必须忍受对马克·欧杰提出的那些现代空间中的“非场所”式典型建筑的厌恶。

博塔的回答听起来令人惊讶，却也令人信服，其重要性可在罗韦雷托和旧金山（加州）的博物馆案例陈述中得以证实。

在第一个案例中，建筑师关心的是通过衔接并强调街道的连续性来代入城市所在的时代，阿尔贝蒂和德尔格拉诺两座历史建筑的前景可比照历史上的本蒂尼大道，分隔两者的街道融入一个圆形广场，广场由表面光洁的三层楼围拢而成，通过明确的功能闭合空间。在第二个案例中，博塔需要在一处沉寂的建成区内进行建造，为避免与环境相冲突，他选用陈旧的材料、石头和砖块构筑起平行六面体建筑，他弃用了传统的立面，代之以巨大的视野，捕捉耀眼的户外自然光线并将其引入内部。对于博塔而言，当以“国际建筑师”身份面临他所谓的沙漠——这个任何角落都会出现狂热客户的全球化世界时，会有某种推动力鼓舞着他，在沉默的漩涡之中，在可能的风险之中发挥自己的作用，在未来即将成为过去之时为其指引方向（这往往是一场赌博）。

如果是这些压倒性的“表达需求”“超越任何理由和风险的因素”使得马里奥独树一帜（他本人也认可），它们却与自负的“明星建筑师”开拓式的傲慢态度毫无关联甚至大相径庭。这更多地是一种伦理态度，在博塔看来，是美学研究所不能够忽视的。很显然，这也包含着将宗教意识看作“文化挑战”，这种挑战是建筑师面对教堂和犹太教会堂的显著问题时加诸于自身的。因此，如果他能够将第二个和第三个千年之间最真实的宗教空间表达传递给我们，他必定会意识到宗教意识必与当下相关，建筑师面对的是世俗问题。因为存在是记忆和历史的实体，存在并不排斥对神秘事物的认识：存在既是开端，也终将不朽。

利奥内洛·普皮

1931年生于贝卢诺，1958年毕业于帕多瓦大学艺术系之后一直在系里担任中世纪艺术史的助理讲师，至1966年。1964年获得中世纪与现代艺术史博士学位，担任建筑与城市规划史讲师，后又担任艺术史科目的讲师。他曾是专科学校的艺术史主任（1972~1973年），随后在艺术史研究院任职（1974~1978年）；1974~1990年间，他担任建筑与城市规划史讲师。1990年，他成为威尼斯卡佛斯卡利大学的教员，并担任多项职务；除此以外，他也曾是现当代艺术史的专职教授、文化遗产保护学位课程主席、艺术史系主任及艺术史方法论教授。2005年成为艺术史方法论名誉教授。曾担任国外多家大学的讲师以及多个重大国际团体和意大利与国外机构的咨询顾问。作为研究人员先后在哈佛大学、佛罗伦萨的塔蒂别墅和华盛顿的敦巴顿橡树园开展多项研究活动，并前往普林斯顿和日本担任访问学者。他曾是多项重大艺术展览的策展人，并负责协调多个国际研究会议；曾是多家科学期刊的编辑人员，并在数本重要的国际杂志上发表文章。他的研究成果发表在超过一千本刊物上，主要研究方向集中为14~20世纪的威尼斯文明以及艺术收藏、文献版本、城市规划、景观、园林等和维罗纳、帕多瓦、维琴查、威尼斯、布宜诺斯艾利斯、蒙德维的亚和巴西利亚的建筑文化等课题。他曾于1985~1987年间担任意大利共和国的参议院议员，目前是前议会成员协会文化委员会的成员。

GEOMETRIES OF LIGHT AND COLOR; IN TIME

Lionello Puppi

"I could have become a photographer or a painter – is what Mario Botta told Antonio Gnoli in a long interview, published in the daily 'La Repubblica' on November 23, 2009 - but in the end I decided to draw and plan. At the age of 15 I discovered that building had some kind of magic. And I built my first house": which turned out to be the incredible surprise of the parish house in Genestrerio, a task commissioned to the aspiring architect in his early adolescence by Tita Carloni, who had "taken him on to work as an apprentice in his studio".

"Not a single day would go by without me going to the construction site to check that work was in progress and being carried out the way I had planned it, and there discover building techniques and processes I had not known about up to then. And, furthermore, I could feel the pleasure and emotion in observing how a *place* was being transformed". Of course: "with all the linguistic doubts due to the *naivety* of the very first work, but nonetheless with the awareness of the role of the creativity present in a work of architecture". And, indeed, in his career, the so-called institutional studies were anticipated by wide-ranging "building site experience". His journey appears to be "inverted" compared to the customary path, but it is at the same time reminiscent at least of the multiple and centuries-old history of the stonecutters from his small homeland Ticino, who achieved supreme and glorious success in the major cultural centers in Italy and Europe after leaving the valleys and the lakes of their native land, their only baggage being the artisan expertise accumulated through the practice of the basic building techniques.

It would be superficial to underestimate the atmosphere that teenage Botta had to breathe in Carloni's studio, permeated by neo-rationalist humors fuelled by Aldo Rossi's teachings, claiming the primacy of composition over function, the recovery of the typology issue, and paying attention to the relationship with the urban texture. Such a climate exhorted to a lack of scruples in the composition practice, but before that, to the consideration and admiration of the historic and natural heritage of the *place*: the rural houses as well as the dramatic spatiality of the small Romanesque churches; a "landscape", according to Dante Isella, with the "sparkling and nearly Manzonian air of the Pre-Alpine lakes and the sharp and at the same time friendly mountain cliff sides". Consequently, Botta's initial "naivety" is only apparent.

And this aspect deserves a note that recalls the peculiarity of Botta's training: the "inverse path", which he himself has never failed to point at with the appropriate emphasis and the assiduous presence on the building site which developed with a "greediness for doing", bound to become a joyful daily habit, but that in the meantime represented a privileged

Excerpted from Mario Botta. *Architecture and Memory*, Bechtler Museum of Modern Art, Silvana Editoriale, Cinisello Balsamo, Milan 2013, pp. 86-95

occasion to accumulate a "wide-ranging experience" before starting his academic course of studies, and that would subsequently become an urge, an ineludible, binding need: the conquest, and practice of *timing*, i.e. the ability that distinguishes the artist.

When Antonio Gnoli provokingly asked Botta to what extent chance had counted for him, in the interview we have taken the cue from, Mario gave an eloquent answer. "Chance always plays an important role. But every one of us has to be able to orient it. You cannot simply succumb to it. One day everything seems to be predictable, then you come across an image that you were not expecting; at that point you have to know if you want to use it, develop it or let it be": and it is necessarily the ability to master *timing*, the achievement of which requires a training and a trial and error period that "cannot take place in the academic-school system, but on the technical field, so to say of practice: the artist can only 'form' by learning the trade in the most technical sense of the term, until he reaches that technical automatism that grants him the *freedom* to repeat his colors incessantly, until 'something' warns him that he cannot change anything anymore: that he has seized the *timing,* precisely". Therefore, this is all there is to "the difference between the engineer and the architect (just like between the prose writer and the poet; the illustrator and the painter; et cetera), for example. The engineer measures and calculates within a 'given' time; whereas the architect applies the 'discretion' of his own *timing*": and therefore he does not verify, he creates "through that process which was already the rush of teenage Botta from the drawing table, where he felt at ease on his own, to the building site", "territory of constant learning", "a difficult, rewarding but sometimes also unforgiving attempt" to *become* irreversible and indelible in architectural space: where, eventually, *timing* cannot do anything else but exclude any "wrong gesture" to materialize as a "right gesture".

When Mario, upon concluding the studies in Milan which gave him the necessary degree to enter university, has to choose the location for his university career, he will not hesitate to recognize Venice as the place of his choice. There he had the *chance* to meet and become friendly with a volcanic figure who taught art history, but also directed one of the city's cultural institutions, the Foundation Querini Stampalia: Giuseppe Mazzariol. He was the man who could introduce Botta to the depths of Venice, explaining to him that if it is true that "all non-common cities are works of art: no other city has such an openness, an inexhaustible interpretability like Venice". Thanks to the incomplete structure of its shape, it is not the object of mere and inert contemplation but rather of immediate participation. As such, "it is possibly the most present city among all: because it has never been a 'classic' city – such as, for example Florence; it has always been and still is an open shape,

versed in *time*, thus sorted out in color and rhythm", and "the city cannot be understood by means of classic contemplation, as a closed shape", it has to be "lived", since the secret of its *modernity* lies in its power of identification between our present time and its shape. And as young Botta's familiarity with Venice gradually increased, he could not help perceiving an "expression of spatial *continuum* and therefore of a mainly urban value", and reach the irrevocable conviction that architecture "is not the tool to build in a place, but to build *that* place. It has to take into account its features, its identity, its being origin, in its own way", and this leads "to working on the territory of memory".
Along these lines and from the very beginning, Botta exorcised the obscene seductions of the song of the mermaids of post-modernism in the omen of the vertigo of globalization. Of post-modernism he despised the confusion of styles with history, thus turning it into a caricature, and a need of memory limited to the remake of the tympanum and the column; of globalization he denounced the negation of the concept of place and the proclamation of the end of history. This is the moment he became aware of the need, in the spatial organization of human *Lebensraum*, of the indissolubility of the ethical and esthetic components; which entailed a lucid and ineludible consciousness of the architect's social responsibility, precisely verified by his awareness of being in the time of history.
In this respect, the meeting of the young talent from Ticino with Le Corbusier - brought about by the usual Mazzariol, who had vehemently wanted the "giant" in Venice to plan the new hospital *on the borders* - must have been exciting, or even shocking. Last but not least, the ripening of the "sense of reality and of nature" that had guided Mario upon his debut in architecture will find further solace and suggestions in Venice; once more through personal meetings.
With Louis Kahn, when the Estonian master arrived in Venice to plan the congress center, without success. He stands at his side day and night, progressively discovering "his strength, intuition, intelligence", convincing himself that he "was a messianic figure of twentieth-century architectural culture".
Then with Carlo Scarpa: he will take Mario to his graduation, fascinating him with his almost obsessive attention for detail, a combination of rigid artisan probity and aristocratic elegance; with his unspent and stubborn attention to the graphic testing of his *organic* spatial intuitions, as they claimed not to be staged in a dimension to be contemplated, but lived in.
If, on the one hand, Botta did not refrain from his independent design work during the period of the so-called academic training, which approached the end of the sixties, on

the other hand, his work could not fail to be affected by the events the *student* was experiencing, almost enduring: and yet, a work like the residential house in Stabio, invented in 1965 and realized two years later, though being an evident "tribute to Le Corbusier", conceals the germs of future original developments (the multi-story structure of the interior; the in-between connections created by light effects rather than plastic elements; the use of unpolished reinforced concrete; the tension aimed at dynamizing the compositional geometry): seeds that would blossom between the mild, green, rolling hills and in the quiet diffused light of Ticino, during the seventies and in the following decade up to the nineties, in a sequence of true masterpieces, inaugurated by the family house in Cadenazzo, invented and realized between 1970 and 1971.

And, one after the other, the houses, with an inexhaustible effusion of creative imagination but always in the relationship with the natural and historical landscape, which was never sidestepped, will materialize and lead to the creation of an extremely original language in the open form of an authentic, and new and innovative, architectural poetry, characterized by dialectics of geometry, color and light. Thus, the buildings in Pregassona, Massagno, Viganello, Morbio, Vacallo, Daro, Bernareggio, have to be reviewed and compared to the apartment building in Novazzano, the Ransila building, the Banca del Gottardo and the Cinque Continenti Center in Lugano, the UBS headquarters in Basel, the library of the Capuchin Convent in Lugano, the audiovisual library in Villeurbanne, the Watari-um gallery in Tokyo, the theater and André Malraux Cultural Center in Chambéry, the churches San Giovanni Battista in Mogno, Beato Oderico in Pordenone, San Pietro Apostolo in Sartirana.

In fact, these works are the result of about two decades of architectural activity; during this, while having to tackle and realize the most manifold and elaborate typology issues, resulting in works of unmistakable originality and authentic architectural poetry, Botta gradually defines the basic structure of a geometrical language with variable shapes, which are never prospectively fixed in the purely contemplatable absolute of a closed plastic *individuum*, temporally tested in light and aroused by the *timing* hazard - and, therefore, dynamic, active, existential - which they establish with the natural and historical *site*. Thus a language, as we have already stated beforehand, that cannot be expressed by abstractions in the logic of being, fixing the certainty of an idea, but bound to justify itself first and foremost as being capable of materializing, with the will of *being* and through and at the head of an exhausting, graphic and building trial and error, in the time of existence. We are hence faced with a process that, in the moment it detracts the artistic quality of the result from the adjustment to an eternal and, so to say, neo-platonic canon, and

connects it to the ethical need for the correct function ("a house - but it could also be a hotel, an office building, a bank - it is not only the square meters that constitute it", is what Botta will say in his interview with Gnoli); he cannot do anything else but retrace and realize it, in fact, in the *hic et nunc* of a *place*, since - and it is worthwhile reiterating a recurring expression used by Mario - doing architecture does not mean building *in a* place, but building *that* place, thus going down in the temporal flow of history.
Now, however, it is evident that such an attitude had a privileged opportunity of being applied in the first two decades of activity which, progressing from the universe of Ticino to the European scale, dealt and communicated with a territory rich in history and memory; "when you go to build in Siena, Venice, Amsterdam, you feel as if you were in paradise. These cities are the formal expression of history". But when the activity of the architect becomes *global*, and this is a condition that Mario will start facing, *more or less*, in the early nineties, the disorientation (no time, no place) could have been devastating; it could have caused the capitulation or the escape in the irresponsible expedients of post-modernism, even though acquired and practiced with irony. But this "is interesting only in literature. If done in stone and concrete it can turn into a serious problem" because "architecture is ineludible" and "cannot be switched off as if it were a program you don't like or put on the side like a disappointing book".
So what? how is it possible to accept the condition of global architect, willing to take on a supranational clientele, in a time when the subjection to a global point of view of architecture is challenged, in the consideration that - for example - "in Korea you can travel for hours and hours within a city where the oldest building is thirty years old", and in the disgust for the spaces of a contemporaneity, which *representing* the *non place*, according to Marc Augé denies time; and memory?
Botta's answer sounds surprising and convincing, and its importance can be perceived by observing the elaboration of the *Museum* issue in Rovereto and in San Francisco (California).
Now, in the first case, the architect is concerned with entering the *time* of the city, by

connecting and emphasizing the *continuum* of the streets - by making the street that separates the two *historical* buildings Alberti and del Grano, whose prospects look on the *historical* Corso Bettini, flow into a circular square, sealed by the bright discourse of the walls of the three stories, which enclose the spaces with explicit functions, whereas in the second case, having to build within an inert built-up area, he avoids any confrontation with it, by choosing *old* materials, stones and bricks, that realize the assembly of the parallelepipeds constituting the building, by even denying the façade, replaced by the great *eye* that catches the dazzling *natural* outdoor light to channel it into the interior paths. In Botta, when he happens to be faced, as "global architect", with the deserts where he is called to by a furiously active clientele in every single corner of the globalized world, there is a sort of tension which animates him to play in a place where there is only a whirling silence of absence, the hazard of a possible present, capable of orienting a future (which is always a gamble) in the moment it develops into a past.

If this pertains to the overwhelming "need for expression", "stronger than any reason, than any risk" that distinguishes Mario (and that he himself recognizes), it is nevertheless unrelated, indeed contrary to any temptation of the colonizing arrogance that moves the conceited "star architect". It rather belongs to an ethical attitude that, in Botta's opinion, esthetic research cannot ignore. Which, obviously - and eventually - includes the awareness of the sacred as a "cultural challenge"; a challenge that the architect has imposed upon himself by facing the explicit issues of the church and the synagogue. And so, if he has entrusted some of the most authentic expressions of religious space between the second and the third Millennium to us, he is aware that the consciousness of the sacred must be present even when the architect faces *civil* issues, because existence, which materializes in memory and history, does not exclude the awareness of mystery: which is threshold and eternity.

LIONELLO PUPPI

He was born in Belluno in 1931 and graduated in 1958 from the Arts Faculty at the University of Padua, where he was assistant lecturer in the History of Medieval Art from then to 1966. In 1964 he earned his Doctorate in the History of Medieval and Modern Art and was lecturer of the History of Architecture and Town Planning, then lecturer of the historical subjects of art. He was director of the Scuola di specializzazione in History of Art (1972-73) and then at the Institute of History of Art (1 974-78); from 1974 to 1 990 he was lecturer of History of Architecture and Town Planning. In 1990 he was appointed to the staff of the University of Ca' Foscari in Venice, where he had various functions; among those he was full-time professor of History of Contemporary and Modern Art, president of the degree course in Conservation of Cultural Property, director of the Department of History of Arts and professor of Methodology of History of Art. In 2005 he was appointed emeritus professor in Methodology of History of Art. He was also a lecturer at several foreign universities and member and consultant of important international bodies as well as of Italian and foreign institutions. He carried out periods of research as fellow at Harvard University, Villa Tatti in Florence and at Dumbarton Oaks in Washington, then as visiting scholar in Princeton and in Japan. He was curator of important art exhibitions and coordinator of international study conventions; he was on the editorial staff of scientific journals and published articles in major international magazines. His works of research have appeared in over one thousand publications, concentrating on Venetian civilization from the 14th to the 20th centuries, art collection, editions of historiographical sources, on town planning, landscape, gardens and the topics of architectural culture in Verona, Padua, Vicenza and Venice and also in Buenos Aires, Montevideo, Brasilia. He was Senator of the Italian Republic from 1985 to 1987 and is a member of the Cultural Commission of the Association of ex-Parliamentarians.

居住空间
LIVING SPACES

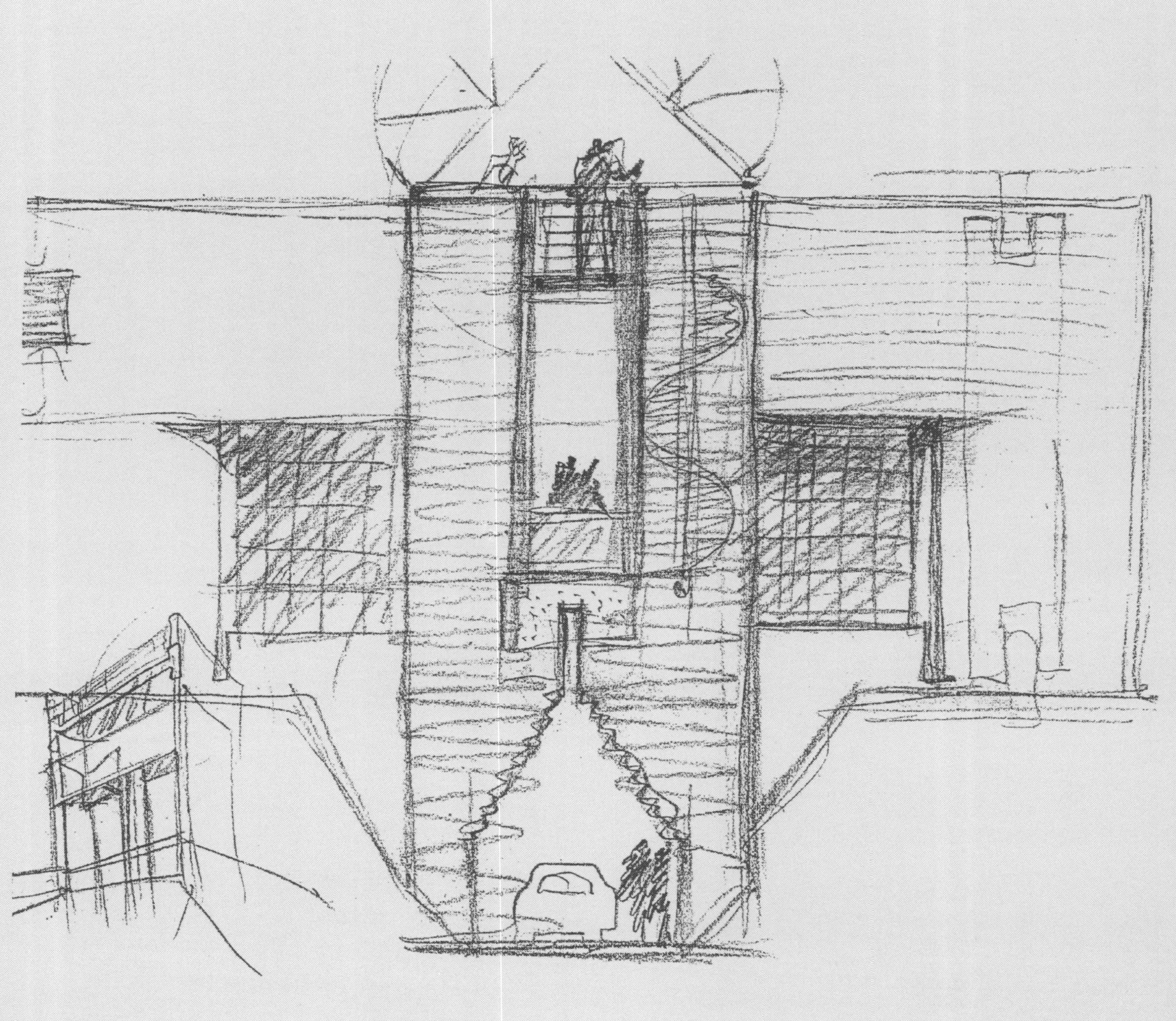

牧师住宅
瑞士，杰内斯特雷里奥

PARISH HOUSE
GENESTRERIO, SWITZERLAND

1961-1963

项目时间：1961年
建造时间：1962～1963年
顾问：提塔·卡尔洛尼
委托方：杰内斯特雷里奥教区
占地面积：750 平方米
建筑面积：190 平方米
建筑体积：900 立方米

Project: 1961
Construction: 1962-1963
Consultant: Tita Carloni
Client: Parish of Genestrerio
Site area: 750 m²,
Useful surface: 190 m²
Volume: 900 m³

这个项目的产生缘自原有教区牧师住宅的拆除，因杰内斯特雷里奥村庄主干道的拓宽所致。新的牧师住宅背倚教堂，全部由琢石建造而成，通过柱廊凸显出与教堂相连的广场。除了两个相反的坡屋顶，建筑主体严格顺应了原有的地形特点，以屋顶斜坡呼应地形的起伏。广场一侧的建筑入口处具有连续不断的水平混凝土线脚装饰，并形成了与众不同的挑台、门廊和房间。

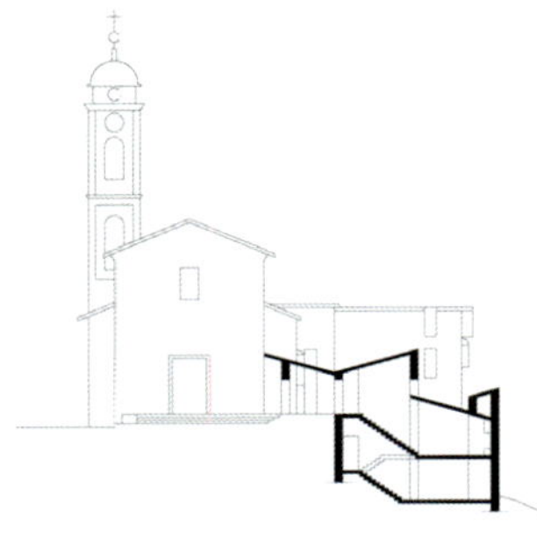

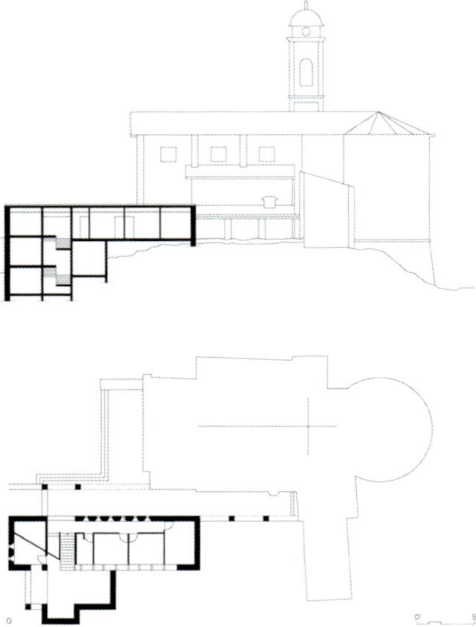

The project came about as a result of the demolition of the old parish house, caused by the widening of the main road passing through the village of Genestrerio. The new parish house leans against the Church and is entirely built in cut stone. It enhances the square joined to the neighboring church by a colonnade. The primary volumes articulate the composition in precise relationships that, except for the two opposing roof structures, follow the lay of the land with the slope of the roof. The empty spaces individuate the loggia, the portico and the rooms, where the concrete architrave runs uninterruptedly in the long horizontal cut of the principal opening.

© ENRICO CANO

© ENRICO CANO

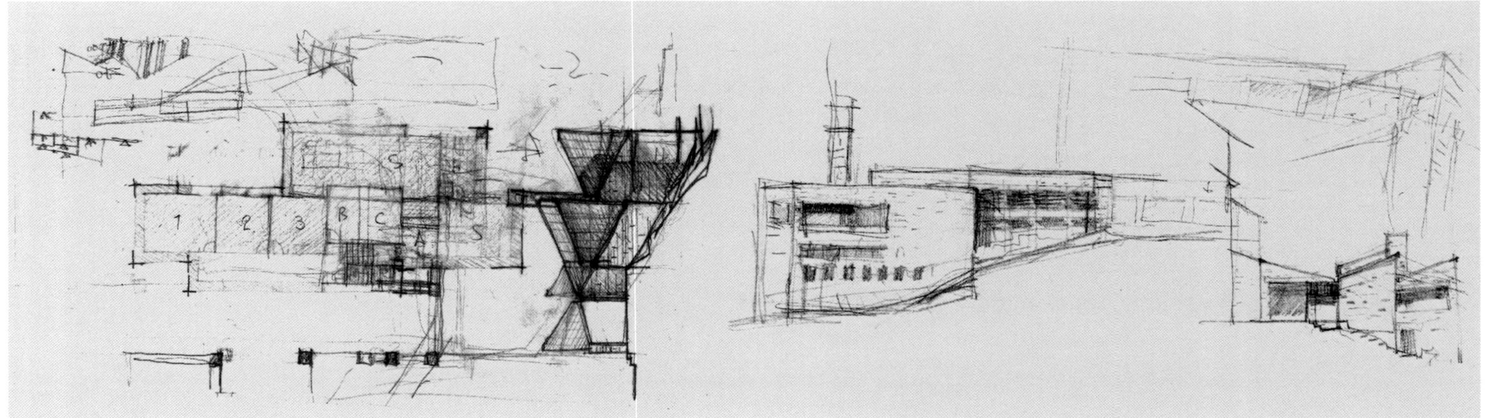

独栋住宅

瑞士，斯塔比奥

SINGLE-FAMILY HOUSE

STABIO, SWITZERLAND

1965-1967

项目时间：1965年
建造时间：1966～1967年
委 托 方：里诺·德拉卡萨
占地面积：1,200 平方米
建筑面积：240 平方米
建筑体积：1,200 立方米

Project: 1965
Construction: 1966-1967
Client: Lino Della Casa
Site area: 1,200 m²
Useful surface: 240 m²
Volume: 1,200 m³

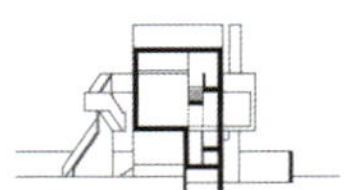

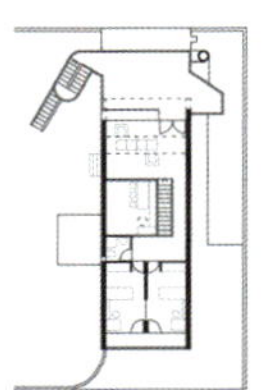

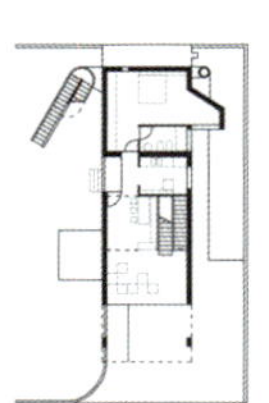

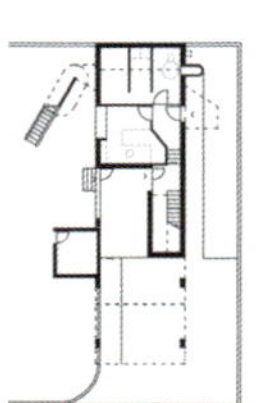

这栋住宅建在城镇中心北部一个长方形地块上，连续的墙体划定了建筑与乡村的边界。该住宅被视为“居住的细胞”，它从北立面开始沿着地块的短边展开。两道平行的墙体限定出建筑的室内空间，墙体两端分别有一个狭窄的北侧开口和一个宽敞的南侧开口。在其另一侧，建筑向东完全敞开，通道和狭小的开口被大面积的玻璃取代。住宅共分为3层：底层为带有游戏室的入口门廊、服务空间和储藏空间；二层分布有起居室、用餐空间、卫生间、厨房和主卧室；围绕着二层通高挑空空间的则是顶层的书房和儿童房，这里可以通往朝西的露台。

The house rises to the north of the town center, on a rectangular site delimited by a continuous wall that defines its borders with respect to the countryside. Thought of as an "inhabited cell", the house is laid out behind the north façade, along the smaller side of the lot. Two parallel lines control the interior development of the building, incised by a narrow opening to the north and by a more ample one to the south. In contrast, the house opens up toward the east; the cuts and the small openings are replaced by a glass plane. The dwelling is organized on three levels: on the ground floor the entrance portico with a playroom, the services, the storage areas; on the second floor, the living room, the dining area, the bathroom, the kitchen and the master bedroom; on the upper floor – around the two-story central space – the study and the children's bedrooms, leading to the west-facing terrace.

© ENRICO CANO

© ALO ZANETTA

© PAOLO PEDROLI

独栋住宅

瑞士，卡代纳佐

SINGLE-FAMILY HOUSE

CADENAZZO, SWITZERLAND

1970-1971

项目时间：1970年
建造时间：1970～1971年
委托方：福尔维奥·卡恰
占地面积：950 平方米
建筑面积：270 平方米
建筑体积：1,150 立方米

Project: 1970
Construction: 1970-1971
Client: Fulvio Caccia
Site area: 950 m²
Useful surface: 270 m²
Volume: 1,150 m³

建筑沿南北向中轴线坐落在切耐里山的北面山坡上，建筑中的室内空间与外部景观巧妙地融合在一起。建筑东侧的视野完全封闭，西侧则被玻璃砖墙分割为几个相同的单元。两个短面的结构形成了独特的建筑构图，巨大的圆形开洞建立起室外空间和两个廊式过渡空间的联系。室内空间的连续性贯穿整个3层建筑：从门廊后的入口可以进入起居室，二层设有两个小型游戏室和书房，可以纵览下层空间和上层露台，卧室则位于顶层。

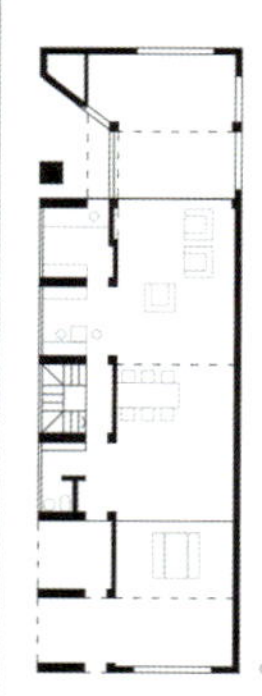

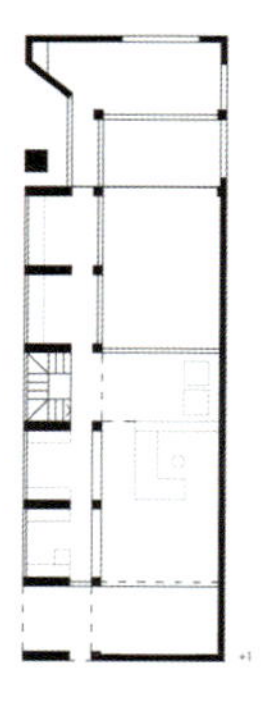

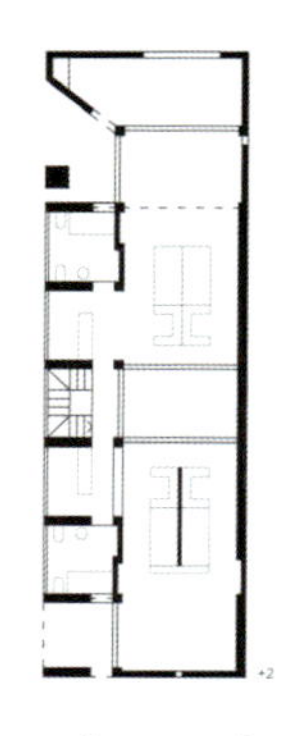

Set on a slope on the north side of Monte Ceneri, the house is laid out along the north-south axis, to best relate the interior space to the landscape. The view to the east is completely blind, while to the west there is a glass block wall, divided up into equal sections. The composition is controlled by the two short ends of the structure, where large circular openings establish a relationship between the exterior and the intermediary spaces of the two loggias. The spatial continuity of the interior is articulated over three floors: from the entrance – preceded by the portico – one enters the living room; the second floor is reserved for two small playrooms and a study that looks out over the space below and the terrace of the raised floor. The top floor houses the bedrooms.

© ALO ZANETTA

© ALO ZANETTA

© MAURIZIO PELLI

© ALO ZANETTA

© ALO ZANETTA

© MAURIZIO PELLI

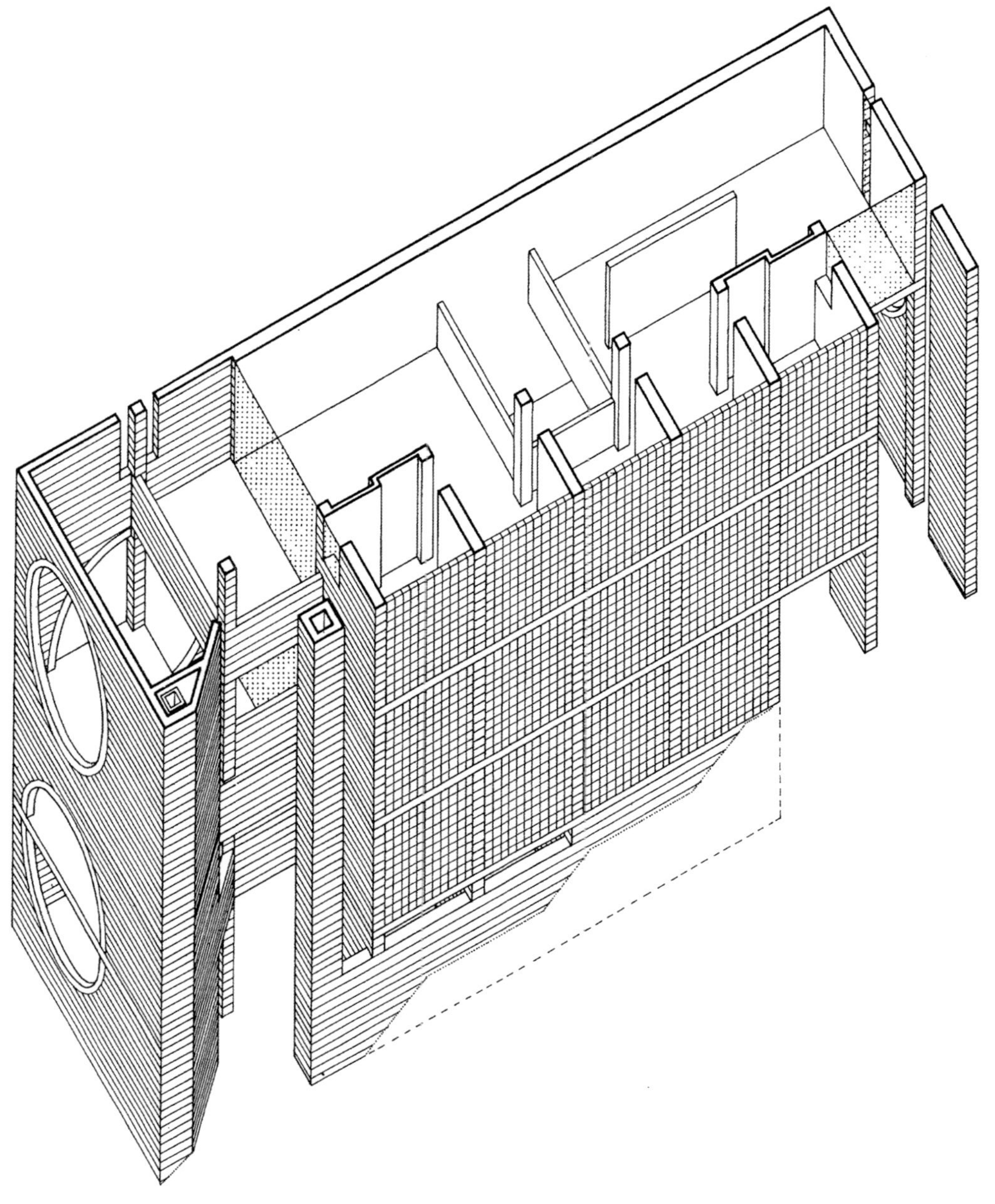

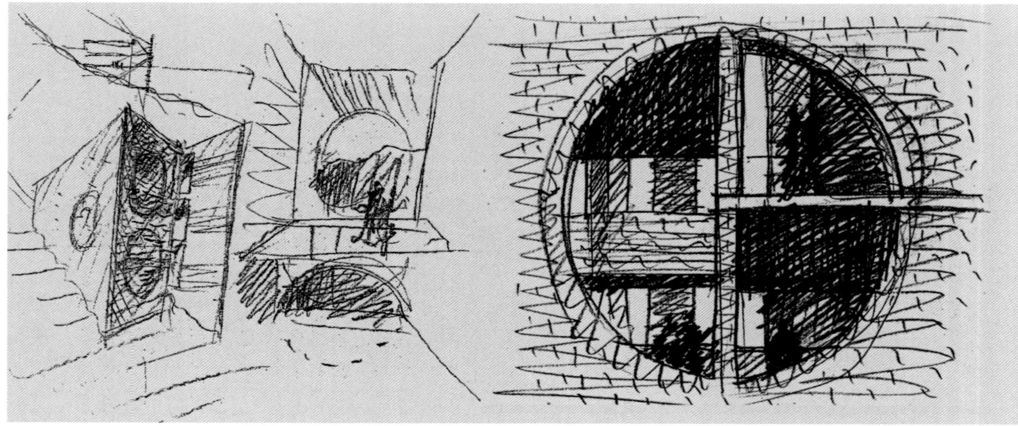

© MAURIZIO PELLI

独栋住宅

瑞士，圣维塔莱河村

SINGLE-FAMILY HOUSE

RIVA SAN VITALE, SWITZERLAND

1971-1973

项目时间：1971年
建造时间：1972～1973年
委托方：莱奥汀娜和卡尔洛·比安奇
占地面积：850 平方米
建筑面积：220 平方米
建筑体积：1,000 立方米

Project: 1971
Construction: 1972-1973
Client: Leontina and Carlo Bianchi
Site area: 850 m²
Useful surface: 220 m²
Volume: 1,000 m³

该建筑位于老村中心靠北环山道路的边缘。道路的北面是一片树林，勾勒出地平线。住宅坐落在地势较低的部分，多层布局构成类似“塔”的形式，与周边地形形成一种辩证关系。一座刷成红色的小型金属桥通向住宅，整栋房子使用了简单、常见的建筑材料：墙壁使用双层混凝土砖，仅将内部漆成白色；地板则为赤陶材料。住宅的功能分区以垂直的维度展开：在建筑上部，也就是第四层，分布着大厅、书房和通向下层的楼梯；三层是主卧；儿童房则设在二层。这些空间部分开敞并与底层的起居空间相连。

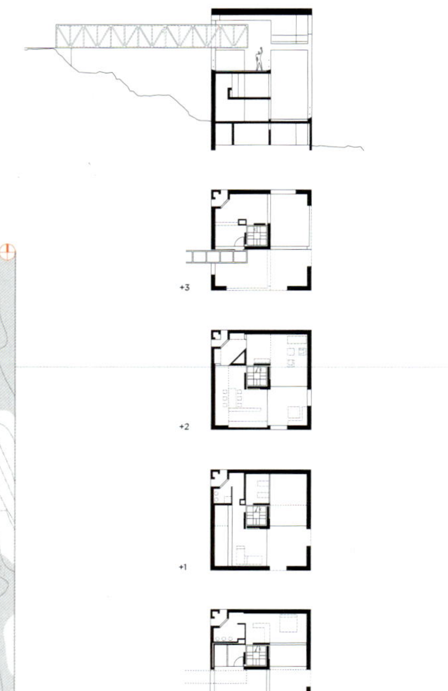

The site lies to the north of the old village center, on the edge of a village road which runs along the mountain slope. Beyond the road, to the north, stretches a wood which delineates the horizon. The house is set in the lower part of the plot and laid out on different levels like a "tower", so as to establish a dialectic relation between the house and its orographic context. A small metal bridge, painted red, leads to the house. The whole house is built with simple and common materials: the walls consist of blocks of double-thick concrete and are painted white only on the inside, the floors are in terracotta. The vertical dimension is maintained even in the functional distribution: in the upper part, corresponding to the third level, there are the hall, the study and the staircase leading to the lower floors. On the second level there is the master bedroom whereas the children's bedroom is on the first floor. These spaces are partially open and linked to the living area on the ground floor.

© MARCO D'ANNA

© MARCO D'ANNA

© ALO ZANETTA

© ALO ZANETTA

© ALO ZANETTA

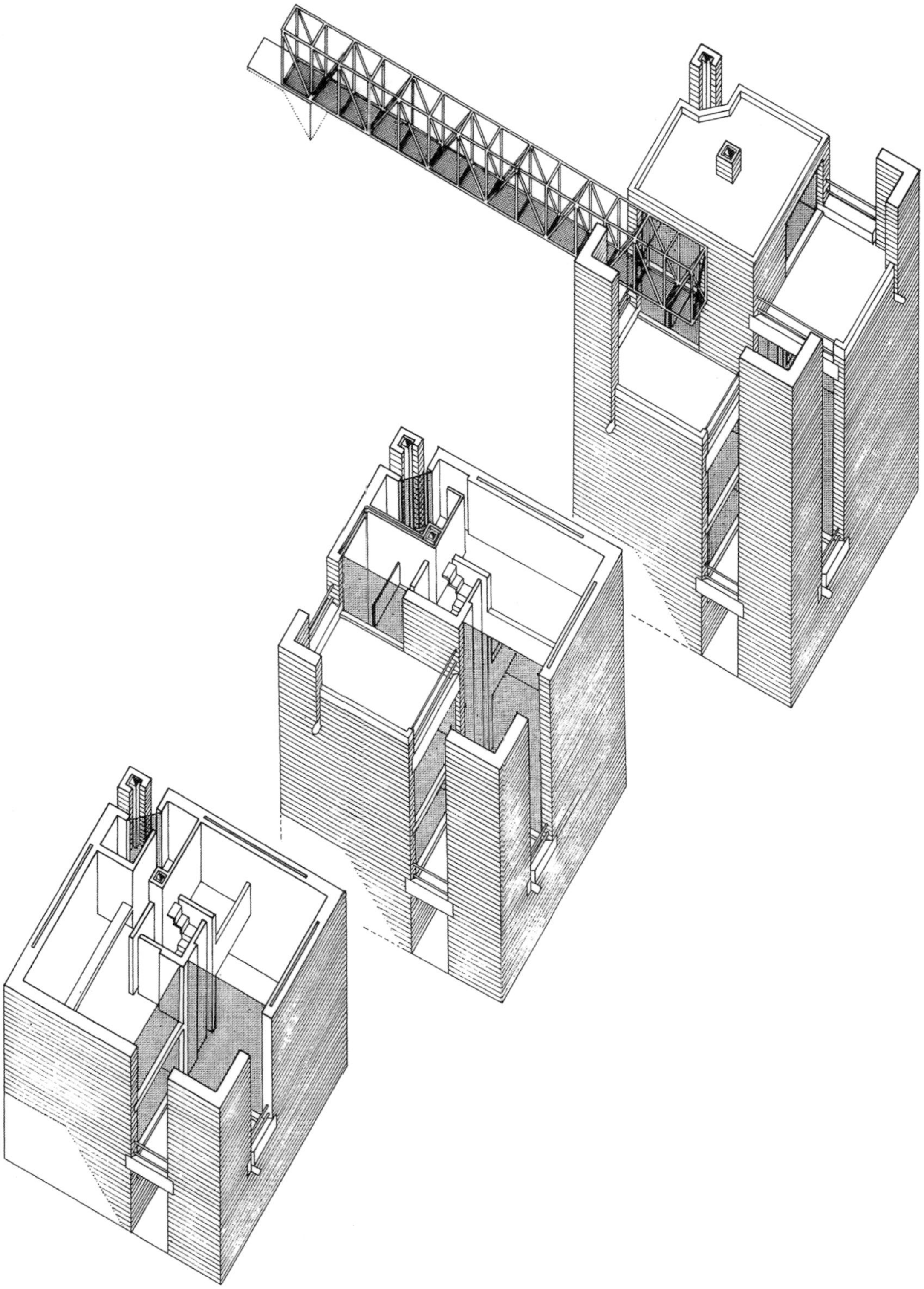

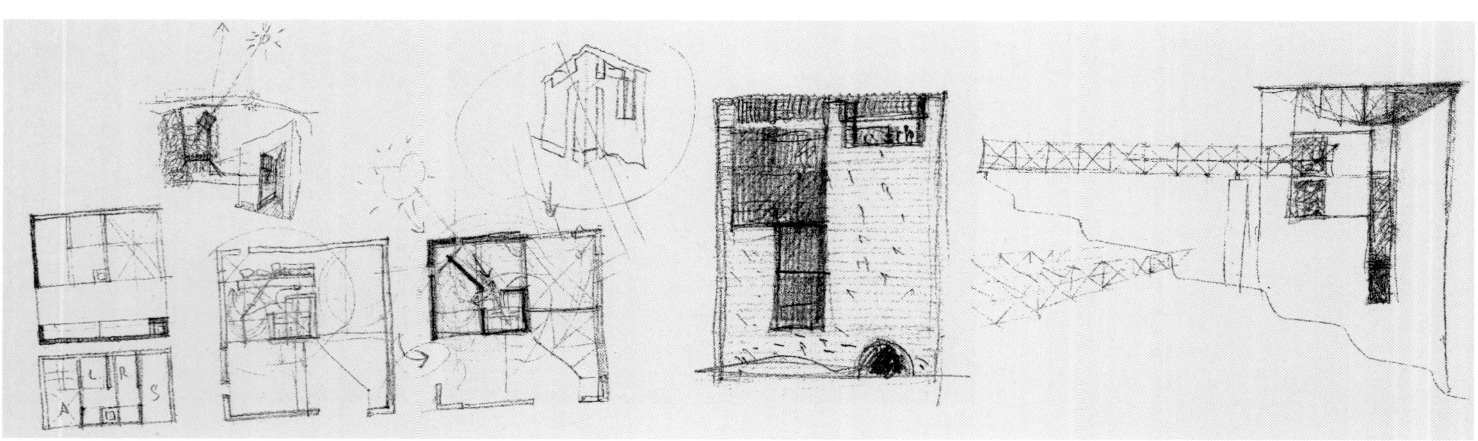

独栋住宅

瑞士，利戈尔内托

SINGLE-FAMILY HOUSE

LIGORNETTO, SWITZERLAND

1975-1976

项目时间：1975年
建造时间：1975～1976年
委托方：朱赛皮娜和达尼洛·比安奇
占地面积：1,800平方米
建筑面积：180平方米
建筑体积：900 立方米

Project: 1975
Construction: 1975-1976
Client: Giuseppina and Danilo Bianchi
Site area: 1,800 m²
Useful surface: 180 m²
Volume: 900 m³

建筑的构想是由两片墙体框定出一座独立的、厚重的扁平建筑物。建筑体量结实，面向野外的立面被一条垂直的中央狭长开口打破，朝向村庄的一面则分成两个横向体块，两个体块高度不同，它们之间被玻璃窗和阳台隔断。建筑分为3层：门廊、入口和地下室位于底层，客厅、厨房和儿童房设在二层，主卧室和工作室则位于顶层。西侧的门廊是该侧惟一的出入口，两道纵向狭缝突出了位于两面墙之间的壁炉，东侧的墙体被两间儿童房的阳台隔断。建筑采用双层混凝土块墙体，外立面的砌块每3层为一组，形成灰色和淡红色交替的水平条状饰面。

The building, conceived as a single, thick screen, is bound by two walls; its compact volume on the side facing the countryside is broken only by a thin vertical cut in the center, while toward the village it opens into two lateral blocks. The space between them, on different levels, is given over to glass windows and balconies. The house has three floors. The porch, the entrance and the cellar are on the ground floor; the living room, the kitchen and the children's bedroom on the first; the master bedroom and the studio on the last floor. The only opening toward the west is provided by the porch, while two thin vertical cuts underline the presence of the fireplace located between two walls. Toward the east the wall is cut by the balcony of the two rooms for the children. The building has walls made of concrete blocks of double thickness. The layer of blocks on the outside consists of three bands made of strips of alternating color, grey and reddish.

© ALO ZANETTA

© ALBERTO FLAMMER

© ALO ZANETTA

© ALO ZANETTA

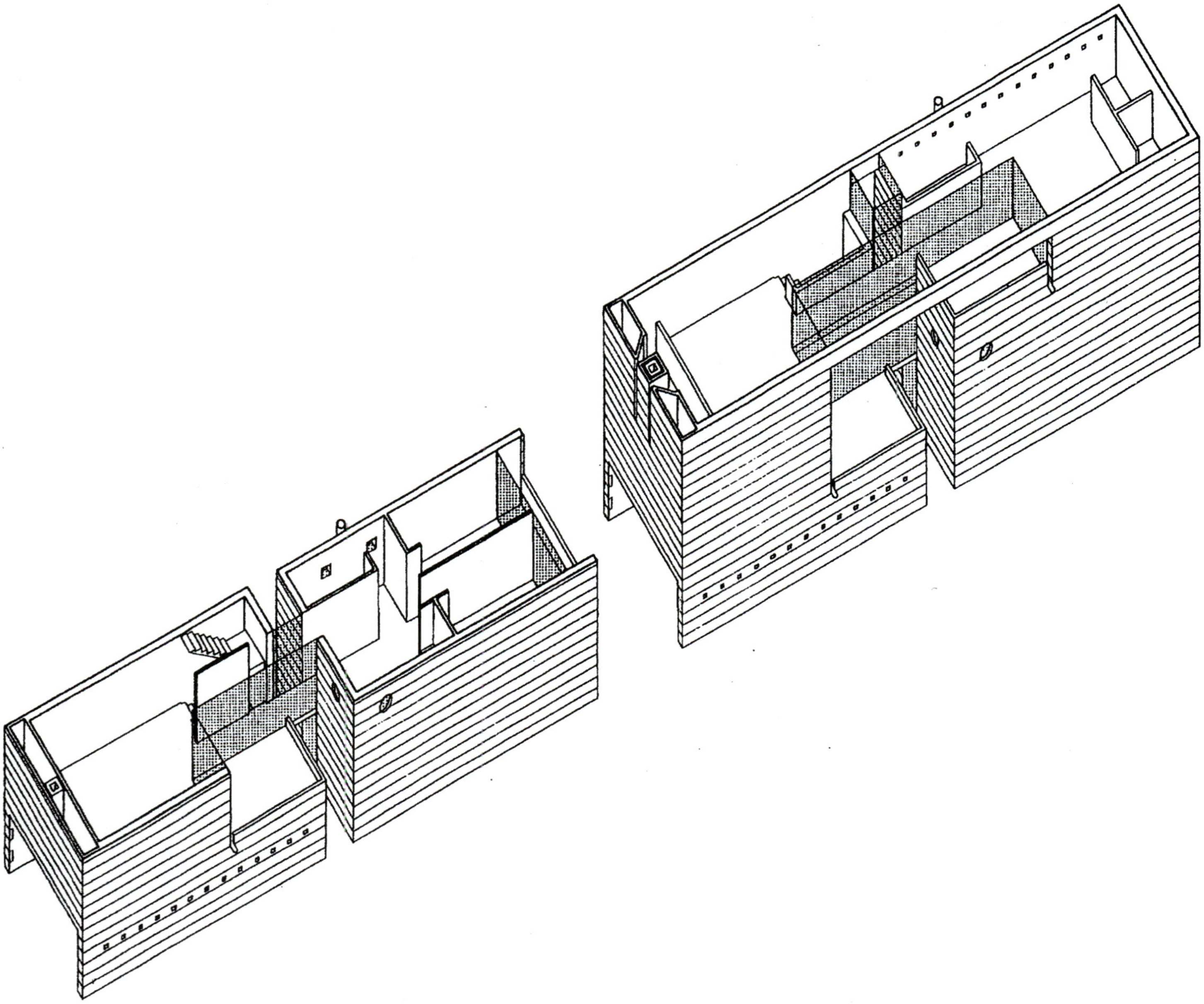

独栋住宅

瑞士，普乐嘉桑那

SINGLE-FAMILY HOUSE

PREGASSONA, SWITZERLAND

1979-1980

项目时间：1979年
建造时间：1979～1980年
委托方：莉莉安娜和多明戈·桑皮埃特罗
占地面积：600 平方米
建筑面积：260 平方米
建筑体积：1,100 立方米

Project: 1979
Construction: 1979-1980
Client: Liliana e Domingo Sampietro
Site area: 600 m^2
Useful surface: 260 m^2
Volume: 1,100 m^3

这座建筑坐落在卢加诺北部山坡住宅区中的一小块土地上。立方体建筑的正立面被深邃的开口在垂直方向上分割，愈高愈窄，直至正中顶部的天窗。半圆柱形楼梯位于建筑轴线上，从北部凸出于建筑立面之外，北立面后侧则是服务空间。入口门廊位于一层；二层为起居室以及面朝南向和西向的餐厅；顶层设有书房和带有露台的卧室。

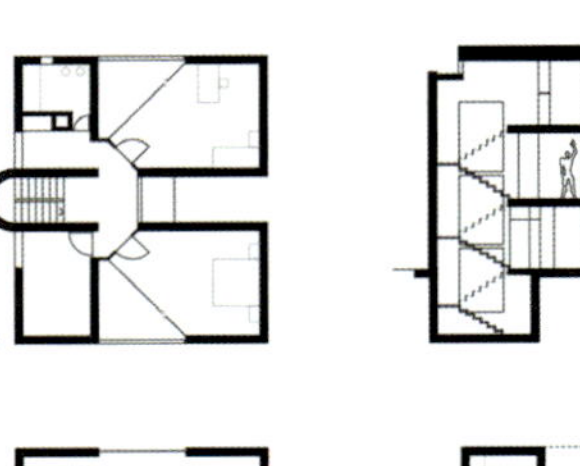

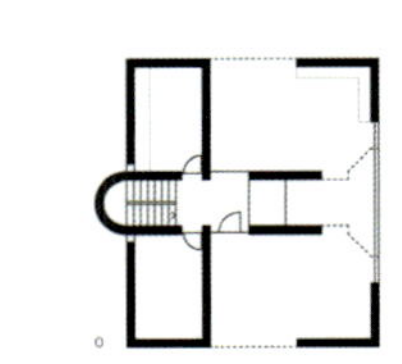

The building is located on a small piece of land on a hillside north of Lugano, amid a residential area. The cubic volume is vertically excavated out of the principal façade by deep openings that tend to close off toward the top before terminating in the roof skylight over the central space. The semicylindrical stairway element is the organizational axis of the house and emerges from the north façade, along which the services are laid out. The porticoed entries are on the ground floor; the second floor holds the living room and the dining room with its windows facing the south and the west; the top floor holds a study and the bedrooms with a terrace.

© ALO ZANETTA

© ALO ZANETTA

© ALO ZANETTA

© ALO ZANETTA

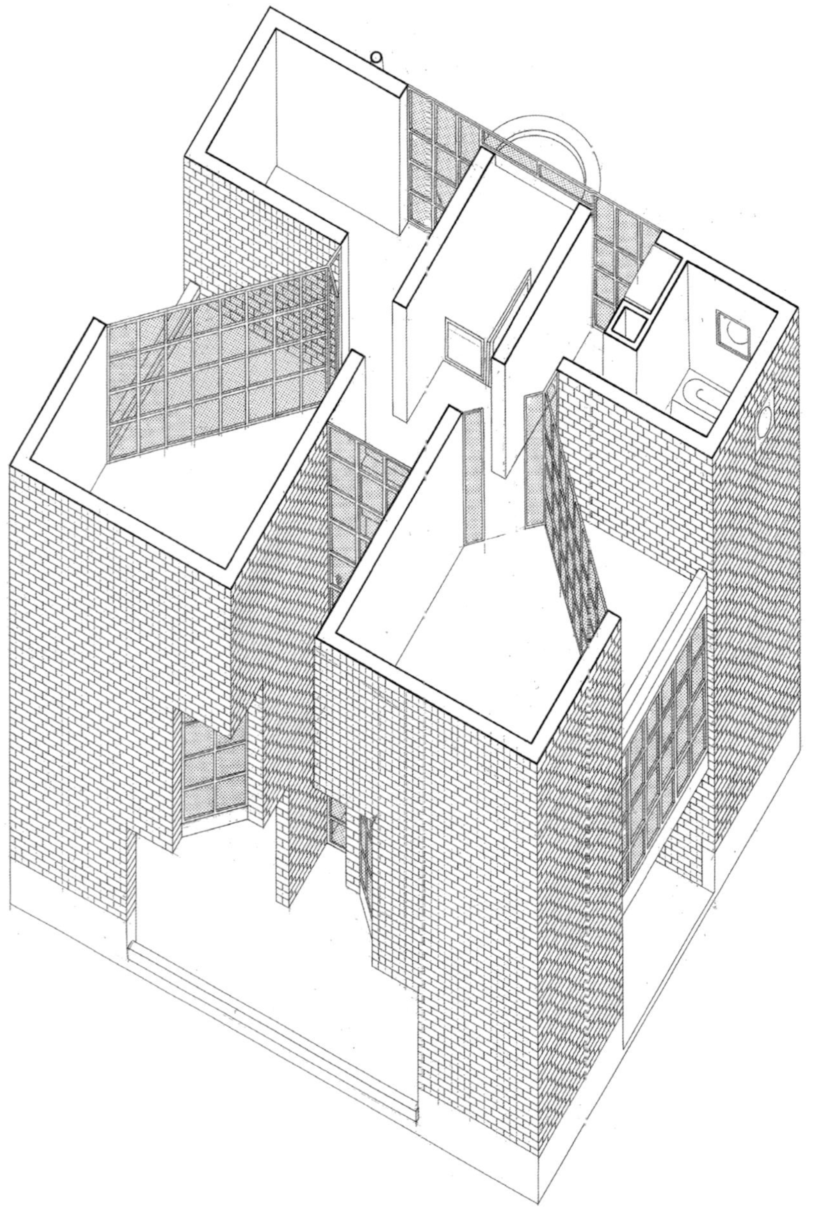

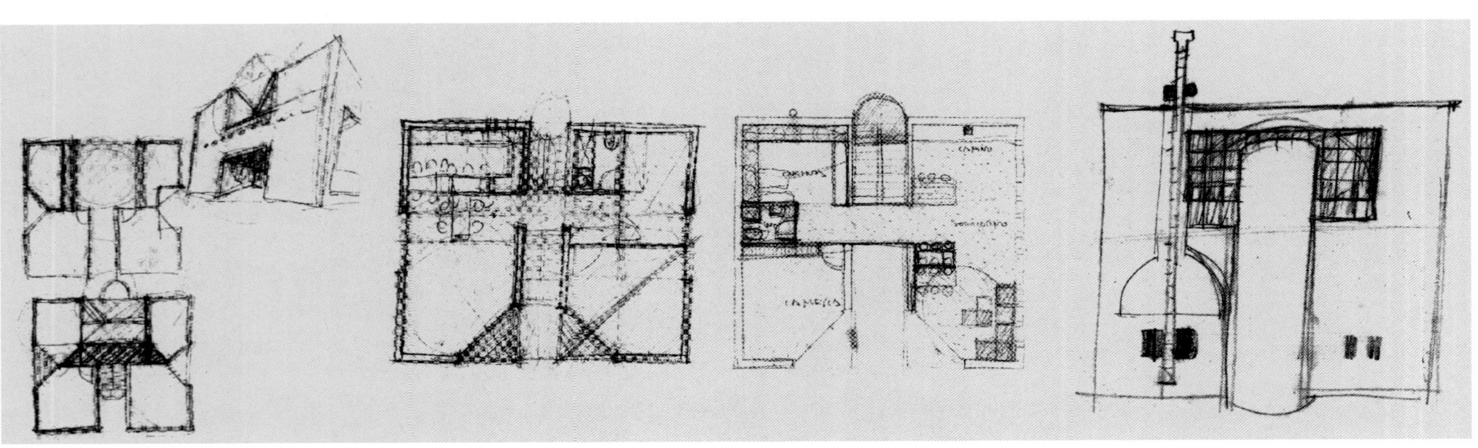

独栋住宅

瑞士，马萨尼奥

SINGLE-FAMILY HOUSE

MASSAGNO, SWITZERLAND

1979-1981

项目时间：1979年
建造时间：1980～1981年
委托方：玛丽埃拉和赫利奥斯·罗比亚尼
占地面积：620 平方米
建筑面积：300 平方米
建筑体积：1,300 立方米

Project: 1979
Construction: 1980-1981
Client: Mariella and Helios Robbiani
Site area: 620 m²
Useful surface: 300 m²
Volume: 1,300 m³

这栋住宅坐落在卢加诺附近的山坡上。分割了东部立面的圆形开口连接起不同的内部空间，交替的粉色和灰色砖块使立面极具特色。建筑的中轴线使空间的纵向连续性更加清晰：双向开放的阳台，向内退进的玻璃墙以及向外探出的楼梯间贯通起3层空间：一层为入口中庭，立面45度切角标示出地下室位置；二层是起居空间；三层则为面朝下方空间的卧室区域。

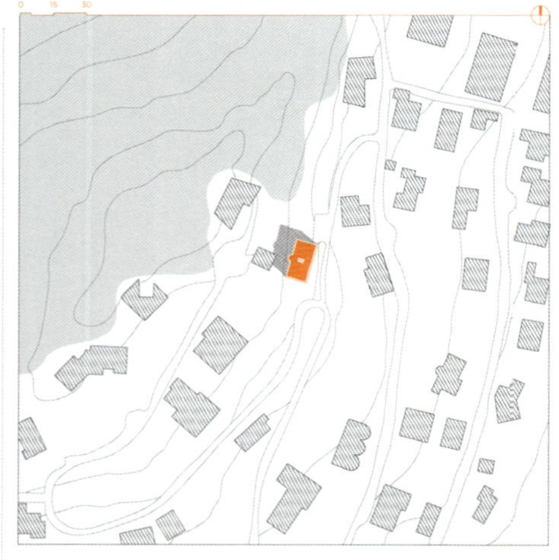

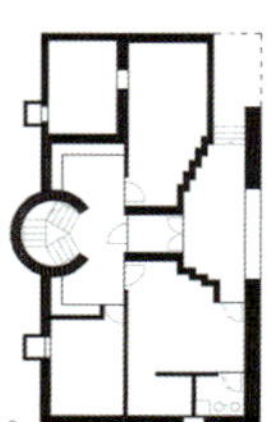

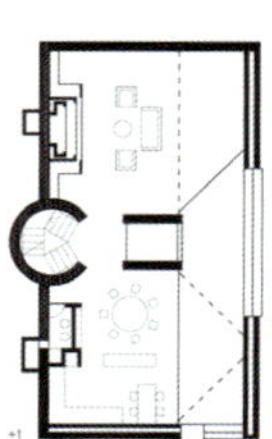

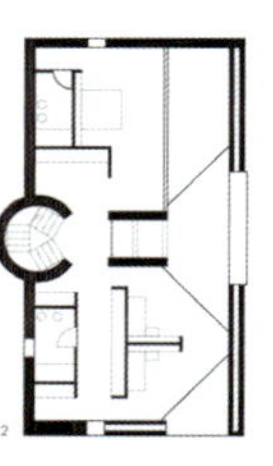

The house rises on the slope of a hill near Lugano. A circular opening, spatially uniting the various interior spaces, is cut out of the plane of the east façade, which is individuated by alternating courses of pink and grey bricks. The central axis articulates in depth a succession of spaces: the loggia open on both sides; the recessed glass windows and the stairwell, which juts out towards the exterior and connects the three levels: the ground floor with the entrance atrium carved out of the basement and marked on the façade by a corner cut at 45 degrees; the first floor with the living area and the second floor with the sleeping area, facing into the space below.

© ALO ZANETTA

© ALO ZANETTA

© ALO ZANETTA

© ALO ZANETTA

© ALO ZANETTA

© ALO ZANETTA

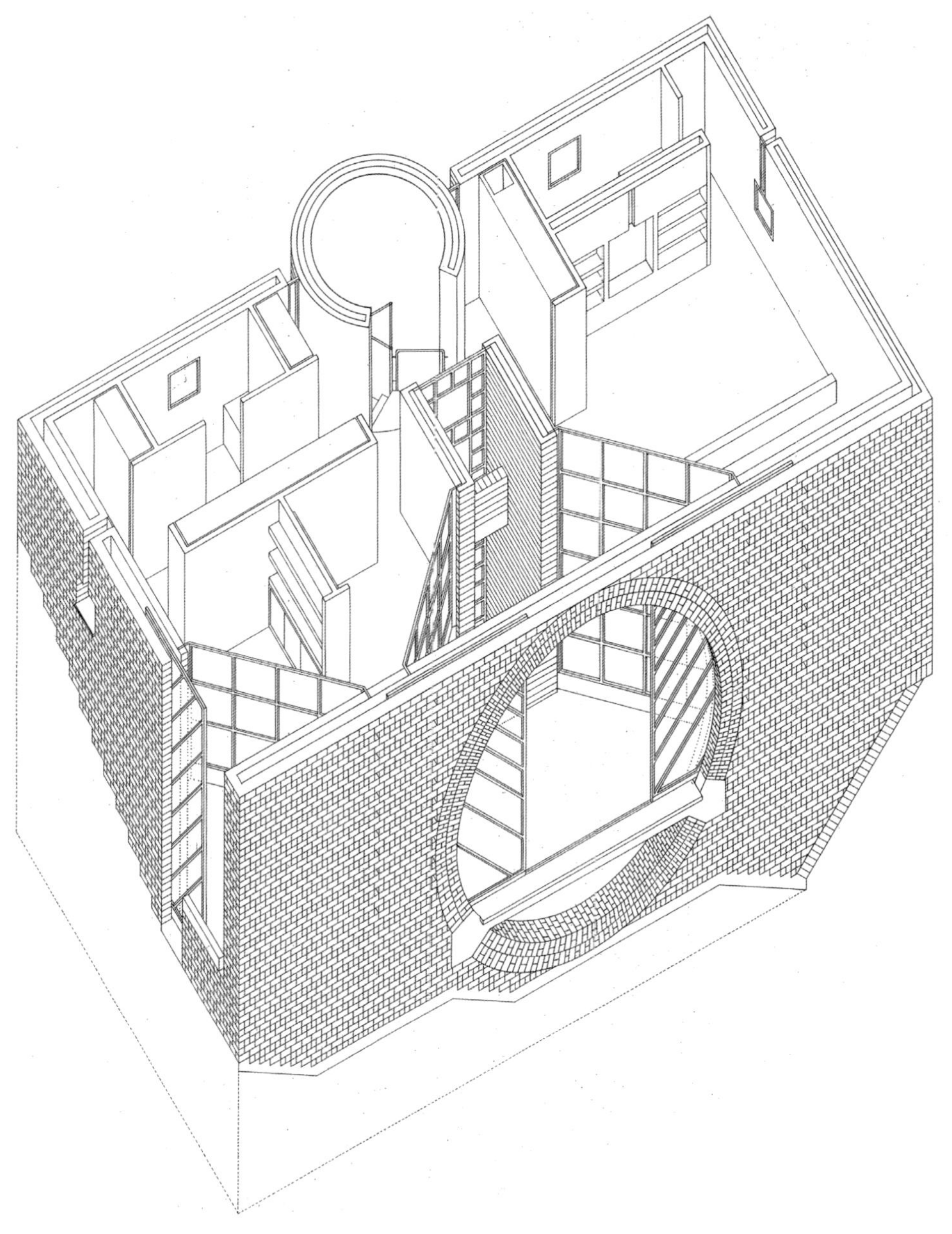

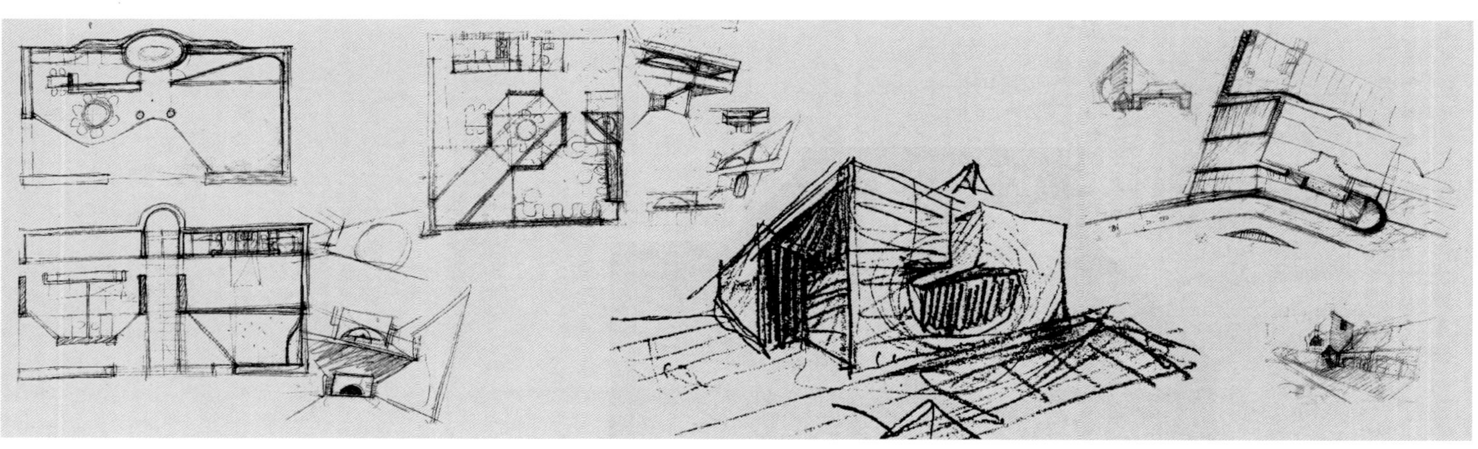

独栋住宅

瑞士，维嘉内罗

SINGLE-FAMILY HOUSE

VIGANELLO, SWITZERLAND

1980-1981

项目时间：1980年
建造时间：1980～1981年
委托方：西尔维娜和汉斯皮特·佩福利
占地面积：1,050平方米
建筑面积：225平方米
建筑体积：1,000立方米

Project: 1980
Construction: 1980-1981
Client: Silvana and Hanspeter Pfäffli
Site area: 1,050 m²
Useful surface: 225 m²
Volume: 1,000 m³

建筑坐落在面向卢加诺市的山坡上，一条步道从公路通向住宅。从一个小型的圆形休息台，经过几级踏步便可到达住宅的三角形主入口。入口内的一根立柱贯通了上下层的楼板，正面用混凝土砖呈45度角铺就，并装有一扇通至玻璃拱顶的大型可移动玻璃窗。宽敞的拱形门廊构成了一个由具备不同功能的3层空间所围合的中心区：一层是入口门厅和辅助空间，二层是起居空间，三层则是卧室区域。

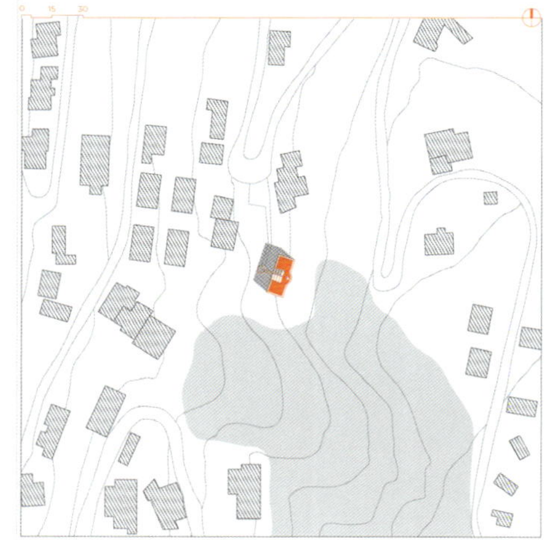

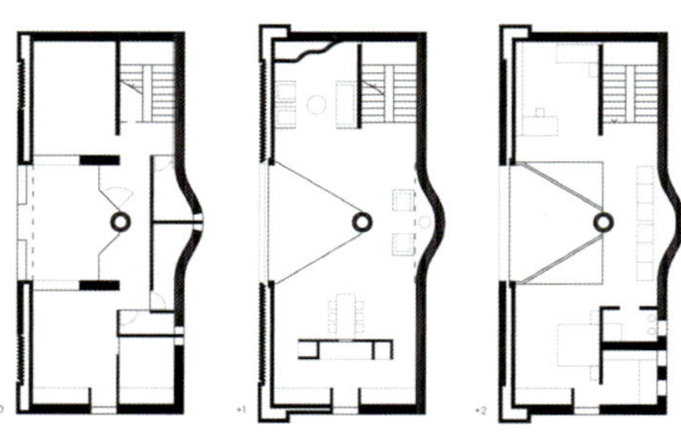

The property on which the house is located slopes toward the city of Lugano. A walk leads from the road to the house. From a small circular lay-by, a few steps lead to the triangular-shaped entrance with the central column piercing the horizontal floors. The blind front, clad in concrete blocks of 45 degrees, is interrupted by a big mobile window ending in a glassy vault. The wide arcaded loggia becomes the centre around which the different spaces, distributed on three levels, are organized: at ground floor the entrance hall and the secondary spaces; on the first floor the living area; on the second floor the sleeping area.

© LORENZO BIANDA

© ALO ZANETTA

© ALO ZANETTA

© ALDO BALLO

© ALDO BALLO

© ALDO BALLO

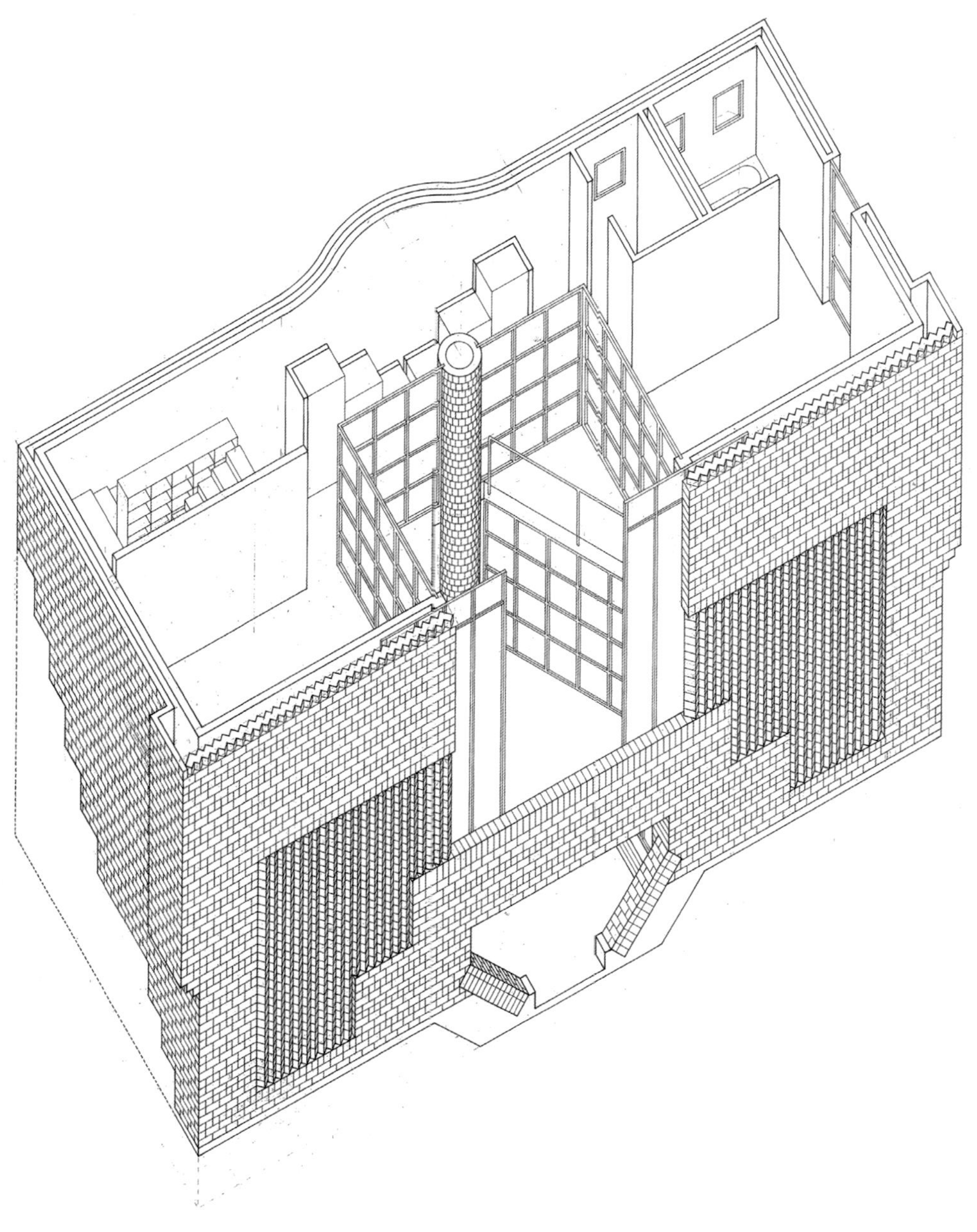

独栋住宅

瑞士，斯塔比奥

SINGLE-FAMILY HOUSE

STABIO, SWITZERLAND

1980-1981

项目时间：1980年
建造时间：1980～1981年
委托方：莉莉安娜和奥维迪奥·美蒂奇
占地面积：700平方米
实用面积：295平方米
建筑体积：1,400立方米

Project: 1980
Construction: 1980-1981
Client: Liliana and Ovidio Medici
Site area: 700 m^2
Useful surface: 295 m^2
Volume: 1,400 m^3

建筑采用圆形平面，因此没有明确的正立面。一条深深的凹槽标示出南北轴线，也明确了峡谷中的建筑朝向。在建筑南面，凹槽将天窗与两条侧面开口连通；在建筑北面，圆柱体楼梯间打破了圆形外墙的连续性。建筑分为4层：设备及服务用房设于地下；一层为门廊和入口；二层为起居室，三层设有卧室。

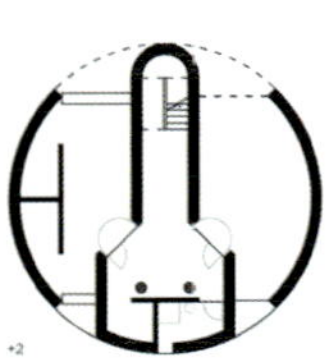

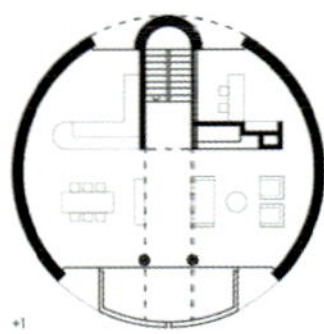

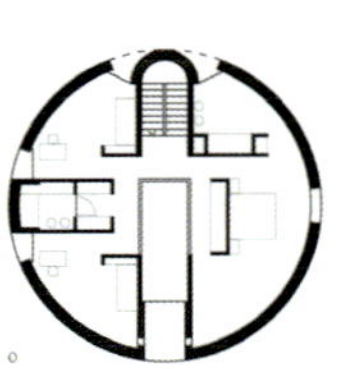

The house has a circular layout and thus it has no real façade. The north-south axis, marked by a deep cut, determines the orientation of the house in the valley. South, the cut links the skylight to the two big side openings; north, the stairs volume, rising like a column, interrupts the continuous wall of the cylinder. The house is on four levels: the basement with the technical and service premises; the ground floor with the portico and the entrance; the first floor with the living area and the second floor with the sleeping area.

© ALBERTO FLAMMER

© ALO ZANETTA

© ALO ZANETTA

© ALO ZANETTA

© ALO ZANETTA

C. LO RISO 10.7.81 PER M. BOTTA

G CALDELARI 11.12.80 PER M. BOTTA

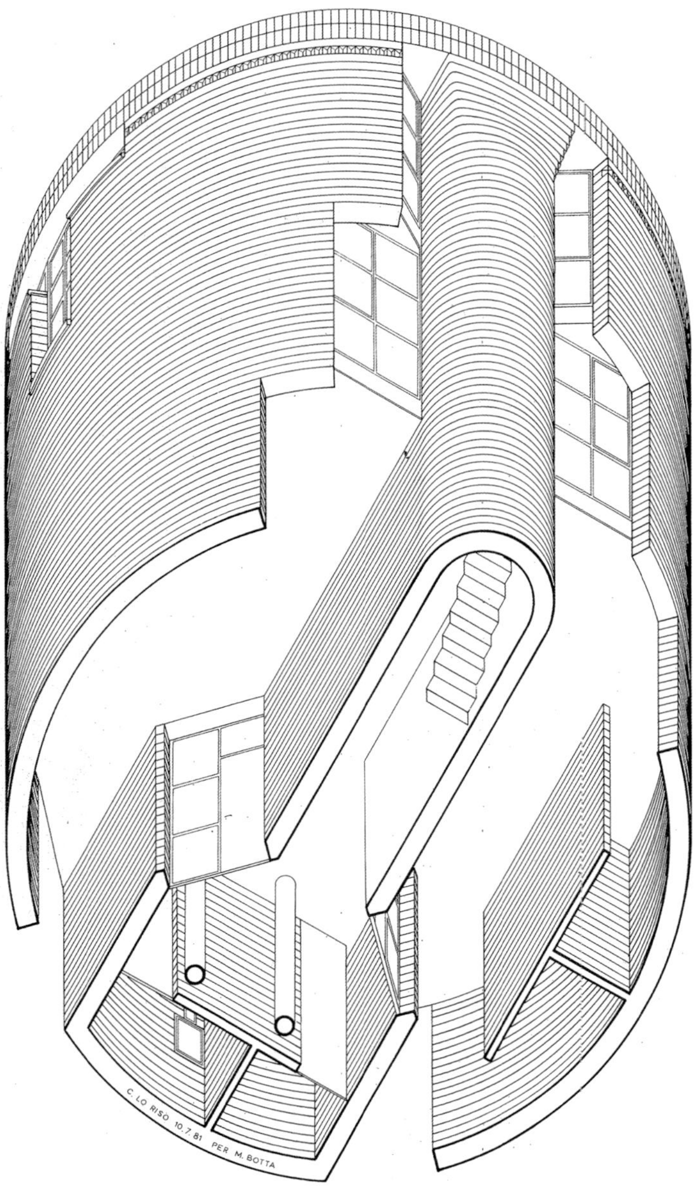

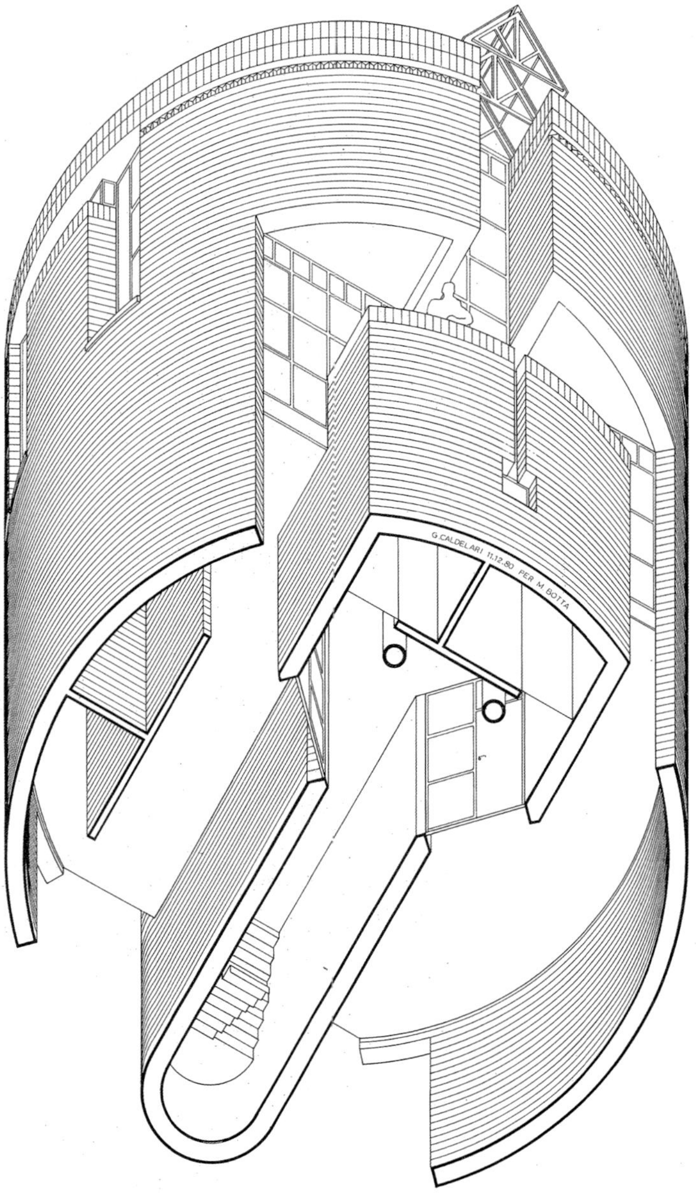

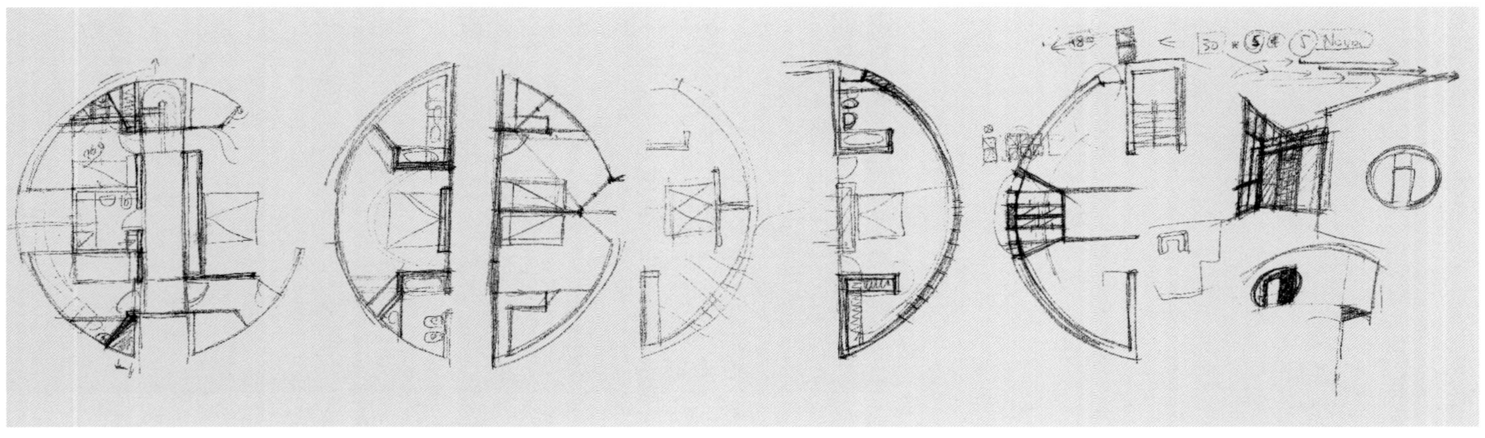

独栋住宅

瑞士，上莫尔比奥

SINGLE-FAMILY HOUSE

MORBIO SUPERIORE, SWITZERLAND

1982-1983

项目时间：1982年
建造时间：1982～1983年
委托方：埃德蒙多·普斯特尔拉
占地面积：2,500平方米
建筑面积：300平方米
建筑体积：1,300立方米

Project: 1982
Construction: 1982-1983
Client: Edmondo Pusterla
Site area: 2,500 m²
Useful surface: 300 m²
Volume: 1,300 m³

住宅坐落在山体与村庄之间的斜坡上，银灰色饰面的南向主立面向内凹，平铺砖层与45度角斜铺砖层交替砌筑，呈现出独特的外观。一道垂直开口将主立面一分为二，在下方形成一个矩形开口，在顶端则构成天窗，可以为楼上的两个楼层提供采光。入口位于建筑背面，被圆弧形服务空间切割，三角形侧廊通向卧室。起居空间位于靠近山坡的一侧，带有一个面向山坡的露台。地下室则包含服务用房和2间办公室，通过主立面下部的圆形开窗获得采光。

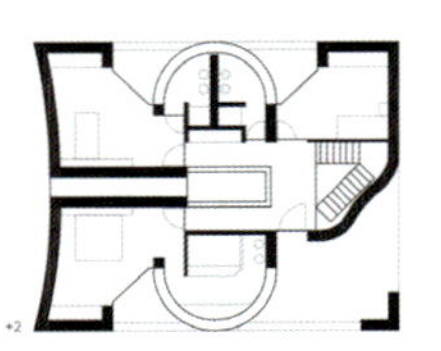

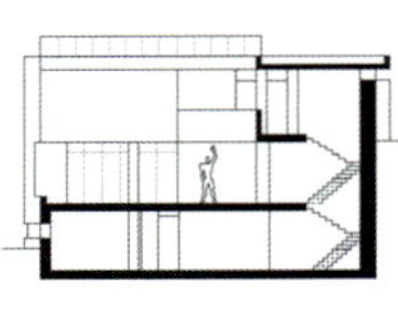

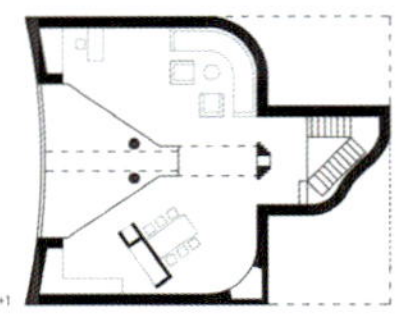

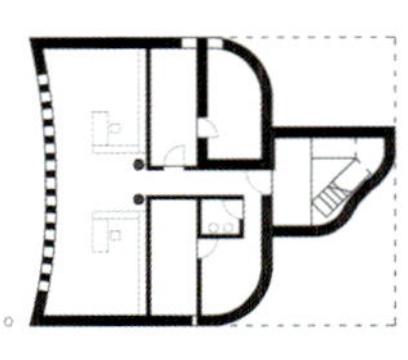

Set on a declivity between the hill and the village, the house shows a southwards concave façade, clad with a silver-colored texture characterized by the alternation of flat courses of bricks and courses laid at 45 degrees. A vertical cut splits the unity of the main façade into two volumes. It creates a rectangular entrance ending with a skylight that illuminates the two upper floors. The entrance is on the back, where the bedrooms open into the triangular side loggias, cut by the cylindrical bodies of the service rooms. The living area is in the direction of the hill with a terrace projecting on it. The basement houses the service rooms and two offices lighted by the circular windows in the lower part of the main façade.

© PINO MUSI

© ALO ZANETTA

© MARIO CARRIERI

© ALO ZANETTA

© ADRIANO HEITMANN

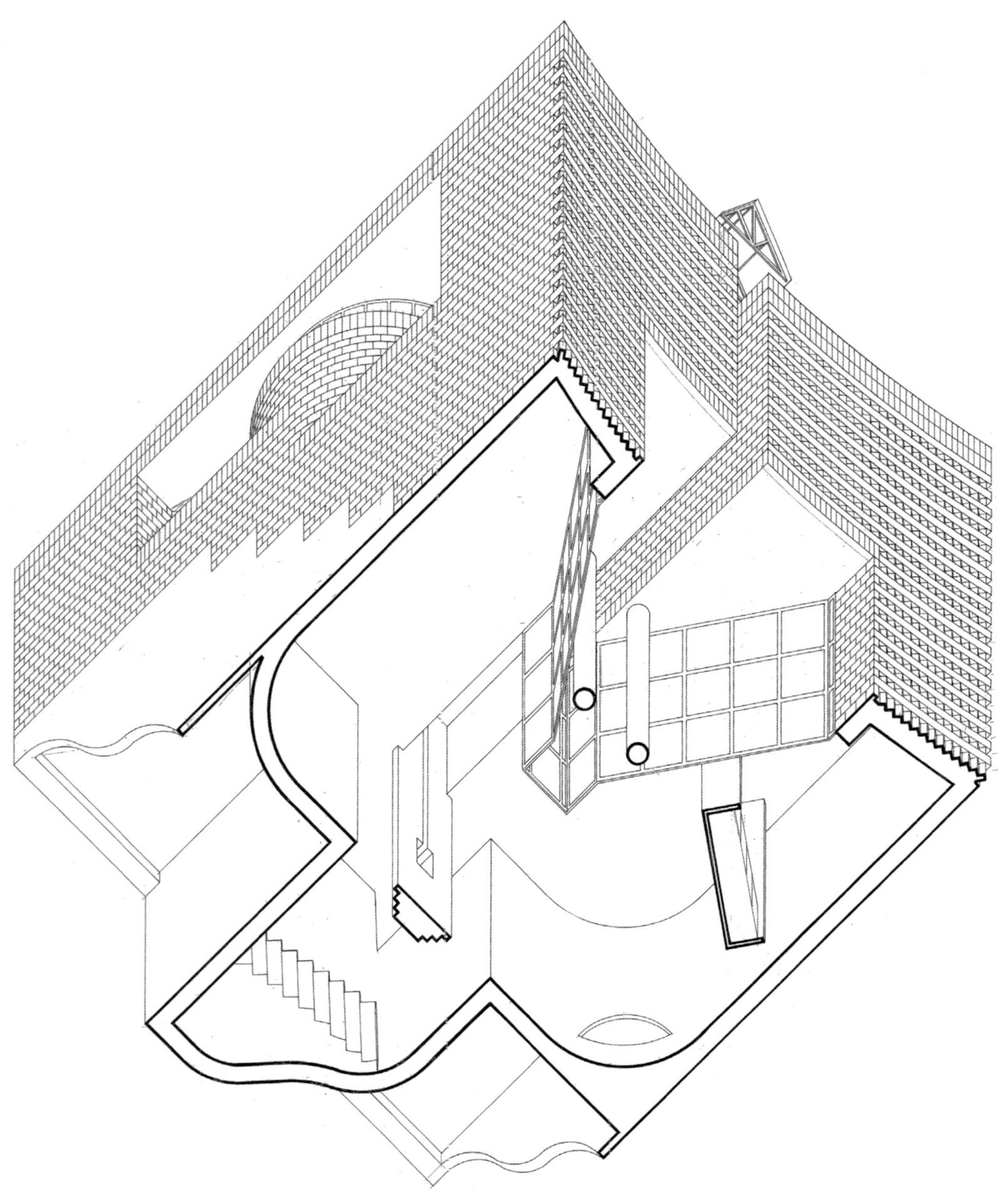

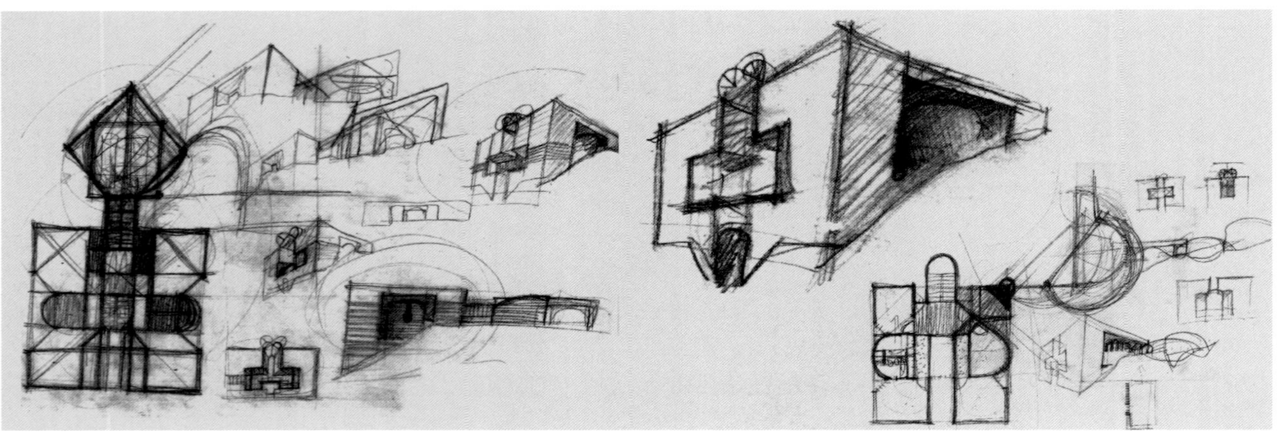

独栋住宅

瑞士，布雷甘佐拉

SINGLE-FAMILY HOUSE

BREGANZONA, SWITZERLAND

1984-1988

项目时间：1984年
建造时间：1986～1988年
委托方：索尼娅和里奥内罗·杰尼尼
占地面积：930平方米
建筑面积：240 平方米
建筑体积：1,100立方米

Project: 1984
Construction: 1986-1988
Client: Sonia and Lionello Genini
Site area: 930 m²
Useful surface: 240 m²
Volume: 1,100 m³

建筑建于卢加诺周边的丘陵地带，位于两条道路的交汇处。所处的转角位置使建筑呈现为“L”形，建筑主体部分嵌入其中形成方形平面。两面并排的墙体向上支撑起双拱形天窗，形成一个高高的拱廊。拱廊过渡了室内外空间，并为二层提供了观景平台。建筑整体的3层空间由转角处的楼梯相连。首层分布有入口、书房以及服务用房，二层是起居空间，三层是卧室区域。建筑墙体由混凝土砌块和白色硅酸钙砖砌筑，条纹式图案令建筑的空间组织形式更加突出。

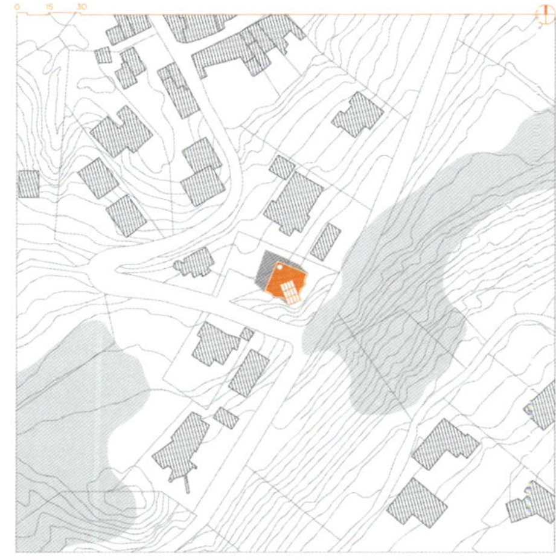

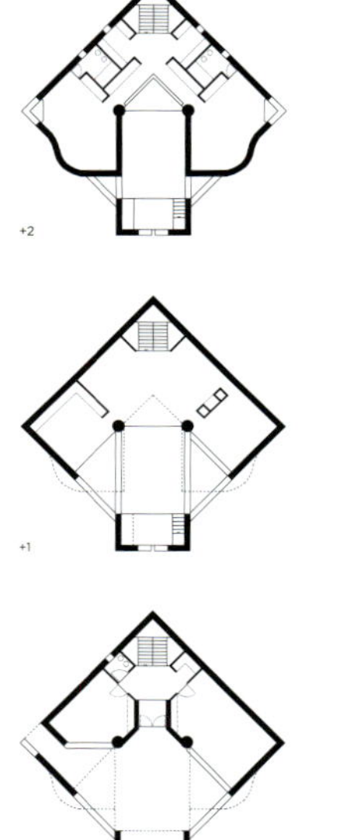

The house stands on a hilly area near Lugano at the crossing of two roads. This corner position originates an L-shaped body whose main volume is inserted into a square plan. Two side by side walls, surmounted by a double skylight, form a high portico – a kind of filter between the exterior and the interior –a terrace at the level of the first floor and a belvedere. The house is on three levels linked by a corner staircase along the diagonal. On the ground floor there is the entrance, a study and the service rooms; on the first floor the living area whereas, on the second one, the sleeping area. The house organization is underlined by the striped pattern of the wall, made of concrete blocks and white calcium silicate bricks.

© PINO MUSI

© PINO MUSI

© PINO MUSI

© PINO MUSI

© PINO MUSI

© FINO MUSI

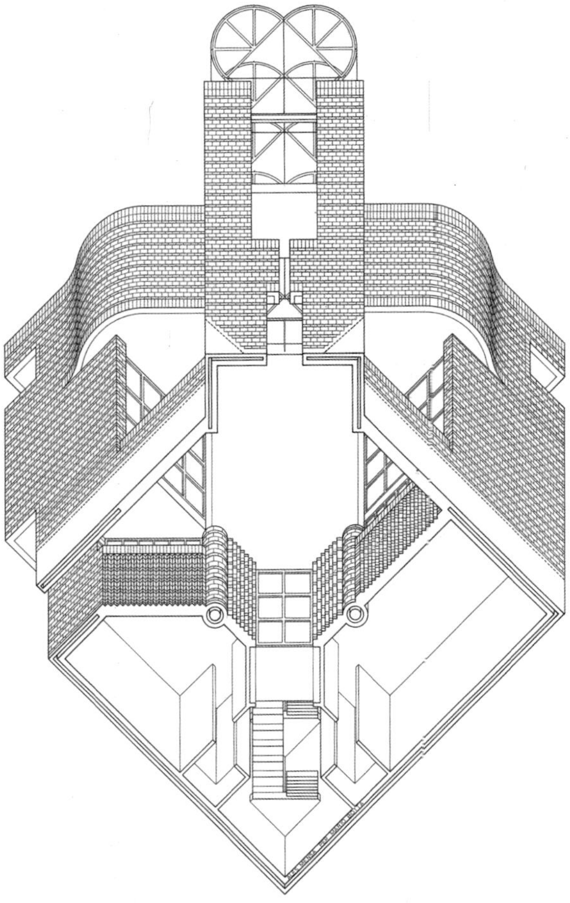

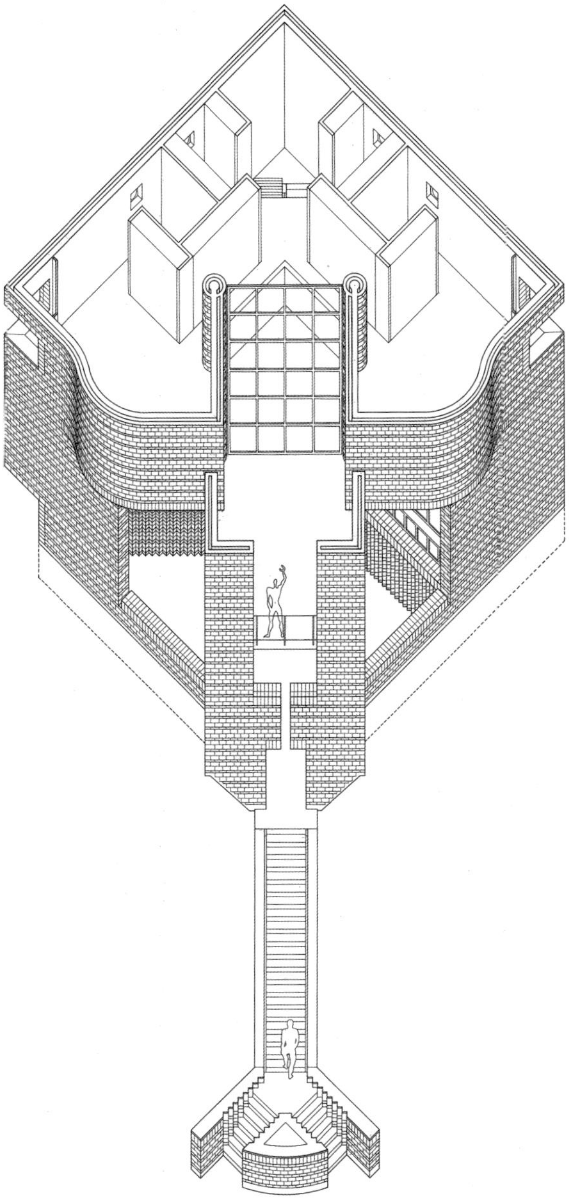

独栋住宅

瑞士，瓦卡洛

SINGLE-FAMILY HOUSE

VACALLO, SWITZERLAND

1986-1988

项目时间：1986年
建造时间：1987～1988年
委托方：乔治·阿尔菲里
占地面积：2,400 平方米
建筑面积：310平方米
建筑体积：2,000立方米

Project: 1986
Construction: 1987-1988
Client: Giorgio Alfieri
Site area: 2,400 m^2
Useful surface: 310 m^2
Volume: 2,000 m^3

建筑坐落于基亚索平原上，为了保护面前大面积的草坪，建筑退到了基地的后侧。这座三角形住宅的最长边朝向南方，内部空间沿中轴线对称组织。透明的玻璃天窗分割出建筑角落的楼梯间，并为2层高的中心空间提供了采光。该建筑最独特的元素是主立面上相交叉的两个圆拱，它形成了一种双重立面的效果，并构筑出一个通往主要房间的巨大门廊。建筑的短边，即西侧和东侧，与主立面脱离且不设窗户。住宅分为2层：一层为起居空间与露台；二层为卧室区域。

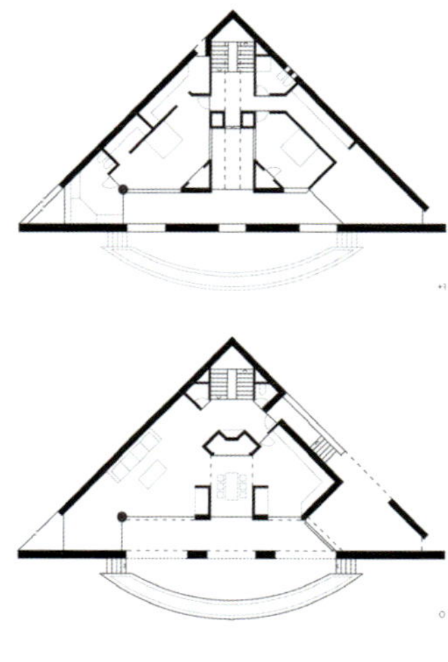

Situated on a terrain that falls to the plain of Chiasso, the house has been relegated to the rear of the site in order to conserve the large meadow opposite. The triangular house has its longest side southward and is organized along a central axis of symmetry. A transparent skylight cuts the house to the staircase corner and illuminates the double-height central space. The distinctive element are two crossed arcades that form a kind of double façade and frame the wide portico onto which all the main rooms give. The short sides, west- and eastward, are detached from the main façade and have no windows. The dwelling is on two levels: the living area and the terrace on the ground floor; the sleeping area on the upper level.

© ENRICO CANO

© PINO MUSI

© ENRICO CANO

© PINO MUSI

© PINO MUSI

© PINO MUSI

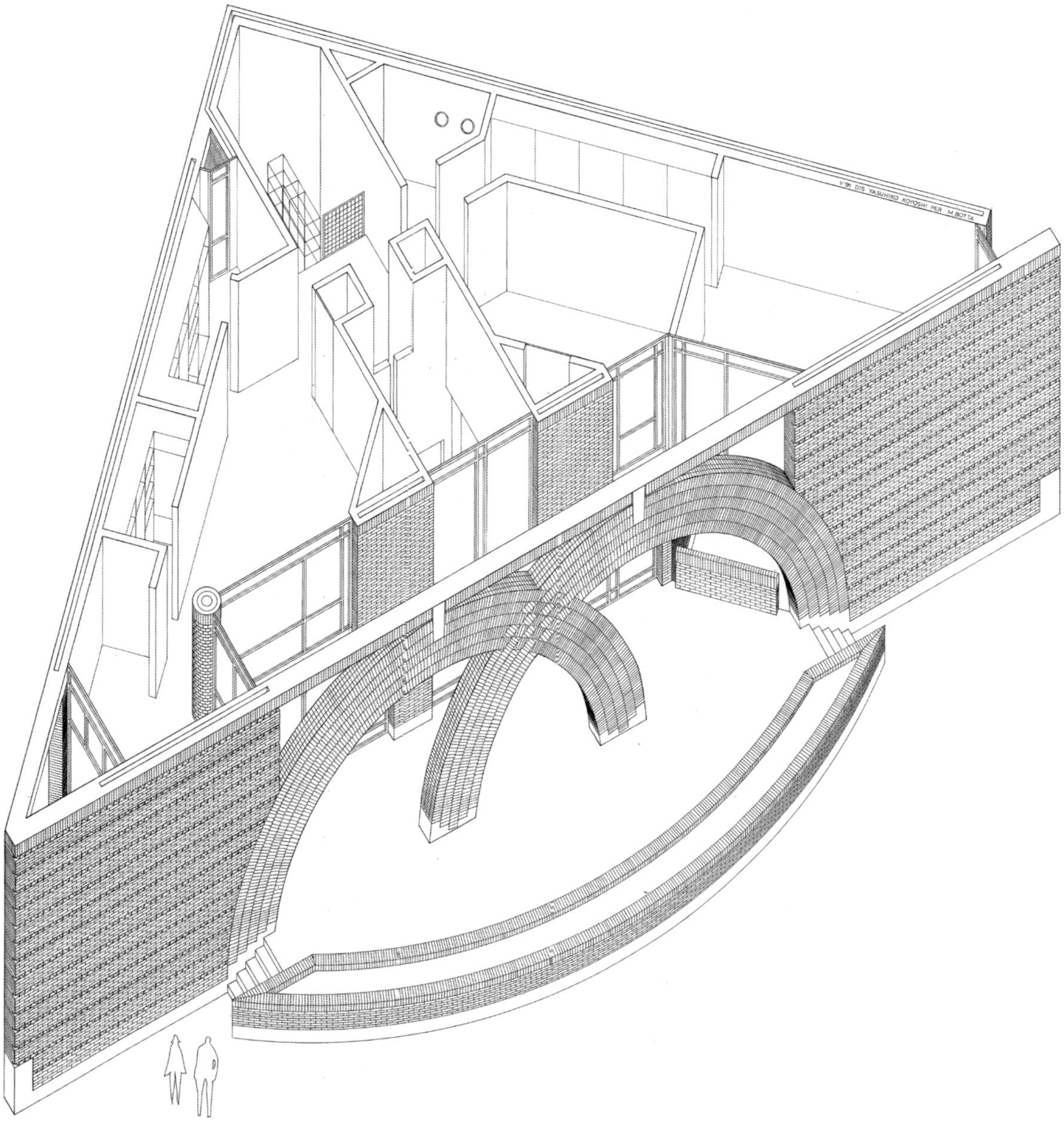

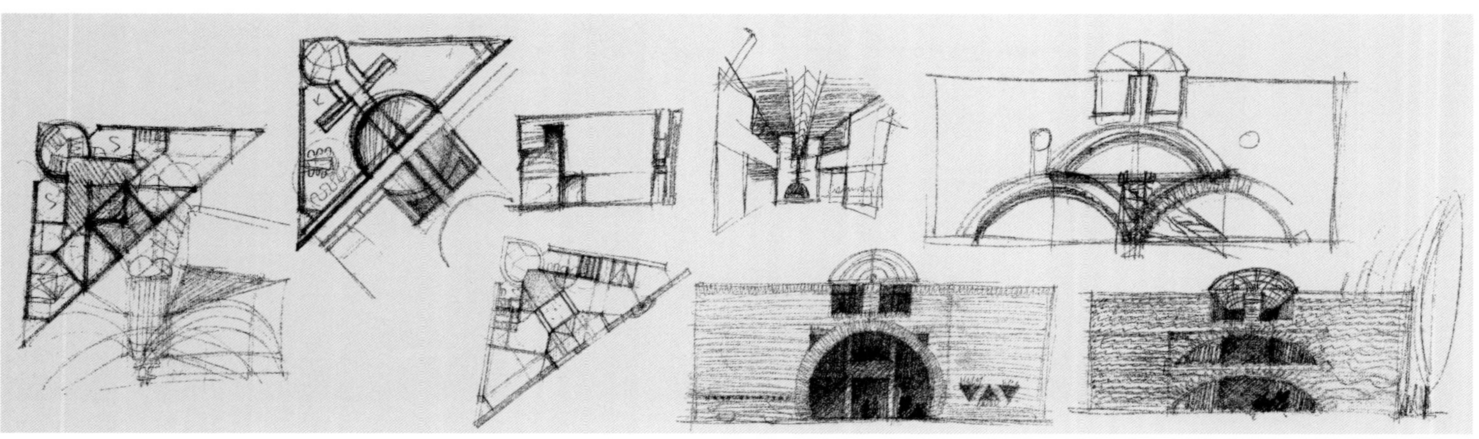

独栋住宅

瑞士，曼诺

SINGLE-FAMILY HOUSE

MANNO, SWITZERLAND

1987-1990

项目时间：1974/1987年
建造时间：1989～1990年
委托方：多丽丝和皮埃费利切·巴尔奇
占地面积：2,500平方米
建筑面积：380平方米
建筑体积：1,200立方米

Project: 1974/1987
Construction: 1989-1990
Client: Doris and Pier Felice Barchi
Site area: 2,500 m^2
Useful surface: 380 m^2
Volume: 1,200 m^3

这座三角形的住宅面朝该地段的东北角。建筑主立面的特点是一个巨大的圆拱，所有活动区域、空间以及开口都围绕着它进行布局。两根正交的横梁贯穿整个建筑直至后部的墙体，划定出一个由天窗照亮的双层空间。另外一面墙体收尾于车道处并围合出外部空间。住宅由2层组成：一层是起居空间，二层是卧室空间。

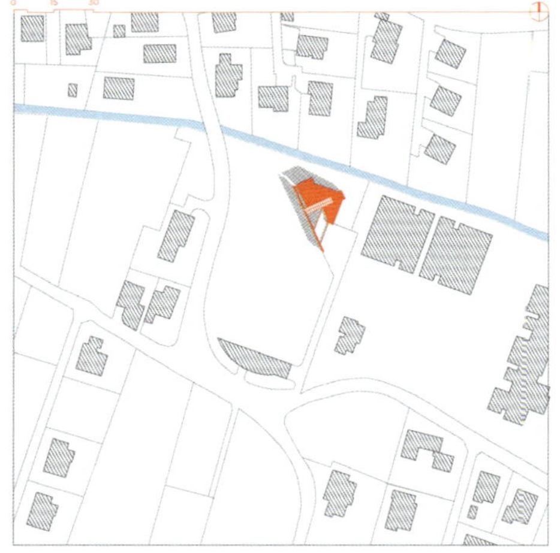

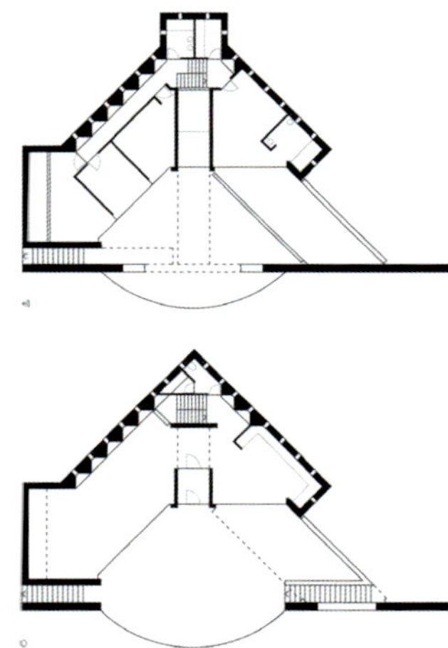

The triangular house faces the north-east corner of the site. The main façade is characterized by the great arch around which all the activities, the spaces and the openings are arranged. Two orthogonal beams that run through the whole of the building to the rear wall define a double volume illuminated by a skylight. Another wall, ending by the driveway, encloses the outer sides. The house is organized on two levels: the living area on the ground floor and the sleeping area on the first floor.

© PINO MUSI

© PINO MUSI

© PINO MUSI

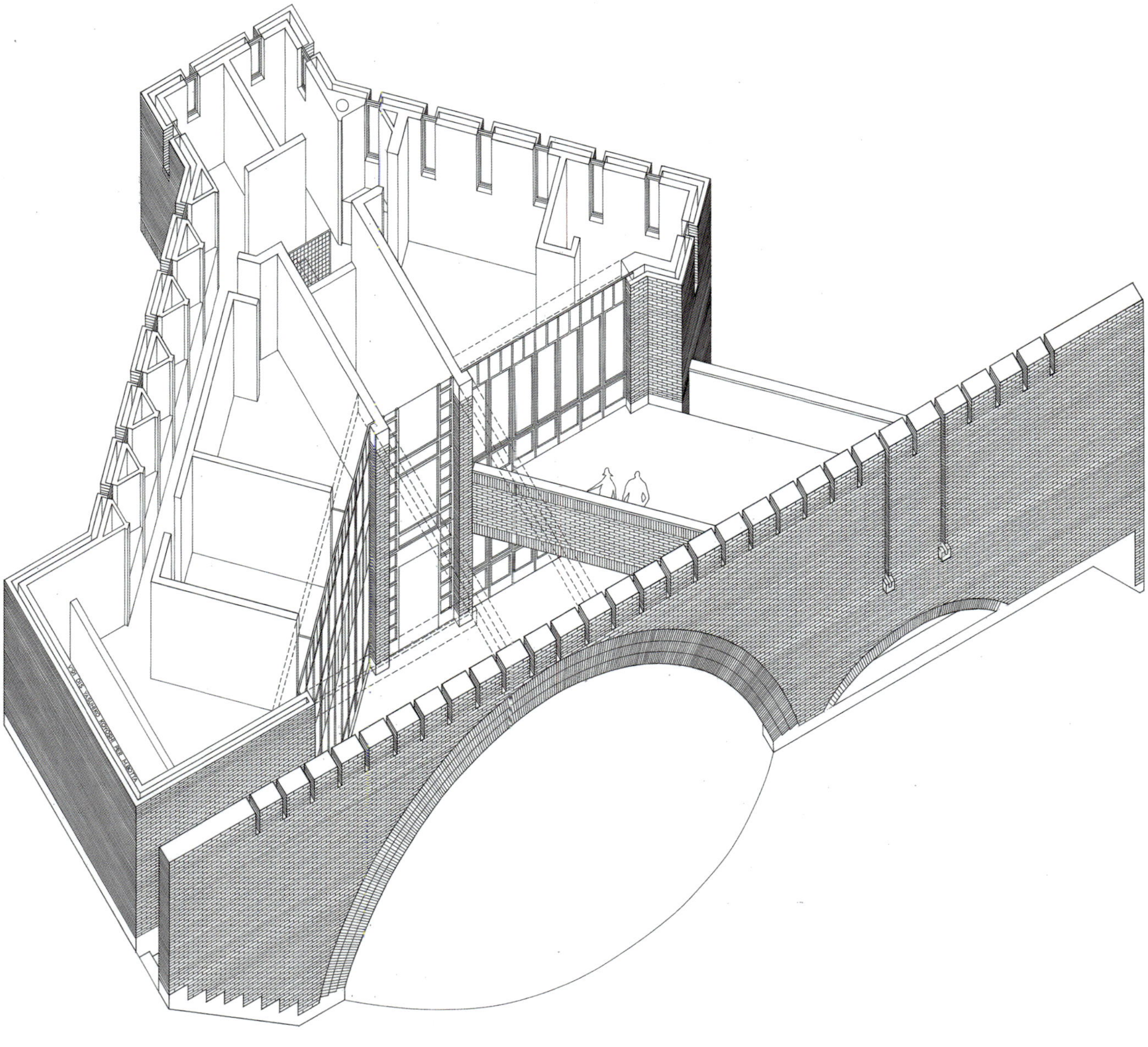

© PINO MUSI

© PINO MUSI

© PINO MUSI

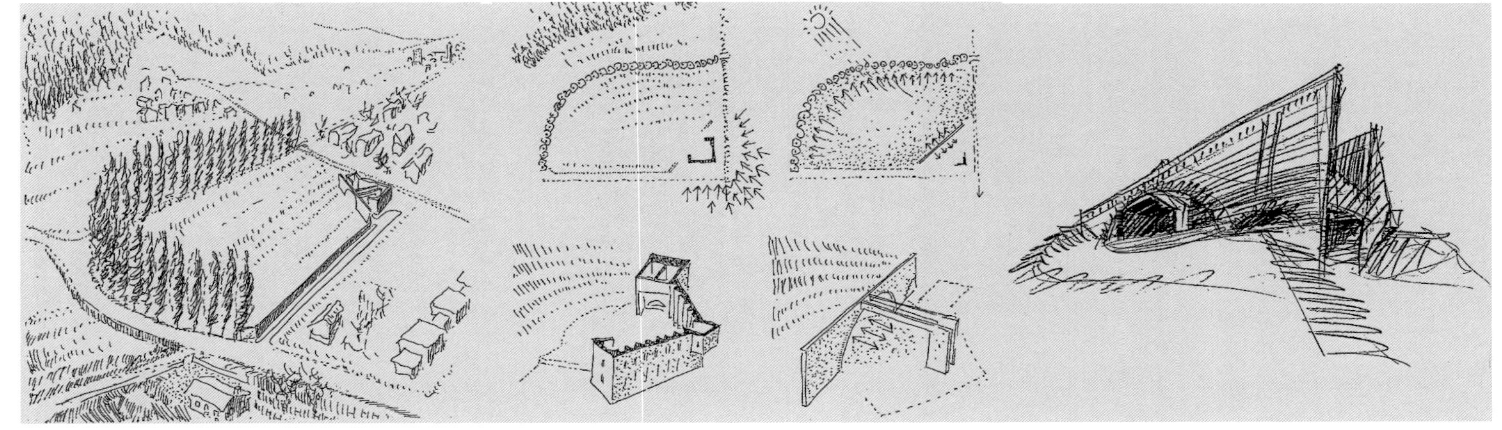

独栋住宅

瑞士，洛索内

SINGLE-FAMILY HOUSE

LOSONE, SWITZERLAND

1987-1989

项目时间：1987年
建造时间：1988～1989年
委托方：罗贝塔和加布里埃尔·比安达
占地面积：1,075平方米
建筑面积：220平方米
建筑体积：960立方米

Project: 1987
Construction: 1988-1989
Client: Roberta and Gabriele Bianda
Site area: 1,075 m^2
Useful surface: 220 m^2
Volume: 960 m^3

建筑体呈圆柱形，入口朝向东南方，建筑正面的独特之处为两面高至圆形屋顶的墙体以及中间一道深邃的切口，向内延伸至楼梯间旁的灵活区域。南侧的梯田式平台将房间区域延伸到室外的覆顶露台。建筑分为4层：卧室设在二层，三层及四层为起居空间。

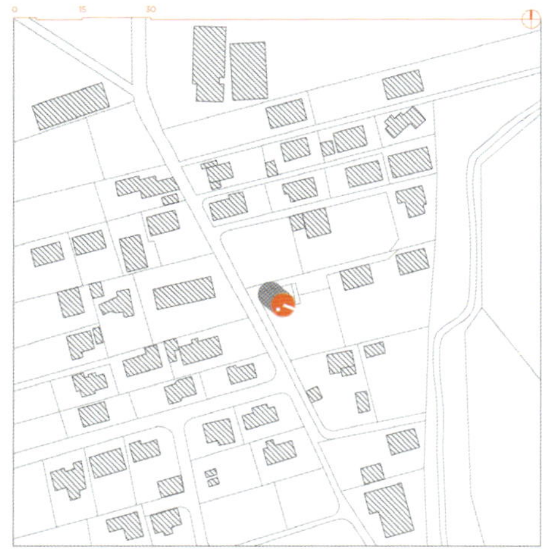

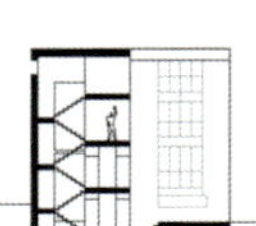

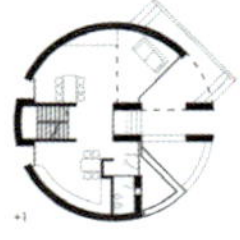

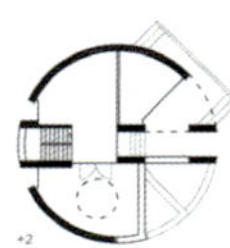

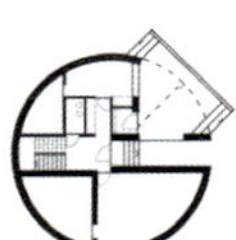

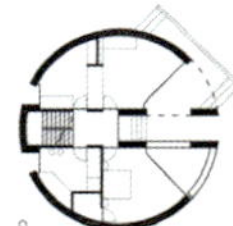

The house has a cylindrical shape with the openings facing south-east. The main front is characterized by two separated walls rising to the circular roof and framing the deep cut that extends inwards to the glazed circulation area next to the stairs. On the south side the stepped volumes form terraces that extend the rooms outdoors, sheltered by the roof. The building is on four levels: the sleeping area is on the first floor while the second and the third floors house the living area.

© PINO MUSI

© PINO MUSI

© PINO MUSI

© PINO MUSI

© PINO MUSI

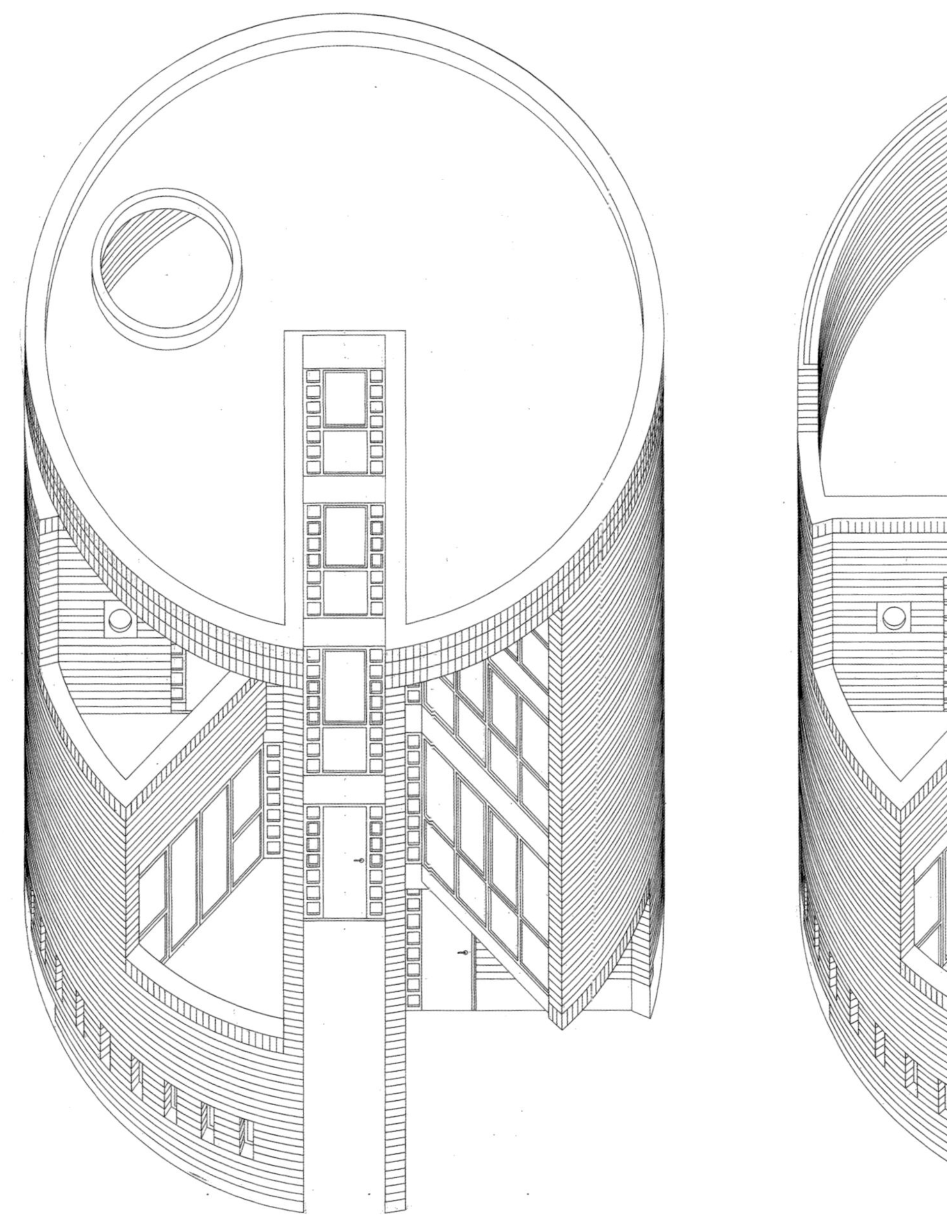

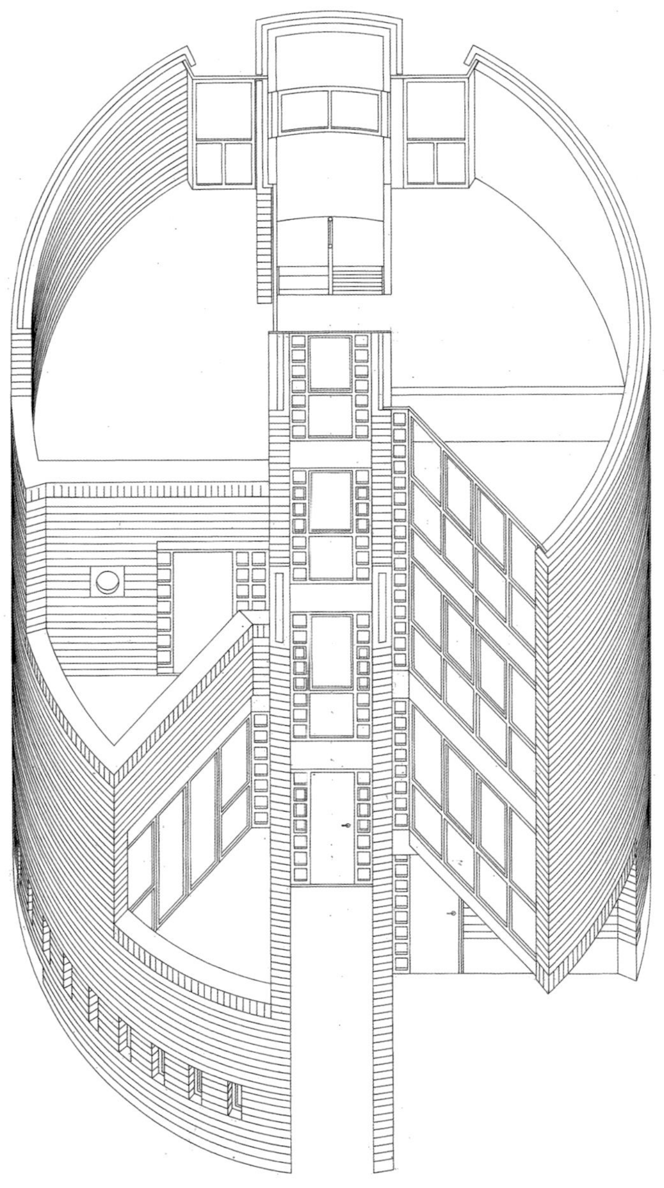

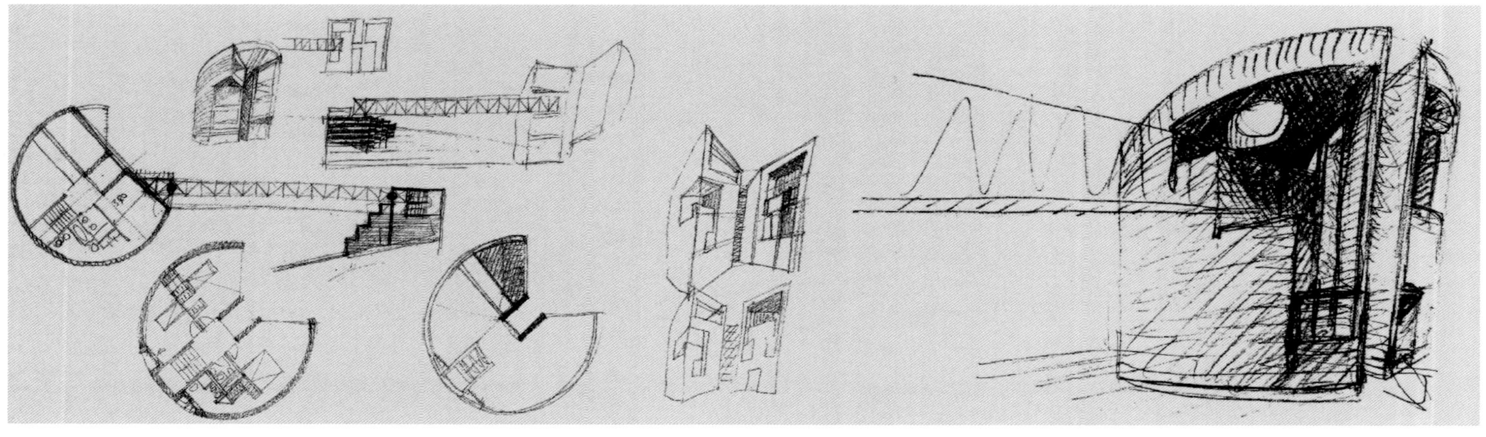

独栋住宅

瑞士，达罗

SINGLE-FAMILY HOUSE

DARO, SWITZERLAND

1989-1992

项目时间：1989年
建造时间：1990～1992年
委托方：罗桑杰拉和克劳迪奥·马洛内
占地面积：927平方米
建筑面积：230平方米
建筑体积：1,420立方米

Project: 1989
Construction: 1990-1992
Client: Rosangela and Claudio Marone
Site area: 927 m²
Useful surface: 230 m²
Volume: 1,420 m³

住宅坐落在一面陡峭的山坡上，俯瞰着贝林佐纳平原。楔形的建筑轮廓面向山脉一侧。主立面朝向西北，设有露台与窗口以及两面支撑着巨大玻璃顶棚的墙体。住宅分为4层：一层是入口，二层为卧室区域，起居区域在三层，面朝起居室的图书室在四层。

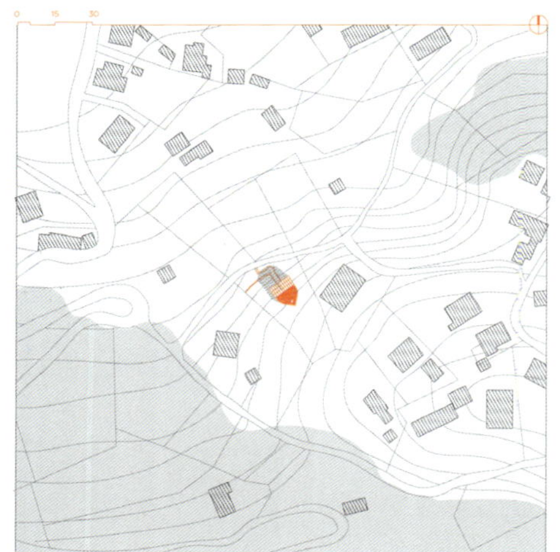

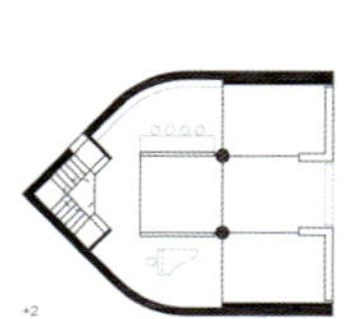

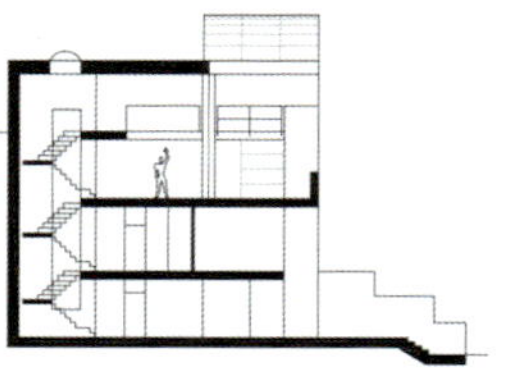

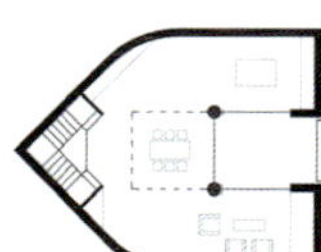

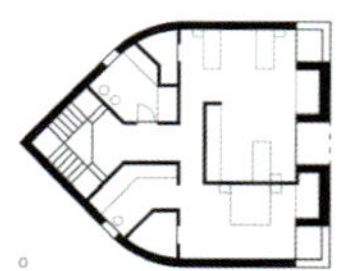

The house is located on a steep slope overlooking the plain of Bellinzona. The wedge-shaped outline defines the side towards the mountain. The main front, facing north-west and showing terraces and windows, consists of two walls supporting the big transparent roof. The dwelling is organized on four levels: the entrance at ground floor, the sleeping area on the first floor, the living area on the second floor and the library that gives onto the living room, on the third floor.

© PINO MUSI

© PINO MUSI

© PINO MUSI

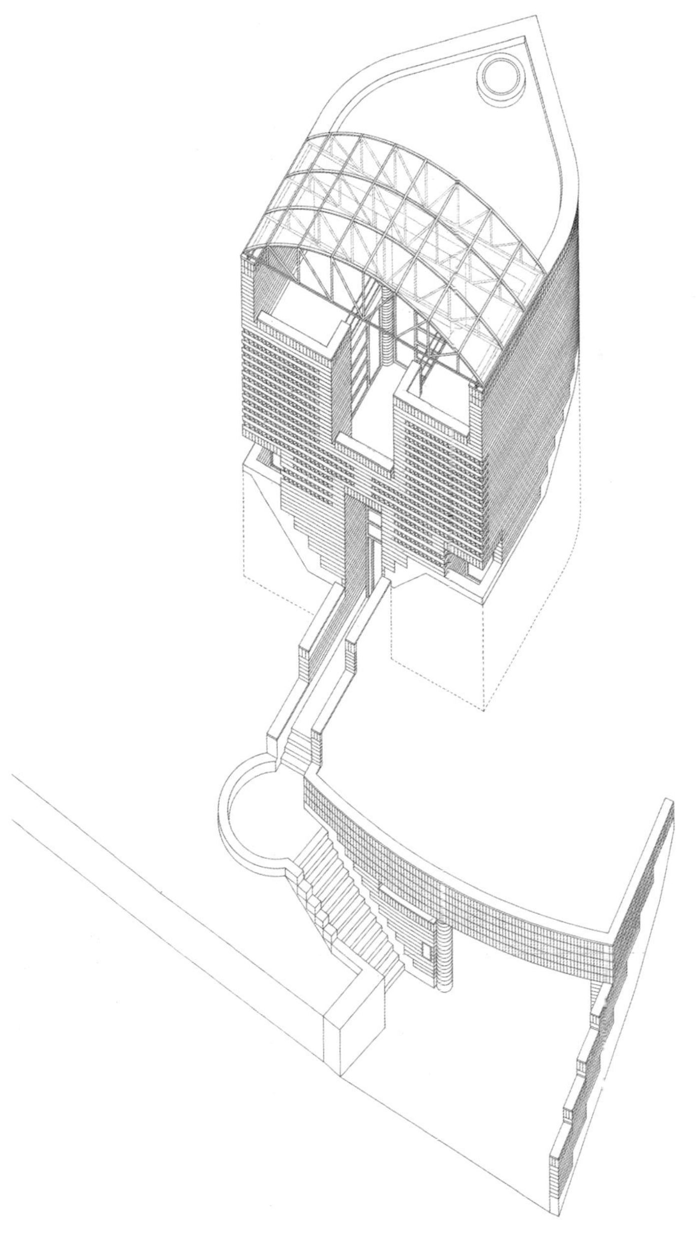

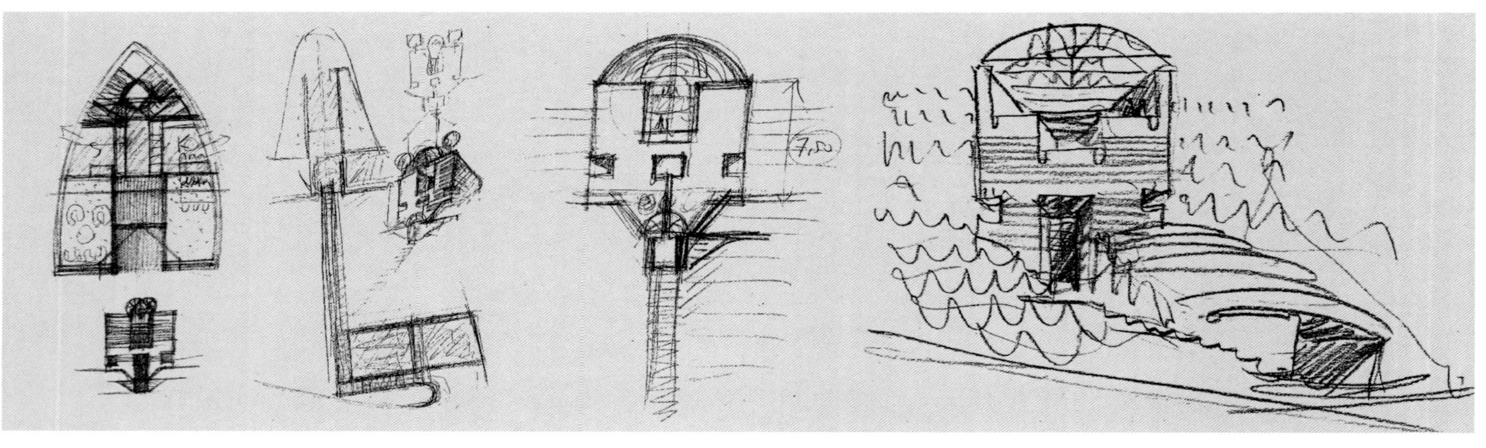

独栋住宅
瑞士，蒙塔格诺拉

SINGLE-FAMILY HOUSE
MONTAGNOLA, SWITZERLAND

1989-1994

项目时间：1989年
建造时间：1991~1994年
委托方：乔治·布隆兹
占地面积：3,666平方米
建筑面积：670平方米
建筑体积：房屋体积为2,760立方米
室内游泳池体积为2,085立方米

Project: 1989
Construction: 1991-1994
Client: Giorgio Bronz
Site area: 3,666 m^2
Useful area: 670 m^2
Volume: house 2,760 m^3,
indoor swimming pool 2,085 m^3

住宅坐落在一个小型公园内，由一个高半圆形建筑体和一个包含健身、游泳功能的直线形建筑体组成。一扇落地窗将具有收藏功能的车库与其他区域分隔开。建筑的居住空间分布在半圆形建筑体的3层空间内。卧室在底部2层，顶层起居空间可以通过舷窗以及嵌入式游廊远眺山谷的美景。

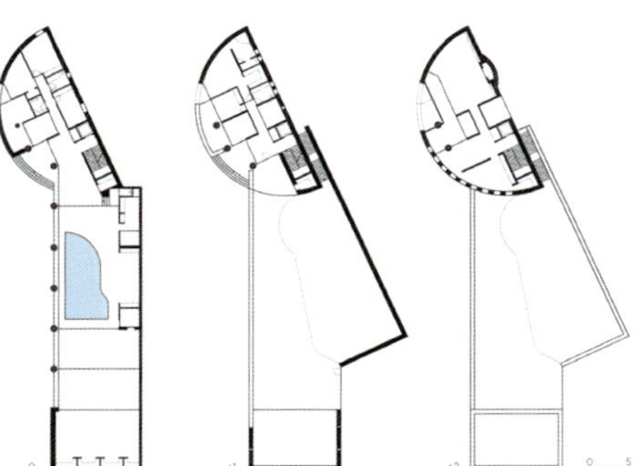

The house lies in a small park. It is composed of a tall semicircular volume and of a rectilinear body housing the gym and the swimming pool. A full-length window separates these facilities from the garage with the car collection. The dwelling spaces are arranged in the semicircular building which is organized on three levels. The sleeping area is on the lower floors and the living area on the upper one, with views of the valley from the portholes and the recessed loggia.

© MARCO D'ANNA

© MARCO D'ANNA

© PINO MUSI

© MARCO D'ANNA

© MARCO D'ANNA

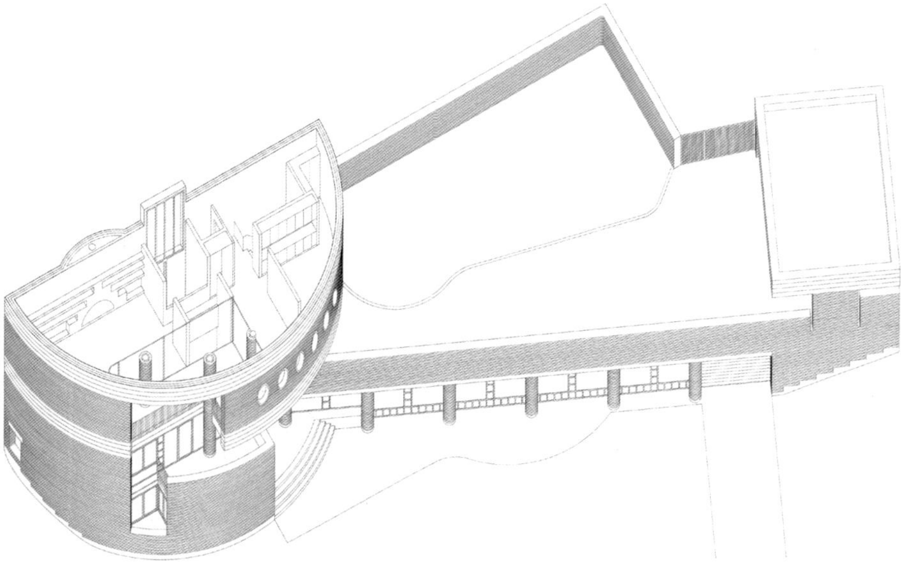

© ENRICO CANO

雷达埃利别墅

意大利，贝尔纳雷焦

VILLA REDAELLI

BERNAREGGIO MI, ITALY

1991-2001

项目时间：1991/1997年
建造时间：1999～2001年
委托方：法比亚诺·雷达埃利和布鲁纳·维特马蒂
占地面积：2,560平方米
建筑面积：713平方米
建筑体积：1,800立方米

Project: 1991/1997
Construction: 1999-2001
Client: Fabiano Redaelli and Bruna Vertemati
Site area: 2,560 m²
Useful surface: 713 m²
Volume: 1,800 m³

别墅坐落在米兰省柏纳瑞吉奥镇北部的居民区，属于独栋单元住宅聚集的典型郊区。博塔在此设计了一系列联排住宅，这栋别墅位于这一排住宅的最北端，共有3层：一层为入口和面向花园开放的室内游泳池及相关设施；起居空间和主卧位于二层；图书馆和其余的卧室设置在三层。别墅的东立面平行于道路，双层墙体以赤陶砖饰面，外部设有连接花园和图书馆的楼梯。朝向花园的西立面具有复杂的凹凸形态，屋檐下的回缩空间形成了连通3个楼层的宽阔门厅和3层的游廊。

The villa is located in a residential area north of the town of Bernareggio, in the province of Milan, in a typical suburban setting with single-family houses. It was designed as the northern header for a series of row houses, also designed by Botta, and is organized on three levels. The ground floor is completely open onto the garden and, in addition to the entrance, features the indoor swimming pool and the connected facilities. The living area and the master bedroom are on the first floor; the library and the rest of the sleeping area are on the second floor. The east façade, set parallel to the road, has double walls faced with terracotta bricks and features external stairs connecting the garden with the library. The convex west façade, which faces the garden, is particularly complex, with recessed areas in relation to the eaves that create a broad portico on three floors and loggias on the second storey.

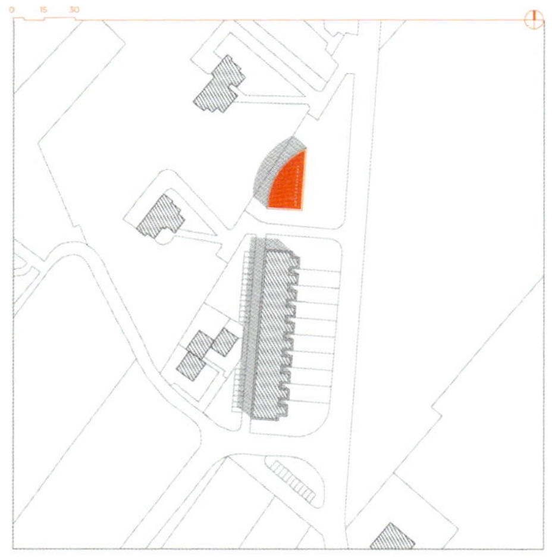

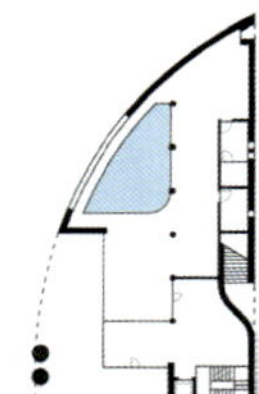

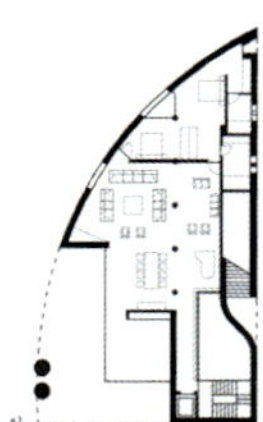

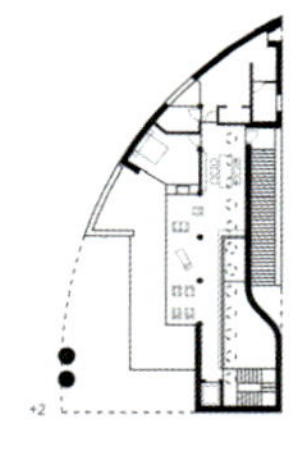

© ENRICO CANO

© PINO MUSI

© PINO MUSI

© PINO MUSI

© PINO MUSI

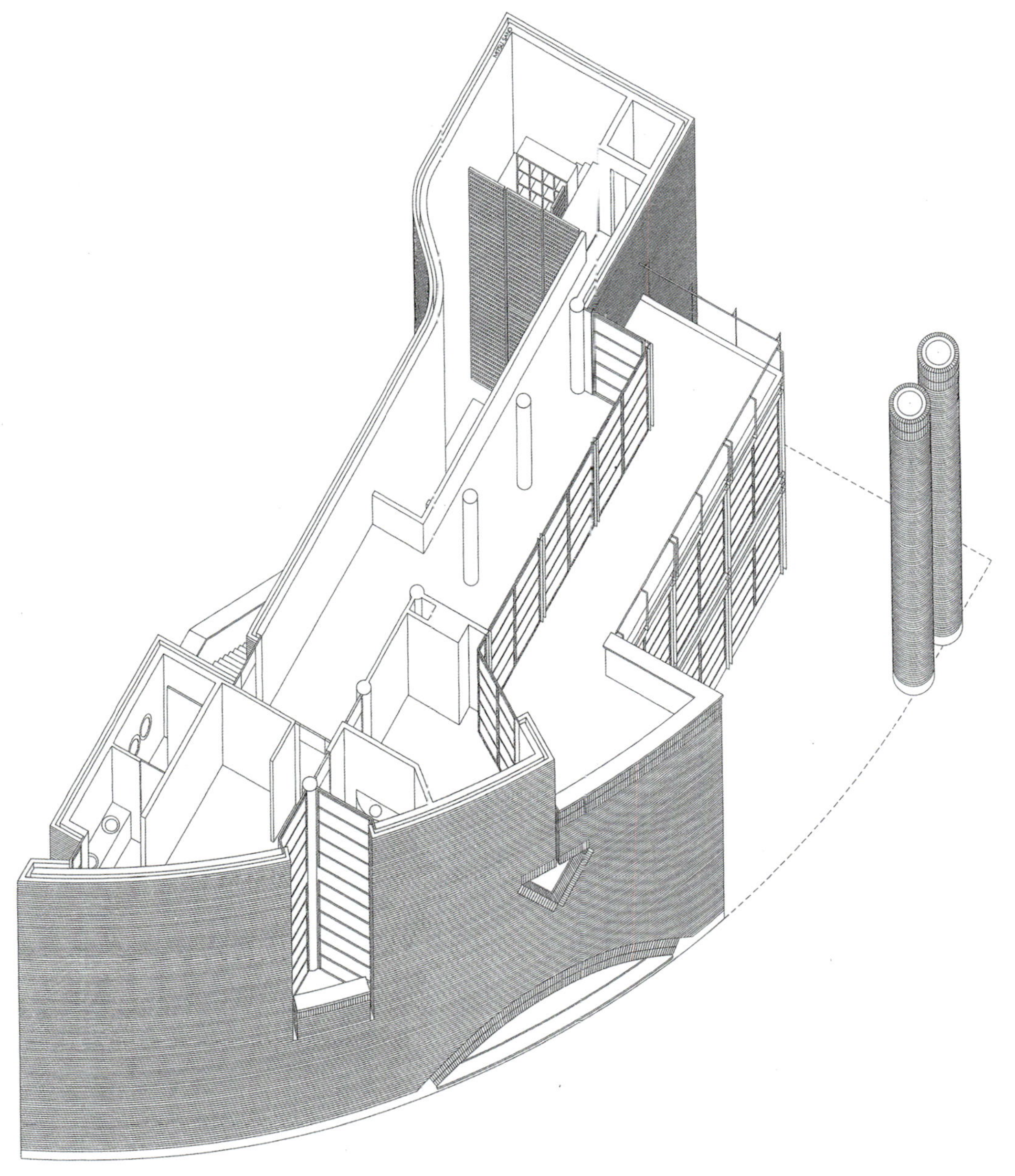

© PINO MUSI

© ENRICO CANO

住宅区

瑞士，诺瓦扎诺

RESIDENTIAL SETTLEMENT

NOVAZZANO, SWITZERLAND

1988-1992

项目时间：1988年
建造时间：1989～1992年
合作建筑师：费鲁乔·罗比亚尼
委托方：塞尔吉奥·蓬齐奥
占地面积：19,200平方米
建筑面积：11,600平方米
建筑体积：58,000立方米

Project: 1988
Construction: 1989-1992
With: arch. Ferruccio Robbiani
Client: Sergio Ponzio
Site area: 19,200 m^2
Useful surface: 11,600 m^2
Volume: 58,000 m^3

该建筑综合体是一个专为低收入家庭而开发的小型地产项目，规模在100套住房左右。这些低成本的4层公寓呈现U形体块的形态，位于地块较高处。建筑围合出一处铺有地砖的庭院，庭院下方是地下停车场，而两座翼楼相对而立形成另一处开放的庭院。一座连桥连接起低处的庭院和一个小型购物中心。建筑由一层的背面进入，入口门廊内分布着诸多带有圆形开孔的连续立面，形成独特的视觉效果。带有门廊的建筑成为庭院的第三条封闭边界，而第四条边则完全开放。不同颜色的使用令建筑别具一格：外立面为三文鱼粉色，内凹区域的柱子为赭石色，中间的服务区域则为蓝色。

The complex is a small estate developed to provide subsidized housing, a proper settlement of one hundred dwellings. These low-cost, four-story apartment blocks are organized in a U-shaped block on the upper part of the site. The block surrounds a paved yard which lies on top of an underground parking-area, while the two wings form the opposite sides of a second open courtyard. A bridge connects the lower courtyard to a small shopping centre. The estate is entered on the ground floor from the back. It opens up to reveal a covered portico created through a succession of round openings on vertical planes giving a surprising visual effect. The block with the portico forms the third closed side of the courtyard, while the fourth remains open to view. The use of different colours characterizes the façades: salmon pink for the outer façades, ochre for the recessed volumes and blue for the intermediate service areas.

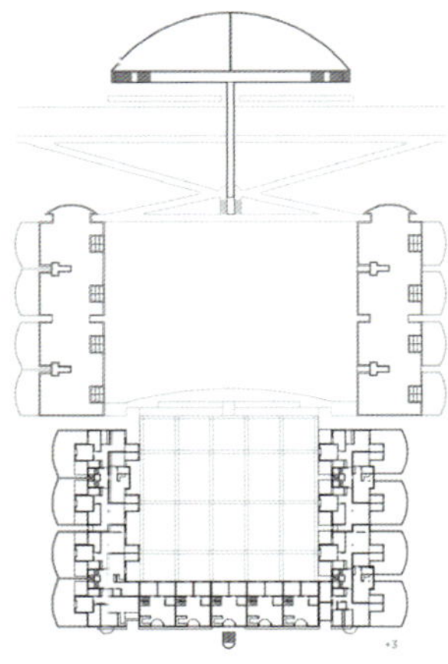

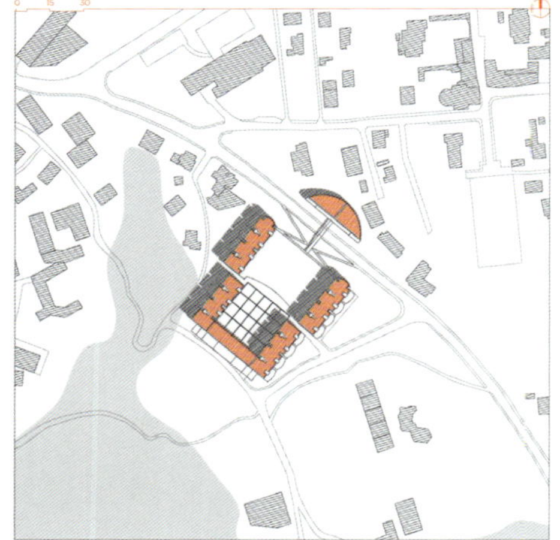

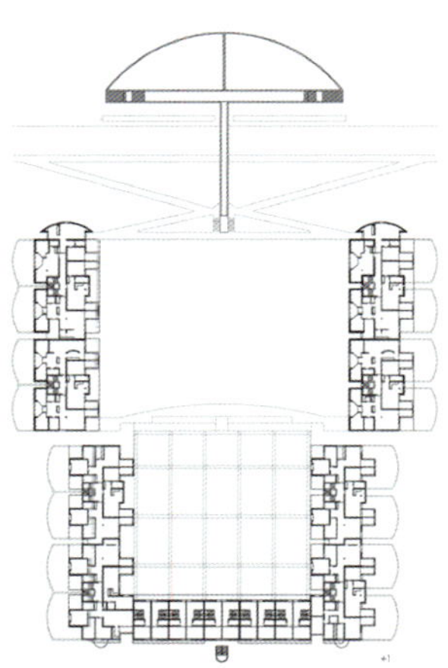

© PINO MUSI

© PINO MUSI

© PINO MUSI

© PINO MUSI

© PINO MUSI

© PINO MUSI

© ENRICO CANO

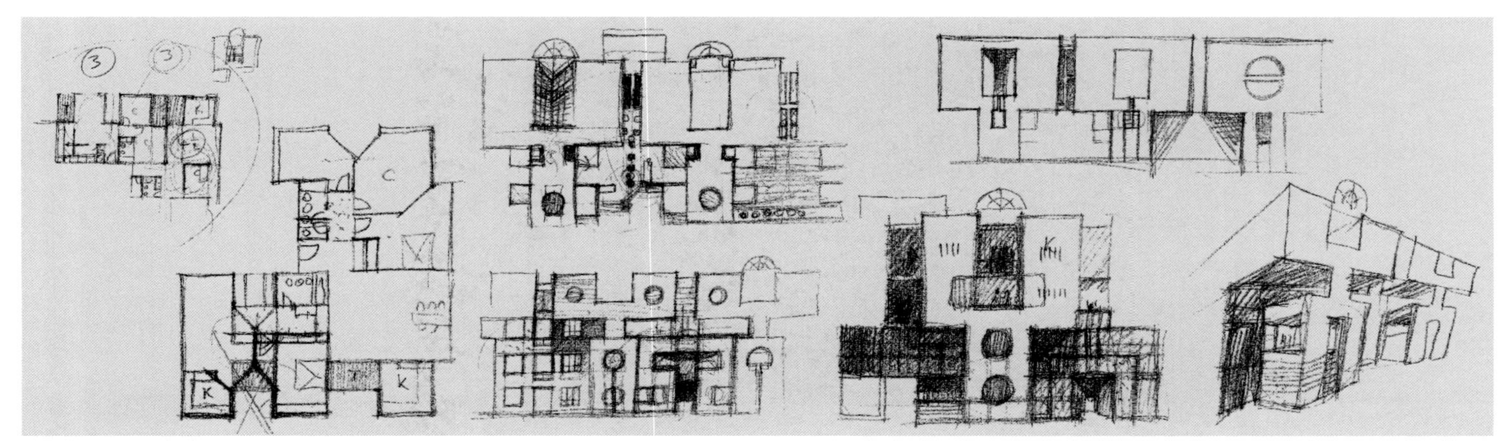

住宅区

瑞士，蒙特卡拉索

RESIDENTIAL SETTLEMENT

MONTE CARASSO, SWITZERLAND

1992-1996

项目时间：1992年
建造时间：1994～1996年
委托方：安东尼尼和奇多西，贝林佐拉
占地面积：2,874平方米
建筑面积：2,490平方米
建筑体积：12,775立方米

Project: 1992
Construction: 1994-1996
Client: Antonini&Ghidossi, Bellinzona
Site area: 2,874 m²
Useful surface: 2,490 m²
Volume: 12,775 m³

这处拥有30座公寓住宅的建筑综合体包括2个体块：一个为矩形体块，立面有小型凸起圆柱；另一个体块的弧形侧边形成了巨大的锐角。二者由一条巨大的白色铅板合金制造的采用透明聚碳酸酯板屋顶的露天走廊相连，并在入口上方形成拱门。矩形体块沿街建造，弧形体块面向周边区域。弧形体块略微后退，因此在庭院一侧能够欣赏风景，而矩形体块的长边则将开放空间与街道隔离开来。阳台构成建筑综合体的连续中空结构，最终形成弧形体块的锐角；而矩形体块短边的两个垂直结构形成建筑的正面。

The housing complex for thirty apartments consists of two volumes: an orthogonal one with small cylindrical extrusions and another with a curved side that points to a sharp edge, connected by an open-air corridor. The two volumes are brought together by a large, white-painted, grid metal structure with a transparent polycarbonate strip roof that arches above the entrance space. The orthogonal volume follows the street line, while the curved one opens up to the surroundings. The courtyard opens to the view at one side as the curved building stands more to the back, while the elongated side of the orthogonal volume protects the open space from the street. Terraces create a successive hollowing out of the volume, culminating in the sharp corner of the curved block, while an articulation of double vertical elements on the short side of the orthogonal part point to the front of the building.

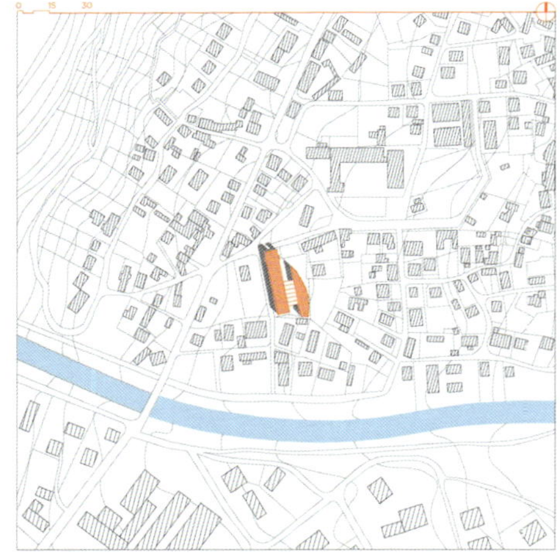

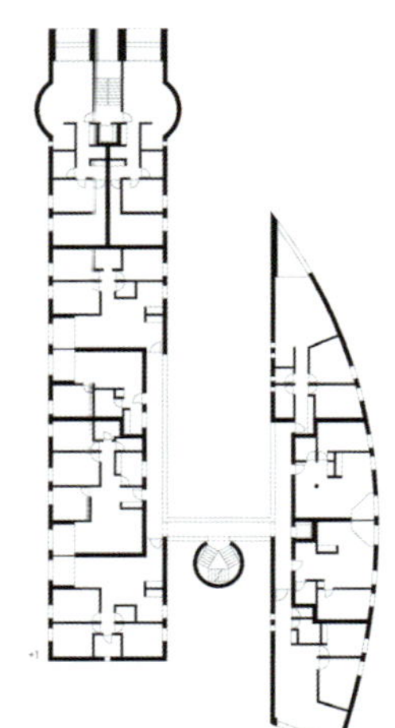

© ENRICO CANO

© ENRICO CANO

© ENRICO CANO

© ENRICO CANO

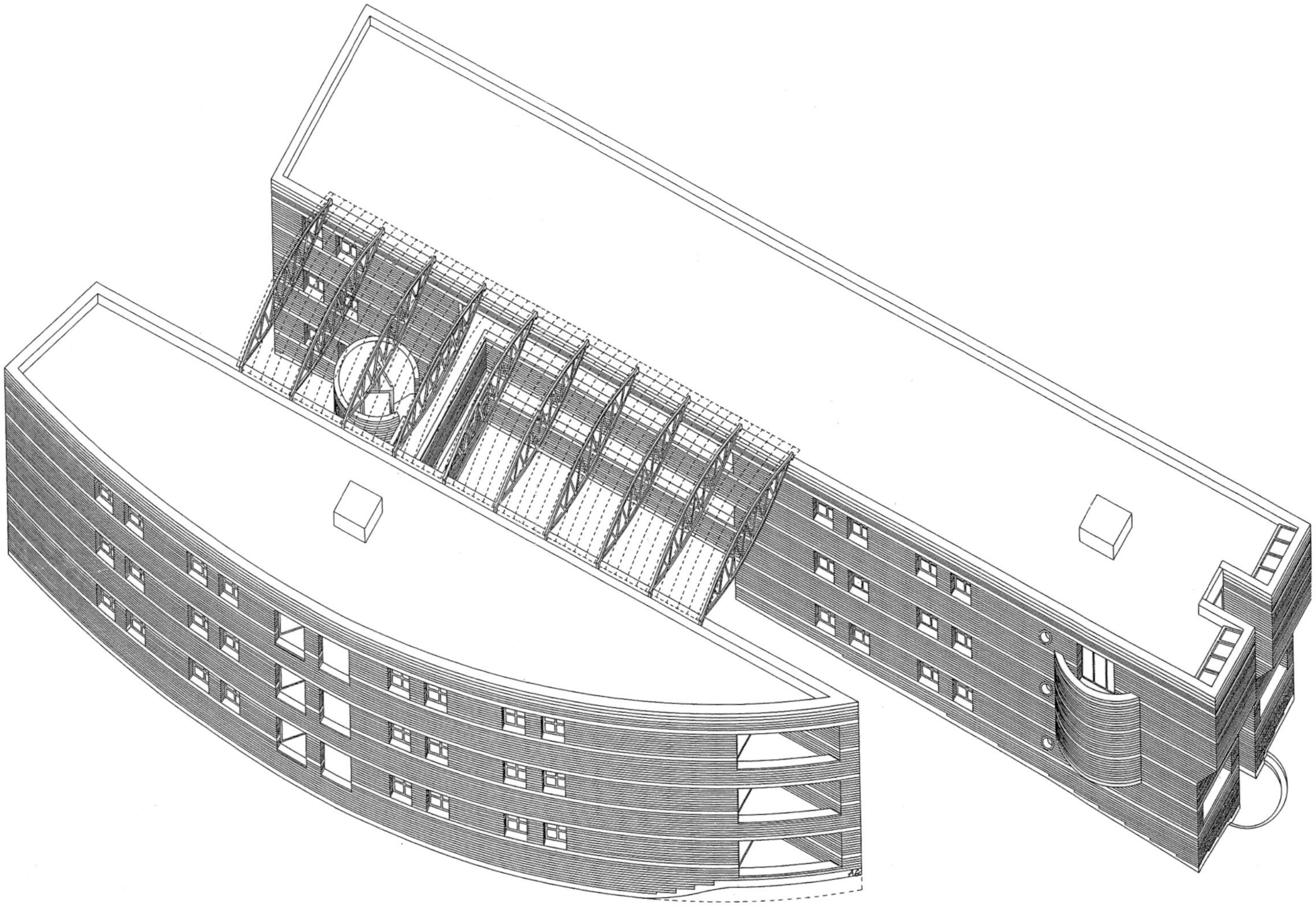

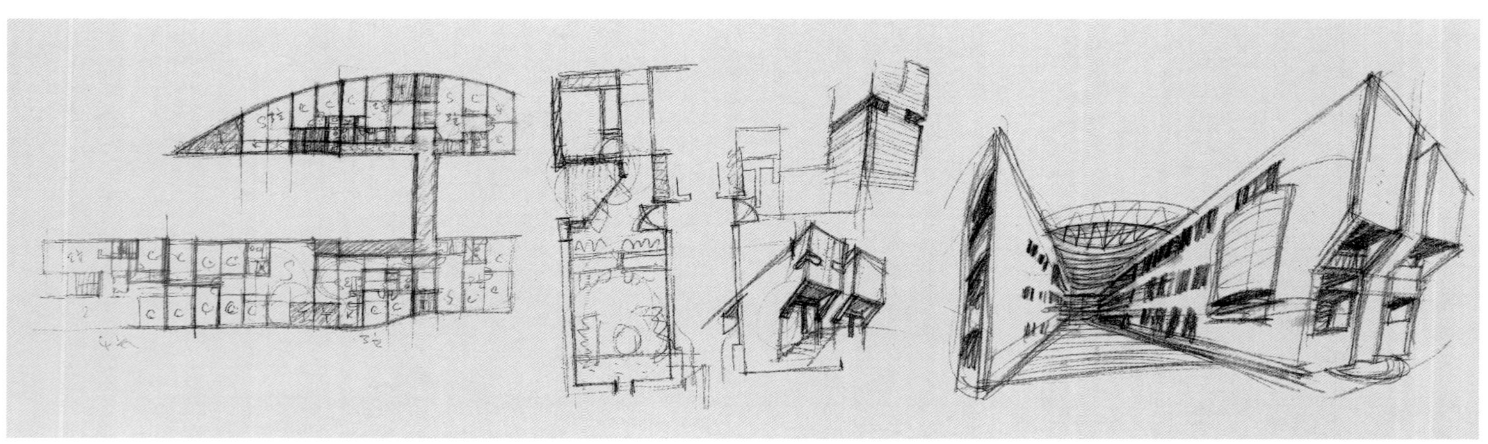

疗养院

瑞士，诺瓦扎诺

REST HOME

NOVAZZANO, SWITZERLAND

1992-1997

项目时间：1992年
建造时间：1995~1997年
委托方：杰内斯特雷里奥市，诺瓦扎诺当局疗养院
占地面积：6,448平方米
建筑面积：3,271平方米
建筑体积：16,577立方米

Project: 1992
Construction: 1995-1997
Client: Rest home Consortium, local authorities of Genestrerio, Ligornetto, Novazzano
Site area: 6,448 m^2
Useful surface: 3,271 m^2
Volume: 16,577 m^3

这家老年疗养院位于一个略有角度的斜坡上，俯瞰着门德里西奥平原的城市风景。规则的凸面石头外墙使得疗养院能够很好地融入周边环境。这座建筑水平铺开，形状类似一个外部覆以砖块的低矮圆柱体。圆柱体的一部分由视野开阔的开口替代，创造出过渡空间。这座建筑入口在背面，经过连接通道到达视野开阔的正面。高高的门廊从地面升起，比圆形墙体略高，阴影处吸引人们前来探索该建筑与自然环境之间的联系。中部柱廊环绕，一个入口引向宽阔的中央地带，并通向一层的复健室和公共空间，如餐厅和小型礼拜堂。这座建筑共有3层，共25个房间，有遮蔽的小型阳台位于每层楼的外围，环绕着中心。大厅尽头有一扇巨大的高窗，尽显杰内罗索山壮阔的美景。圆柱体块中空部分被设计成一个内庭院，在延长的金属拱顶的遮挡下，中央空间向外延伸，通过建造在斜坡上的一系列坡道和楼梯与花园相接。虚空间与实空间仿佛在此融为一体。建筑的正立面通过简洁的建筑语言强化了空间的牢固性，并使得室内外空间更加靠近。建筑并未通过扩张去侵占外部世界，反而使外部世界成为了建筑自身的一部分。45度墙体立面、嵌入式空间、中央圆柱体和双拱形天窗共同构造出了这座既独立又完美融于周边景观的建筑。

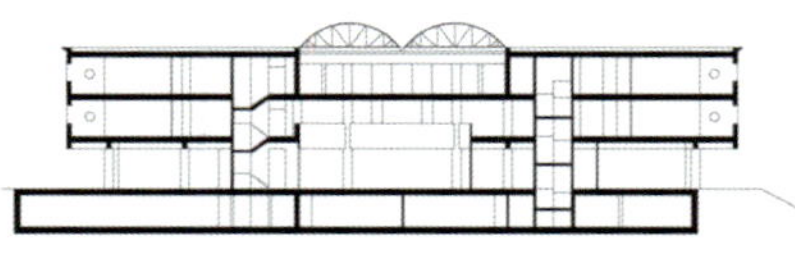

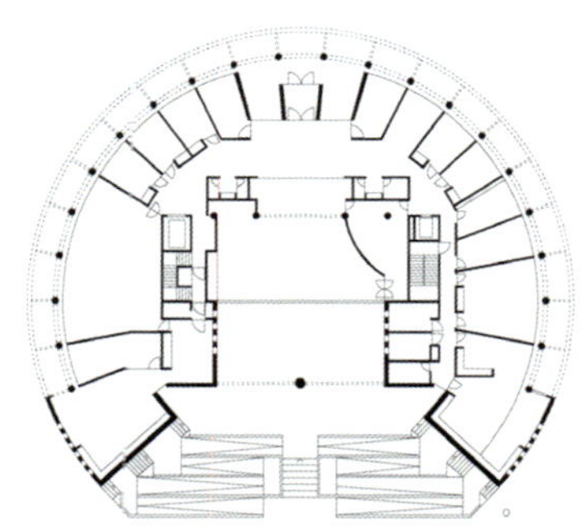

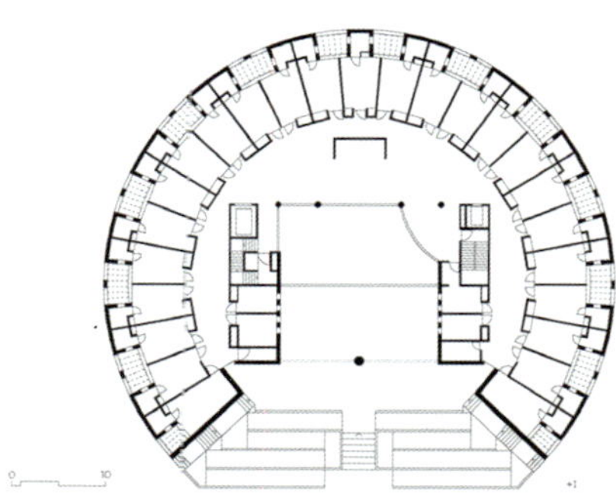

© ENRICO CANO

© ENRICO CANO

© ENRICO CANO

© ENRICO CANO

© ENRICO CANO

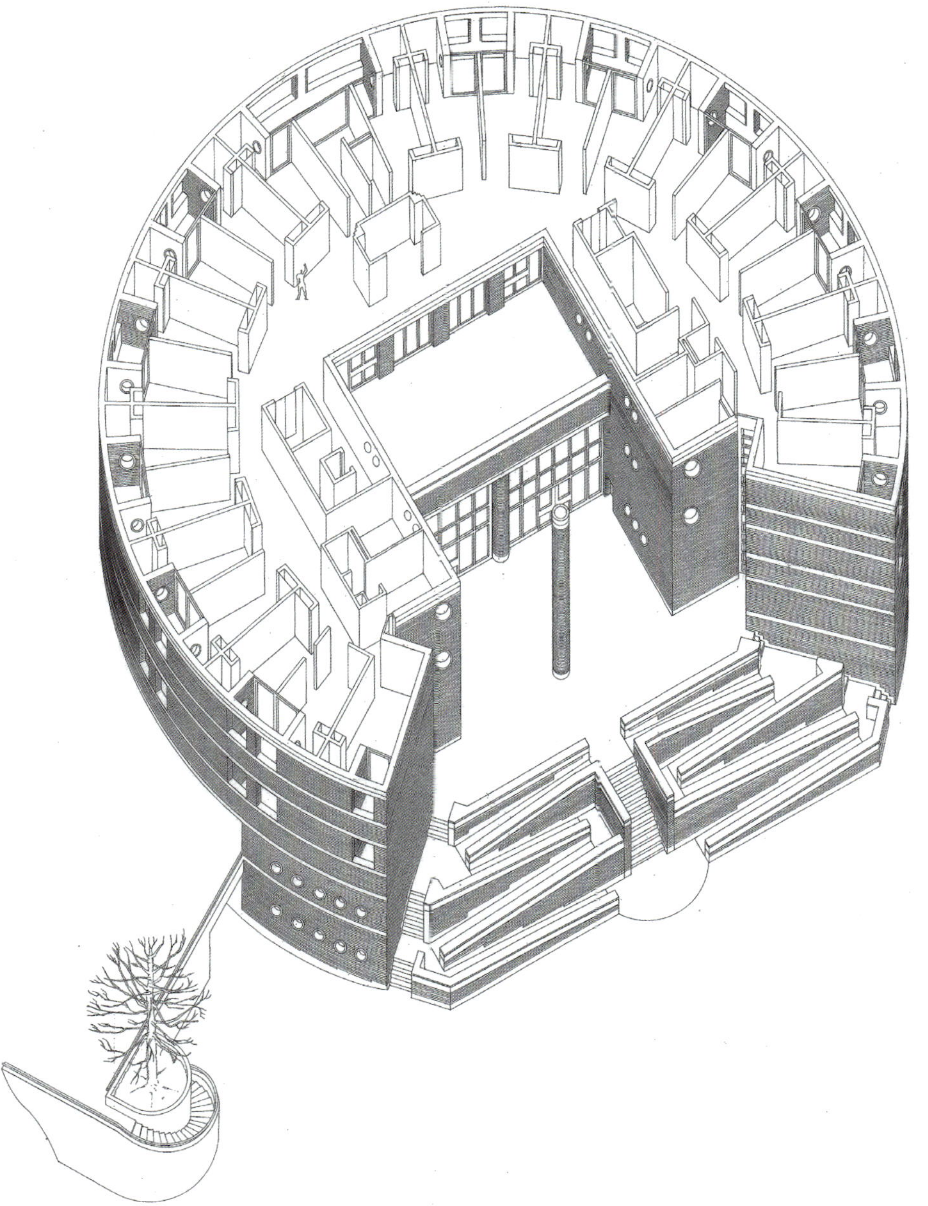

On a slight slope, overlooking the urbanized landscape of the plain of Mendrisio, the rest home for the elderly is inserted in the context primarily due to its regular convex stone walls. The building extends on the horizontal and takes the form of a low cylinder clad in brick. Part of the cylinder is missing, revealing an impressive opening to the view, creating a transitional space. The building is entered from the back and opens up to the view through the articulation of its front. The tall portico is slightly raised from the ground compared to the circular wall and its shadow becomes an invitation to explore the relationship with the natural setting. At the middle of the colonnaded perimeter, the entrance provides access to a vast central space, leading on the ground floor to rehabilitation rooms and the common areas, such as the dining room and the chapel. Apart from the ground floor, the building develops on two levels. Twenty-five rooms, with small, protected terraces, are placed on the perimeter on each level, while circulation winds around the core. At the end of the hall a huge window stretching upwards frames the stunning landscape of Monte Generoso. The emptying out of the central core of the cylinder creates an inner courtyard. A space sheltered by the extended vaults of the metal roof structure continues the central volume, connected to the garden by a system of ramps and stairs modeled in the sloping ground. As if the void has gained an existence of its own, the negative volume penetrates into the real one. Subtraction emphasizes the solidity of the volume, creates a front, and brings the inside close to the outside. Instead of the building expanding to include parts of the external world, the external world becomes part of the building itself. The surfaces of the walls set at a forty-five-degree angle, the recessed volumes, the circular column in the middle, the twin cylindrical form of the skylight create a self-contained building in dialogue with the landscape.

© MARCO D'ANNA

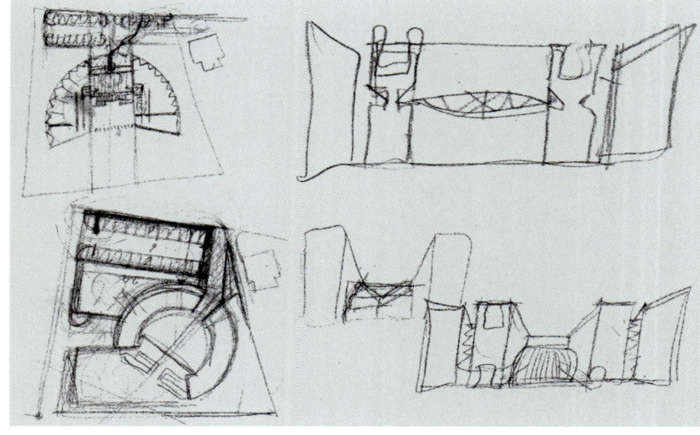

“卡特里娜”住宅区

瑞士，洛索内

RESIDENTIAL SETTLEMENT “CATERINA”

LOSONE, SWITZERLAND

2010-2015

项目时间：2010年
建造时间：2013～2015年
委托方：达尼埃莱和帕特里克·皮诺亚
占地面积：1,830平方米
建筑面积：1,245平方米
建筑体积：地上4,300立方米
地下4,570立方米

Project: 2010
Construction: 2013-2015
Client: Daniele and Patrick Pinoja
Site area: 1,830 m^2
Useful area: 1,245 m^2
Volume: 4,300 m^3 above ground,
4,570 m^3 underground

住宅区在旧城区与其下方平原之间扮演了桥梁角色。建筑构图的特征是其矩形基座被划分为4个3层高的体块，每个独立的体块暗示着公寓的分布。建筑将均匀的体量分解为独立的单元，并与周围建筑形成一种平衡关系。外墙的装饰使人联想起位于历史中心区的石雕建筑。

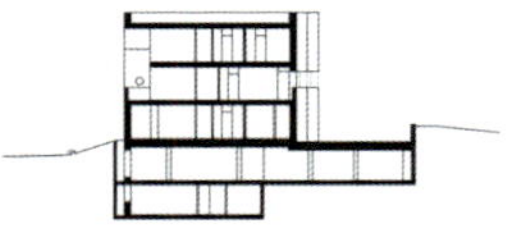

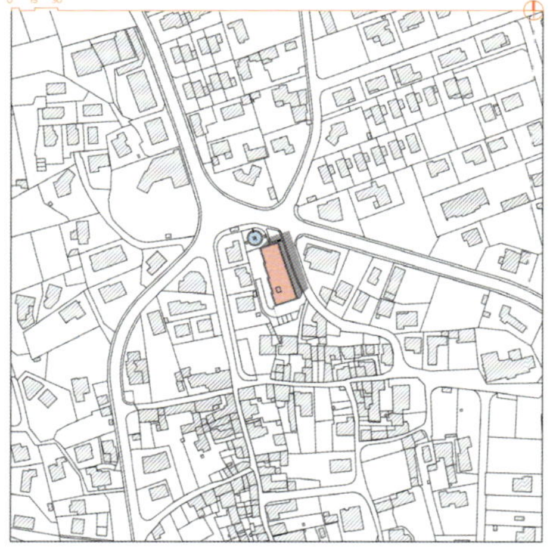

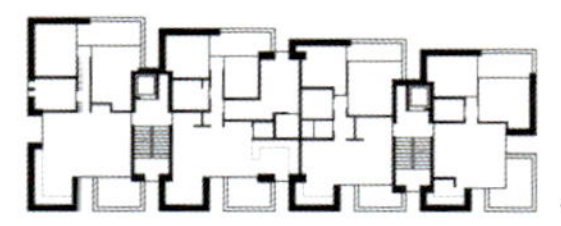

The residential settlement acts as a bridge between the old town and the plain below. The architectural composition is distinguished by a rectangular base divided into four three-story units. The single volumes also suggest the organization of the apartments. The breaking of the homogeneous volume into distinct units permits a balanced relationship with the surrounding buildings. The cladding recalls the stonework of the houses in the historic centre.

© ENRICO CANO

© ENRICO CANO

© ENRICO CANO

© ENRICO CANO

宗教空间
SACRED SPACES

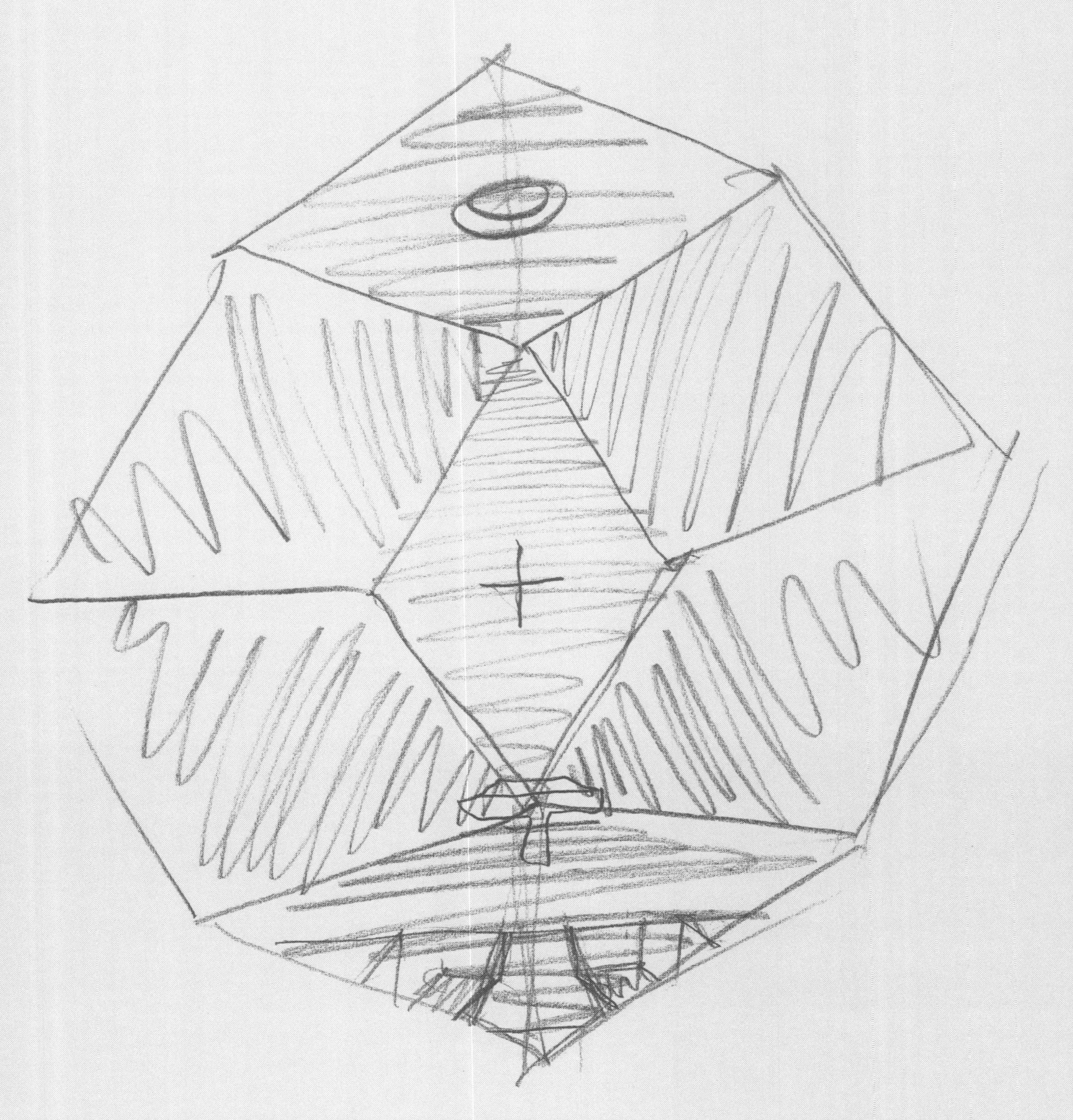

圣乔瓦尼巴蒂斯塔教堂

瑞士，蒙哥诺

CHURCH SAN GIOVANNI BATTISTA

MOGNO, SWITZERLAND

1986-1996

项目时间：1986/1992年
建造时间：1990～1996年
监理：吉安路易吉·达奇奥
委托方：蒙哥诺教堂翻修协会
占地面积：178平方米
建筑面积：123平方米
建筑体积：1,590立方米

Project: 1986/1992
Construction: 1990-1996
Site supervision: Gianluigi Dazio
Client: Mogno Church Reconstruction Association
Site area: 178 m^2
Useful surface: 123 m^2
Volume: 1,590 m^3

1986年的一场雪崩覆没了位于马吉亚峡谷的蒙哥诺村庄，摧毁了一座17世纪的小教堂。新建的圣乔瓦尼巴蒂斯教堂坐落在原教堂的旧址上，虽然保持了原建筑相对较小的体量，却呈现出全新的形象与建筑语言。这种当代性的语言和表达方式通过基本形体间的相互作用获得了一种古朴的内涵：内接于椭圆外形的矩形平面延伸至屋顶时演变为一个圆形。圆柱体的体量和厚重的石墙使得建筑足以抵抗未来可能出现的自然灾害。

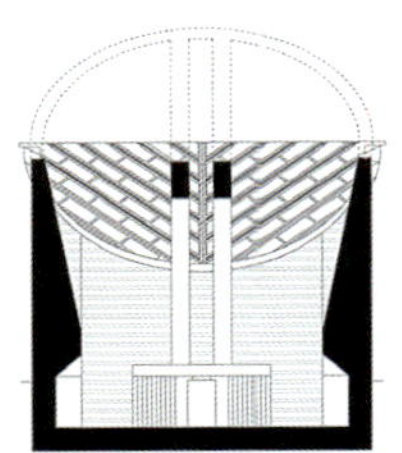

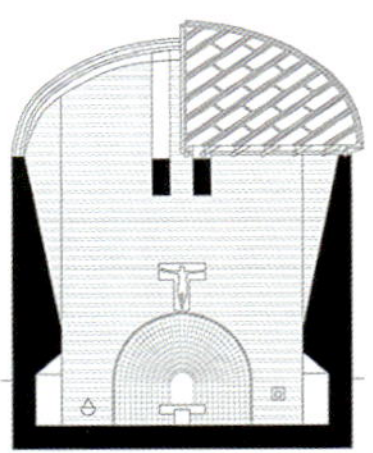

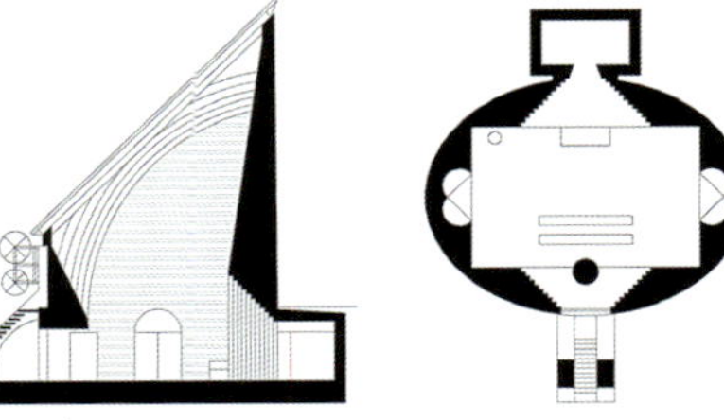

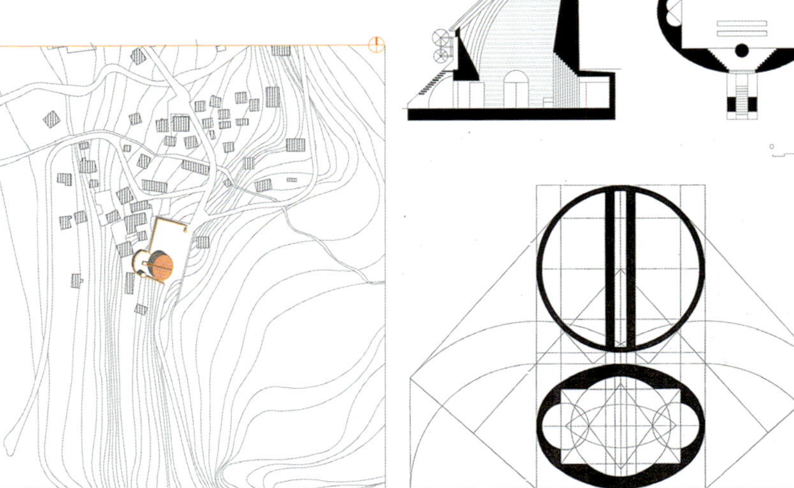

In 1986 an avalanche overwhelmed the village of Mogno in the Maggia Valley and carried the small 17th-century chapel away. The new church rises up on the same site of the former chapel and, though it preserves the relatively modest dimensions of the hall, it introduces a new image and architectural language. A language and expression that conveys a contemporary dimension, yet mediated by an archaic meaning thanks to the interplay of essential shapes: a rectangle inscribed within an external ellipse that widens into a circle at roof level. By means of its cylindrical volume and the massive stone walls, the building aims to resist any future natural disaster.

© PINO MUSI

© ENRICO CANO

© PINO MUSI

© PINO MUSI

© PINO MUSI

© ENRICO CANO

© PINO MUSI

© ENRICO CANO

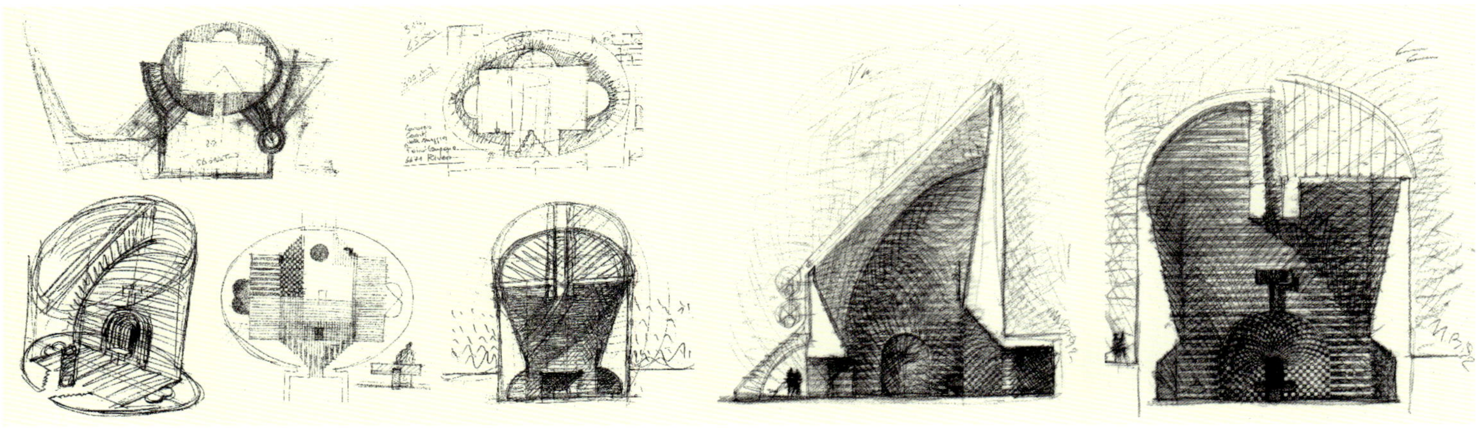

奥德利柯小教堂

意大利，波代诺内

CHURCH BEATO ODORICO

PORDENONE, ITALY

1987-1992

项目时间：1987年
建造时间：1988～1992年
委托方：圣鄂多立克教区
工程管理：工程师皮耶罗·贝尔特拉梅，乔治·拉芬
占地面积：3,800平方米
建筑面积：1,020平方米
建筑体积：8,800立方米

Project: 1987
Construction: 1988-1992
Client: Parish of Beato Odorico di Pordenone
Construction management: Eng. Piero Beltrame, Giorgio Raffin
Site area: 3,800 m²
Useful surface: 1,020 m²
Volume : 8,800 m³

该教堂以简洁而统一的结构为特点，基座如街区般大小，将庭院、回廊、配套服务设施和高处的截角锥形教堂围合在内。方形基座上的内切圆形成强烈的向心性。沿回廊形前院而建的廊柱形成一处僻静的空间，逐渐过渡到外部城市环境中。环绕四周的拱廊中，垂直的缝隙切断了连续的墙体。与周边杂乱无章的环境相比，建筑外观具有突出的同质性。建筑内部空间位于中央锥体结构之中，低矮的基座将外部空间纳入到建筑划定的矩形范围内。

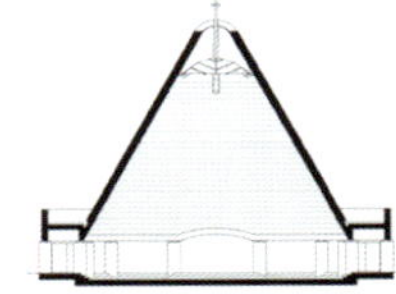

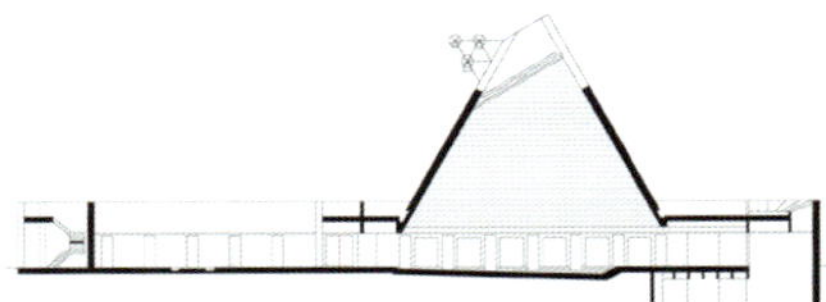

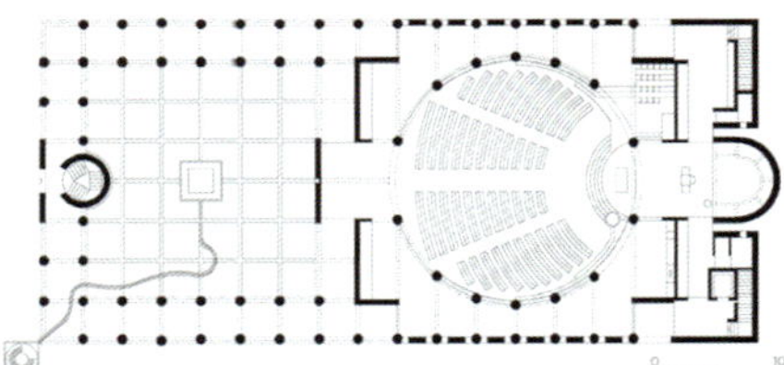

The church is characterized by a simple and unified structure, a kind of urban block enclosing the courtyard, the ambulatory, the ancillary services and the high part of the church in the shape of a truncated cone. The theme of the centrality, achieved by inscribing a circle on a square base, is linked to a clear direction. The colonnade borders of the cloise-shaped parvis create a secluded space as filter towards the urban surroundings. Within the four-sided portico a vertical slit on the main axis interrupts the continuous wall. The exterior image highlights the homogeneous character of the building with respect to the fragmentariness of the urban context. Inside, the space acts between the central conical volume and the lower side areas that merge outside into the rectangular boundary delimiting the building.

© PINO MUSI

© PINO MUSI

© PINO MUSI

© PINO MUSI

© PINO MUSI

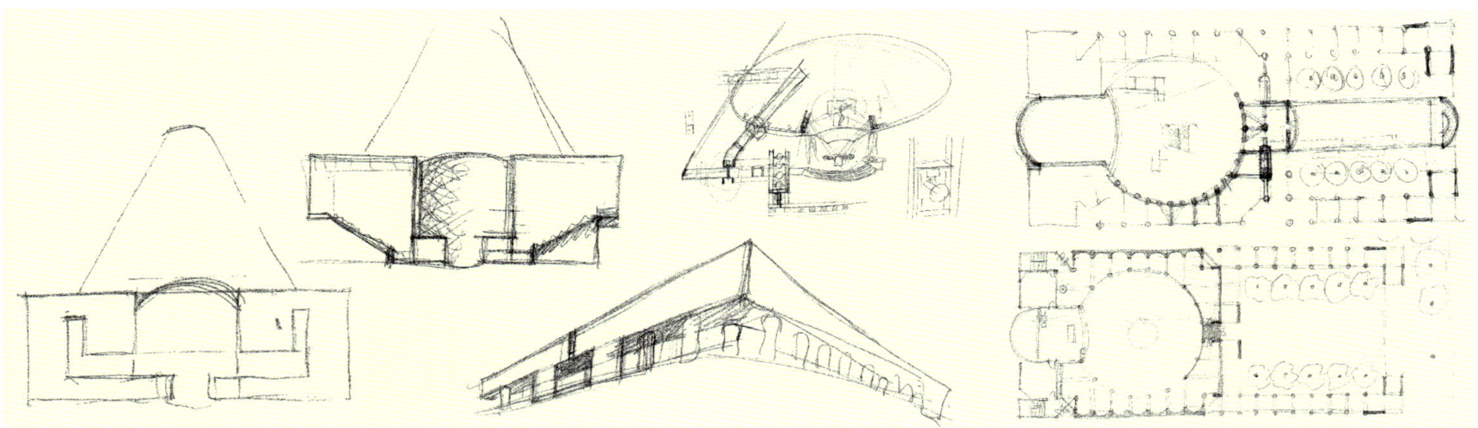

圣彼得使徒教堂

意大利，萨尔迪拉纳

CHURCH SAN PIETRO APOSTOLO

SARTIRANA, ITALY

1987-1995

项目时间：1987/1992年
建造时间：1992～1995年
合作建筑师：法比亚诺·雷达埃利，安娜·布鲁纳·维尔特马蒂
委托方：Parish San Pietro Apostolo, Sartirana
占地面积：1,600平方米
建筑面积：620平方米
建筑体积：9,800立方米

Project: 1987/1992
Construction: 1992-1995
Partner: arch. Fabiano Redaelli, Anna Bruna Vertemati
Client: Parish San Pietro Apostolo, Sartirana
Site area: 1,600 m²
Useful surface: 620 m²
Volume : 9,800 m³

圣彼得教堂的建筑理念是创造一个立方体与圆柱体相互贯通的几何结构的外形。由棱角分明的立方体构成，而朝圣空间则被设计为圆柱体。一个巨大的门切入建筑主体，标示出两侧楼梯上方的入口位置。简洁的主立面因钟塔的嵌入而被打破。立方体块内的圆柱体从一层升起，转变为一个2层高的女性回廊。一系列花格嵌板构成了与外立面分离的屋顶，重新塑造了下部的方形空间。直射光来自圣坛背后宽阔的拱形玛瑙滤窗，间接光源则来自三层回廊上方的天窗。

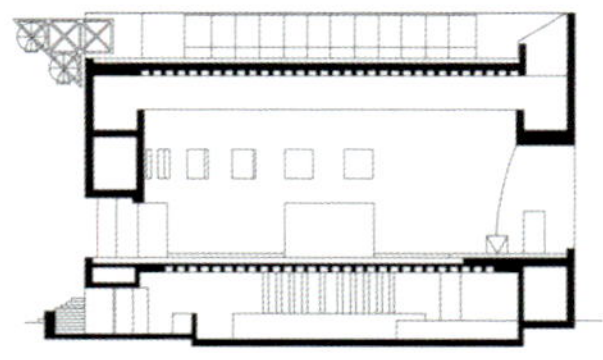

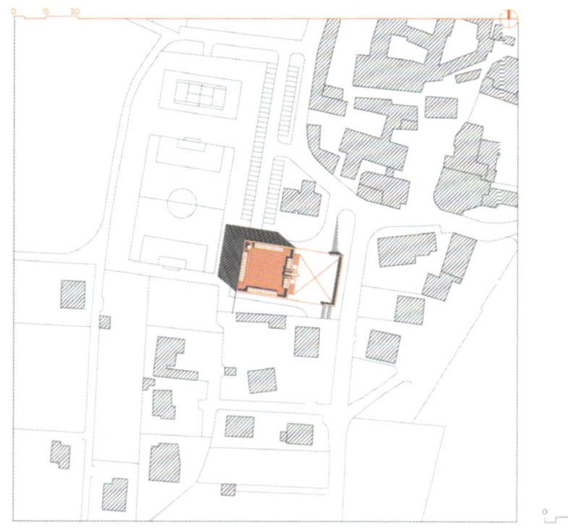

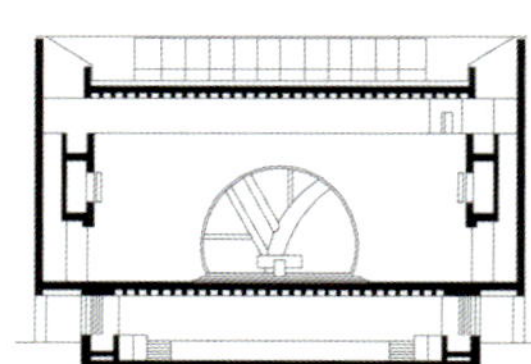

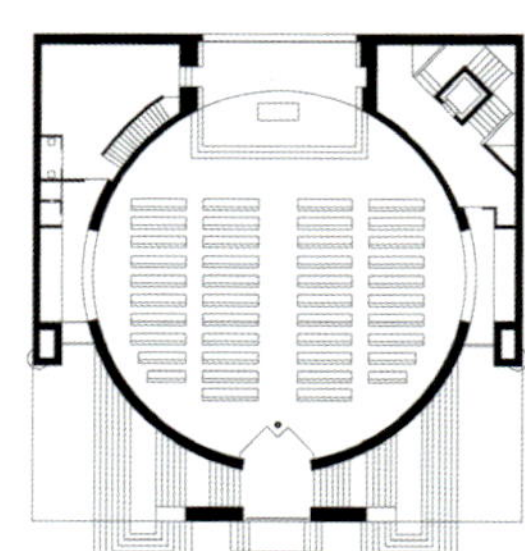

The architectural idea for the Church San Pietro Apostolo is based on a geometrical construction generated by the interpenetration of a cube and a cylinder. The prism forms the outer envelope while the cylinder defines the space designed for the faithful. A large portal, cut into the primary form of the mass, marks the entrance that is accessible from two side staircases. The main front tidiness is only interrupted by the cut with the belfry. The mass of the cylindrical ring within the cube rises from the floor, transforming itself into a two-floor women's gallery. The roof, detached from the external shell, is characterized by a series of coffers that recreates the base cube. Direct light comes in through the onyx filter of the wide arch-shaped opening behind the altar, and indirect light through the skylights set above the galleries.

© ENRICO CANO

© ENRICO CANO

© PINO MUSI

© ENRICO CANO

© ENRICO CANO

© PINO MUSI

© ENRICO CANO

艾维复活大教堂

法国，艾维

CATHEDRAL OF THE RESURRECTION

ÉVRY, FRANCE

1988-1995

项目时间：1998～1992年
建造时间：1992～1995年
项目管理：菲利普·塔尔伯特事务所
委托方：科尔贝埃松教区主管协会
占地面积：1,600平方米
建筑面积：4,800平方米
建筑体积：45,000立方米

Project: 1988-1992
Construction: 1992 -1995
Project management: Philippe Talbot&Associés
Client: Associazione Diocesana Évry Corbeil Essonnes
Site area: 1,600 m²
Useful surface: 4,800 m²
Volume: 45,000 m³

"我在设计上帝之家时，怀揣着一种为人建造房子的愿望。"这是一个简洁且均匀的结构：一个斜切的圆柱体。建筑的上部可以俯瞰广场，下部则毗邻一个住宅群。教堂通过圆形基座与三角形屋顶之间所连接的玻璃向天空开放。建筑顶部植有树木，犹如一个悬于城市上空的绿色光环。圆柱体自身并不具备正立面，一个内接于圆形的三角形倾斜面表明了教堂的朝向。在建筑内部，用于朝圣的中部区域和周边各层的服务区域有着明确的主次关系。圆柱体与屋顶一侧交接的线条赋予教堂后殿特殊的形态，砖决的肌理加强了这种效果。

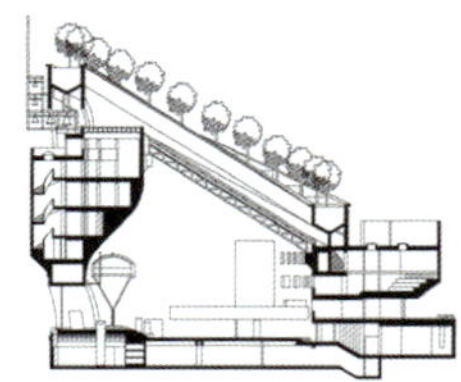

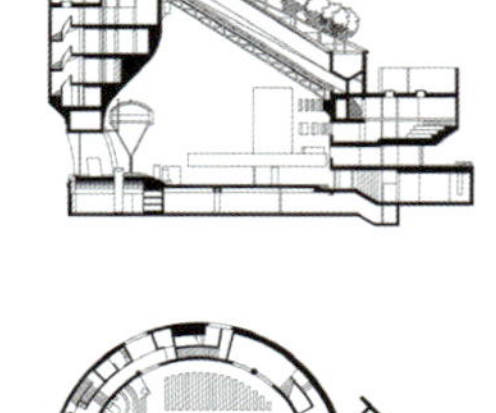

"I thought of the design for the House of God in the hope of making a house for man." It is a simple and homogeneous structure, formed by a cylinder cut diagonally. The uppermost part of the building overlooks the square while the lowest part borders with a residential complex. The cathedral opens towards the sky by means of the glass connection between the circle of the base and the triangle of the roof. The choice of placing a series of trees at the top of the building evokes a green halo suspended above the city. The cylindrical volume negates the very idea of a façade: it is the inclined surface of the triangle inscribed within the circle that indicates the church orientation. Inside, there is a given hierarchy between the central space designed for the faithful and the border areas for services on the different levels. The intersection of the cylinder with the linear connection of one side of the roof provide the apse with a particular shape , all enhanced by the texture of the bricks.

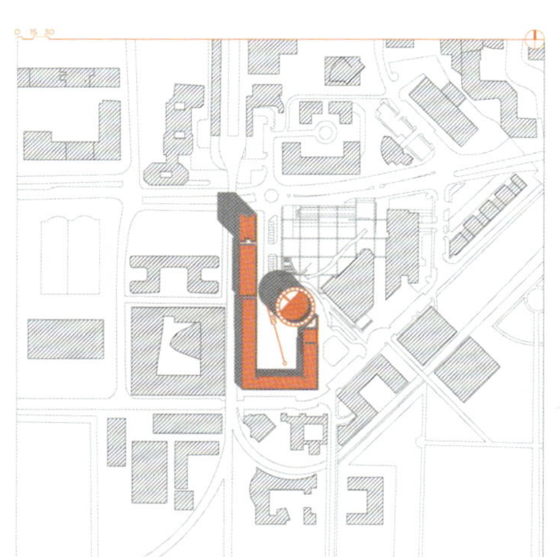

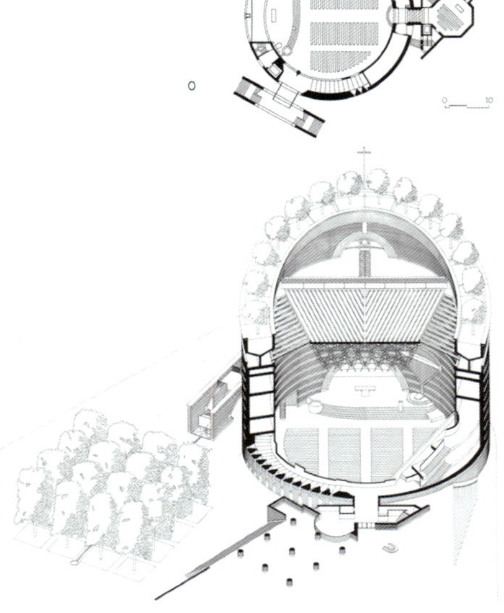

© PINO MUSI

© PINO MUSI

© PINO MUSI

© PINO MUSI

© PINO MUSI

© PINO MUSI

© PINO MUSI

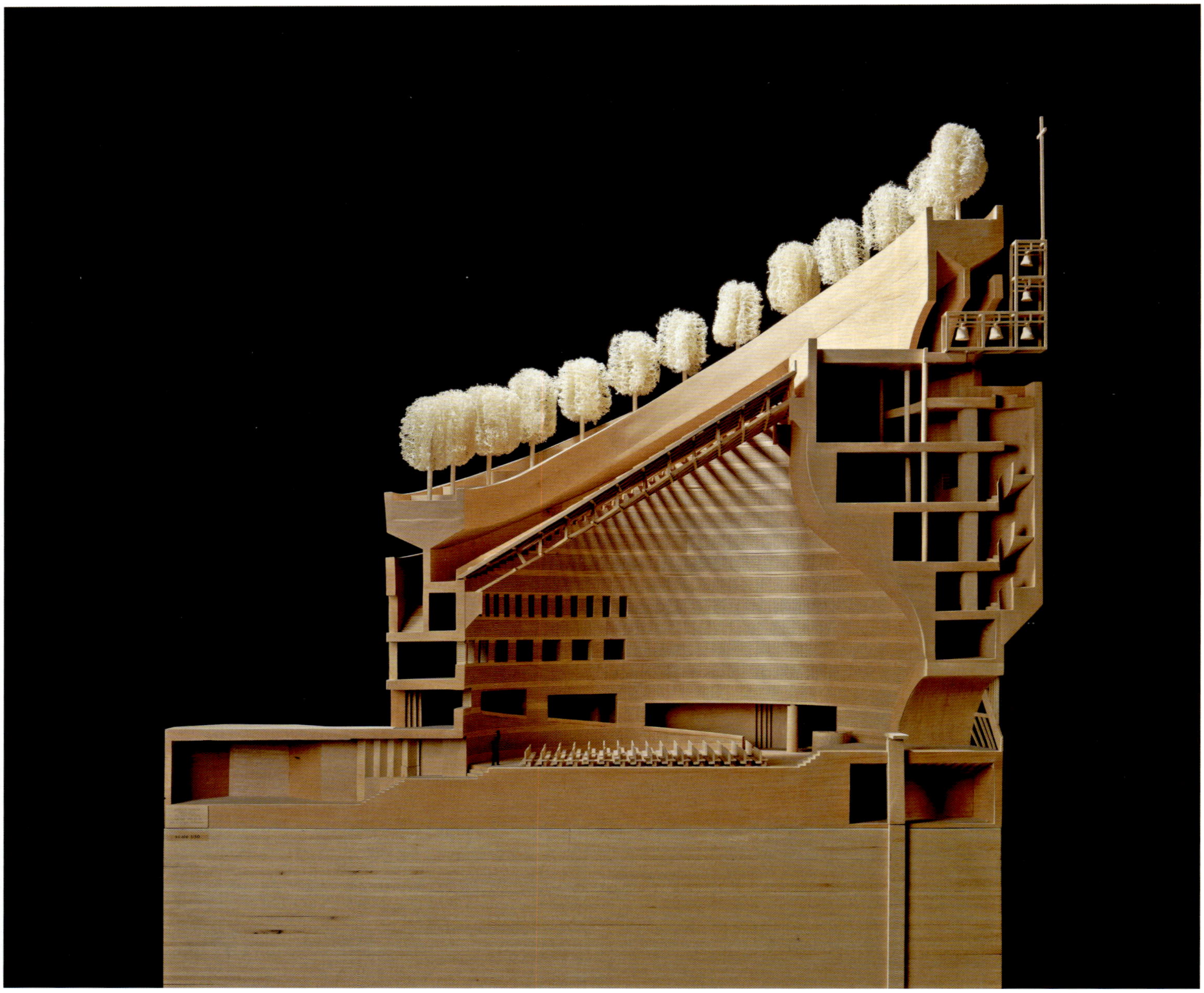

© ENRICO CANO

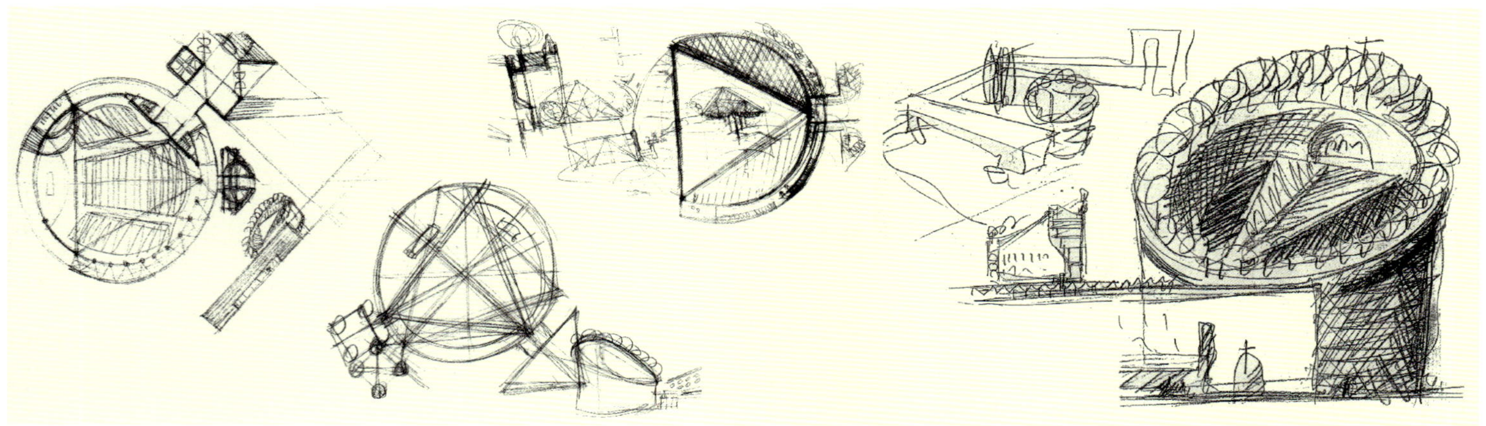

圣洁天使玛利亚教堂

瑞士，塔玛洛山

CHAPEL SANTA MARIA DEGLI ANGELI

MOUNT TAMARO, SWITZERLAND

1990-1996

项目时间：1990～1992年
建造时间：1992～1996年
委托方：埃吉迪奥·卡塔内奥
艺术家：恩佐·库奇
教堂面积：184平方米
外部走道面积：150平方米
建筑体积：2,820立方米

Project: 1990-1992
Construction: 1992-1996
Client: Egidio Cattaneo
Artist: Enzo Cucchi
Chapel: 184 m^2
Outer walkway: 150 m^2
Volume: 2,820 m^3

该建筑位于一处山坡上，延山体伸展，结束于一个结实的圆柱形体块。参观者有两条路线可以选择：一条路线通向可以远观整个山谷的观景台，另一条路线从墙体中间穿过，并通向下方的教堂入口。教堂内部空间被分为3个中殿，室内环形墙体为灰黑色石灰砂浆表面，与白色直线造型的顶棚形成鲜明的对比。两个较大的中殿起始于较低中殿的入口处，结束于从主体建筑体中伸出的半圆形后殿。在这个小空间里，强烈的光线将人们的注意力吸引到祷告区的壁画上，那是意大利画家恩佐・库奇的作品，描绘了一位双手合十的祈祷者。弧形墙上22个小型垛口内的雕刻也由恩佐・库奇创作而成。清晰的建筑结构和简洁的形式语言使教堂很好地融于自然形态之中，表现出对周围环境全新的、意想不到的理解。

From a natural slope of the mountain the building extends into space to reach solidity in a cylindrical volume. Visitors can walk two paths: either along the walkway leading to a lookout across the valley or, following a path in between the walls downstairs towards the church entrance. The internal space is divided into three naves and characterized by the contrast between the circular walls, covered with blackened lime mortar, and the linear white outlines of the ceiling. Two heavy columns are set at the entrance of the lower central nave, which ends in the small apse that protrudes from the main volume. In this small space, the intense zenithal light draws attention to the sign of prayer displayed by two hands depicted on the wall by Enzo Cucchi, the Italian artist who also realized the engravings applied in the embrasures of the twenty-two small openings along the curved walls. The chapel by means of its articulated building work and the simple forms set within a natural morphology, defines a new and unexpected perception of the surrounding landscape.

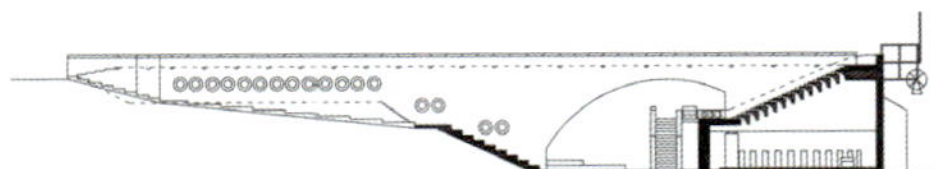

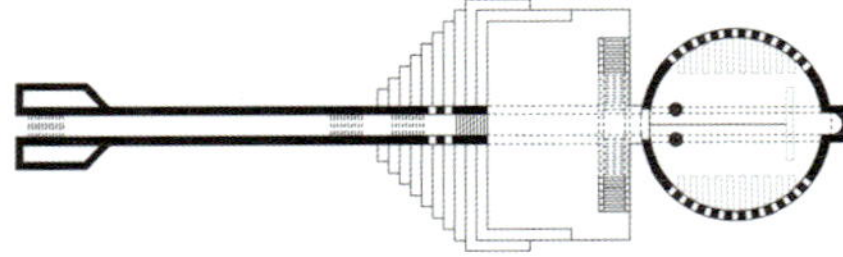

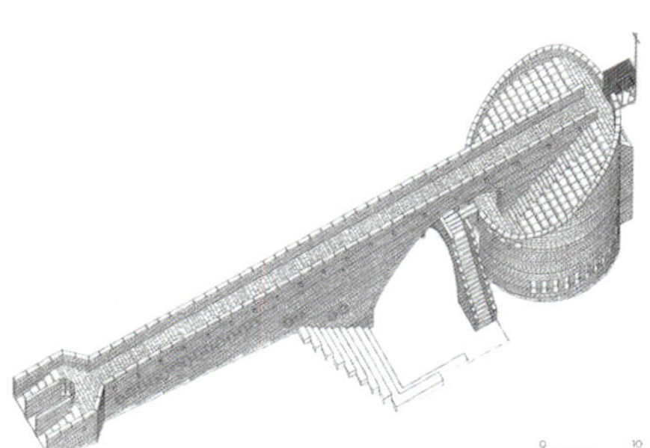

© ENRICO CANO

© ENRICO CANO

© PINO MUSI

© ENRICO CANO

© ENRICO CANO

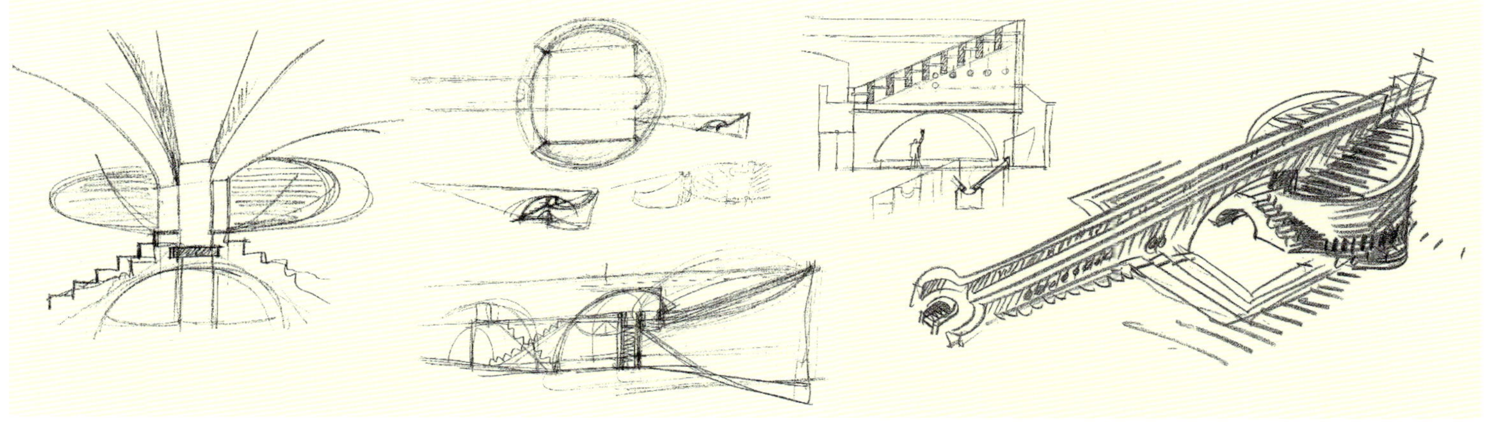

教皇若望二十三世教堂

意大利，塞里亚泰

CHURCH PAPA GIOVANNI XXIII

SERIATE BG, ITALY

1994-2004

项目时间：1994/2000年
建造时间：2001～2004年
委托方：塞里亚泰S.S. 救赎者教区
合作建筑师：古列尔摩·克里瓦蒂
雕塑家：朱利亚诺·万吉
占地面积：26,300平方米
建筑面积：2,137平方米
建筑体积：16,500立方米

Project: 1994/2000
Construction: 2001-2004
Client: Parish S.S. Redentore, Seriate
Partner: arch. Guglielmo Clivati
Sculptor: Giuliano Vangi
Site area: 26,300 m^2
Useful surface: 2,137 m^2
Volume: 16,500 m^3

塞里亚泰位于意大利北部贝加莫市南侧的一个小城镇。为教皇乔凡尼二十三世修建的新教堂坐落于17世纪圣亚历山德罗烈士教堂附近。项目由位于中央的正方体教堂和被两排柱廊围绕的长条形教会空间组合而成，长条形空间内设置了服务用房和教区工作用房。为提高建筑体的统一性，所有外立面都饰以带有裂痕的维罗纳石。自然光从屋顶的四扇天窗进入，沿四周墙面倾泻而下，形成完整、纯粹的内部空间。抛光的维罗纳石被运用在教堂内部，包括地板、四周墙面的护墙板和一些礼拜仪式性家具（祭坛、讲坛和椅子），使用镀金木板条做墙板支撑，这些都唤起了人们对古老技术和传统的记忆。有石材饰面双拱的内殿陈列着意大利艺术家朱利亚诺·万吉的浅浮雕作品。

The site of the new church dedicated to Holy Pope Giovanni XXIII is located close to the 17th-century church of San Alessandro Martyr in Paderno-Seriate, south of the city of Bergamo. The complex is composed of a square volume of the church, set in the center of the assigned area, and a long linear body surrounded on two sides by a colonnade that houses the services and the parish works. To enhance the unity of the complex, all volumes are clad with a split Verona stone. The interior of the church space offers itself as a one and only volume marked off by the perimeter walls and filled with daylight generated by the four roof lights. Polished Verona stone is also part of the interior finishing, not only for the floors but also as a high plinth running along the walls and the liturgical furnishings (altar, pulpit and chair) and supporting the wall panels made of gold-plated wooden lath, that evoke an ancient technique and tradition. A stone clad twin apse completes the presbytery and reveals a bas-relief by the Italian artist Giuliano Vangi.

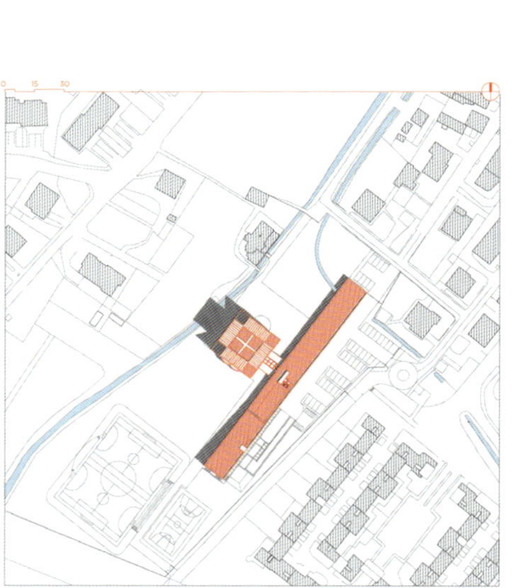

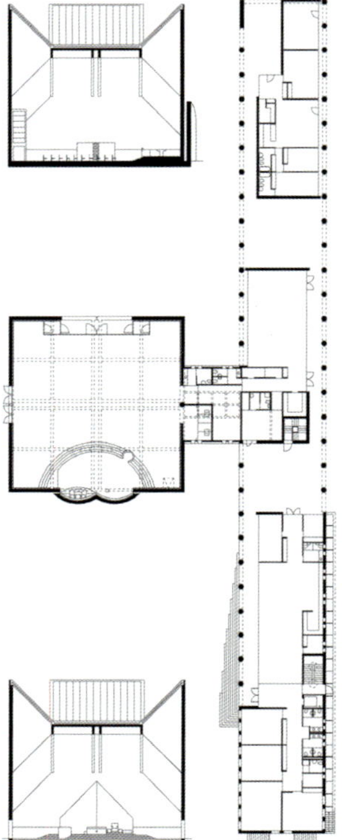

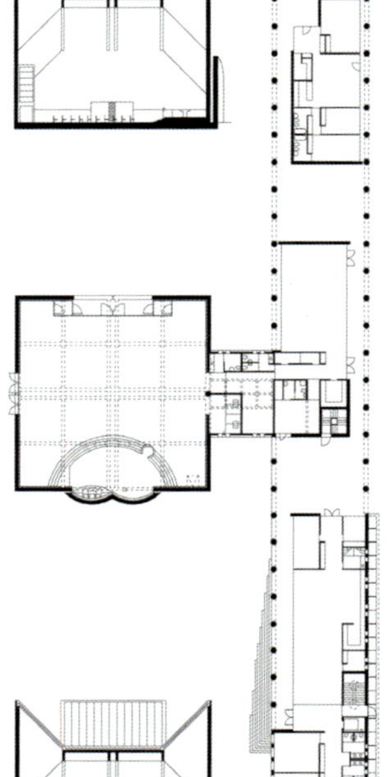

© ENRICO CANO

© ENRICO CANO

© PINO MUSI

© ENRICO CANO

© ENRICO CANO

© PINO MUSI

© ENRICO CANO

© ENRICO CANO

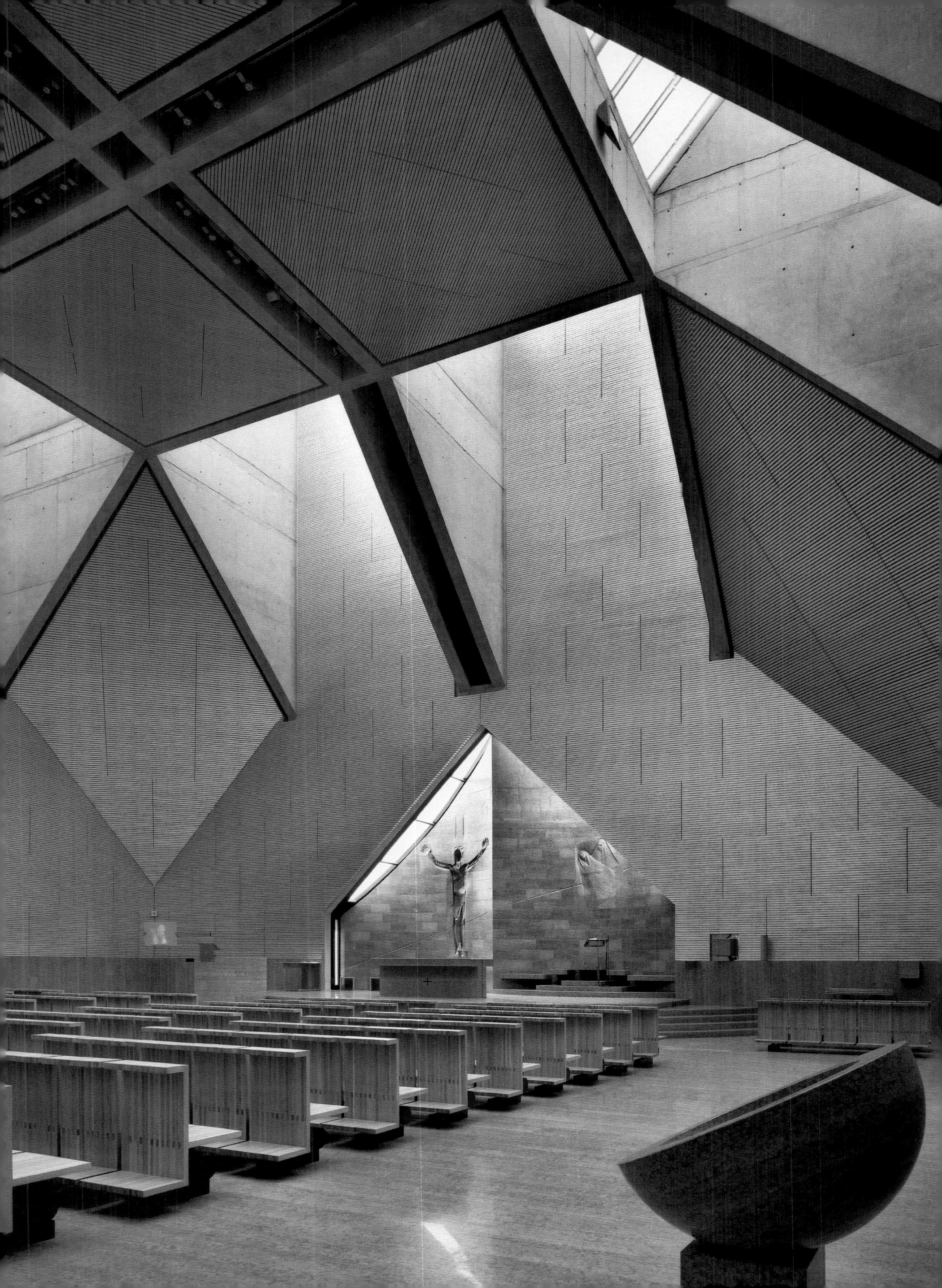

辛巴立斯达犹太教堂和犹太遗产中心

以色列，特拉维夫

CYMBALISTA SYNAGOGUE AND JEWISH HERITAGE CENTRE

TEL AVIV, ISRAEL

1996-1998

项目时间：1996年
建造时间：1997～1998年
委托方：宝莱特和诺伯特·辛巴立斯达
当地建筑师：亚瑟·辛波扎克
土木工程：什玛雅·本-亚伯拉罕
建筑面积：800平方米
建筑体积：7,325立方米

Project: 1996
Construction: 1997-1998
Client: Paulette and Norbert Cymbalista
Local architect: Arthur Zylberzac
Civil engineering: Shmaya Ben-Abraham
Useful surface: 800 m²
Volume.: 7,325 m³

这是一个祈祷的地方、一个讨论的地方，是一座犹太会堂、一座会议礼堂，是一处将宗教和世俗融合的地方。项目的概念来源于委托方给出的清晰想法：在特拉维夫大学校园内建造两个能满足精神需求的空间，它们在功能上分离，但在形式上要能一致地表达对精神的共同追求。独特的矩形基座上升起两个相同的方形体块，旋转并打开形成圆形。每个圆形体块在筒壁和内切方形屋顶之间形成了四个拱形天窗，光线由此泻下，洒在室内特有的金色砂石墙面上，形成独特的内部空间。所有的外立面都饰以带有裂痕的红色维罗纳石。底部空间中共用服务和活动设施精心分布在两个主要空间的周围。只有通过室内的装饰才能辨别出两个大厅的不同功能。

A place for prayer and a place for discussion, a synagogue and a conference hall, a crossroads for the religious and the secular. The concept for the project - to be built within the campus of Tel Aviv University - was helped by the clients' clear ideas about what they wanted: two spaces that were separate in functions but united as a symbol expressing the common quest for spirituality. From a unique rectangular base two identical square volume arise, both turning and open up into a circular shape. On top of each body the inscribed square roof creates four arch segments to let daylight in and flood down the interior gold sandstone walls, that characterizes the interior spaces. All exterior façade are clad in split red Verona stone. The base gathers the shared services and activities, well distributed around the two main spaces. Only the interior fittings reveal the different functions of the two halls.

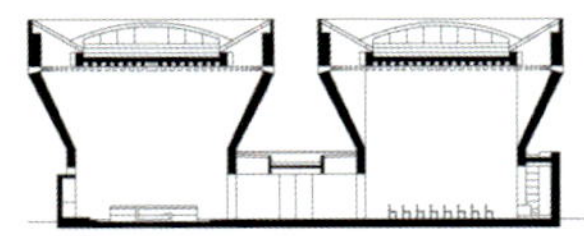

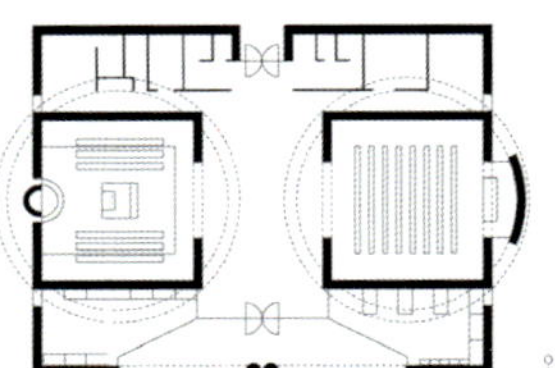

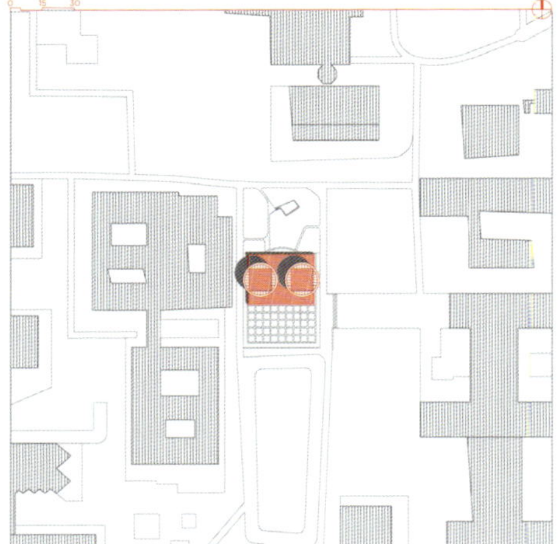

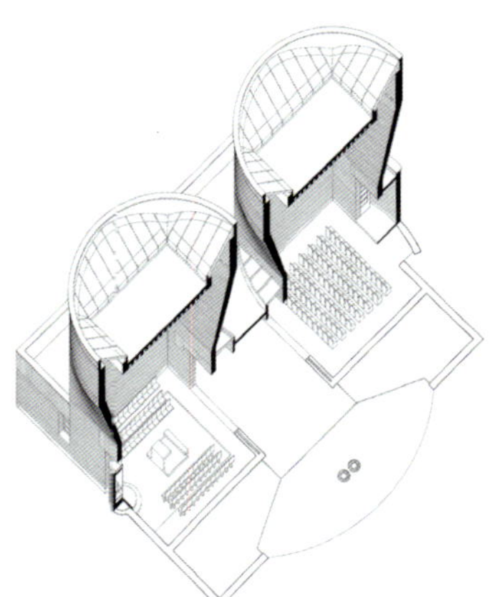

© PINO MUSI

© PINO MUSI

© PINO MUSI

© PINO MUSI

© PINO MUSI

© ENRICO CANO

圣安东尼教堂正立面

瑞士，杰内斯特雷里奥

FAÇADE OF THE CHURCH SANT'ANTONIO ABATE

GENESTRERIO, SWITZERLAND

1999-2003

项目时间：1999年
建造时间：2002~2003年
委托方：杰内斯特雷里奥教区
土木工程：瑞士，瓦卡诺，埃拉尔多·皮亚内蒂
工程管理：瑞士，杰内斯特雷里奥，弗拉维奥·波奇
结构和材料：钢筋混凝土承重结构，外部覆维罗纳石

Project: 1999
Construction: 2002-2003
Client: Parish of Genestrerio
Civil engineering: Eraldo Pianetti, Vacallo, Switzerland
Construction management: Flavio Pozzi, Genestrerio, Switzerland
Structure and materials: reinforced concrete bearing structure; cladding in blocks of split Verona stone.

该项目意图使用带有裂痕的维罗纳石去完成新的石头立面，打造出一件与后方的17世纪教堂建筑形成对比的当代工艺品。新的入口大门通过一个层次切割分明的宽大喇叭形结构加深了3米，并与现有的教堂立面明确分离。在对教堂前柱廊进行改造的同时，项目也实现了新的入口与现有广场的连接，提高了教区用房（博塔的第一件建筑作品）的品质。2009年，本地艺术家阿卜杜拉创作的青铜门取代了旧的木制门。

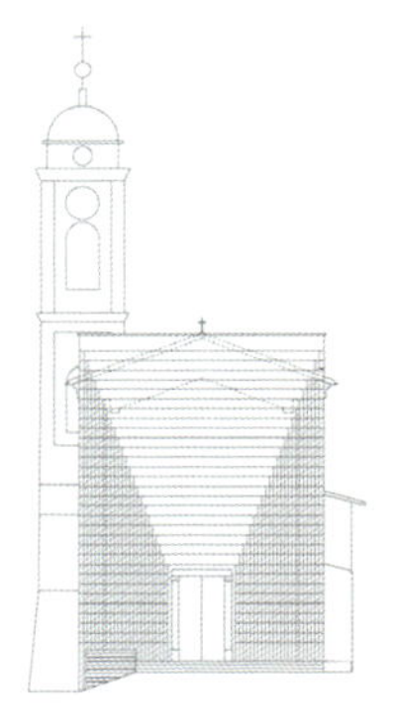

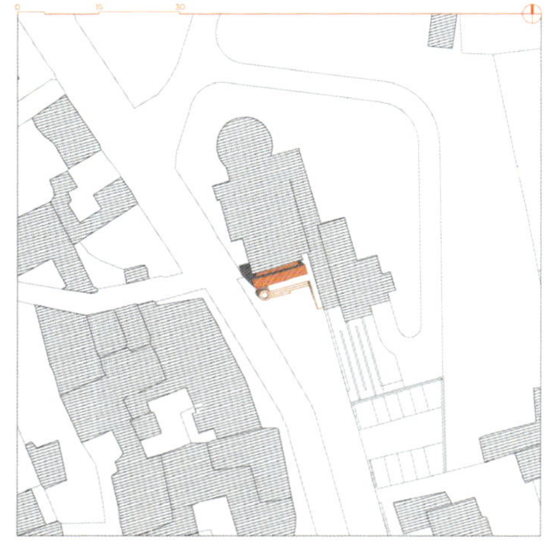

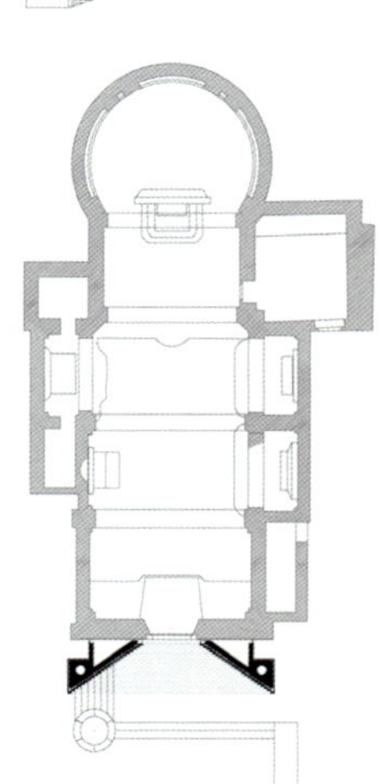

The intention was to realize a new stone façade, worked in split Verona stone, to create a contemporary artefact in contrast to the 17thcentury church building at the back. The new entrance gate is detached from the existent church front by a clear cut and widens on all side like a bellow up to a depth of three meters. This project was paralleled by the renovation of the parvis to create the levels required to link the new entrance with the existing square and the parish house, Botta's first architectural work. In 2009, the local artist Selim Abdullah created a bronze door to replace the former wooden one.

圣卡尔利诺

瑞士，卢加诺湖

SAN CARLINO

LAKE LUGANO, SWITZERLAND

1999-2003

项目时间：1999年
建造时间：1999年
项目拆除：2003年
筹办方：卢加诺大学；门德里西奥建筑学院
土木工程：卢加诺，奥雷里奥·穆敦尼
工程管理：基亚索，艾里奥·奥斯蒂内利

Project: 1999
Construction: 1999
Dismantling: 2003
Promoters: University of Lugano;
Academy of architecture of Mendrisio
Civil engineering: Aurelio Muttoni, Lugano
Construction management: Elio Ostinelli, Chiasso

这个与实物一样大小的木制模型展示了罗马四喷泉圣卡罗教堂的剖面。该教堂模型建于1999年，是为纪念弗朗切斯科·博罗米尼诞辰400周年以及庆祝卢加诺艺术博物馆的展览而建。得益于卢加诺大学和门德里西奥建筑学院就业计划的支持，也感谢临时工人、建筑师、绘图员、木工以及手工匠的付出，这个计划因此得以在短时间内取得非凡的成就。这个木制模型放置在卢加诺一个离湖岸几米远的平台上。将近33米高的木质结构由35000块4.5厘米厚的木板构成，通过1厘米的空缝进行模块化组装，并用钢索固定在钢结构上。该展览在卢加诺湖边展出直到2003年10月结束。

The life-size wooden model represented the cross section of the San Carlo alle Quattro Fontane Church in Rome. It was built in 1999 to commemorate the 400th anniversary of the birth of Francesco Borromini and to celebrate the exhibition at the Museo Cantonale d'Arte in Lugano. The contribution of an employment programme, supported by the University of Lugano and the Academy of architecture of Mendrisio made it possible to achieve an extraordinary undertaking in very little time thanks to the involvement of dozens of unemployed workers, as well as architects, draftsmen, carpenters and craftsmen. The wooden model was placed on a square platform anchored a few meters from the shore, on the lakefront of Lugano. The wooden structure, nearly 33 m high, was composed of 35'000 planks with thickness of 4.5 cm, modularly mounted with a hollow joint of 1 cm and held together with steel cables fixed to an important steel frame. San Carlino graced Lugano lakeside until October 2003.

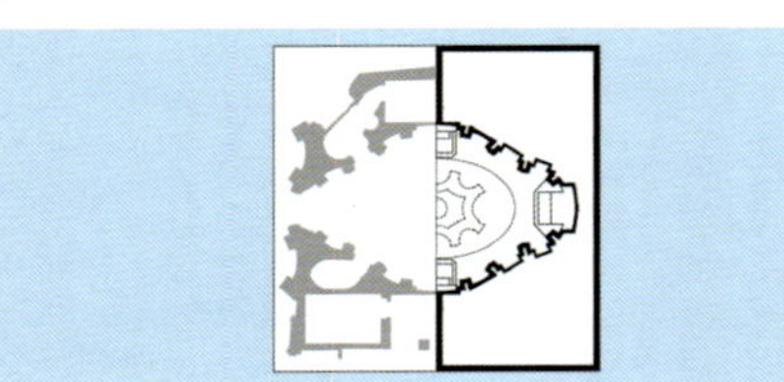

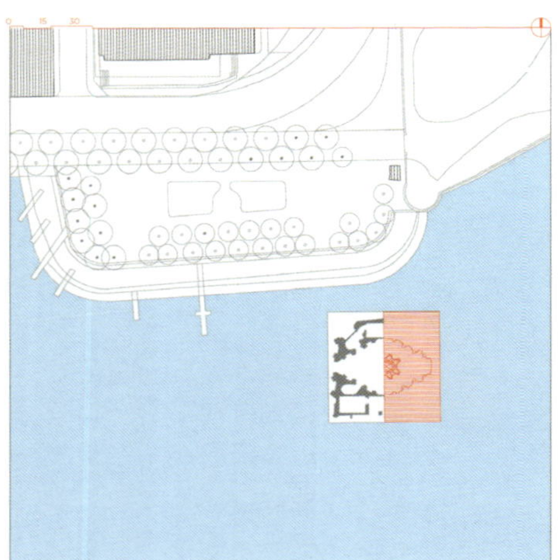

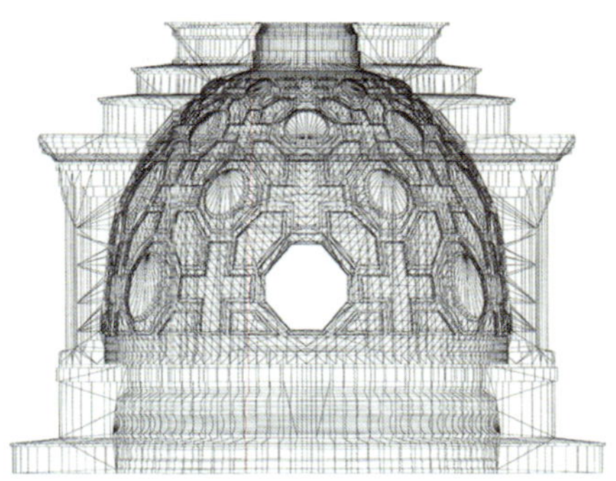

© PINO MUSI

© PINO MUSI

© PINO MUSI

© PINO MUSI

© PINO MUSI

圣容教堂

意大利，都灵

CHURCH SANTO VOLTO

TURIN, ITALY

2001-2006

项目时间：2001年
建造时间：2004～2006年
委托方：都灵大主教，红衣主教塞维利诺·伯莱托
项目管理：都灵O·西尼斯卡尔科工作室
占地面积：10,000平方米
建筑面积：26,300平方米
建筑体积：125,000立方米

Project: 2001
Construction: 2004-2006
Client: Archbishopric of Turin, Cardinal Severino Poletto
Project management: Studio O. Siniscalco, Turin
Site area: 10,000 m²
Useful surface: 26,300 m²
Volume: 125,000 m³

教堂由围绕中心的七座塔楼组成，塔下各连接着略矮一些的小型礼拜堂，将这些礼拜堂的顶部截面形成天窗。在空间内部，金字塔形的屋顶覆盖着宽阔的大厅，在空间中央通过虚实交替制造出光影交错的效果。依照委托方的要求，以交错安装不同质地石材的方法重塑耶稣圣像的面部，这种肌理在日光的照射下效果更为强烈。原钢厂的烟囱是这个区域工业文化的象征，被保留下来并添加了明亮的螺旋钢环。通过沿两侧展开的矮楼，教堂与城市连接，这里分布有城市元老院的办公室、公寓、工作日礼拜堂、长老会、各种教育娱乐机构和地下会议厅。

The central plan of the church is surrounded by seven towers added with lower bodies of the chapels that, through their truncated top, also act as skylights. Inside, the pyramidal roof shape embraces the wide hall and through the alternation of solids and voids generates a suggestive play of light and shadow in the central space. Following the clients' requests, the face of Jesus impressed on the "holy shroud" has been reproduced through a skillful interweaving of stone worked as a texture, enhanced by the daylight. As a reminder of the workers' culture on this area, the smokestack from the former steelworks has been conserved and added with a lightening steel spiral. The church connects to the urban surrounding by the lower building running along two sides with offices of the metropolitan curia, apartments, a weekday chapel, a presbytery and various structures for education and recreation as well as an underground conference hall.

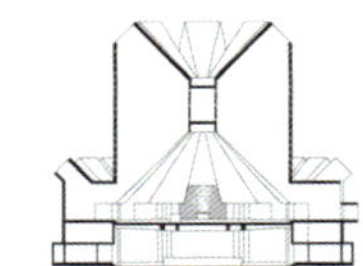

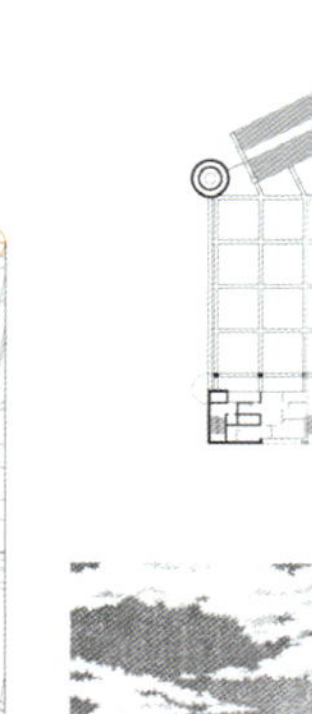

© ENRICO CANO

© ENRICO CANO

© ENRICO CANO

© ENRICO CANO

© ENRICO CANO

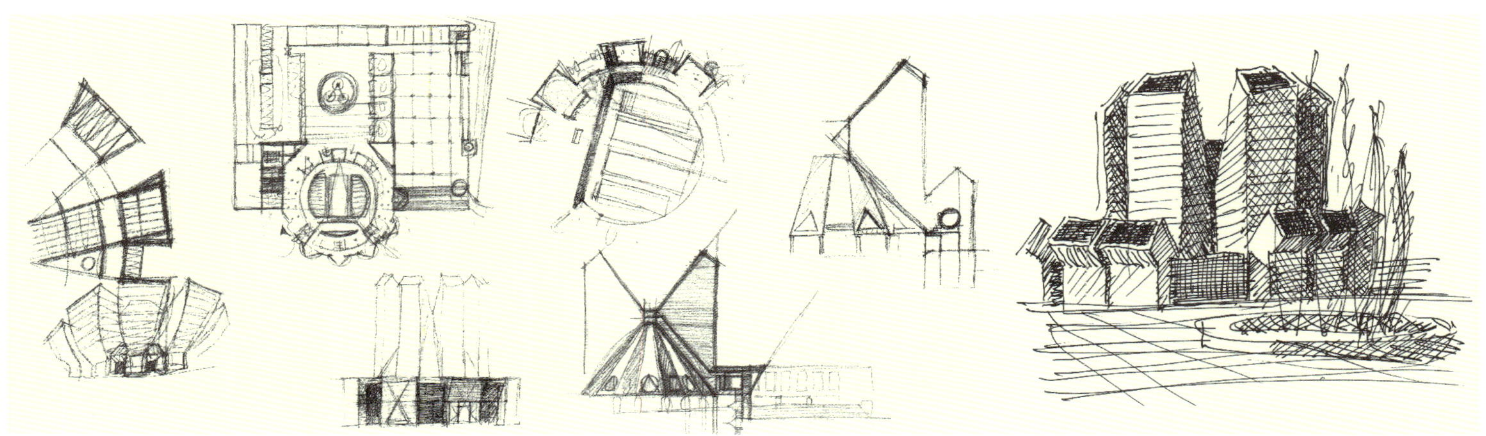

© ENRICO CANO

© ENRICO CANO

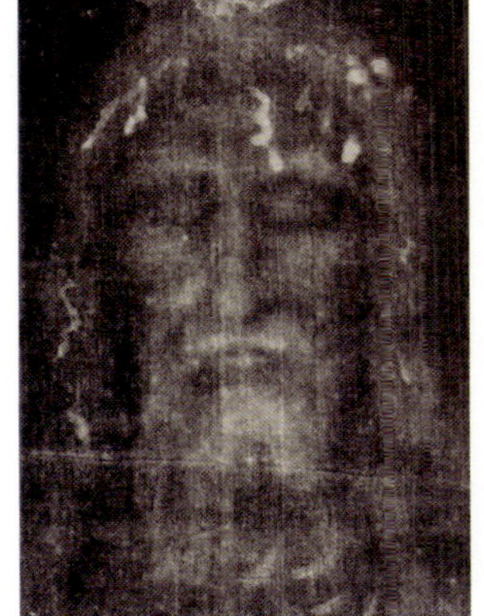

© ENRICO CANO

丧葬礼教堂

意大利，赛拉维扎的阿扎诺

FUNERARY CHAPEL

AZZANO DI SERAVEZZA, ITALY

1999-2001

项目时间：1999年
建造时间：2000～2001年
委托方：吉安内蒂·达安杰洛基金会
雕塑家：朱利亚诺·万吉
结构设计：马可和乌戈·达维尼
建筑体积：约170立方米

Project: 1999
Construction: 2000-2001
Client: Fondazione Mite Gianetti D'Angiolo o.n.l.u.s.
Sculptor: Giuliano Vangi
Structures: Marco and Ugo Davini
Volume: approx. 170 m^3

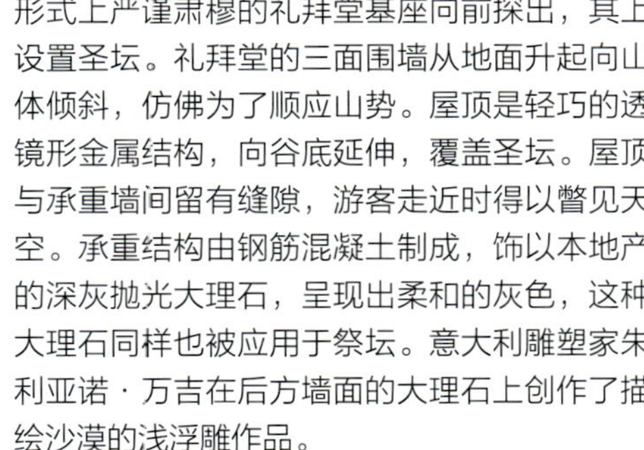

形式上严谨肃穆的礼拜堂基座向前探出，其上设置圣坛。礼拜堂的三面围墙从地面升起向山体倾斜，仿佛为了顺应山势。屋顶是轻巧的透镜形金属结构，向谷底延伸，覆盖圣坛。屋顶与承重墙间留有缝隙，游客走近时得以瞥见天空。承重结构由钢筋混凝土制成，饰以本地产的深灰抛光大理石，呈现出柔和的灰色，这种大理石同样也被应用于祭坛。意大利雕塑家朱利亚诺·万吉在后方墙面的大理石上创作了描绘沙漠的浅浮雕作品。

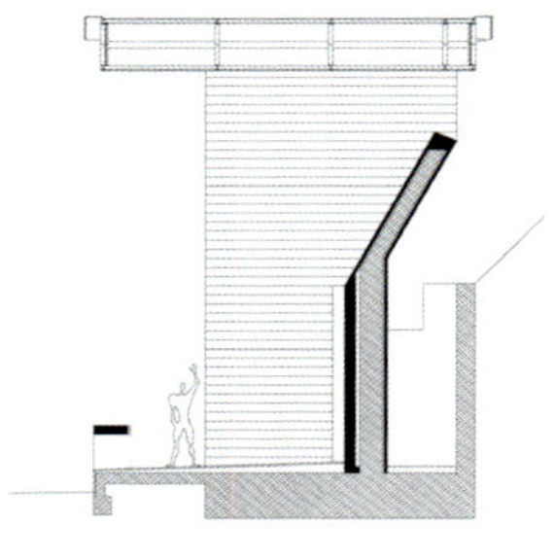

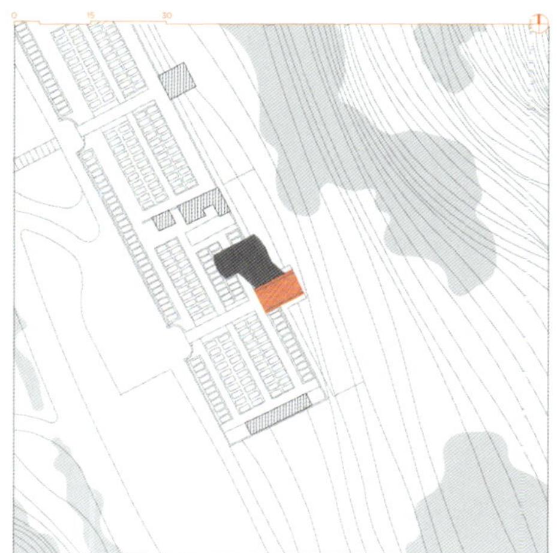

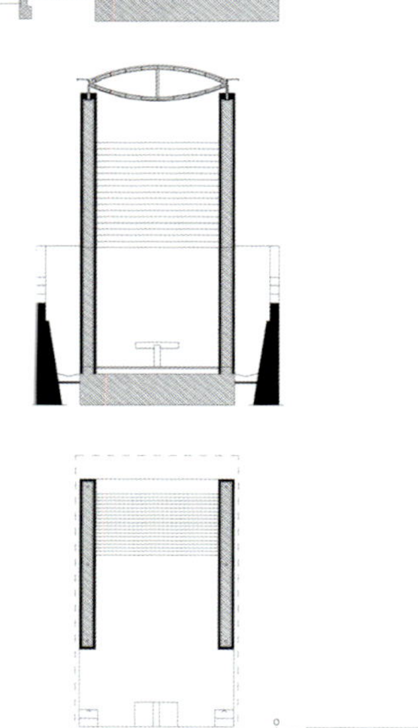

Extremely austere in form, the chapel is set on a base from which the altar juts out along the front. On three sides, it is defined by walls that rise impressively from the ground to tilt towards the mountain, as if following its slope. The roofing is a lightweight lens-shaped metal structure that extends towards the valley to cover the altar, and it is slightly detached from the bearing walls to offer visitors a glimpse of the sky as they approach. The bearing structure is made of reinforced concrete clad with polished local Bardiglio Cappella marble that is velvety grey in colour, also used for the altar. The Italian Sculptor Giuliano Vangi used the marble of the back wall as a bas-relief portraying Job in the desert.

© PINO MUSI

© PINO MUSI

© PINO MUSI

© PINO MUSI

MAZZUCCHELLI

新圣母玛利亚教堂

意大利，泰拉诺瓦 布拉乔利尼

CHURCH SANTA MARIA NUOVA

TERRANUOVA BRACCIOLINI, ITALY

2005-2010

项目时间：2005～2007年
建造时间：2007～2010年
合作建筑师：马里奥·马斯奇
委托方：圣母圣婴大主教教区
艺术家：桑德罗·奇亚
占地面积：2,459平方米
建筑面积：595平方米
建筑体积：4,700立方米

Project: 2005-2007
Construction: 2007-2010
Partner architect: Mario Maschi
Client: Parish archbishopric S. Maria Bambina
Artist: Sandro Chia
Site area: 2,459 m²
Useful surface: 595 m²
Volume : 4,700 m³

在历史街区旁的中央城市广场上，人们可以看到这座新建筑。建筑北面简洁的双拱形结构形成单一的内部空间，纵向天窗将该空间分成两个中殿。项目旨在突出拱形的体量，同时弱化中殿空间。外墙覆盖着陶土砖，而内部则饰以白色灰泥。版画艺术家桑德罗·奇亚创作的一系列玻璃雕刻作品沿纵向天窗展开，无形中构成了又一个中殿。

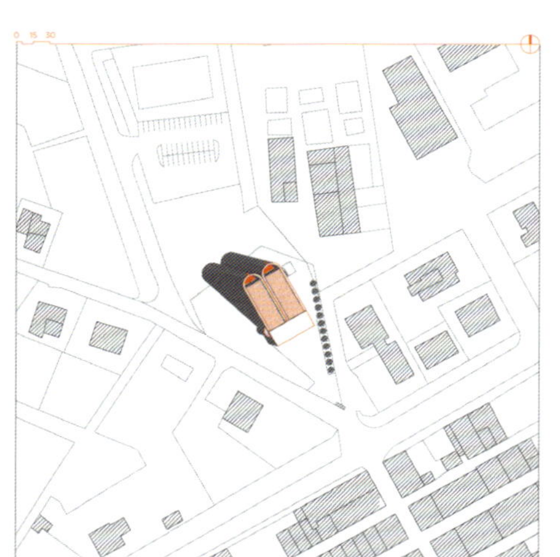

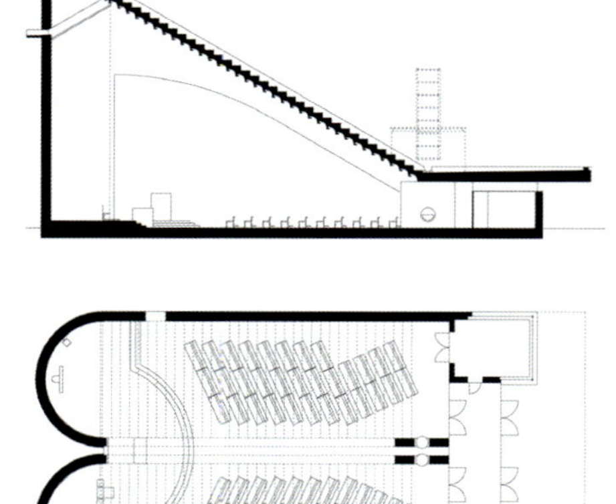

One can make out the new construction from the central square of the city, just beyond the historic center. The simple north-facing bi-apsidal structure defines a single internal space that is divided into two naves by a longitudinal skylight. The project aims to highlight the presence of the apsidal bodies and, meanwhile, to make the naves disappear. The exterior cladding is in terracotta bricks while the interior is in white stucco. Along the longitudinal skylight, a series of glass engravings by the Italian artist Sandro Chia virtually outlines a third nave.

© ENRICO CANO

© ENRICO CANO

© ENRICO CANO

© ENRICO CANO

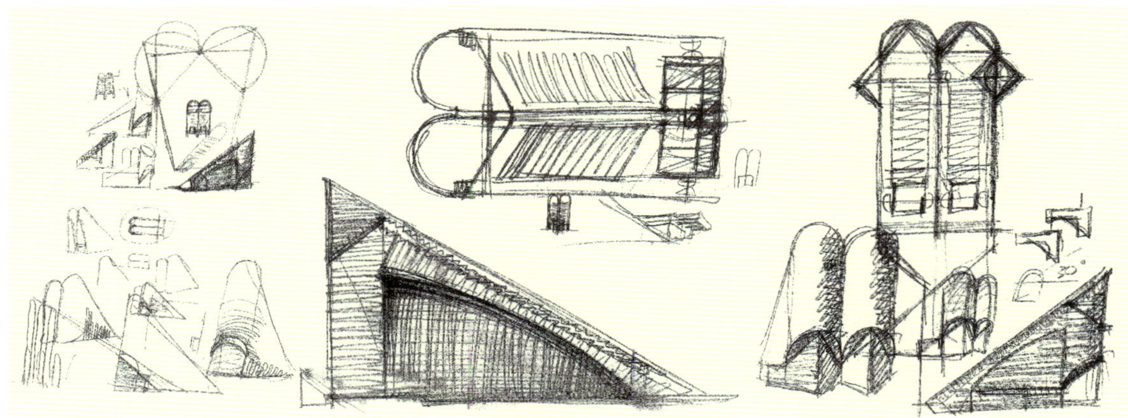

“圣洛克”教堂

意大利，圣吉奥瓦尼泰阿蒂诺

CHURCH “SAN ROCCO”

SAN GIOVANNI TEATINO, ITALY

2006-IN PROGRESS

项目时间：2006年
建造时间：2011年至今
委托方：奇艾迪-瓦斯托大主教管区
占地面积：7,700平方米
建筑面积：3,000平方米
建筑体积：25,000立方米

Project: 2006
Construction: 2011 - in progress
Client: Archdiocese of Chieti-Vasto
Site area: 7,700 m²
Useful surface: 3,000 m²
Volume: 25,000 m³

项目有意构筑水平圆形体和垂直有机形体间的对比，一方面连接起教区和居住社区，另一方面强调教会的存在及其在城市中发挥的宗教作用。建筑位于区域的西北侧，重塑了加富尔路和罗马路之间的街区。相对于整个建筑综合体，教堂呈现出旋转的形态，高30米，30度倾斜于地面，是凸出于整个综合体的独立体块。它向前院伸出，在顶部设有巨大的十字形开口。平日的礼拜活动在教堂的一侧举行，教区的中心垂直于罗马大街，另一侧被柱廊覆盖，前院作为社交聚会的场所以及整个综合体的中心。

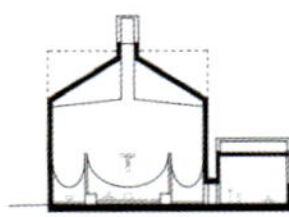

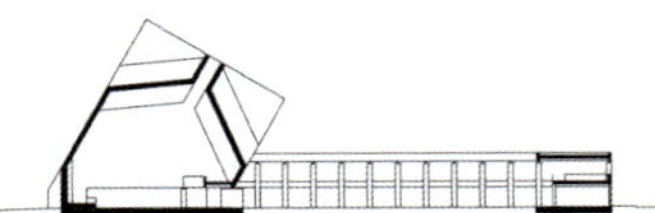

The play on the contrast between a horizontal parametrical complex and a plastic vertical body, was a choice made with the intention, on the one hand, of linking the parish services to the fabric of the neighbourhood and on the other, of reaffirming the presence of the church as a sacred space in the city. The building lies on the northwest side of the ground, redefining the corner of the block between Via Cavour and Via Roma. The church, rotated with respect to the entire complex, was conceived of as a single volume 30 meters high and inclined at 30 degrees with respect to the ground. It reaches out towards the parvis and is cut at the top only by a great cross-shaped opening. The weekday chapel is on the side of the church; the parish centre is perpendicular to Via Roma and the covered colonnade is on the other end of the parish centre. The parvis becomes the place of social gathering and the central element of the entire complex.

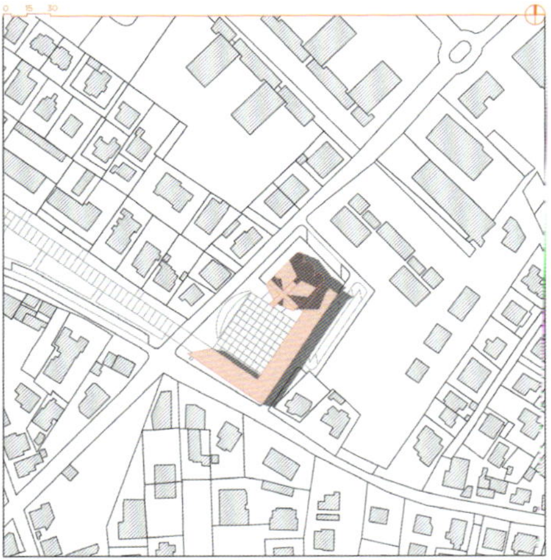

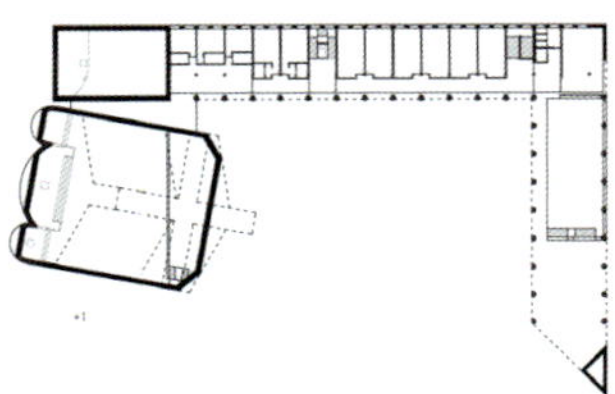

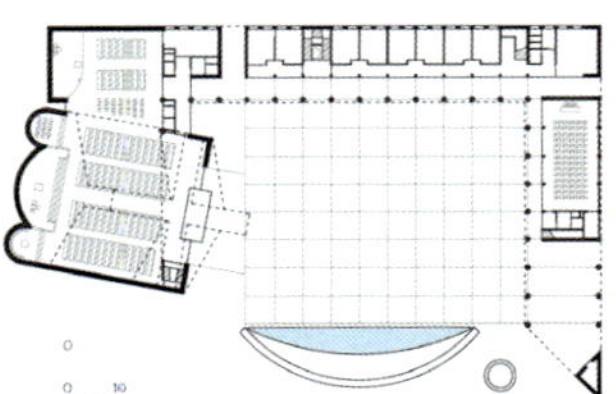

© ENRICO CANO

© ENRICO CANO

© ENRICO CANO

© ENRICO CANO

© ENRICO CANO

© ENRICO CANO

“石榴石”教堂

奥地利，齐勒佩恩约克

“GARNET” CHAPEL IN PENKENJOCH

ZILLERTAL, AUSTRIA

2011-2013

项目时间：2011~2012年
建造时间：2013年
地点：奥地利，齐勒佩恩约克，芬肯山，朋肯洛
委托方：约瑟夫·布林得林那，克里斯塔和乔格·克罗尔-布林得林那
合作建筑师：伯恩哈德·斯托汉弗，贝思托有限责任公司
占地面积：分隔区600平方米
建筑面积：40平方米
建筑体积：750立方米

Project: 2011-2012
Construction: 2013
Location: Penkenjoch, Municipality of Finkenberg, Zillertal, Austria
Client: Josef Brindlinger, Christa and Georg Kroell-Brindlinger
Partner: Architect Bernhard Stoehr, Besto zt gmbh
Site area: delimited area 600 m^2
Useful surface: 40 m^2
Volume: 750 m^3

教堂得名于一种在自然状态下为菱形多面体的特殊矿石（石榴石）。教堂坐落于海拔2087米的山顶，毗邻一处池塘，向北可俯瞰齐勒河谷。这座新建筑呈菱形多面体形态，矗立在一个混凝土基座上，外部为耐候钢包裹的木质结构。一层楼梯将参观者引入内部空间，参观者在这里能立刻感知到几何空间的均匀性。由顶部开口进入的光线，照亮落叶松板条覆盖的墙体表面。墙壁上流动的光线随着时间的变化刻画出不同的空间形态，为空间赋予了持续的魔力。

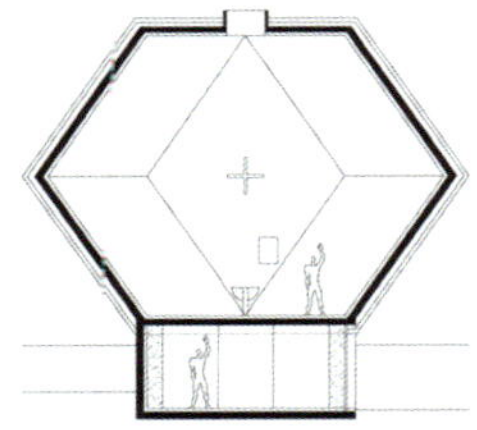

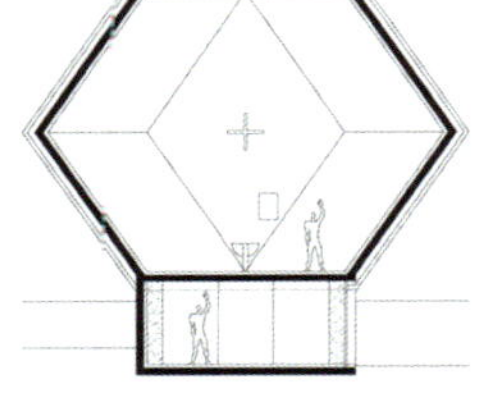

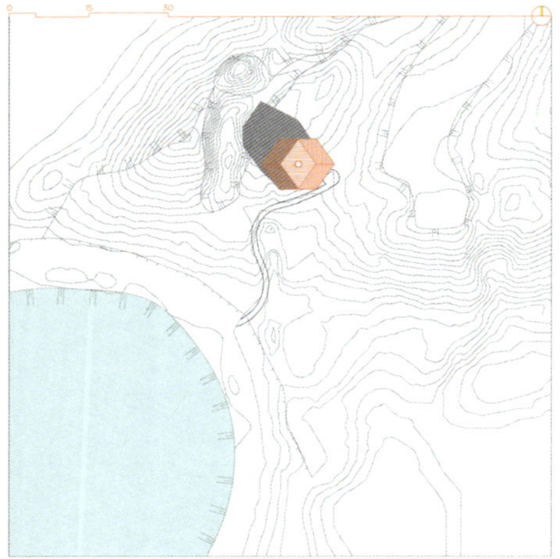

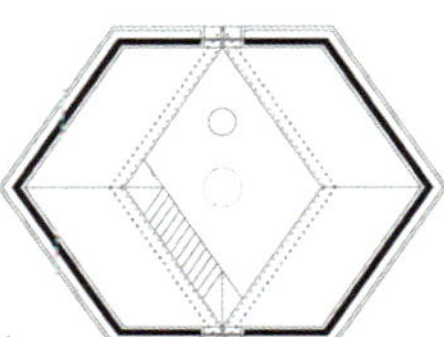

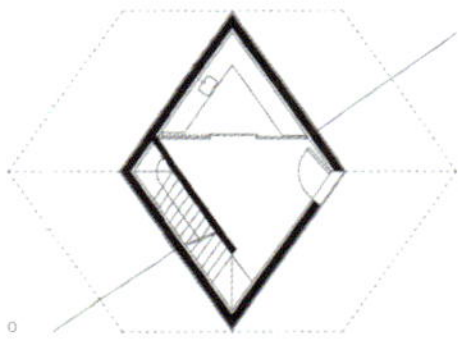

The chapel gets its name from the particular mineral (garnet) that, in nature reminds a rhombic dodecahedron. The construction is set on top of a mountain at 2087m amsl, next to a pond and overlooking to the north the lower Zillertal. The new building comes in the shape of a rhombic dodecahedron , set on a concrete base, with a wooden structure and covered in sheets of corten steel. From the base at ground level a staircase leads to the interior space where the visitor perceives at a single glance the evenness of the geometrical space. One single opening on the top offers a light source that brings to life the even surfaces of the walls, clad in larch wood lath. The magic of this space is the uninterrupted thanks to the light that comes streaming on the walls whose identical regular shapes produce different effects depending on the hours of the day.

© FRANZ DENGG

© ENRICO CANO

© ENRICO CANO

© ENRICO CANO

© ENRICO CANO

© ENRICO CANO

© ENRICO CANO

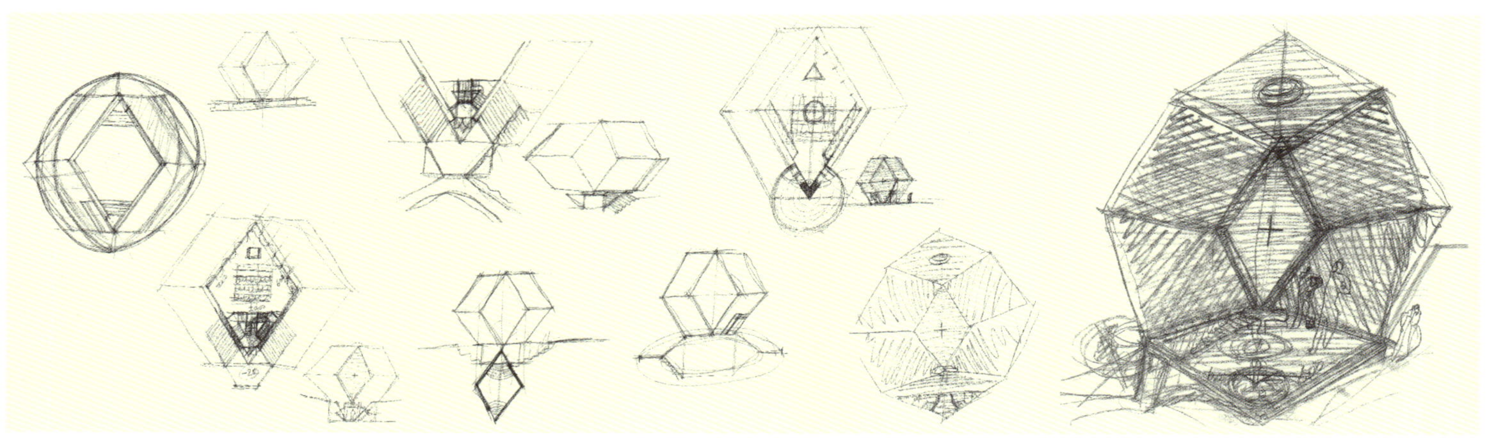

博物馆
MUSEUMS

和多利美术馆
日本，东京

ART GALLERY WATARI-UM
TOKYO, JAPAN

1985-1990

项目时间：1985～1988年
建造时间：1988～1990年
合作方：东京竹中工务店
委托方：渡洋史
占地面积：157平方米
建筑面积：627平方米
建筑体积：3,650立方米

Project: 1985-1988
Construction: 1988-1990
With: Takenaka Corporation
Client: Hiroshi Watari
Site area: 157 m^2
Useful surface: 627 m^2
Volume: 3,650 m^3

美术馆位于涩谷区一个人口稠密的地段，所在的三角形地块意味着需要应对三种不同的环境要素：一条主干道、一条支路，和建筑后方另一个体量较小的建筑。建筑主立面由条状的黑色石材和预制的素混凝土交替构成，一条纵向竖缝将立面从中部切开，底部则以矩形的开口结束。主入口位于建筑的一角，正面紧邻切割出轮廓的疏散楼梯。楼梯被推向外侧，超出建筑体并沿边墙展示出独特的立面。建筑顶部开有圆形窗洞的混凝土圆柱体块内整合了技术设施。建筑地上5层，地下1层，由单一的纵向通道连接。展览空间位于1~3层，尽管面积有限，但由于布局简约，空间仍旧显得较为宽敞。

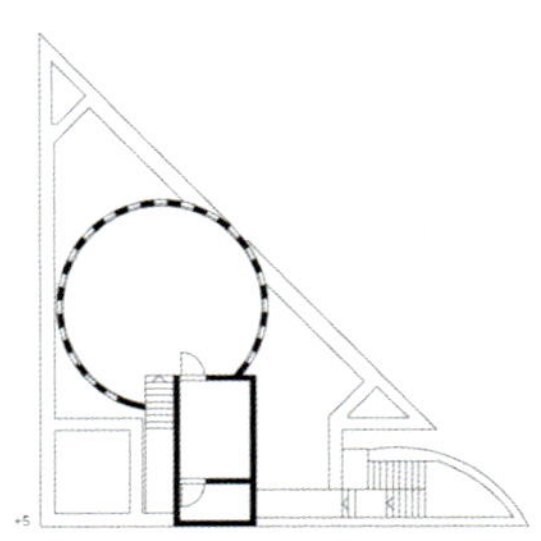

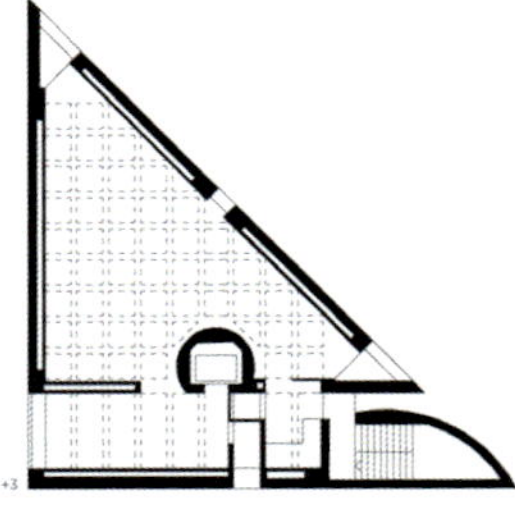

The art gallery stands in a densely populated urban area, in the Shibuya-ku district. It occupies a triangular plot and is confronted with three different situations: a major thoroughfare, a side street and a smaller construction to the rear. The main façade is characterized by the alternation of black stone slabs with unfinished, precast concrete elements and by a long vertical cut ending at the base in a rectangular opening. The entry is on the corner where the front meets the cut-out silhouette of the emergency stairway. This latter is pushed outward, beyond the building's size, so to gain exhibition surface along the side walls. The top of the building is crowned by cylinder with round wholes that incorporates technical facilities. The building is articulated over five levels above ground and a basement, linked by a single vertical connection. The exhibition spaces are on the first three levels and, in spite of their limited dimensions, they appear larger thanks to the simple layout.

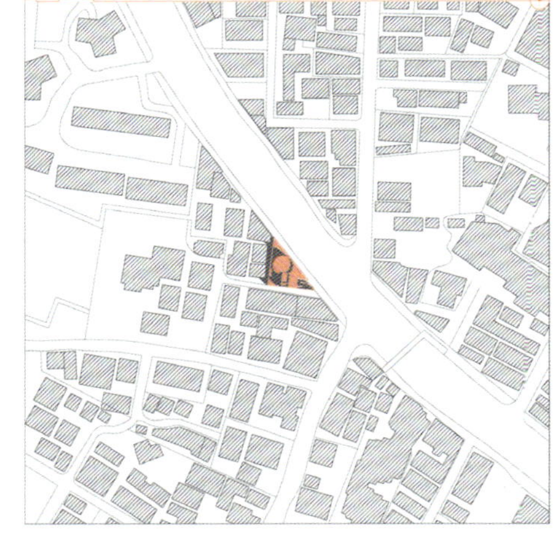

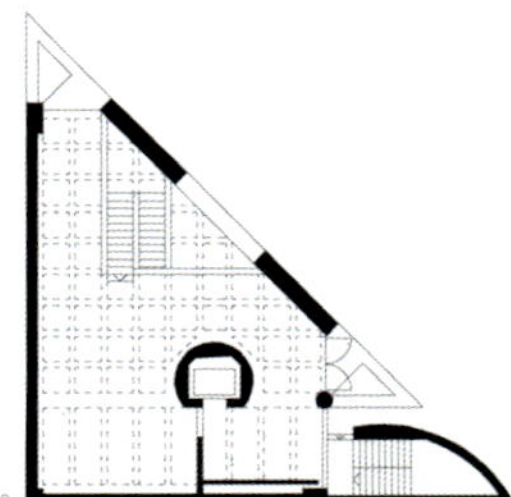

© PINO MUSI

© PINO MUSI

© PINO MUSI

© PINO MUSI

© PINO MUSI

© PINO MUSI

© ENRICO CANO

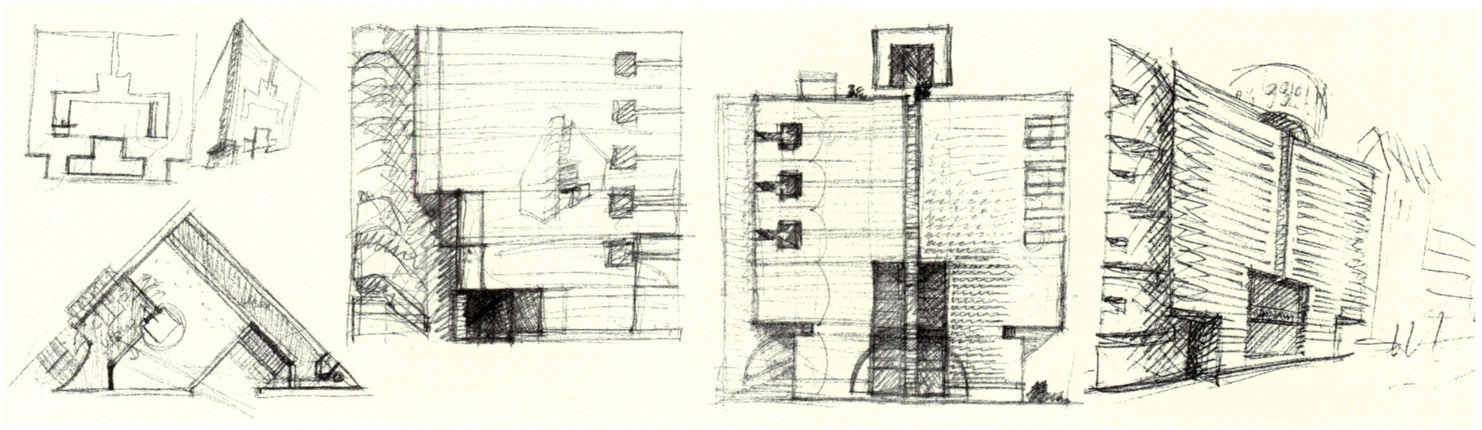

MART现当代艺术博物馆
意大利，罗韦雷托

MART-MUSEUM OF MODERN AND CONTEMPORARY ART
ROVERETO, ITALY

1988-2002

项目时间：1988～1992年
建造时间：1996～2002年
合作工程师：朱里奥·安德雷奥利
委托方：罗韦雷托市特兰托自治省
占地面积：29,000 平方米
建筑面积：20,800平方米
建筑体积：140,000立方米

Project: 1988-1992
Construction: 1996-2002
Partner: Eng. Giulio Andreolli
Client: City of Rovereto, autonomous province of Trento
Site area: 29,000 m^2
Useful surface: 20,800 m^2
Volume: 140,000 m^3

这座当代艺术博物馆部分藏匿于地下，因此人们对它的惊人体量无法一览无余。项目遵循中轴布局，沿两座历史建筑之间的小巷而建。小巷通往具有玻璃穹顶的圆形广场，广场周边可以开展各类活动。宽阔的空间成为博物馆的入口，巨大的展示空间位于建筑一层，二层设有较小的展厅。楼上两层画廊围绕中庭展开，楼梯位于中庭四周正方形平面的角落处。光线来自顶部一系列的天窗。建筑与城市的连接方式、公共空间向室内空间的过渡以及对空间结构的理解，都在这座博物馆的设计中至关重要。博物馆对现有的城市肌理进行了感性的阐释，通过空间和形式形成复杂的相互作用。

The impressive mass of the museum of modern and contemporary art is not revealed at first sight but remains partially hidden underground. The project follows an axial composition and is organized along the lane between two historical buildings. The lane leads to the circular plaza covered by a glass dome, around which all the activities are arranged. The spacious plaza gives access to the museum. The large exhibition rooms are located on the first level, while the second floor houses smaller exhibition spaces. Circulation through the galleries on the two upper floors takes place around the central courtyard, while staircases occupy the end corners of a square that is formed around it. Light comes from above through a series of skylights. The way the building relates to the city, the transition from the public space to the interior and the ability to understand the spatial structure, are important in the design of the museum. The museum offers a sensitive interpretation of the existing urban texture, and composes a complex interplay with space and form.

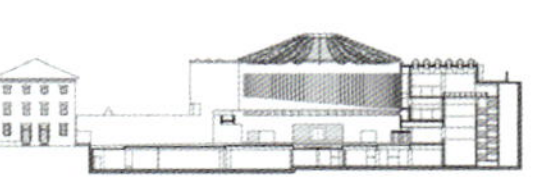

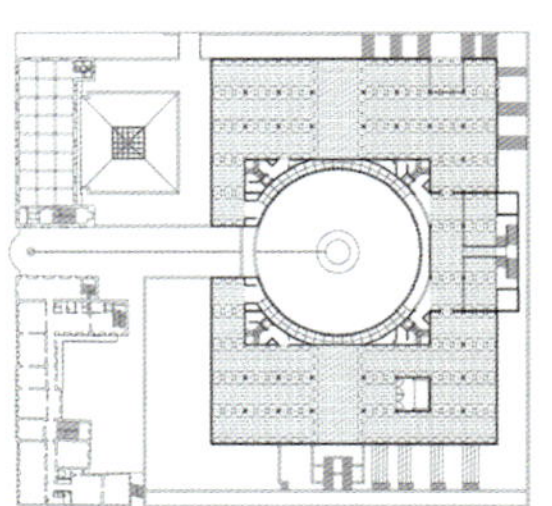

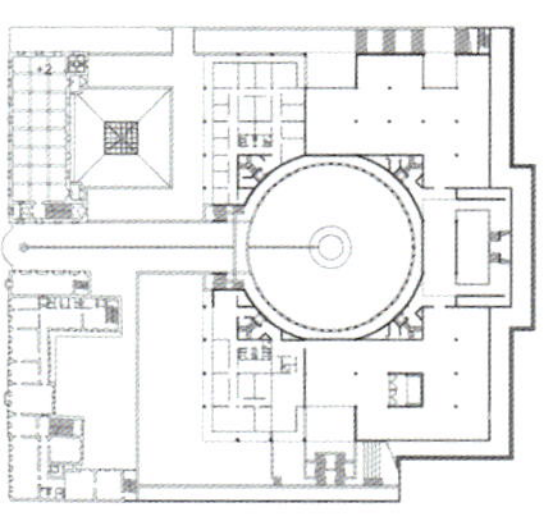

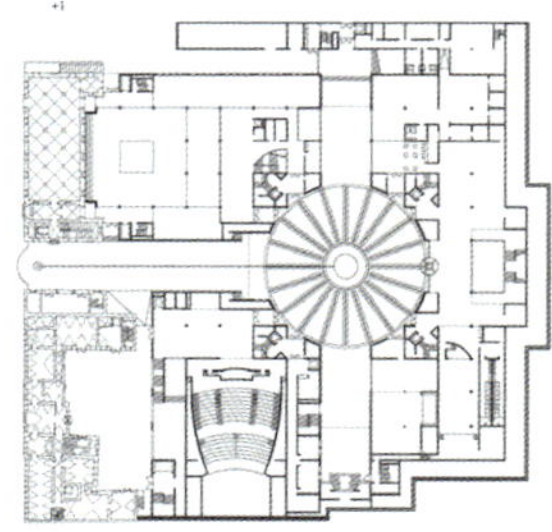

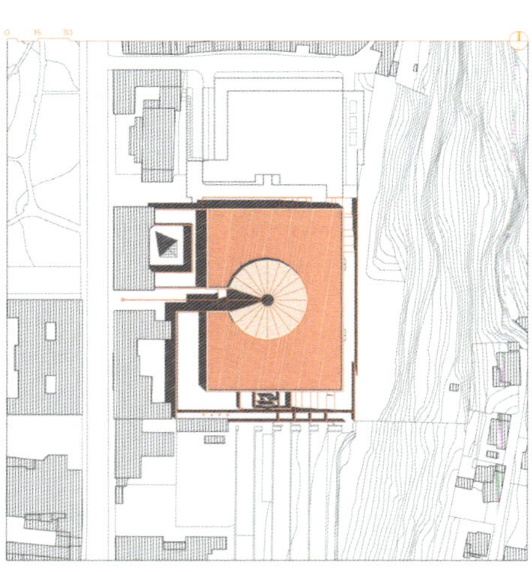

© ENRICO CANO

© ENRICO CANO

© PINO MUSI

© PINO MUSI

© PINO MUSI

© PINO MUSI

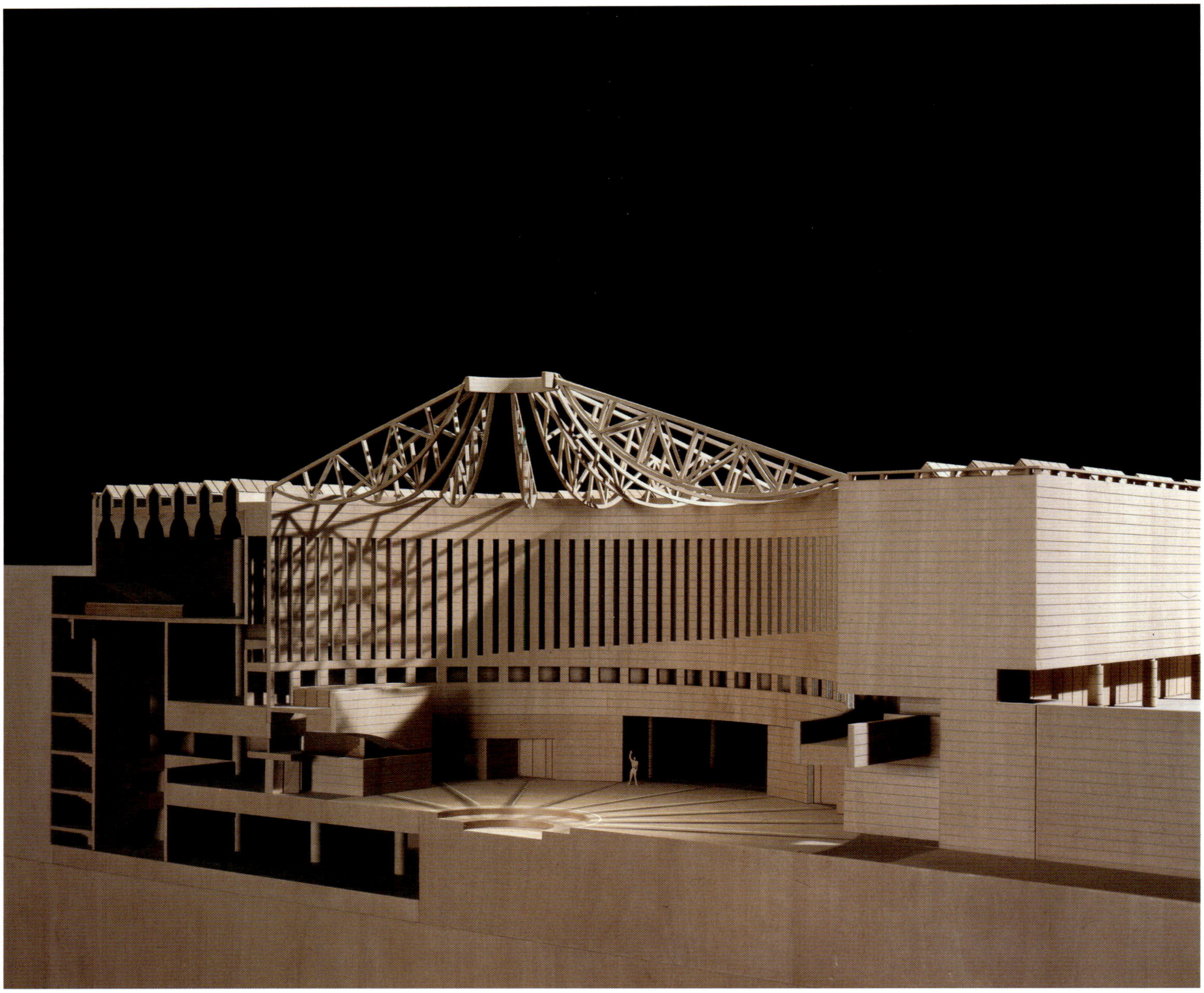

© NICOLA ECCHER

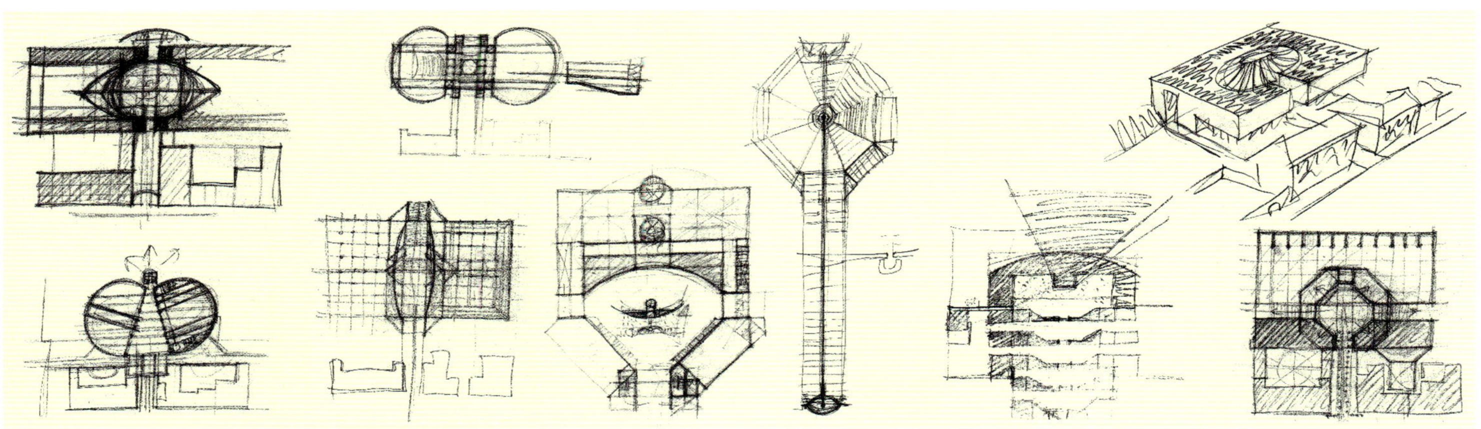

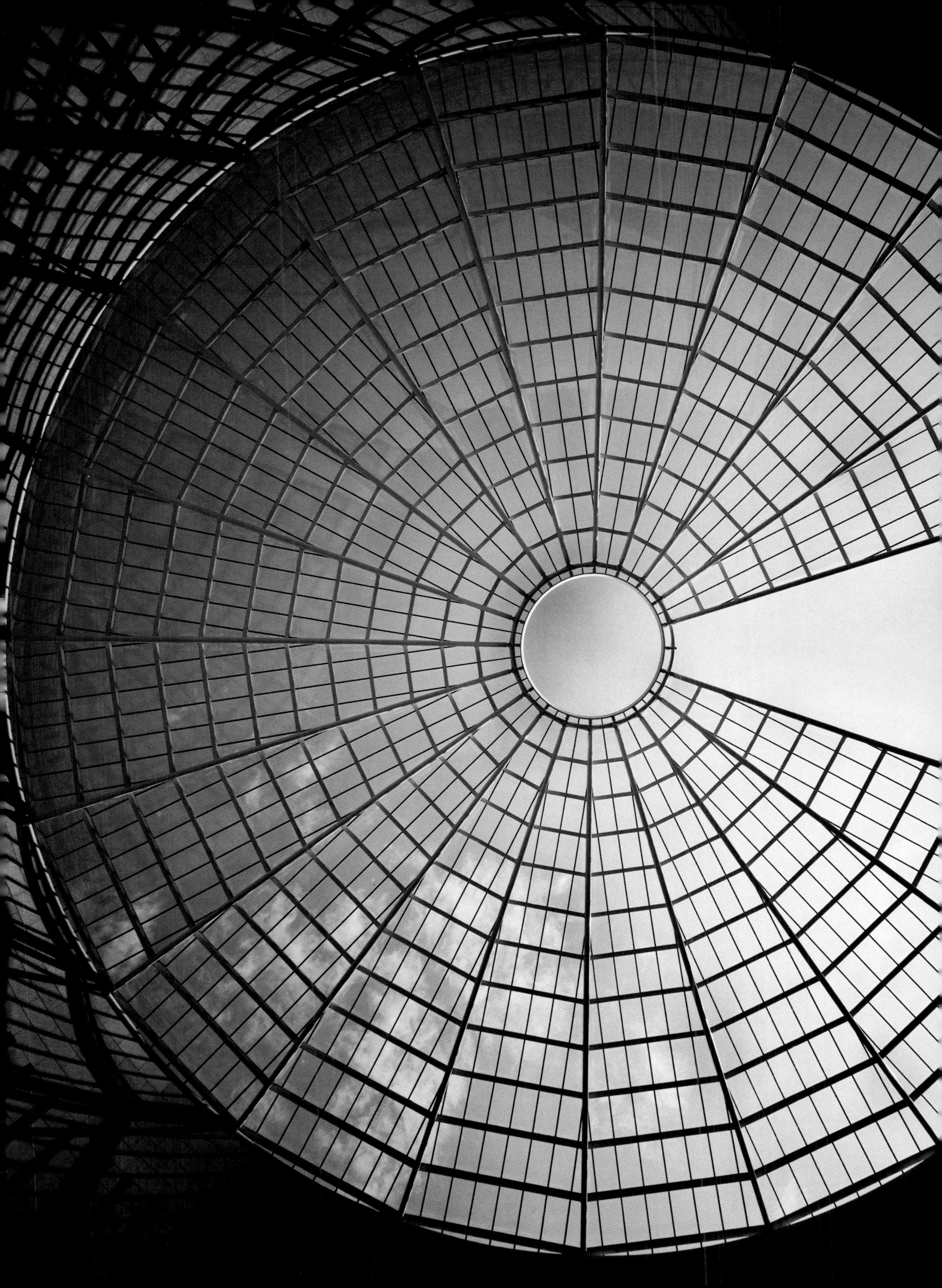

MOMA现代艺术博物馆

美国，旧金山

MOMA-MUSEUM OF MODERN ART

SAN FRANCISCO, USA

1989-1995

项目时间：1989/1990～1992年
建造时间：1992～1995年
合作方：旧金山HOK公司
委托方：旧金山现代艺术博物馆
占地面积：5,575平方米
建筑面积：18,500平方米
建筑体积：100,000立方米

Project: 1989/1990-1992
Construction: 1992-1995
Partner: Hellmuth, Obata & Kassabaum Inc., San Francisco
Client: San Francisco Museum of Modern Art
Site area: 5,575 m^2
Useful surface: 18,500 m^2
Volume: 100,000 m^3

建筑位于耶尔瓦布埃纳区，四周摩天大楼林立，与其纵向的高度相比，博物馆像是稳固地盘踞在地面上。矩形体量横向延展，由钢结构建造并覆以预制砖饰面。斜向圆柱体形状的硕大天窗如同面向城市的一只“眼睛”，为下方的大厅带来了自然光。博物馆地上5层，地下1层。地面层的室内大厅设有咨询台、图书馆、咖啡厅、活动空间与教育设施。中央的空旷空间贯穿了每个楼层，被认为是建筑的重心所在。与背后市区的“抽象”面貌相比，该建筑体现出一种强烈的“具象”特点。

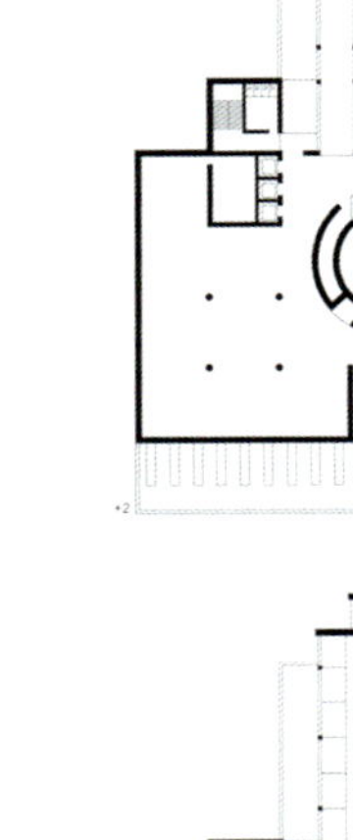

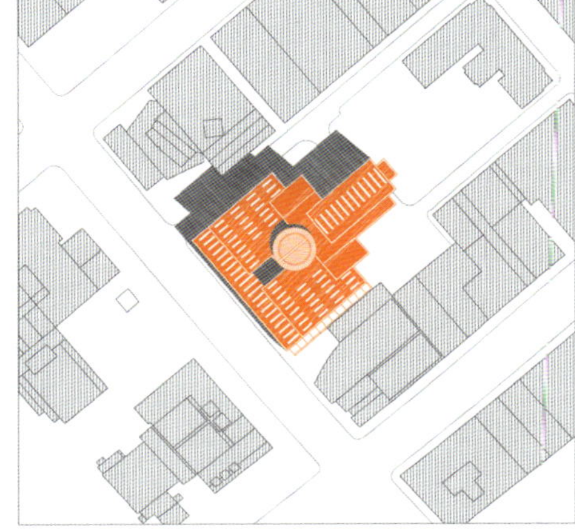

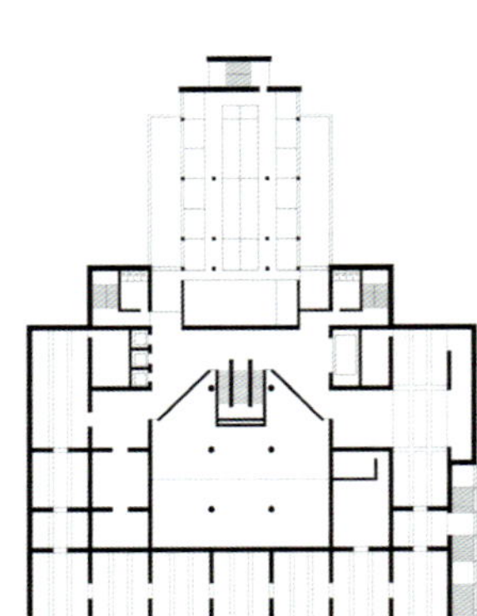

The museum is in the Yerba Buena district with the city skyscrapers in the background. In contrast with the vertical tension of this latter, the MOMA seems anchored to the ground. Its orthogonal volume, formed by a steel structure covered with brick clad precast panels, expands horizontally. The impressive skylight in the shape of a truncated cylinder becomes an “eye” towards the city and illuminates the lobby beneath. The museum develops on five floors above ground and a basement. The ground floor dominated by the sculptural presence of the staircase offers a wide hall with the reception and information desk, library, cafeteria, event space and educational facilities. The central void rises through all levels and is to be considered the gravity center of the museum. Compared to the “abstract” image of the downtown at the back, the building shows a strong “figurative” feature.

© PINO MUSI

© ROBERT CANFIELD

© PINO MUSI

© ROBERT CANFIELD

© PINO MUSI

scale 1/100

© ENRICO CANO

迪伦马特中心

瑞士，纳沙泰尔

DÜRRENMATT CENTRE

NEUCHÂTEL, SWITZERLAND

1992-2000

项目时间：1992/1995～1997年
建造时间：1997～2000年
委托方：瑞士联邦财政部
合作方：纳沙泰尔市厄沙勒和阿里戈建筑事务所
占地面积：4,200平方米
使用面积：820平方米
建筑体积：4,700立方米

Project: 1992/1995-1997
Construction: 1997-2000
Client: Swiss Confederation, Federal Department of Finance
Partner: arch. Urscheler & Arrigo SA
Site area: 4,200 m²
Useful surface: 820 m²
Volume: 4,700 m³

这座小型博物馆保存着瑞士作家弗雷德里希·杜伦玛特的绘画和图像作品。建筑坐落在山地中，毗邻杜伦玛特的故居，旁边是原有的图书馆，现在容纳了一些公共服务设施、办公室和咖啡厅。这样的结合使新的空间可以完全用于展览。博物馆嵌入山体，形成3个楼层，呈弧形向山谷的方向伸展，在急剧倾斜的地形上筑造出一个凸出的体块。从外部只能看到建筑的石质弧墙，塔楼暗示了下方博物馆空间的存在，而全景大露台仿佛在邀请人们到此享受面向湖泊的美景。外层灰色石板的使用增强了建筑的体量感和墙面的肌理效果。访客从后方街道前来，通过一个位于故居和塔楼之间的小厅进入博物馆，沿着宽敞的楼梯向下抵达展厅所在的楼层。沿建筑边缘设置的顶部照明照亮了整个地下展览空间。

The small museum conserves the graphic work and paintings by the Swiss author Friedrich Dürrenmatt. Set on a hilly site, the museum is built underground, next to Dürrenmatt's former private house that beside the author's original library now hosts several public services, the offices and the coffee shop, to allow the new spaces to be totally used for exhibition purposes. The construction penetrates the body of the mountain through three levels and expands downward in an arc towards the valley as "bowels" whose convex form resurfaces from the steeply sloped terrain. On the outside just the curved stone wall and the tower reveal the presence of the museum spaces beneath, while the large terrace invites to enjoy the great panoramic view towards the lake. The use of grey slate blocks as exterior cladding enhances the massiveness and texture of the walls. Visitors approach from the street in the back, enter the museum through a small lobby between the house and the tower and move downstairs to the main exhibition floor. Roof lights along the edge of the building illuminate the underground exhibition spaces.

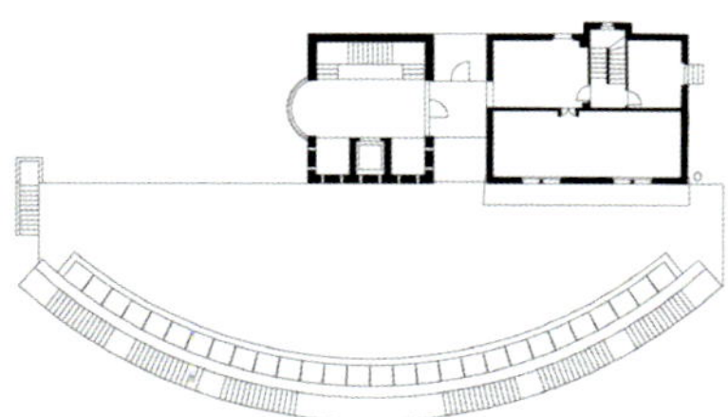

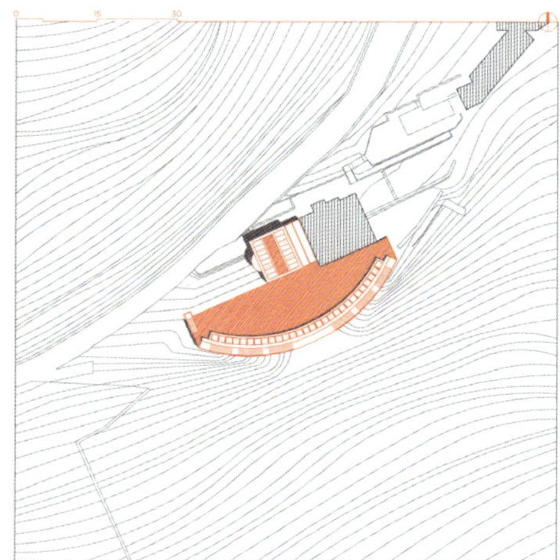

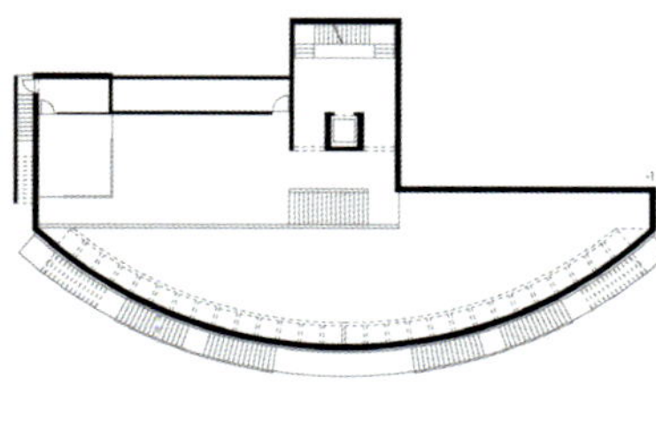

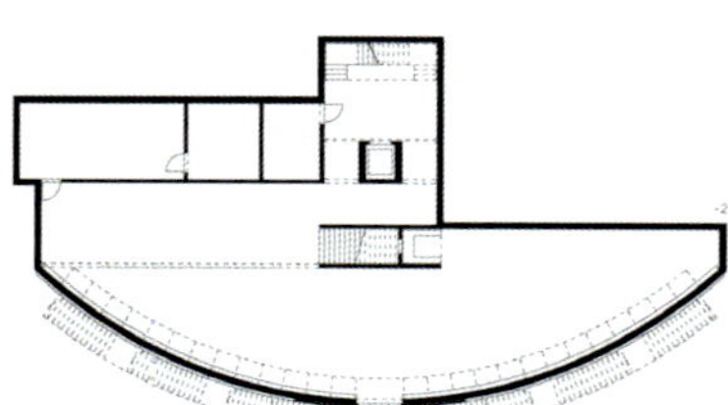

© PINO MUSI

© PINO MUSI

© PINO MUSI

© PINO MUSI

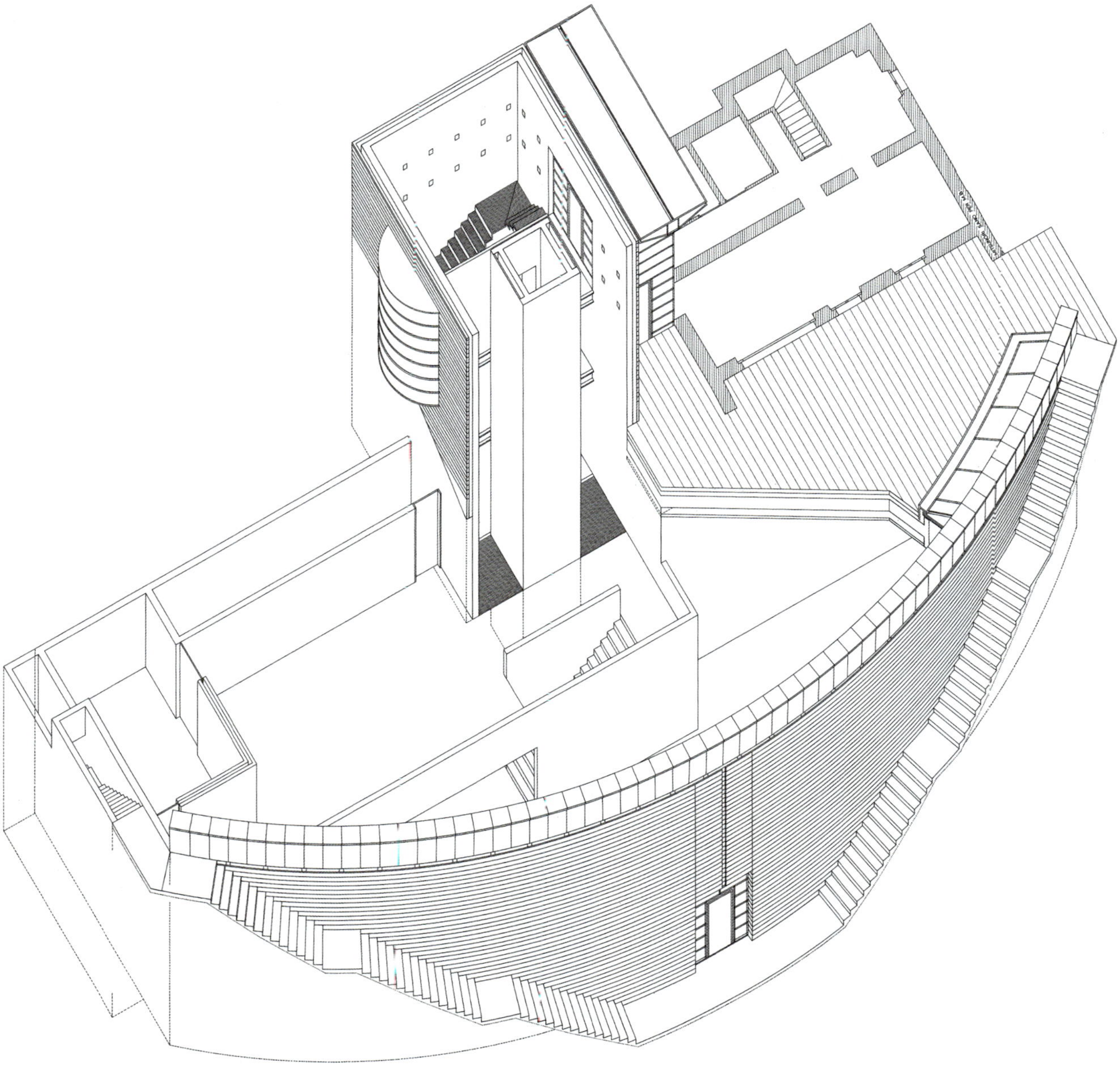

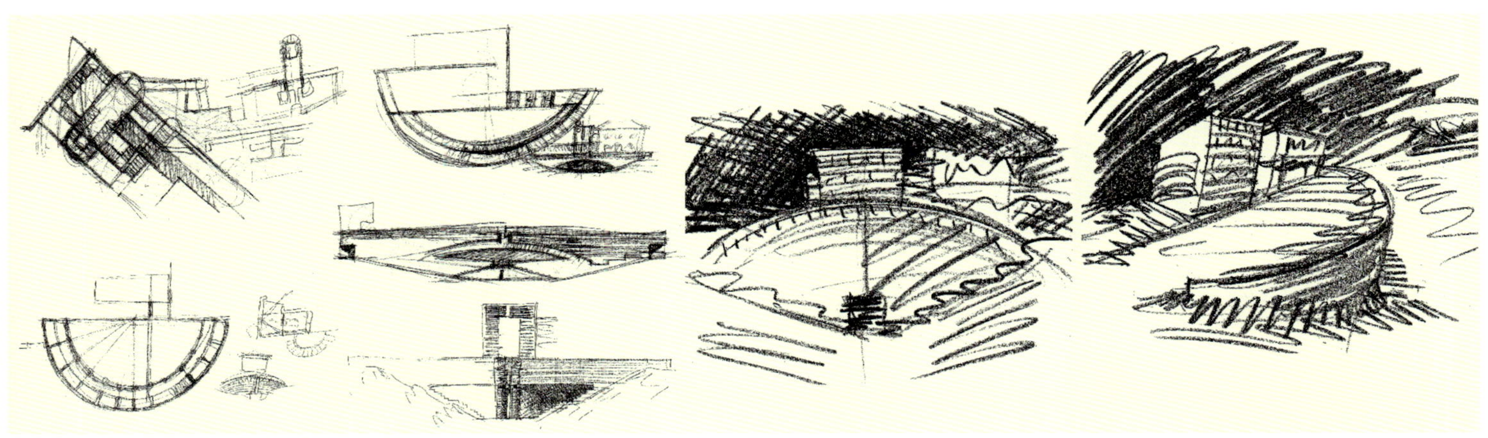

丁格利博物馆

瑞士，巴塞尔

MUSEUM TINGUELY

BASEL, SWITZERLAND

1993-1996

项目时间：1993年
建造时间：1994~1996年
委托方：巴塞尔，罗氏公司
合作方：巴塞尔，GSG 建筑公司
占地面积：28,450 平方米
建筑面积：6,057平方米，其中展厅面积2,866平方米
建筑体积：54,150立方米

Project: 1993
Construction: 1994-1996
Client: Hoffmann-La Roche AG, Basel
Construction management: GSG Baucontrol, Basel
Site area: park 28,450 m^2
Useful surface: 6,057 m^2, of which 2,866 m^2 for exhibition purposes
Volume: 54,150 m^3

博物馆坐落在19世纪的索利图德公园东侧沿，面向莱茵河，位于高速公路桥梁的尽头。项目因此尝试对这片位于20世纪城市肌理和高速公路边缘之间的空地进行重新设计。每个建筑立面以不同的方式回应其面对的城市状态：在靠近高速公路的东侧，建筑物以巨大的墙壁和高耸的体量形成了保护博物馆的屏障；面向公园的西立面是一排宽阔的拱廊，向公园完全开放；北侧设置了一个通向公园和博物馆的覆顶入口；南立面朝向河流，使用了形式感强烈的设计元素，观众在进入美术馆之前，可以通过这条弯曲的玻璃通道欣赏河流周边的壮丽景色。贯穿4层楼的展览线路结束于底层的开阔空间。

The museum is set along the eastern side of the 19th-century Solitude Park, facing the Rhine River and at the end of a motorway bridge. Thus, the building is an attempt to redesign the urban void between the 20th-century fabric of the city and the edge of the motorway. Each building front responds in a different way to the prevailing urban conditions. On the east, next to the traffic lane, the building's massive wall and elevated volume are shaped to create a barrier protecting the museum's area. On the west side, facing the park, the volume opens towards the garden with a wide portico, characterized by a series of arches. The north side provides a covered entrance to the park and the museum. The south front faces the river with a strong formal element: a slightly curved glass walkway takes the visitor along the magnificent river view before entering the galleries. The itinerary through the exhibition spaces on four different levels ends in the large open space on the ground floor.

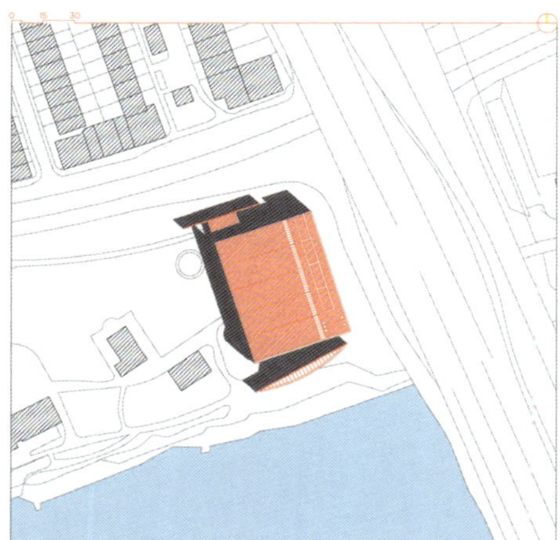

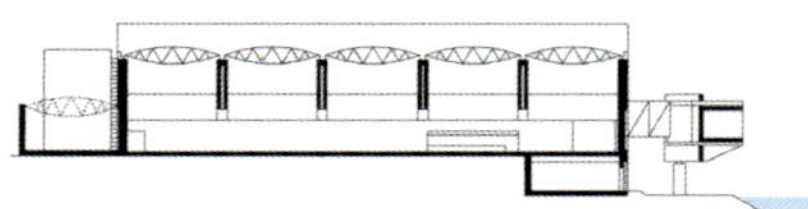

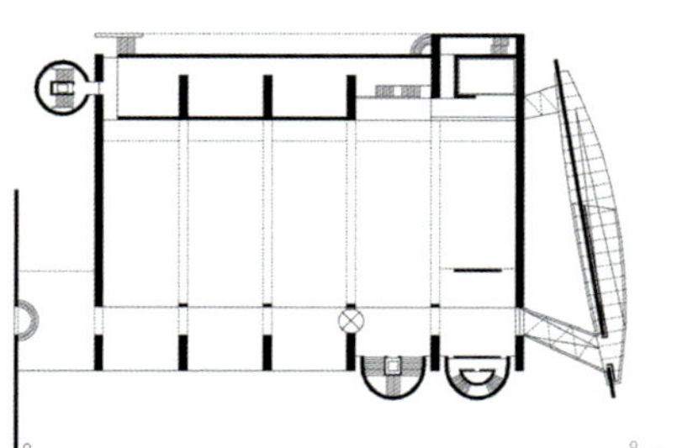

© PINO MUSI

© PINO MUSI

© PINO MUSI

© PINO MUSI

© PINO MUSI

© PINO MUSI

© PINO MUSI

诺亚方舟

以色列，耶路撒冷

NOAH'S ARK

JERUSALEM, ISRAEL

1995-2001

项目时间：1995～1998年
建造时间：1999～2001年
委托方：耶路撒冷基金会，耶路撒冷市政，动物园主管，沙·多隆
艺术家：尼基·德桑菲尔
建筑面积：670平方米
建筑体积：地下体积2,700立方米

Project: 1995-1998
Construction: 1999-2001
Client: The Jerusalem Foundation, City of Jerusalem, director of the zoological gardens, Shai Doron
Artist: Niki de Saint Phalle
Useful surface: 670 m^2
Volume: 2,700 m^3 underground

马里奥·博塔和尼基·桑法勒之间深厚的友谊造就了这个诺亚方舟计划。这个想法被看做一次机会，通过互补的才能和表达方式完成一个共同的构想，能够超越世界上不同的意识形态和文化诉求。方舟坐落于耶路撒冷的动物园内，设计采用的浅浮雕如同铭刻在黄色石头上的化石印记。延续空间为游客呈现出一条犹如梦境交织的小道，有一条小溪和连续的拱门，向下通往主要的地下空间，如同进入一个石头“腹腔”，巨大的彩色动物雕塑布满建筑周围的草坪。人体尺度的地下空间和带有许多圆洞的雕塑使得项目的效果接近原本的构想。

The project for Noah's Ark was sparked by the profound friendship with Niki de Saint Phalle. The idea was taken as an opportunity to exploit the complementary talents and the feeling of expression with a sense of complicity, going beyond the ideological and cultural disquisitions that characterise different worlds. The ark is located in the zoological gardens of Jerusalem has been thought in low-relief, as an imprint in the ground and fossilised in the yellow local stone. The ensuing space is presented to visitors as a path marked by a tempo of dream-like moments, with a descent into the main underground volume that resembles a shady stone "belly" crossed by a rivulet and marked by the regular succession of arches. Big colored animals fill the patch of grass around the structure. The man-sized underground spaces of the ark and the hollows in the sculptures promote the play for which the project was conceived.

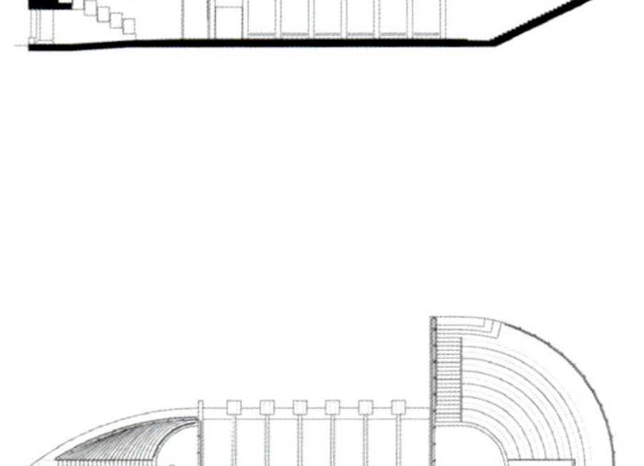

© PINO MUSI

© PINO MUSI

© PINO MUSI

© PINO MUSI

© ENRICO CANO

© PINO MUSI

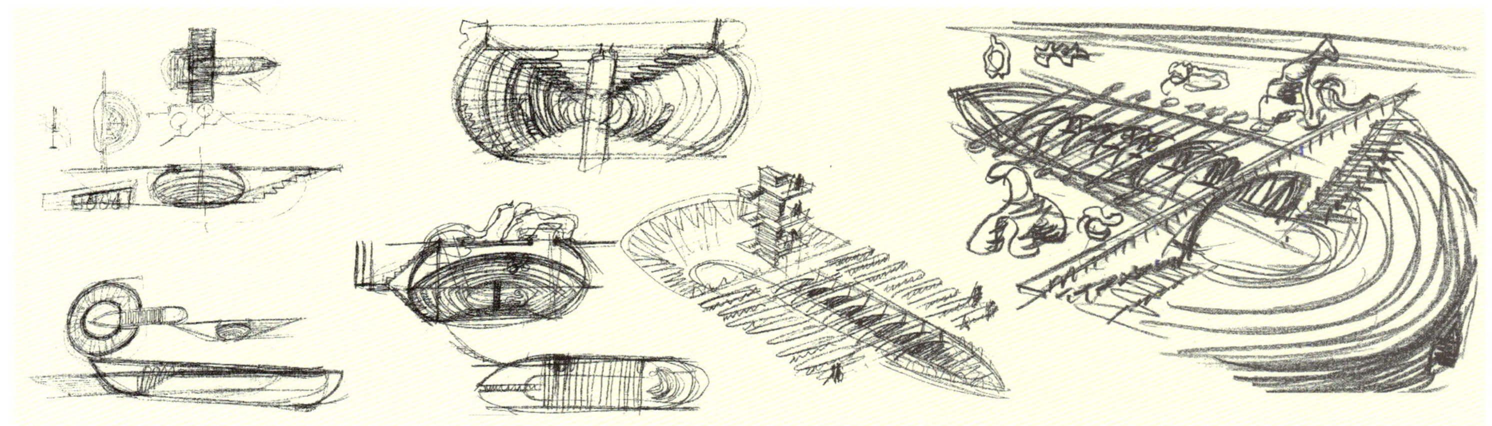

三星美术馆

韩国，首尔

LEEUM – SAMSUNG MUSEUM OF ART

SEOUL, SOUTH KOREA

1995-2004

项目时间：1995～1997/2002年
建造时间：2002～2004年
委托方：三星文化基金会
合作方：首尔三友建筑工程事务所
占地面积：2,333 平方米
建筑面积：10,000 平方米
建筑体积:42,000平方米

Project: 1995-1997/2002
Construction: 2002-2004
Client: Samsung Foundation for Culture
Partner: Samoo Architects & Engineers, Seoul
Site area: 2,333 m²
Useful surface: 10,000 m²
Volume: 42,000 m³

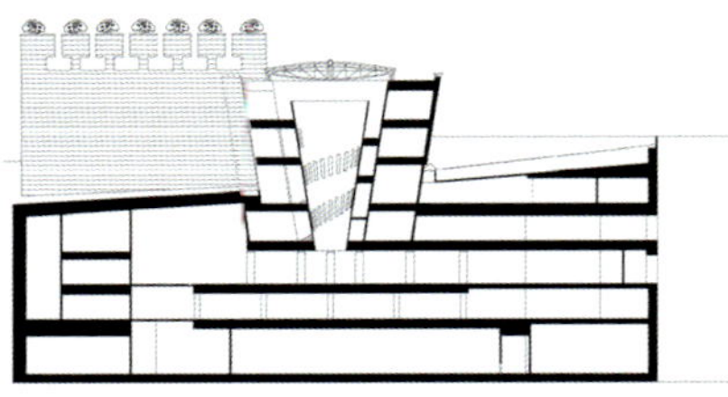

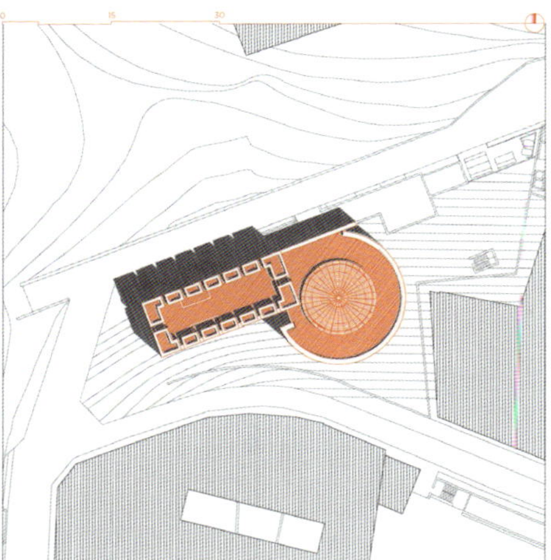

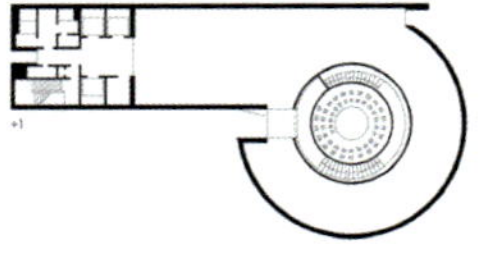

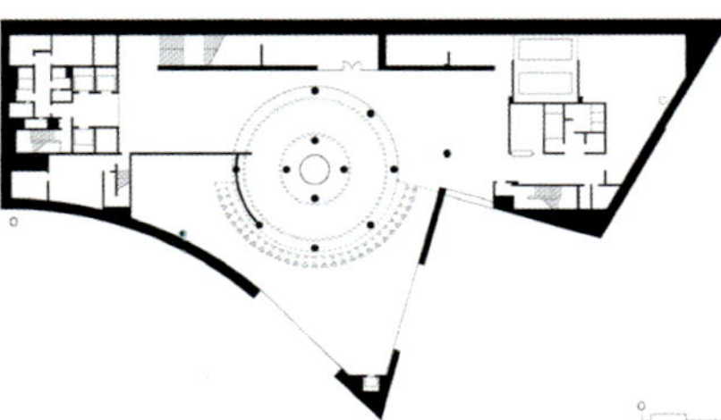

这个由三星基金会创立的新型文化中心位于韩国汉南洞的半山腰上，包含三座不同的建筑——两座博物馆和一座儿童教育中心。与其他两座建筑相比，这座古代艺术博物馆修建在后方更高的位置，成为基金会所倡导的新型城市化计划中的地标性建筑。博物馆的大部分空间位于地下，是三个文化实体的聚合。从外部看就像一个从绿色斜坡中升起的孤立体块，连接起上下的道路。整座建筑包含两个主要部分：一个平行六面体和一个倒锥体。具有表现力的建筑肌理进一步强化了立面节奏：外立面结合平整的红色陶土砖与特殊的“V”形截面，在自然光下营造出微妙的色调效果。在倒锥形建筑体内，观众可以沿明亮的中央楼梯由顶层拾级而下，光线透过巨大的圆形玻璃屋顶洒向内部空间，与展览空间较暗的光线形成对比。

Half way up a hill in Hannam-dong, three different buildings, two museums and one educational center for children create the new cultural center of Samsung foundation. Leeum Museum for Ancient Art is set back and on higher ground compared to the other buildings and therefore becomes the landmark of the new urbanization plan proposed by the Foundation. The museum, with an important part underground where the three cultural entities meet, is an isolated object rising from a green slope that connects the roads above and below. The building consists of two primary shapes: a parallelepiped coupled with an inverted cone. The exterior is further enhanced by the expressive language of the façade texture: smooth, flat terracotta tiles combined with special V-sectioned elements create a natural effect of subtle shades under the natural light. The visit starts on the top floor and steps down the bright central stairs that unwinds along the curved walls of the cone. In contrast to the dim light of the exhibit spaces, the large glass roof enlightens the central core down to main lobby.

© PIETRO SAVORELLI

© PIETRO SAVORELLI

© PIETRO SAVORELLI

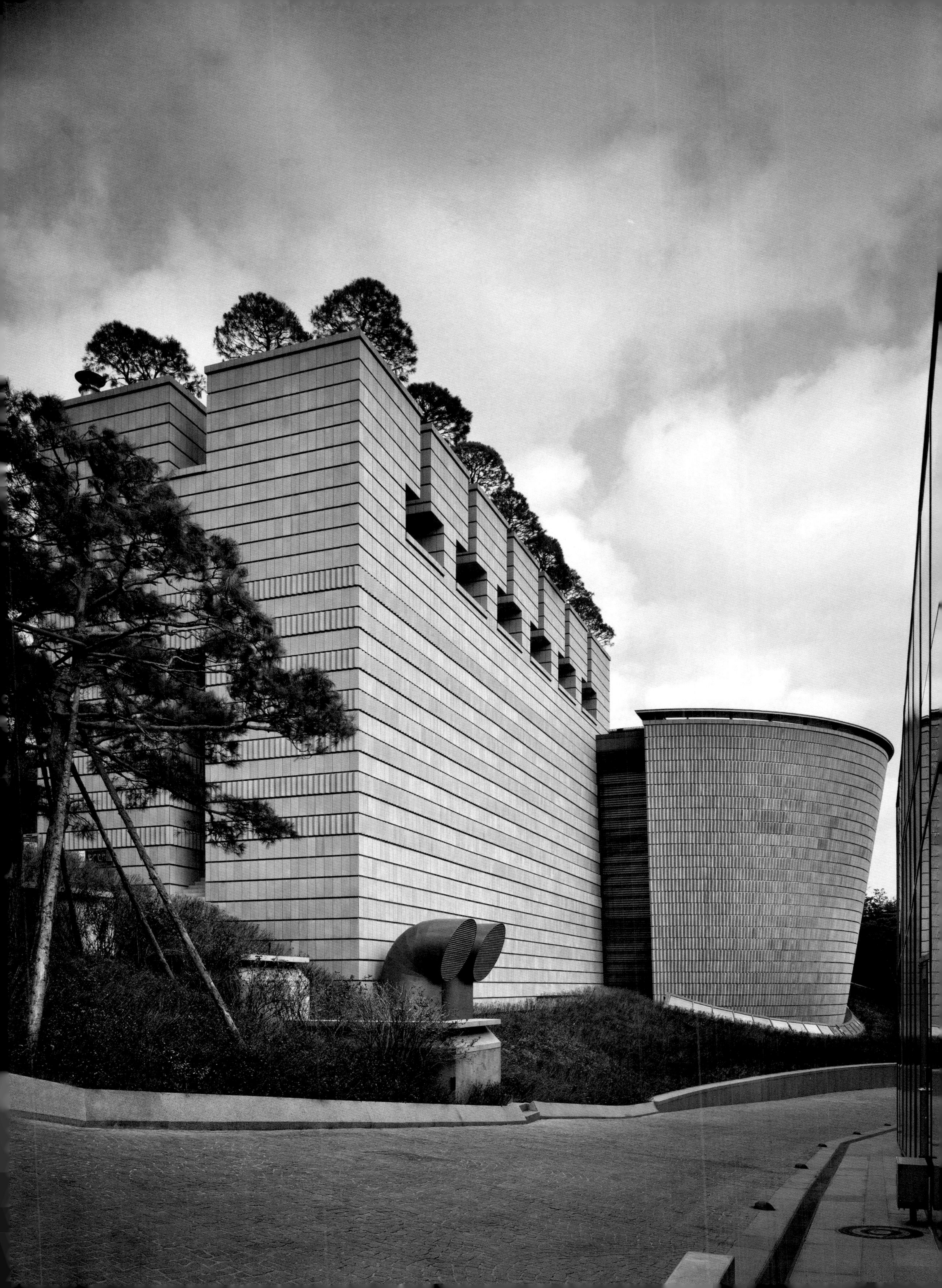

贝希特勒现代艺术博物馆

美国，夏洛特

BECHTLER MUSEUM

CHARLOTTE, NORTH CAROLINA, USA

2000/2005-2009

项目时间：2000～2005年
建造时间：2007～2009年
委托方：安德鲁·贝希特勒
合作方：瓦格纳·穆雷建筑事务所，夏洛特
占地面积：1,912 平方米
建筑面积：2,490 平方米
建筑体积：16,992 立方米

Project: 2000-2005
Construction: 2007-2009
Client: Andreas Bechtler
Partner: Wagner Murray Architects PA, Charlotte
Site area: 1,912 m^2
Useful surface: 2,490 m^2
Volume: 16,992 m^3

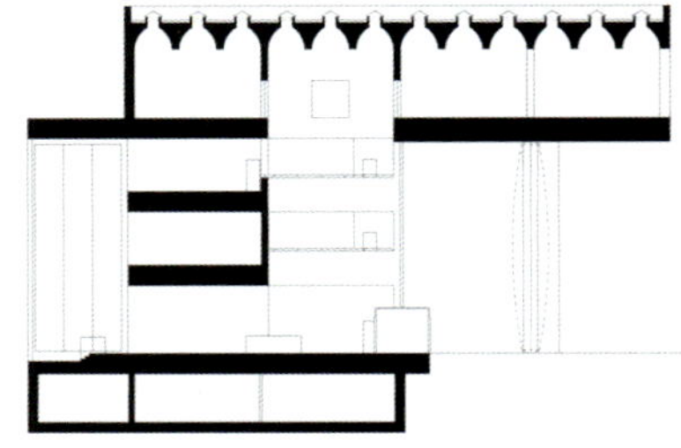

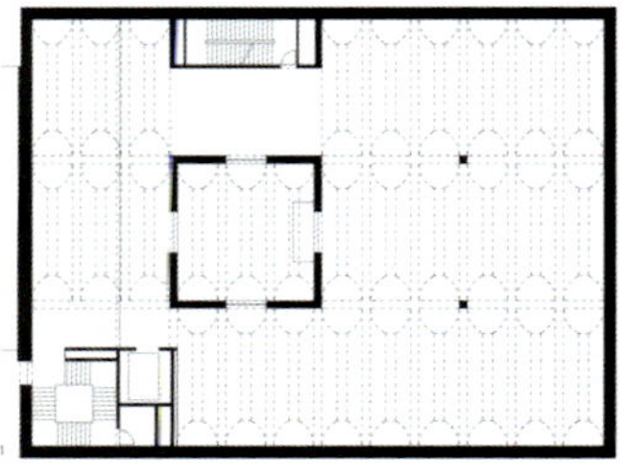

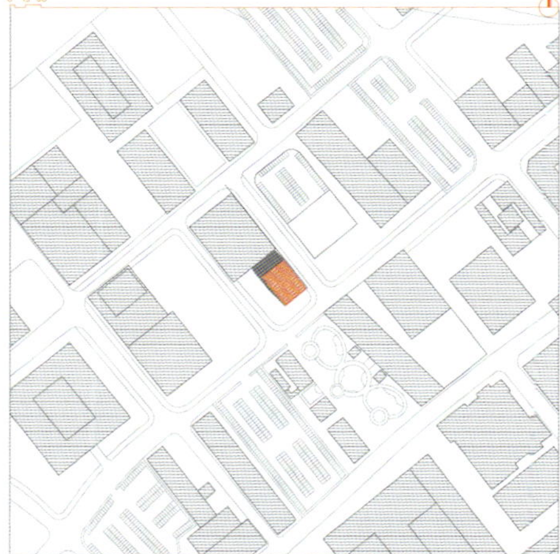

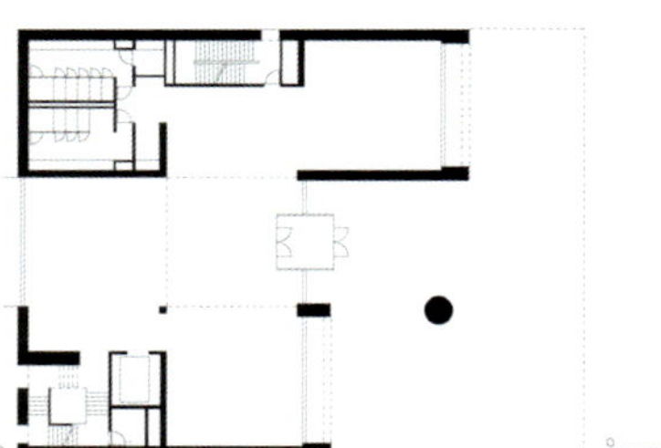

博物馆坐落于夏洛特市中心，这座城市近年来经历了迅速的城市化发展。该博物馆收藏了安德烈斯·本奇特勒的藏品，包括尚·丁格利、妮基·桑法勒、毕加索、贾科梅蒂、马蒂斯、米罗、德加、安迪·沃霍尔、勒·柯布西耶、莱热等重要艺术家的作品。这座立方体建筑的中部是空的，为后部提供了一个体量可塑的室外公共庭院。四层建筑的特别之处在于高耸的玻璃中庭，延伸穿过博物馆核心，通过拱形天窗系统为整个建筑提供良好的自然采光。尽管建筑体量不大，但虚实关系的巧妙运用充分体现出建筑的可塑性。它甚至可以被看作一尊建筑雕塑，四层画廊从建筑中部挑出，由一根巨大的立柱支撑，在其遮蔽下形成全新的城市空间。室内空间选择的材料和室外的赤土陶饰面为博物馆塑造出了简约、严谨而又优雅的形象。

The museum is located in downtown Charlotte, a city that has undergone a rapid urban development in recent years. It houses the works of art of the Andreas Bechtlers' collection with important artists such as Tinguely, Niki de Saint Phalle, Picasso, Giacometti, Matisse, Mirò, Degas, Warhol, Le Corbusier, Léger. The cube-shaped building is hollow inside to offer an outdoor public courtyard that is outlined by the plastic volumes at the back. The four-storey structure is characterized by the soaring glass atrium that extends through the core of the museum and diffuses natural light throughout the building thanks to a system of vaulted skylights. Despite its modest dimensions, a great plastic force is created by the play of solids and voids. It can be thus defined as an architecture-sculpture where the voids mark a new urban space sheltered by the fourth floor gallery jutting out from the core of the building and supported by a huge single column rising from the plaza below. The choice of the materials for the interior spaces and the terra cotta exterior cladding provide the museum with a rigorous, though elegant simplicity.

© JOËL LASSITER

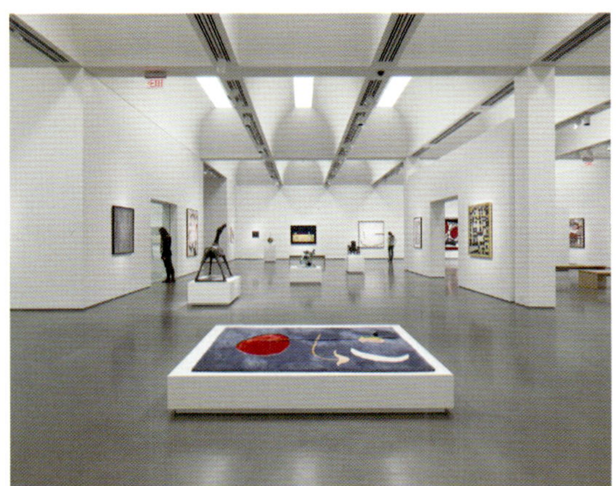

© ENRICO CANO

© ENRICO CANO

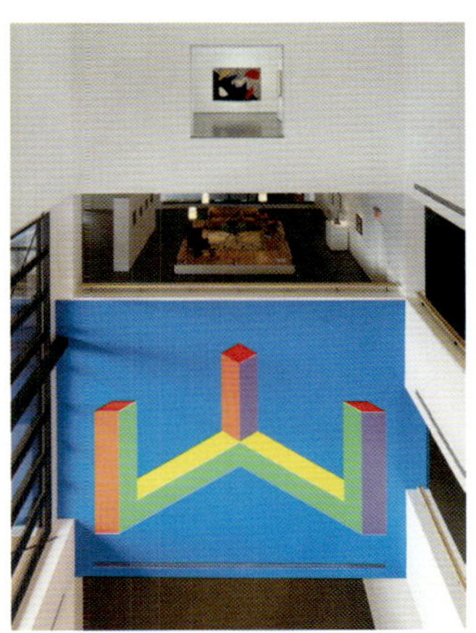

© ENRICO CANO

清华大学艺术博物馆

中国，北京

TSINGHUA UNIVERSITY ART MUSEUM

BEIJING, P.R. CHINA

2002-2016

竞赛项目时间：2002年
建造时间：2012～2016年
委托方：清华大学
责任建筑师与工程师：中国建筑科学研究院，北京
占地面积：16,000 平方米
建筑面积：30,000 平方米
建筑体积：156,000立方米

Competition project: 2002
Construction: 2012-2016
Client: Tsinghua University, Beijing
Architect: Mario Botta Architect and Ass. LLC
Architect of record and engineers:
CABR Building Design Institute, Beijing
Site area: 16,000 m²
Useful surface: 30,000 m²
Volume: 156,000 m³

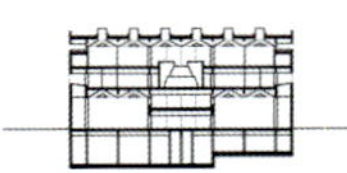

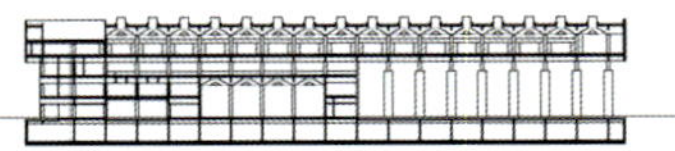

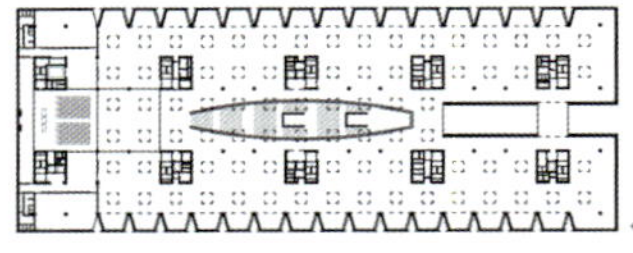

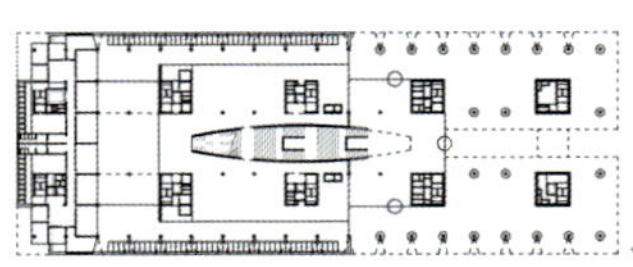

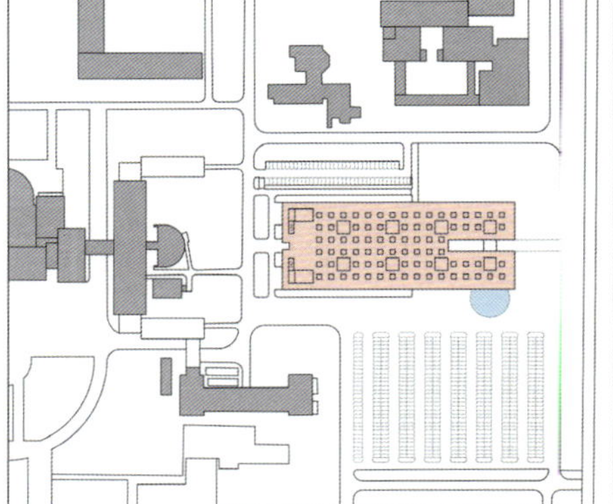

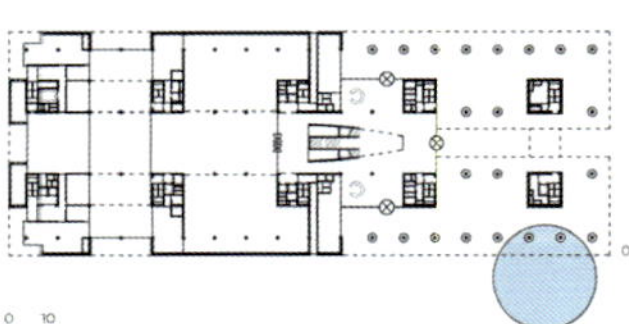

清华大学艺术博物馆是2002年的一个竞赛项目，它位于北京市清华大学校园内，于2016年9月落成开幕。该建筑为一个长方形体块，位于学校主楼的东侧，西接校园的内部道路。外立面采用光滑和粗糙相间的水平条形粉色花岗石饰面。建筑拥有4层展览空间，大体量的柱廊朝向南面的开阔空间。柱廊向大厅延伸，宏伟的楼梯纵向贯穿了整座建筑，一直通至建筑顶层。楼梯所形成的巨大中心空间成为整座建筑的核心及最为显著的特征，仿佛空间得以停顿，观众可以感受到从一层到顶层的整体氛围。顶层的格栅天窗将自然光线引入展览空间。这一系列天窗占据了整个顶面，并可以根据展览和路线需要进行分隔操作。在校园里，这座建筑构建出了开放空间和室内空间的平衡关系，如同一个慷慨迎接观众的覆顶广场。

The building housing the Tsinghua University Art Museum is the result of a competition project held in 2002. It is on the campus of Tsinghua University in Beijing and was inaugurated in September 2016. The building is a long parallelepiped placed between the rectorate building to the west and the campus boundary road to the east. It is clad in horizontal bands of pink granite, smooth or split. It consists of four exhibition levels and is characterized by a large portico with huge columns facing the broad open space to the south. The portico leads to the lobby, where a majestic staircase crosses the whole building lengthwise and leads to the upper exhibition floors. The large central space created by the staircase is the distinctive feature and the heart of the building: a kind of spatial caesura that allows visitors to perceive the space between the ground floor and the ceiling, characterized by a grid of skylights that let natural light flood the last exhibition floor. It occupies the whole surface and can be divided into different rooms according to the exhibition programs and paths. On the campus, the building gives a balanced relationship between the open spaces and the interiors: a covered plaza that generously welcomes visitors.

© ENRICO CANO

© ENRICO CANO

© ENRICO CANO

© ENRICO CANO

© ENRICO CANO

© ENRICO CANO

© ENRICO CANO

© ENRICO CANO

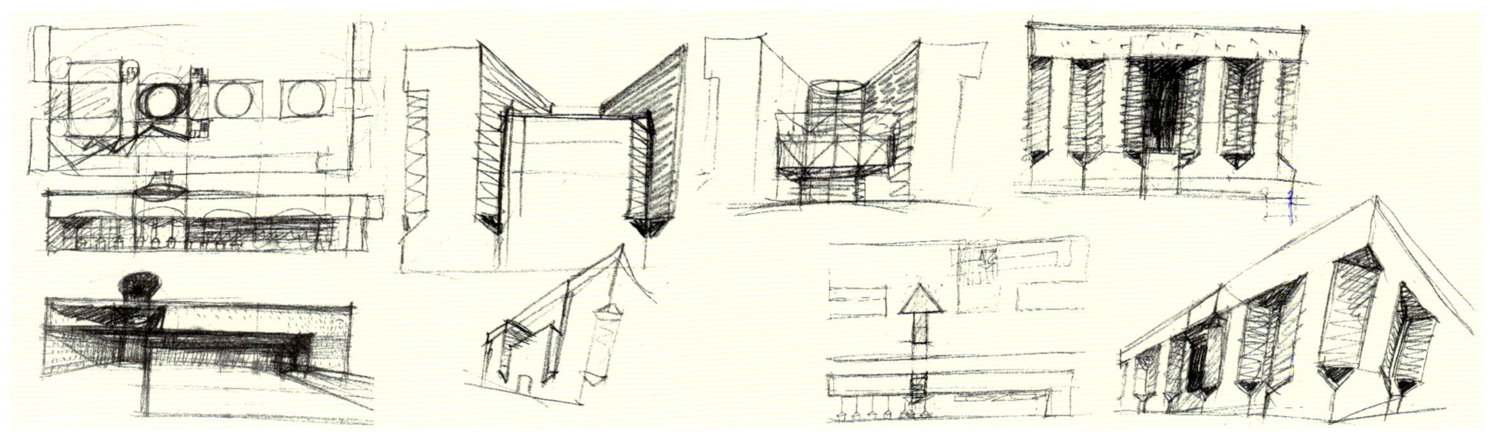

剧院
THEATERS

马尔罗文化中心

法国，尚贝里

ESPACE MALRAUX

CHAMBÉRY, FRANCE

1982-1987

竞赛项目时间：1982年
建造时间：1983~1987年
委托方：尚贝里市
占地面积：7,600平方米
建筑面积：9,800平方米
建筑体积：82,000立方米

Competition project: 1982
Construction: 1983-1987
Client: City of Chambéry
Site area: 7,600 m²
Useful surface: 9,800 m²
Volume: 82,000 m³

项目来自一次建筑设计竞赛，竞赛内容包括修复一座19世纪拿破仑时期的军营以及新建一座多功能建筑综合体。新建部分位于一个现有四方体结构的外部，作为建筑的外部门厅，紧贴着历史建筑，以突出两部分体量所营造的紧张感。综合体的不同功能被组织在三个建筑体中：技术设施用房、舞台塔以及艺术家休息室，圆形的剧院是整体布局的重点，紧急楼梯作为第三要素与剧院上下两层相连，将这座独立建筑定义为全新的城市广场。行政管理用房位于拿破仑时期四方体结构东翼，公众入口连接着一条通道，可穿越历史悠久的庭院。

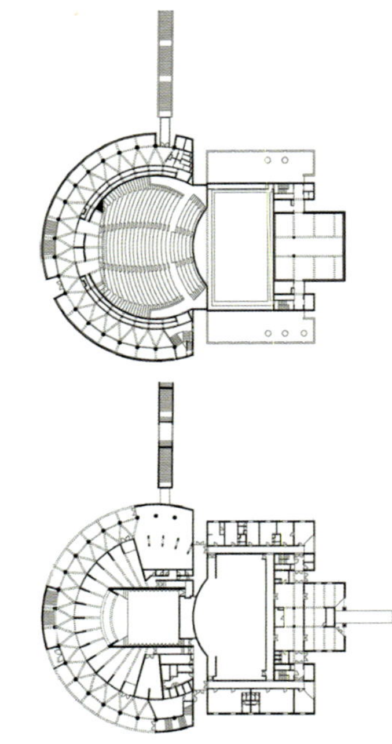

The project arises from an architecture competition calling for the restoration of a 19th-century Napoleonic military barracks and for the construction of a multi-use complex. The new building is set outside the existing quadrilateral, interpreted as an external foyer. It only just touches the historical building to accentuate the perception of tension created by the two volumes. The different functions of the complex are organized within three volumes: the parallelepiped that houses the technical facilities, the stage tower and artist's room, the circular volume of the theatre itself that represents the key point in the layout and as a third element, the emergency stairs, linked to the two levels of the theater hall and delimiting as an autonomous construction an new urban square. Whereas the administrative services are located within the east wing of the Napoleonic quadrilateral, the public entrance follows a path through the historical courtyard.

© PINO MUSI

© ENRICO CANO

© ENRICO CANO

© PINO MUSI

© PINO MUSI

© ENRICO CANO

© PINO MUSI

瑞士联邦700周年庆祝帐幕

瑞士，贝林佐纳

TENT FOR THE 700TH ANNIVERSARY OF THE SWISS CONFEDERATION

BELLINZONA, SWITZERLAND

1989-1991

项目时间：1989年
建造时间：1990～1991年
委托方：瑞士联邦内政与经济部
建筑面积：1,540平方米
建筑体积：13,000立方米

Project: 1989
Construction: 1990-1991
Client: Swiss Confederation, Federal Interior and Economics Department
Useful surface: 1,540m²
Volume : 13,000m³

“我设想这座建筑能够在景观中展现出一种原始形象——拱顶——简单而精致，现代又古老，足以抵抗脆弱的‘现代’文化这一令人困惑的术语，并成为参照的标准，以及不同语境之下的话题。”巨大的帐篷是为庆祝1991年瑞士联邦成立700周年而设计的，它的半径超过40米，高度33米，内设约1900个座席，由13根钢管构成的金属结构肋支撑，加以绳索固定。在建筑皇冠般的拱顶结构上方，飘扬着瑞士联邦的旗帜。在一年的时间里，多座瑞士城市和其他欧洲城市都建造过这种帐篷。

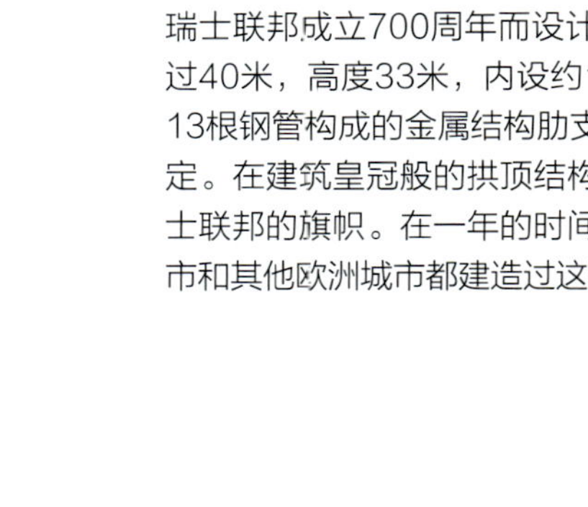

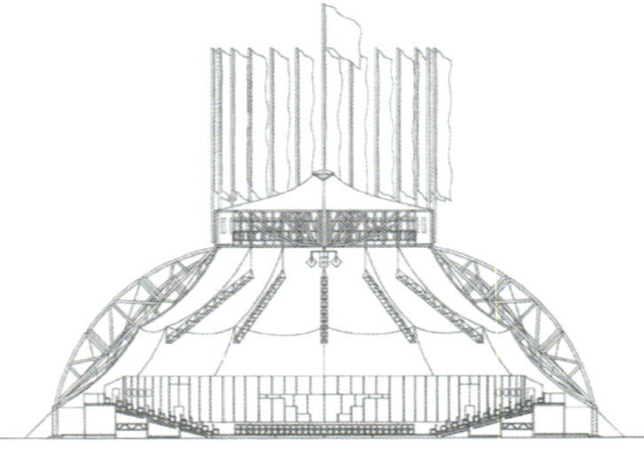

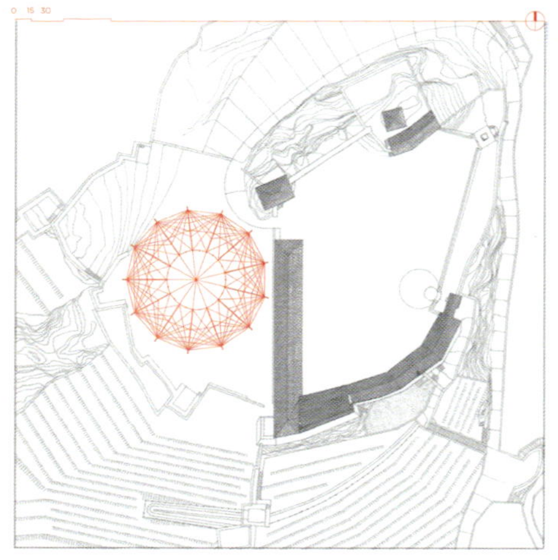

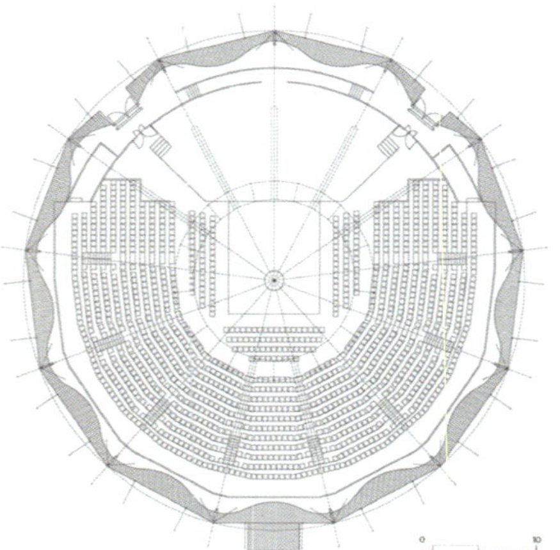

“I imagined a structure able to shape a primary image in the landscape - a dome - something simple and precise, contemporary and archaic at the same time, thus capable to resist the confused jargon of the fragile “modern” culture and to become a point of reference and of dialogue in the different contexts”. The large tent was designed on the occasion of the celebrations for the 700th anniversary of the Swiss Confederation in 1991, with a diameter of more than 40 meters, a height of 33 meters, it offered approximately 1900 seats. The reticular frame of thirteen metals ribs and stabilized with guy-wires, consisted of white tubular steel elements that held the suspended bright tent. On top the structure converged into a crown surmounted by the colored flags of the Swiss Cantons. Within the space of a year, the tent was set up in several Swiss and European cities.

© ALO ZANETTA

© PINO MUSI

© ALO ZANETTA

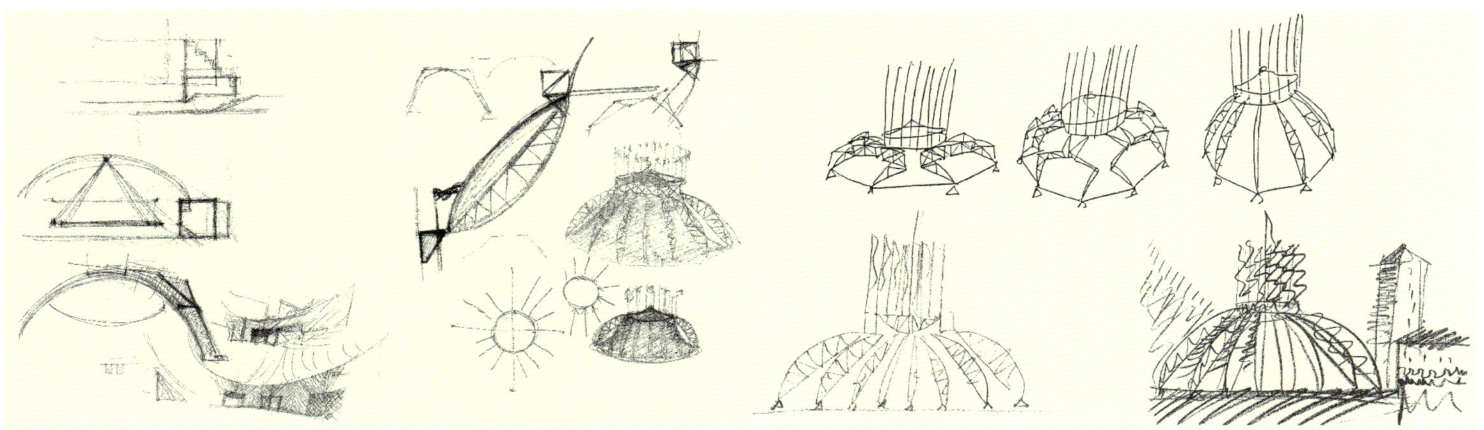

斯卡拉剧院修复

意大利，米兰

RESTORATION OF THE THEATER ALLA SCALA

MILAN, ITALY

2001-2004

项目时间：2001年
建造时间：2002～2004年
委托方：米兰市
新增体积：130,000 立方米
（地上95,000立方米，地下35,000立方米）

Project: 2001
Construction: 2002-2004
Client: City of Milano
Volume new part: 130,000 m^3
(above ground: 95,000 m^3, underground: 35,000 m^3)

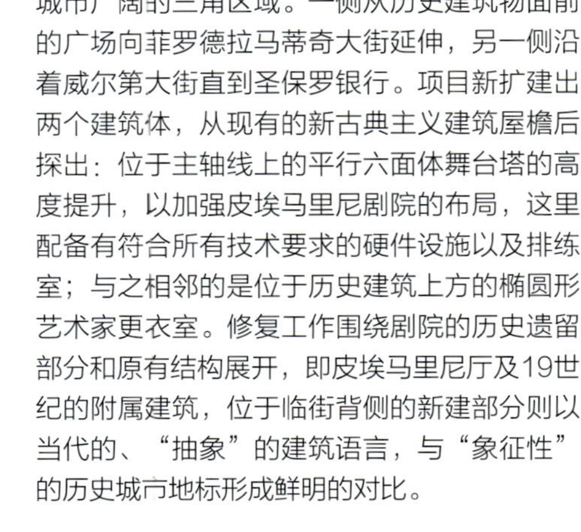

斯卡拉大剧院的修复和扩建工程影响了其周边城市广阔的三角区域。一侧从历史建筑物面前的广场向菲罗德拉马蒂奇大街延伸，另一侧沿着威尔第大街直到圣保罗银行。项目新扩建出两个建筑体，从现有的新古典主义建筑屋檐后探出：位于主轴线上的平行六面体舞台塔的高度提升，以加强皮埃马里尼剧院的布局，这里配备有符合所有技术要求的硬件设施以及排练室；与之相邻的是位于历史建筑上方的椭圆形艺术家更衣室。修复工作围绕剧院的历史遗留部分和原有结构展开，即皮埃马里尼厅及19世纪的附属建筑，位于临街背侧的新建部分则以当代的、“抽象”的建筑语言，与“象征性”的历史城市地标形成鲜明的对比。

The restoration and extension of the Theater alla Scala affected a wide triangle of the city. From the square in front of the historic building the lot extends along Via Filodrammatici on one hand, and along Via Verdi until the former San Paolo bank on the other. The architectural project regarding the extension developed two new volumes surmounting the eaves of the existent neoclassical building: the raising of the stage tower in the shape of a parallelepiped, -with all technical requirements and rehearsal rooms to fit -, set in the main axis to reinforce the layout of the Piermarini theater, and next to it, an elliptic volume housing the artists' dressing room that hovers above the historical buildings. A conservative restoration was provided for the monumental parts of the theater and its original structure as the Piermarini hall and the nineteenth century annex buildings, whereas the new parts, that are set back from the street front, want to express a contemporary and "abstract" architectural language to contrast with the "figurative" one of the historical urban landmark.

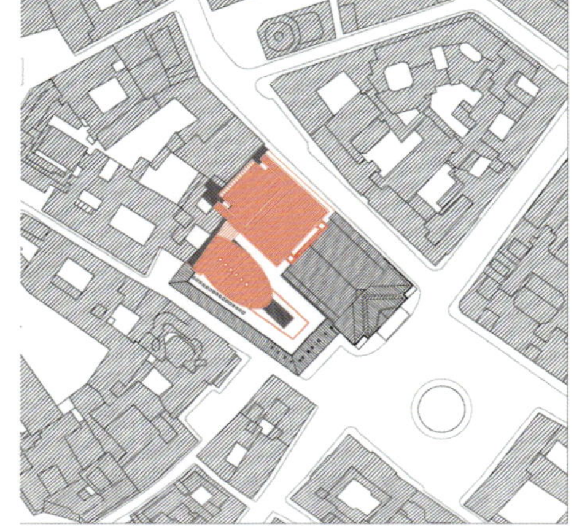

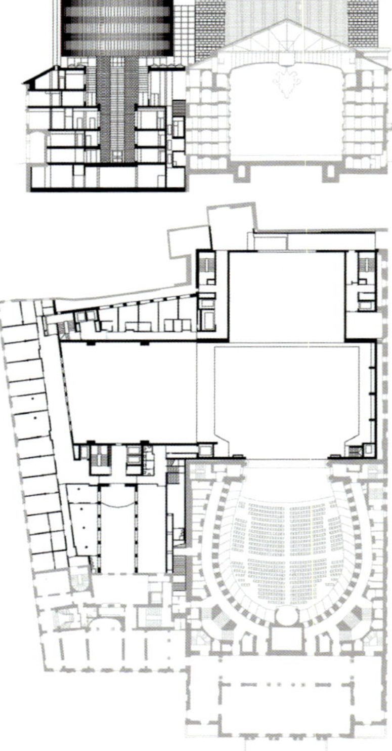

© PINO MUSI

© PINO MUSI

© PINO MUSI

© PINO MUSI

© ENRICO CANO

图书馆
LIBRARIES

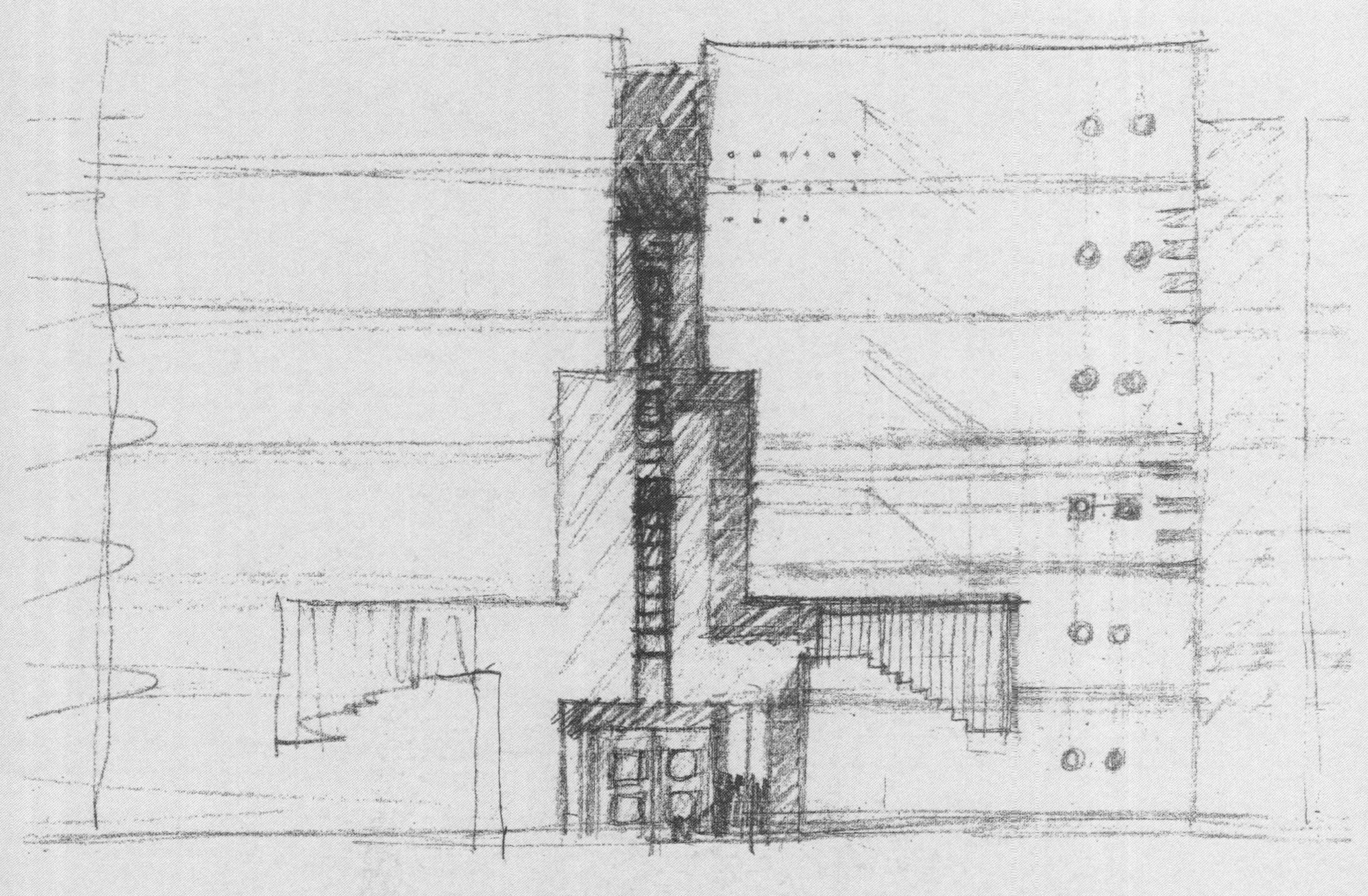

嘉布遣会修道院图书馆

瑞士，卢加诺

LIBRARY IN THE CAPUCHINS CONVENT

LUGANO, SWITZERLAND

1976-1979

项目时间：1976年
建造时间：1976~1979年
委托方：卢加诺，嘉布遣会修道院
占地面积：7,200平方米
建筑面积：900平方米
建筑体积：3,800立方米

Project: 1976
Construction: 1976-1979
Client: Monastery of the Capuchin Friars, Lugano
Site area: 7,200 m^2
Useful surface: 900 m^2
Volume: 3,800 m^3

这座建于17世纪的修道院坐落于该城市历史中心与车站建成区之间的山坡上。项目旨在重现整个组织的聚合作用，建立一所公用图书馆，之后修复整个修道院。该建筑为地下结构，保留了原修道院的规划。内部包含上下两层的资料阅览室，围绕中央区域展开。花园里的天窗使得人们可以直接观赏地面上的教堂，并照亮了图书馆的中心区域，加深了中轴墙面的垂直纵深感。长长的藏书室划出朝向城市的地下结构，运用垂直元素配合升降梯，将图书馆与地面的修道院办公室连通。

The 17th - century monastery lies on the hill-side between the historic centre of the city and the built-up area around the station. The aim of the project was to revive the collective character of the entire structure, realizing a public library, and later the restoration of the convent. The building is set underground and leaves unchanged the plan of the old convent. The interior offers a reading and reference room on two floors that opens around a central space. A skylight that emerges from the garden and establishes an immediate visual relationship with the church above illuminates the core and highlights the axis of the library marked by a deep vertical cut in the wall. The long book storeroom delimits the underground structure towards the city and while a vertical element with the elevator links the library to the offices located in the above convent.

© ALO ZANETTA

© ALO ZANETTA

© ALO ZANETTA

© ALO ZANETTA

© ALO ZANETTA

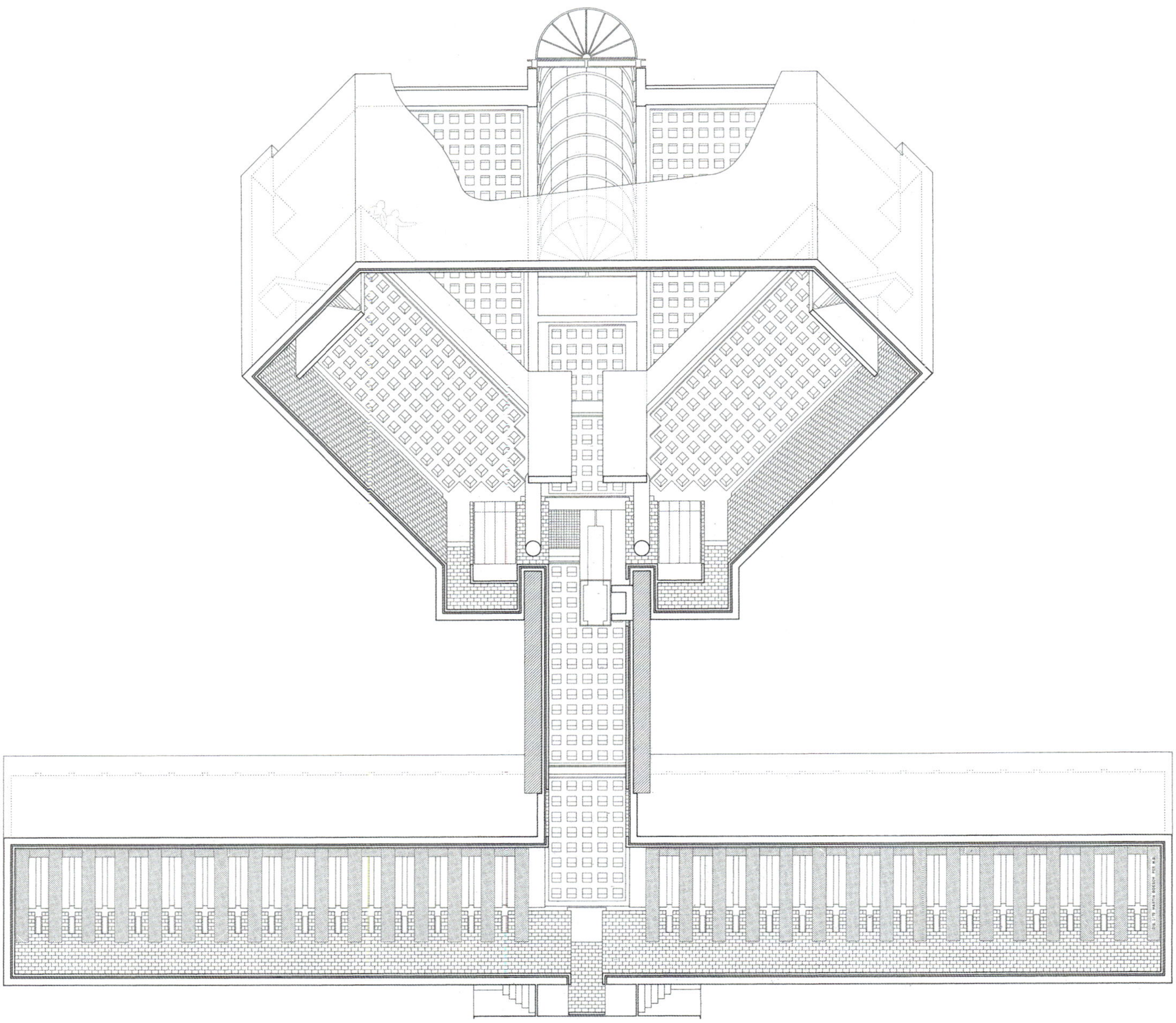

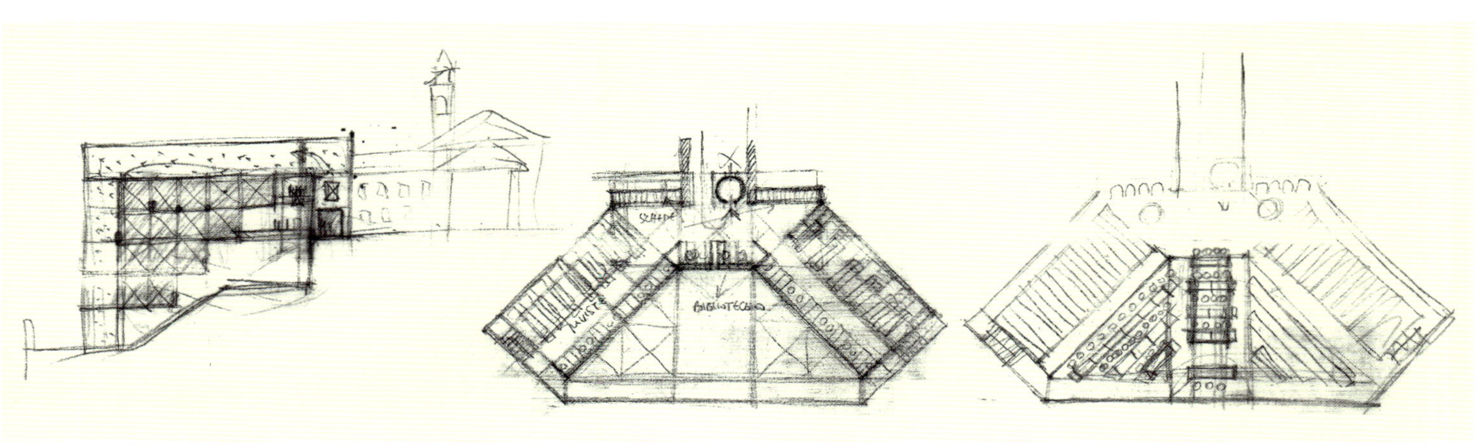

书籍、影像与声音之家

法国，维勒班

MAISON DU LIVRE, DE L'IMAGE ET DU SON

VILLEURBANNE, FRANCE

1984-1988

竞赛项目时间：1984年
建造时间：1985～1988年
委托方：维勒班市
占地面积：5,400平方米
建筑面积：5,580平方米
建筑体积：18,000立方米

Competition project: 1984
Construction: 1985-1988
Client: City of Villeurbanne
Site area: 5,400 m²
Useful surface: 5,580 m²
Volume: 18,000 m³

该建筑沿埃米尔·佐拉大道而建，位于城市前部。入口一侧的立面略向外凸出，连接起周围建筑的玻璃砖墙。垂直开口的设计形成了两面对称的墙体，墙体的角落设有楼梯井。街道立面的图案由多种颜色的石头打造而成，同时突显出后院的圆柱形建筑体。与主立面一样，圆柱形建筑体通过由玻璃砖装饰的部分与周围建筑分隔开，内部空间的挑空从一层直达屋顶，形成了一个同心环构成的采光井，周围分布着资料室，用玻璃围合出用于放置图书馆员工办公桌的区域。

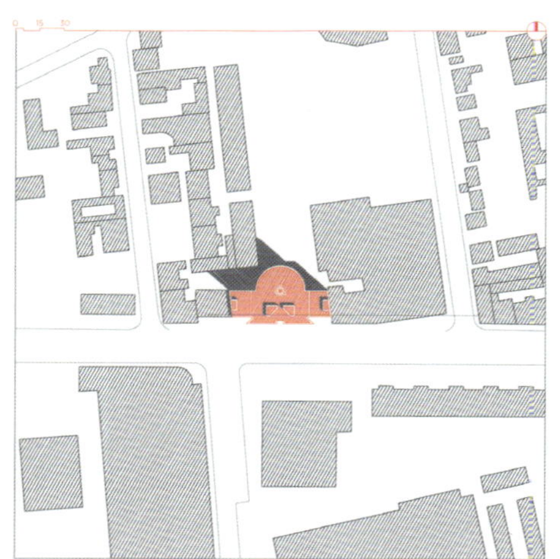

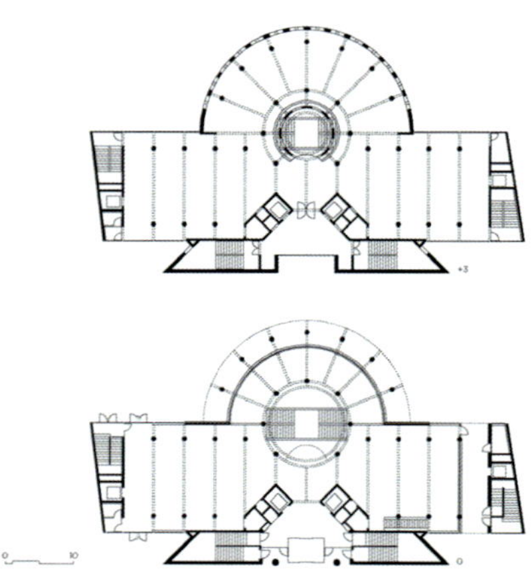

The building is set within the continuous urban front along avenue Emile Zola. The entrance façade projects itself forward with respect to the glass brick walls connecting with the neighboring buildings. A deep vertical cut forms two symmetrical walls, in whose corners the stairwells are set. The pattern of the street façade, clad in alternated colored bands of stone, also characterizes the cylindrical volume on the rear courtyard. Same as the main front, the cylindrical volume is detached from the surrounding buildings by means of connecting parts faced with glass bricks. The interior space presents a central cavity, rising up from the ground floor to the roof. It shapes a light well made of concentric rings, around which the reference rooms are located and from which the glassed-in volumes containing the librarians' desks emerge.

© PINO MUSI

© PINO MUSI

© PINO MUSI

© PINO MUSI

© ENRICO CANO

提拉波斯奇图书馆

意大利，贝加莫

LIBRARY TIRABOSCHI

BERGAMO, ITALY

1995-2004

项目时间：1995年
建造时间：2004年
委托方：贝尔加莫市
合作建筑师：乔治·奥尔西尼
占地面积：9,360平方米
建筑面积：3,130平方米
建筑体积：17,500立方米

Project: 1995
Construction: 2004
Client: City of Bergamo
Partner: arch. Giorgio Orsini
Site area: 9,360 m^2
Useful surface: 3,130 m^2
Volume: 17,500 m^3

提拉波斯奇图书馆是联合图书馆系统的核心部分，这个系统囊括了贝尔加莫的所有图书馆。出于战略考虑，该建筑位于大学附近，在一条城市主要街道与一片绿地之间。厚重而坚固的砖墙结构面向主干道，仅在入口附近设置一个小小的开口。建筑内部共有5层，均面朝一处由采光屋顶照亮的中央空间。入口对面开阔的通高玻璃窗将阅览席的视野引至种植着树木的后院。

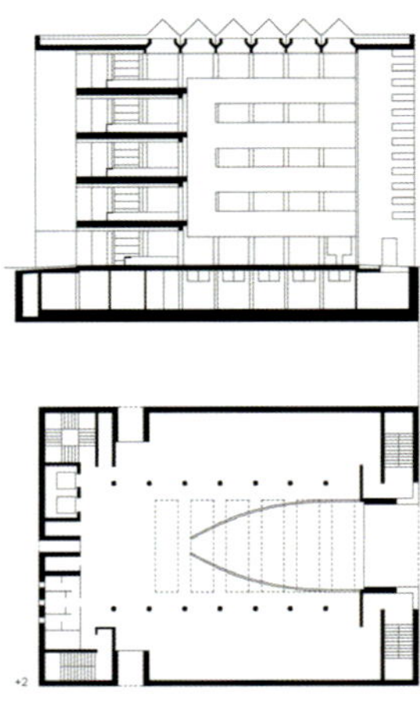

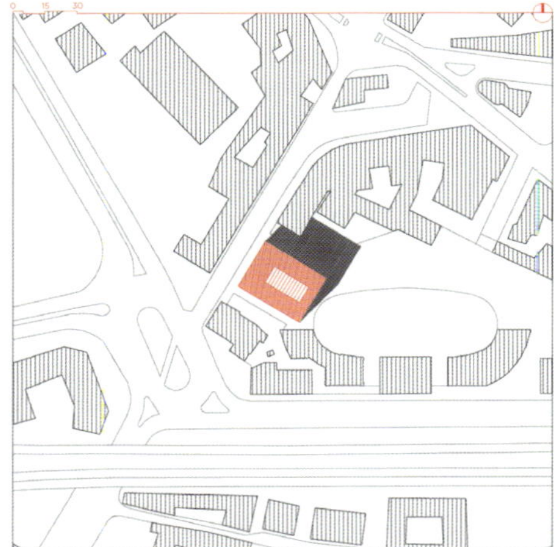

The Tiraboschi library is the core of the inter-librarian system including all the Bergamo-based libraries. The building is strategically located near the university, between a major city street and a green area. Towards the main road, the solidity of the massive brick wall is only interrupted by a thin cut that widens near the entrance. Inside, the building develops on five levels all facing the central void illuminated by roof lights. Opposite the entrance, a wide window front along the whole height of the building opens the reading galleries towards the backyard planted with trees.

© ENRICO CANO

© ENRICO CANO

© ENRICO CANO

© ENRICO CANO

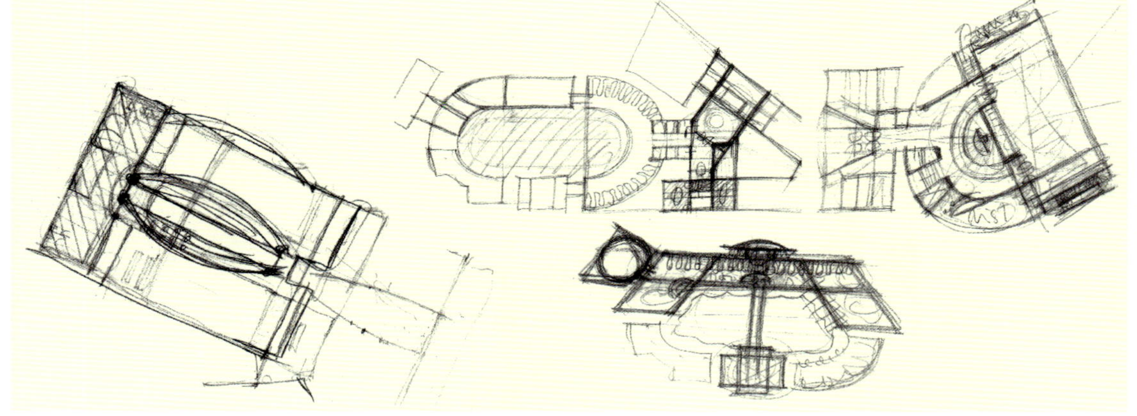

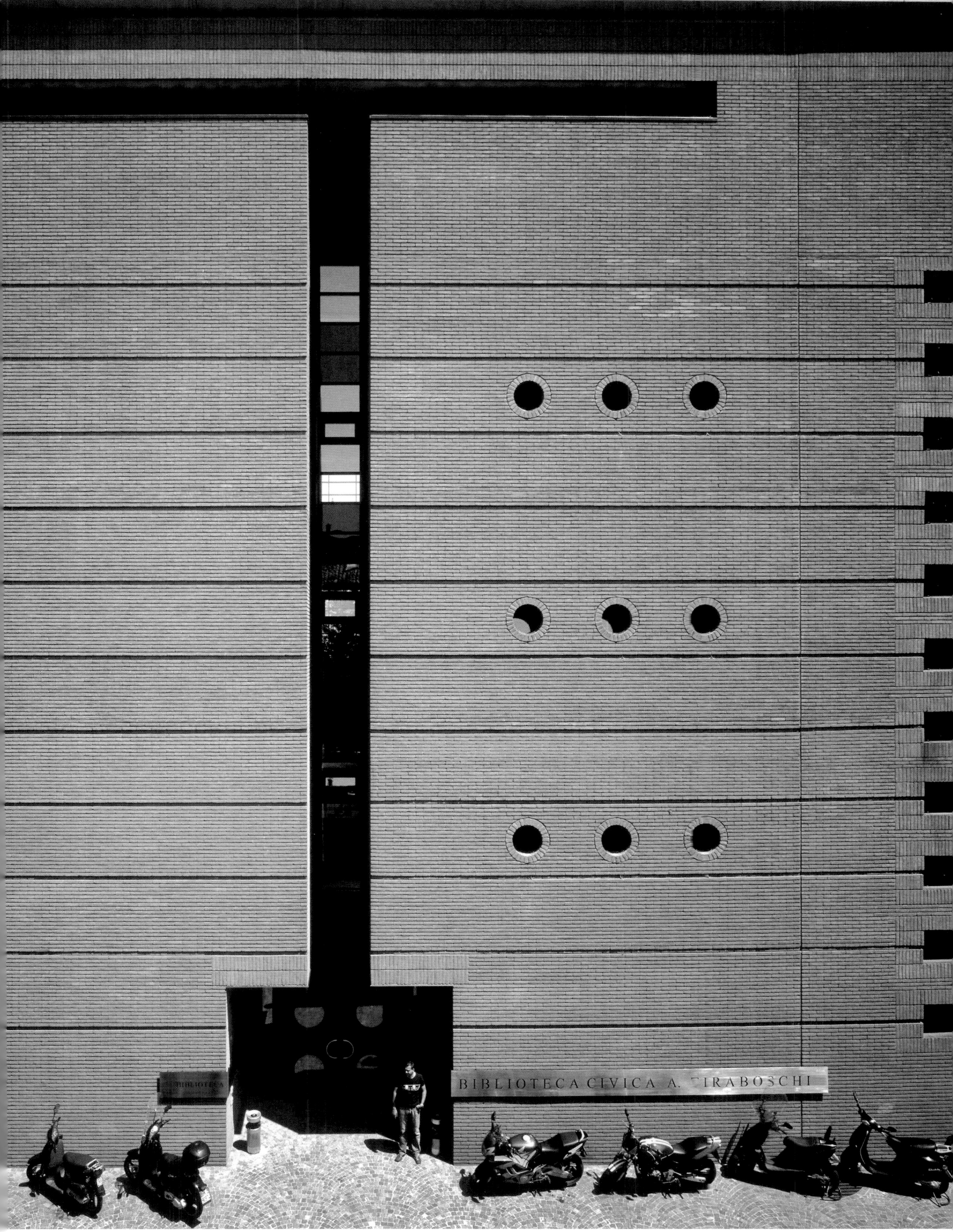
BIBLIOTECA
BIBLIOTECA CIVICA A. TIRABOSCHI

市政图书馆
德国，多特蒙德

MUNICIPAL LIBRARY
DORTMUND, GERMANY

1995-1999

竞赛项目时间：1995年
建造时间：1997～1999年
委托方：多特蒙德市
合作建筑师：杰尔·维特，克勒门斯·佩勒（工程师）
占地面积：7,000平方米
建筑面积：14,130平方米
建筑体积：53,735立方米

Competition project: 1995
Construction: 1997-1999
Client: City of Dortmund
Partner: arch. Gerd Vette, eng. Klemens Pelle
Site area: 7,000 m^2
Useful surface: 14,130 m^2
Volume: 53,735 m^3

图书馆位于老城区与19世纪修建的火车站前的空地之间。图书馆由两个在体量与形态上完全不同的建筑组成，各自的功能和使用材料也不同。其中之一是被切割成一半的倒锥形体块，在开放空间的不同楼层设有咨询台、检索处和阅读室。另一个则是长长的矩形体块用作办公室和藏书库。图书馆的入口在这两个建筑的首层连接处。图书馆的内部设计使得各层的道路以及各部分的联系都可以容易地被识别。

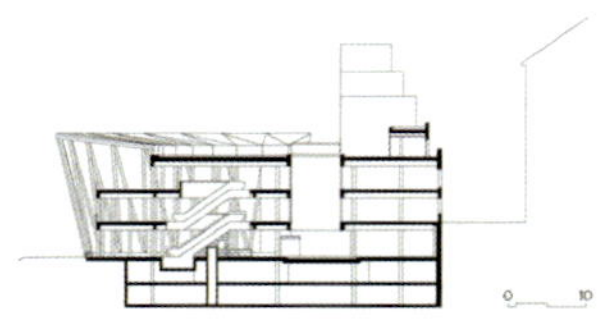

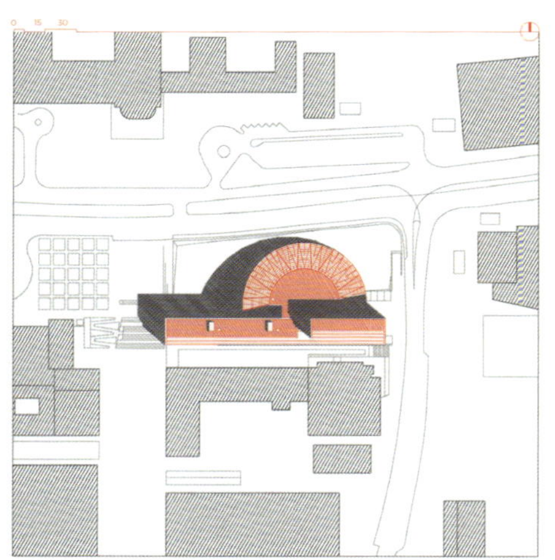

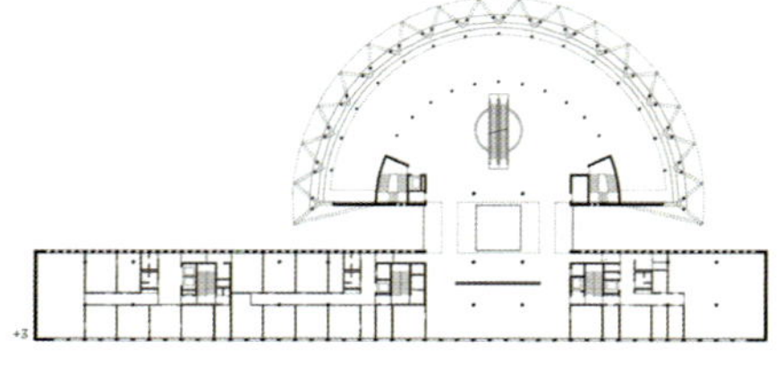

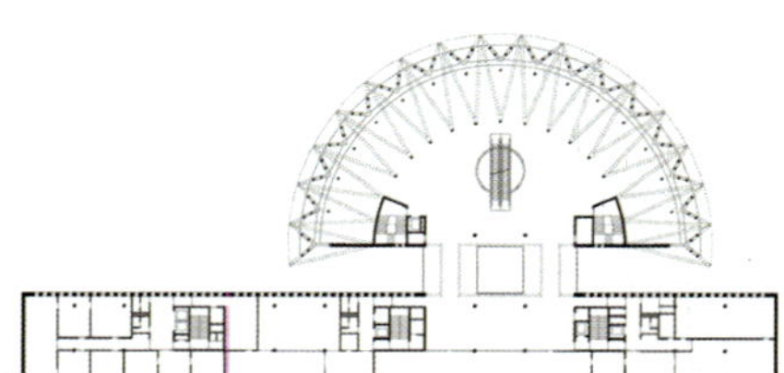

The library is located between the historic town and the empty urban space in front of it with the 19th century railway station. It consists of two distinct buildings, in shape and volume, in material as well as in use. One, an upside down truncated half-cone houses in a one and open space different floors with the reception area, the library catalogues and the reading rooms. The other, a long orthogonal building for offices and storages, is characterized by a progressive tapering on the different floors. The entrance to the library is set at ground floor in the junction of the two different volumes. The interior allows at a glimpse the distribution of paths on the two floors of the library and the connection to the facilities located in the body next to it.

© MARKUS STEUR

© CORNELIA SUHAN

© CORNELIA SUHAN

© RALPH RICHTER

© RALPH RICHTER

© ENRICO CANO

马丁·柏德梅基金会图书馆与博物馆

瑞士，科洛尼

MARTIN BODMER FOUNDATION, LIBRARY AND MUSEUM

COLOGNY, SWITZERLAND

1998-2003

项目时间：1998年
建造时间：2000～2003年
委托方：马丁•柏德梅基金会
现场监理：皮利建筑实验工作室
占地面积：5,500平方米
建筑面积：1,280平方米
建筑体积：9,000立方米

Project: 1998
Construction: 2000-2003
Client: Fondation Martin Bodmer
Site supervision: Studio Archilab, Pully
Site area: 5,500 m^2
Useful surface: 1,280 m^2
Volume : 9,000 m^3

马丁·柏德梅基金会在靠近日内瓦的城市科洛尼，收藏有大量手稿和文件，这些藏品的品质和稀有程度使其成为受人瞩目的文化遗产。基金会扩建项目选址在一处大型地产内，位于两栋20世纪初建造的别墅之间。建筑包含两层地下结构并与两座别墅相连，地面上仅显露出5个玻璃元素，天窗使得自然光能够进入地下展区。扩建后的博物馆入口设在花园里，通过建筑在湖边的一个下沉式庭院进入。建筑内部的展览空间通过光线所形成的鲜明对比而得以区分：自然光散落在悬垂于新建筑中部的艺术品上，柔和而精确的人工光则照在嵌墙式展柜深处那些稀有的书籍上。整个空间看起来无边无际、充满变化，仅通过书籍的摆放划定界限，每本书都配备有特制的铁质支架。

Martin Bodmer Foundation in Cologny, near Geneva, hosts the collection of manuscripts and documents that constitutes a cultural heritage remarkable for its quality and rarity. The extension of the foundation is set between two early 20th century villas in a large estate and consists of a two-story hypogeal construction linked to both of the villas. Only five glass elements emerge from the ground. Skylights enables natural light flow into the underground exhibition area. The access to the new museum's extension happens from the garden, crossing a sunken courtyard on the lakeside of the property. Inside, the exhibition spaces are distinguished by the contrast of the daylight tangling the suspended artworks that are placed in the centre of the new building, and the soft punctual light on the rare books behind the showcases along the walls. The space appears almost boundless and mutable, only delimited by the arrangements of the books, each of them held by a specific designed iron support.

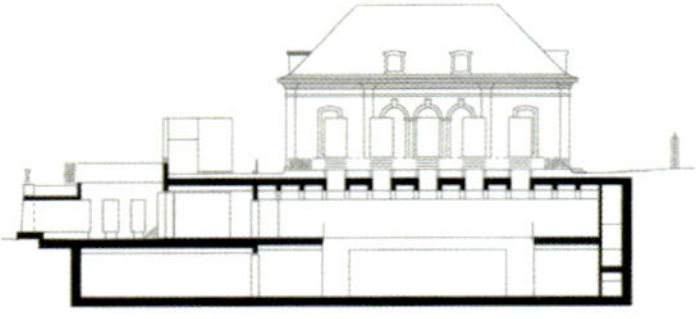

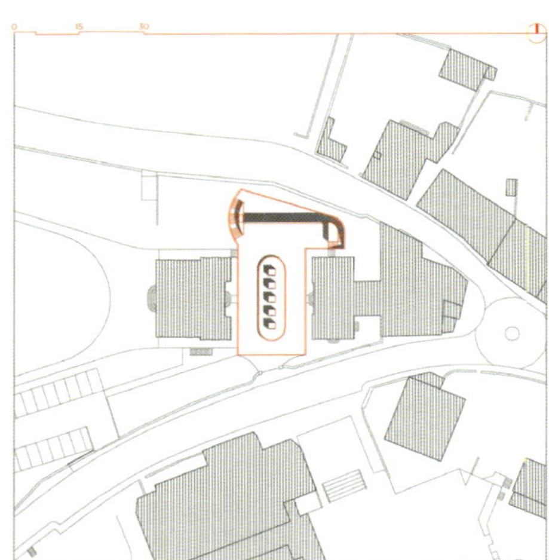

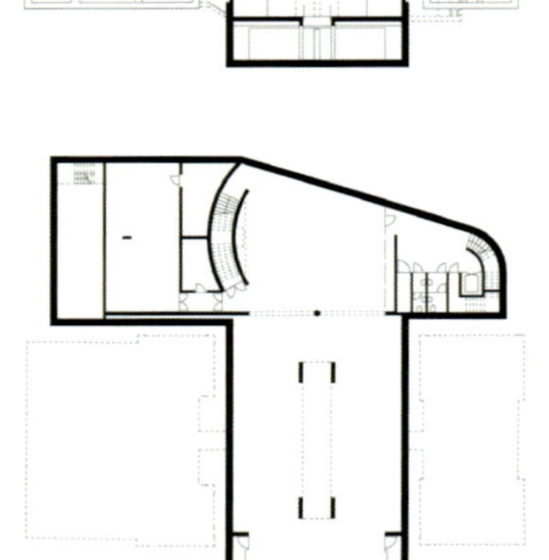

© PINO MUSI

© PINO MUSI

© PINO MUSI

© MARIO BOTTA

© PINO MUSI

© PINO MUSI

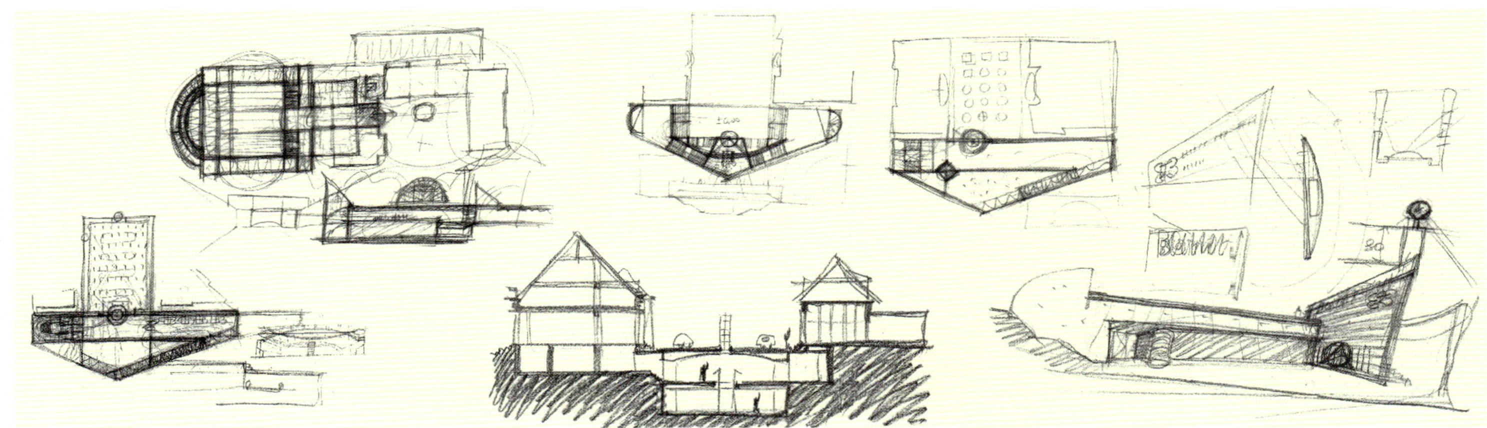

清华大学图书馆

中国，北京

TSINGHUA UNIVERSITY LIBRARY

BEIJING, CHINA

2008-2011

项目时间：2008年
建造时间：2009~2011年
委托方：上海地产集团
上海申通地铁资产管理有限公司
合作建筑师：华东建筑设计研究院
占地面积：20,000平方米
建筑面积：地上16,000平方米
建筑体积：地上70,000立方米

Project: 2008
Construction: 2009-2011
Client: Shanghai Real Estate (Group) Co. Ltd.
Shanghai Shentong Underground Railway Assets Managements CO. Ltd
Partner architect: Ecadi, East China Architectural Design & Research Institute Co., Ltd
Site area: 20,000 m²
Useful surface: 16,000 m² above ground
Volume: 70,000 m³ above ground

图书馆首先具有一个直线形建筑体，分布均匀的一系列高窗形成了富有节奏感的外立面，该建筑体相对独立的同时嵌入了一个巨大的、具有凹入式开口的倒圆锥体。建筑内部中央区域是图书馆的核心空间，配有可以仰望天空的巨大天窗；通高的内庭正对着三个楼层的阅览室，阅览室被木板条组成的屏风遮蔽起来。隔热砖石结构与石块饰面保证了全年高效的能源性能，可以良好地适应北京炎热的夏季和寒冷的冬季；同时，所有室内空间都使用温和的线形材料，为这个致力于提供知识和回忆的场所营造出温馨踏实的氛围。

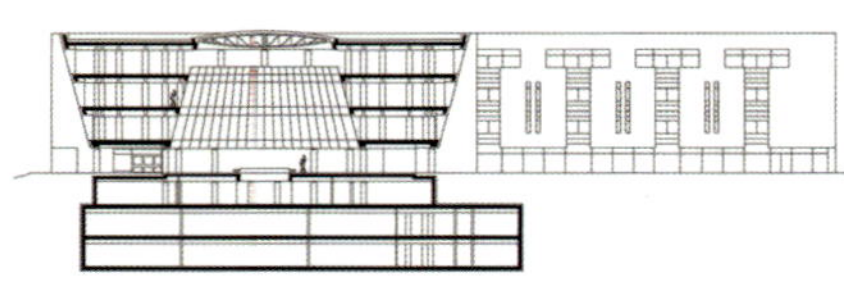

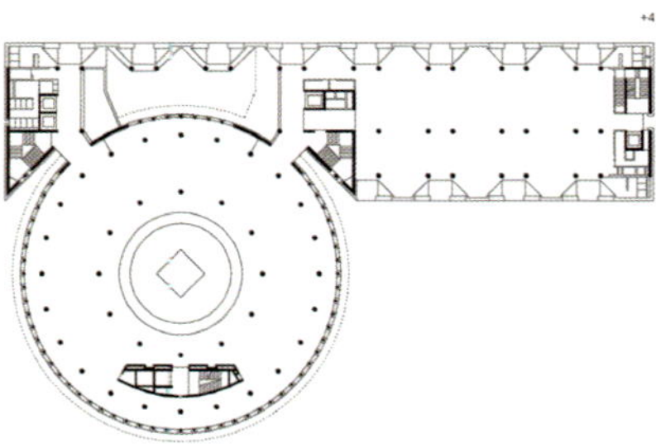

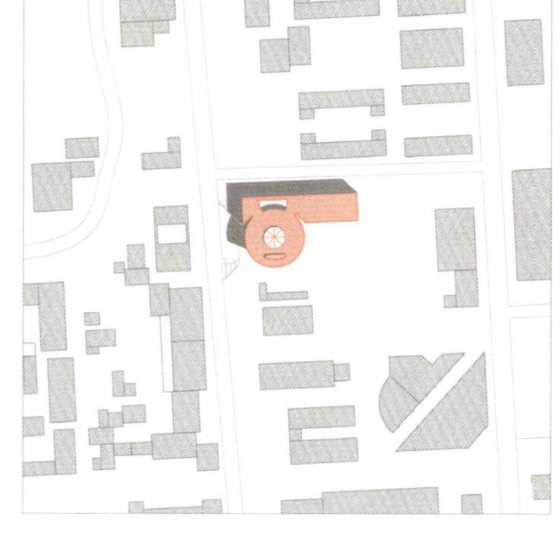

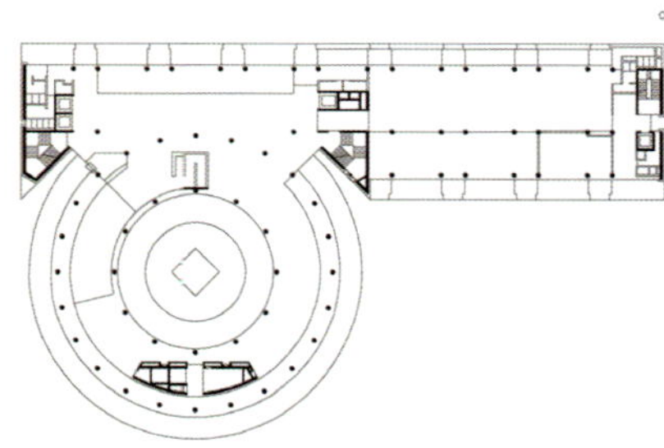

The library is composed of a rectilinear volume marked by a balanced sequence of large windows used to form the rhythmical composition of the façade. It is treated as a single, full-height body in which to insert the large circle of an overturned conical volume with recessed openings. The library features an inner central space, the library's core, covered by a large skylight, forming a perspective toward the sky and a full-height courtyard faced by the three levels of the reading rooms, that are sheltered by a screen composed of wooden slats. The insulated masonry and the stone cover guarantee a good energy performance throughout the year, adapting to the hot summers and the cold winters of Beijing, while all interior spaces feature linear and tempered materials to enhance a warm and essential atmosphere of a place devoted to knowledge and memory.

© FU XING

© FU XING

© FU XING

© FU XING

© FU XING

© ENRICO CANO

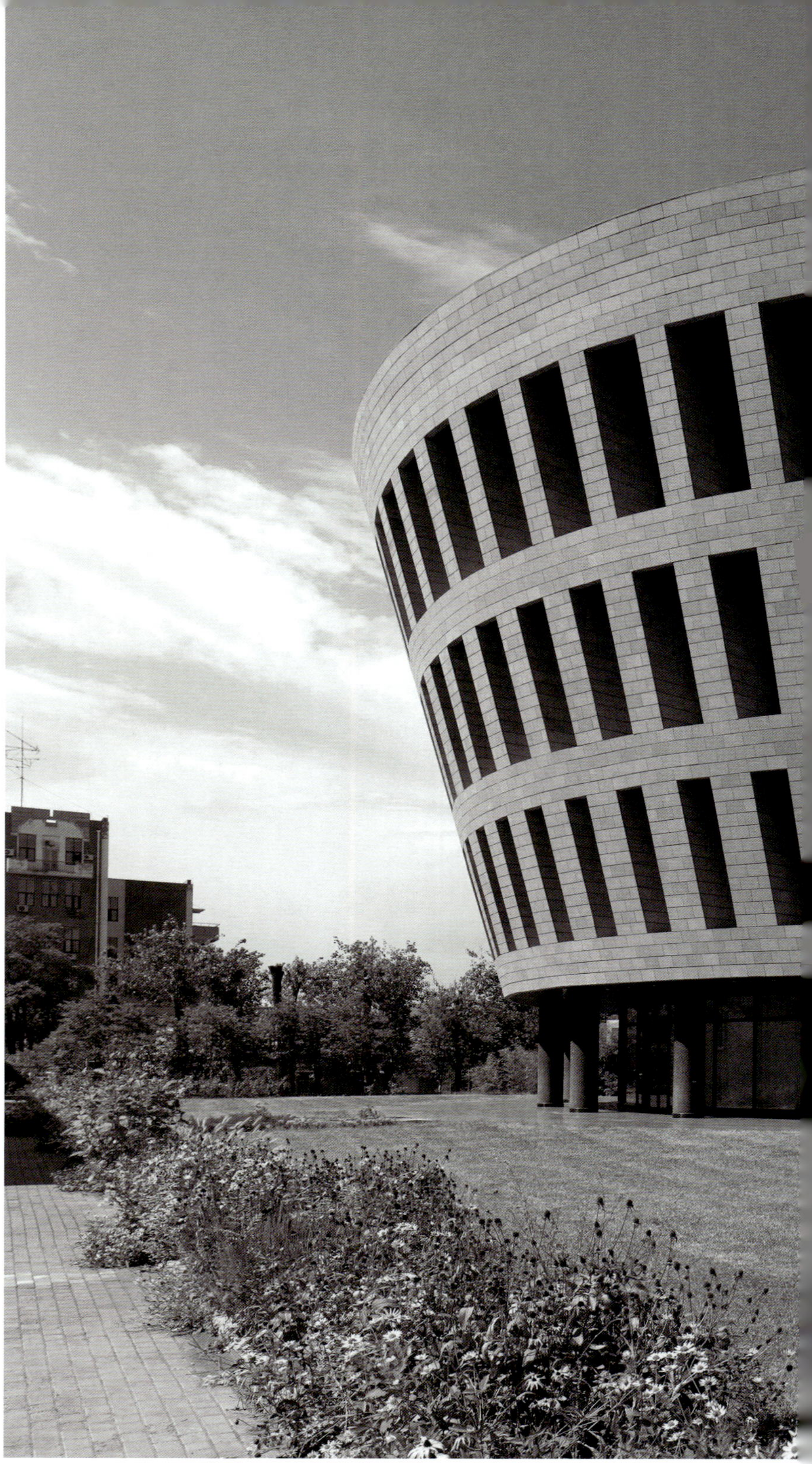

© ENRICO CANO

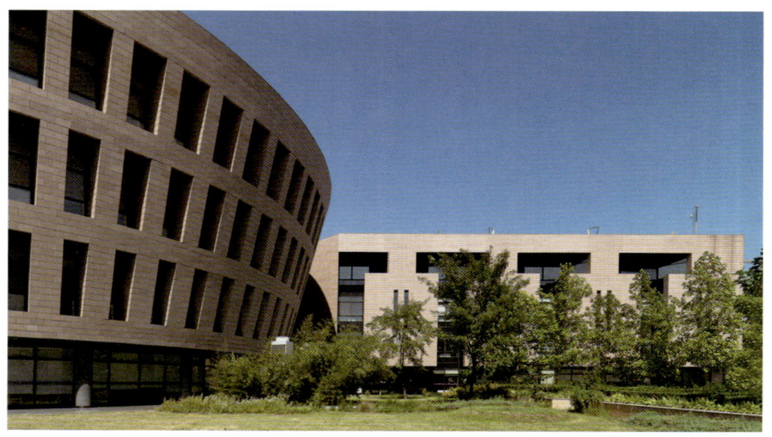

办公空间
WORK SPACES

国家银行

瑞士，弗里堡

STATE BANK

FRIBOURG, SWITZERLAND

1977-1982

项目时间：1977年（竞赛项目）
建造时间：1982年
客户：弗里堡国家银行
占地面积：1,800 平方米
建筑面积：18,500平方米
建筑体积：64,000立方米

Project: 1977 (competition project)
Construction: 1982
Client: State Bank, Fribourg
Site area: 1,800 m²
Useful surface: 18,500 m²
Volume: 64,000 m³

建筑坐落于城市中一处重要的三角形地块，位于一条大道和一条街之间，二者交汇于火车站对面的广场。建筑由沿街道方向平行展开的两翼和中心的圆柱体组成。两翼尽头的下沉空间标示出人行步道的起点，同时也是建筑的入口。在一层，光线透过建筑中央的天窗照亮了大厅和银行营业部，以及咖啡厅和餐馆。地下层包括停车场、银行服务区和一个迪斯科舞厅。楼上数层则是办公空间，顶层包含了银行的特殊服务功能区域、一间会议室和一个宽敞的露台。

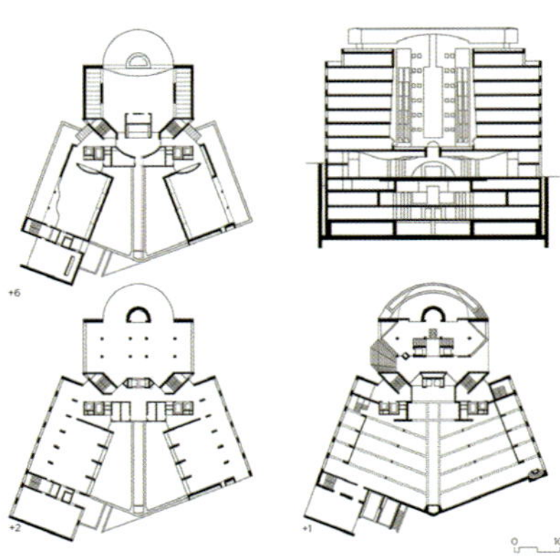

The building occupies an area of particular urban significance: the triangular lot is delimited by a boulevard and a street that converge in the large piazza in front of the railroad station. The building is composed of two lateral wings aligned with the street, and a central cylindrical element. The concave end is detached from the lateral wings at the point where the pedestrian walkway appears, a point that marks the organization of the entrances. On the ground floor, in addition to the bank counters which occupy the covered courtyard illuminated by the central skylight, there are a café and a restaurant. The floors below ground level contain a parking area, the service areas for the bank and a discotheque. The upper floors hold offices, and the top floor contains the special services of the bank, a meeting room and a wide terrace.

© ALO ZANETTA

© ALO ZANETTA

© ALO ZANETTA

© ALO ZANETTA

© ALO ZANETTA

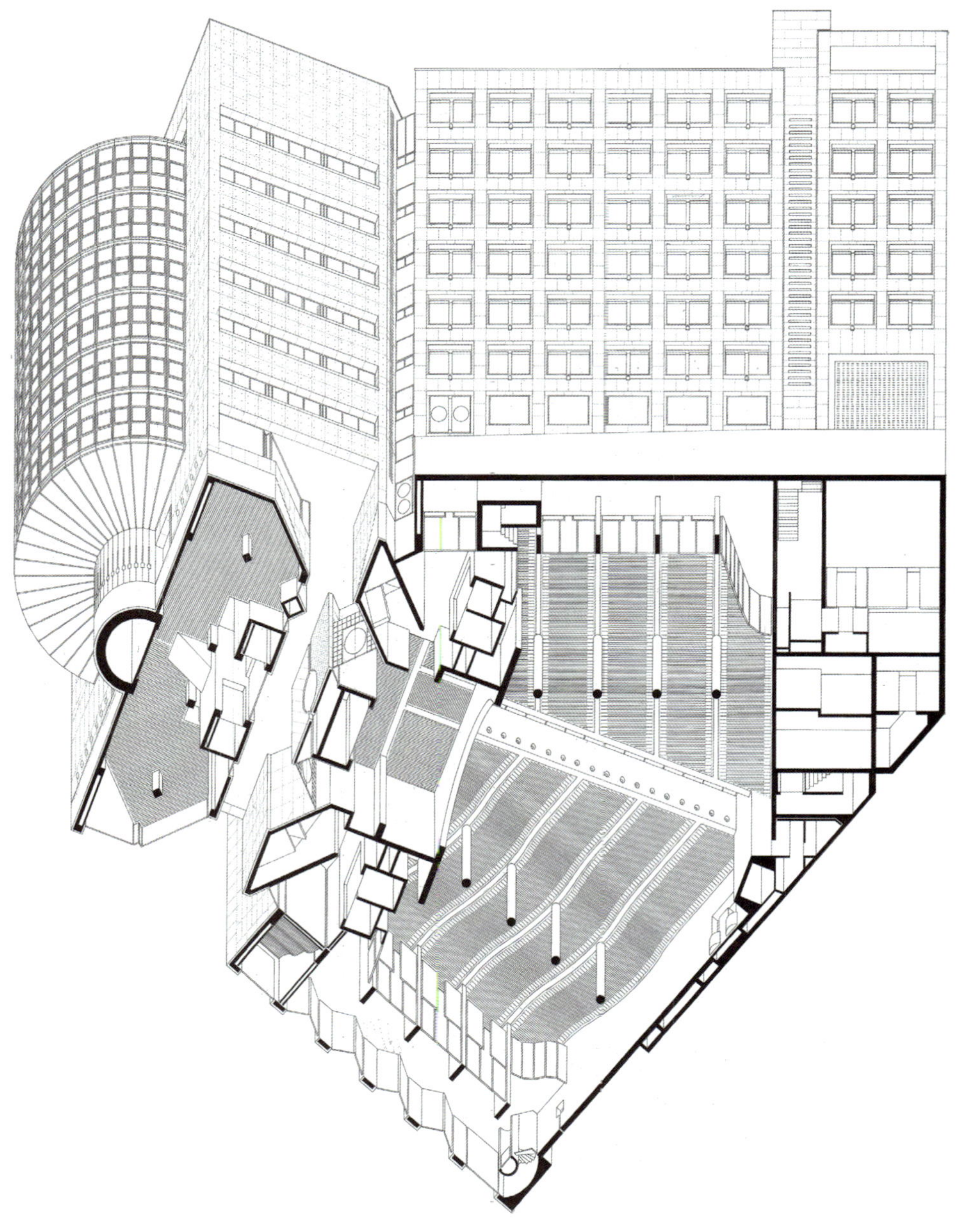

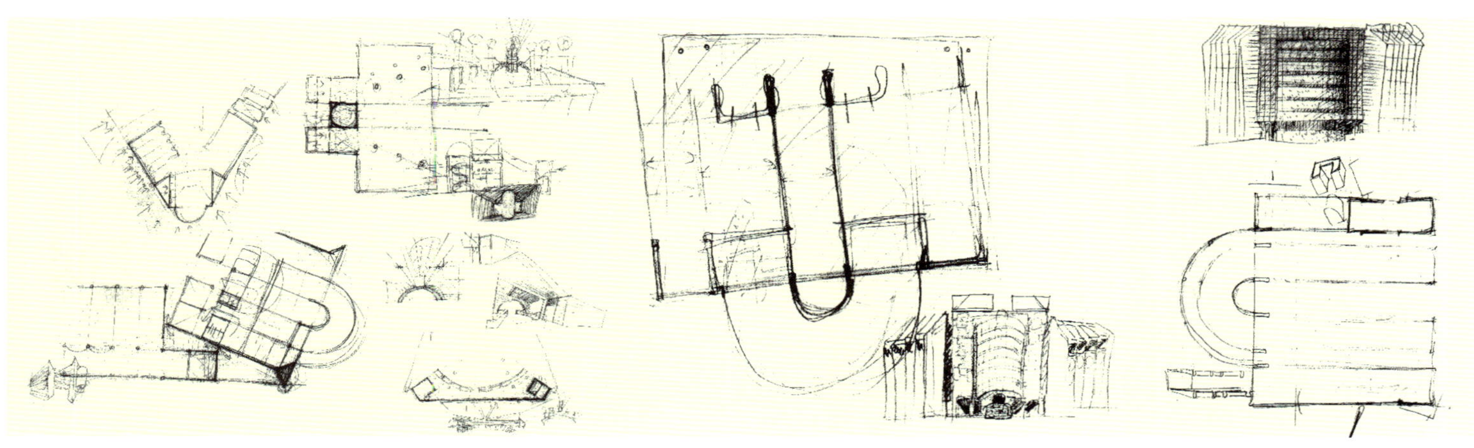

兰希拉1号楼

瑞士，卢加诺

BUILDING RANSILA 1

LUGANO, SWITZERLAND

1981-1985

项目时间：1981年
建造时间：1982～1985年
委托方：卢加诺，费迪南公司
占地面积：850平方米
建筑面积：4,000平方米
建筑体积：20,000立方米

Project: 1981
Construction: 1982-1985
Client: Fidinam, Lugano
Site area: 850 m^2
Useful surface: 4,000 m^2
Volume: 20,000 m^3

建筑坐落于卢加诺历史中心区的20世纪新城区内，位于两条重要道路的交汇处，由两座翼楼组成。翼楼的交汇处形成一座转角塔楼，角楼顶部的一棵树成为该建筑的标志物。建筑的力量感通过墙体的厚度充分体现，并因沿外墙边线退进的双层窗户得以增强。同时，翼楼连续的玻璃外墙与角楼厚重的砖墙形成鲜明对比。服务用房及垂直交通体系设置在角楼内，办公室布置在两翼。建筑的一层门廊下分布着多个商铺的入口。

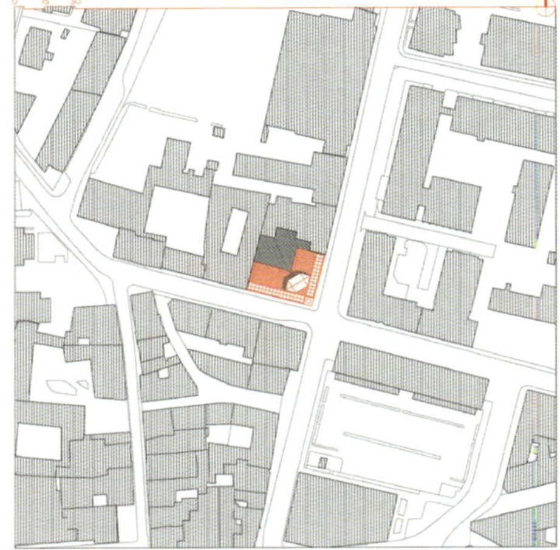

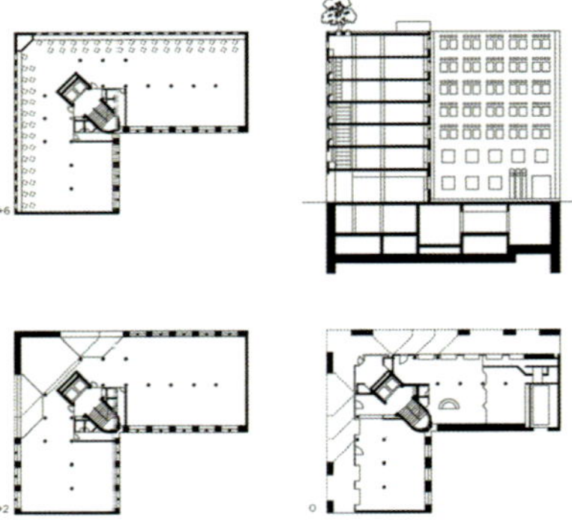

The building stands on the corner of two important streets in the 20th century fabric of the historic centre of Lugano. It is composed of two wings that, at their meeting point, form a sort of corner tower, marked at the summit by the presence of a tree. The building force lies in the thickness of the walls, emphasized by the presence of double windows which are set back with respect to the exterior wall line. The side volumes display continuous glassed walls in contrast with the massive brickwork of the corner tower. The tower houses the services and the vertical distribution system; the offices are in the side wings. On the ground floor, the portico provides the access to the different stores.

© ALBERTO FLAMMER

© ALO ZANETTA

© PINO MUSI

Società di Banca Svizzera
Società di Banca Svizzera
Società di Banca Svizz
Cambio
Bata
Bata
Bata

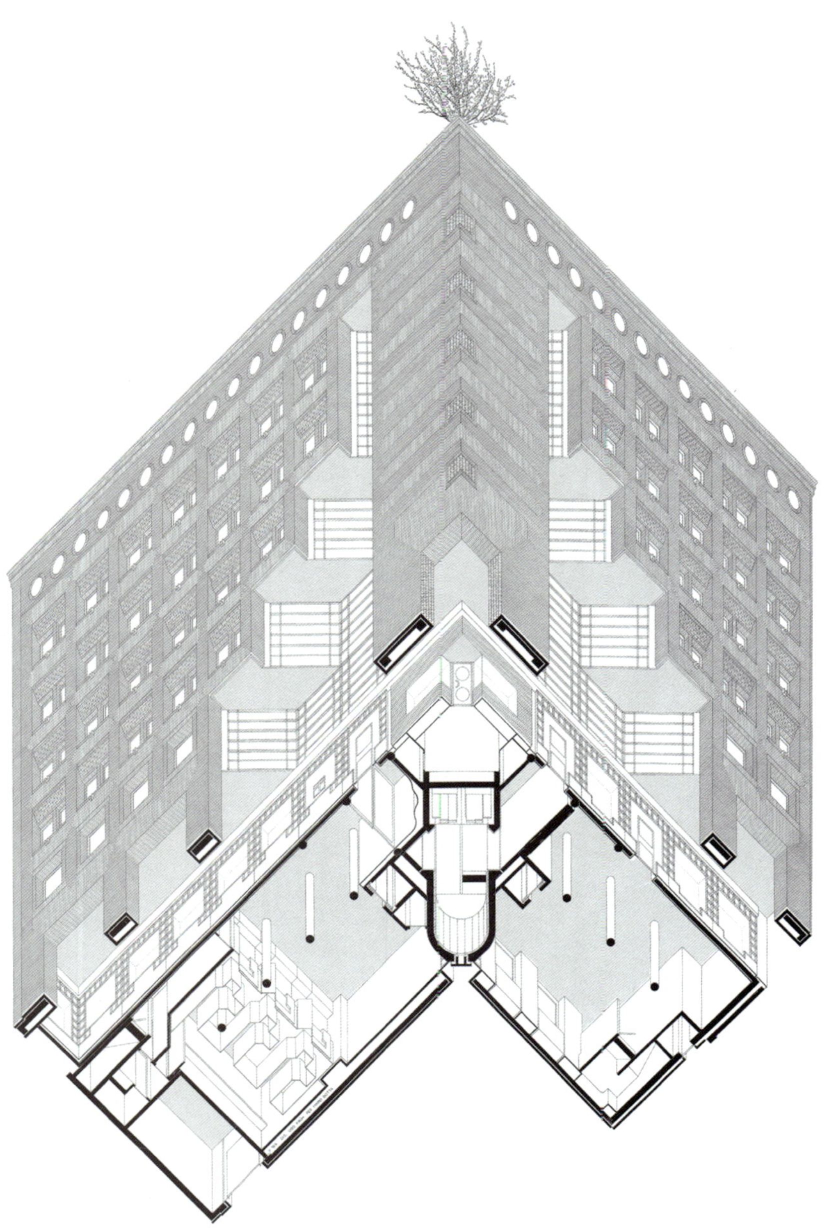

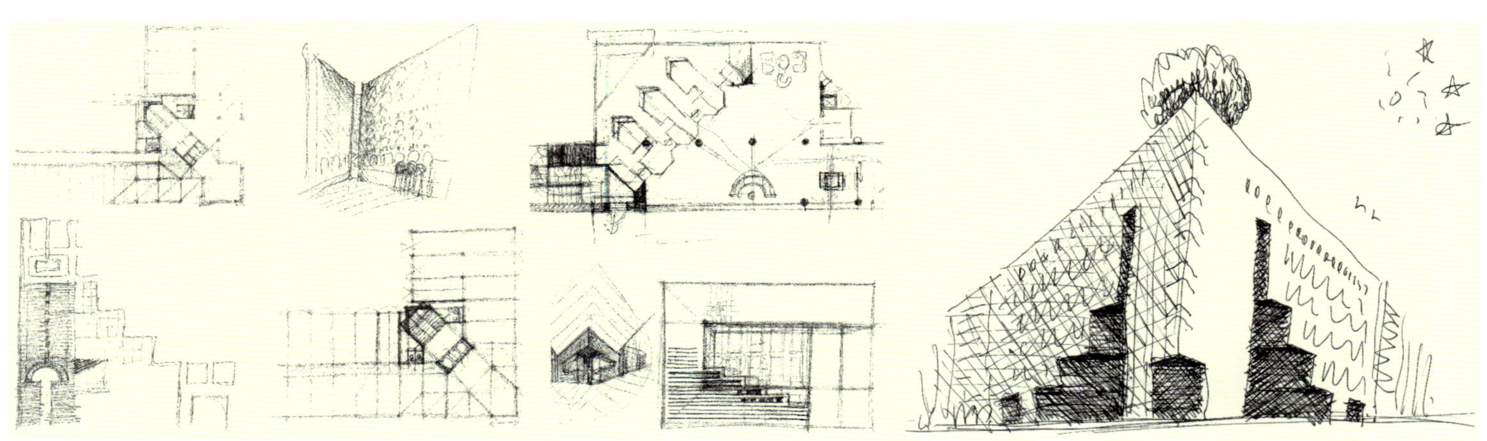

Via Pretorio
9
Bata

格塔多银行旧址

瑞士，卢加诺

FORMERLY BANCA DEL GOTTARDO

LUGANO, SWITZERLAND

1982-1988

竞赛项目时间：1982年
建造时间：1984～1988年
委托方：卢加诺，格塔多银行
占地面积：8,800平方米
建筑面积：14,000平方米
建筑体积：114,000立方米

Competition project: 1982
Construction: 1984-1988
Client: Banca del Gottardo Lugano
Site area: 8,800 m^2
Useful surface: 14,000 m^2
Volume: 114,000 m^3

银行大厦建筑综合体建于连接卢加诺历史老城中心与20世纪城市新区的重要连接线上，由4个具有垂直交通循环系统的建筑体块构成。每个体块的尽端都面向大街，由此形成一座外部庭院，创造出虚实交替的空间节奏。一条绿荫带将城市道路与步行廊道分隔开，廊道通向不同功能区的独立入口：银行办公室、多功能大厅及餐厅。每个建筑体块均围绕一个三角形大厅展开平面，以走廊相连通，穿过大厅天窗倾洒而下的自然光线丰富了空间效果。办公空间依靠玻璃外墙采光，石材与水泥交错的结构形成建筑的外墙特征。

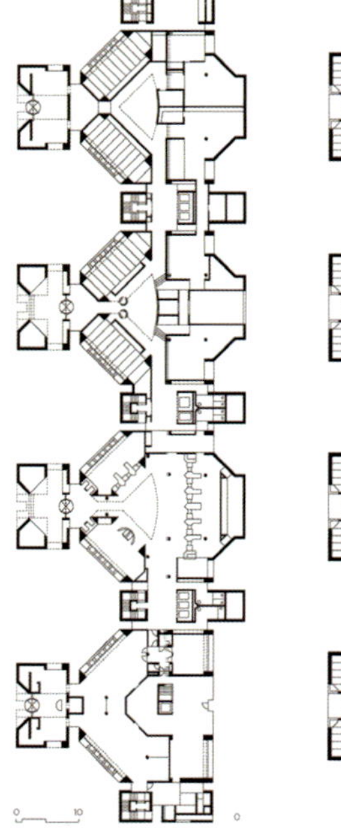

The complex, built along an important connecting axis between the historic centre of Lugano and the areas of 20th-century expansion, is articulated in four building blocks marked by the areas of vertical circulation. The end of all the blocks faces onto the avenue so to give shape to the exterior courts, which punctuate the alternation of solids and voids. A tree-lined strip separates the street from the partially porticoed pedestrian path, leading to independent entrances for the various activities: bank offices, multi-use hall, restaurant. Each of the four buildings is developed around a triangular hall onto which give the distribution pathways, enriched by natural light from the overhead skylight. The offices receive light from the exterior glass walls, characterized on the façade by the large brise-soleil screens in stone and cement.

© ENRICO CANO

© PINO MUSI

© ENRICO CANO

© ENRICO CANO

Banca
Gottar
Ingresso
principale
Lunedi - Vene
8.30 - 12.30
13.30 - 16.30
24 ore su 24

瑞银集团

瑞士，巴塞尔

UBS BANK

BASEL, SWITZERLAND

1986-1995

竞赛项目时间：1986年
建造时间：1989～1995年
合作方：巴塞尔，布克哈特建筑事务所
委托方：苏黎世瑞银集团
占地面积：3,847平方米
建筑面积：8,700平方米
建筑体积：92,700立方米

Competition project: 1986
Construction: 1989-1995
Partner: Burkhardt+Partner, Basilea
Client: UBS Zurich
Site area: 3,847 m^2
Useful surface: 8,700 m^2
Volume: 92,700 m^3

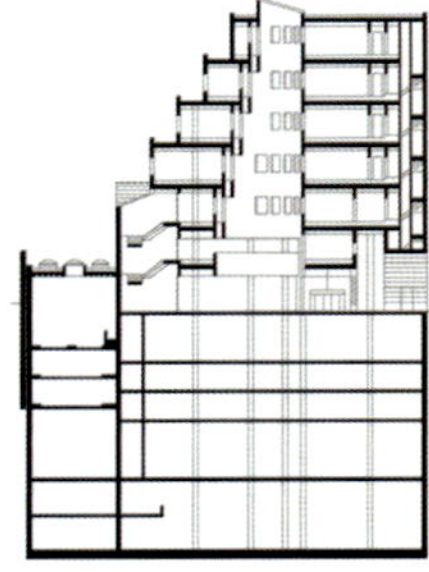

这座7层建筑坐落在两条重要道路轴线的交汇处：建筑街区接连分布的埃申格拉本大街，以及散布着独立住宅楼的圣雅戈布斯特拉大街。建筑主立面向外凸起，表面采用色彩交替的水平横条石材，与一栋用作餐厅的小别墅相连。在街道拐角处，建筑的圆柱体块切割成背面的阶梯形态，垂直狭缝和表面石材的处理加强了效果。大型中央圆柱体以及位于外侧边缘阶梯状的空腔共同构成巨大的弧形主立面。室内空间逐渐缩小直至顶部，自然光从中央天井进入，照亮每层楼的方形开孔。

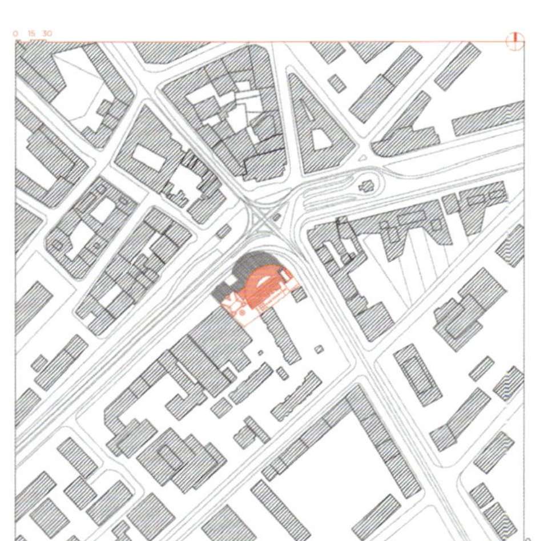

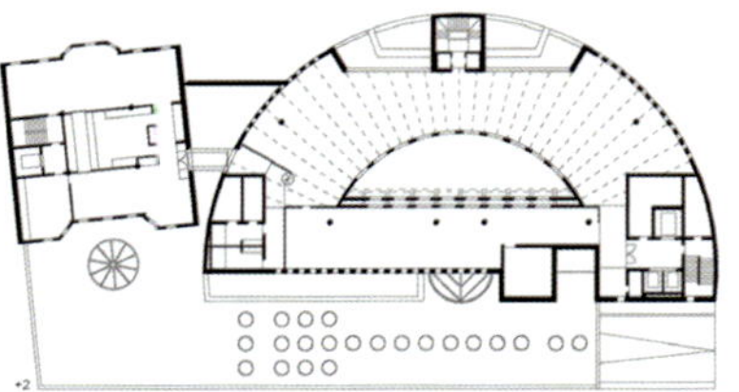

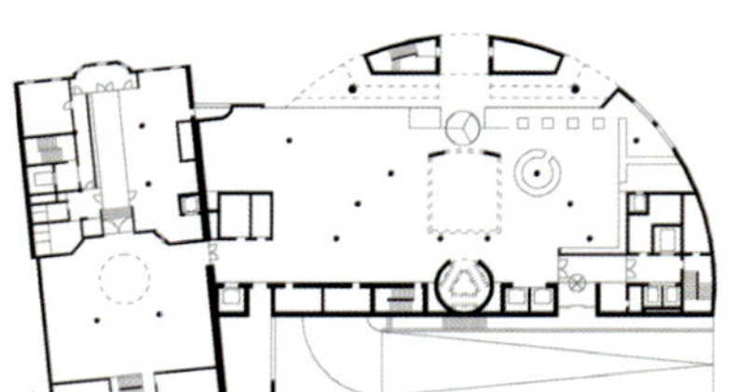

The seven-storeyed building lies at confluence of two important road axis: Aeschengraben street, with the continuity of the building blocks, and St. Jakobsstrasse, with the discontinuity of separate houses. The front is composed of a convex surface clad in stone with horizontal strips that alternate in color. It is linked to the small villa housing the restaurant. At the corner of the streets, the cylinder is cut to create a rear stepped surface, accentuated by vertical slits as well as by the treatment of the stone cladding. The large curved front is marked by the massive central column and by the wide cavity made of edges and stepped elements. The interior space tapers at the top and the skylight illuminates the sequence of square openings placed on each floor overlooking the pit.

© PINO MUSI

© PINO MUSI

© PINO MUSI

© PINO MUSI

© PINO MUSI

© PINO MUSI

© ENRICO CANO

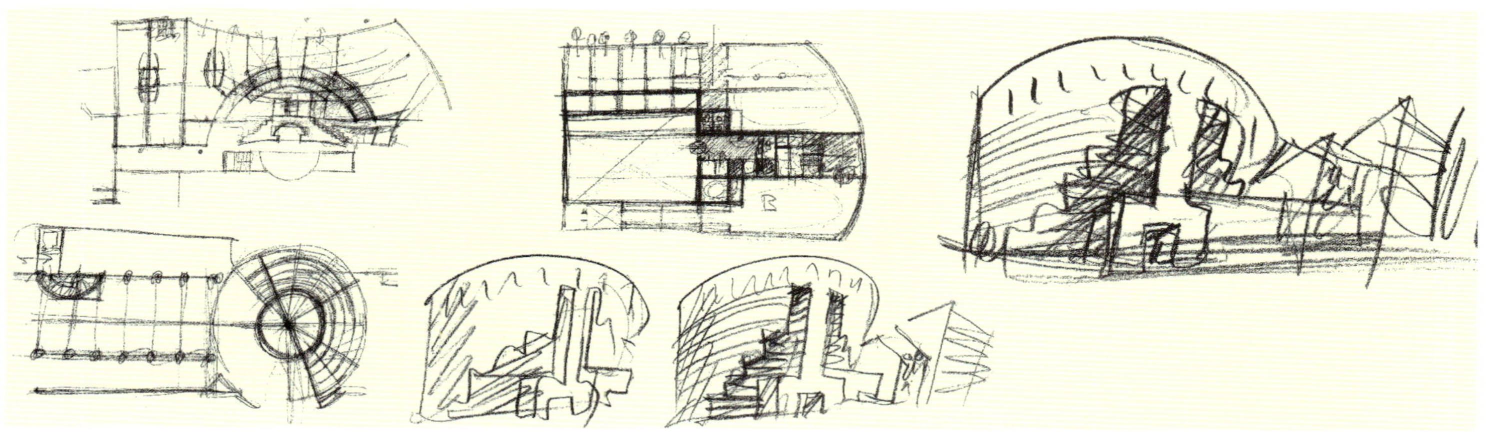

五大洲中心
瑞士，卢加诺

CENTRE CINQUE CONTINENTI
LUGANO, SWITZERLAND

1986-1992

项目时间：1986年
建造时间：1989～1992年
合作建筑师：卢加诺，吉安弗兰克·阿加齐
委托方：罗尔夫·法斯本德
占地面积：2,865平方米
建筑面积：4,300平方米
建筑体积：13,000立方米

Project: 1986
Construction: 1989-1992
Partner: arch. Gianfranco Agazzi, Lugano
Client: Rolf J. Fassbind
Site area: 2,865 m^2
Useful surface: 4,300 m^2
Volume: 13,000 m^3

以砖为表面材料的圆柱形建筑坐落于卢加诺-帕拉迪索的一处居民区中，拥有被玻璃和金属结构覆盖的巨大方形广场，面向湖面开放。广场背面有一个弧形圆柱建筑体，以玻璃砖为饰面材料，设置有通向阳台的楼梯井。这座建筑地上6层，地下2层。一层的广场空间设置了多个商店的入口，不同形状和大小的入口将一层以上的行政空间（设在2~4层）与楼上的公寓区分开来。

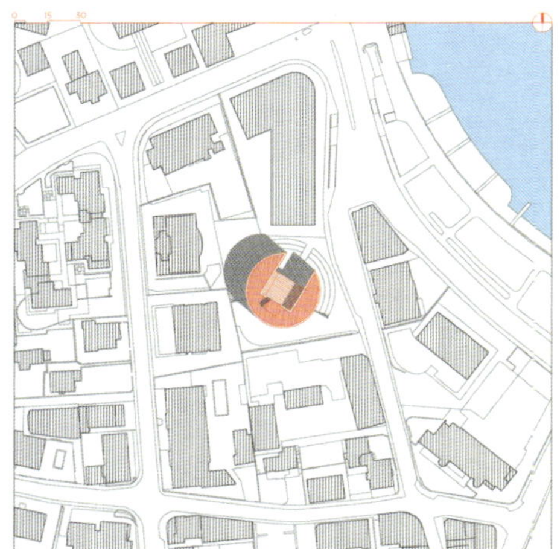

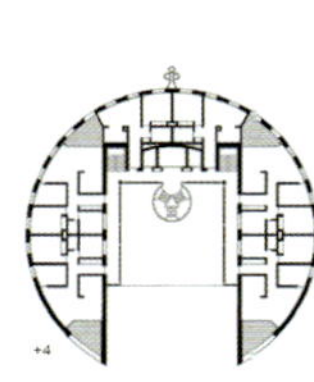

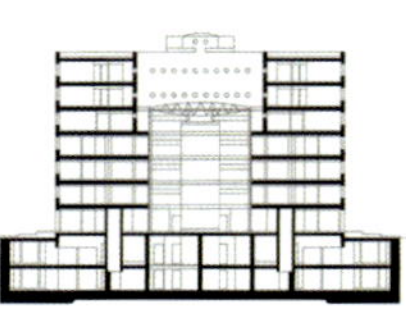

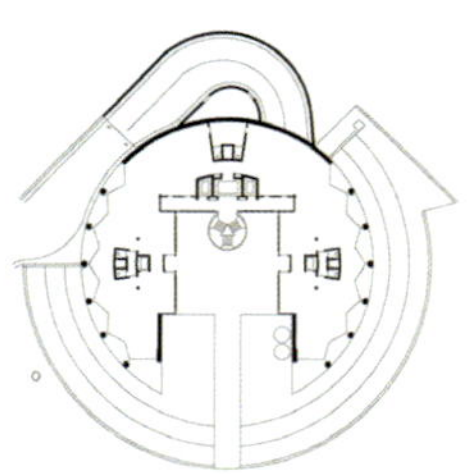

The cylindrical building, clad in brick, is set in a residential area of Lugano-Paradiso. It opens towards the lake thanks to the presence of a large square-shaped plaza covered by a glass and metal structure. At the back of the plaza is another cylindrical body made of glass housing the stairwells to the balconies. The building is composed of two floors underground and six floors above ground. On the ground floor the plaza provides access to the different stores. The openings, of different shapes and sizes, distinguish the administrative spaces (set in F2-F4) from the apartments on the upper levels.

© PINO MUSI

© PINO MUSI

© PINO MUSI

© PINO MUSI

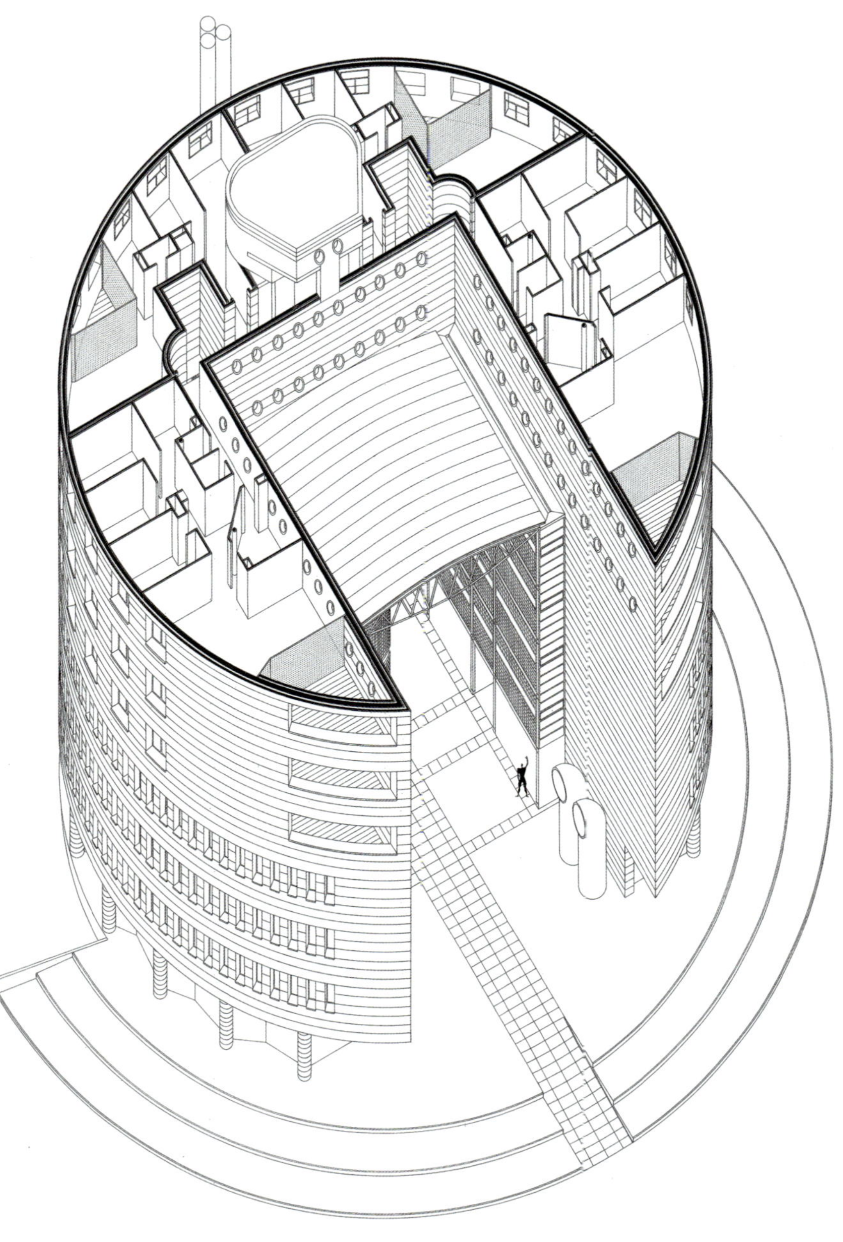

“卡伊马托”大楼

瑞士，卢加诺

BUILDING “CAIMATO”

LUGANO, SWITZERLAND

1986-1993

项目时间：1986年
建造时间：1989～1993年
委托方：卢加诺，费迪南公司
占地面积：4,633平方米
建筑面积：12,150平方米
建筑体积：51,000立方米

Project: 1986
Construction: 1989-1993
Client: Fidinam Lugano
Site area: 4,633 m^2
Useful area:12,150 m^2
Volume: 51,000 m^3

这座办公建筑坐落在卢加诺市卡萨拉泰河岸边的林荫道上，建筑综合体平面呈“U”形。“U”形末端的侧墙互成对称的45°角并围合出一个内部庭院，朝向河流和城市。北侧连接处的开口是一个巨大的、设置在中轴线上的中空区域。一个低矮的圆柱体块标志出地下停车场的入口，通过一架轻质金属桥连接到建筑的东侧翼楼上。东西两侧为办公区，顶层后退并形成俯瞰庭院的“阳台”。两侧翼楼底部设有柱廊，面朝公寓的东翼楼结构紧凑而封闭，面向河流的西翼楼则为进入内部庭院提供了一条人行通道。

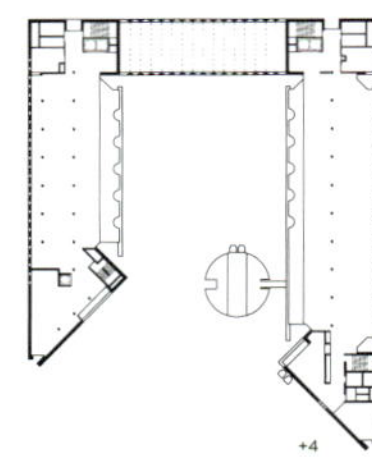

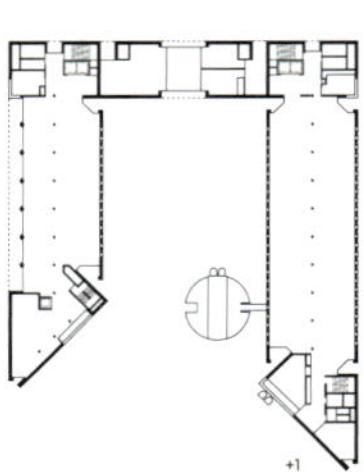

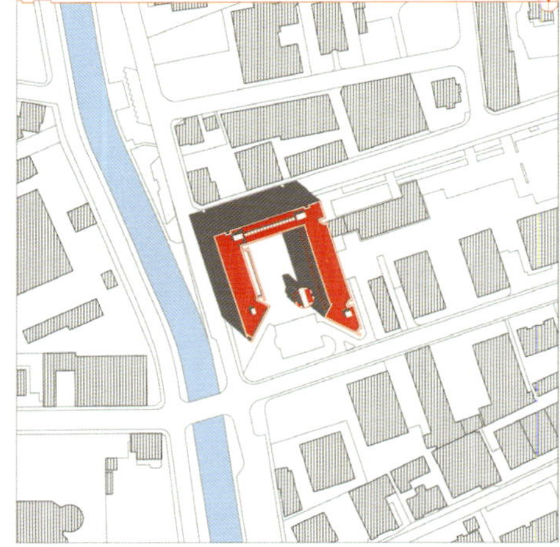

The office building is located along the tree-lined bank of the River Cassarate in Lugano. The complex takes the form of a U-shaped block. The symmetrical side walls, set at 45° to one another, create an inner courtyard and their triangular ends open it up to the city and the lake. The north-facing connecting block opens up through a grand void placed on the axis of symmetry of the whole complex. A low cylindrical volume marks the access to the underground parking lot and is connected to the east wing via a lightweight metal bridge. The east and west façades house the offices and the last floor is set back and gives onto the courtyard by means of a “balcony”. At the base of the side wings there are columned passages, while the east wing is compact and closed towards the apartment blocks, the west one, towards the river, provides a further pedestrian crossing to the interior courtyard.

© ENRICO CANO

© ENRICO CANO

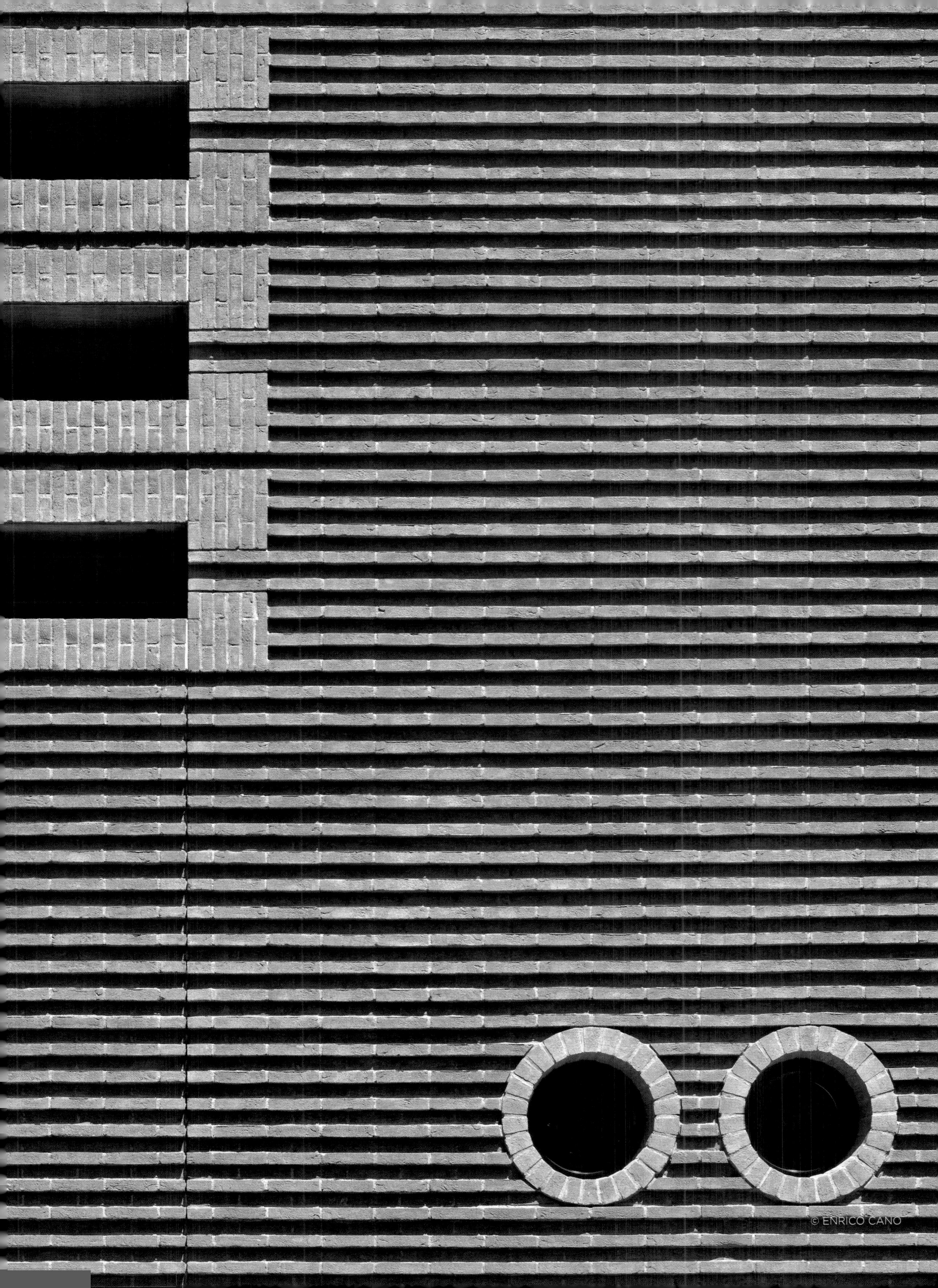

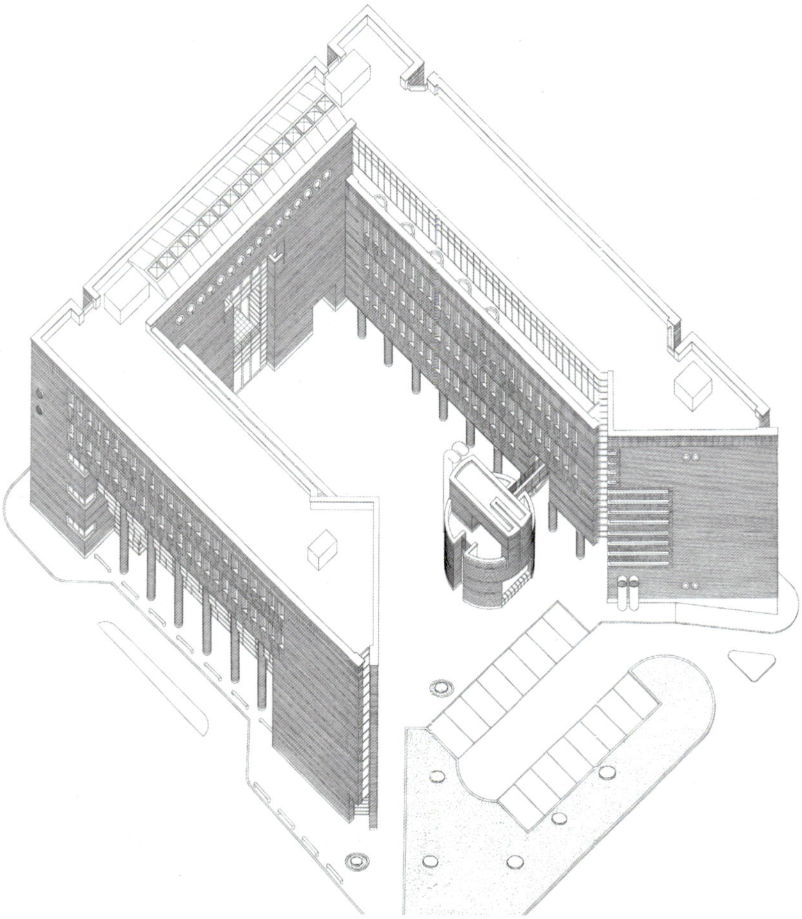

© ENRICO CANO

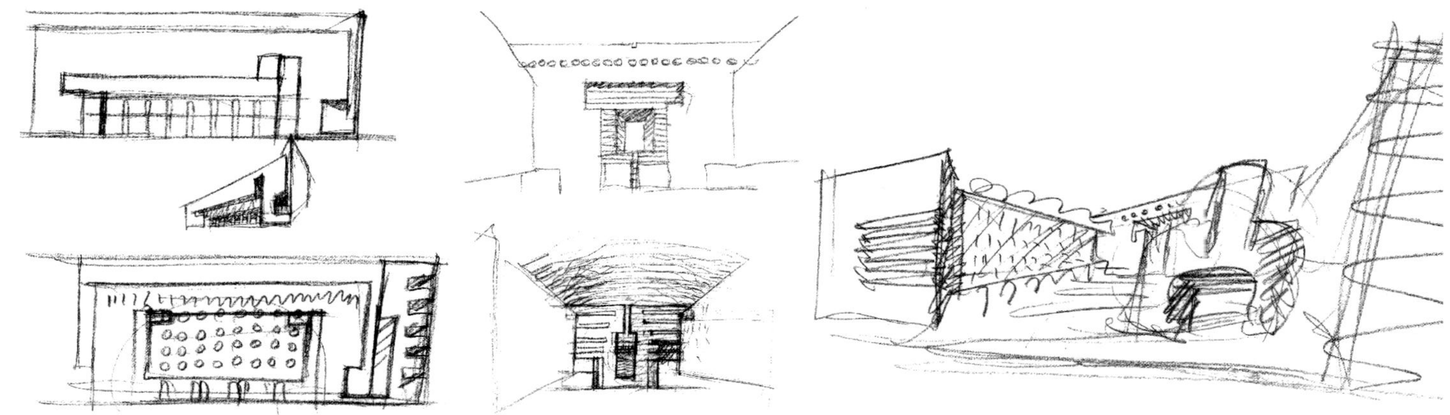

布鲁塞尔-朗贝银行

瑞士，日内瓦

BANQUE BRUXELLES LAMBERT

GENEVA, SWITZERLAND

1987-1996

项目时间：1987（竞赛项目）/1993年
建造时间：1993~1996年
合作建筑师：乌尔斯·屈米
委托方：日内瓦，布鲁塞尔，朗贝银行
占地面积：7,084平方米
建筑面积：656平方米
建筑体积：20,000立方米

Project: 1987 competition project/1993
Construction: 1993-1996
Partner: arch. Urs Tschumi
Client: BBL Geneva
Site area: 7,084 m²
Useful surface: 656 m²
Volume: 20,000 m³

银行大楼位于一处面朝先主教公园的四边形地块北端。建筑由天然石材覆面，地上7层，地下3层。由于建筑体宽度有限，不同功能区域分布在东西两侧。第六层和第七层的垂直切口分别为圆形洞口和拱形天窗。底层的两根柱子决定了出入口的位置，延伸向上打破了两侧立面的延续性。建筑的北立面沿冯特奈大街而展开，以中心一条深缝而彼此相连的两座塔楼为特点。这种空间组织手法创造出直通建筑顶部的中空空间。在连续而光滑的墙体之外，每一层通过有角度的中空循环路线建立联系。

The bank occupies the north end of a quadrangular plot which fronts onto the park of the Pré l'Évêque. It is clad in natural stone and is made up of seven above-ground floors and three underground floors. The small width led to the arrangement of the different functions in the east and west façades. On the sixth and seventh floor the close line of small vertical incisions changes, respectively, into circular openings and the skylights of the vaulted roof. The continuity of the side façades is interrupted by the incisions that start from the pair of columns framing the entrances. The north front along Avenue de Frontenex is characterized by two twin towers linked to each other by a deep central slit. The organizational principle led to the creation of a central void stretching up to the top of the building. The circulation paths branching off from the void at every level establish a series of relations with right-angled intersecting views out, beyond the continuous glazed walls.

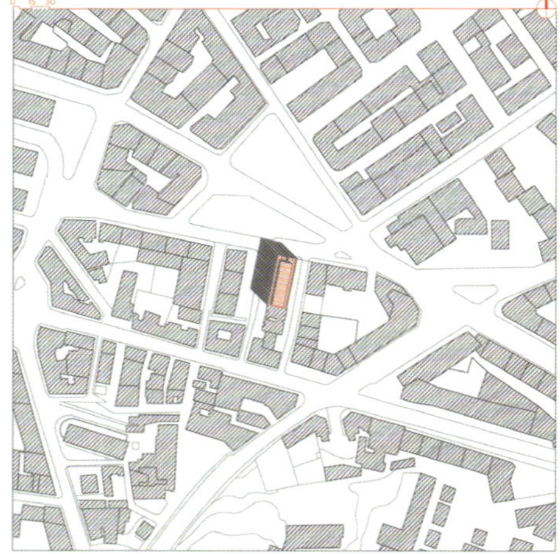

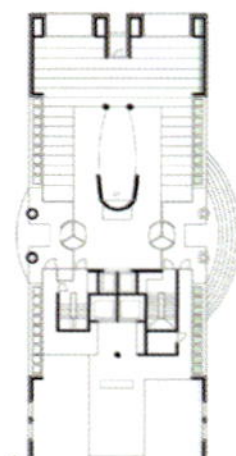

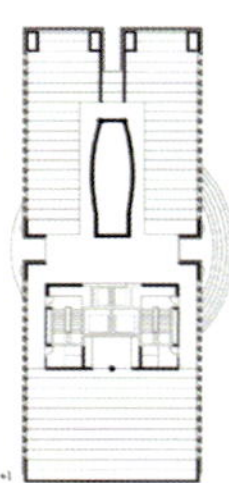

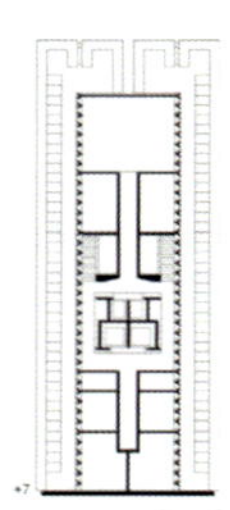

© ENRICO CANO

© ENRICO CANO

© ENRICO CANO

© ENRICO CANO

© ENRICO CANO

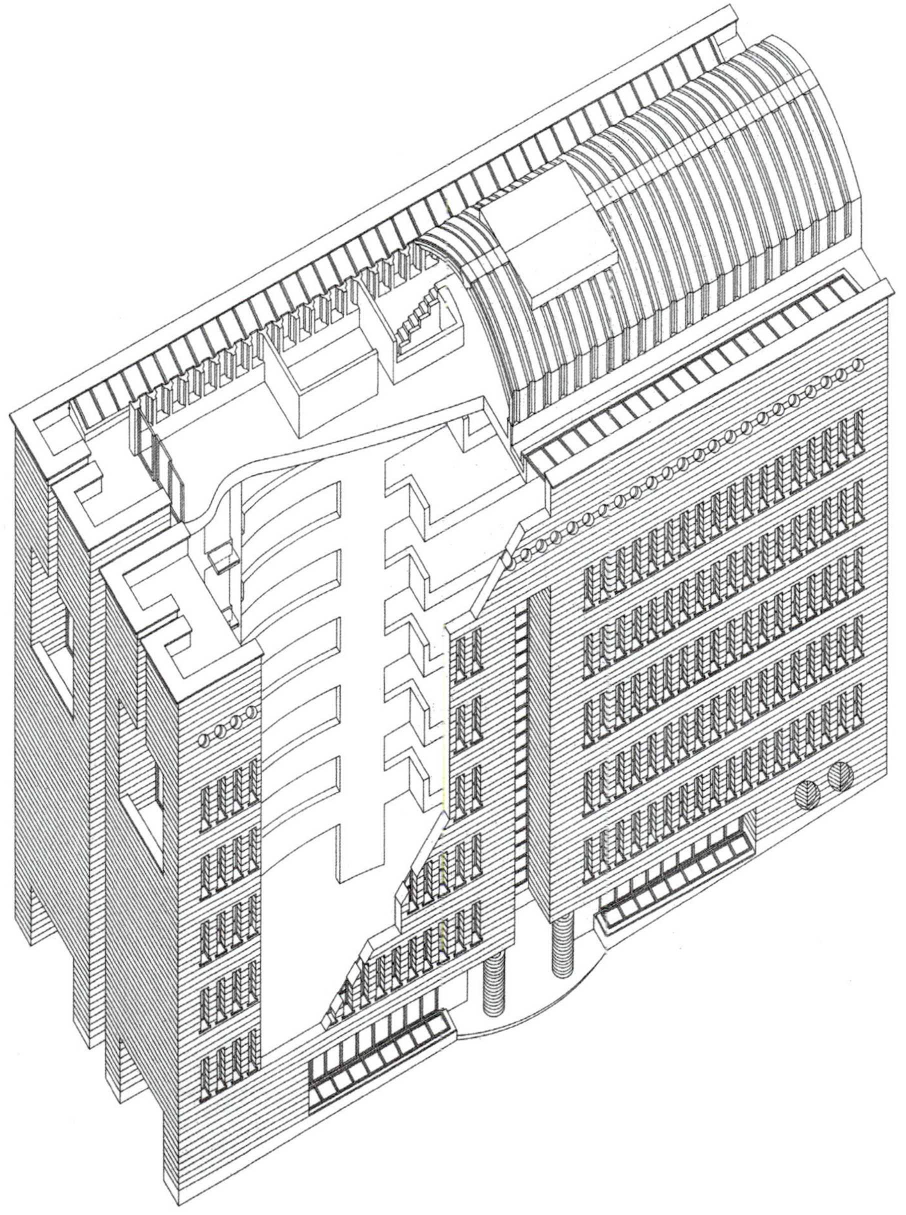

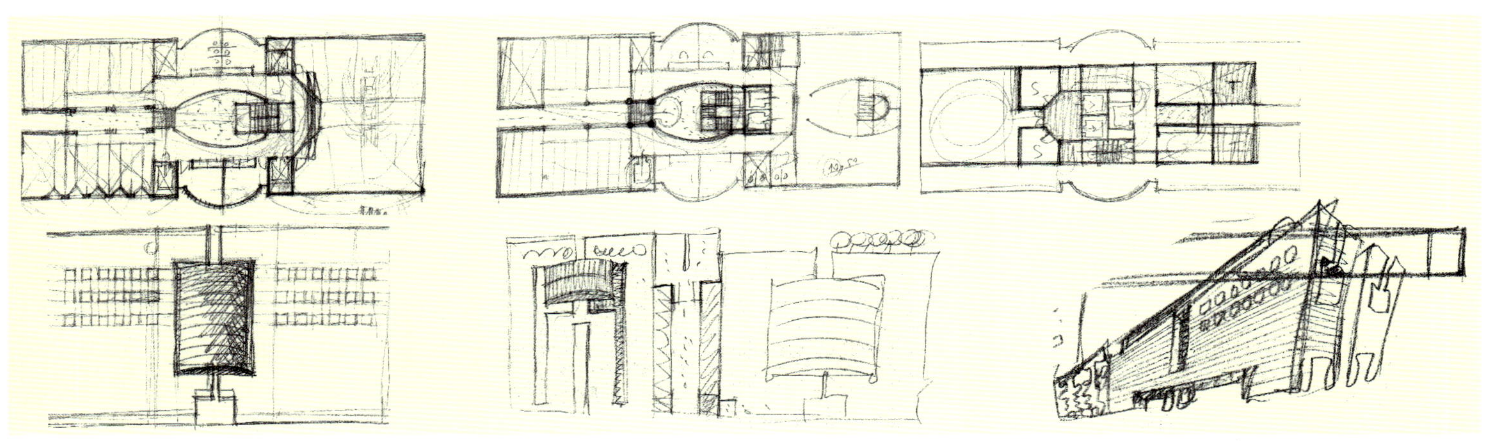

restaurant

瑞士电信大楼

瑞士，贝林佐纳

SWISSCOM BUILDING

BELLINZONA, SWITZERLAND

1988-1998

项目时间：1988年
建造时间：1992～1998年
委托方：伯尔尼瑞士电信公司
占地面积：20,770平方米
建筑面积：27,800平方米
建筑体积：125,100立方米

Project: 1988
Construction: 1992-1998
Client: Swisscom Bern
Site area: 20,770m²
Useful surface: 27,800 m²
Volume: 125,100 m³

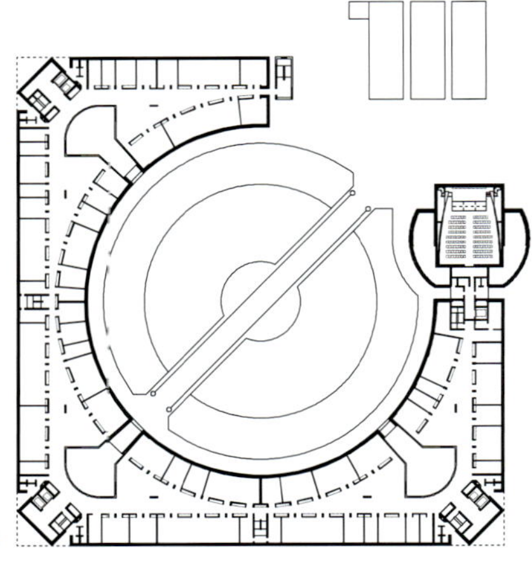

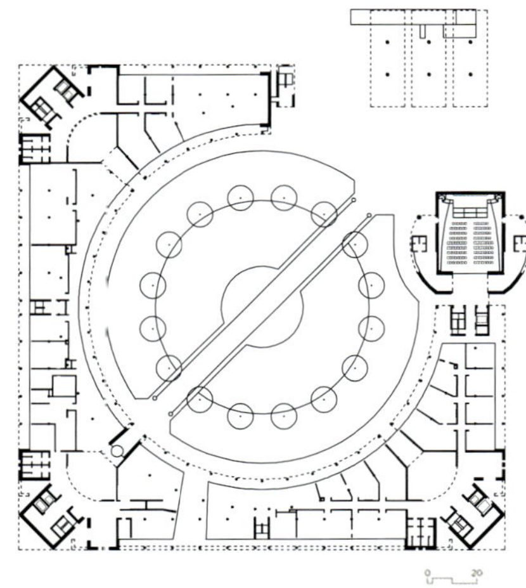

这座体量庞大的红砖饰面建筑旨在修复贝林佐纳市“哥伦白亚”区破损的城市肌理。建筑形成一个巨大的四边形，每条边长均为100米。它被成排的树木围绕，入口朝向城堡区以及历史老城中心的方向，从入口处可以看到弧形内墙划分出的内部庭院。在入口的尽端，一侧是贯通各楼层的楼梯，另一侧是对外开放的礼堂以及餐厅。办公空间沿外立面和面向庭院的立面分布，建筑的内曲线交汇于内部楼梯附近，这一设计使该空间更为宽敞。外立面比内侧庭院立面高出一层，通向内侧庭院立面入口的桥梁。

The large scale building clad in red bricks intends to restore order inside the ragged urban fabric of “La Colombaia” district, in Bellinzona. The building forms a big quadrilateral 100 meters long on each side. It is surrounded by rows of trees and open in the direction of the castles and the historic centre of the city so to reveal a circular courtyard defined by the curving line of the building's inner wall. At the end of the breach there are, on the one side, a stair that joins all the floors and, on the other one, the façade with the services open to the public, such as the assembly hall and the cafeteria. The office spaces are distributed on the exterior façade as well as on the façade overlooking the courtyard and converge in the vicinity of the internal stairs, where the building's inner curve leaves a broader volume. The exterior façade is a story higher than the one facing the courtyard, this latter cut on the diagonal from the access bridge.

© PINO MUSI

© PINO MUSI

© PINO MUSI

© PINO MUSI

© ENRICO CANO

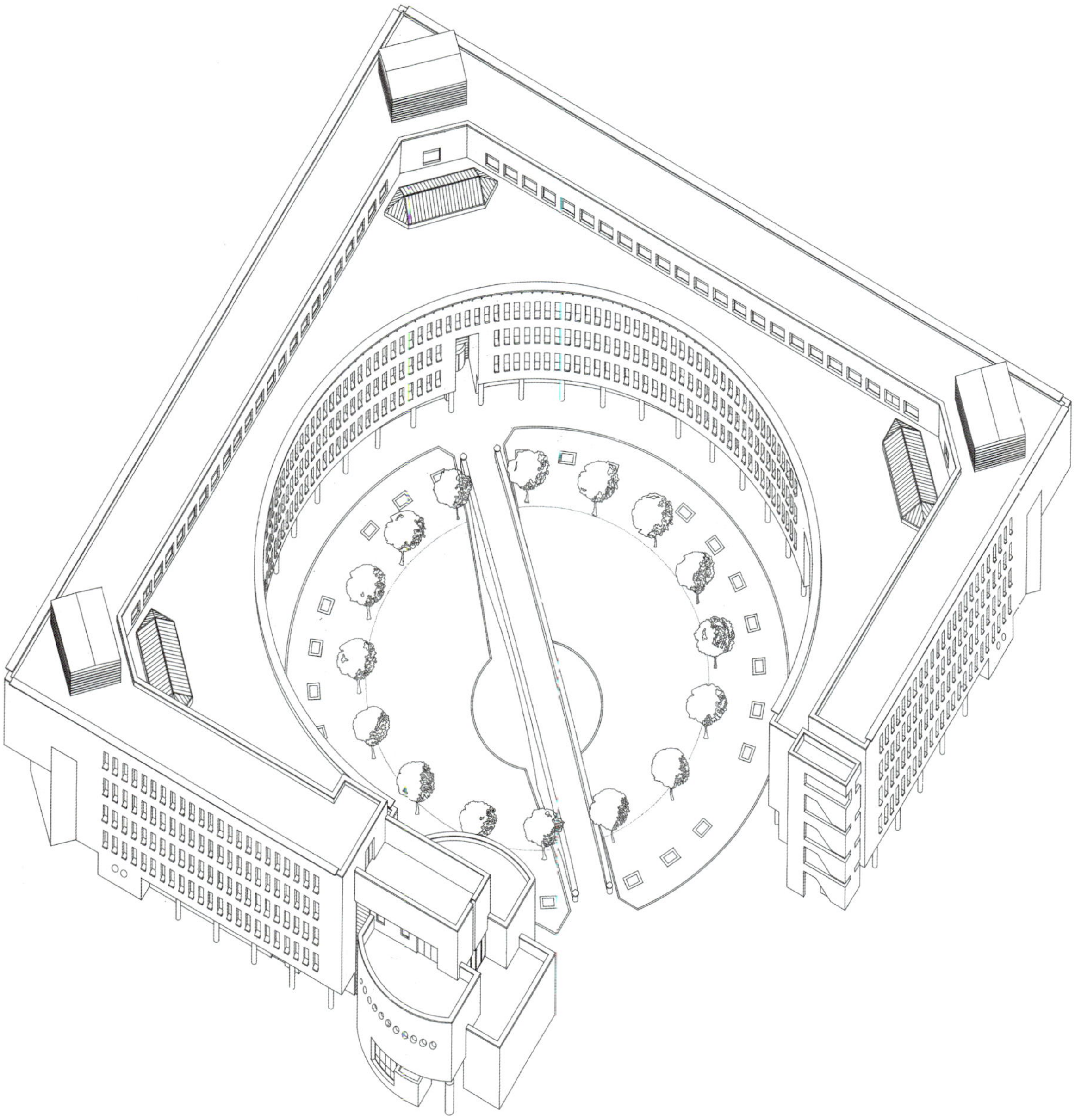

塔塔咨询服务公司办公室

印度，新德里

TCS OFFICES

NEW DELHI, INDIA

1996-2002

项目时间：1996～1997年
建造时间：1999～2002年
委托方：塔塔咨询服务公司
合作建筑师：斯内哈·沙阿
占地面积：15,340平方米
建筑面积：11,300平方米
建筑体积：50,000立方米

Project: 1996-1997
Construction: 1999-2002
Client: Tata Consultancy Services
Partner: arch. Snehal Shah
Site area: 15,340 m^2
Useful surface: 11,300 m^2
Volume: 50,000 m^3

建筑综合体是软件制造商TCS（塔塔咨询服务公司）设在诺伊达的行政办公室总部，距新德里大约30公里。除了为保护该地区免受季风期暴雨洪灾而建的直线形障碍物外，这片土地几乎完全平坦，此项目旨在诠释这片土地的潜力。在新市区的规划中，这一屏障成为开发区与乡村之间的边界。一栋4层高的建筑垂直于边界而建，如同一个长达150米的平行六面体横在这个区域之上。在面朝入口道路的北侧，一个圆柱形建筑体清晰地矗立在线性建筑体一侧，顶部设置的凸起通风塔可满足通风和采光需求，一层则完全通透开放。阿格拉石材外墙与玻璃幕墙相隔超过2米，可避免当地恶劣天气对室内空间的影响。

The complex for the administrative offices of the software producer TCS (Tata Consultancy Services) is headquartered in Noida, at about thirty kilometers from New Delhi. The work seeks to interpret the potential of a territory that is completely flat, with the exception of a straight barricade to protect the area from flooding caused by the heavy rains of the monsoon season. In the plans for the new urban district, this barrier becomes the border between the constructed area and the countryside. The four-story building is set perpendicular to this border, like a parallelepiped expressed as a 150-meter-long beam suspended over the terrain. On the northern side, towards the access road, a cylindrical volume stands clear off the linear building. At the top of this volume small openings in the projecting ventilation tower provide overhead day lighting. The ground floor is completely clear. The outside walls in red Agra stone are set more than two meters away from the glass walls, which are thus protected from the harsh weather typical of the region.

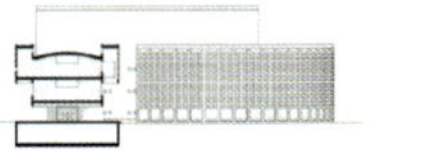

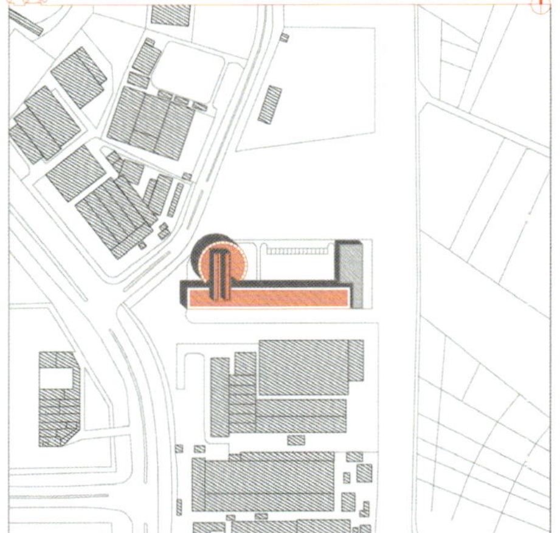

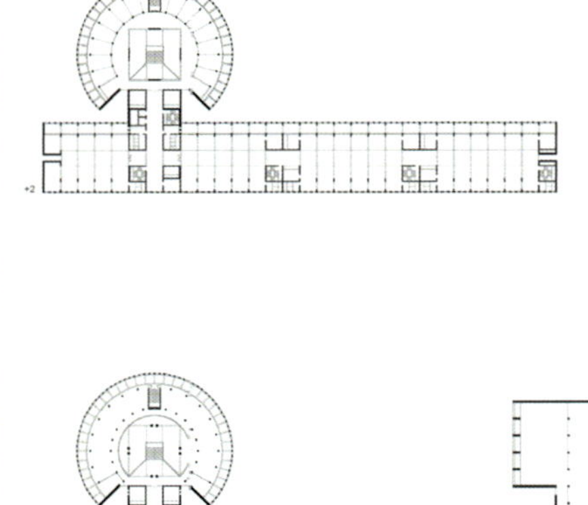

© ENRICO CANO

© ENRICO CANO

© ENRICO CANO

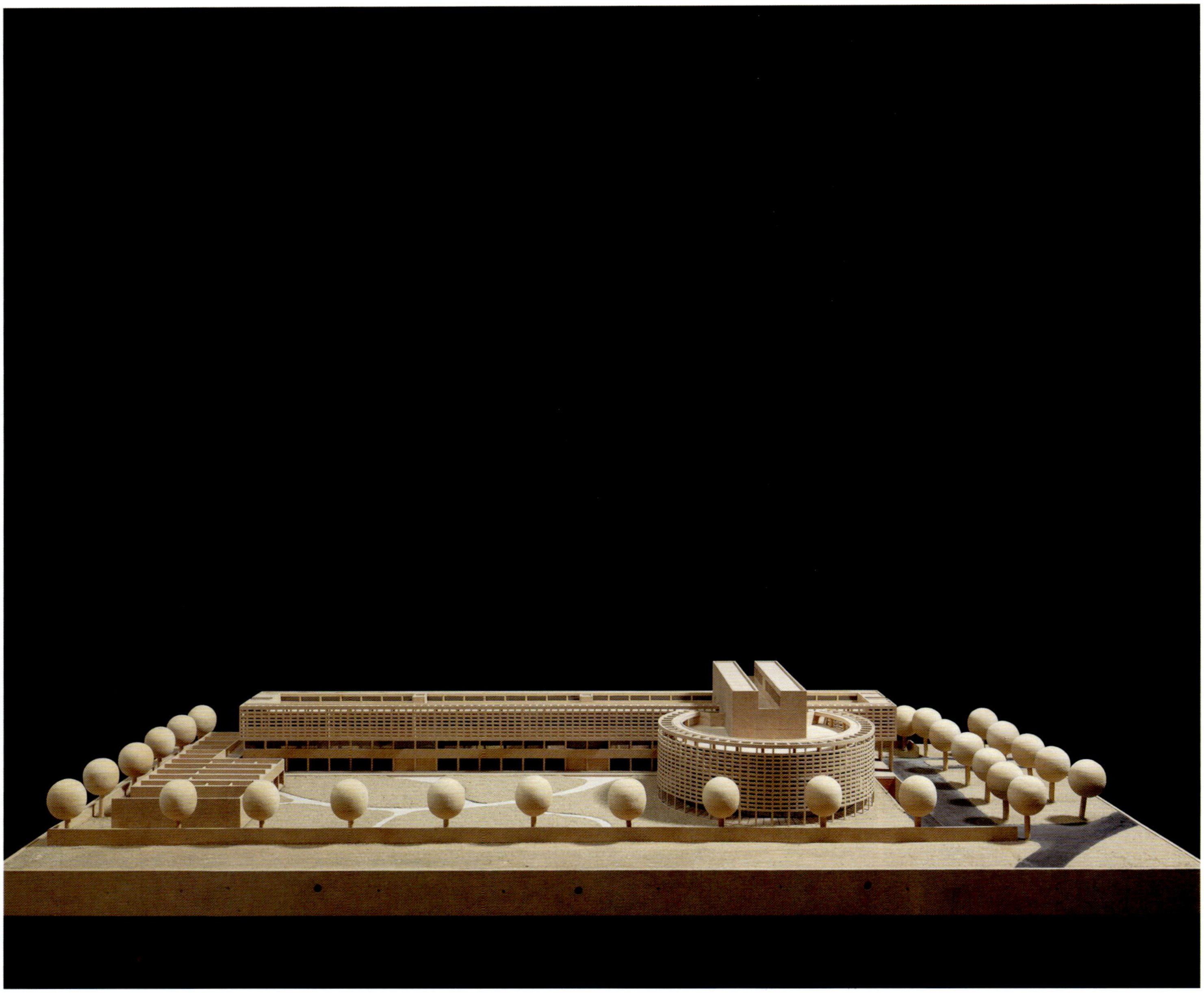

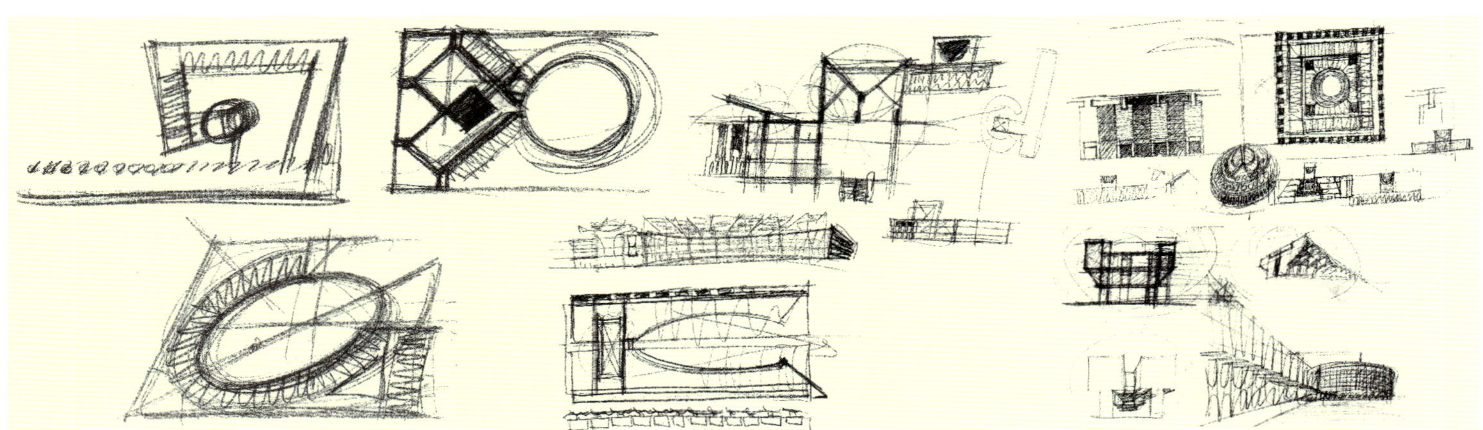

© ENRICO CANO

教保塔楼

韩国，首尔

KYOBO TOWER

SEOUL, SOUTH KOREA

1989-2003

项目时间：1989年
建造时间：1999～2003年
合作建筑师：首尔昌乔建筑事务所
委托方：教保人寿保险公司
占地面积：6,770平方米
建筑面积：92,717平方米
建筑体积：350,000立方米

Project: 1989
Construction: 1999-2003
Partner: Chang-Jo Architects, Inc, Seoul
Client: Kyobo Life Insurance Co. Ltd.
Site area: 6,770 m²
Net floor area: 92,717 m²
Volume: 350,000 m³

教保保险公司大楼位于首尔瑞草区的重要交汇处，此处联系着城市的各个部分。该建筑由一个3层高的裙房和2个双子塔组成。位于建筑核心位置的中央大厅被设计成室内广场，环绕它的3层裙房空间得以享受从玻璃天窗射入的自然光。两座塔楼表面覆砖，其上划分的垂直切口强调了建筑的垂直走向。水平带状的百叶窗平衡了这一上升的立面趋势。一条狭窄的玻璃走廊连接着两座塔楼，成为建筑的透明心脏。它创造出不同寻常的景观，犹如一个可以从不同楼层欣赏的大花园。建筑顶部设有一个透镜状的屋顶，保护着顶层的宽敞露台。

The building of the Kyobo insurance company in the Seocho district is located at an important intersection that links the various parts of the city. It is composed of a lower section of three stories and of two twin towers. The main lobby, in the core of the building, is designed as an interior piazza so that the three floors arranged around it can benefit from the natural light coming from the glass ceiling. Each tower is clad in brick and is subdivided through vertical cuts to underline the vertical development of the construction. The up thrust is counterbalanced by the horizontal bands of the brise-soleil. The towers are connected by a narrow glassed-in passageway that becomes the transparent heart of the building. It affords an unusual vista, a kind of large constructed garden that can be enjoyed from the different levels. The arrangement of the upper portion of the building features a lens-shaped roof that protects the wide terraces of the rooftop floors.

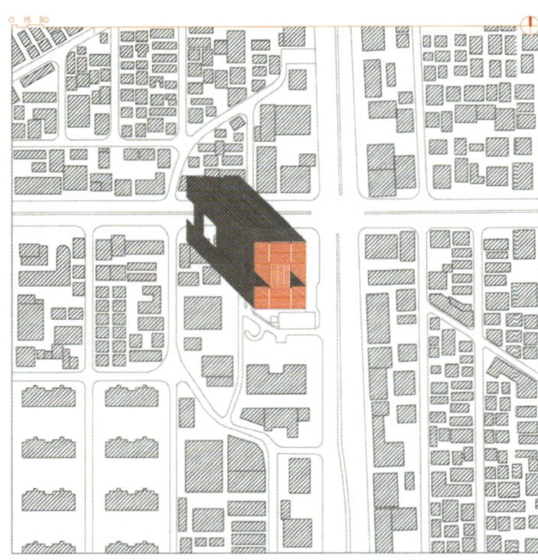

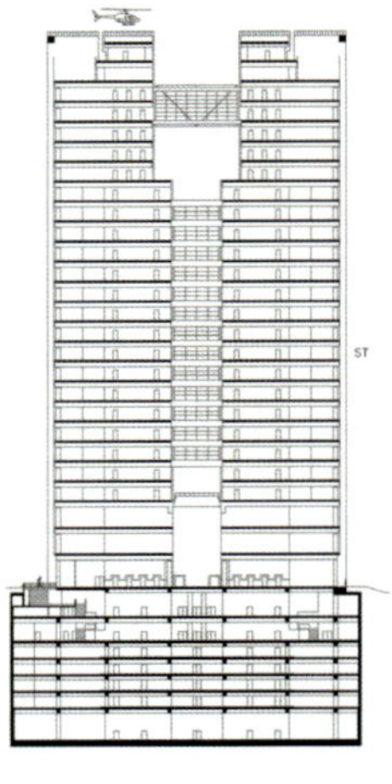

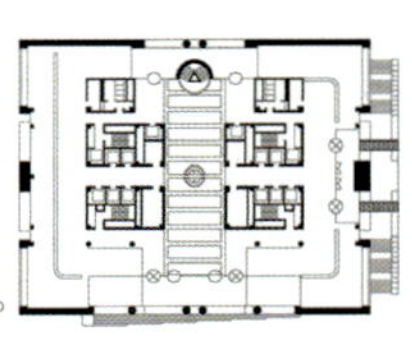

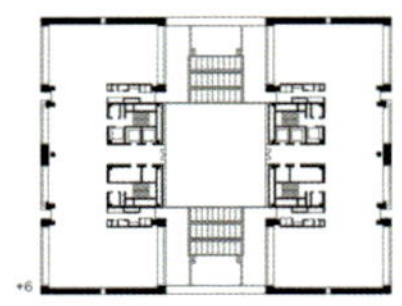

© YOUNG CHEA PARK

© YOUNG CHEA PARK

© YOUNG CHEA PARK

© PINO MUSI

希腊国家银行

希腊，雅典

NATIONAL BANK OF GREECE

ATHENS, GREECE

1998-2001

竞赛项目时间：1998年
建造时间：1999～2001年
委托方：希腊国家银行
合作建筑师：摩尔佛·帕帕尼克拉乌，伊莲娜·帕帕尼克拉乌和玛利亚·宝兰尼
占地面积：1,452平方米
建筑面积：5,000平方米
建筑体积：28,900 立方米

Competition project: 1998
Construction: 1999-2001
Client: National Bank of Greece
Partner: arch. Morfo Papanikolaou, Irena Sakellaridou and Maria Pollani
Site area: 1,452 m²
Useful surface: 5,000 m²
Volume: 28,900 m³

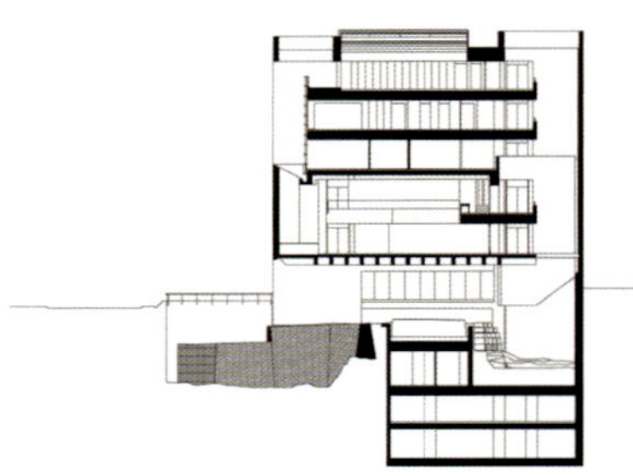

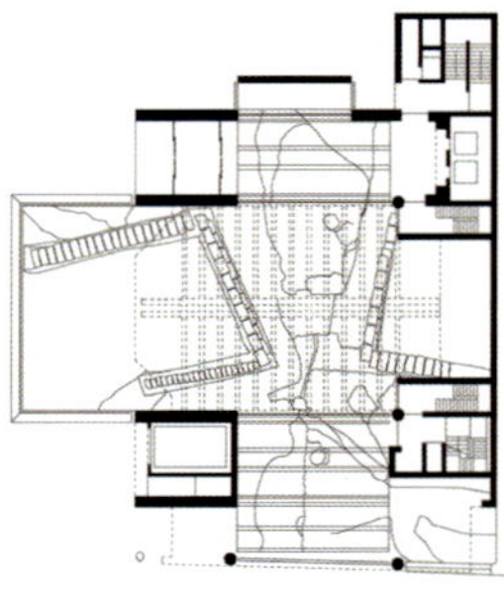

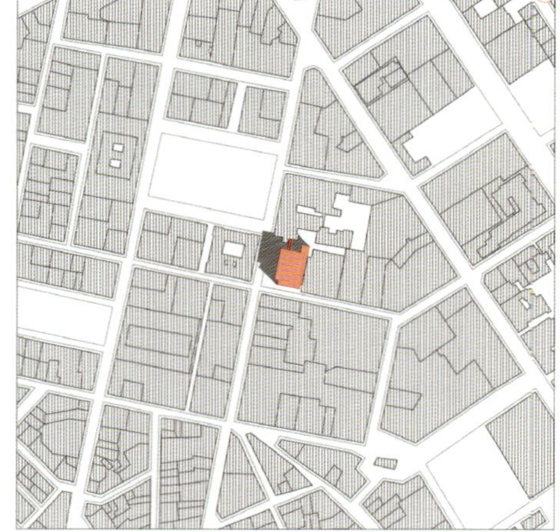

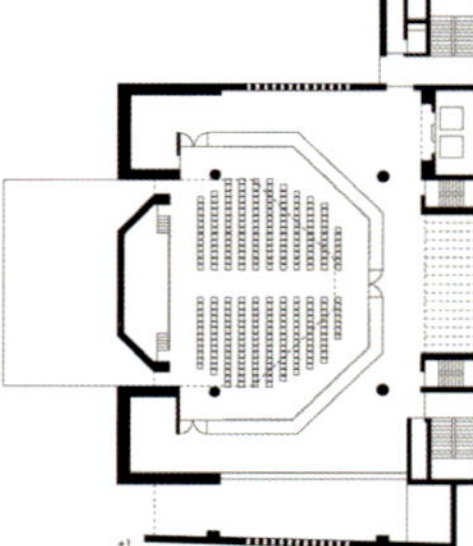

该建筑占据了雅典历史老城中心艾洛街区南端的一个转角，可以欣赏到雅典卫城的景色。尽管立面在一层有个开口，但建筑体量整体上呈现出严谨朴实的形式，通过正立面与周围的新古典建筑进行对话。建筑空旷的内部空间使得自然光可以通过一系列天窗在室内流动，并从顶层一直倾泻到底部的发掘坑。人们可以从用金属和玻璃制成的桥上观察考古的路径，有效地使底层空间变成了一座室外博物馆。建筑的新地基保留了阿卡尼基路的古老分层。除底层之外，新建筑还包括地上部分5层和地下部分4层。建筑外立面以及内部公共区域以自然的沙色石材覆盖，地板选用黑色抛光花岗石，建筑内部墙体和人造天花板则选用木材建造而成。

The building completes the corner of an important block in the historic centre of Athens at the southern end of Eolou Street, with a view of the Acropolis. The volume presents a very austere primary form, despite the cavity on the ground floor, with a single façade that dialogues with the neoclassical buildings nearby. A void inside the building lets in natural light via a series of skylights and lends movement to the circulation areas from the top floor down to the excavations. The archeological road can be viewed from metal-and-glass bridges, effectively making the ground floor an outdoor museum. The new foundations of the building have preserved the ancient stratification of Acharniki Street. In addition to the ground floor, the new building has five stories above the ground and four basement levels. Natural sand-colored stone was used to clad the exterior and the public areas inside the building. Polished black granite was chosen for the floors, while the interior walls and the false ceilings are made of wood.

© PINO MUSI

© PINO MUSI

© PINO MUSI

© PINO MUSI

© PINO MUSI

新港大楼

荷兰，代芬特尔

DE NIEUWE POORT

DEVENTER, THE NETHERLANDS

1998-2009

项目时间：1998/2006年
建造时间：2006~2009年
委托方：克莱克项目开发公司
合作建筑师：代芬特尔 I' M 建筑事务所
占地面积：16,365平方米
建筑面积：5600平方米

Project: 1998/2006
Construction: 2006-2009
Client: Le Clercq Planontwikkeling b.v.
Partner: I'M Architects, Deventer
Site Area: 16,365 m²
Useful surface: 5,600 m²

这个项目的构想是建造22座联排房屋和2栋行政大楼。项目选址于贝腾拉赫大桥的两端，属于战略性区域。这个毗邻运河的综合体项目正是城市的入口。

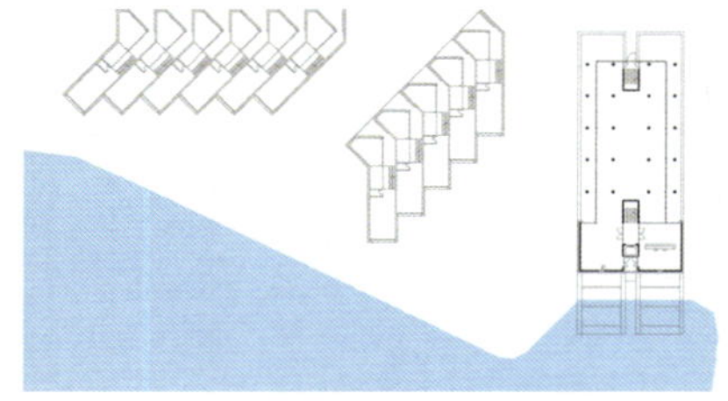

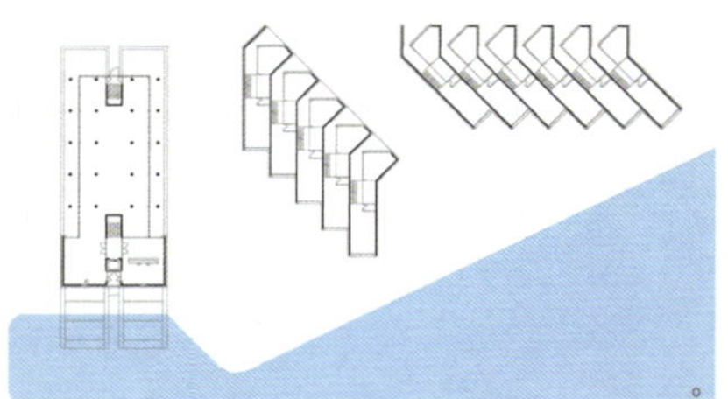

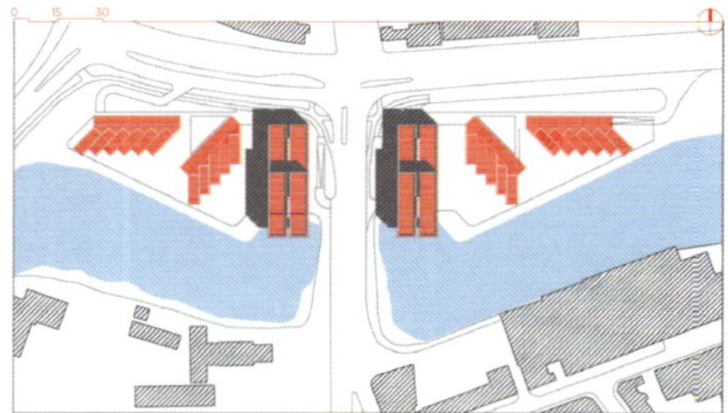

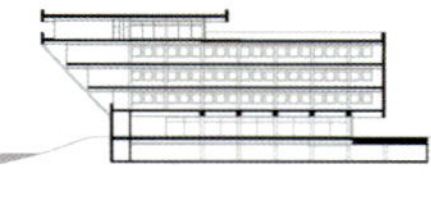

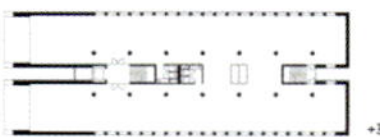

The project envisages the construction of twenty two row houses and two blocks of administrative buildings. They are in a strategic area as the site lies on both sides of the Buitengracht bridge. The new complex is alongside the canal bank and represents the entrance to the city.

© ENRICO CANO

© ENRICO CANO

© ENRICO CANO

© ENRICO CANO

© ENRICO CANO

德国浩亭公司总部办公室

德国，明登

HARTING SALES HEADQUARTERS

MINDEN, GERMANY

1999-2001

项目时间：1999年
建造时间：2000～2001年
委托方：洪狄马和洪玛嘉，浩亭埃斯珀尔坎普公司
合作方：明登规划公司
土木工程：多特蒙德，克莱门斯·佩尔
技术工程：弗伦斯堡，彼得森工程公司
占地面积：5,000平方米
建筑面积：2,800平方米
建筑体积：22,000立方米

Project: 1999
Construction: 2000-2001
Client: Margrit and Dietmar Harting, Harting Espelkamp Company
Partner: Planungsgruppe Minden
Civil engineering: Klemens Pelle, Dortmund
Technical engineering: Petersen Ingenieure, Flensburg
Site area: 5,000 m²
Useful surface: 2,800 m²
Volume: 22,000 m³

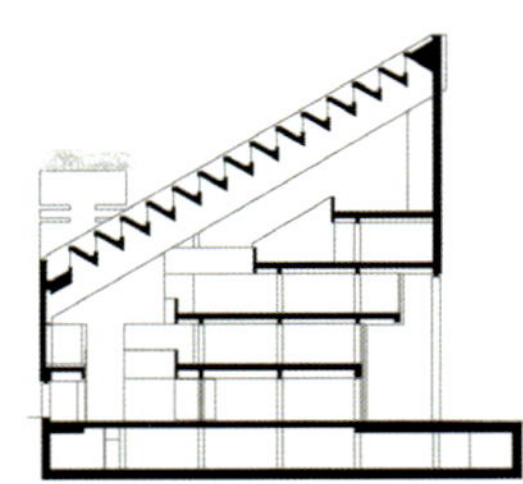

德国浩亭公司销售总部建立在旧普鲁士堡垒的一个战略之地，那里现在依然有大片绿地——西门斜坡。沿着通往明登镇历史中心的主干道，新建筑力求将历史背景与当代语境连接。建筑开口面向南侧的主要道路，与巨大倾斜屋顶的方向相同。屋顶（约1000平方米）呈现出棚状的横截面，可以捕获和过滤自然光，增加下方工作区域的舒适度。面朝北侧的开阔窗户增强了南向光线的流动特质。

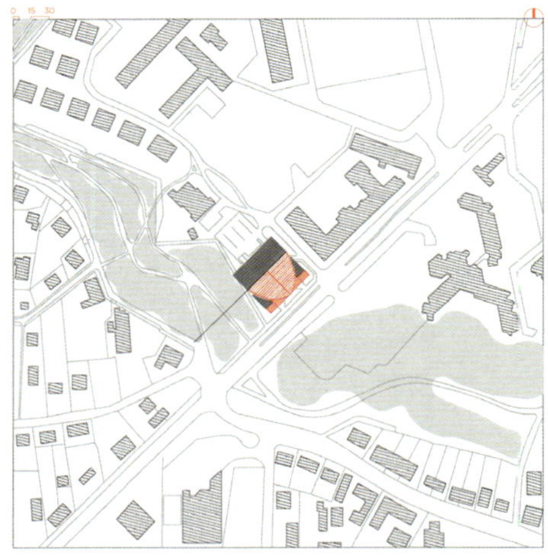

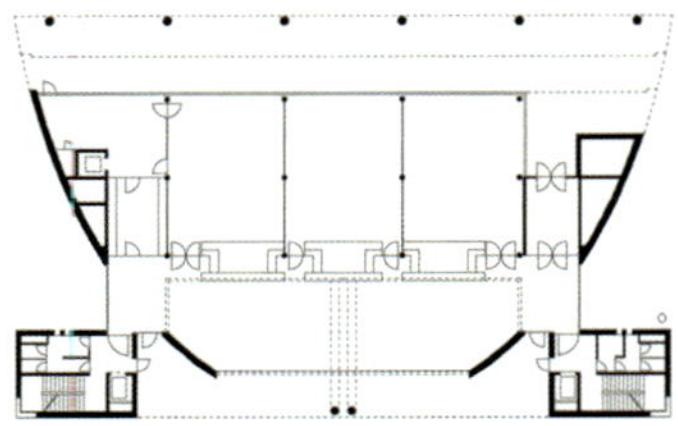

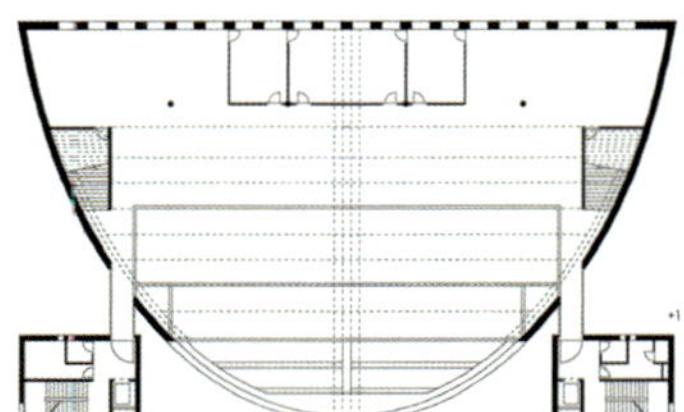

The building for the German sales headquarters of the Harting Company is set in a strategic spot on the site of an old Prussian bastion, which is still present with a green area – Simeons Glacis. Extending along the main thoroughfare leading into the historic centre of the town of Minden, the new building strives to link its contemporary content with the existing historic surroundings. It opens southward along the main road at the level of the enormous sloped roof. This surface - noteworthy in size (approximately 1000 m²) - presents a shed-shaped cross-section that captures and filters natural light to enhance the comfort of the work areas beneath it. The unique quality of the southerly light streaming in from above is augmented by the broad windows facing north.

© RAINER HOFMANN

© ENRICO CANO

© ENRICO CANO

© RAINER HOFMANN

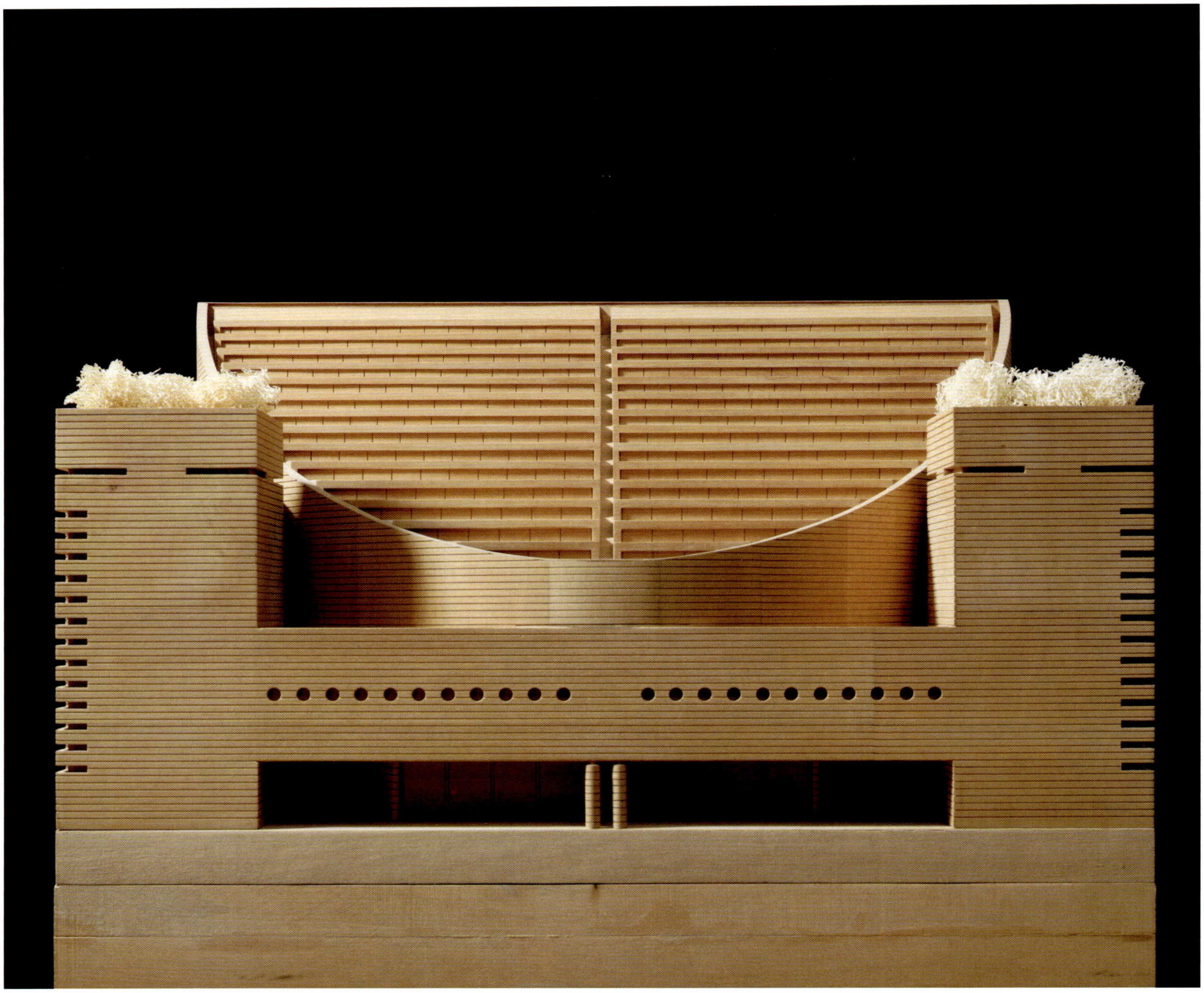

© ENRICO CANO

弗奥利波塔大楼

瑞士，门德里西奥

BUILDING FUORIPORTA

MENDRISIO, SWITZERLAND

2005-2011

项目时间：2005年
建造时间：2007～2011年
委托方：建筑师马里奥·博塔
占地面积：3,336平方米
建筑面积：3,300平方米
建筑体积：地上14,000立方米，地下6,500立方米

Project: 2005
Construction: 2007-2011
Client: Arch. Mario Botta
Site area: 3,336 m^2
Useful surface: 3,300 m^2
Volume: 14,000 m^3 above ground
6,500 m^3 underground

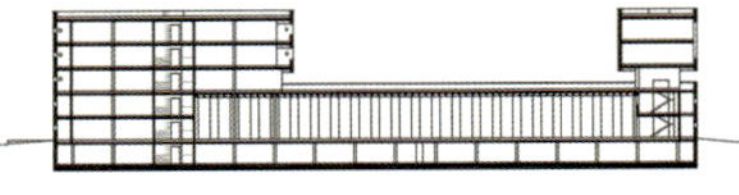

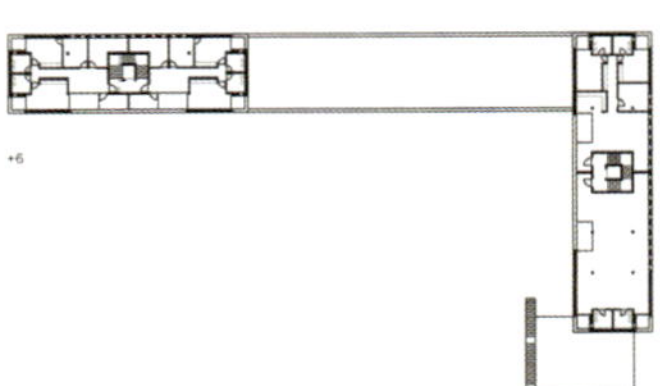

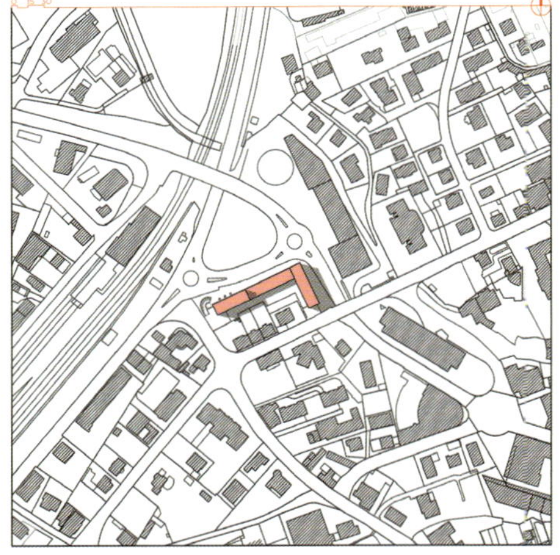

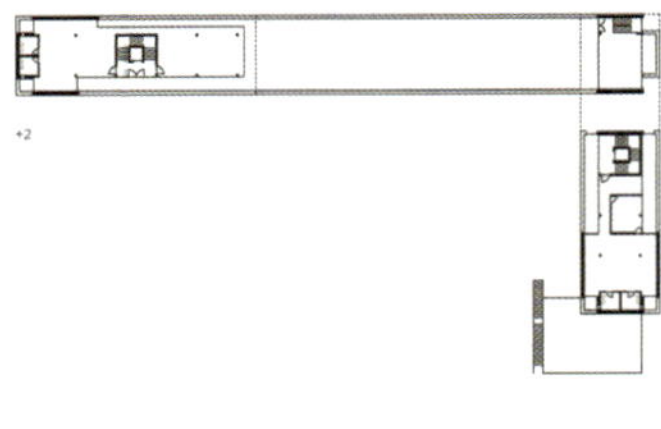

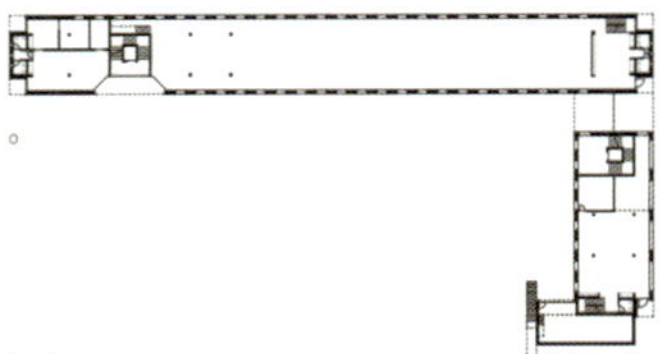

该项目可以诠释为代表了老城区山坡上实现20世纪城市化的成果。新建筑代表着圣马提诺平原及其南部村镇面貌与北部交通设施（公路、火车站和主干道）之间的界线（关口）。这座5层楼的建筑平面呈“L”形，长边面向山谷且平行于通往火车站的道路；短边则与通往历史中心的佐尔齐路对齐。马里奥·博塔建筑事务所位于建筑长边的一层，上层空间则用作办公室或公寓。工作区域为一个两层通高的空间，长约80米，宽约10米。一整排通高的开窗使得空间南北通透。室外穿孔的金属百叶可以控制斜射光线，以达到调节室内光线的目的。建筑外墙材质为约旦石灰石板。

The project can be interpreted as the completion of the 20th century urbanization that has spread on the hillside around the old town. The new building represents a limit (a gateway) between the village fabric to the south and the plain of San Martino with the traffic infrastructures (highway, railway station and main road) to the north. The five-storey building is in the shape of an L with the long side towards the valley, parallel to the road that leads to the railway station, and the short side aligned on via Zorzi, that leads to the historic centre. The new Arch. Mario Botta's architecture practice is on the ground floor in the long side of the building while the spaces on the upper levels are used as offices or apartments. The office is a double-height parallelepiped approx. 80 meters long and 10 meters wide. It opens towards south and north thanks to a row of full-height windows. The control of the light is from the outside by means of perforated metal shutters that let in a plain light. The exterior cladding is in slabs of Jordan travertine.

© ENRICO CANO

© ENRICO CANO

城市空间
URBAN FABRIC

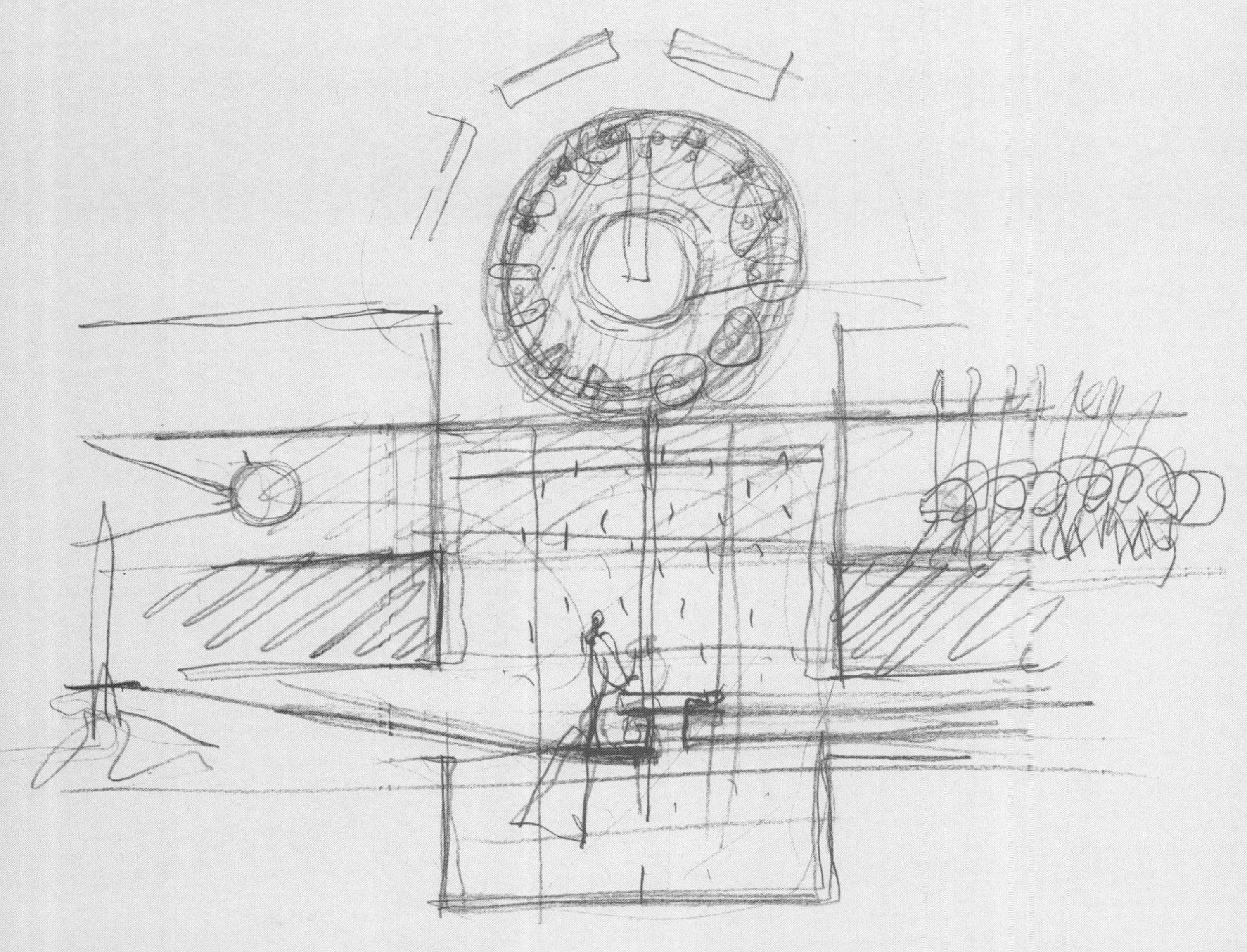

和平广场

意大利，帕尔玛，皮洛塔花园

PIAZZALE DELLA PACE

GIARDINO DELLA PILOTTA, PARMA, ITALY

1986/1996-2001

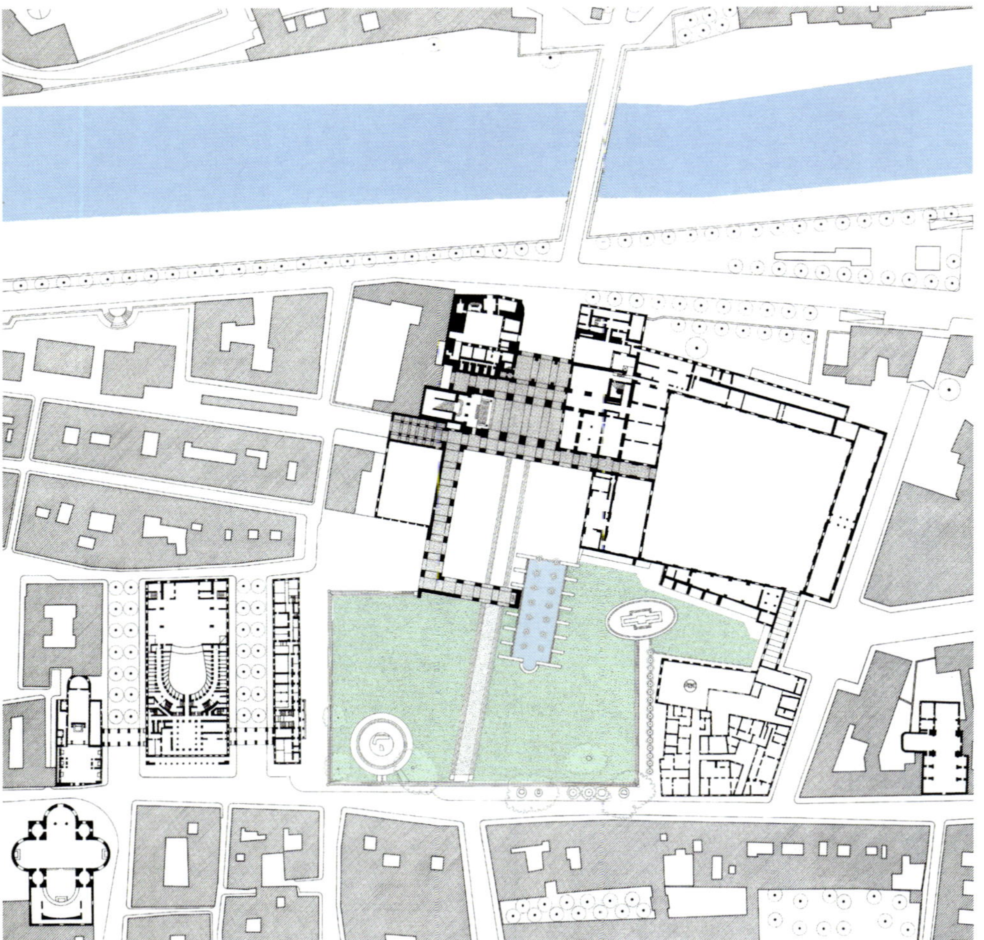

项目时间：1986/1996年
建造时间：1998～2001年
合作建筑师：乔治·奥尔西尼
委托方：帕尔马市

Projects: 1986/1996
Construction: 1998-2001
Partner: arch. Giorgio Orsini
Client: City of Parma

项目意识到皮洛塔历史结构的“未完成”状态是帕尔马城市肌理的一大特色。设计基本思路是将这片区域转换成“精心设计过”的绿色空间，通过不同元素唤起历史中的特定瞬间，共包括5个极具特色的部分：“围墙”由双层线性石块构成，界定了花园与其周边城市景观的区界；“水池”几乎完全再现了圣彼得殉难教堂的平面；“信徒纪念碑”置于略高于广场的初始位置；还有强调斜向布局的“威尔第纪念区”以及慢跑小路延伸至加里波第大街的“皮洛塔庭院”。

The project acknowledges the “unfinished” condition of the Pilotta’s historical structure as a feature of the urban fabric of Parma. The basic idea was the transformation of the area into a “designed” green space characterized by different elements evoking particular moments of its history. Five distinctive elements can be identified: the “enclosure”, realized by means of a double linear edge made of stone that defines the boundary between the Giardino and the adjoining urban landscape; the “pond” that virtually redraws the plan of the church San Pietro Martire; the “Monument to the Partisan”, which has been left in its original elevated position with respect to the level of the piazza; the oblique orientation of the “Verdi area” highlighted by the new layout and the “Pilotta courtyard” emphasized by the extension of the trotting tracks to the Via Garibaldi.

© PINO MUSI

© PINO MUSI

© PINO MUSI

© PINO MUSI

© PINO MUSI

赌场
意大利，意大利金皮庸

CASINO
CAMPIONE D'ITALIA, ITALY

1990-2006

项目时间：1990/1998年
建造时间：1998～2006年
合作建筑师：乔治·奥尔西尼
委托方：意大利金皮庸市
占地面积：15,000平方米
建筑面积：63,550平方米
建筑体积：237,830立方米

Project: 1990/1998
Construction: 1998-2006
Partner: arch. Giorgio Orsini
Client: City of Campione d'Italia
Site area: 15,000 m^2
Useful surface: 63,550 m^2
Volume: 237,830 m^3

该赌场及其配套服务设施所在的地区紧邻历史中心地带，位于小镇所在的山脚下。多样化的地理环境与城市肌理共存于此：一侧是历史老城，另一侧是21世纪发展起来的新城区。建筑综合体划分为3个部分：中央的9层建筑体和2个较低的边翼。边翼的楼梯径直通向湖泊，留出现有行人通道的同时形成一个广阔的中间地带。两个边翼通过悬桥与中央建筑体相连，设有行政办公室、技术用房和储藏室。建筑的主体部分则容纳了赌场，餐厅设在第七层，覆顶平台从建筑中部分离出来，构成了贯穿至建筑背后的造型以及位于第九层宽阔的接待大厅，使得建筑面向卢加诺湖的一侧形成图腾般的外观。

The area for the casino and its corollary services is positioned next to the historical centre, at the foot of the hill where the town rises. This area is a place where diverse geographical and architectural fabrics coexist: on the one side the old town and on the other the development realized in this century. The complex is divided into three different parts: the central nine-story volume and two lower side wings with stairs leading to the lake so to keep the existing pedestrian links and form a great void in the middle. The side wings, connected to the central volume by means of suspended bridges, house the administration offices, the technical rooms and the storages. The main body houses the games, a restaurant on the seventh floor, a covered terrace carved from the centre of the building providing a view which penetrates to the back of the construction and a wide reception hall on the ninth floor, which crowns this totem-like presence facing Lake Lugano.

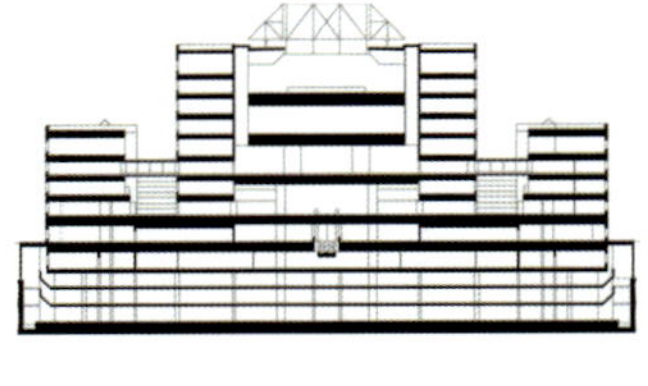

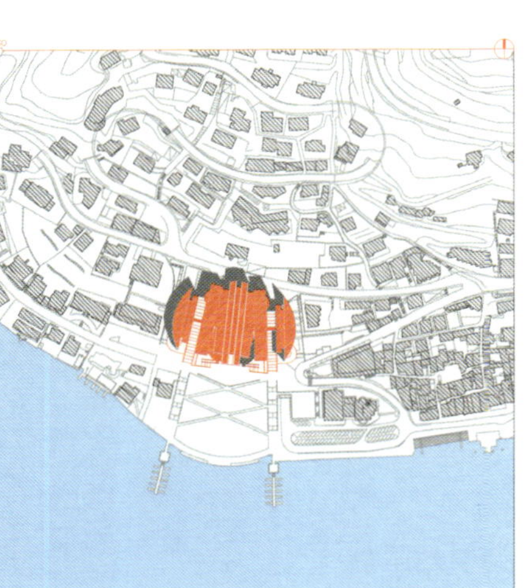

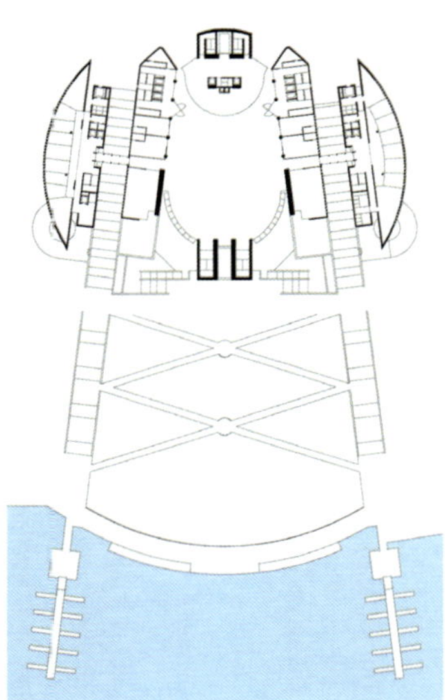

© PINO MUSI

© ENRICO CANO

© PINO MUSI

© PINO MUSI

© ENRICO CANO

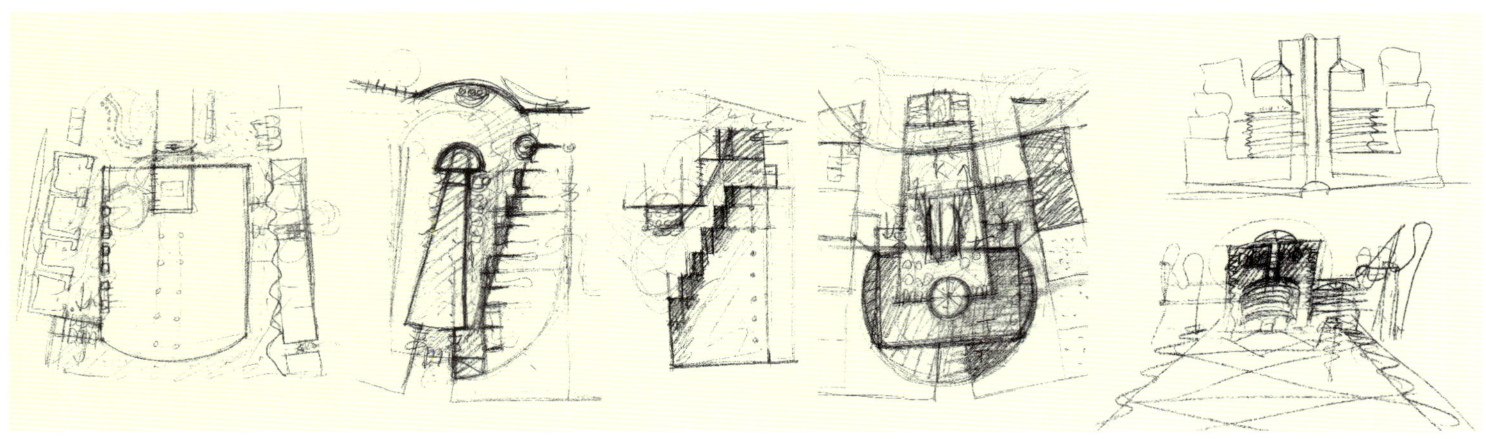

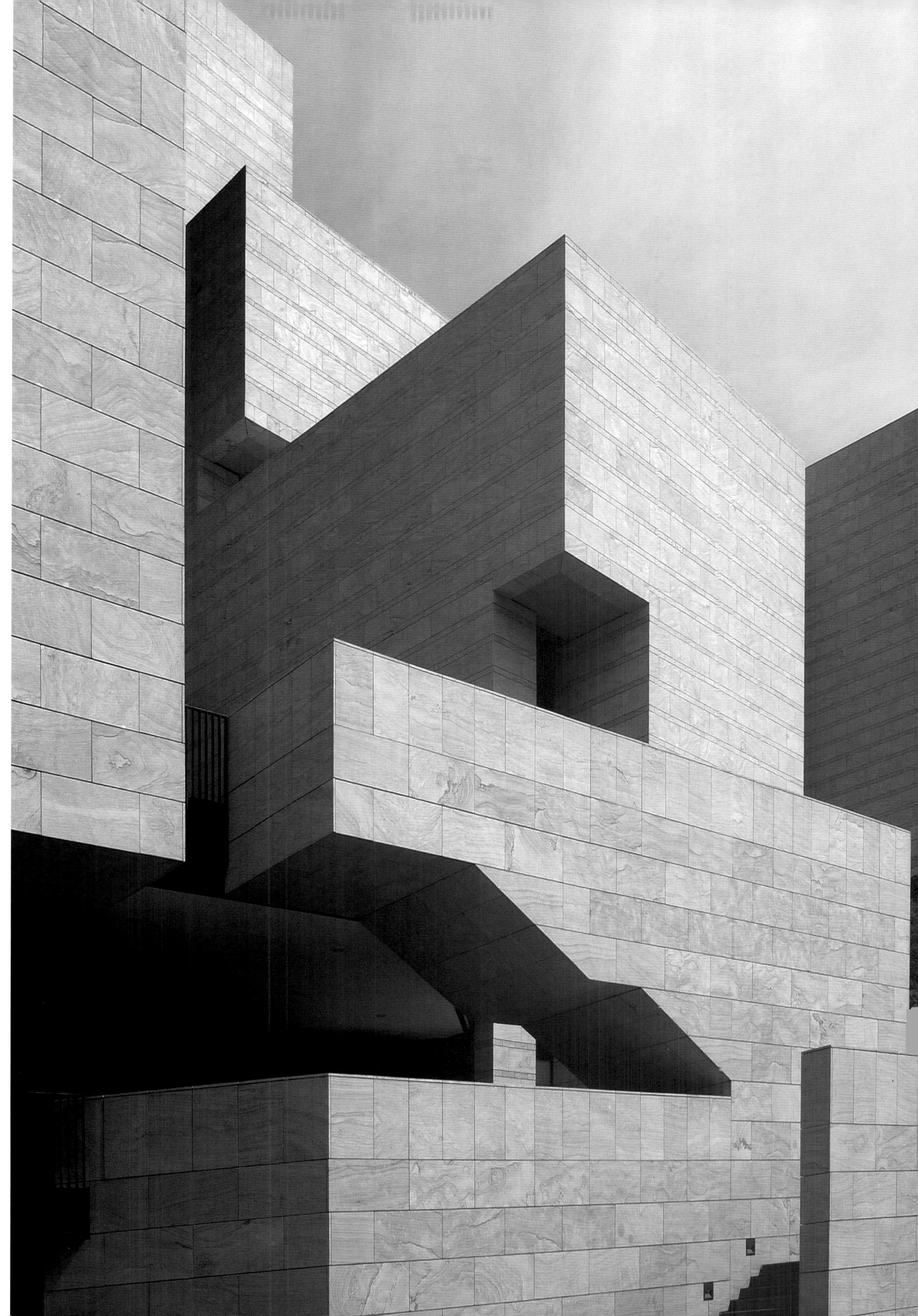

前阿皮亚尼城市发展区域

意大利，特雷维索

URBAN REDEVELOPMENT OF THE AREA EX-APPIANI

TREVISO, ITALY

1994-2013

委托方：特雷维索，卡萨玛卡基金会
项目管理：皮埃特罗·塞门扎托工程师
景观建筑师：苏珊娜·马塞特
占地面积：70,000平方米
建筑体积：230,000 立方米
公共建筑：48,000平方米
私人建筑：23,000平方米
礼堂：1,360平方米，500座席
广场和绿化带：15,000平方米
玫瑰花园：1,260平方米（70米×18米），11个花坛

Client: Fondazione Cassamarca; Treviso
Project management: Eng. Pietro Semenzato
Landscape architect: Susanna Maset
Site area: 70,000 m^2
Built volume: 230,000 m^3
Public buildings: 48,000 m^2
Private buildings: 23,000 m^2
Auditorium:1,360 sq.m, seats 500
Piazza and green areas: 15,000 m^2
Rose garden: 1,260 sq.m (70 m x 18 m) divided in 11 beds

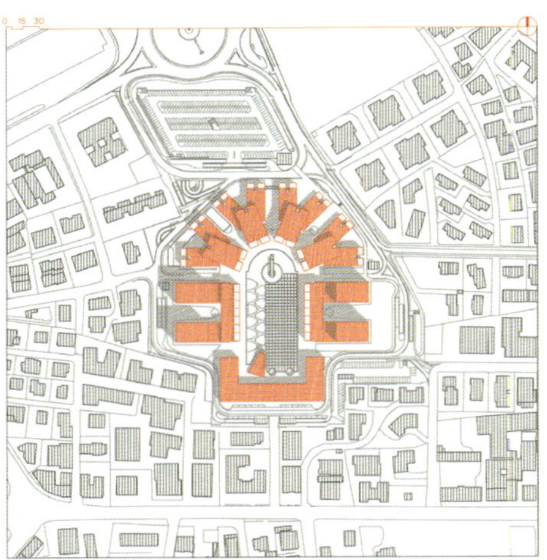

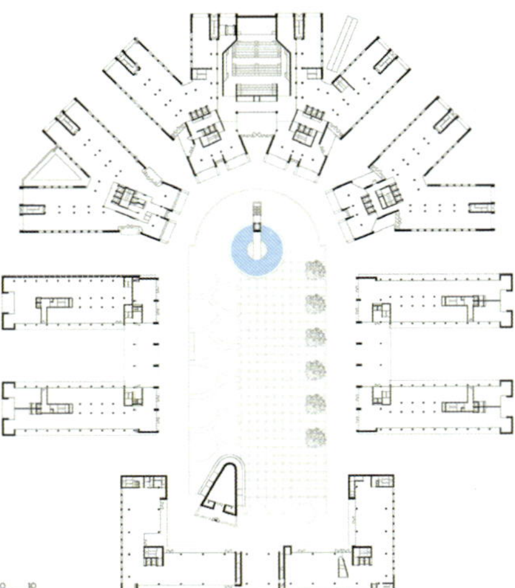

© ENRICO CANO

这个庞大的建筑群是“当局大本营”（公共机构的总部）的所在地，占地面积达7万平方米，曾经是格拉齐亚诺·阿皮亚尼于1910年创立的陶瓷工厂。与市中心的独特位置关系是该地块的一大特点：距离标出城市中心区域的16世纪城墙仅400米。项目构想是设计一座可以俯瞰连接城市中心主要步行街的，集行政和商业活动于一体的4层建筑，以及4座容纳主要城市机构的8层放射状建筑。这些放射状建筑包括一间可容纳500余座席的礼堂，以及一座表面覆砖且具有铜屋顶的小教堂。位于建筑群中心的大广场以红色阿夏戈石材铺就，最大的特点是一座壮观的喷泉。东面有一处划分了11个苗圃的玫瑰园，西面则种植有6棵近30年树龄的朴树。新区的服务设施还包括近2000个停车位。

The huge complex, home to the “Citadel of the Authorities”, stands on an area of 70,000 sq.m., once occupied by the ceramics factory founded by Graziano Appiani in 1910. The area is characterized by its peculiar position with respect to the urban centre, set at approx. 400 m from the sixteenth-century walls that delimit the historic centre. The project envisages the construction of a four-story building for administrative and commercial activities overlooking the main pedestrian entrance from the urban centre and of four radial eight-storey buildings with the main city institutions. Between these latter buildings there is the auditorium with more than 500 seats. It has been also designed a small chapel that presents a brick cladding and a copper roofing. The big plaza is set in the heart of the complex is covered with red Asiago stone and is characterized by a spectacular fountain. The eastern side is defined by a rose garden divided into 11 beds whereas the western side is enriched by the presence of six hackberries of almost 30 years. In the service of the new area there is a network of almost 2000 car parks.

© ENRICO CANO

© ENRICO CANO

© ENRICO CANO

© ENRICO CANO

© ENRICO CANO

© ENRICO CANO

前坎帕里区域总部与住宅

意大利，塞斯托·圣乔凡尼

CAMPARI HEADQUARTERS AND RESIDENCES, AREA EX - CAMPARI

SESTO SAN GIOVANNI, ITALY

2004-2009/2010

业主/委托方总部：大卫·坎帕里公司
委托方所在地：莫雷蒂地产公司
合作建筑师：吉安卡尔洛·马佐拉蒂
占地面积：22,000平方米
办公空间建筑面积：10,200平方米
地上办公空间体积：38,400立方米
住宅空间建筑面积：12,400平方米
住宅空间建筑体积：41,500立方米

Client Campari headquarters: Davide Campari, SpA
Client residences: Moretti Real Estate
Partner: arch. Giancarlo Marzorati
Site area: 22,000 m²
Useful surface offices: 10,200 m²
Volume above ground offices: 38,400 m³
Useful surface residences: 12,400 m²
Volume residences: 41,500 m³

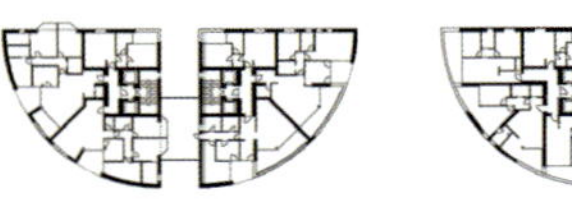

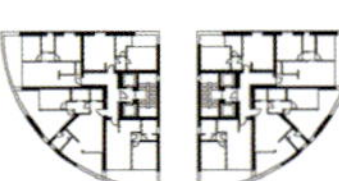

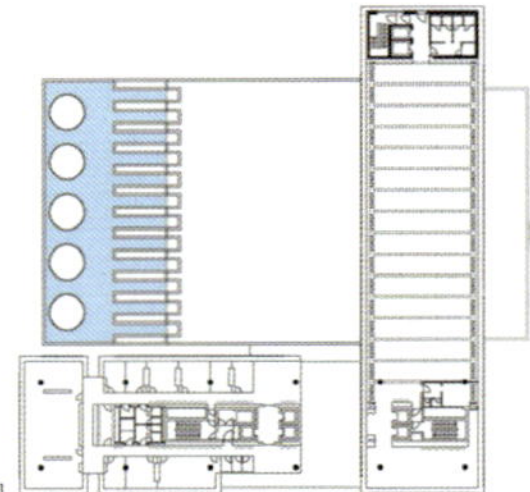

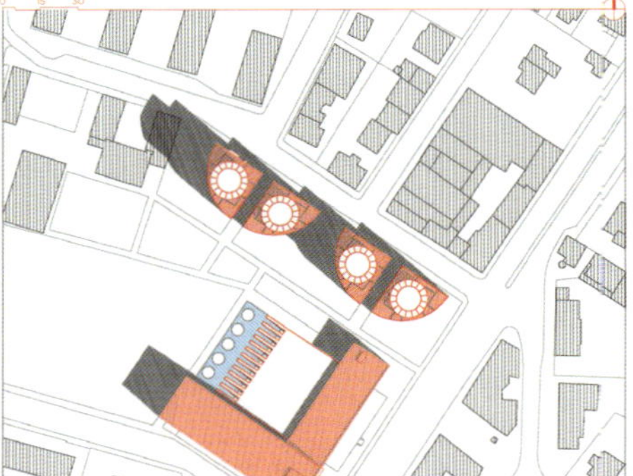

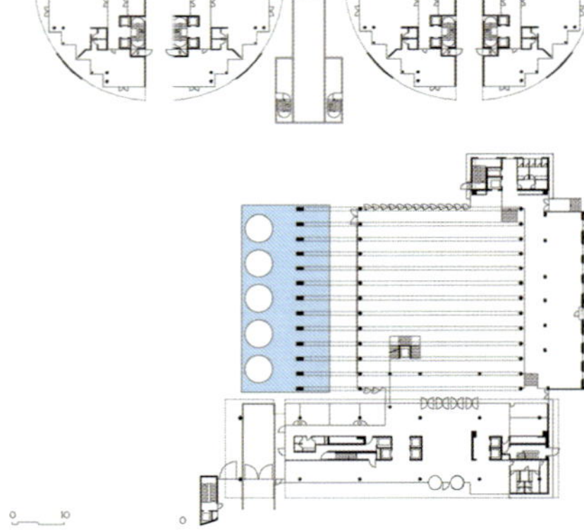

坎帕里办公楼高38米，由2个巨大的矩形建筑体组成。第一部分包含地上9层以及地下2层，第二部分地上与地下各有2层。历史建筑的外墙被保留了下来，与俯瞰格拉姆西大街的新建筑结构融为一体。历史建筑的侧面由新的红色砖墙封闭，马里奥·博塔在此设计了2处德佩罗（坎帕里的代表人物）的浮雕。2个矩形建筑体以“L”形相交，围合出一处内庭院，大堂的大型草坪屋顶向倒影池倾斜，同时构成了花园的立面，成为标志性特征。住宅楼（约有100间公寓）位于邻近的区域，呈现出¼圆柱形的塔楼形态，高度各不相同，外部皆覆以红砖。

The volume housing the Campari offices has a height of 38 meters and is formed by the intersection of two huge rectangular volumes. The first one has nine floors above-ground and two floors underground while the second one has two floors above-ground and two under-ground. The historic building, whose original façade has been preserved, has been included within the volume overlooking via Gramsci and is closed on the sides by new brick buffer walls, on which Mario Botta has designed two bas-reliefs evoking the icons Depero designed for Campari. The inner courtyard, defined by the L-shaped intersection of the two rectan-gular volumes is characterised by the grassy roof of the lobby which models the elevation of the garden as it slopes down to a reflecting pool. The residential towers (with approx. 100 apartments) stand in the neighbouring area. They are in the form of four quarter circles with different heights and are clad with red brick.

© ENRICO CANO

© ENRICO CANO

© ENRICO CANO

© ENRICO CANO

© ENRICO CANO

© ENRICO CANO

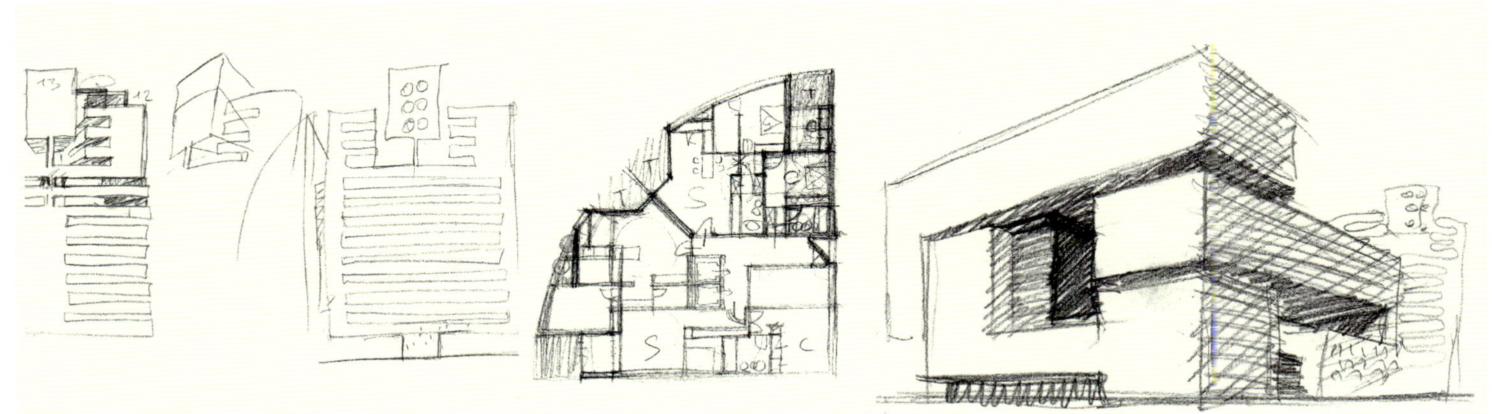

学校与休闲空间
SCHOOLS AND FREE TIME SPACES

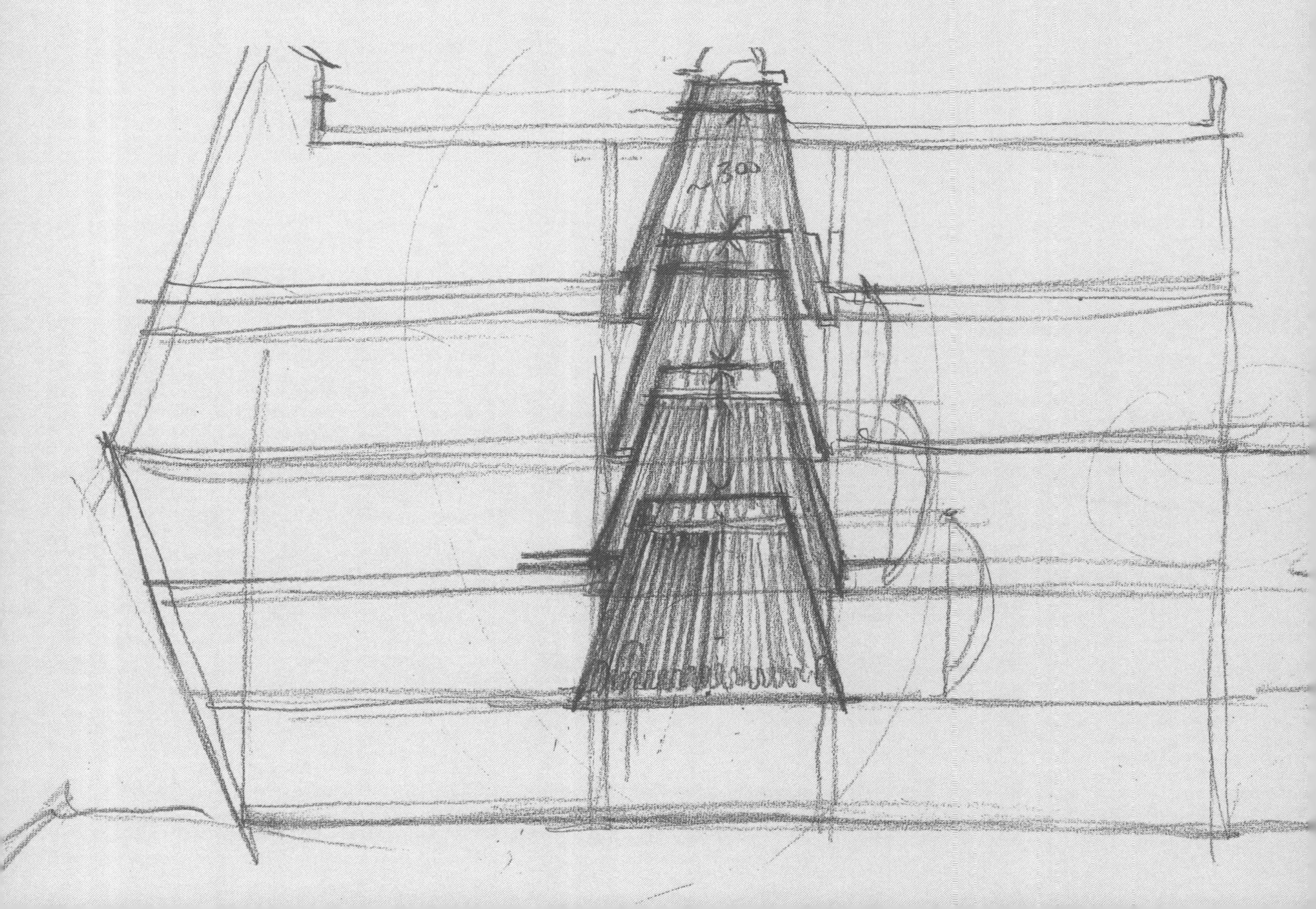

中学

瑞士，下莫尔比奥

MIDDLE SCHOOL

MORBIO INFERIORE, SWITZERLAND

1972-1977

竞赛项目时间：1972年
建造时间：1972～1977年
委托方：提契诺州
占地面积：28,800 平方米
建筑面积：15,000平方米
建筑体积：68,500立方米

Competition project: 1972
Construction: 1972-1977
Client: Canton of Ticino
Site area: 28,800 m²
Useful surface: 15,000 m²
Volume: 68,500 m³

学校由8个富有节奏的单元组成，形成一座长条形的纵向建筑物。每个单元通过位于一层的开放式门廊与环境沟通，横向连接起建筑物前方的大片绿地以及后方的树林。一层分布有过渡室内外空间的大厅、连接各楼层的楼梯以及教师用房。二层均有四间围绕在中央空间四周的教室；建筑开阔的窗户使自身与周围景观建立起视觉和空间上的联系。在三层，特殊功能教室和实验室被屋顶天窗透进的光线照亮。室内画廊与建筑物长度一致，并连接起各个建筑单元。自然光穿过屋顶的玻璃表面，在这个大型纵向空间（虚拟的轴线）内部流动。

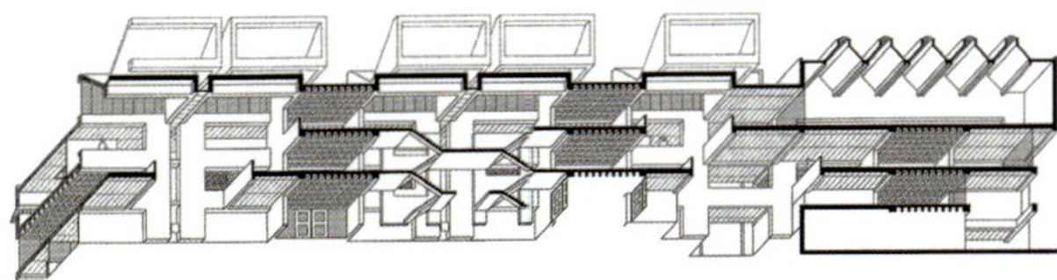

The school looks like a rhythmical sequence of eight units that give shape to a long longitudinal building. Each unit is in dialogue with the context by means of the open portico at ground level and transversally connects the big green area in front of the building with the woods at the back. On the ground floor there are the transition spaces (outside-inside) with the halls, the stairs to the different floors and the rooms for the teachers. On the first floor of each unit there are four classrooms organized around a big central space; broad windows allow establishing visual and spatial relationships with the surrounding landscape. On the second floor, the special classrooms and laboratories are lit from above by means of the skylights on the roof. The interior gallery that runs the length of the building represents the link between the units. Natural light comes streaming in this large longitudinal interior space (a virtual backbone) through glass surfaces set on the roof.

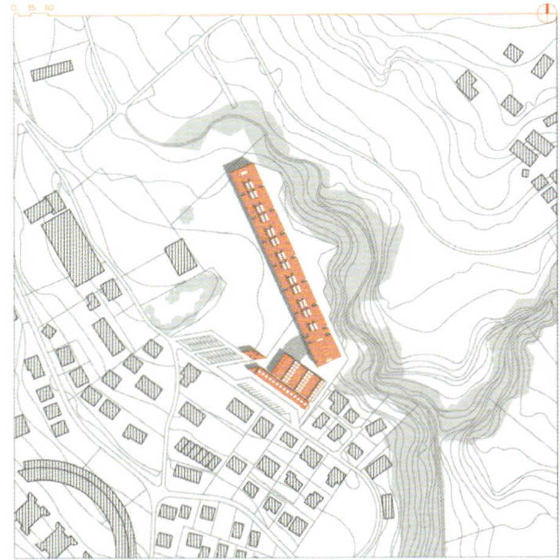

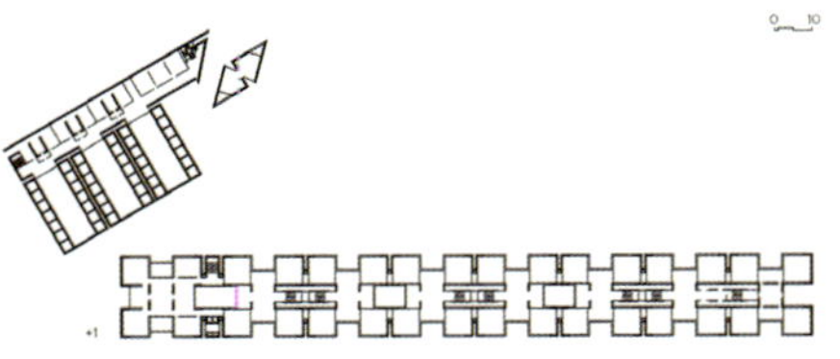

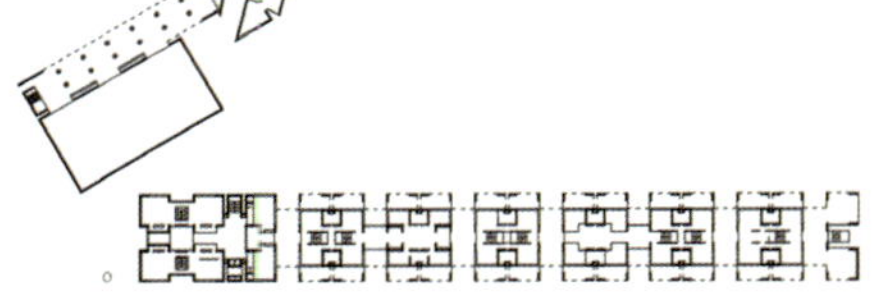

© ALO ZANETTA

© ALO ZANETTA

© ALBERTO FLAMMER

© ALO ZANETTA

© ALO ZANETTA

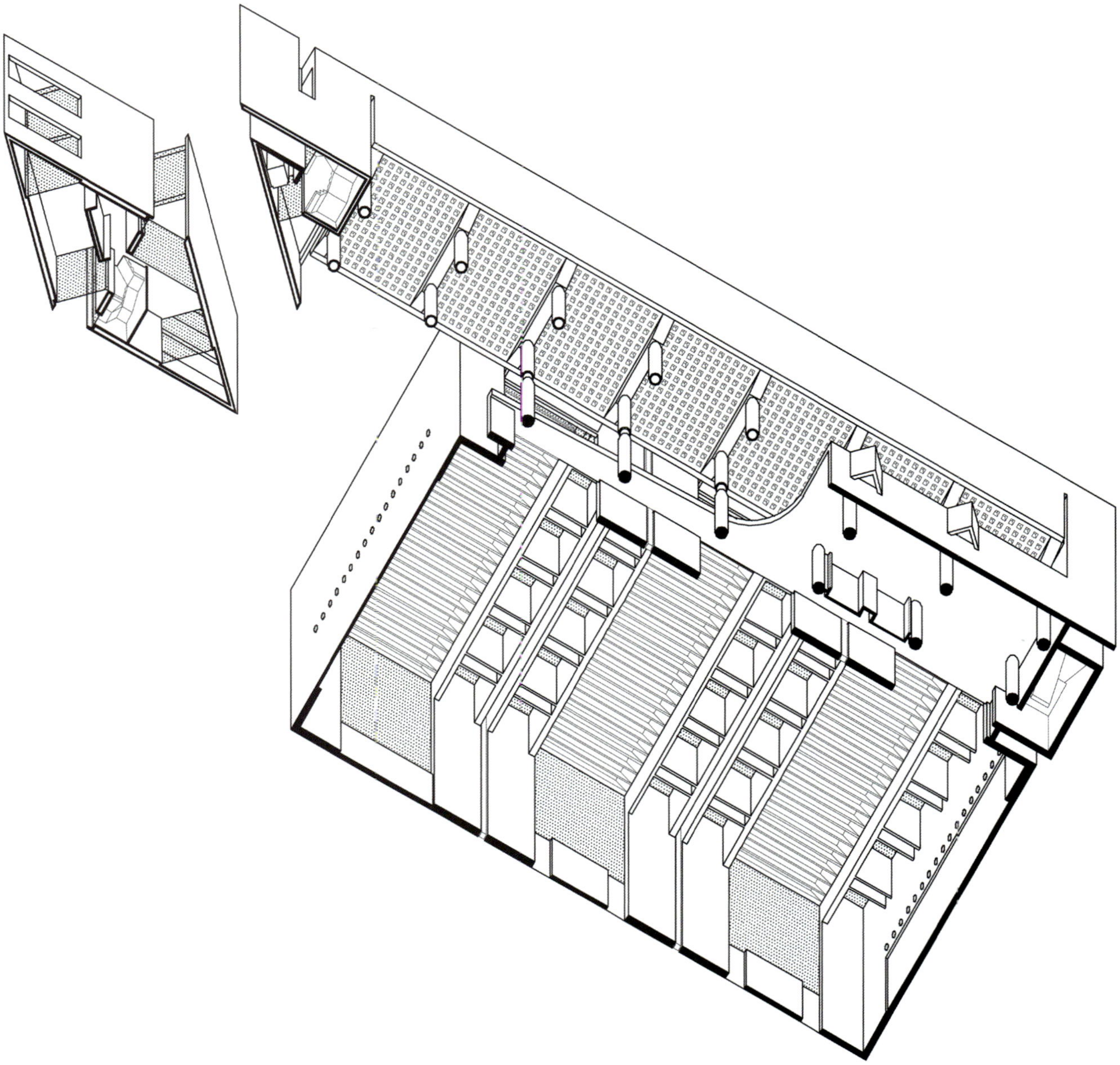

国家青少年体育中心

瑞士，特内罗

NATIONAL YOUTH SPORTS CENTRE

TENERO, SWITZERLAND

1990/1998-2001

竞赛项目时间：1990年
建造时间：1998～2001年
委托方：瑞士联邦体育局UFSPO
占地面积：53,200平方米
建筑面积：10,000平方米
建筑体积：57,300立方米

Competition project: 1990
Construction: 1998-2001
Client: Swiss Confederation, Federal Office of Sport
Site area: 53,200 m^2
Useful surface: 10,000 m^2
Volume: 57,300 m^3

特内罗国家青少年体育中心由运动场和行政住宅设施2个结构紧凑的部分组成，精简节约了场地并使绿化区域得到最优的安排。主建筑体包含体育馆、体育设施和自助餐厅，沿南面宽阔的门廊展开，形成一处有遮挡的阴凉区域，作为室外空间与室内设施的过渡。面向南部湖水的凉廊是行政住宅建筑的正立面，呈半圆形布局，面向主干道的一侧完全封闭。办公空间设置在一层，居住空间则分布于楼上4层。

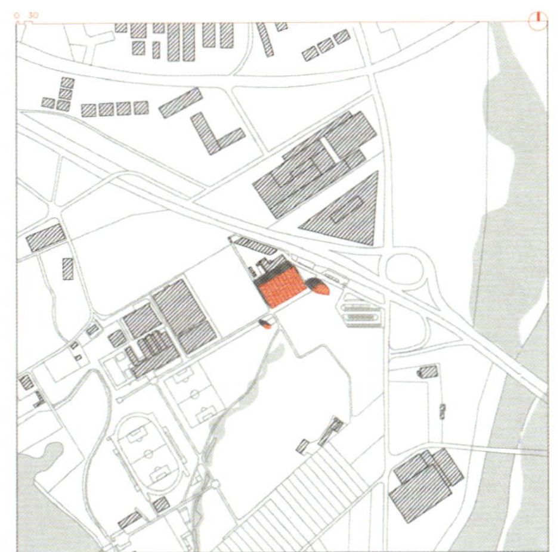

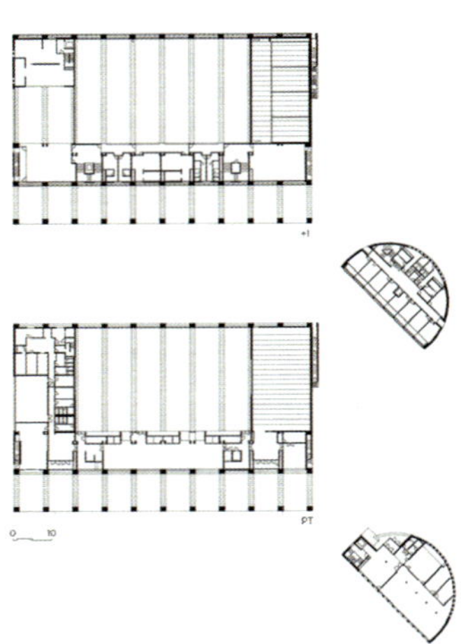

The National Youth Sports Centre in Tenero is organized into two compact structures that group both the sports and the administrative-residential facilities, in order to streamline and economise the site and permit an optimum organization of the green areas. The main volume, which includes the gym, the athletic facilities and the cafeteria, stretches along the south front with a broad portico that provides a shady covered area as a transition point between the outdoor areas and the indoor facilities. The administration-residential building is positioned so that the long façade of the loggias faces south, towards the lake, with a semicircular layout that is completely closed on the side towards the main road. The offices are located on the ground floor, while the lodgings are on the four upper floors.

© ENRICO CANO

© ENRICO CANO

© ENRICO CANO

© ENRICO CANO

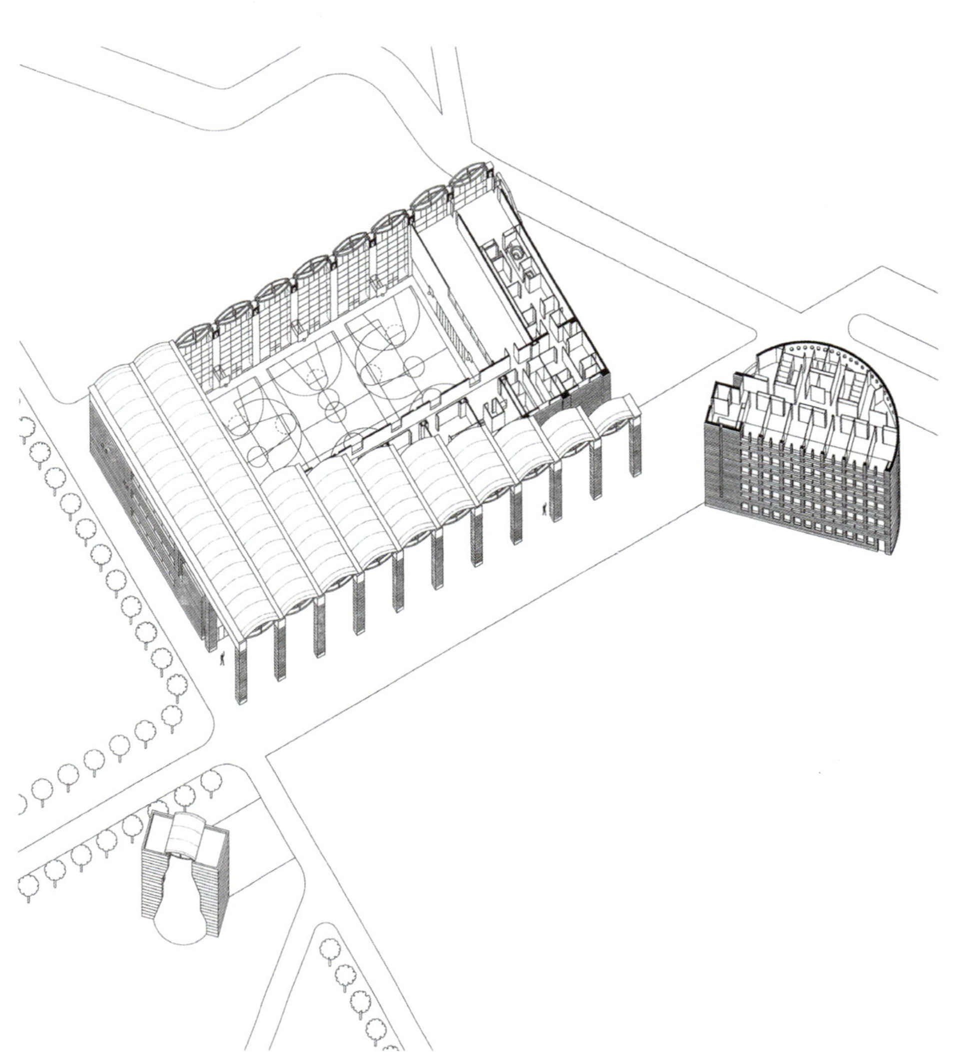

© ENRICO CANO

© ENRICO CANO

“美洲首脑峰会”纪念碑

玻利维亚，圣克鲁斯

MONUMENT FOR THE “CUMBRE DE LAS AMERICAS”

SANTA CRUZ DE LA SIERRA, BOLIVIA

1996

项目时间：1996年
建造时间：1996年
委托方：圣克鲁斯-德拉谢拉市
合作建筑师：路易斯·费尔南德兹·德科多瓦和罗达公司
建筑体积：每座塔楼2,300立方米

Project: 1996
Construction: 1996
Client: City of Santa Cruz de la Sierra
Partner: arch. Luis Fernández de Córdova e Roda s.r.l.
Volume : 2,300 m^3 per tower

这座纪念碑式建筑为1996年12月6日在圣克鲁斯-德拉谢拉市召开的可持续发展峰会而修建。项目想要建造2座多层红砖塔楼，以整合毗邻市区的公园的两角。一连串相连的室内楼梯通向阳台。这2座塔楼展示出一幅拟人的景象：顶部设有技术空间的角楼看起来像建筑的“头部”，夜间通过发射出的激光相连。一层部分墙体被移除，露出2根圆柱，给建筑物带来一丝轻盈感，同时也为公园提供了新的视角。在地面层，23个小型喷泉划分的铺装人行道连接了塔楼，每个喷泉之间的间隔相等，200米的长度从公园前部延伸而来。

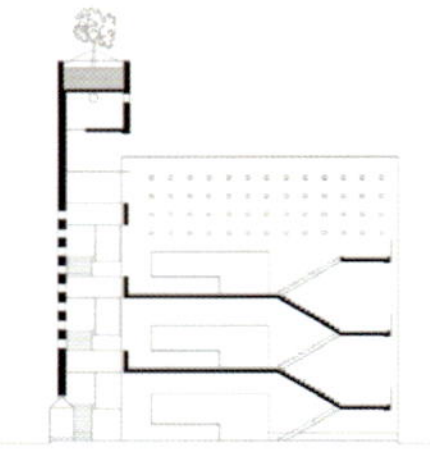

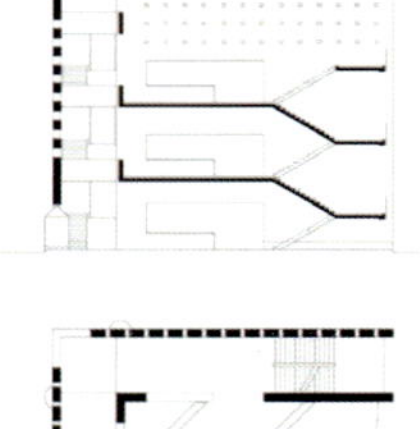

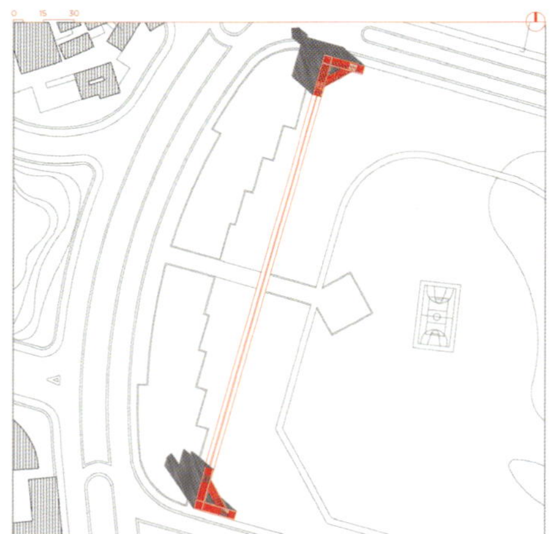

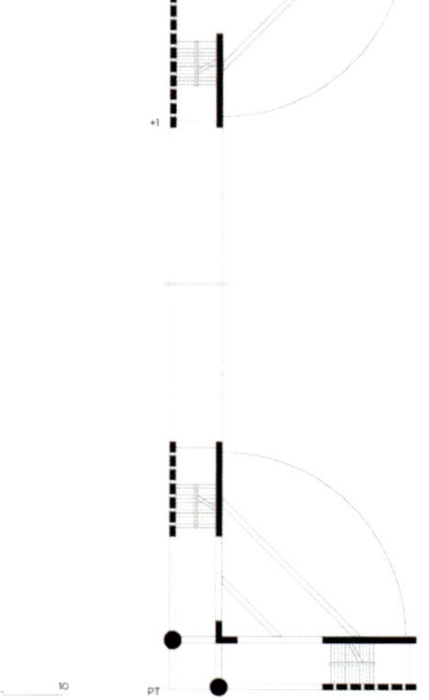

The monument was built on occasion of the Summit on Sustainable Growth that was held in Santa Cruz de la Sierra in 1996. The project entailed consolidating the two corners of the park adjacent to the city by building two multi-storey towers, clad in red bricks. A series of linked interior staircases lead to balconies. The towers display an anthropomorphic image: on their tops, the turrets with the technical spaces look like heads, linked at night by a luminous ray of laser light. On the ground floor, the removal of part of the wall reveals two round columns that bestow a sense of lightness to the structures and offer, at the same time, new viewpoints on the park. At ground level, the towers are connected by a paved walkway marked by twenty-three fountains, set at regular intervals, that runs the entire two-hundred-metre length of the front of the park.

© PINO MUSI

© PINO MUSI

© PINO MUSI

© PINO MUSI

© PINO MUSI

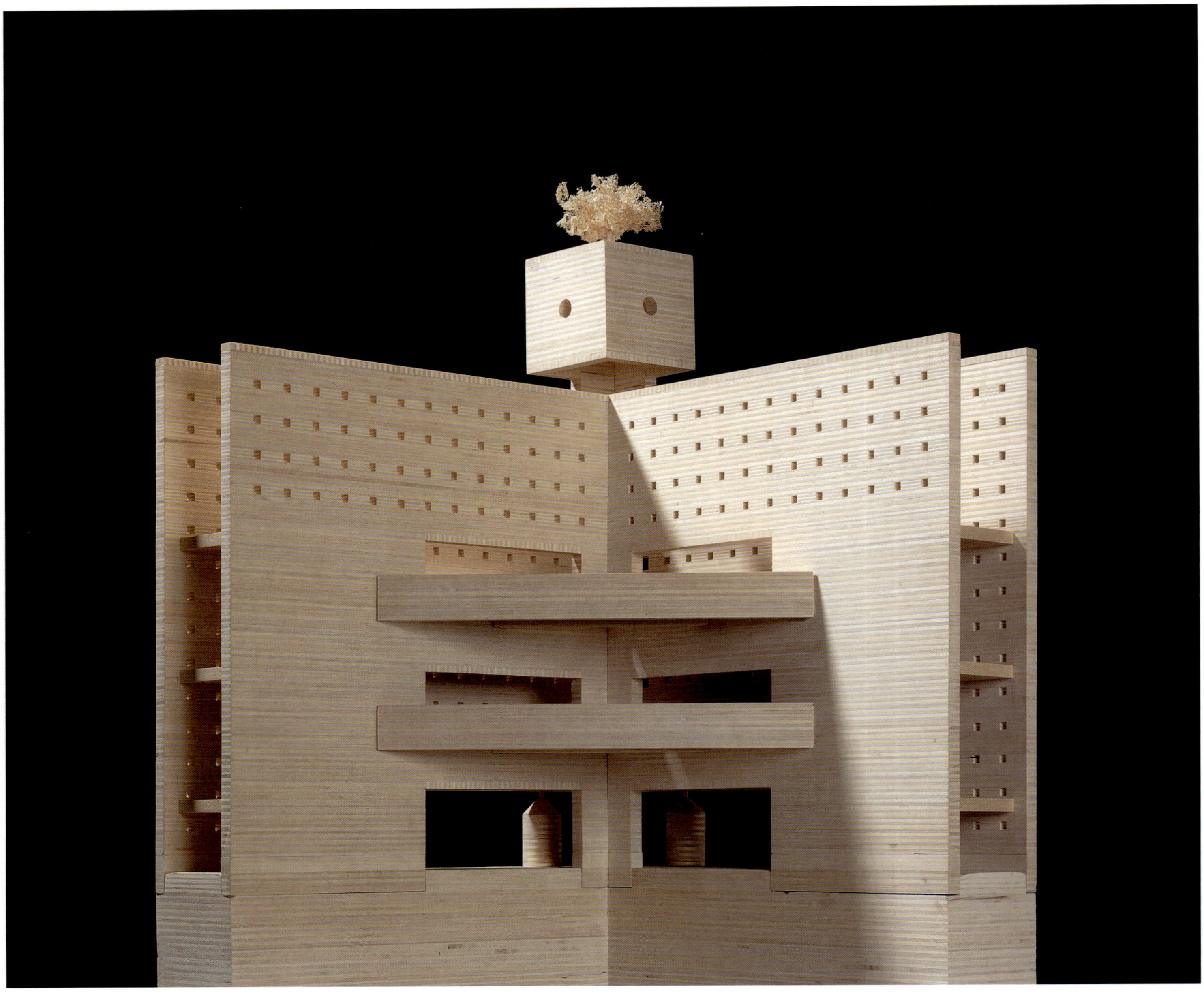

莫隆塔

瑞士，马勒赖

MORON TOWER

MALLERAY, SWITZERLAND

1998-2004

项目时间：1998年
建造时间：2000～2004年
委托方：马勒赖莫隆观光基金会
筹办方：穆捷建筑师学会监督委员会；安东内·贝尔纳斯科尼，亨利·西蒙，提奥·杰瑟
土木工程：德莱蒙，施特兰巴赫股份公司

Project: 1998
Construction: 2000-2004
Client: Tour de Moron Foundation, Malleray
Promoter: Surveillance commission, Moutier Builders Society
Antoine Bernasconi, Henri Simon, Théo Geiser.
Civil engineering: Stampbach SA, Delémont

莫隆塔位于伯内斯尤拉，坐落在从瑞士北部延伸至上萨瓦省和黑森林的高地上。这座瞭望塔结构的灵感源于几百名学徒在石匠职业培训中打造作品的画面。塔高26米，直径约6米。坚固的石阶悬挑于中空的中央承重结构。每级台阶由2块插入立板的楔形石头组成，立板起到栏杆的作用。瞭望塔顶部是一处可以360° 观赏乡村景色的钢制平台。如要到达观景台，游客必须爬上位于圆筒形承重结构内的狭窄梯子。2个平面锥形体组成的金属圆盘位于石砌结构上方，构成瞭望塔的屋顶。

The Moron Tower is located in the Bernese Jura on the highlands stretching from the northern edge of Switzerland towards Haute-Savoie and the Black Forest. The construction of this belvedere tower was inspired by the intention of giving an image to the work done by several hundred apprentices as part of their vocational training to become masons/stonecutters. The tower is tall 26 meters and has a diameter of about 6 metres. The solid stone steps are cantilevered around a hollow central bearing structure. Each step is characterized by two stone wedges embedded into vertical slabs that act as a railing. The tower is topped by a steel lookout platform that offers a 360-degree view of the surrounding countryside; to reach the belvedere, the visitor must climb up a narrow ladder inside the bearing cylinder. A metal disc composed of two flattened cones creates a roof over the stone structure.

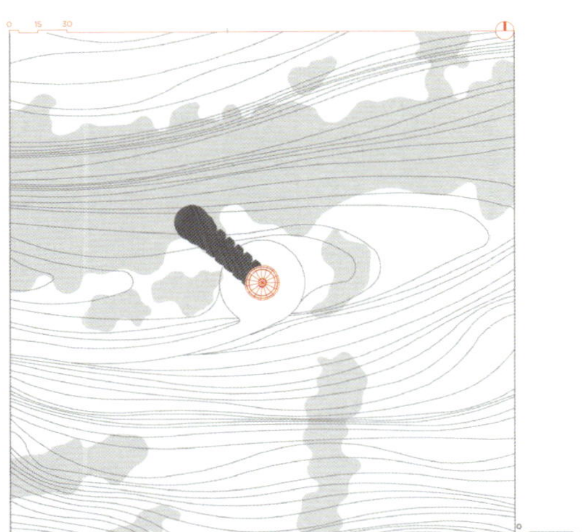

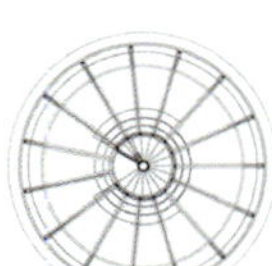

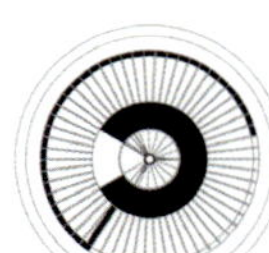

© THOMAS JANTSCHER

© THOMAS JANTSCHER

© CLAUDE WEHRLI

© THOMAS JANTSCHER

© THOMAS JANTSCHER

© CLAUDE WEHRLI

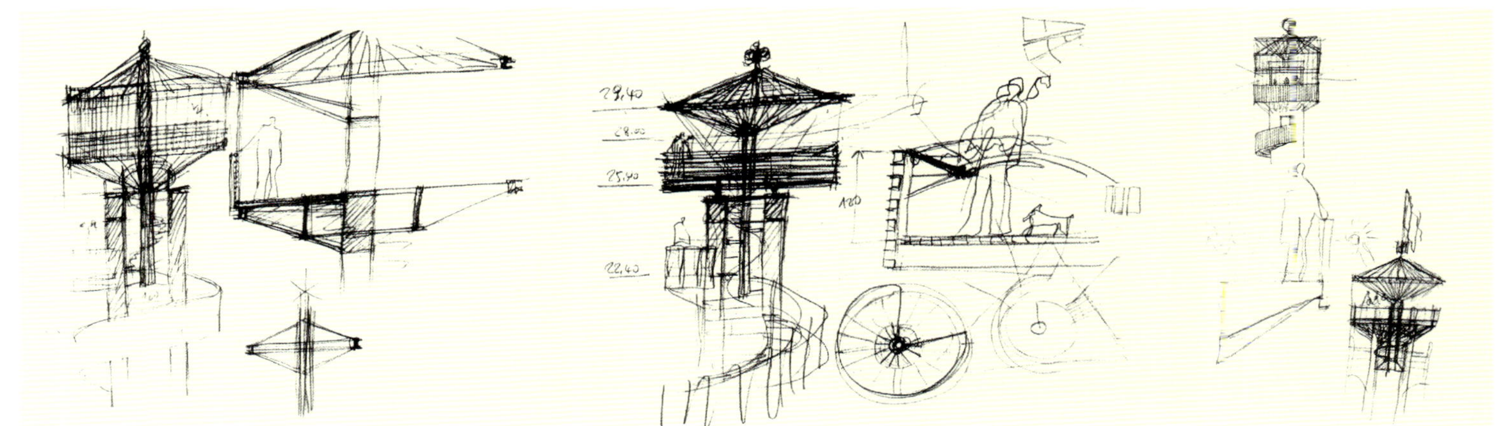

“图亨山地绿洲”健康中心
瑞士，阿罗萨

SPA “TSCHUGGEN BERG OASE”
AROSA, SWITZERLAND

2003-2006

项目时间：2003年
建造时间：2004～2006年
委托方：阿罗萨，图亨大酒店股份公司
合作建筑师：库尔吉安方尊股份公司
建筑面积：5,300平方米
建筑体积：27,000立方米

Project: 2003
Construction: 2004-2006
Client: AG Grandhotel Tschuggen, Arosa
Partner: Arch. Gian Fanzun AG
Useful surface: 5,300 m^2
Volume: 27,000 m^3

图亨山地绿洲健康中心毗邻五星级图亨大酒店，坐落在被森林包围的一处自然盆地内。将大部分建筑物安置于地下是减少占地的一种方式，保护非凡自然景观的同时表示出对周围村庄的充分尊重。9个突出地面的大型天窗是地下建筑结构的唯一显现。健康中心分布在4层空间中，视觉上互相联系：一层是健身设施、技术用房和外部宾客入口；二层是美容护理隔间；三层通过玻璃桥连接到酒店入口，这里设有接待处、宾客衣帽间和“桑拿世界”；四层则是“水上乐园”。室外桑拿浴室、日光浴室和游泳池位于大型露台上，与大自然亲密接触。

The Tschuggen Berg Oase Wellness Center is placed next to the five-star Tschuggen Grand Hotel, in a natural basin surrounded by a forest. The choice to place most of the building underground was a way to reduce the surface above ground, to preserve an extraordinary part of the landscape and to establish a respectful relationship with the nearby village. Nine large skylights emerge from the ground and represent the only signs of the hypogeal construction. The wellness center spreads over four levels visually linked to each other. On the first level are the fitness facilities, the technical rooms, and the entry for the external guests; on the second level are the cabins for beauty treatment. The third level represents the entrance level connected to the hotel via a glass bridge. Here there are the reception, guest cloakrooms, and the 'sauna world'. The fourth level houses the 'water world'. The exterior sauna, solarium, and swimming pool are on a large terrace in direct relationship with nature.

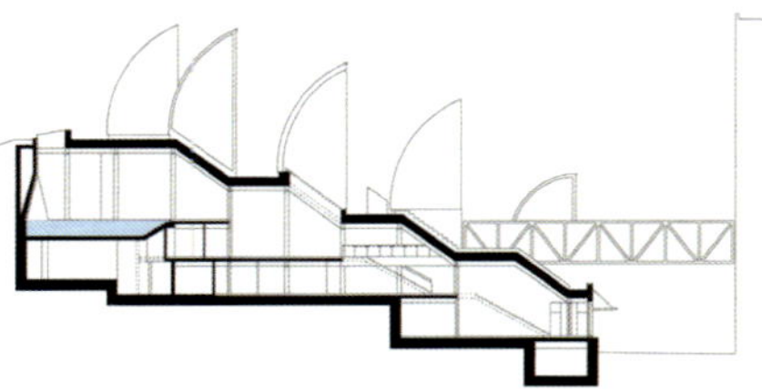

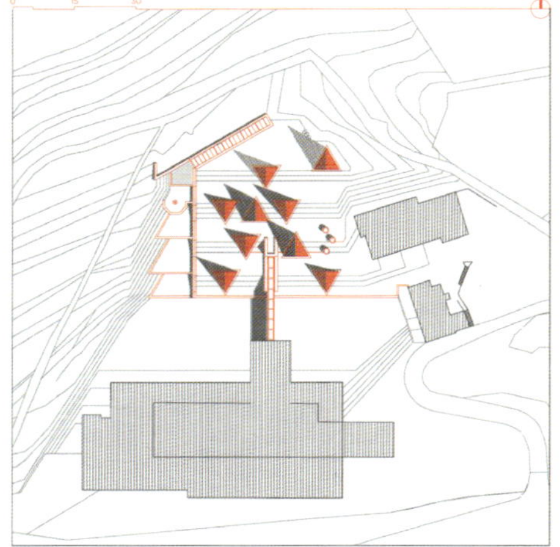

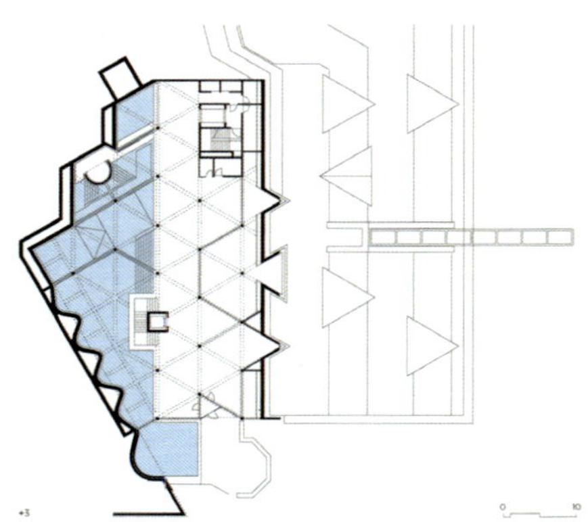

© URS HOMBERGER

© ENRICO CANO

© ENRICO CANO

© ENRICO CANO

© ENRICO CANO

© URS HOMBERGER

© URS HOMBERGER

广场与温泉中心

瑞士，瑞吉

SQUARE AND SPA

RIGI KALTBAD, SWITZERLAND

2004-2012

项目时间：2004年
建造时间：2012年
委托方：瑞士信贷集团投资基金会
使用方：伯恩发展与管理公司水疗度假村
项目管理：MLG 建筑承包商
工程师：卢塞恩，普鲁斯·美亚公司
占地面积：2,400 平方米（其中绿地面积 650平方米）
温泉面积：2,540平方米
建筑体积：17,000立方米

Project: 2004
Construction: 2012
Client: Credit Suisse Anlagestiftung, Zurich
User: Aqua-Spa-Resorts, Development & management AG, Bern
Project Management: MLG Generalunternehmung AG, Bern
Engineer: Plüss Meyer Partner AG, Lucerne
Square surface: 2,400 m^2 (of which 650 m^2 green area)
Spa surface: 2,540 m^2
Volume: 17,000 m^3

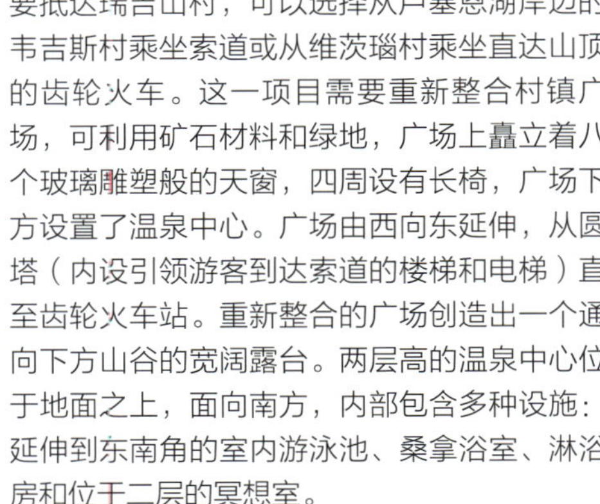

要抵达瑞吉山村，可以选择从卢塞恩湖岸边的韦吉斯村乘坐索道或从维茨瑙村乘坐直达山顶的齿轮火车。这一项目需要重新整合村镇广场，可利用矿石材料和绿地，广场上矗立着八个玻璃雕塑般的天窗，四周设有长椅，广场下方设置了温泉中心。广场由西向东延伸，从圆塔（内设引领游客到达索道的楼梯和电梯）直至齿轮火车站。重新整合的广场创造出一个通向下方山谷的宽阔露台。两层高的温泉中心位于地面之上，面向南方，内部包含多种设施：延伸到东南角的室内游泳池、桑拿浴室、淋浴房和位于二层的冥想室。

The mountain village of Rigi Kaltbad is reachable by cableway from the village of Weggis on the shores of Lake Lucerne, or by cogwheel train from the village of Vitznau. The project entails both the reorganization of the village square by means of mineral parts and green areas from which emerge eight skylights conceived as glass sculptures surrounded by benches, and the creation of a spa below the village square. The square extends from west to east, from the cylindrical tower (with a staircase and lift to lead the visitors to the cableway) to the way station of the cogwheel train. The reorganization of the square creates a wide terrace opening out to the valley beneath. The spa opens southwards with two levels above ground and offers many facilities: from the inside swimming pool that prolongs outwards to the south-east corner, to the saunas, the showers and the meditation room on the second floor.

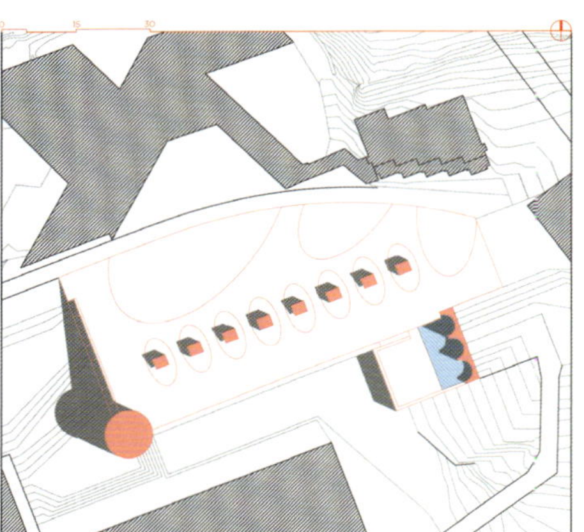

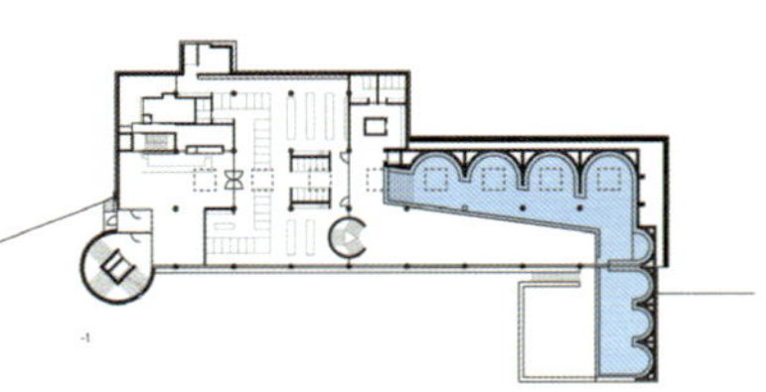

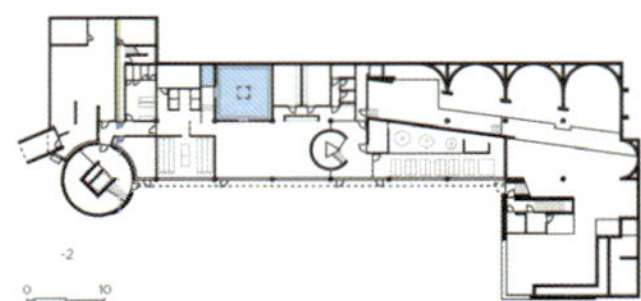

© ENRICO CANO

© ENRICO CANO

© ENRICO CANO

© ENRICO CANO

© ENRICO CANO

© ENRICO CANO

AGORÀ俱乐部会所

韩国，济州岛

CLUB HOUSE AGORÀ

JEJU ISLAND, SOUTH KOREA

2006-2008

项目时间：2006年
建造时间：2008年
合作方：首尔，三友建筑事务所
委托方：普光有限公司
使用面积：1,000平方米
建筑体积：7,000立方米

Project: 2006
Construction: 2008
Partner: Samoo Architects, Seoul
Client: Bokwang JeJu Co., Ltd
Useful Surface: 1,000 m^2
Volume: 7,000 m^3

项目处于新的住宅城市化背景下，力求通过理性的选址把建筑与起伏的自然景观有机结合，形成更密切的滨海关系。建筑为附近入住的游客提供服务，除了室外游泳池外，还有体育、健身设施、厨房、休息室和接待处。整个建筑的平立面均基于正方形网格设计，显示出一种立方体序列。严谨的几何形体与透明的内部空间形成对比，金字塔形透明玻璃体面朝广阔的地平线，巨大的棱镜结构将室内外设施连接在同一水平高度上。由当地艺术家安中源设计的大型不锈钢球体装置悬挂在透明结构中，成为此度假胜地的显著标志。通过使用该岛屿自产的熔岩石材，建筑与周围环境之间的密切关系更近了一步。

The project stands in the context of a new residential urbanization and rises out of the reasoned choice of the place in order to merge in a balanced way with the winding natural landscape and gain a privileged relationship with the sea. The building houses the services for the tourists of the adjoining residential complex. Besides the outdoor swimming pool, there are sports and wellness facilities, kitchens and resting rooms and a reception. The building is designed on a square grid, both in plan and elevation, and appears as a sequence of cubes. The rigorous geometry contrasts with the transparency of the interior spaces that open towards the horizon thanks to the pyramid-shaped glass prism. The big prism links the indoor and outdoor facilities that follow each other on a single level. A big sphere in stainless steel by the local artist Ahn Jong Yuen hangs from the transparent structure and is a clear sign of the resort. The integration of the building within the surrounding environment is further highlighted by the use of the same lava stone the island is made of.

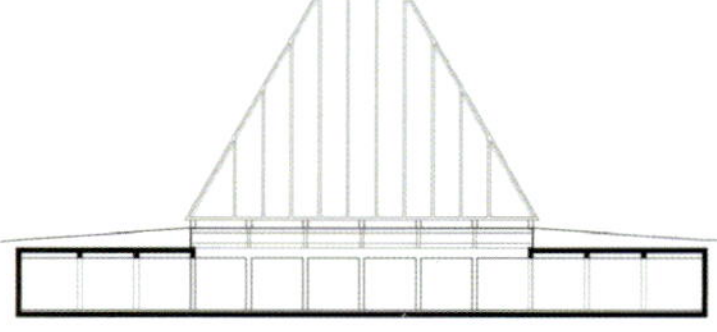

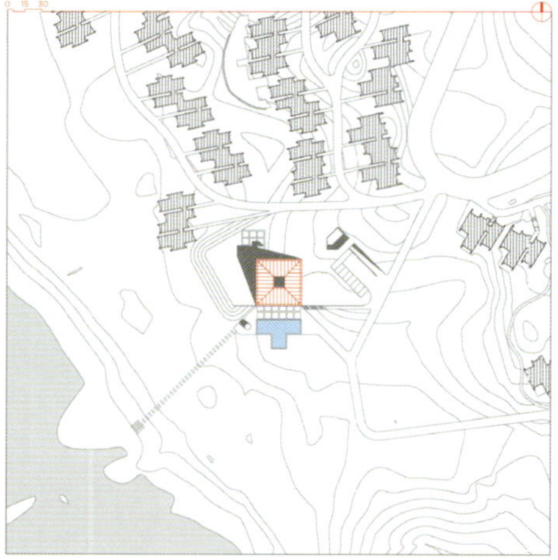

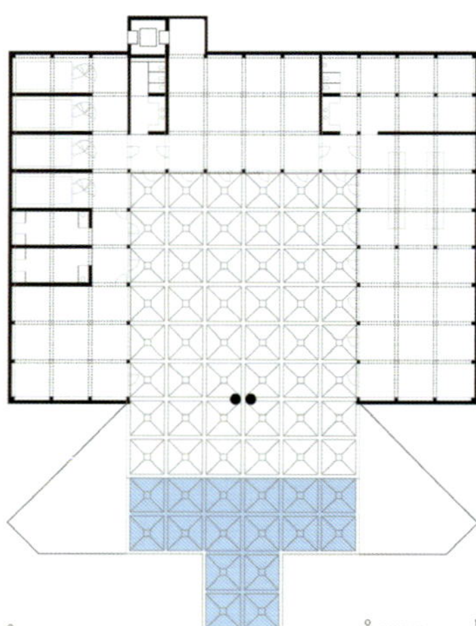

© YUM SEUNG-HOON

© YUM SEUNG-HOON

© YUM SEUNG-HOON

© YUM SEUNG-HOON

© YUM SEUNG-HOON

© YUM SEUNG-HOON

衡山路12号酒店

中国，上海

HOTEL TWELVE

HENGSHAN, SHANGHAI, PRC

2006-2012

项目时间：2006年
建造时间：2012年
项目地点：上海衡山路12号
委托方：上海地产集团
合作建筑师：李瑶
建筑面积：51,094平方米

Project: 2006
Construction: 2012
Place: No. 12 Hengshan Road, Shanghai
Client: Shanghai Land Group
Partner: arch. LI Yao
Useful Surface: 51,094 m²

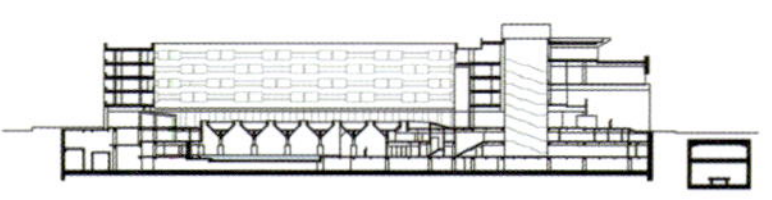

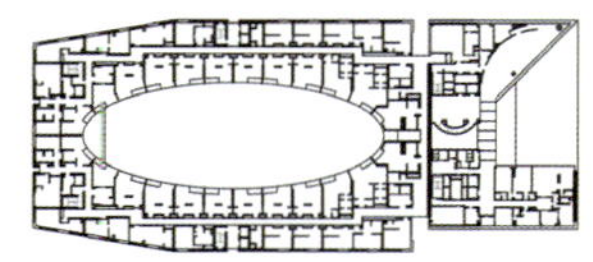

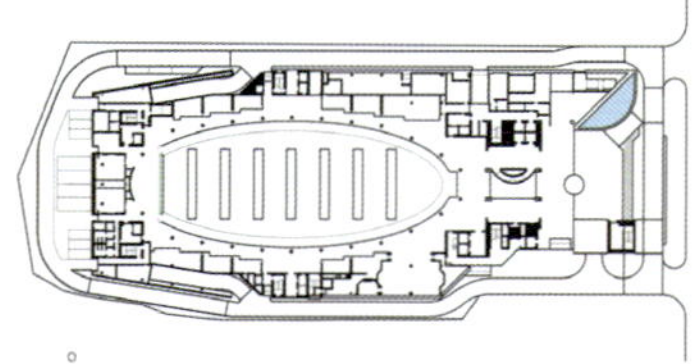

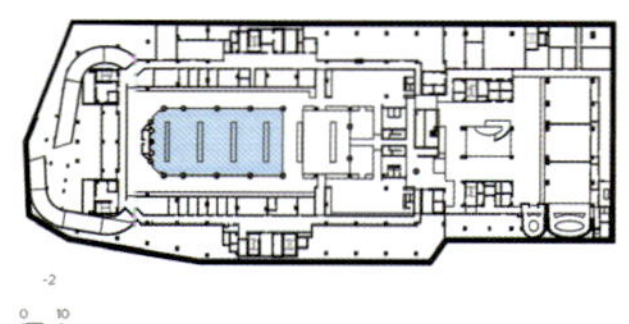

12号酒店坐落在上海市衡山路住宅区的主干道上，是一栋地上有5层的平行六面体建筑。酒店入口处的旋转楼梯通向楼上，楼上包含餐厅、休息室和活动区域，地下则设有健康中心、室内游泳池和多功能厅。项目基于原有的城市语境，同时出于对尊贵感和高品质的追求，围绕两个主要概念展开：首先，衡山路上的入口门廊被诠释为扩展的舞台，为客人提供可以停留的庇护场所；此外，从客房的阳台和窗户可以俯瞰带有中央花园的椭圆形庭院。因为下方有健身中心，所以该花园的位置比酒店大堂略高。酒店屋顶围绕着椭圆形庭院，并构建出一处独特的屋顶花园。

Hotel Twelve stands on the main road in the residential quarter of Shanghai, Hengshan. It is a paral elepiped of five floors above ground. At the entrance of the hotel a spiral staircase leads to the upper floors, which contain the restaurant, lounge, and the events space. The basements house the wellness center, the indoor swimming pool, and the lecture hall. The urban conditions and the search for exclusiveness and high standards made the project develop according to two main outlines. The first one interprets the entrance portico on Hengshan Road like an external stage - a concave volume where guests can stop in the big sheltered hall. The second designs an elliptical courtyard embellished by a garden in its center. The balconies and the windows of the rooms overlook the garden, which is slightly raised with respect to the lobby to reveal the hypogeal space with the wellness center. The roof of the hotel follows the perimeter of the courtyard and is characterized by another garden.

© FU XING

© FU XING

© FU XING

© BENOIT FLORENÇON

© FU XING

© FU XING

© FU XING

石花餐厅

瑞士，杰内罗索山

RESTAURANT FIORE DI PIETRA

MONTE GENEROSO, SWITZERLAND

2013-2017

项目时间：2013年
建造时间：2015~2017年
委托方：杰内罗索山铁路公司
土木工程：路易吉·布雷尼工程工作室
占地面积：28,000平方米
建筑面积：2,500平方米（其中2,140平方米为新建面积，360平方米为现有面积）
建筑体积：9,200立方米（其中8,000立方米为新建体积，1,200立方米为现有体积）

Project: 2013
Construction: 2015-2017
Client: Ferrovia Monte Generoso SA
Civil Engineering: Studio d'Ingegneria Luigi Brenni
Site area: 28,000 m^2
Useful Surface: 2,500 m^2 (of which 2,140 m^2 new + 360 m^2 existing)
Volume: 9,200 m^3 (of which 8,000 m^3 new + 1,200 m^3 existing)

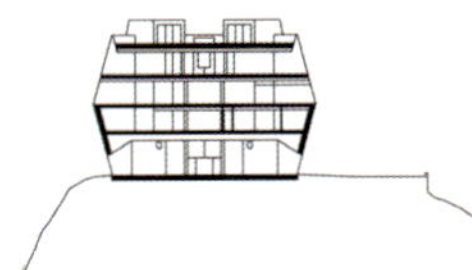

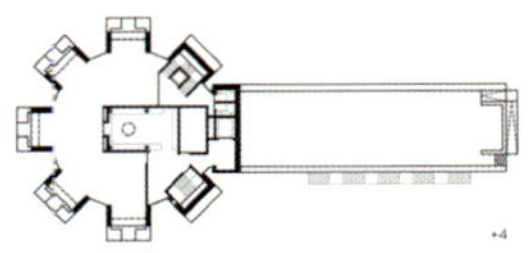

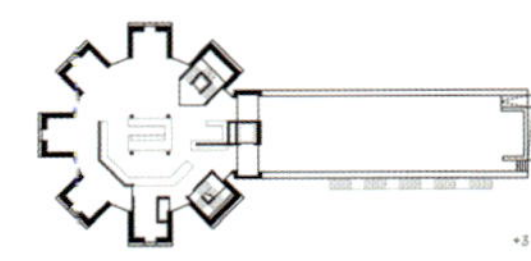

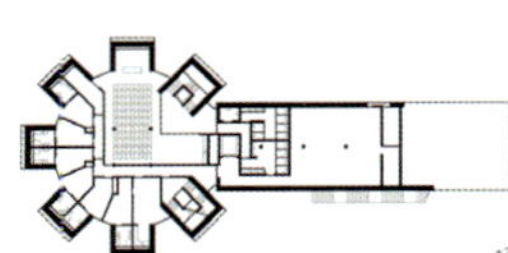

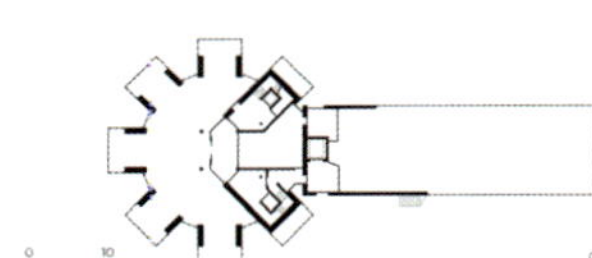

© ENRICO CANO

杰内罗索山顶曾坐落着一座20世纪早期的酒店，如今这里因坐落了新的地标建筑而越显尊贵。此处的地理位置不同寻常：一块小小的高地俯瞰着山体北侧的悬崖；山上有一块巨大的岩石，陡峭的山坡长达300~400米。这块令人望而生畏的岩石正是创造“石花”的决定性因素，“石花”是一座八角形建筑，具有独立的“花瓣”。在东侧正面，这个圆形的皇冠顺着山脊脉络形成一个观景区域。独立的“花瓣”结构组合形成一组5层塔形建筑，中部略向外突出，到高层的位置则重新聚拢。在齿轨铁路站这一层（地面层），一条宽敞的入口通道将室内外连接起来，经由通道可以进入展厅。展厅中，许多信息屏展示着杰内罗索山的历史，还陈列着这座建筑的模型以及建筑师马里奥·博塔绘制的方案草图。服务空间位于二层；三层有一间可容纳近90人的会议室；最高的两层设有一间自助餐厅（可通往大阳台）和一间高级餐厅。建筑的承重结构由钢筋混凝土制造，交叉点缀着灰色天然石材和平滑的条形装饰带。看似相互独立的几座塔楼实际上由几个大型的玻璃表面联结在一起，人们可以360°饱览全景，包括南侧的位于米兰附近的波河河谷和北侧的卢加诺湖以及阿尔卑斯山。

The new landmark at the top of Mount Generoso now graces the spot where an early 20th-century hotel once stood. The location is extraordinary: a small plateau overlooking the precipice on the north side of the mountain, characterised by a mighty rock with a steep 300-400-meter drop. The impressive rock formation was the deciding factor for creating the 'stone flower'—an octagonal building with individual 'petals'. On the east front this circular crown provides the space for an observation deck that follows the ridge of the mountain. The arrangement of the individual components (or 'petals') creates a group of five-story towers that project out slightly, to close again on the upper floors. On the level of the rack railway station (ground level), a spacious entrance area with an entryway connects the exterior with the interior. The exhibition room, which can be accessed via the entryway, is home to information boards with the history of Mount Generoso and a model of the current building with plans and sketches drawn by architect Mario Botta. The service rooms are located on the first floor, a conference room that seats up to approximately 90 people is on the second floor, and the upper two floors contain a self-service restaurant (with access to the large terrace) and a refined upscale restaurant. The bearing structure is in reinforced concrete clad in grey natural stone with alternate smooth and split bands. The seemingly self-contained towers are interconnected by large glazed surfaces that afford 360-degree panoramic views—of the Po Valley around Milan to the south and Lake Lugano and the Alps to the north.

© LUCA FERRARIO

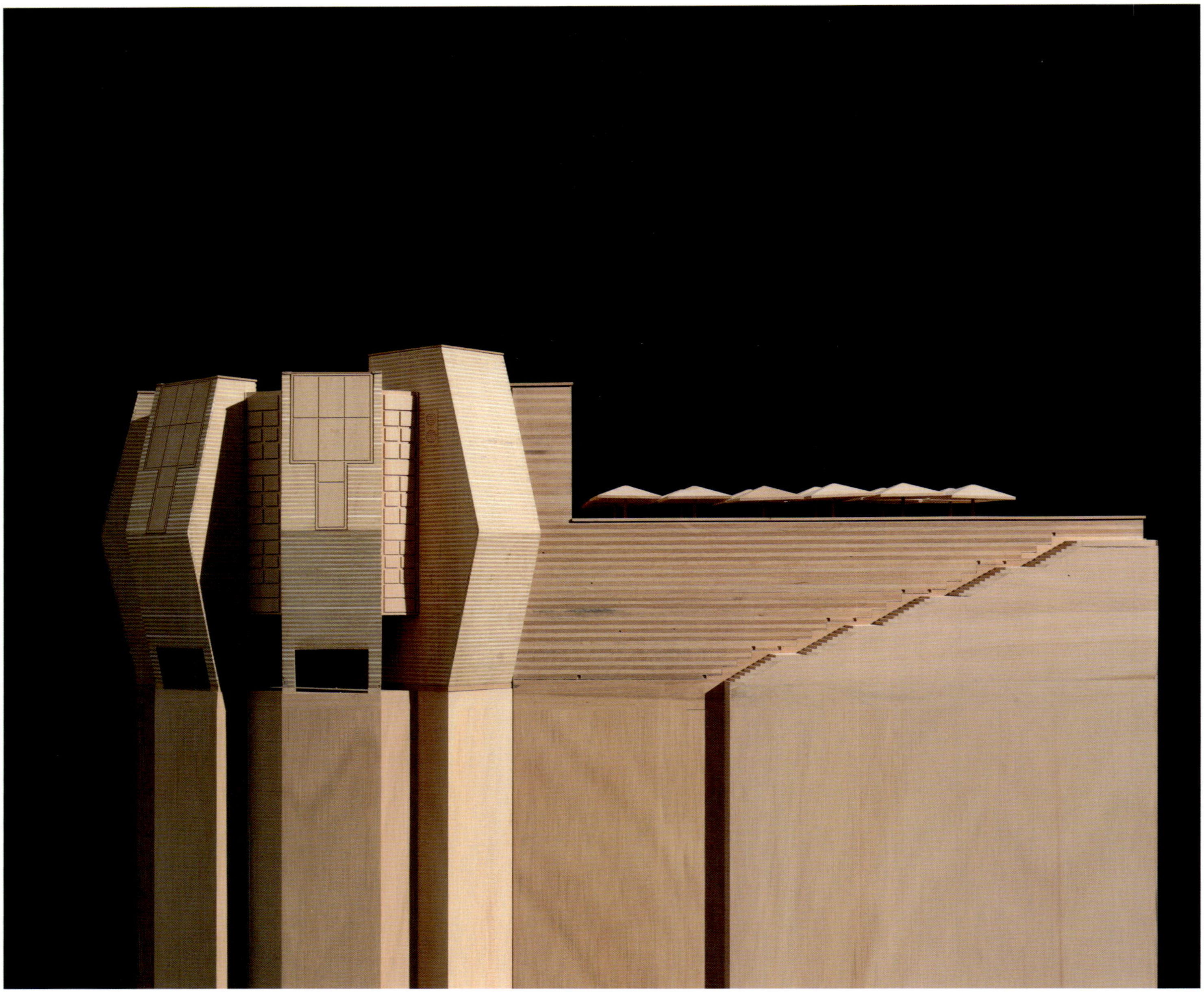

© ENRICO CANO

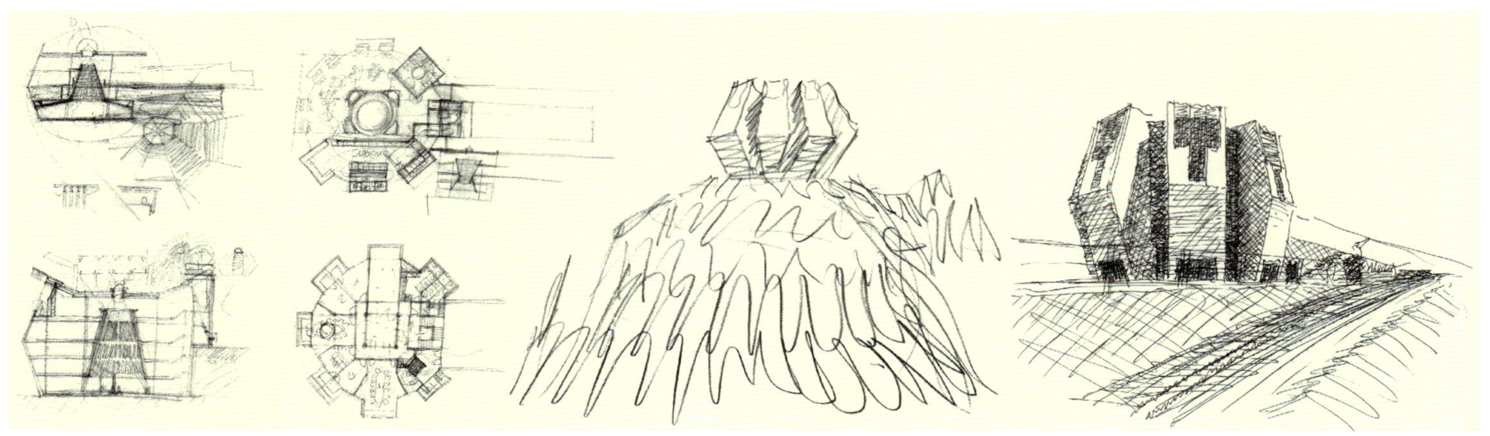

酒庄
WINERIES

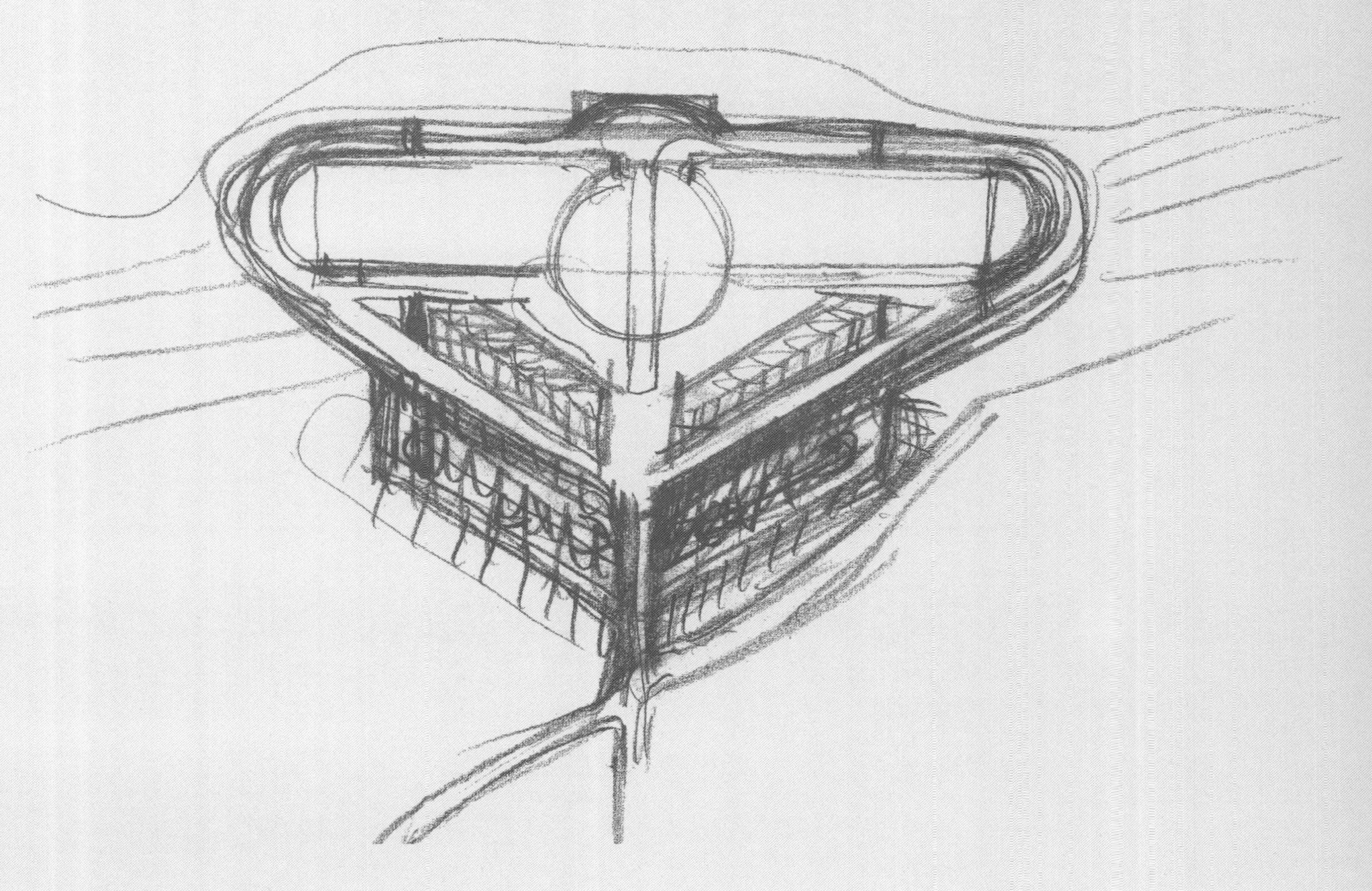

佩特拉酒庄

意大利，苏韦雷托

PETRA WINERY

SUVERETO, ITALY

1999-2003

项目时间：1999年
建造时间：2001~2003年
委托方：维多利奥·莫雷蒂
结构设计：意大利，布雷西亚，莫雷蒂建筑工业公司
占地面积：10,000平方米
使用面积：7,200平方米
建筑体积：63,000立方米
柱形体积：高25米，直径42米

Project: 1999
Construction: 2001-2003
Client: Vittorio Moretti
Structural design: Moretti Industrie delle Costruzioni, Brescia, Italy
Site area: 10,000 m^2
Useful surface: 7,200 m^2
Volume: 63,000 m^3
Cylindrical volume: height 25 m, diameter 42 m

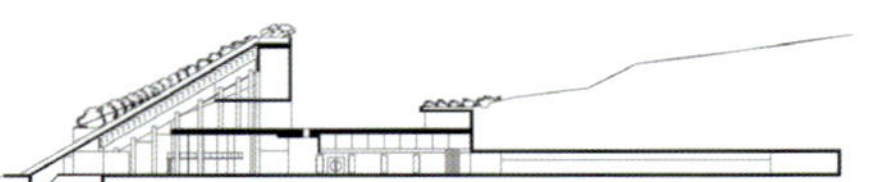

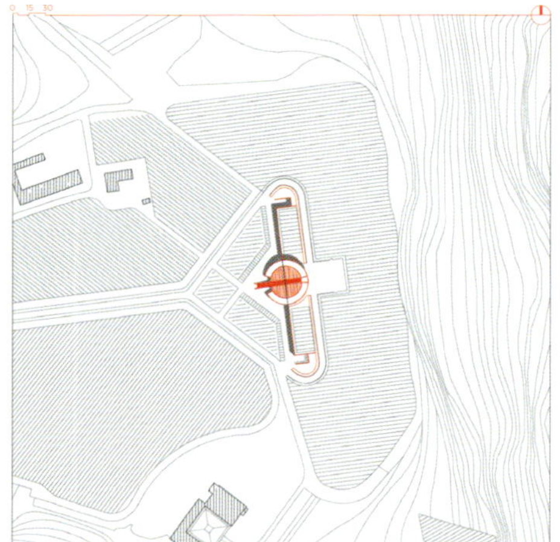

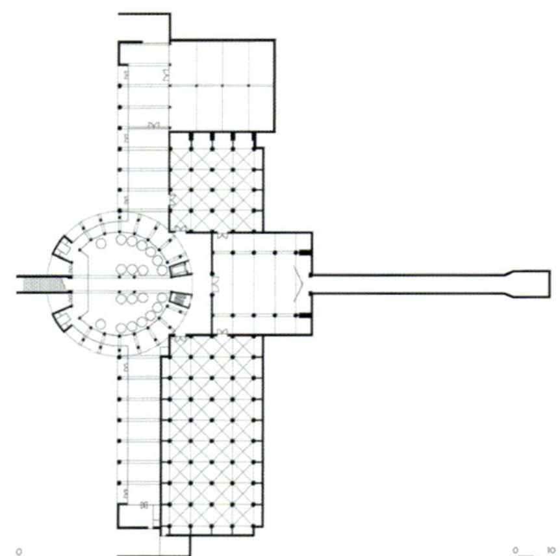

酒庄位于苏维莱托，托斯卡纳马雷玛地区一个田园诗歌般的地方。该酒庄以普兰石材料建造的圆柱体形式展现在游客面前，仿佛被一个平行于山坡的斜面切开，形成面朝大海的双翼。建筑像一个“巨大的花朵”立于山中，为此处的景观赋予了新的涵义。圆柱形建筑体内部设有接待处，压花钢发酵罐位于空间的中心，顶层用于葡萄的运输和压榨、葡萄酒罐装以及其他与葡萄酒生产及管控相关的活动。在一层中心区域和为橡木桶预留区的深处，有一条长长的隧道穿过山体并终止于岩壁，此处可供游客品尝葡萄酒。该隧道是通往山体中心的神秘通道，好似一条脐带将我们与大地母亲连接起来。

The winery is in Suvereto, an idyllic spot of the Tuscan Maremma. Petra presents itself to visitors as a cylinder in Prun stone, cut across by a diagonal plane set parallel to the slope, with two porticoed wings facing seaward. The building appears like a "big flower" extending over the hill and redefining the landscape. The cylinder houses the reception activities and has at its centre the embossed steel fermentation tanks. Its top floors host the areas for the delivery and the pressing of the grapes, the bottling of wine and all the activities related to the production and the controls. On the ground floor, in the depths beyond the central area and the space reserved for the oak barrels, a long tunnel pierces the hill ending in front of a rock wall, where a tasting area for visitors has been arranged. The tunnel is a mysterious path that leads to the centre of the mountain, an umbilical cord that connects us with Mother Earth.

© ENRICO CANO

© ENRICO CANO

© ENRICO CANO

© PINO MUSI

© PINO MUSI

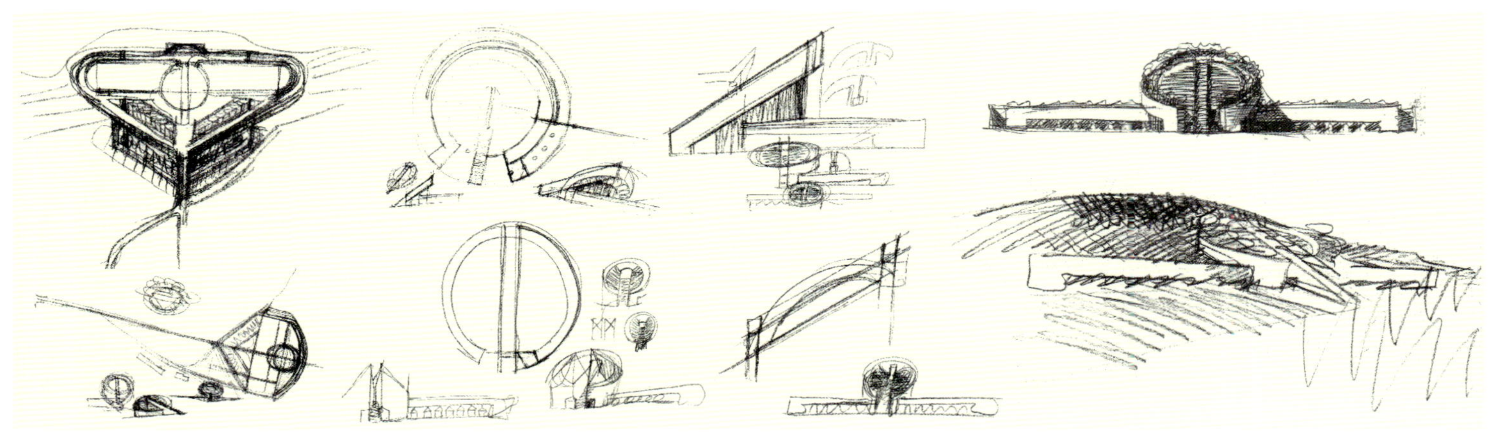

蒙库切托酒庄

瑞士，卢加诺

WINERY MONCUCCHETTO

LUGANO, SWITZERLAND

2005-2010

项目时间：2005年
建造时间：2007～2010年
委托方：莉塞塔和尼科洛·卢基尼
占地面积：18,164平方米
使用面积：酒庄1,300平方米，建筑500平方米
建筑体积：酒庄6,000立方米，建筑2,400立方米

Project: 2005
Construction: 2007-2010
Client: Lisetta and Niccolò Lucchini
Site area: 18,164 m^2
Useful surface: winery 1,300 m^2 / house 500 m^2
Volume: winery 6,000 m^3 / house 2,400 m^3

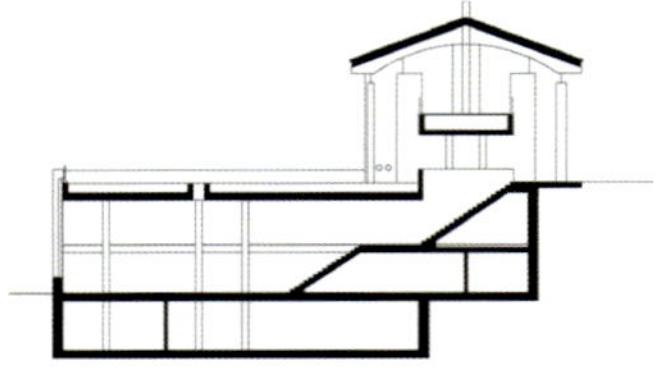

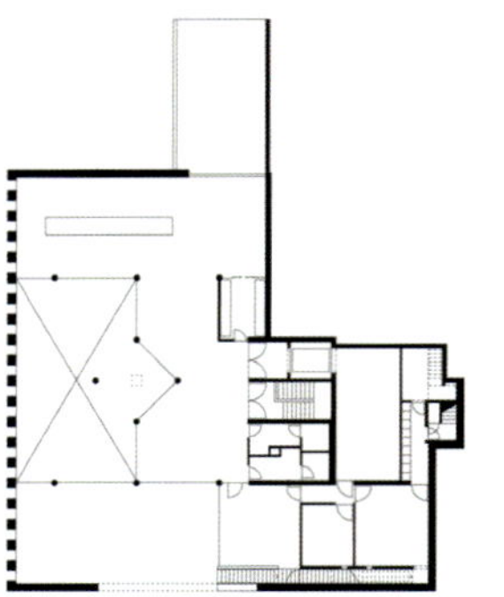

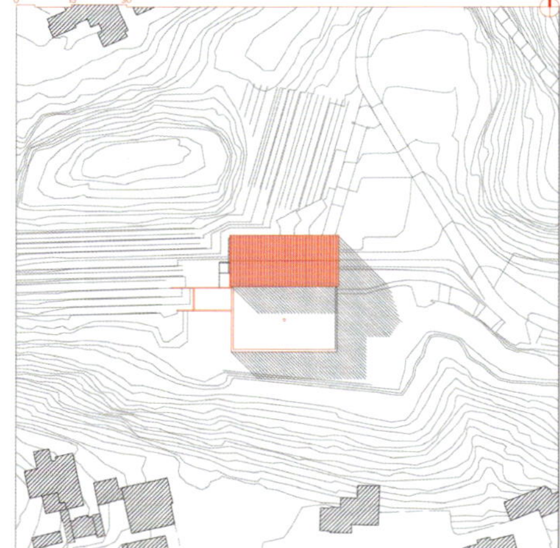

酒庄坐落在卢加诺市内的蒙库切托山上，这里原本只是一间古老的农舍，现在农舍的一部分融入新的建筑结构之中，旨在创造建筑与环境之间的全新平衡。项目分为2个部分：位于地面之上的建筑有着与古老农舍相同的曲面瓷砖屋顶，地面以下则是三层酒庄（上层设有品尝室和厨房，中间层包含葡萄酒成品区和管理员宿舍，底层则是技术用房和木桶储藏室）。面向山谷的外墙从地面中显露出来，仿佛一具石头基座。酒庄入口前的方形广场地面用花岗岩铺就，作为卸货区域，主要用于开展与酒庄运行相关的所有活动。

The winery is in the innermost part of the city of Lugano, on the hill Moncucchetto. It is where an old farmhouse - now partly integrated in the new construction - once stood. The project aimed at establishing a new balance between the construction and the environment. The project is divided into two parts: the house that rises above ground and has the same curved tiled-roof as the old house and the winery that is underground and is organized on three levels (the upper part with the tasting room and the kitchen, the middle part with the wine production area and the keeper's apartment, the lower part with the technical rooms and the barrels stockrooms). The façade towards the valley emerges from the ground and appears as a stone socle. In front of the entrance to the winery a big square paved with granite serves as loading dock for all the activities linked to the functioning of the winery.

© ENRICO CANO

© ENRICO CANO

© ENRICO CANO

© ENRICO CANO

© ENRICO CANO

© ENRICO CANO

© ENRICO CANO

富爵酒庄

法国，圣埃米利翁

CHÂTEAU FAUGÈRES

ST.EMILION, FRANCE

2005-2009

项目时间：2005～2006年
建造时间：2007～2009年
合作建筑师：法国，利布尔纳埃，布雷建筑社，塞吉·兰萨洛
委托方：富爵酒庄
占地面积：32,625平方米
使用面积：3,500平方米

Project: 2005-2006
Construction: 2007-2009
Partner: arch. Serge Lansalot, agency Epure, Libourne, France
Client: Sarl Château Faugères
Site area: 32,625 m^2
Useful surface: 3,500 m^2

酒庄位于波尔多地区圣埃米利翁附近起伏的山峦上，这里有大片葡萄园向游客开放，葡萄藤整齐地排列在耕犁过的土地上。酒庄以条理性和简约为特征，建筑结构露出很大一部分石质基座。一层是踩榨葡萄汁的区域，地下部分则用来生产及陈酿葡萄酒。一座塔楼矗立在建筑中部，以规则的开口为显著特征，内部设有行政服务空间和舒适的葡萄酒品尝区。在顶层，一个面向东南的覆顶式露台可俯瞰整个村落。天然黄色石质外墙勾勒出建筑的几何轮廓。

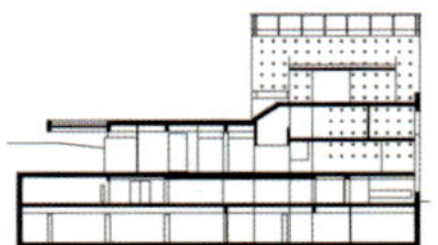

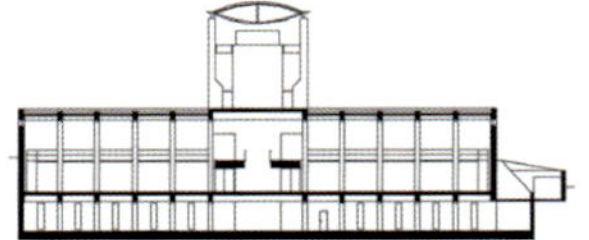

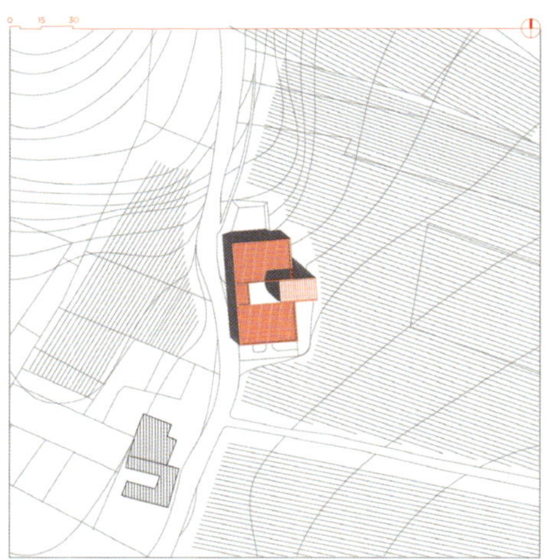

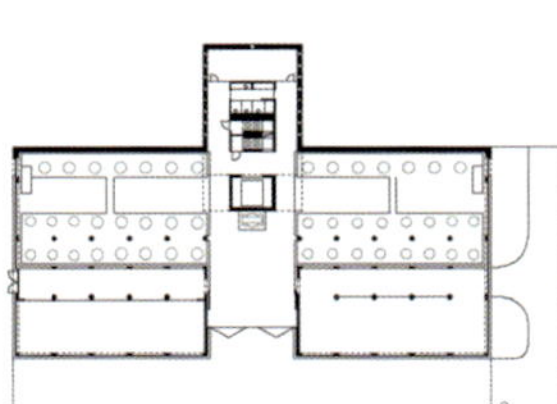

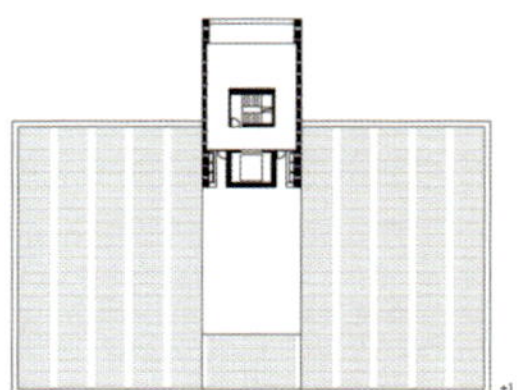

Situated atop the undulating hills near Saint Emilion, in the Bordeaux area, swathes of vineyards open out to the visitor in neat rows of vines rooted in the furrowed surfaces of the earth. Characterized by formal simplicity, the construction presents a big partly underground stone base. On the ground floor there is the area for the treading of the grapes while on the underground levels there are the areas for the production and the ageing of wine. A tower, characterized by a regular pattern of openings, rises up in the centre of the building. It houses the administrative services and a cosy space for wine-tasting. At the top, a covered terrace oriented towards south-east overlooks the countryside. The external facade in natural yellow stone accentuates the geometric outline of the composition.

© ENRICO CANO

© ENRICO CANO

© ENRICO CANO

© ENRICO CANO

© ENRICO CANO

© ENRICO CANO

© ENRICO CANO

设计
DESIGN

“布鲁门泽”台钟 (1995)	**450**	**WATCH “BLUMENZEIT”** (1995)
孟提亚・丹修道院挂毯 (1997)	**451**	**TAPESTRY FOR THE MONASTERY MOUTIER D’AHUN** (1997)
“马里奥・博塔”手表 (1998/2008)	**452**	**WATCHES MARIO BOTTA** (1998 / 2008)
13只花瓶 (1998/2001/2005/2012)	**453**	**13 VASES** (1998/2001/2005/2012)
国铁手表系列 (1995/1998)	**454**	**MONDAINE WATCHES** (1995 / 1998)
“我的&你的”壶具 (1997)	**455**	**JUGS “MIA & TUA”** (1997)
穆纳里玻璃杯 (2000)	**456**	**MUNARI GLASSES** (2000)
“特隆科”花瓶 (2001)	**457**	**VASE “TRONCO”** (2001)
移动剧院 (2004-2007)	**458**	**TRAVELLING THEATRE** (2004 - 2007)
“马里奥・博塔为凯兰帝设计”钢笔 (2004)	**459**	**PEN “MARIO BOTTA FOR CARAN D’ACHE”** (2004)
“美丽”桌 (2004)	**460**	**TABLE “BELLO”** (2004)
“壳”装置，意大利米兰三年展 (2007)	**461**	**GUSCIO, TRIENNALE DI MILANO, ITALY** (2007)
“桥”桌 (2008)	**462**	**TABLE “PONTE”** (2008)
马克杯组合 (2009)	**463**	**MUGS** (2009)
“沙漏”高脚凳 (2010)	**464**	**STOOL “CLESSIDRA”** (2010)
“安那托利亚” 毯 (2009)	**465**	**CARPET “ANATOLIA”** (2009)
“现成品” (2010)	**466**	**“BRICOLAGES”** (2010)
基因药房 (2013)	**467**	**REST FOR GENES GENETIC PHARMACY** (2013)
“莫雷拉托”椅 (2013)	**468**	**CHAIR “MORELATO”** (2013)
“吉欧”花瓶 (2014)	**469**	**VASE “GEO”** (2014)
凯兰帝铅笔 (2014)	**470**	**FIXPENCIL CARAN D’ACHE** (2014)
“胜利”喷泉，意大利之胜利 (2016)	**471**	**FONTANA “VITTORIALE”, VITTORIALE DEGLI ITALIANI** (2016)

“一号”椅和“二号”椅
CHAIRS “PRIMA” AND “SECONDA”

1982

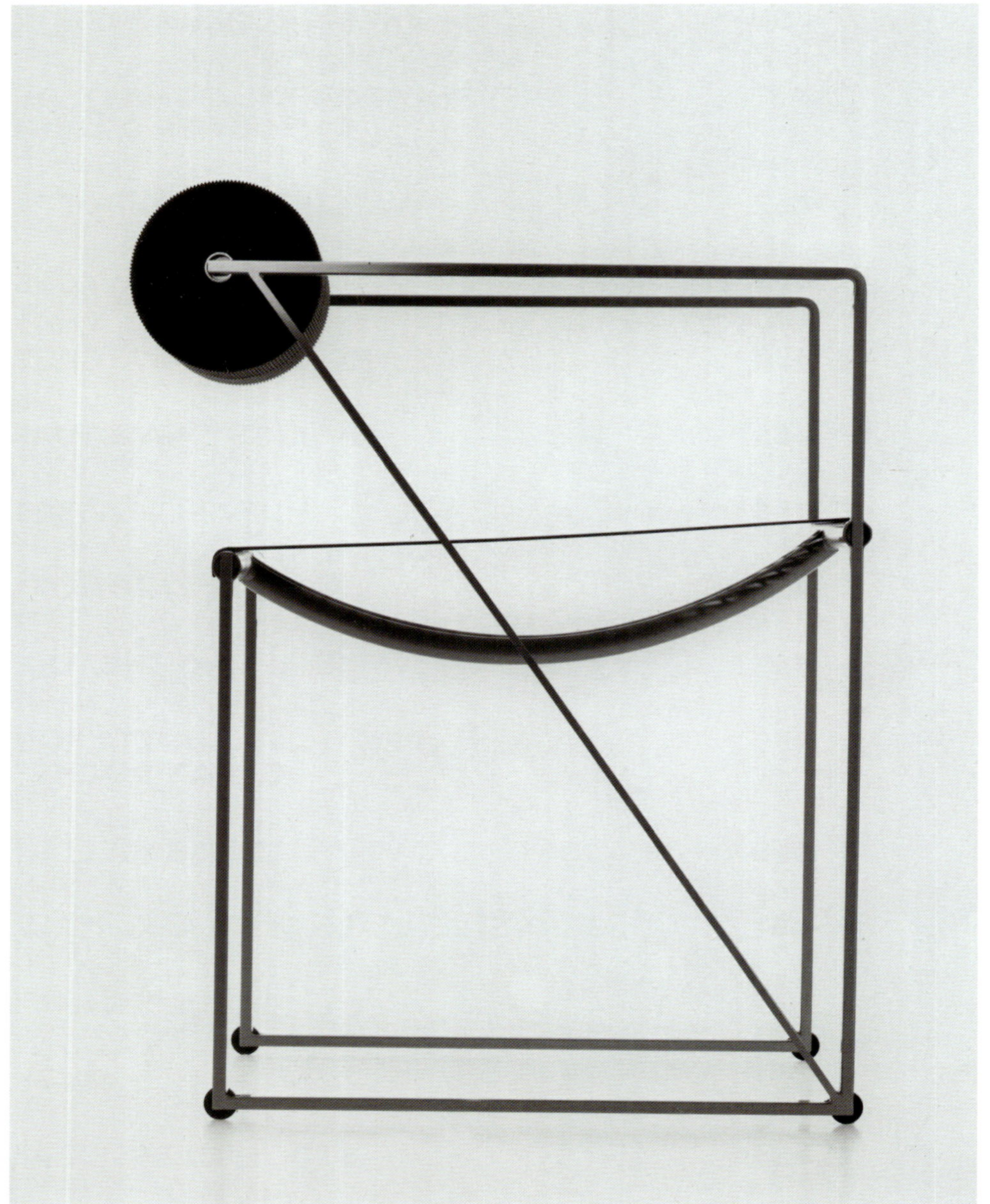

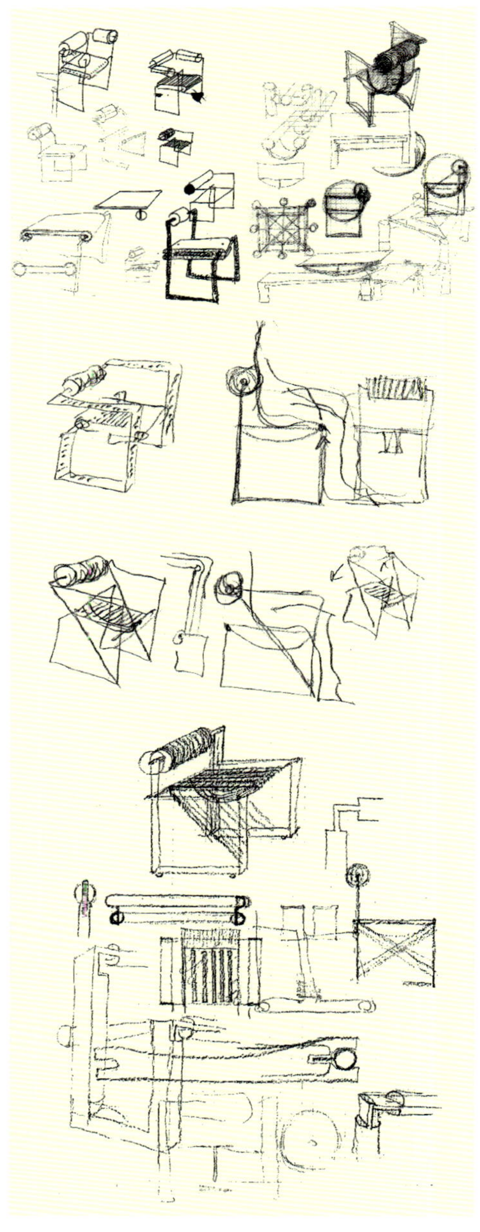

© ALDO BALLO

© ALDO BALLO

设计时间：1982年
生产时间：自1982年起
制造商：阿利亚公司
尺寸：48厘米×58厘米，高72厘米
重量：5千克
结构：钢管，银灰色或漆不透明的黑色环氧树脂涂料
椅面：银灰色或亚光黑色穿孔钢板
椅背：2个可旋转的黑色松软聚氨酯泡沫塑料圆柱体

Design: 1982
Production: since 1982
Manufacturer: Alias S.p.A.
Dimension: 48 cm × 58 cm, 72 cm H,
Weight: 5 kg
Structure: steel tubing, metallic grey or opaque black epoxy resin coating
Seat: slotted steel plate, metallic grey or matt black
Back: two rotating cylindrical sections in soft black polyurethane foam

“三号”桌
TABLE “TERZO”

1983

© ALDO BALLO

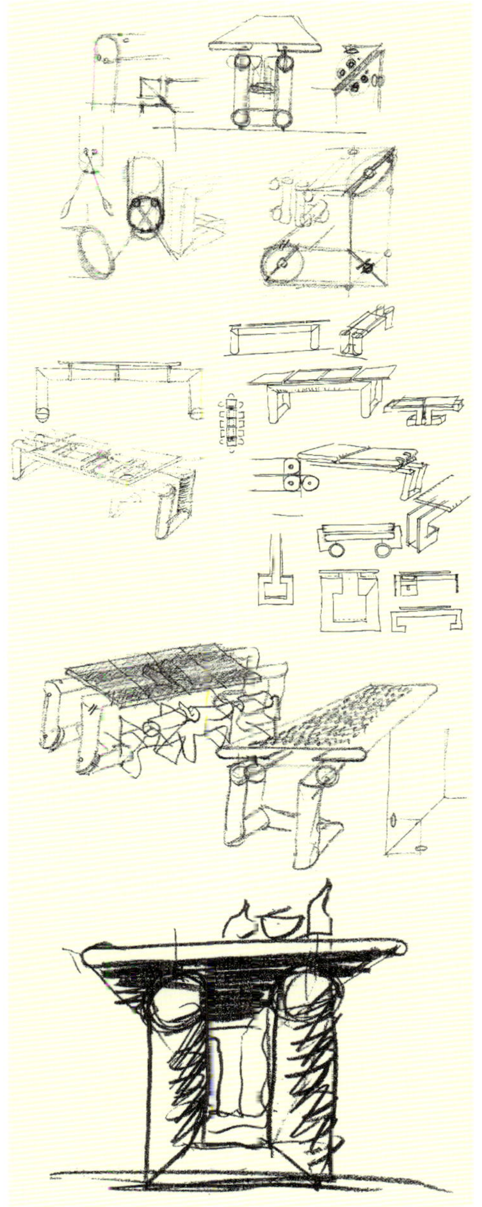

© ALDO BALLO

项目时间：1983年
生产时间：1983年
制造商：阿利亚公司
尺寸：长237厘米 × 宽86厘米 × 高76厘米，桌面长度189/237/299厘米
结构与材料：钢管，亚光黑环氧树脂涂层；12根黑色支撑细钢管，配可调节螺丝。
桌面：角砾岩、维罗那大理石或灰色片麻岩，实心金属基座（固定尺寸）支撑不同尺寸和石材的桌面

Project: 1983
Production: 1983
Manufacturer: Alias S.p.A.
Dimension: 237×86×76 H cm; top 189/237/299 cm
Structure and materials: Steel tubing, matt black epoxy resin coating; 12 small steel supports, painted black, with adjusting screw.
Top: “Breccia medicea”, Verona marble or grey Beola. The solid metal base (constant size) supports stone tops of different sizes and materials.

“四号”椅
CHAIR “QUARTA”

1984

© ALDO BALLO

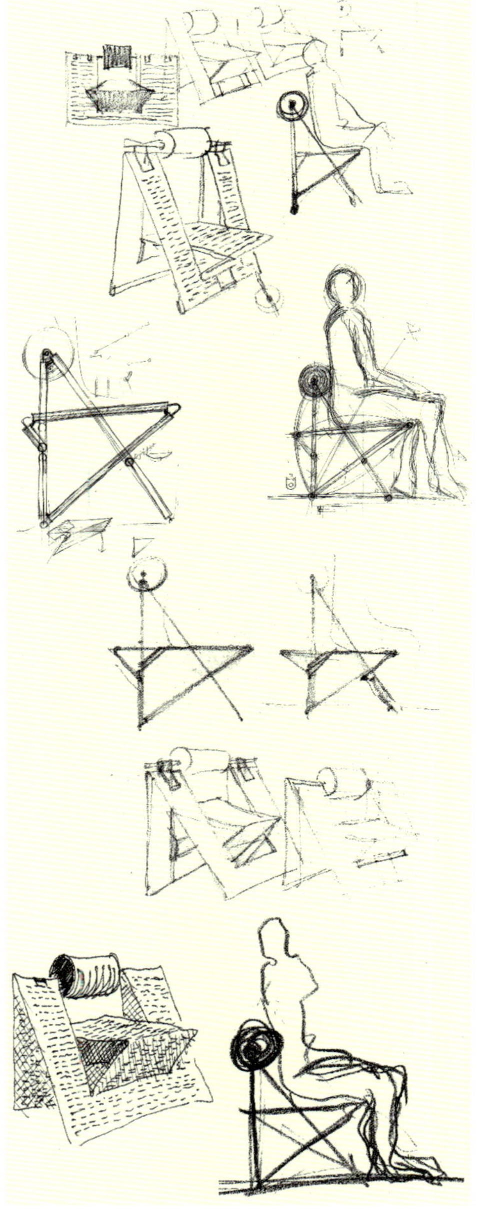

© MARIO CARRIERI

© ALDO BALLO

设计时间：1984年
生产时间：自1984年起
制造商：阿利亚公司
尺寸：98厘米×65厘米，高67厘米
结构：铝管，镀铬或黑色环氧粉末涂层的PVC垫片，黑色聚氨酯椅背

Design: 1984
Production: since 1984
Manufacturer: Alias S.p.A.
Dimension: 98 cm × 65 cm, 67 cm H
Structure: aluminum tubing with PVC spacers finished in chromium plate or black epoxy powder coating. Back in black polyurethane.

“壳”家具组合，为17届米兰三年展设计
“GUSCIO” (SHELL) DESIGN FOR THE 17TH TRIENNALE DI MILANO

1984-1985

© STUDIO 2000, LISSONE

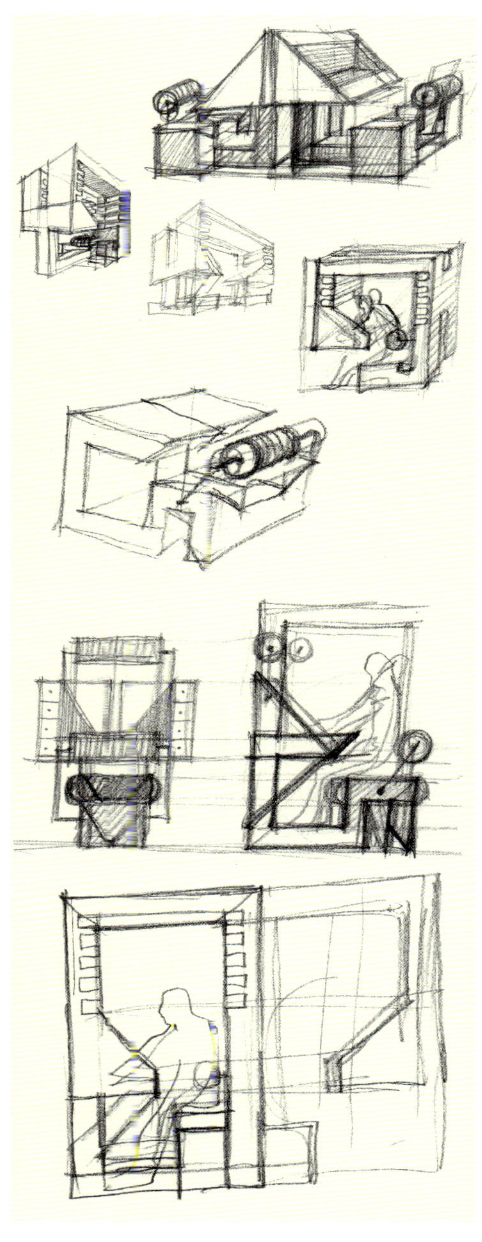

© STUDIO 2000, LISSONE

© STUDIO 2000, LISSONE

项目时间：1984～1985年
生产时间：1985年
展览：1985年2月第十七届米兰三年展
制造商：梅亚尼兄弟，利索内
尺寸：圆柱高226厘米，直径226厘米
材质：榉木板条

Project: 1984-1985
Production: 1985
Presentation: XVII Triennale di Milano, February 1985
Manufacturer: Fratelli Meani, Lissone
Dimension: cylinder 226 cm high and 226 cm in diameter
Material: spaced beech slats.

“五号”椅
CHAIR “QUINTA”

1985

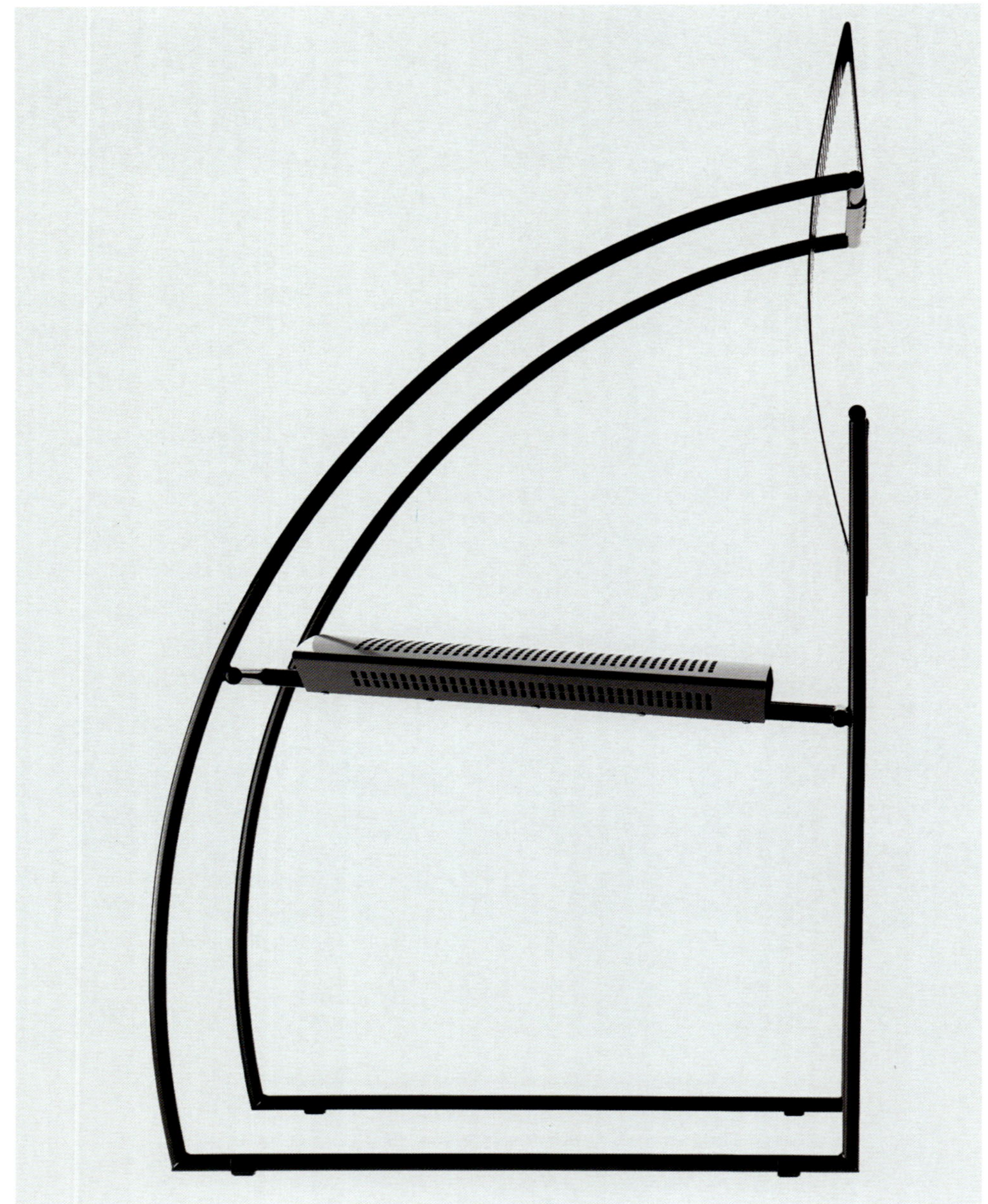

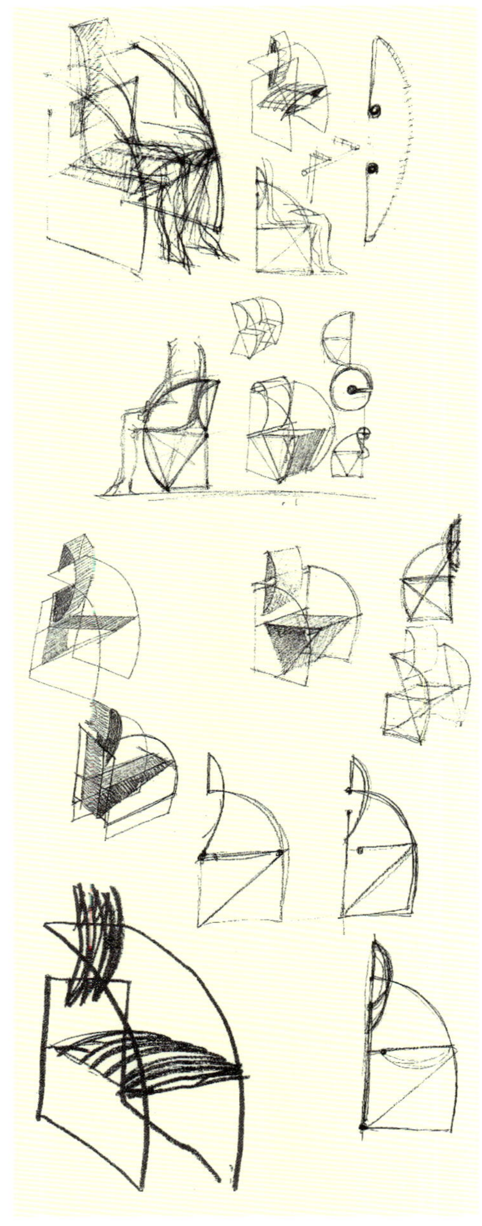

© ALDO BALLO

© ALDO BALLO

设计时间：1984年
生产时间：自1985年起
制造商：阿利亚公司
尺寸：45厘米×52厘米，高92厘米
结构：直径14毫米的喷漆钢管
椅背与椅面：薄喷漆金属，黑色或铜绿色

Design: 1984
Production: since 1985
Manufacturer: Alias S.p.A.
Dimension: 45 cm × 52 cm, 92 cm H
Structure: painted steel tubing 14 mm in diameter.
Seat and back: sheet metal painted either black or verdigris.

“六号”扶手椅
ARMCHAIR SESTA

1985

© PETER PAIGE

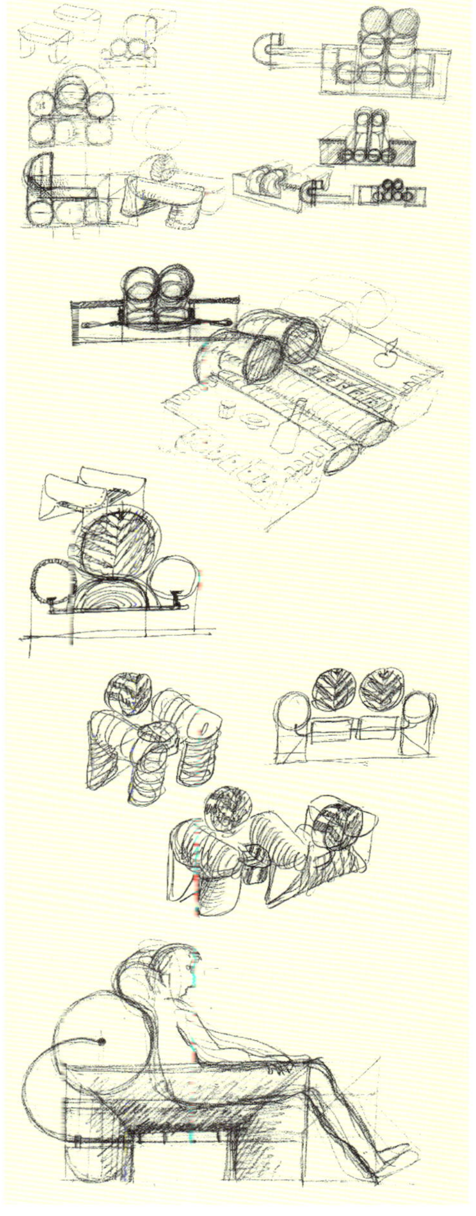

© ALDO BALLO

设计时间：1985年
生产时间：自1985年起（现已停产）
制造商：阿利亚公司
三种型号：王子、国王和王后、东方和西方
尺寸：100厘米×100厘米，高85厘米
结构：穿孔金属板
椅面与椅背：聚氨酯泡沫塑料，覆盖双色皮革

Design: 1985
Production: since 1985 (now out of production)
Manufacturer: Alias S.p.A.
Three models: Prince, King and Queen, East and West
Dimension (Prince): 100 cm × 100 cm, 85 cm H
Structure: perforated sheet metal.
Seat and back: polyurethane foam covered in two-tone leather.

“将军”灯具
LAMP “SHOGUN”

1985

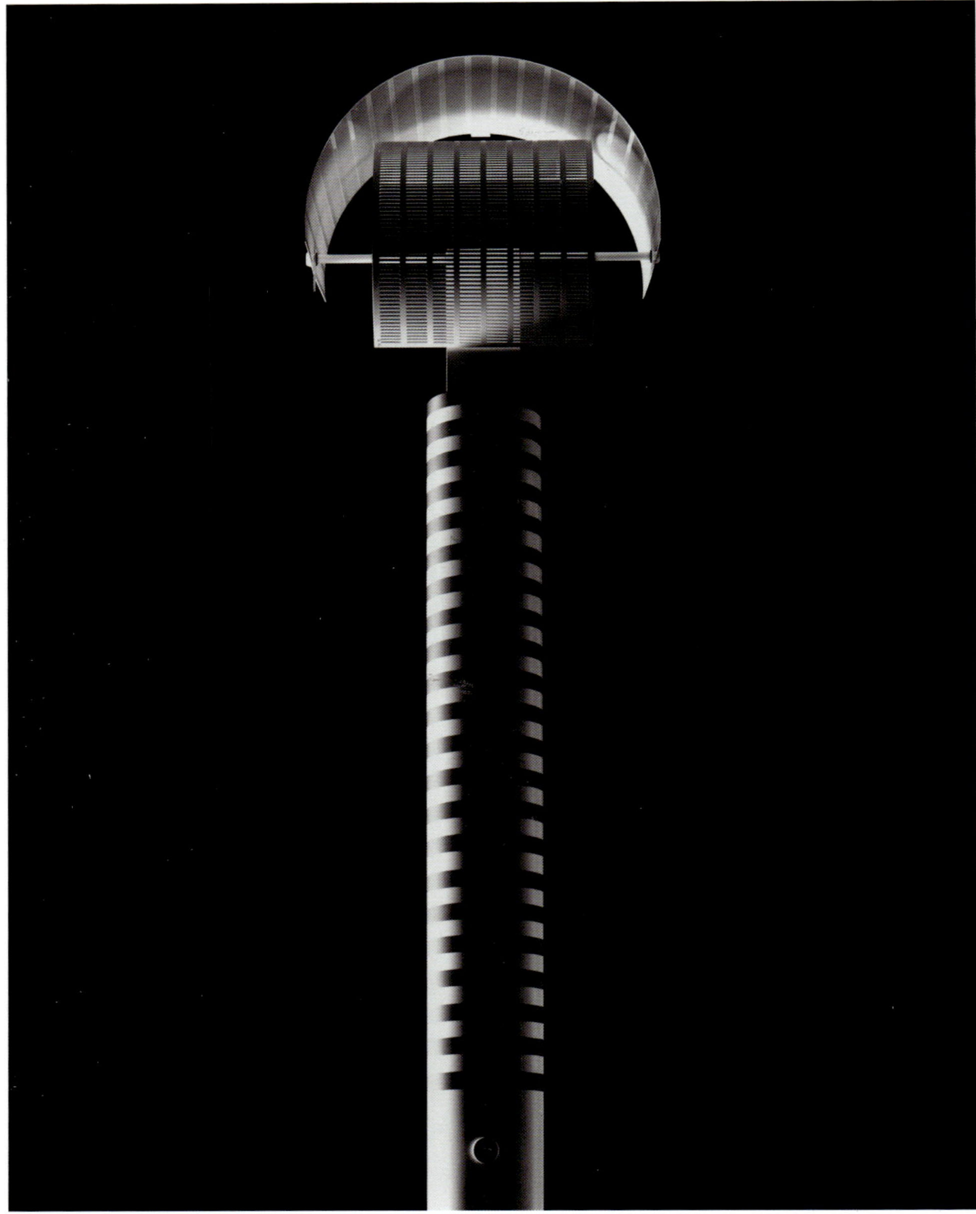

© GIASCO BERTOLI

© ALDO BALLO

© ALDO BALLO

设计时间：1985年
生产时间：1985年（现已停产）
制造商：雅特玥特照明
型号：三种型号，分为落地灯、桌面灯与壁灯
尺寸（落地灯）：宽33厘米，深16厘米，灯杆高183/226厘米
结构：白色喷漆穿孔金属薄板，白色喷漆铝制灯管

Design: 1985
Production: 1985 (now out of production)
Manufacturer: Artemide S.p.A.
Three models. floor, table and wall.
Dimension (floor model): width 33 cm; depth 16 cm; stem 183/226 cm H
Structure: white painted perforated sheet metal; stem in aluminum painted white.

双瓶组合一号
DOUBLE CARAFE 1

1985

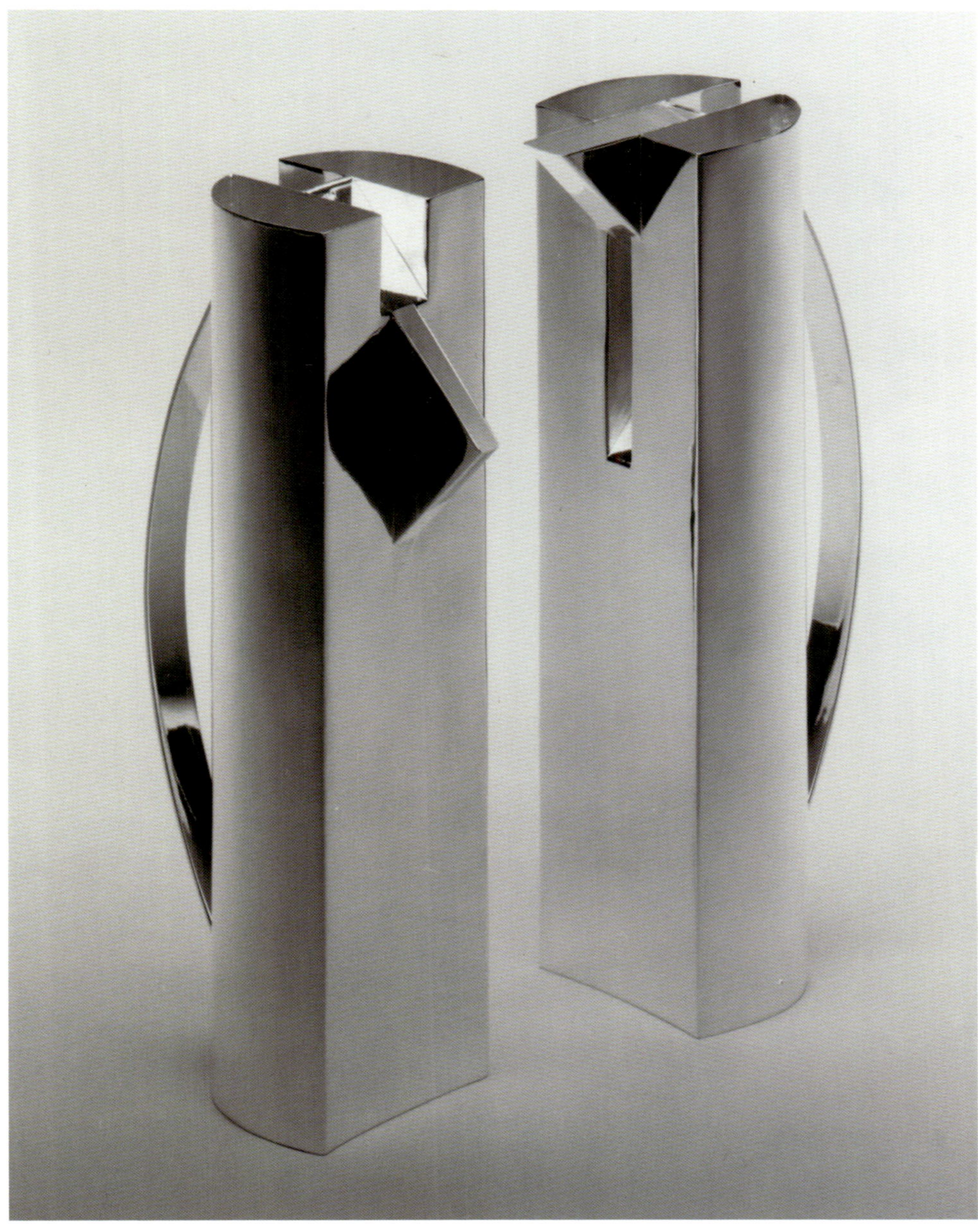

© CLETO MUNARI

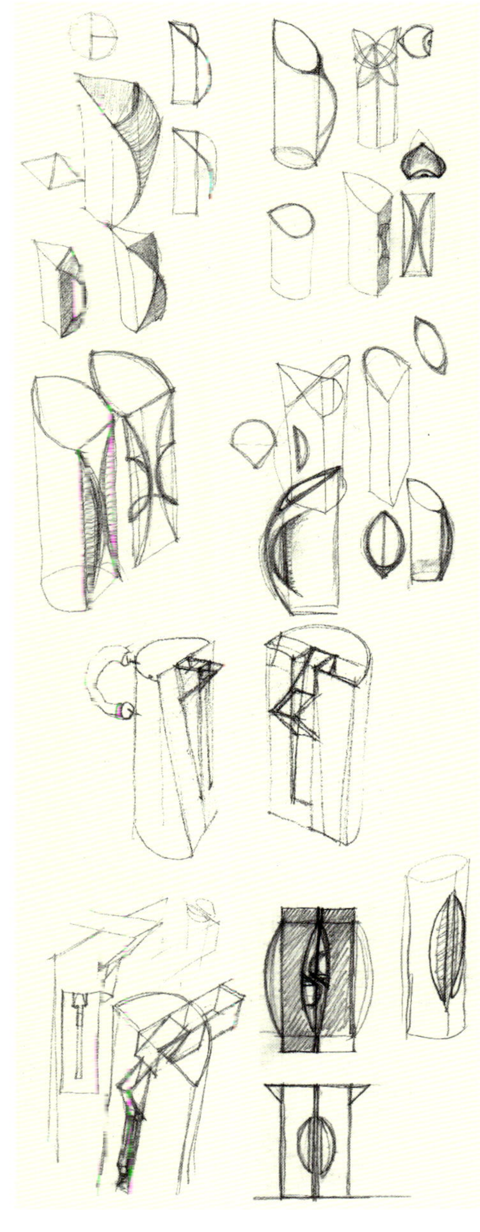

© ENRICO CANO

© ENRICO CANO

设计时间：1985年
生产时间：自1985年起
制造商：克莱托·穆纳里，意大利维琴察
尺寸：高30厘米，重1750克
材质：抛光银器

Design: 1985
Production: since 1985
Manufacturer: Cleto Munari, Vicenza
Dimension: 30 cm height, 1750g weight
Material: polished silver.

双瓶组合二号
DOUBLE CARAFE 2

1989

© CLETO MUNARI

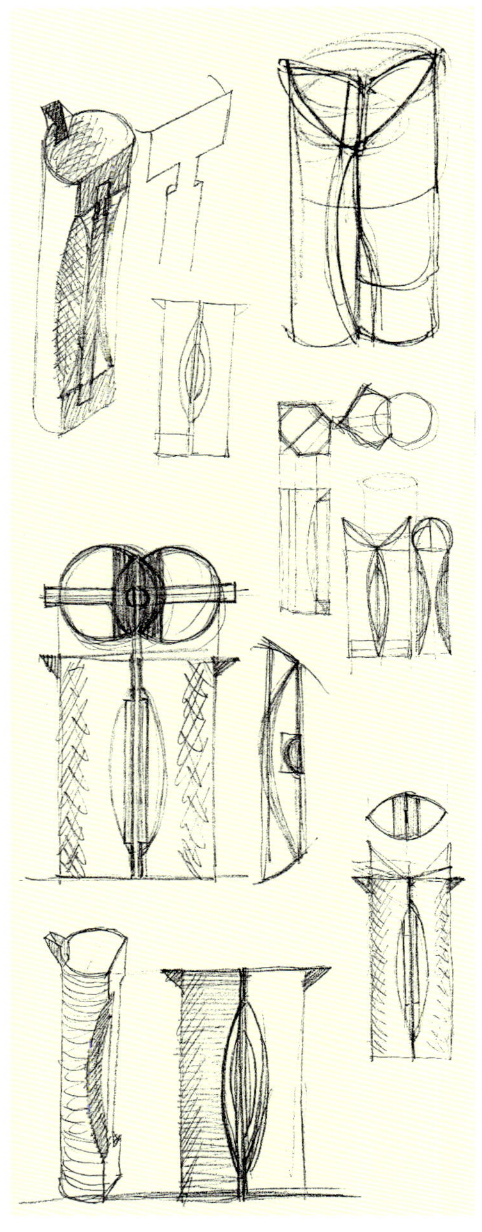

© ENRICO CANO

© ENRICO CANO

设计时间：1989年
生产时间：自1989年起
制造商：克莱托·穆纳里，维琴察
尺寸：高29厘米，重1950克
材质：抛光银器

Design 1989
Production: since 1989
Manufacturer: Cleto Munari, Vicenza
Dimension: 29 cm height, 1950 g weight
Material: polished silver.

“菲迪亚”壁灯
WALL LAMP “FIDIA”

1986

© MICHEL DARBELLAY

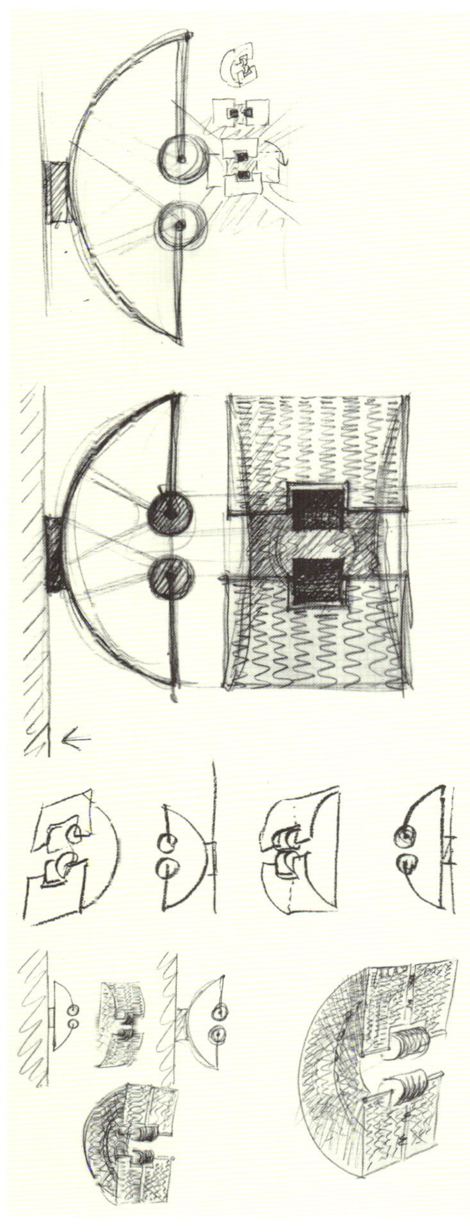

© ALDO BALLO

设计时间：1986年
生产时间：1987年（现已停产）
制造商：雅特[illegible]特照明
尺寸：26.5厘米×21.5厘米，高46厘米
结构：弧形白色喷漆穿孔金属薄板

Design: 1986
Production: 1987 (now out of production)
Manufacturer: Artemide S.p.A.
Dimension: 26.5 cm × 21.5 cm, 46 cm H
Structure: bent, perforated steel sheet, painted white.

“TESI”桌
TABLE “TESI”

1986

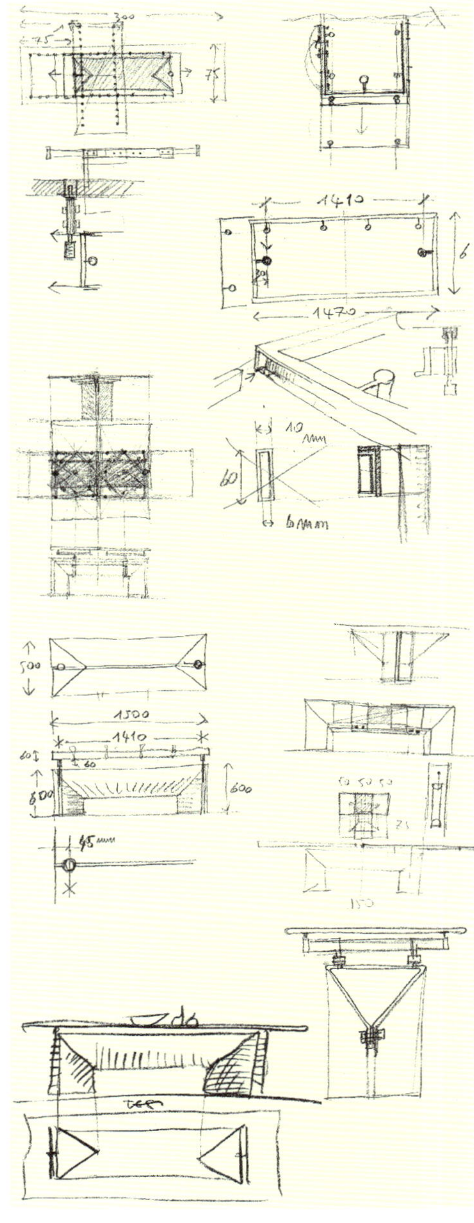

© ALDO BALLO

© ALDO BALLO

设计时间：1986年
生产时间：自1987年起
制造商：阿利亚公司
尺寸：桌面玻璃长180/240/300×宽86厘米，高74厘米
结构与材质：钢管结构，黑色或银色穿孔金属薄板，退火玻璃桌面

Design: 1986
Production: since 1987
Manufacturer: Alias S.p.A.
Dimension: length of glass top 180/240/300 × 86cm; 74 cm H
Structure and materials: tubular steel structure, perforated black or silver metal sheet; annealed glass top.

圈椅
CHAIR "LATONDA"

1987

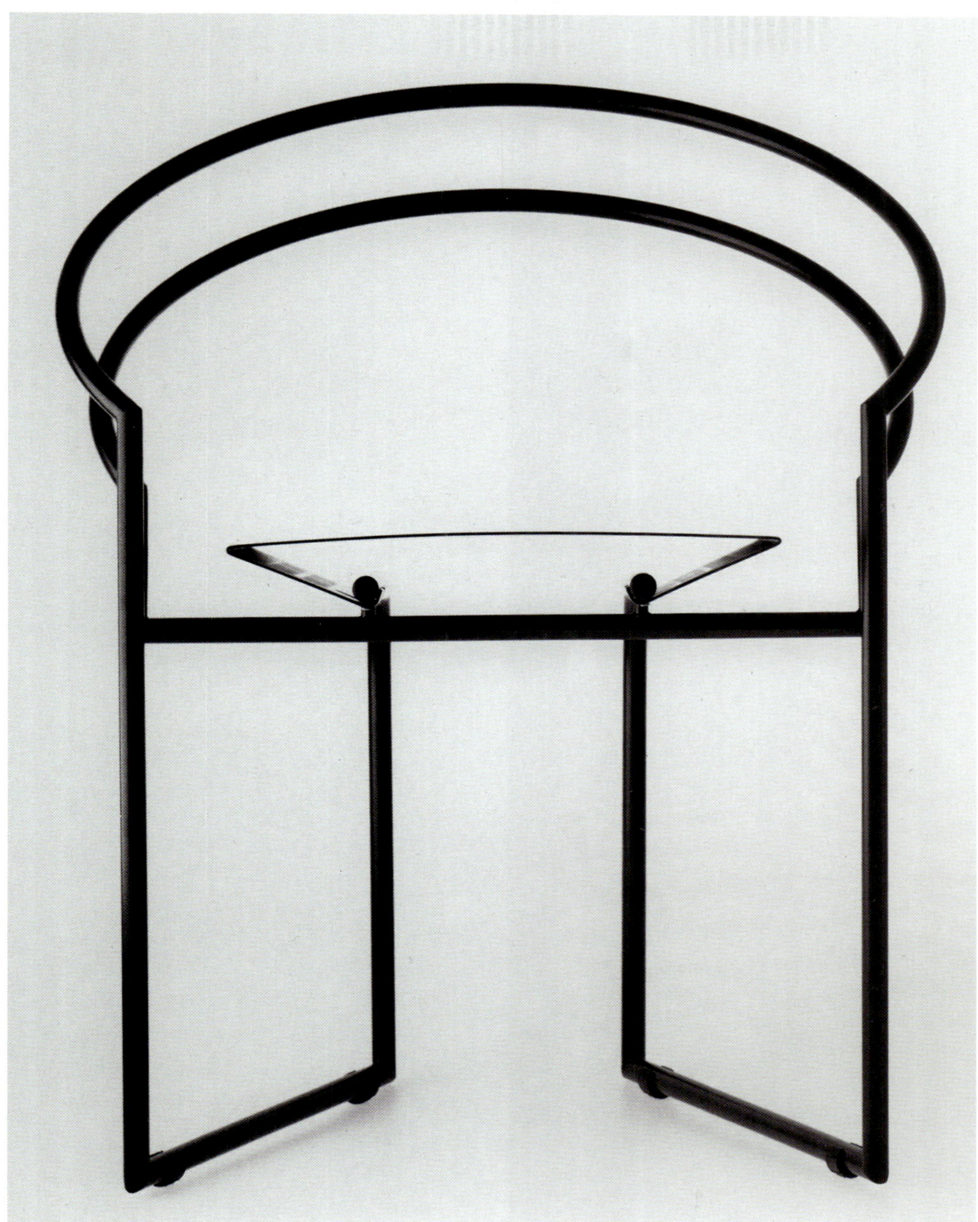

© ALDO BALLO

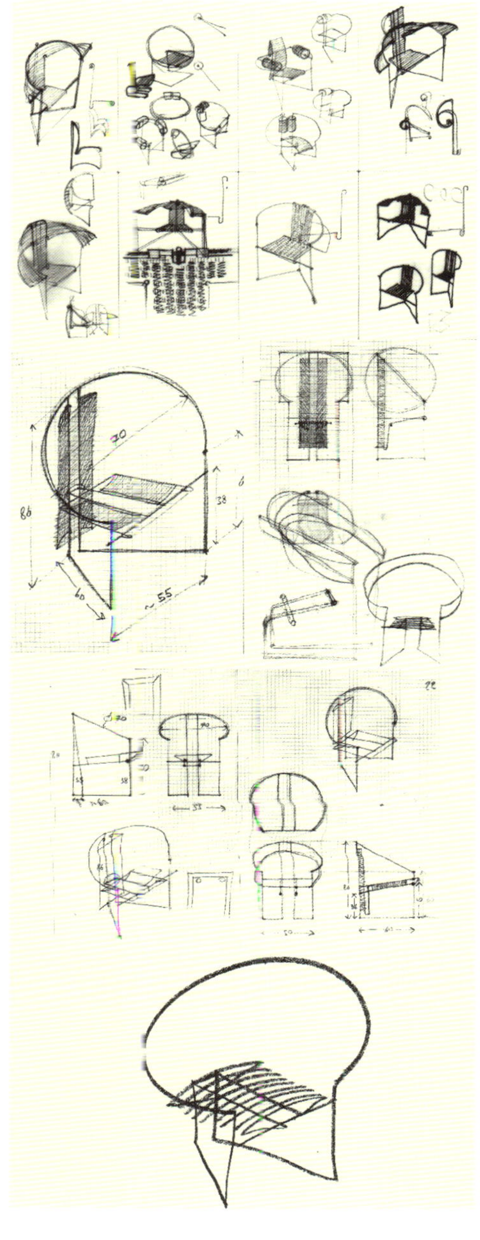

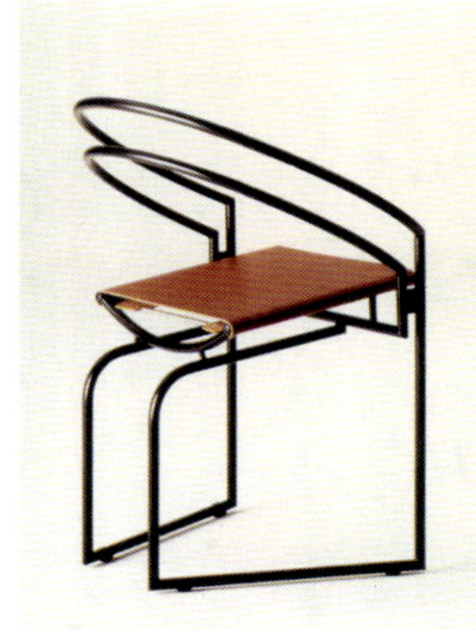

© ROBERTO SELLITTO

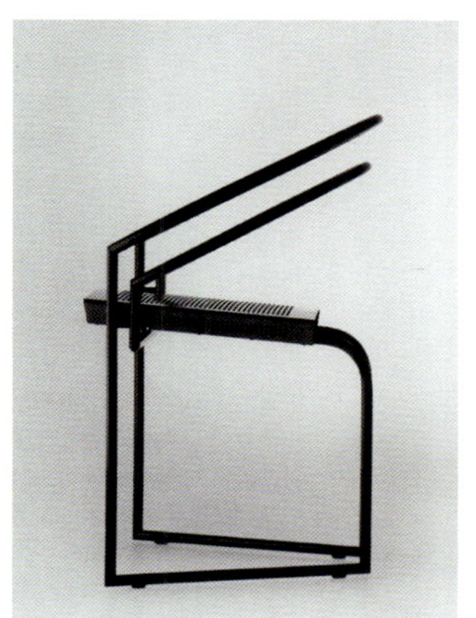

© ALDO BALLO

设计时间：1987
生产时间：自1987年起（现已停产）
制造商：阿利亚公司
尺寸：63厘米×48厘米，高47/77厘米
结构：黑色或银色喷漆钢管，黑色或铜绿色环氧涂层穿孔薄金属板座面，或红色或黑色皮革座面

Design: 1987
Production: since 1987 (now out of production)
Manufacturer: Alias S.p.A.
Dimension: 63 cm × 48 cm, 47/77 cm H,
Structure: painted steel in black or silver. Epoxy-coated perforated sheet seat in black or copper green; or in red or black leather.

"倾斜"单人沙发
ARMCHAIR "OBLIQUA"

1987

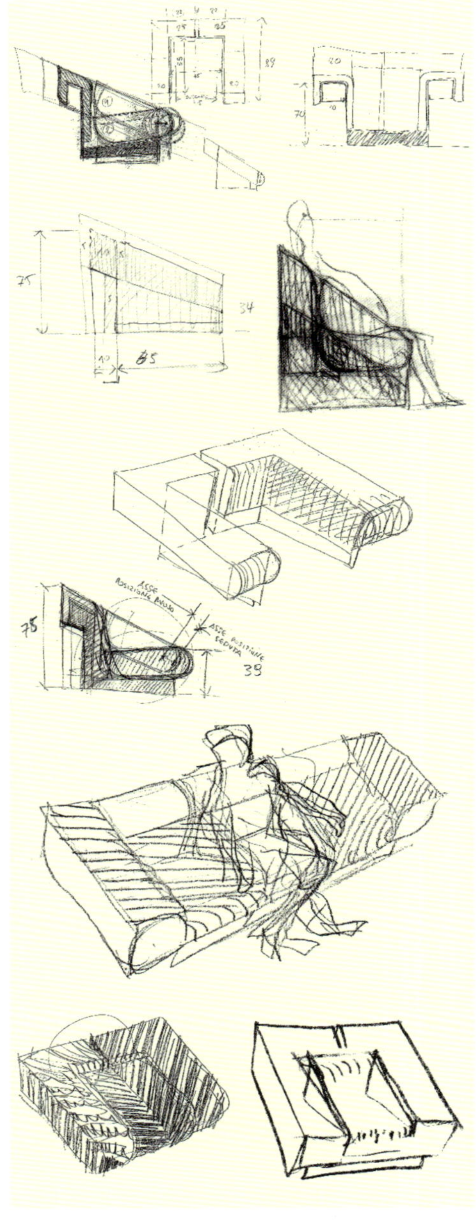

© ROBERTO SELLITTO

© ALDO BALLO

设计时间：1987年
生产时间：自1988年起（现已停产）
制造商：阿利亚公司
尺寸：88厘米×88厘米，高38/70厘米
结构：基座框架为高密度聚氨酯结构，表面涂覆聚氨酯清漆；椅面、靠背以及扶手可选择聚氨酯织物、麂皮或其他皮革；椅面部分可移动

Design: 1987
Production: since 1988 (now out of production)
Manufacturer: Alias S.p.A.
Dimension: 88 cm × 88 cm, 38/70 cm H
Structure: basic frame of structural polyurethane, pressed to high density and coated with polyurethane varnish. Seat, backrest, armrests in optional polyurethane fabric, shammy or leather. Movable seat.

“黑色”灯具
LAMP “MELANOS”

1986

© ALDO BALLO

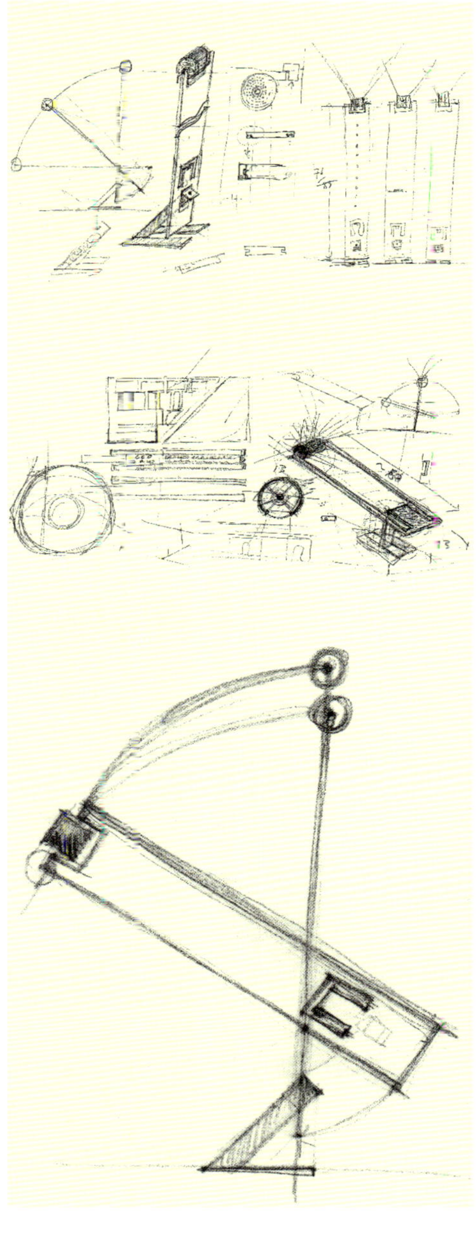

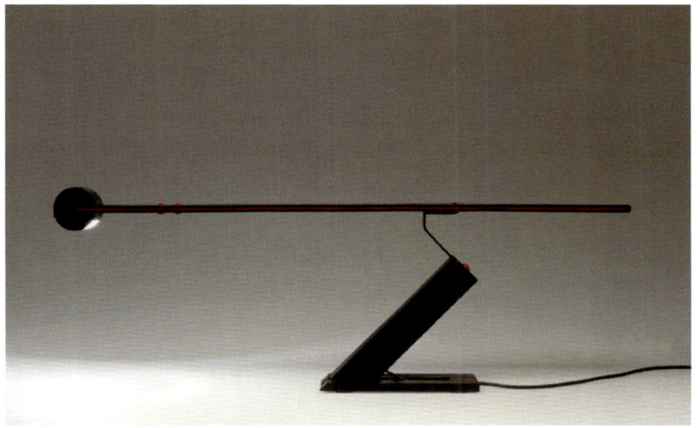

© ALDO BALLO

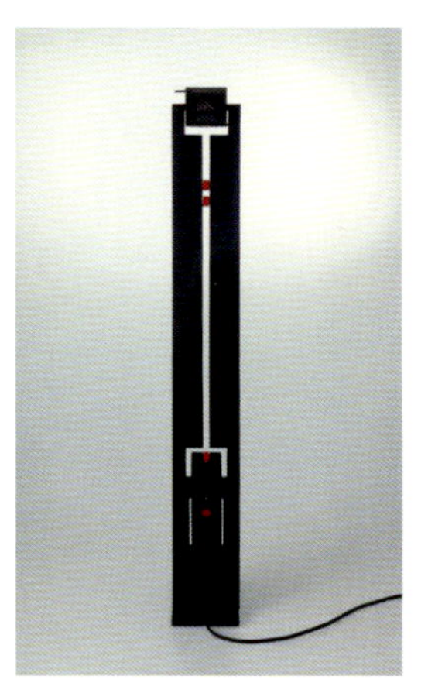

© ALDO BALLO

设计时间：1986年
生产时间：自1987年起（现已停产）
制造商：雅特明德照明
尺寸：可调节灯臂长度85厘米；最高高度86.5厘米
结构：黑色金属压铸灯臂，黑色瓷釉钢底座

Design: 1986
Production: since 1987 (now out of production)
Manufacturer: Artemide S.p.A.
Dimension: adjustable arm 85 cm, 86.5 cm max. H
Structure: lamp arm in black die-cast metal; base in black enameled steel.

“微风”灯具
LAMP “ZEFIRO”

1988

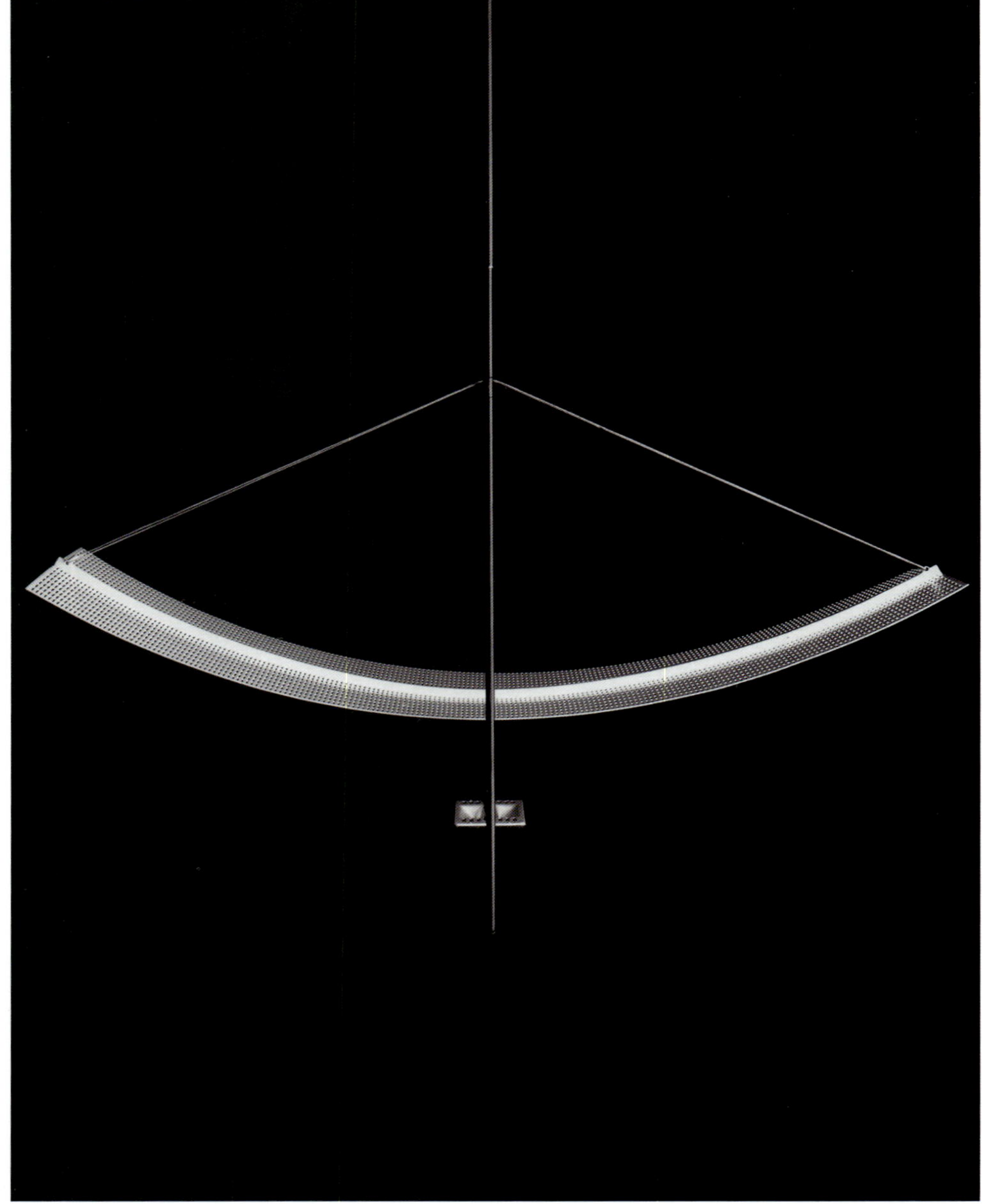

© GIASCO BERTOLI

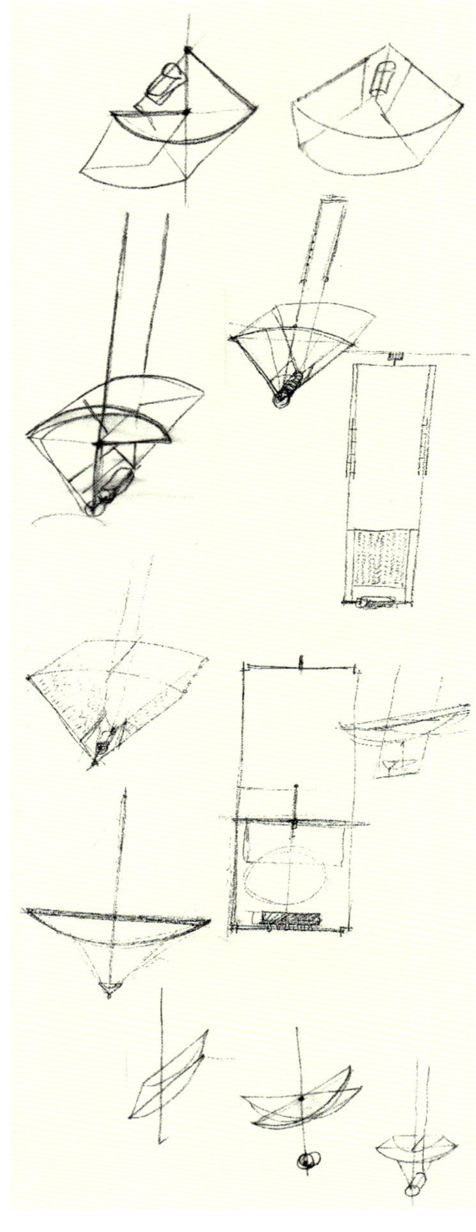

© ALDO BALLO

设计时间：1988年
生产时间：1988年（现已停产）
制造商：雅特明特照明
尺寸：90厘米×92厘米，高111厘米
结构：黑色钢管框架，白色穿孔金属板

Design: 1988
Production: 1988 (now out of production)
Manufacturer: Artemide S.p.A.
Dimension: 90 cm × 92 cm, 111 cm H
Structure: black tubular steel frame; white perforated metal sheet.

“博塔91号”椅子
CHAIR “BOTTA 91”

1989-1991

设计时间：1989年
生产时间：自1991年起（现已停产）
制造商：阿利亚公司
尺寸：宽52厘米，深53厘米，高84厘米
结构：黑色或镀铬钢管，真皮椅面和椅背

Design: 1989
Production: since 1991 (now out of production)
Manufacturer: Alias S.p.A.
Dimension: width 52, depth 53 cm, 84 cm H,
Structure: tubular steel with black or chrome finish. Seat and back in natural leather.

“机器人”抽屉柜
CHEST OF DRAWERS “ROBOT”

1989

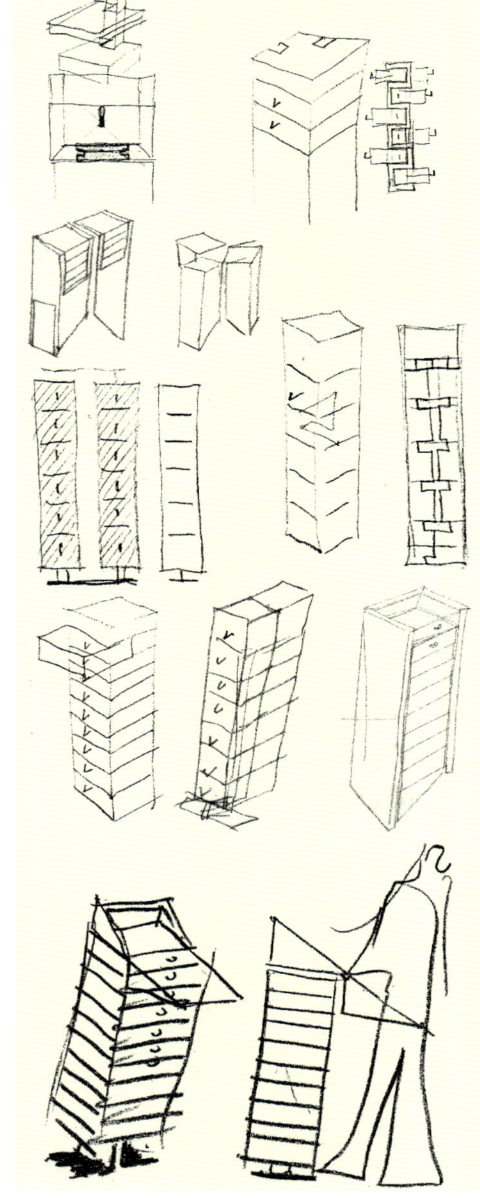

项目时间：1989年
生产时间：自1992年起（现已停产）
制造商：阿利亚公司
尺寸：35厘米 × 35厘米，高121厘米
结构和材质：支撑结构为黑色喷漆钢材，抽屉为黑色中密度木材或天然梨木

Project: 1989
Production: since 1992 (now out of production)
Manufacturer: Alias S.p.A.
Dimension: 35 cm × 35 cm; 121 cm H
Structure and materials: support structure in black painted steel, drawers in black painted medium density wood or natural pear wood.

“眼睛”手表
WATCH “EYE”

1989

© ALESSI

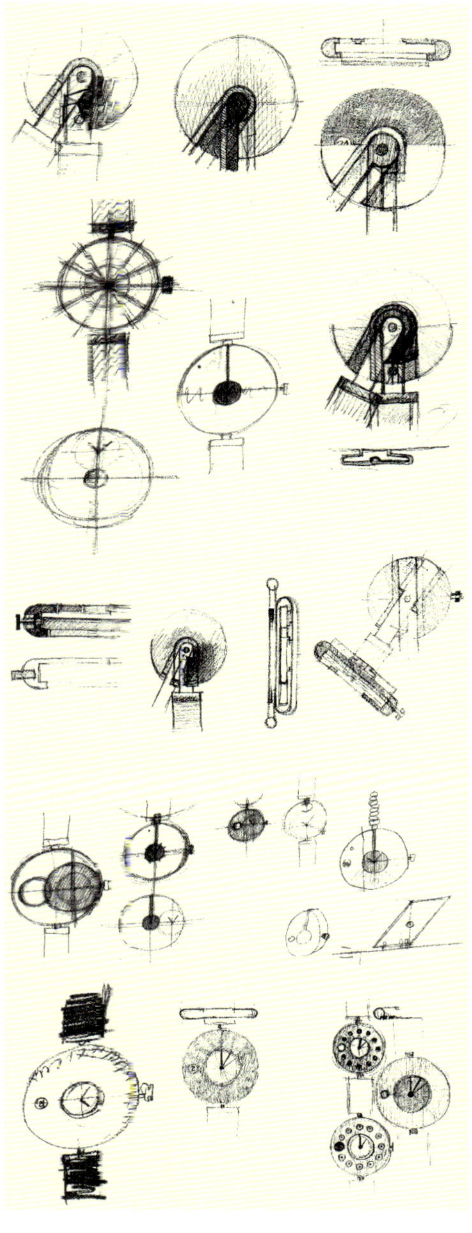

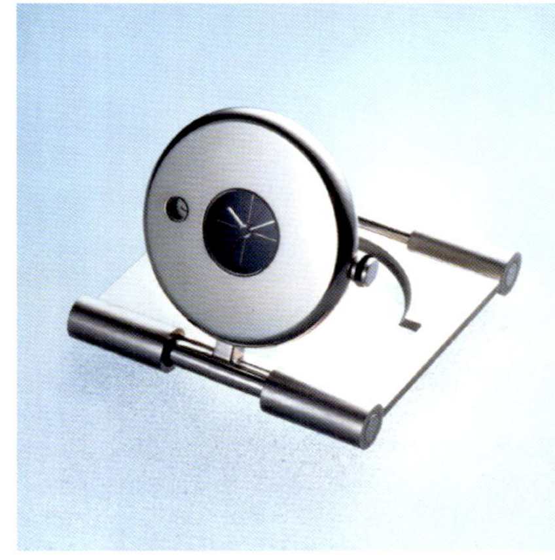

© ALESSI

© ALESSI

项目时间：1989年
生产时间：自1990年起
制造商：阿莱西公司
材料：钢，石英机芯，平玻璃罩面

Project: 1989
Production: since 1990
Manufacturer: Alessi S.p.A.
Material: steel, quartz mechanism, plate glass.

“大教堂”“483黑色”“483铜绿”“马伦扎”毯
CARPETS “LA CATTEDRALE” ,“483NERO”, “483 VERDE RAME”, “MARENZA”

1990

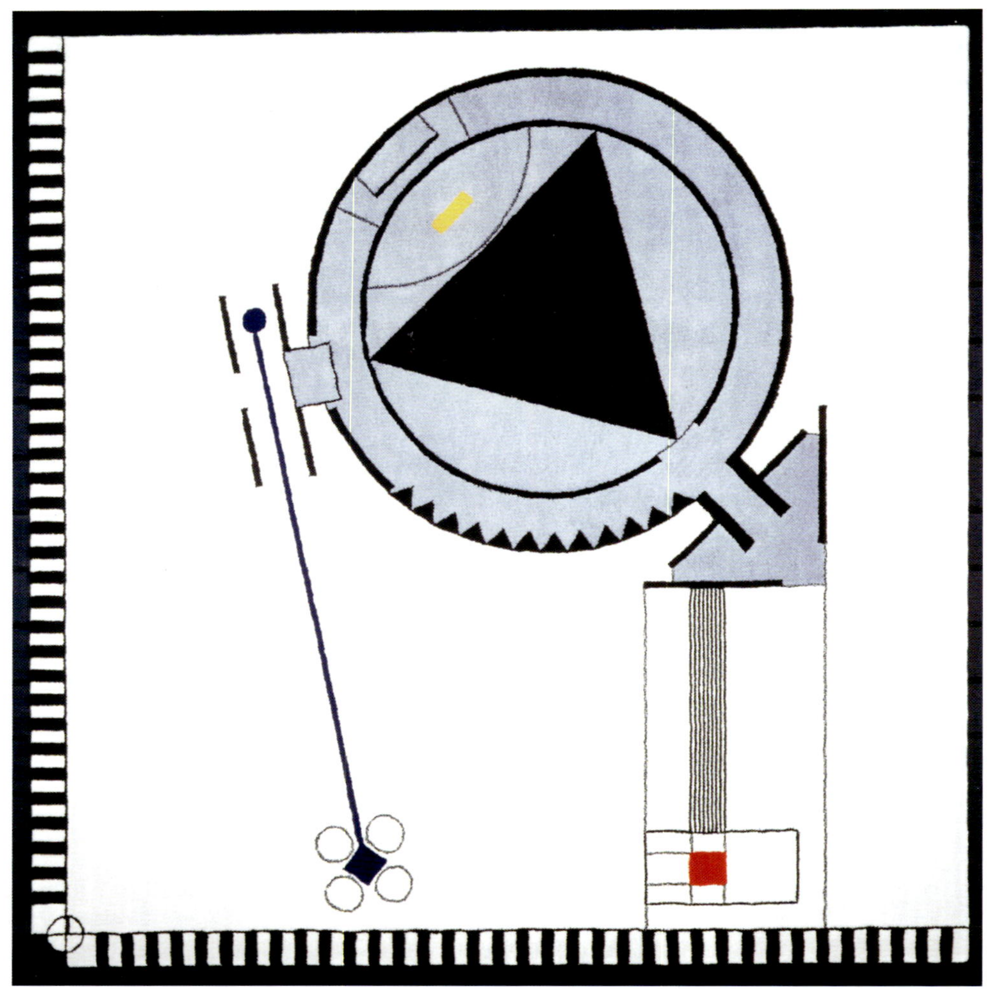

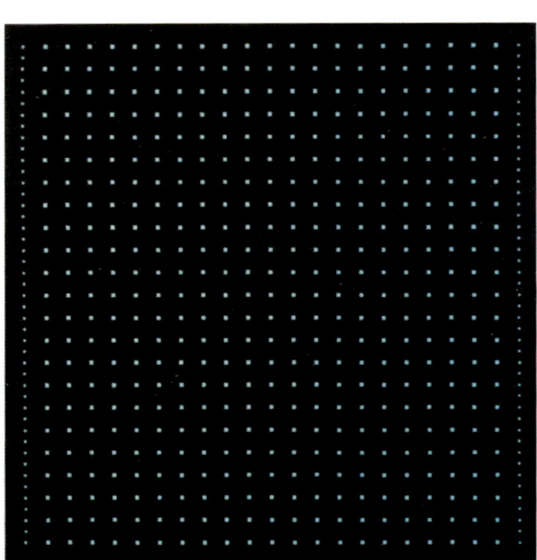

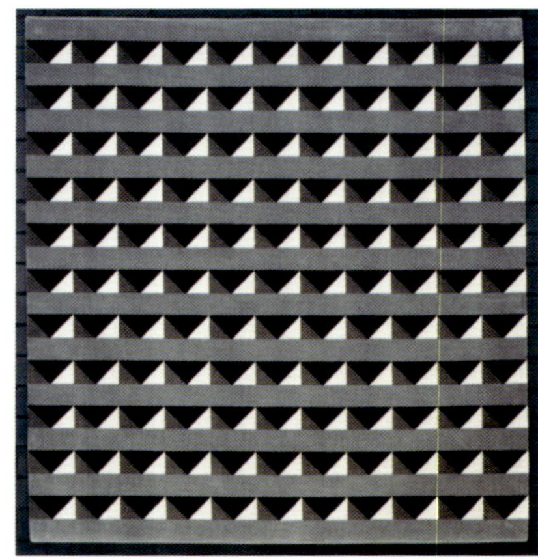

项目时间：1990年
生产时间：1991年
制造商：兰陶尔纺织股份公司，朗根塔尔
尺寸：“大教堂”245厘米×245厘米，“483黑色”“483 铜绿”“马伦扎”245厘米×250厘米
材质：威尔顿织羊毛，限量版

Project: 1990
Production: 1991
Manufacturer: Lantal Textiles AG, Langenthal
Dimension: “La cattedrale” 245 cm × 245 cm , “483 nero”, “483 verde rame”, “marenza” 245 cm × 250 cm
Material: Wilton weave wool. Limited edition

“尼拉·洛萨”屏风
SCREEN “NILLA ROSA”

1992

© PINO MUSI

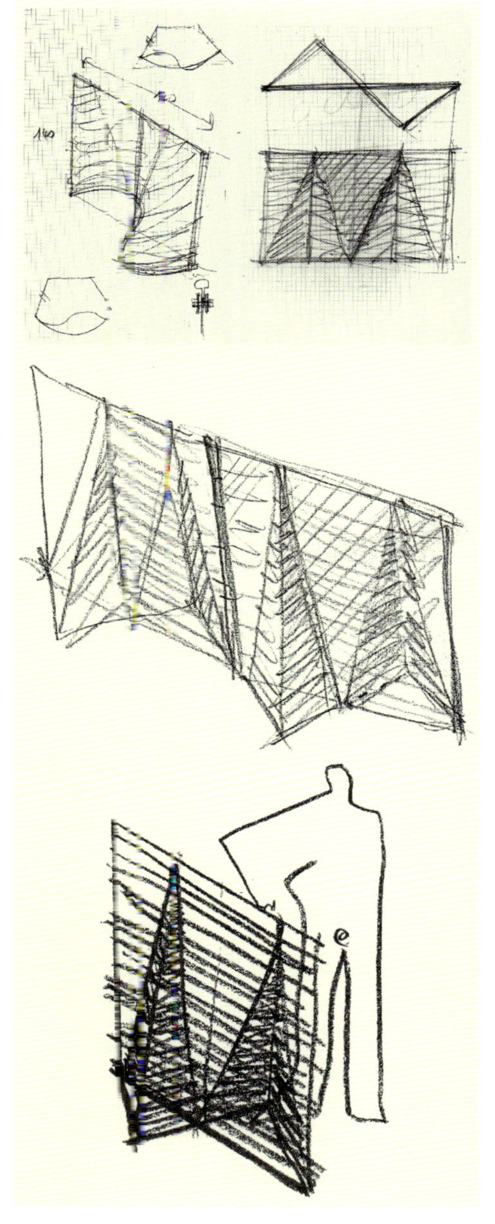

© PINO MUSI

项目时间：1992年
生产时间：自1992年起
制造商：阿利亚公司
尺寸：140厘米×70厘米，高140厘米
材质：涂黑色或铜绿色漆的冷拉钢板

Project: 1992
Production: since 1992
Manufacturer: Alias S.p.A.
Dimension: 140 cm × 70 cm, 140 cm H
Material: stretched steel sheet, painted black or verdigris.

花瓶
FLOWER VASE

1992

© MARCO D'ANNA

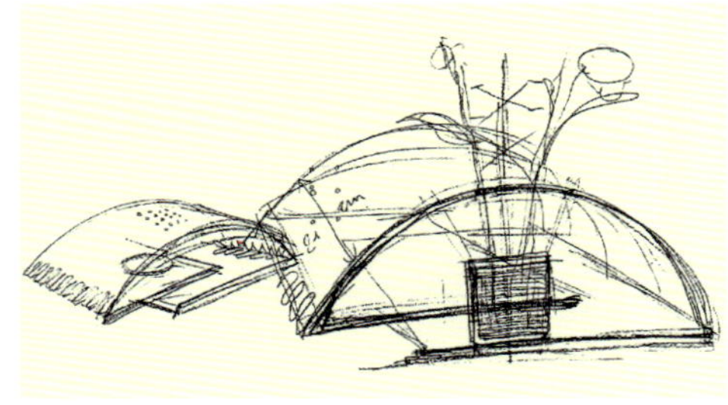

© MARCO D'ANNA

项目时间：1992年
生产时间：自1992年起
制造商：克莱托·穆纳里，维琴察
尺寸：18厘米×13厘米，高13厘米
材质：银板，水晶玻璃

Project: 1992
Production: since 1992
Manufacturer: Cleto Munari, Vicenza
Dimension: 18 cm × 13 cm; H. 13 cm
Material: silver sheet, crystal glass.

“夏洛特”椅
CHAIR CHARLOTTE

1994

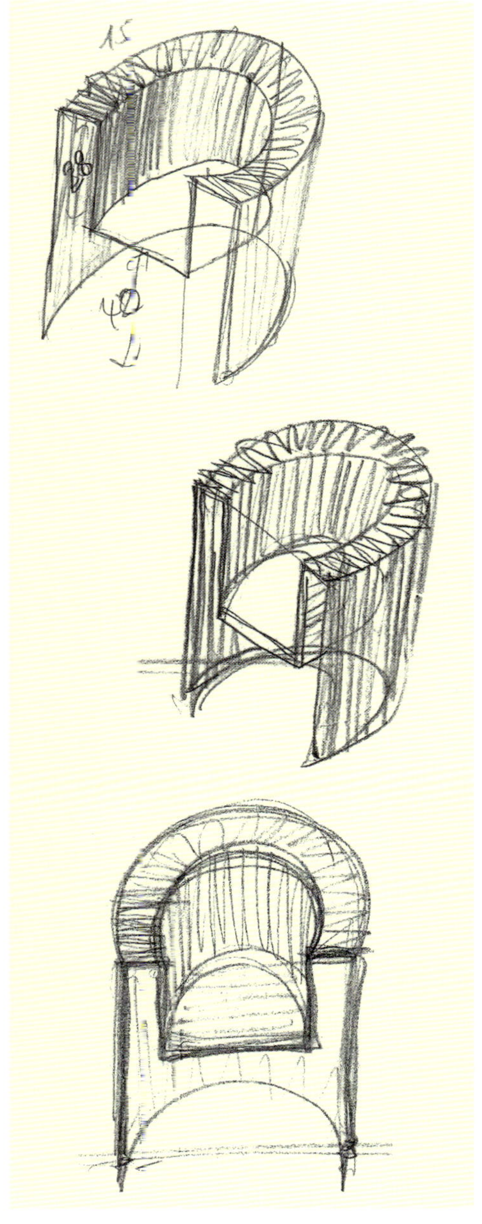

© HORM srl

© HORM srl

项目时间：1994年
生产时间：自1994年起
制造商：Horm公司
尺寸：90厘米×72厘米，高70厘米

Project: 1994
Production: since 1994
Manufacturer: Horm s.r.l.
Dimension: 90 cm × 72 cm, H. 70 cm

“布鲁门泽”台钟
WATCH “BLUMENZEIT”

1995

© MARCO D'ANNA

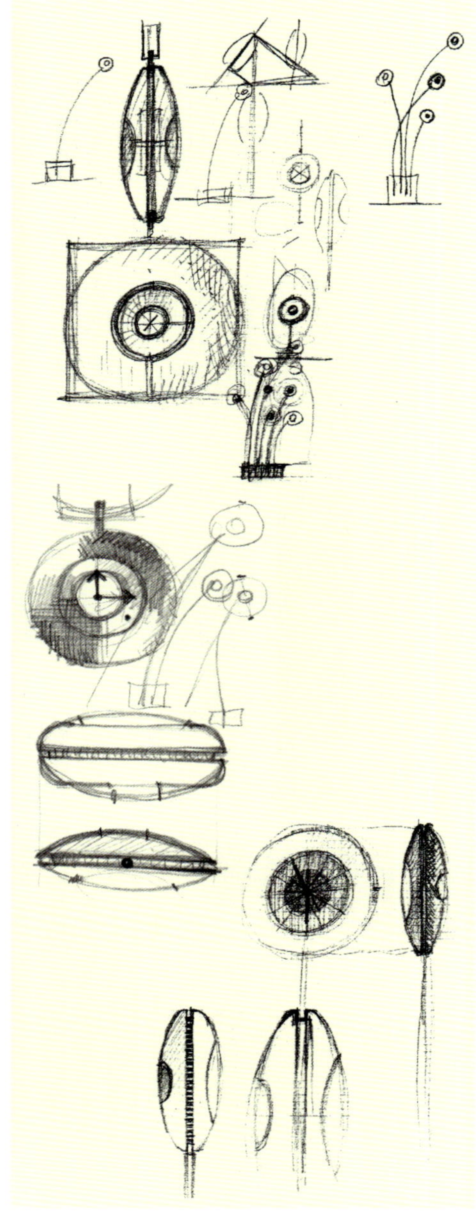

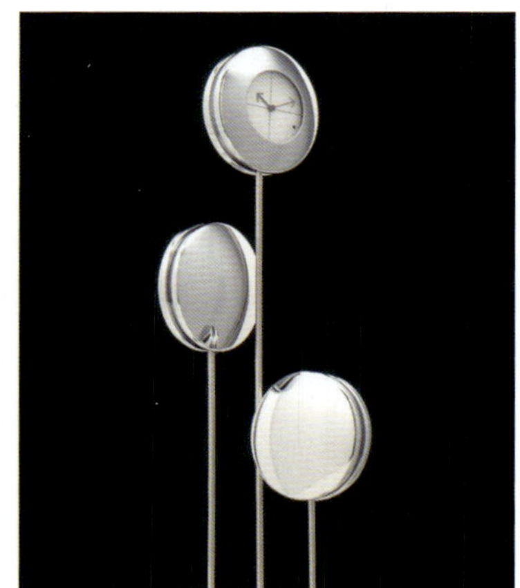

© MARCO D'ANNA

项目时间：1995年
生产时间：1996年（限量版）
制造商：瑞士国铁表有限公司
尺寸：正方体5厘米 × 5厘米 × 5厘米，表面直径3.6厘米；宽1.4厘米；高28.5厘米
材质：黑钢立方体，铬钢指针和时钟

Project: 1995
Production: 1996 (Limited edition)
Manufacturer: Mondaine Watch, Switzerland
Dimension: cube 5 cm × 5 cm × 5 cm; clock face diameter 3.6 cm; width 1.4 cm; height 28.5 cm
Material: black steel cube; stalks and clock in chromium steel.

孟提亚·丹修道院挂毯
TAPESTRY FOR THE MONASTERY MOUTIER D'AHUN

1997

© ARCHIVE MARIO BOTTA

© ARCHIVE MARIO BOTTA

项目时间：1997年
生产时间：1997年
委托方：法国孟提亚·丹修道院，巴黎文化部
制造商：奥比松挂毯
尺寸：272厘米×272厘米

Project: 1997
Production: 1977
Client: Monastery Mout er d'Ahun, France, Ministry for culture, Paris
Manufacturer: Tapisseries de Aubusson
Dimension: 272 cm × 272 cm.

“马里奥·博塔”手表
WATCHES MARIO BOTTA

1998/2008

© PIERRE JUNOD

MBL 98 手表
项目时间：1997年
生产时间：自1998年起
制造商：瑞士皮埃尔•朱诺德公司
尺寸：直径34毫米
材质：不锈钢、蓝宝石水晶、皮革、石英机芯

Watch MBL 98
Project: 1997
Production: since 1998
Manufacturer: Pierre Junod Switzerland
Dimension: diameter 34 mm
Material: stainless steel, sapphire crystal, leather, quartz movement

© PIERRE JUNOD

MBL 08手表
项目时间：2007年
生产时间：自2008年起
制造商：瑞士皮埃尔•朱德诺公司
尺寸：直径28毫米
材质：不锈钢，蓝宝石水晶，皮革，石英机芯

Watch MBL 08
Project: 2007
Production: since 2008
Manufacturer: Pierre Junod Switzerland
Dimension: diameter 28 mm
Material: stainless steel, sapphire crystal, leather, quartz movement

13只花瓶
13 VASES

1998/2001/2005/2012

© MARCO D'ANNA

© ENRICO CANO

© ENRICO CANO

© ENRICO CANO

项目时间：1998年
生产时间：（梨木）1998年，（赤陶）2001年，（白镴）2005年，（大理石）2012年
限量版：梨木样品
赤陶：哑光黑色法琅陶器
制造商：朱塞佩·罗西科内，陶瓷艺术，意大利米兰
白镴：铸造锡板，手工建模和焊接
制造商：Numa design，尚尼公司，意大利布雷西亚
大理石：法国红大理石
制造商：GVM大理石文明，意大利卡拉拉

Project: 1998
Production: (pear wood) 1998; (terracotta) 2001; (pewter) 2005; (marble) 2012
Limited editions: Prototypes in pear wood
Terracotta: matte black enamel terracotta
Manufacturer: Giuseppe Rossicone, Arte della ceramica, Milan, Italy.
Pewter: slabs of cast pewter, modelled and welded by hand
Manufacturer: Numa design, trademark Serafino Zani di Zani Roberto & C., Brescia, Italy.
Marble: marble Rosso Francia
Manufacturer: GVM La Civiltà del Marmo, Carrara, Italy.

国铁手表系列
MONDAINE WATCHES

1995/1998

© MONDAINE WATCH ltd

© MONDAINE WATCH ltd

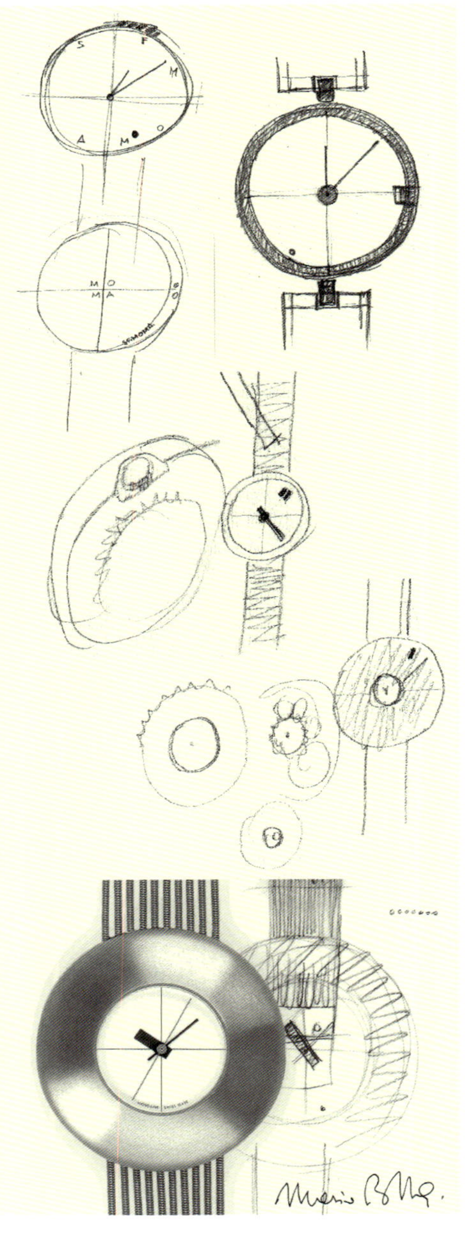

© MONDAINE WATCH ltd

制造商：瑞士国铁表有限公司

“旧金山现代艺术博物馆”台钟
项目时间：1998年
生产时间：自2000年起
尺寸：直径50毫米
材质：石英机芯，铝制外壳，无机玻璃

“博塔-旧金山现代艺术博物馆”手表
项目时间：1998年
生产时间：自1999年起
尺寸：直径32毫米
材质：石英机芯、无机玻璃钢、金属或皮革

“博塔-迪斯科”手表
项目时间：1995年
生产时间：自1996年起
尺寸：直径35毫米
材质：石英机芯、拉丝钢、无机玻璃、钢丝

Manufacturer: Mondaine Watch, Switzerland

Table clock SFMOMA
Project: 1998
Production: since 2000
Dimension: diameter 50 mm
Material: quartz movement, aluminium case, mineral glass.

Watch Botta SFMOMA
Project: 1998
Production: since 1999
Dimension: diameter 32 mm
Material: quartz movement, mineral glass, metal or leather.

Watch Botta DISCO
Project: 1995
Production: since 1996
Dimensions: diameter 35 mm
Material: quartz movement, brushed steel, mineral glass, steel wires.

“我的&你的”壶具
JUGS “MIA & TUA”

1997

© ENRICO CANO

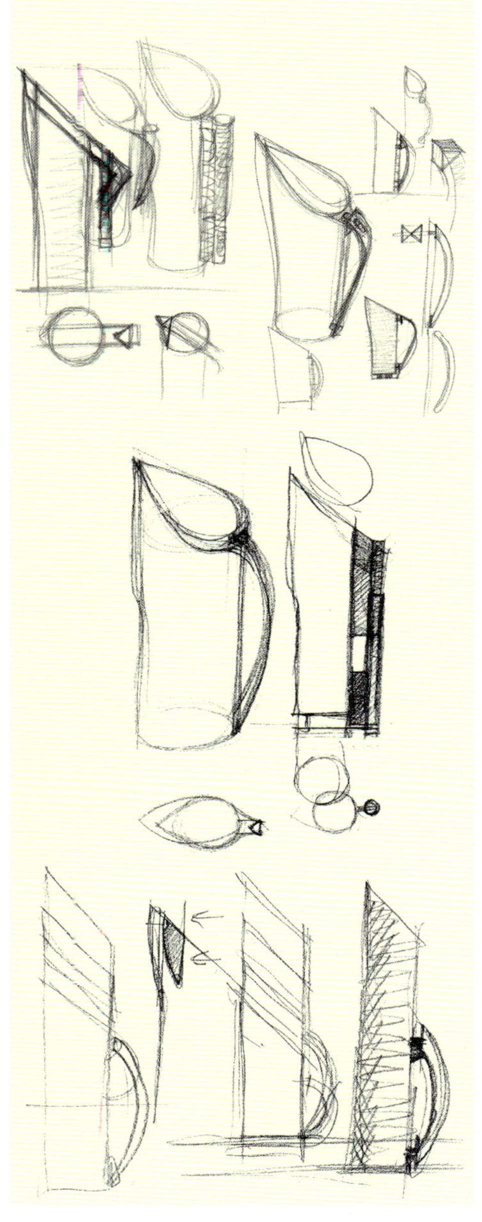

项目时间：1997年
生产时间：自1998年起
制造商：阿莱西公司
尺寸：
“我的”（葡萄酒壶）高23.5厘米，直径9厘米，70厘升
“你的”（水壶）高29厘米，直径9厘米，100厘升
材质：18/10抛光不锈钢，黑色尼龙手柄

Project: 1997
Production: since 1998
Manufacturer: Alessi S.p.A.
Dimension:
Mia (wine jug) H 23.5cm, diameter 9 cm, cl 70
Tua (water jug) H 29 cm, diameter 9 cm, cl 100
Material: polished stainless steel 18/10, handle in black polyamide.

穆纳里玻璃杯
MUNARI GLASSES

2000

© ENRICO CANO

© ENRICO CANO

项目时间：2000年
生产时间：2000年（限量生产）
制造商：克莱托·穆纳里，维琴察
尺寸：高22厘米，直径4-11厘米
材质：穆拉诺玻璃

Project: 2000
Production: 2000 (limited production)
Manufacturer: Cleto Munari, Vicenza
Dimension: 22 cm height, diameter from 4 to 11 cm
Material: Murano glass.

“特隆科”花瓶
VASE “TRONCO”

2001

© ENRICO CANO

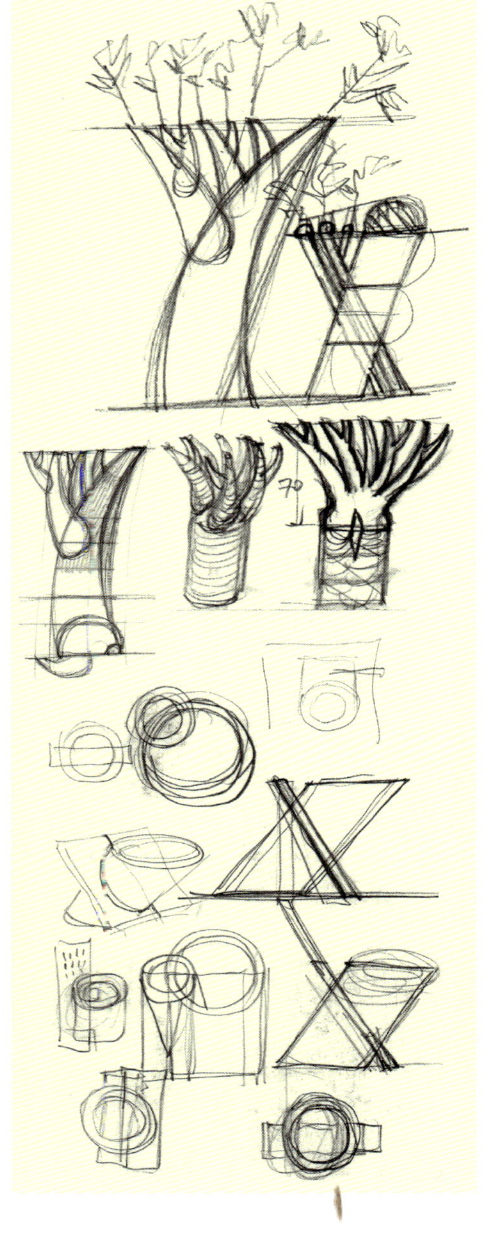

项目时间：2001年
生产时间：自2002年起
制造商：阿莱西公司
尺寸：22厘米 × 24厘米；高28.8厘米
材质：不锈钢

Project: 2001
Production: since 2002
Manufacturer: Alessi S.p.A.
Dimension: 22 cm x 24 cm, H. 28.8 cm
Material: stainless steel.

移动剧院
TRAVELLING THEATRE

2004 - 2007

© ARCHIVE MARIO BOTTA

© ARCHIVE MARIO BOTTA

项目时间：2004年
生产时间：2007年
结构与材质：钢轴承结构，竹条覆盖的木信封；
四个自行车轮和灯光系统；
带木质毛发的可拆卸顶盖；
后部由可拆卸的脚踏板和门帘组成；
机械运动时钟。
尺寸：宽150厘米 × 长140厘米（打开后长度275厘米），总高度（含木质毛发）410厘米

Project: 2004
Construction: 2007
Structure and materials: bearing structure in steel, wood envelope with bamboo list cover.
Four bicycle wheels and light system.
Removable covering with wooden hair.
The rear is composed of a removable footboard and a curtain.
Clock with mechanical movement.
Dimension: width 150 cm x depth 140 cm (275 cm open) total height (with wood hair): 410 cm.

“马里奥·博塔为凯兰帝设计”钢笔
PEN “MARIO BOTTA FOR CARAN D’ACHE”

2004

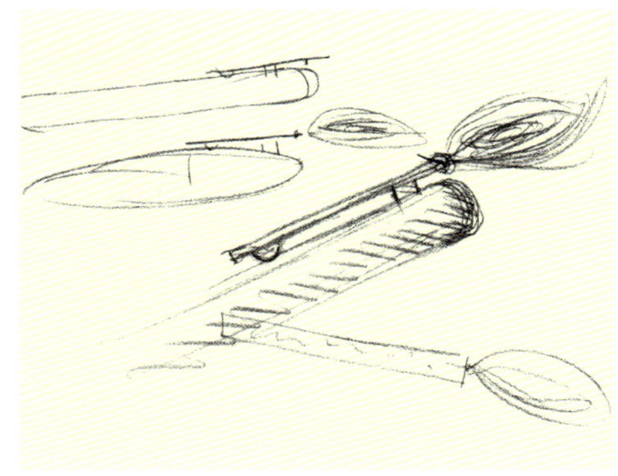

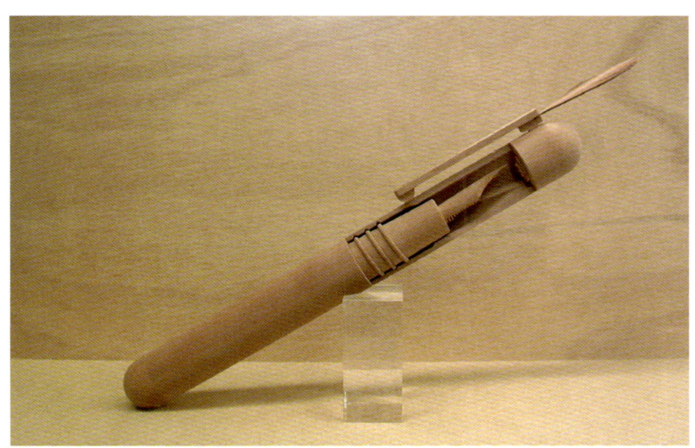

项目时间：2004年
生产时间：2005年（限量版）
制造商：凯兰帝，瑞士日内瓦
材质：镀银，铑涂层镜面笔身，铑涂层18K金笔尖，孔雀羽毛

Project: 2004
Production: 2005 (limited edition)
Manufacturer: Caran d’Ache, Switzerland
Material: silver-plated, rhodium-coated mirror body, rhodium coated 18 carat gold nib, peacock feather.

“美丽”桌
TABLE “BELLO”

2004

© HORM srl

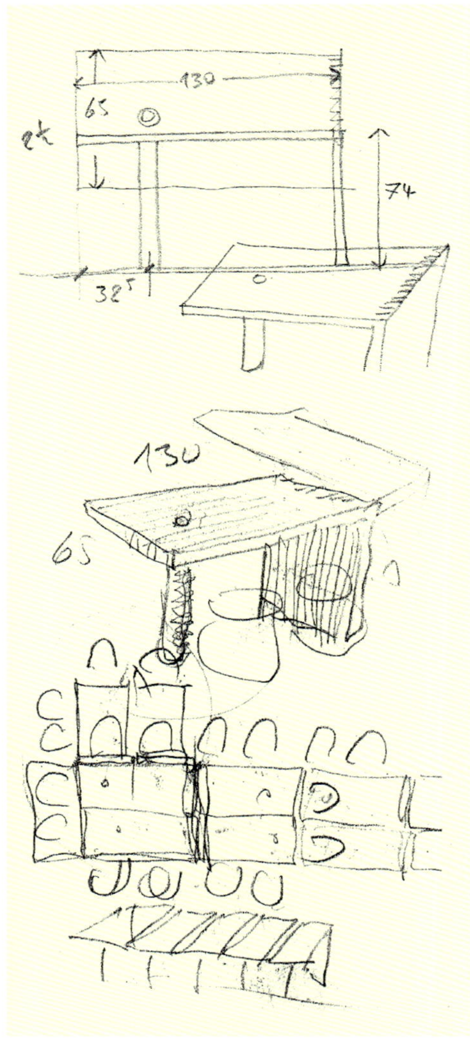

© HORM srl

设计时间：2004年
生产时间：自2004年起
制造商：意大利霍姆有限公司
尺寸：134厘米×67厘米，高72厘米
材质：实心山毛榉木，钢制桌腿

Design: 2004
Construction: since 2004
Manufacturer: Horm Italia srl
Dimension: 134 cm × 67 cm; H 72 cm
Material: table made of solid beech wood and steel leg.

“壳”装置，意大利米兰三年展
GUSCIO, TRIENNALE DI MILANO, ITALY

2007

设计时间：2007年
建造时间：2007年
制造商：格雷地板，意大利摩德纳
材质：陶瓷

Design: 2007
Construction: 2007
Manufacturer: Floor Gres, Modena, Italy
Material: ceramic.

“桥”桌
TABLE “PONTE”

2008

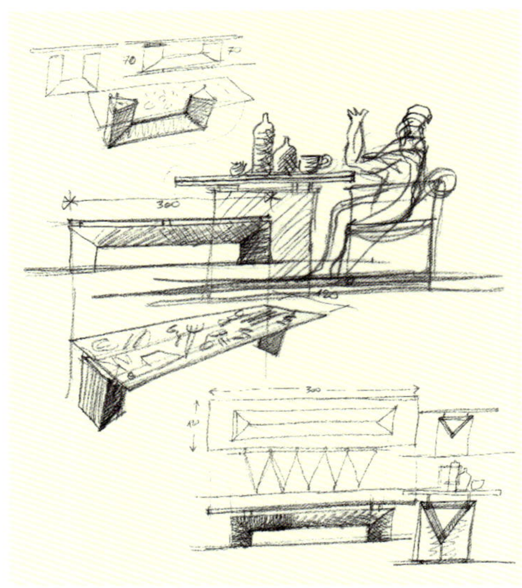

项目时间：2008年
生产时间：2009年（限量99张）
生产商：克莱托·穆纳里，维琴察
尺寸：底座高70厘米，长宽60厘米×80厘米，顶部120厘米×300厘米
材质：底座为涂黑色亮漆的中密度纤维板，桌面为漆面夹层玻璃

Project: 2008
Production: 2009 (limited edition: 99 pieces)
Manufacturer: Cleto Munari, Vicenza
Dimension: H 70 cm, base 60 cm × 180 cm; top 120cm × 300 cm
Material: base: black enameled MDF wood; top: varnished and laminated glass.

马克杯组合
MUGS

2009

© ENRICO CANO

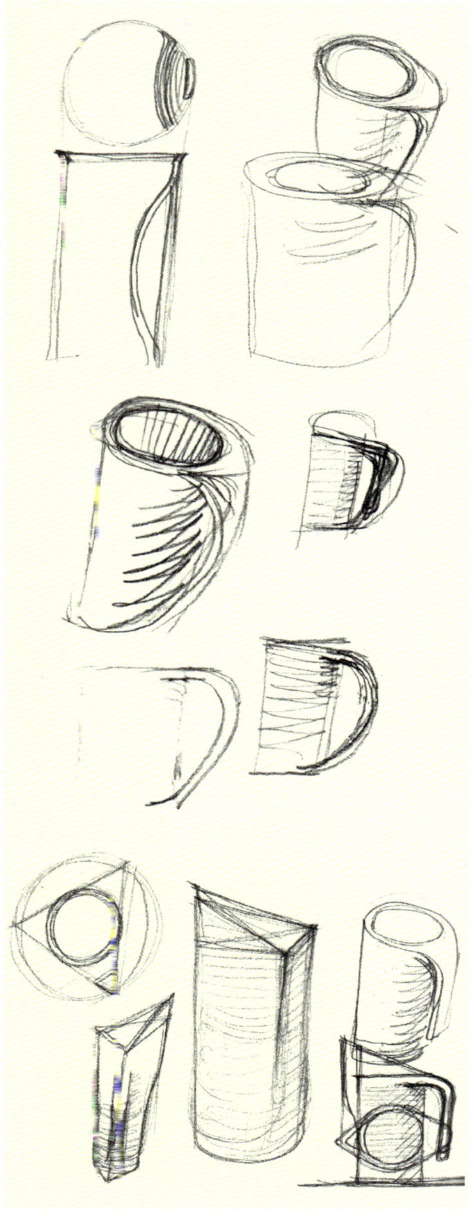

项目时间：2009年
生产时间：自2010年起
制造商：马克杯公司，库尼茨·伯茨兰
尺寸：高11.5/14.9厘米，直径8/9厘米
材质：白色、灰色和黑色陶瓷

Project: 2009
Production: since 2010
Manufacturer: Mug Company, Könitz Porzellan
Dimension: 11.5/14.9 cm height, diameter 8/9 cm
Material: white, grey and black china.

“沙漏”高脚凳
STOOL “CLESSIDRA”

2010

© RIVA MOBILI 1920

© RIVA MOBILI 1920

项目时间：2010年
生产时间：自2010年起
制造商：丽瓦1920家具，意大利坎图
尺寸：高41.5厘米，直径40厘米
材质：雪松木块

Project: 2010
Production: since 2010
Manufacturer: Riva 1920, Cantù, Italy
Dimension: H 41.5 cm, diameter 40 cm
Material: block of cedar-wood.

"安那托利亚"毯
CARPET "ANATOLIA"

2009

© FRANCESCA TISO, MORET srl

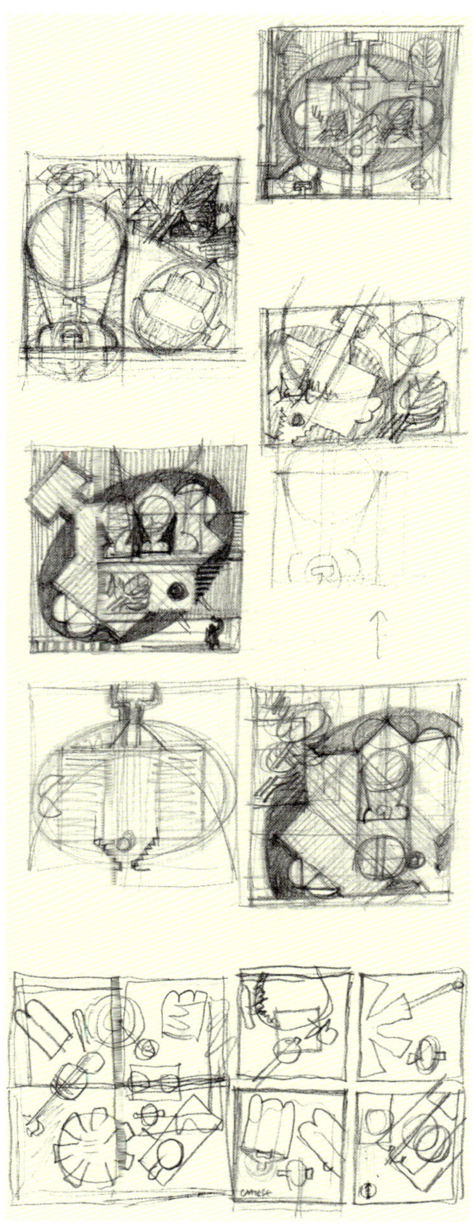

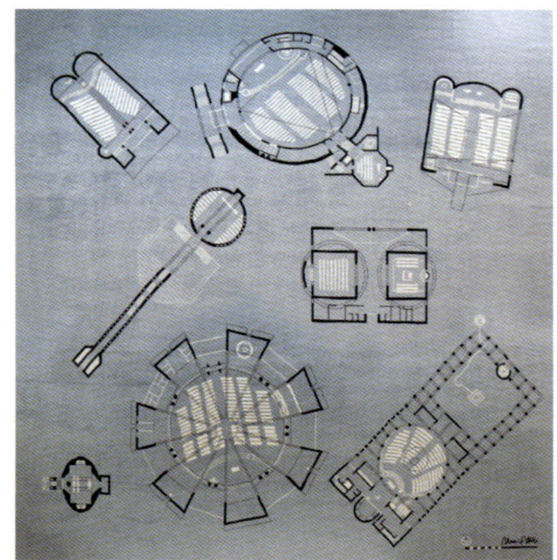

© FRANCESCA TISO, MORET srl

© FRANCESCA TISO, MORET srl

项目时间：2009年
生产时间：自2010年起
合作：克莱托·穆纳里
制造商：莫雷特
制造地：莫雷特工作室，土耳其乌沙克
尺寸：520厘米 × 520厘米，毛皮高度：8毫米
材质：棉质织物，锡韦雷克羊毛皮
编制技术：手编地毯，吉奥迪斯结；打结数量：2,620,800
编制时间：6个月；编织人数：6人

Project: 2009
Production: since 2010
Partner: Cleto Munari
Manufacturer: Moret
Manufacturing process: Moret atelier, Ushak, Turkey
Dimension: 520 cm × 520 cm, fur height 8 mm,
Material: texture and warp in cotton; fur in Siverek wool
Technique: hand-knotted, Ghiordes knot; number of knots: 2,620,800
Knotting time: 6 months; number of weavers: 6 persons.

“现成品”
“BRICOLAGES”

2010

© RIVA MOBILI 1920

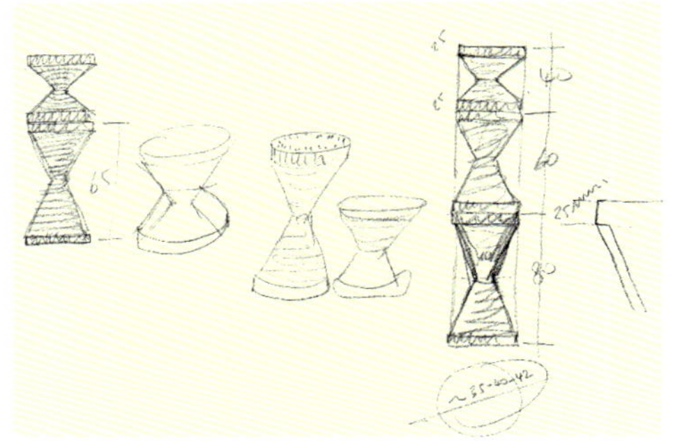

© RIVA MOBILI 1920

项目时间：2010年
生产时间：自2010年起
制造商：丽瓦1920家具，意大利坎图
尺寸：高40/60/80厘米，直径35/40厘米
材质：标记航道所用的威尼斯橡木木柱“现成品”

Project: 2010
Production: since 2010
Manufacturer: Riva 1920, Cantù, Italy
Dimension: H 40/60/80 cm, diameter 35/40cm
Material: “briccole”, oak wood posts on which Venice was built.

基因药房
REST FOR GENES GENETIC PHARMACY

2013

项目时间：2013年
建造时间：2013年
委托方：瑞士巴塞尔基因公司
制造商：丽瓦1920家具，意大利坎图
材质：实心枫树木

Project: 2013
Construction: 2013
Client: Genes Company, Basel, Switzerland
Manufacturer: Riva 1920, Cantù, Italy
Material: solid maple wood.

“莫雷拉托”椅
CHAIR “MORELATO”

2013

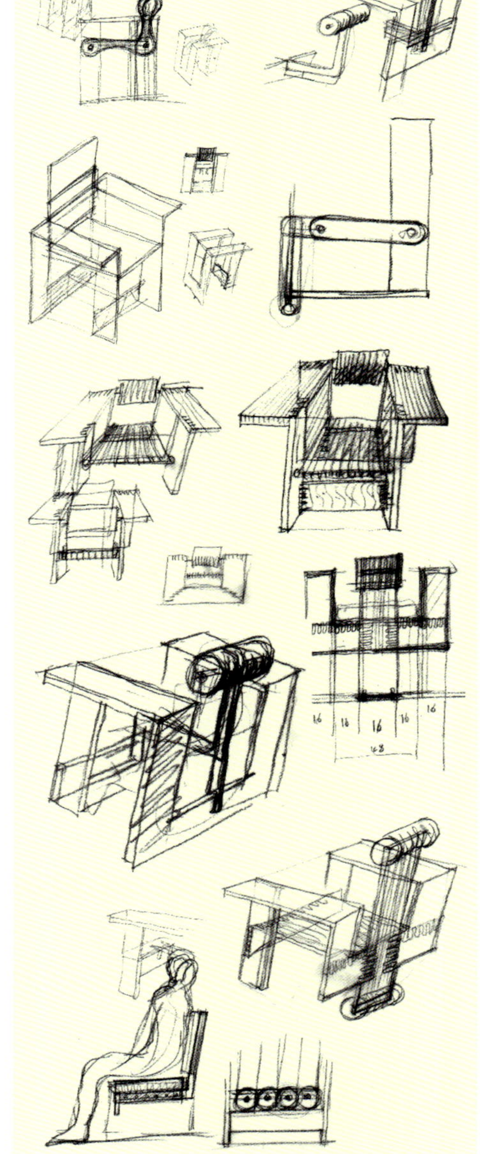

© MORELATO srl

© MORELATO srl

项目时间：2013年
生产时间：样品，未生产
制造商：莫雷拉托公司，意大利维罗纳省切雷亚市
结构：16毫米厚桦木胶合板，黑色皮革坐垫和靠背

Project: 2013
Production: prototype, not in production
Manufacturer: Morelato Company, Cerea (VR), Italy
Material: birch plywood 16mm and upholstered black leather seat and back.

“吉欧”花瓶
VASE “GEO”

2014

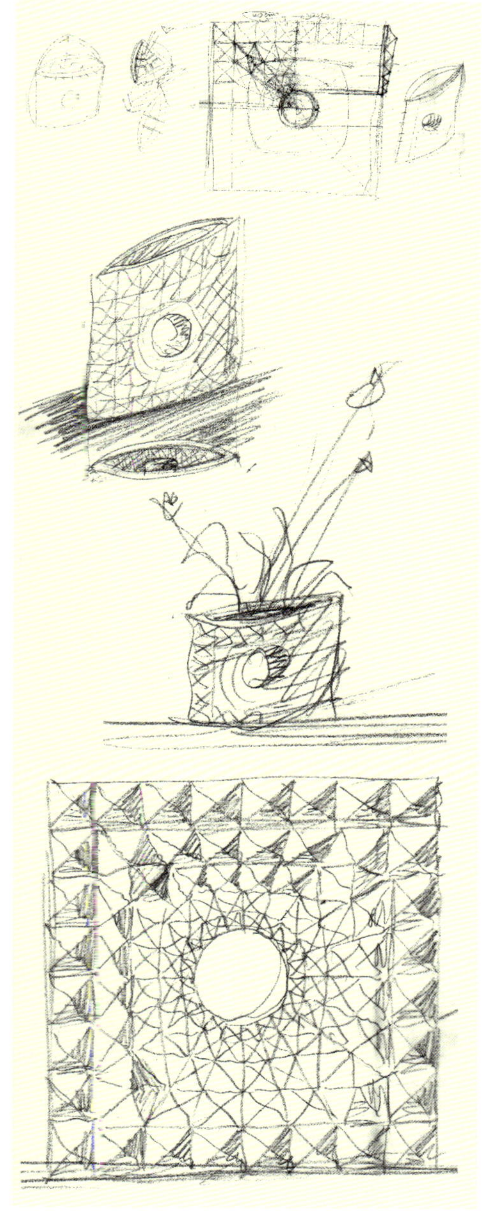

项目时间：2014年
生产时间：2016年（限量编号版本）
制造商：拉利克公司，法国莫代尔河畔温让

大花瓶
尺寸：40厘米×40厘米×17厘米
材质：透明、午夜蓝、黑水晶
技术：失蜡铸造，带编号限量版，每个颜色10件（其中8件供商业销售，2件为非卖品）

小花瓶
尺寸：32.5厘米×32.5厘米×15厘米
材质：透明水晶
技术：钢模限量和签名版250件

Project: 2014
Production: 2016 (limited and numbered edition)
Manufacturer: Lalique S.A., Wingen sur Moder, France

Big vase
Dimension: 40 cm × 40 cm × 17 cm;
Material: clear, midnight-blue, black crystal
Technique: lost wax casting. Limited, numbered edition of 10 pieces for each colour (8 commercially available and 2 not for sale)

Small vase
Dimension: 32,5 cm × 32,5 cm × 15 cm;
Material: clear crystal
Technique: mould in steel Limited and signed edition of 250 pieces

凯兰帝铅笔
FIXPENCIL CARAN D'ACHE

2014

© CARAN D'ACHE © CARAN D'ACHE © CARAN D'ACHE

项目时间：2014年
生产时间：2016年（限量版）
制造商：凯兰帝，瑞士日内瓦
材质：轻型耐蚀铝合金
两个版本：白底黑图案、黑底白图案

Project: 2014
Production: 2016 (limited edition)
Manufacturer: Caran D'Ache, Geneva, Switzerland
Material: light, resistant aluminum
Two versions: black checks on a white background
white checks on a black background

“胜利”喷泉，意大利之胜利

意大利，加尔多内 · 里维埃拉

FONTANA “VITTORIALE”, VITTORIALE DEGLI ITALIANI

GARDONE RIVERA, ITALY

2016

© MARCO BECK PECCOZ

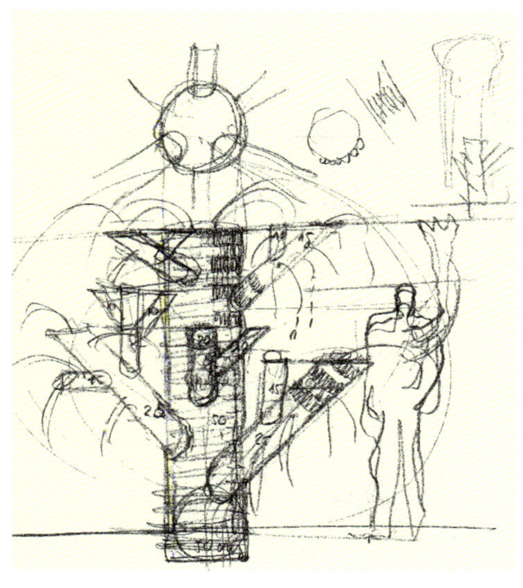

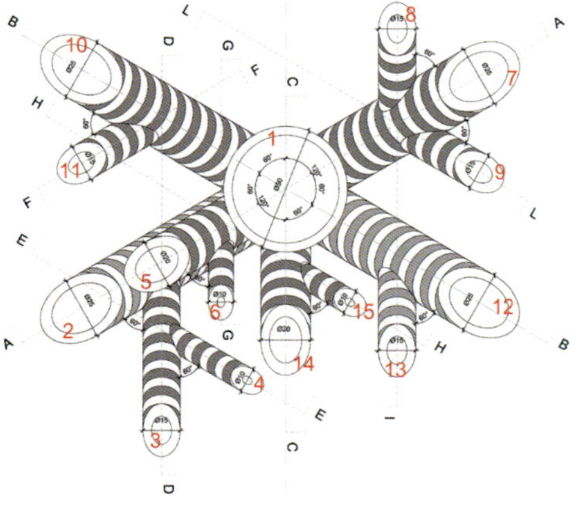

项目时间：2016年
建造时间：2016年
委托方：加尔多内·里维埃拉，意大利之胜利基金会
制造商：弗洛玛和阿雷起亚公司
尺寸：高2.5米，宽2米
材质：钢结构，黑白陶瓷饰面

Project: 2016
Realization: 2016
Client: Fondazione il Vittoriale degli Italiani, Gardone Riviera (BS)
Manufacturer: firms Floema e Arezia
Dimension: H. 2,5 m, width 2 m
Material: steel structure clad with black and white ceramic.

附录
APPENDIX

个人简介

博塔1943年4月1日出生在瑞士提契诺州的门德里西奥。于卢加诺接受学徒训练后，他先进入米兰艺术学院学习，随后又到威尼斯大学建筑学院学习。在卡洛·斯卡帕和朱塞佩·马萨里奥尔的指导下，于1969年取得专业学位。在威尼斯学习期间，他有幸遇见了勒·柯布西耶和路易斯·I·康，并与他们共事。

博塔的职业生涯始于1970年的卢加诺，因在提契诺州设计的独栋住宅而闻名，他的作品还包括许多其他建筑类型，有学校、银行、行政办公楼、图书馆、博物馆和宗教建筑等。除了自身的建筑工作外，他还从事多种教学活动，在欧洲、亚洲和南北美洲的建筑学院开展讲座、研讨会和课程教学等。

他曾于1976年担任洛桑联邦理工学院的客座教授；1987年担任美国纽黑文市耶鲁大学建筑学院的客座教授；自1983年以来被瑞士理工学院聘为教授；1982年到1987年间担任瑞士联邦美术委员会委员。自他的职业生涯开启以来，博塔的作品一直广受国际认可，屡获殊荣。

博塔一直是一名优秀的教师，致力于帮助他人学习专业知识。正因如此，他于1996年成为位于门德里西奥的瑞士提契诺大学的建立者之一，如今他仍在该校担任教授，并于2002年~2003年间和2011年~2013年间出任管理者。他在建筑学院担任教师，同时是英国标准协会建筑基金会的评奖团主席，如今还致力于建筑剧场的实现。在倾注了全部激情的建筑事业中，博塔完全有能力将其所学传授给后人。

BIOGRAPHY

Born in Mendrisio, Ticino, on April 1, 1943. After an apprenticeship in Lugano, he first attended the Art College in Milan and then studied at the University Institute of Architecture in Venice. Directed by Carlo Scarpa and Giuseppe Mazzariol he received his professional degree in 1969. While studying in Venice, he had the opportunity to meet and work for Le Corbusier and Louis I. Kahn.

Botta's professional career began in 1970 in Lugano. Known for his single-family houses in Ticino, his work encompasses many other building types including schools, banks, administration buildings, libraries, museums and sacred buildings. Along his work he teaches extensively in giving lectures, seminars and courses in architectural schools in Europe, Asia, North- and South America.

He served as visiting professor at the Ecole Polytechnique Fédérale in Lausanne in 1976, and at the Yale School of Architecture, New Haven, USA in 1987 and since 1983 he is entitled professor of the Swiss Polytechnic Schools. From 1982 to 1987 he was a member of the Swiss federal commission of fine arts. Since the beginning of his career, Botta's work has been recognized internationally and honored with prestigious awards.

Botta has always been an excellent instructor and is committed to helping others learn his trade, which led him, in 1996, to become one of the founders of the Academy of architecture of the Università della Svizzera Italiana in Mendrisio (Switzerland). Today he continues to teach there as a Professor and he held the directorship in 2002-2003 and 2011-2013. By teaching at the Academy of architecture, his role as chairman of the award jury of the BSI Architectural Foundation and his current commitment in the realization of the Theatre of architecture, Botta is able to impart his knowledge of a profession that is, first and foremost, his passion.

儿童时期的马里奥·博塔（1959年）。

Mario Botta as a child in 1959.

资历与荣誉

名誉会员

1983年

BDA-德国建筑师联合会

1984年

AIA-美国建筑师协会

1991年

巴黎法国建筑学会（瑞士代表委员）

1993年

米兰布雷拉美术学院

1994年

CAM-SAM墨西哥城建筑师协会

1996年

瑞士工程科学院

1997年

-索非亚国际建筑学院院士

-RIBA-伦敦英国皇家建筑师协会名誉会员

1999年

-罗马圣卢卡学院海外专员

-伯尔尼国际艺术哲学学院

2000年

索非亚国际建筑学院

2002年

瓦雷泽英苏布里亚-吉罗拉莫·卡尔达诺高等研究院普通会员普通会员

2003年

SIA-提契诺瑞士工程师与建筑师学会

2006年

RIBA伦敦（英国皇家建筑师协会）国际会员

2009年

SIA-苏黎世瑞士工程师与建筑师学会名誉会员

2010年

比利时建筑师协会会员

2012年

-威尼斯科学、文学与艺术研究院海外成员

-罗马教皇文学与艺术学院“万神殿艺术大师”成员

名誉教授

1989年

布宜诺斯艾利斯艺术与传媒中心高等研究学院

1995年

塞萨罗尼基亚里士多德大学建筑学院

1996年

国立科尔多瓦大学建筑学院

1997年

布宜诺斯艾利斯巴勒莫大学建筑学院

1998年

布加勒斯特建筑技术大学

2001年

若昂佩索阿公立大学

2002年

布加勒斯特建筑与城市规划大学

2006年

弗里堡大学神学系

2007年

纳沙泰尔大学艺术系

2016年

索非亚建筑、土木工程与地质大学

所获奖项

1985年

苏黎世贝顿建筑奖

1986年

芝加哥建筑奖

1988年

巴黎艺术和文学大骑士勋章

1989年

-荷兰皇家组织巴克斯顿奖

-国际建筑双年展国际建筑评论家委员会奖，布宜诺斯艾利斯

1991年

1991年度奖-基亚索伊赛德与切萨雷·拉维扎利基金会

1993年

-欧洲大理石建筑奖，意大利卡拉拉，获奖项目是位于贝林佐纳的办公与居住大楼

-国际建筑双年展国际建筑评论家委员会CICA奖，布宜诺斯艾利斯

1995年

-设计优秀大奖特别奖—AIA，加利福尼亚州，获奖项目是旧金山现代艺术博物馆

-国际石材建筑奖，维罗纳国际大理石展

-卡尔斯鲁厄欧洲文化奖

1997年

-SACEC奖（瑞士与美国文化交流协会）

-卡拉拉美国大理石建筑奖，获奖项目是旧金山现代艺术博物馆

1999年

-意大利卡拉拉欧洲大理石建筑奖，获奖项目是位于莫格诺的圣乔凡尼巴蒂斯塔教堂

-巴黎国家荣誉军团骑士勋章

2000年

-美洲千禧年奖，第21届泛美建筑师学会，墨西哥城

-获2000年古比奥奖，获奖项目是位于帕尔马的皮洛塔花园（和平广场）

2002年

-博洛尼亚，欧罗波利斯“王子与建筑师，重新思索城市的新思想”奖项，获奖项目是位于帕尔马的皮洛塔花园（和平广场）

-意大利卡拉拉中东大理石建筑奖，获奖项目是位于特拉维夫市的犹太教堂和犹太遗产中心

- 瓦雷泽艺术家事业奖

2003年

-维罗纳建筑师一等奖：大理石作品；维罗纳Progetto marmo & CCIAA项目

-苏黎世2003年瑞士文化奖

2004年

-第22届首尔年度建筑奖大奖：首尔教保塔楼

-国际高层建筑奖荣誉奖：首尔教保塔楼

2005年

-意大利共和国大军官勋位功绩勋章，罗马

马里奥·博塔在威尼斯IUAV进行毕业论文答辩（1969年7月31日）。左起依次为：毛罗·莉娜，朱塞佩·萨莫纳，卡洛·艾蒙诺，康斯坦诺·达迪，卡洛·斯卡帕，瓦莱里安诺牧师，吉安乌戈·博莱赛罗，伊格纳齐奥·加迪拉，马里奥·博塔。

Mario Botta during the defense of his graduation thesis at the IUAV in Venice (31 July 1969). From left: Mauro Lena, Giuseppe Samonà, Carlo Aymonino, Constantino Dardi, Carlo Scarpa, Valeriano Pastor, Gian Ugo Polesello, Ignazio Gardella, Mario Botta.

-国际奥委会（科隆）颁发的IOC/IAKS奖，获奖项目是位于泰内罗的国家青少年运动中心
-阿尔巴，加富尔-阿尔巴·庞培亚区奖
-“民用建筑设计优秀奖”，获奖项目是首尔市政府的三星美术馆
-意大利共和国大军官勋位功绩勋章，罗马

2006年

-2005年IAA年度大奖，国际建筑学会，保加利亚索非亚，获奖项目是首尔教保塔楼
-芝加哥雅典娜建筑与设计博物馆国际建筑奖，获奖项目是米兰斯卡拉剧院重建
-海牙“欧盟文化遗产奖”，获奖项目是米兰斯卡拉剧院重建
-“信仰与形式”单元的“设计荣誉奖”，获奖项目是塞里亚泰的若望二十三世教堂

2007年

-壁纸设计奖，获奖项目是都灵圣沃尔托教堂
-基耶蒂圣乔凡尼泰亚迪诺名誉公民
-芝加哥雅典娜建筑与设计博物馆国际建筑奖，获奖项目是图亨山地绿洲健康中心及圣沃尔托教堂
-卡拉拉欧洲大理石建筑奖，获奖项目是塞里亚泰的教皇圣若望二十三世教堂
-曼多瓦Vergilius d’Oro奖

2008年

-金色斯卡拉国际大奖，米兰狮子俱乐部，获奖项目是斯卡拉大剧院翻新工程
-2007年里吉普斯金奖杯，获奖项目是阿罗萨山地绿洲健康中心

2009年

-亚洲国际房地产大奖，获奖项目是“凤凰岛别墅公寓及俱乐部房屋”（合作方：韩国三友建筑师与工程师事务所）
-IOC/IAKS奖（银奖），由国际奥委会（科隆）颁发，获奖项目是Tschuggen Berg Oase健康中心

2010年

-“全球建筑贡献金奖”，建筑与设计基金会，吉隆坡

2011年

-2011国际“Sebetia-Ter”建筑奖，艺术与文化研究中心，那不勒斯
-“Alessandro Manzoni-Città di Lecco”国际文学奖，“2011年职业奖”单元
-罗马“维托里奥·德·西卡”建筑奖

2012年

米兰“Myrta Gabardi”国际奖

2013年

上海卓越项目一等奖，获奖项目是“衡山路12号”酒店，上海测绘设计联合会

2014年

-潘普洛纳哈维尔·卡瓦霍尔国际建筑奖
-“Per Artem Ad Deum”奖章，由凯尔采宗座文化委员会颁发
-年度国际设计艺术成就奖，获奖项目是“上海衡山路12号”酒店，中国建筑装饰协会，北京

2015年

-卢加诺BSI百年基金会奖，提契诺大学
-2015年阿纳瓦克设计奖章，阿纳瓦克大学，威斯基鲁康

2016年

-“皮耶罗之梦”奖，佛罗伦萨美术学院
-中国勘察设计协会一等奖，获奖项目是“清华大学图书馆”，北京

马里奥·博塔与梅拉·奥本海姆（1983年）。

Mario Botta with Meret Oppenheim (1983).

QUALIFICATIONS AND AWARDS

Honorary member
1983
BDA - Bund Deutscher Architekten
1984
AIA - The American Institute of Architects
1991
Académie d'Architecture (Swiss representation member), Paris
1993
Accademia delle Belle Arti di Brera, Milan
1994
CAM-SAM Colegio de Arquitectos de la Ciudad de Me-xico-Sociedad de Arquitectos Mexicanos, Mexico city
1996
Swiss Academy of Engineering Sciences
1997
- Academician of the International Academy of Architecture, Sofia
- RIBA- Royal Institute of Bri-tish Architects, Honorary Fellowship, London
1999
- Foreign Correspondent for the Academy of San Luca, Rome
- International Academy of Philosophy of Art, Bern
2000
International Academy of Architecture, Sofia
2002
Ordinary member at the Istituto di Studi Superiori dell'Insubria Gerolamo Cardano, Varese
2003
SIA - Swiss Society of Engineers and Architects, Ticino
2006
RIBA (Royal Institute of British Architects) International Fellowship, London
2009
Honorary member SIA - Swiss Society of Engineers and Architects, Zürich
2010
Member of the Belgian Order of Architects
2012
- Foreign member of the Istituto Veneto di Scienze, Lettere ed Arti, Venice
- Member of the Pontifical Academy of Fine Arts and Letters of the "Virtuosi al Pantheon", Rome

Professor Doctor Honoris Causa
1989
Escuela de Altos Estudios del CAYC, Buenos Aires
1995
School of Architecture, Aristotele University in Thessalonica
1996
School of Architecture, National University of Cordoba
1997
School of Architecture, Universidad de Palermo of Buenos Aires
1998
Institutul de Arhitectura Ion Mincu of Bucarest
2001
Universidade Federal da Paraiba, Joao Pessoa
2002
Universitatea de Arhitectura si Urbanism Ion Mincu of Bucarest
2006
Faculty of Theology, Fribourg University
2007
Arts Faculty, Neuchâtel University
2016
University of Architecture, Civil Engineering and Geo-desy, Sofia

Awards
1985
Architecture Award Prix Beton, Zurich
1986
Chicago Architecture Award
1988
Grade de Chevalier dans l'Ordre des Arts et des Lettres, Paris
1989
- Backsteen Award, Royal Dutch Organization
- CICA Award- International Committee of Architectural Critics, International Biennale of Architecture, Buenos Aires
1991
Award 1991 - Foundation Iside e Cesare Lavezzari, Chiasso
1993
- Marble Architectural Award Europe, Carrara (Italy), for the office and residential building in Bellinzona
- CICA Award - International Committee of Architectural Critics, International Biennale of Architecture, Buenos Aires
1995
- Merit Award for Excellence in Design-AIA, California, for

马里奥·博塔与弗朗西斯科·达尔科和波利斯·博德莱卡在威尼斯的"卡洛·斯卡帕1906-1978"展览布置现场（1984年）。

Mario Botta with Francesco Dal Cò and Boris Podrecca during the installation of the exhibition Carlo Scarpa 1906- 1978 in Venice (1984).

the San Francisco museum of modern art.
- International Award Architecture in Stone, International Marble Exhibition, Verona
- European Prize for Culture, Karlsruhe
1997
- SACEC Award (Swiss American Cultural Exchange Council)
- Marble Architectural Award America, Carrara, for the San Francisco museum of modern art
1999
- Marble Architectural Award Europe, Carrara, Italy, for the church San Giovanni Battista in Mogno
- Chevalier dans l'Ordre National de la Légion d'Honneur, Paris
2000
- Award Millennium America-rum, on occasion of the XXI Congrego Panamericano de Arquitectos, Mexico City
- Gubbio Award 2000 for the design of Il Giardino della Pilotta (Piazzale della Pace) in Parma
2002
- Award The Prince and the Architect, new ideas of rethin-king the city for the design of il Giardino della Pilotta (Piazzale della Pace) in Parma, Europolis 2002, Bologna
- Marble Architectural Award Middle East, Carrara, Italy for the Cymbalista synagogue and Jewish heritage centre in Tel Aviv
- Award Artist's Circle of Varese, Varese
2003
- 1st Prize Architects for Verona: Marble for the project; Progetto marmo & C.C.I.A.A. of Verona
- Swiss Award 2003 for culture, Zurich
2004
- 22nd Annual Seoul Architectural Award: Grand Award for the Kyobo Tower in Seoul
- The International Highrise Award: Mention for the Kyobo Tower in Seoul
2005
- Honour in the grade of Officer grant by the Order to the Merit of the Italian Republic, Rome
- IOC/IAKS Award grant by the Olympic International Committee (Köln) for the National Youth Sport Centre in Tenero
- Award Grinzane Cavour - Sezione Alba Pompeia, Alba
- Award "Excellence in design for civic architecture", Leeum Samsung museum of art Seoul Metropolitan Government
- Honour in the grade of Great Officer grant by the Order to the Merit of the Italian Republic, Rome
2006
- IAA Annual Prix 2005, International Academy of Architecture, Sofia Bulgaria for the Kyobo Tower, Seoul
- International Architecture Award, The Chicago Athena-eum Museum of Architecture and Design for the restructu-ring of the Theatre alla Scala in Milan
- "European Union Prize for Cultural Heritage Europa Nostra", The Hague for the restructuring of the Theatre alla Scala in Milan
- Prize "Faith & Form" section "Design honour award" for the church Papa Giovanni XXIII, Seriate
2007
- Wallpaper Design Award for Church Santo Volto in Turin
- Honorary citizenship, municipality of San Giovanni Teatino, Chieti
- International Architecture Award, The Chicago Athenaeum Museum of Architecture and Design for the wellness centre Tschuggen Berg Oase and the church Santo Volto
- Marble Architectural Awards Europe, Carrara, for the church Papa Giovanni XXIII, Seriate
- Prize Vergilius d'Oro, Mantova
2008
- International Prize Scala d'Oro, Lions Club Milano alla Scala for the refurbishment of the Theatre alla Scala
- Prize "Rigips Gold Trophy 2007" for the wellness centre Bergoase, Arosa
2009
- MIPIM Asia Award for "Phoenix Island Villa Condo & Club House" with Samoo Architects & Engineers
- IOC/IAKS Award (silver) by the Olympic International Committee,(Köln) for the wellness centre Tschuggen Berg Oase
2010
"The Golden Award for Global Contribution in Architecture", Architecture + Design & Spectrum Foundation, Kuala Lumpur

马里奥·博塔携夫人玛利亚与亘理一家在东京（1985年）。

Mario Botta and his wife Maria with Watari family in Tokyo (1985).

© PINO MUSI

2011

- International Award "Sebetia-Ter" for Architecture 2011, Centro Studi di Arte e Cultura, Naples
- International Literary Prize "Alessandro Manzoni - Città di Lecco", section "Career Award 2011"
- Award "Vittorio De Sica" for architecture, Rome

2012

- International Prize "Myrta Gabardi", Milan

2013

Shanghai Excellent Project 1st Prize for the project "Twelve at Henghshan", Shanghai Survey & Design Associate

2014

- Premio Internacional Arquitectura Javier Carvajal, Pamplona
- Medal "Per Artem Ad Deum", Pontifical Council for Culture, Kielce
- Annual International Design Art Achievement Award for the project "Twelve at Hengshan Hotel, Shanghai", China Building Decoration Association, Beijing

2015

- Award "BSI Fondazione del Centenario", Università della Svizzera Italiana, Lugano
- Medalla Anáhuac en Diseno 2015, Universidad Anáhuac, Huixquilucan

2016

- Award "Il Sogno di Piero", Accademia di Belle Arti, Urbino
- China Exploration & Design Association 1st Prize for the project "Library of the Tsinghua University", Beijing

马里奥·博塔和玛利亚·博塔与安藤忠雄（1986年）。

Mario and Maria Botta with Tadao Ando (1986).

个人展览

马里奥·博塔：工程和项目展览
1977年11月14日至11月25日
奥地利维也纳，科技大学
1979年12月
美国纽约，哥伦比亚大学
1979年10月15日至11月20日
美国纽约，锡拉丘兹大学
1979年12月15日至1980年3月2日
意大利，米兰设计三年展
1980年2月
美国夏洛茨维尔，弗吉尼亚大学
1980年3月8日至3月25日
意大利，巴勒莫大学建筑学院
1980年4月3日至4月24日
美国华盛顿州西雅图，蓝图：建筑
1980年4月14日至5月5日
意大利罗马，国家建筑研究院（IN/ARCH）
1980年6月6日至6月20日
瑞士，日内瓦大学建筑学院
1980年11月5日至11月19日
瑞士，洛桑联邦理工学院
1980年12月
德国，布伦瑞克工业大学
1981年1月
德国，不莱梅造型艺术及音乐学院
1981年3月13日至4月10日
荷兰，阿姆斯特丹建筑中心
1981年5月25日至6月11日
瑞士，弗里堡玛拉艺廊
1981年11月9日至11月30日
比利时，布鲁塞尔美术馆
1981年11月24日至12月17日
美国俄亥俄州，旧代顿邮局美术馆

马里奥·博塔的建筑
1980年9月至10月
阿根廷，布宜诺斯艾利斯艺术与交流中心
1981年8月10日至8月20日
巴西贝洛奥里藏特市米纳斯热莱斯联合大学，建筑学院

居住的圆筒
1981年9月21日至9月23日
意大利米兰，马可尼工作室

马里奥·博塔的建筑
1981年12月10日至12月24日
匈牙利佩奇活动之家
1982年3月5日至3月30日
匈牙利布达佩斯，J画廊（约瑟法洛奇·吉利托特莱博物馆）

遇见阿尔伯特·萨托里斯
1982年5月27日
瑞士，斯塔比奥国际艺术中心

马里奥·博塔
1982年6月2日至6月16日
巴西里约热内卢，国家建筑研究所爱博艺廊

“一号与二号”：马里奥·博塔的双椅
1982年9月17日至9月22日
意大利米兰，马可尼文化研究中心

马里奥·博塔 恰似桌上之拳的风景
1982年12月7日至1983年2月12日
巴黎国际时装学院与法国尚贝里萨瓦博物馆

建筑师马里奥·博塔
1983年3月12日至3月28日
巴西圣保罗，巴西建筑学院

马里奥·博塔
1983年5月7日至5月31日
意大利，安科纳神甫大厅

马里奥·博塔1961-1982
1983年9月3日至10月12日
德国，科隆历史档案馆

初步研究：马里奥·博塔
1984年9月8日至10月14日
日本东京，涩谷区GA美术馆
1984年10月17日至11月25日
德国，斯图加特魏森霍夫建筑美术馆

建筑师马里奥·博塔
1984年5月16日至6月24日
瑞士佛里堡，艺术与历史博物馆

马里奥·博塔：建筑1960-1985
由马里奥·博塔与阿齐勒·卡斯蒂伊奥尼设计展览
1985年10月12日至12月8日
意大利威尼斯，圣乔瓦尼·埃万杰利斯塔学校
1986年1月4日至1月26日
意大利维琴查，帕拉迪亚大教堂
1986年4月4日至5月10日
西班牙，巴塞罗那建筑师官方学院
1986年6月3日至6月18日
西班牙马略卡岛，巴利阿里群岛建筑师官方学院

马里奥·博塔
1986年11月20日至1987年2月10日
美国纽约，现代艺术博物馆
1987年3月3日至4月17日
美国休斯顿，莱斯大学建筑学院法理什美术馆
1987年8月
美国旧金山，现代艺术博物馆

马里奥·博塔建筑1960-1985
1987年3月
德国，巴登-符腾堡州银行
1987年4月30日至5月15日
德国斯图加特，曲步林豪斯
1987年5月23日至6月10日
德国弗里堡，弗里德里希宫

马里奥·博塔：三人居
1987年3月19日至4月24日
瑞士日内瓦，装饰艺术学院

马里奥·博塔在于卢加诺戈达尔多银行旧址上新建的建筑中（1986年）。

Mario Botta on the building site of the ex Banca del Gottardo in Lugano (1986).

马里奥·博塔：帕尔马与都灵
1987年6月18日至6月25日
意大利帕多瓦，拉马达莱纳教堂

马里奥·博塔——做家具的建筑师
1988年1月
德国拉芬斯堡Solus
1988年6月
德国威斯巴登Casa Nova Galerie

马里奥·博塔：项目与实施1972-1985
1988年3月
哥伦比亚，波哥大现代美术馆
1988年5月
哥伦比亚，梅德林现代美术馆
1988年10月
秘鲁，利马大区米拉弗洛雷斯文化中心
1989年4月至5月
阿根廷，布宜诺斯艾利斯艺术与传媒中心

书，图像和声音之家 维勒班
1988年6月8日至9月3日
法国巴黎，IFA法兰西建筑学院

马里奥·博塔
1988年9月30日至10月29日
瑞士日内瓦，提奥•雅各布公司

阿德里亚诺·海特曼：马里奥·博塔的建筑
1988年11月7日至11月24日
法国巴黎，国际摄影书店画廊

马里奥·博塔：对卢加诺市哥达尔多银行的初步研究
1988年11月22日至1989年2月18日
瑞士卢加诺，哥达尔多银行

马里奥·博塔 I 1989年备忘录的53幅设计草图
1988年11月29日至1989年1月7日
意大利米兰，阿奇沃尔托画廊

马里奥·博塔：构建客体
1989年7月1日至8月27日
瑞士马尔蒂尼，路易·莫雷基金会

马里奥·博塔：家
1989年9月23日至11月15日
瑞士，利戈尔内托航海博物馆

椅子
1990年5月14日至5月26日
瑞士弗里堡，阿夫里河畔马特兰阿夫里美术馆

东京和多利项目
1990年9月17日至11月18日
日本东京，涩谷区，和多利当代美术馆

马里奥·博塔建筑设计80-90
1991年2月2日至4月7日
法国巴黎，瑞士文化中心

马里奥·博塔建筑1980-1990
1991年6月20日至9月29日
瑞士日内瓦，拉特艺术与历史博物馆
1991年12月19日至1992年1月26日
德国吕贝克，布尔格修道院
1992年2月27日至3月29日
西班牙马德里，MOPT展览馆
1992年5月21日至6月21日
葡萄牙里斯本，卡卢斯特·格本基安基金会
1992年7月9日至8月16日
德国，杜塞尔多夫州立大众经济博物馆
1992年10月4日至11月21日
德国，罗伊特林根业余大学
1993年3月9日至4月4日
塞萨罗尼基，希腊技术协会，亚里士多德大学建筑学院
1993年9月20日至9月30日
阿根廷布宜诺斯艾利斯，CAYC雷科莱塔文化中心
1994年5月30日至6月26日
巴西圣保罗，巴西家居博物馆
1994年10月23日至10月30日
巴西国际建筑双年展伯南布哥会展中心
1995年2月28日至4月9日
波哥大，哥伦比亚国立大学
“莱奥波多·罗瑟” 建筑博物馆
1995年5月9日至5月30日
厄瓜多尔基多，现代艺术博物馆
1995年7月17日至8月3日
利马美术馆，瑞士大使馆，秘鲁建筑师协会
1995年11月16日至12月8日
圣地亚哥-德智利，智利宗座天主教大学

马里奥·博塔建筑1980-1990
1992年12月12日至1993年1月31日
意大利佛罗伦萨，斯特罗奇宫

马里奥·博塔：蒙哥诺教堂项目
1992年12月15日至1993年1月31日
瑞士洛迦诺，莫雷蒂尼宫，斯帕赛斯画廊
1993年3月31日至5月16日
瑞士锡安，古耐特艺术馆
1994年1月20日至2月13日
瑞士沙夫豪森，阿勒海利根博物馆
1995年1月7日至2月5日
瑞士圣加仑州东瑞士凯瑟琳画家、雕塑家、建筑师和视觉艺术家协会

马里奥·博塔
1994年7月22日至8月10日
意大利佩斯卡拉，Fuori Uso ' 94，前加斯里尼工厂
1994年10月1日至11月30日
意大利特雷维，特雷维闪光艺术馆

马里奥·博塔 恩佐·库奇：塔玛洛山教堂
1994年10月8日至11月6日
瑞士卢加诺，州立艺术博物馆
1995年2月10日至3月19日
瑞士，苏黎世美术馆

赫尔曼·韦埃克，马里奥·博塔和加布里埃·马尔克斯在采尔马特（1991年）。

Herman Vieco, Mario Botta and Gabriel García Marquez in Zermatt (1991).

1995年9月14日至12月2日
加拿大多伦多，意大利文化研究所
1996年1月至2月
加拿大温哥华，意大利文化研究所
1996年3月29日至5月3日
美国洛杉矶，意大利文化研究所

马里奥·博塔
1994年11月18日至11月30日
意大利博洛尼，意法文化协会-法语联盟

马里奥·博塔：旧金山现代艺术博物馆项目
1995年1月18日至6月25日
美国旧金山，现代艺术博物馆

马里奥·博塔：房子1980-1990
1995年4月18日至7月11日
瑞士厄马廷根，瑞银集团沃尔夫斯贝格管理培训中心

马里奥·博塔在巴塞尔：一座城市三个项目
1995年6月10日至8月20日
瑞士巴塞尔，建筑博物馆

马里奥·博塔的博物馆
1995年7月8日至7月22日
意大利佩萨罗，前拉马达莱纳教堂

马里奥·博塔设计
1995年11月3日至12月25日
希腊，塞萨洛尼基设计博物馆

马里奥·博塔，朱利奥·安德雷奥利：罗韦雷托博物馆
1996年4月27日至5月5日
意大利特伦托，建筑画廊
1996年5月8日至8月4日
美国旧金山，意大利文化研究所

马里奥·博塔建筑1980-1995
皮诺·穆西摄影回顾展
1996年8月7日至8月14日
新加坡国立大学建筑学院
1996年9月17日至9月28日
马来西亚吉隆坡，Pam大楼，马来西亚建筑师学会
1996年11月9日至11月23日
印度尼西亚，雅加达大学
1997年2月15日至2月27日
韩国首尔，Rotunda美术馆
1997年4月3日至4月13日
中国香港，香港艺术中心，Pao美术馆五楼
1997年4月17日至4月28日
中国香港，香港大学博物馆与美术馆
1998年1月8日至1月31日
澳大利亚悉尼，乌鲁姆鲁艺术空间美术馆
1998年2月9日至2月20日
澳大利亚堪培拉，澳大利亚高等法院
1998年3月9日至3月20日
佩斯，西澳大学建筑与美术学院，卡利提美术馆
1998年4月1日至4月22日
澳大利亚墨尔本大学，建筑、建造与规划专业，五层美术馆
1999年1月21日至2月5日
黎巴嫩巴拉曼仙埃尔-费尔大学美术学院
2000年2月13日至3月2日
叙利亚，大马士革大学建筑系
2000年10月15日至10月24日
叙利亚，拉塔基亚国家博物馆
2000年11月11日至11月30日
叙利亚，阿勒颇大学建筑系
2001年2月11日
约旦，安曼大学建筑系

马里奥·博塔：五幢建筑
1996年9月15日至11月17日
意大利威尼斯，奎里尼·斯坦帕利亚科学基金会
1998年6月13日至8月30日
瑞士，索洛图恩艺术博物馆

马里奥·博塔建筑：光——物质景象——皮诺·穆西摄影
1997年1月10日至2月9日
德国，勒夫库森摩尔斯布洛里希宫城市博物馆

马里奥·博塔 石头的情绪：公共建筑之间的道路
1997年6月30日至9月28日
意大利，那不勒斯皇宫多利卡庭院大厅
1998年6月27日至9月27日
荷兰，马斯特里赫特伯尼范登博物馆

马里奥·博塔：丁格列美术馆
1998年1月9日至4月19日
瑞士巴塞尔，丁格列美术馆

马里奥·博塔：特拉维夫辛巴利斯塔犹太教堂
1998年9月24日至9月28日
意大利维罗纳，国际天然大理石及技术展览

光与物质：马里奥·博塔 1990-2000
1999年11月12日至2000年1月15日
德国柏林，德国建筑中心

马里奥·博塔：舞美搭建 草图与摄影
1999年12月13日至2000年1月14日
德国萨尔布吕肯，萨尔兰博物馆图片展览室

马里奥·博塔：建筑模型
2000年5月19日至7月2日
意大利博洛尼亚，OIKOS新精神馆

马里奥·博塔：木头与陶瓷
2001年5月25日至6月25日
意大利布雷西亚，天主教大学奇佐里尼堂

马里奥·博塔和让·佩提在卢加诺（1991年）。

Mario Botta with Jean Petit in Lugano (1991).

马里奥•博塔：设计一个犹太教堂
2001年5月至6月
以色列特拉维夫，纳厄姆·戈德曼犹太人流散博物馆

马里奥博塔：13只花瓶、轮廓、木、陶瓷
2001年8月31日至9月29日
瑞士苏黎世，斯塔克美术馆

马里奥•博塔：光线与重心：建筑1993-2003
2003年12月12日至2004年3月21日
意大利，帕多瓦法理宫

斯卡拉剧院的建筑翻新与舞台新机械设计
2005年3月8日至5月31日
意大利米兰，斯卡拉大剧院“奥图洛·托斯卡尼尼包厢休息室”

马里奥·博塔：宗教建筑：石头的祈祷
2005年4月30日至2007年7月30日
意大利佛罗伦萨，国立石膏雕塑艺术陈列馆
2005年11月23日至2006年1月14日
英国伦敦，英国皇家建筑师协会RIBA

斯卡拉大剧院与宗教建筑
2005年10月8日至10月30日
意大利阿尔巴，圣朱塞佩教堂

建筑书籍展
[书籍介绍：《致初学者之天使的语言》马里奥·博塔与达里奥·费提力奥著，2006年米兰斯基拉出版社]
2007年3月15日至4月15日
意大利曼多瓦，贝纳尔德利书店艾迪诺儿童中心美术馆

马里奥·博塔：13只花瓶限量版系列
2007年11月17日至11月25日
比利时，布鲁塞尔美术馆

马里奥·博塔：建筑1960-2010
2010年9月25日至2011年1月23日
意大利，特伦托和罗韦雷托现代与当代艺术博物馆

马里奥·博塔：建筑与回忆
2011年4月2日至8月15日
瑞士，纳沙泰尔Centre Dürrenmatt

马里奥·博塔：以卡拉拉大理石完成的12件独特作品
2011年5月25日至7月25日
法国巴黎，白月美术馆

马里奥·博塔：“13只花瓶”
（13只青灰色花瓶展；花瓶由NUMA限量制造，总数仅33只）
2011年9月23日至10月9日
比利时，布鲁塞尔美术馆

马里奥·博塔“花瓶”
2012年5月8日至6月9日
意大利米兰，安东尼娅·让诺内建筑设计美术馆

马里奥·博塔：速写模型
2013年1月12日至3月2日
瑞士伯尔尼，科恩菲尔德画廊

马里奥•博塔：建筑与记忆
2014年1月30日至7月25日
美国北卡罗来纳州夏洛特，贝赫勒现代美术馆

马里奥•博塔：在物质与记忆之间
2014年3月25日至5月14日
意大利都灵，都灵大学人文学系阿图罗·格拉法图书馆

马里奥•博塔：近乎日记 2003-2013
2014年10月27日至11月7日
意大利米兰，波瓦拉宫艺术厅画展

卡特布兰奇十二世：马里奥•博塔：构筑一个神圣空间
2014年12月11日至2015年2月28日
瑞士，苏黎世建筑论坛

马里奥•博塔“13只花瓶”
2015年11月20日至11月21日
瑞士蒙塔格诺拉，赫尔曼·黑塞基金会

马里奥·博塔和恩佐·库奇在位于塔玛洛山的圣洁天使玛利亚教堂。

Mario Botta with Enzo Cucchi at the Chapel Santa Maria degli Angeli on Mount Tamaro.

PERSONAL EXHIBITION

Mario Botta. Opere e progetti
1977.11.14 - 11.25
Technische Universität Vienna, Austria
1979.12
Columbia University, New York, USA
1979.10.15 - 11.20
Syracuse University, Syracuse NY, USA
1979.12.15 - 1980.03.02
XVI Triennale di Milano, Milan, Italy
1980.02
University of Virginia, Charlottesville, USA
1980.03.08 - 03.25
Facoltà di architettura Università di Palermo, Italy
1980.04.03 - 04.24
Blueprint: For Architecture, Seattle, Washington, USA
1980.04.14 - 05.05
Istituto Nazionale di Architettura (IN/ARCH), Rome, Italy
1980.06.06 - 06.20
École d'Architecture Université de Genève, Switzerland
1980.11.05 - 11.19
École Polytechnique Fédérale Lausanne, Switzerland
1980.12
Technische Universität Braunschweig, Germany
1981.01
Hochschule für Gestaltende Kunst und Musik, Bremen, Germany
1981.03.13 - 04.10
Stichting Architectuur Museum Amsterdam, The Netherlands
1981.05.25 - 06.11
Galerie Mara, Fribourg, Switzerland
1981.11.09 - 11.30
Palais des Beaux-Arts, Brussels, Belgium
1981.11.24 - 12.17
Gallery at the Old Post Office Dayton, Ohio, USA

La arquitectura de Mario Botta
1980.09- 10
Centro de Arte y Comunicacion (CAYC), Buenos Aires, Argentina
1981.08.10 - 08.20
Escola de Arquitectura da UFMG, Belo Horizonte, Brasil

Un cilindro da abitare
1981.09.21 - 09.23
Studio Marconi, Milan, Italy

Architettura di Mario Botta
1981.12.10 - 12.24
Casa del Movimento, Pecs, Hungary
1982.03.05 - 03.30
J. Galeria (Jozsefvarosi Kiallitoterem), Budapest, Hungary

Incontro con Alberto Sartoris
1982.05.27
Centro Internazionale d'Arte, Stabio, Switzerland

Mario Botta
1982.06.02 - 06.16
Instituto de Arquitectos do Brasil, Galeria do IAB*, Rio de Janeiro, Brasil

"Prima & Seconda". Due sedie di Mario Botta
1982.09.17 - 09.22
Studio Marconi Centro Culturale, Milan, Italy

Mario Botta. Dans le paysage comme un poing sur la table
1982.12.07- 1983.02.12
IFA Institut Français d'Architecture, Paris and Musée Savoisien, Chambéry, France

Arquiteto Mario Botta
1983.03.12 - 03.28
Instituto dos Arquitectos do Brasil, San Paolo, Brasil

Mario Botta
1983.05.07 - 05.31
Sala del Rettorato, Ancona, Italy

Mario Botta 1961-1982
1983.09.03 - 10.12
Historisches Archiv, Cologne, Germany

Preliminary studies. Mario Botta
1984.09.08 - 10.14
GA Gallery, Shibuya-ku, Tokyo, Japan
1984.10.17 - 11.25
Architektur - Galerie am Weissenhof, Stuttgart, Germany

Mario Botta Architecte
1984.05.16 - 06.24
Musée d'Art et d'Histoire, Fribourg, Switzerland

Mario Botta. Architetture 1960-1985
Exhibition design by Mario Botta and Achille Castiglioni
1985.10.12 - 12.08
Scuola di San Giovanni Evangelista, Venice, Italy
1986.01.04 - 01.26
Basilica Palladiana, Vicenza, Italy
1986.04.04 - 05.10
Colegio Oficial de Arquitectos, Barcelona, Spain
1986.06.03 - 06.18
Colegio Oficial de Arquitectos de Baleares, Palma de Mallorca, Spain

Mario Botta
1986.11.20 - 1987.02.10
The Museum of Modern Art, New York, USA
1987.03.03 - 04.17
Farish Gallery School of Architecture, Rice University, Houston, USA
1987.08
Museum of Modern Art, San Francisco, USA

Mario Botta Architektur 1960-1985
1987.03
Landeskreditbank, Baden-Württemberg, Germany
1987.04.30 - 05.15
Züblinhaus, Stuttgart, Germany
1987.05.23 - 06.10
Friedrichsbau, Freiburg, Germany

Mario Botta. Une architecture trois habitats
1987.03.19 - 04.24

马里奥·博塔和尼基·德·圣菲尔在圣迭戈（1996年）。

Mario Botta with Niki de Saint Phalle in San Diego (1996).

École des Arts Décoratifs, Geneva, Switzerland

Mario Botta. Parma e Torino
1987.06.18 - 06.25
Ex Oratorio delle Maddalene, Padua, Italy

Mario Botta - Ein Architekt macht Möbel
1988.01
Solus, Ravensburg, Germany
1988.06
Casa Nova Galerie, Wiesbaden, Germany

Mario Botta. Proyectos y realizaciones 1972-1985
1988.03
Museo de Arte Moderno, Bogotá, Colombia
1988.05
Museo de Arte Moderno, Medellín, Colombia
1988.10
Centro Cultural di Miraflores, Lima, Perú
1989.04 - 05
Centro de Arte y Comunicación (CAYC), Buenos Aires, Argentina

Villeurbanne maison du livre, de l'image et du son
1988.06.08 - 09.03
IFA Institut Français d'Architecture, Paris, France

Mario Botta
1988.09.30 - 10.29
Teo Jakob, Geneva, Switzerland

Adriano Heitmann: architectures de Mario Botta
1988.11.07 - 11.24
Galerie de la Librairie Internationale de Photographie, Paris, France

Mario Botta. Studi preliminari per la Banca del Gottardo a Lugano
1988.11.22 - 1989.02.18
Galleria Banca del Gottardo, Lugano, Switzerland

Mario Botta. I 53 disegni dell'agenda 1989
1988.11.29 - 1989.01.07
Galleria L'Archivolto, Milan, Italy

Mario Botta. Construire les objets
1989.07.01 - 08.27
Fondation Louis Moret, Martigny, Switzerland

Mario Botta: una casa
1989.09.23 - 11.15
Museo Vela, Ligornetto, Switzerland

La chaise
1990.05.14 - 05.26
Avry-Art Galerie, Avry-sur-Matran, Fribourg, Switzerland

Watari-um project in Tokyo
1990.09.17 - 11.18
Watari-um, Shibuya-ku, Tokyo, Japan

Mario Botta Architectures & Design 80-90
1991.02.02 - 04.07
Centre Culturel Suisse, Paris, France

Mario Botta architectures 1980-1990
1991.06.20 - 09.29
Musée Rath, Musée d'Art et d'Histoire, Geneva, Switzerland
1991.12.19 - 1992.01.26
Burgkloster, Lübeck, Germany
1992.02.27 - 03.29
MOPT Galeria de Exposiciones Madrid, Spain
1992.05.21 - 06.21
Fundaçao Calouste Gulbenkian, Lisbon, Portugal
1992.07.09 - 08.16
Landesmuseum Volk und Wirtschaft, Düsseldorf, Germany
1992.10.04 - 11.21
Volkshochschule, Reutlingen, Germany
1993.03.09 - 04.04
Aristotele's University - School of Architecture, Technical Chamber of Greece, Thessaloniki
1993.09.20 - 09.30
CAYC BA / 93, Centro Cultural Recoleta, Buenos Aires, Argentina
1994.05.30 - 06.26
Museu da casa brasileira, San Paolo, Brasil
1994.10.23 - 10.30
Bienal Internacional de Arquitectura de Brasil, Centro de Convenciones de Pernambuco Recife, Brasil
1995.02.28 - 04.09
Museo de Arquitectura "Leopoldo Rother", Universidad Nacional de Colombia, Bogotá
1995.05.09 - 05.30
Museo de Arte Moderno, Quito, Ecuador
1995.07.17 - 08.03
Colegio de Arquitectos del Perú, Embajada Suiza, Museo de Arte, Lima
1995.11.16 - 12.08
Pontificia Universidad Catolica de Chile, Santiago de Chile

Mario Botta architetture 1980-1990
1992.12.12. - 1993.01.31
Palazzo Strozzi, Florence, Italy

Mario Botta. Progetti per la chiesa di Mogno
1992.12.15 - 1993.01.31
Galleria SPSAS, Palazzo Morettini, Locarno, Switzerland
1993.03.31 - 05.16
Galerie de la Grenette, Sion, Switzerland
1994.01.20 - 02.13
Museum Allerheiligen, Schaffhausen, Switzerland
1995.01.07 - 02.05
GSMBA Ostschweiz Katharinen, St.Gallen, Switzerland

Mario Botta
1994.07.22 - 08.10

马里奥·博塔和乔万尼·波奇在门德里西奥（1997年）。

Mario Botta with Giovanni Pozzi in Mendrisio (1997).

Fuori Uso ' 94, Ex Opificio Gaslini, Pescara, Italy
1994.10.01 - 11.30
Trevi Flash Art Museum, Trevi, Italy

Mario Botta Enzo Cucchi, la cappella del Monte Tamaro
1994.10.08 - 11.06
Museo Cantonale d'Arte, Lugano, Switzerland
1995.02.10 - 03.19
Kunsthaus, Zürich, Switzerland
1995.09.14 - 12.02
Italian Cultural Institute, Toronto, Canada
1996.01 - 02
Italian Cultural Institute, Vancouver,Canada
1996.03.29 - 05.03
Italian Cultural Institute, Los Angeles, USA

Mario Botta
1994.11.18 - 11.30
Associazione Culturale Italo Francese - Alliance Française, Bologna, Italy

Mario Botta. The San Francisco Museum of Modern Art project
1995.01.18 - 06.25
Museum of Modern Art, San Francisco, USA

Mario Botta. Bauten 1980-1990
1995.04.18 - 07.11
Wolfsberg Management Training Center, Schweizerische Bankgesellschaft, Ermatingen, Switzerland

Mario Botta in Basel. Ein Architekt und drei Projekte für die Stadt
1995.06.10 - 08.20
Architekturmuseum, Basel, Switzerland

I musei di Mario Botta
1995.07.08 - 07.22
Ex Chiesa della Maddalena, Pesaro, Italy

Mario Botta Design
1995.11.03 - 12.25
Design Museum, Thessaloniki, Greece

Mario Botta Giulio Andreolli, il museo di Rovereto
1996.04.27 - 05.05
Galleria d'architettura, Trento, Italy
1996.05.08 - 08.04
Italian Cultural Institute, San Francisco, USA

Mario Botta. Bauten 1980-1995. Eine photographische Retrospektive von Pino Musi
1996.08.07 - 08.14
Faculty of Architecture, National University, Singapore
1996.09.17 - 09.28
Malaysian Institute of Architects, Pam Building, Kuala Lumpur, Malaysia
1996.11.09 - 11.23
University of Jakarta, Indonesia
1997.02.15 - 02.27
Rotunda Gallery, Seoul, South Korea
1997.04.03 - 04.13
Pao Galleries 5/F, Hong Arts Center, Hong Kong, China
1997.04.17 - 04.28
The University Museum and Art Gallery Hku, Hong Kong, China
1998.01.08 - 01.31
Artspace Gallery Woolloomooloo, Sidney, Australia
1998.02.09 - 02.20
The High Court of Australia, Canberra, Australia
1998.03.09 - 03.20
Cullity Gallery, School of architecture and Fine Arts, University of Western Australia, Perth
1998.04.01 - 04.22
5th floor Gallery, Faculty of Architecture, Building and Planning, University of Melbourne, Australia
1999.01.21 - 02.05
Académie Libanaise des Beaux-Arts, Université de Balamand Sin-El-Fil, Libanon
2000.02.13 - 03.02
Faculty of Architecture, University of Damascus, Syria
2000.10.15 - 10.24
National Museum, Latakia, Syria
2000.11.11 - 11.30
Faculty of Architecture, Aleppo University, Syria
2001.02.11
Faculty of Architecture, Amman University, Jordan

Mario Botta. Cinque architetture
1996.09.15 - 11.17
Fondazione Scientifica Querini Stampalia, Venice, Italy
1998.06.13 - 08.30
Kunstmuseum Solothurn, Switzerland

Architektur: Licht-Materie-Landschaft. Mario Botta gesehen von Pino Musi
1997.01.10 - 02.09
Städtisches Museum Schloss Morsbroich, Leverkusen, Germany

Mario Botta. Museum Jean Tinguely
1997.01.09 - 1998.04.19
Museum Jean Tinguely, Basel, Switzerland

Mario Botta. Emozioni di pietra. Un percorso fra le architetture pubbliche
1997.06.30 - 09.28
Palazzo Reale, Sala Dorica-Cortile delle Carrozze, Naples, Italy
1998.06.27 - 09.27
Bonnefanten Museum, Maastricht, The Netherlands

Mario Botta. Sinagoga Cymbalista a Tel-Aviv,
1998.09.24 - 09.28

马里奥·博塔在博洛尼亚的“马里奥博塔，建筑模型”展览现场（2000年）。

Mario Botta during the exhibition Mario Botta. Modelli di architettura in Bologna (2000).

Mostra Internazionale di Marmi Pietre e Tecnologie Verona Fiere, Verona, Italy

Licht und Materie. Mario Botta 1990-2000
1999.11.12 - 2000.01.15
DAZ Deutsches Architektur Zentrum, Berlin, Germany

Mario Botta. Bühnenarchitektur. Entwürfe und Fotografien
1999.12.13 - 2000.01.14
Graphisches Kabinett, Saarland Museum, Saarbrücken, Germany

Mario Botta. Modelli di architettura
2000.05.19 - 07.02
OIKOS Bologna 2000, Padiglione dell'Esprit Nouveau, Bologna, Italy

Mario Botta, legni e ceramiche
2001.05.25 - 06.25
Università Cattolica, Sala Chizzolini, Brescia, Italy

Mario Botta: designing a synagogue
2001.05 - 06
Beth Hatefutsoth, The Nahum Goldmann Museum of the Jewish Diaspora, Tel Aviv, Israel

Mario Botta. 13 Vasen Skizzen Holz Keramik
2001.08.31 - 09.29
Galerie Stuker, Zürich, Switzerland

Mario Botta. Luce e gravità. Architetture 1993-2003
2003.12.12 - 2004.03.21
Palazzo della Ragione, Padua, Italy

La ristrutturazione architettonica e la nuova macchina scenica del Teatro alla Scala
2005.03.08 - 05.31
Teatro alla Scala, Ridotto dei palchi "Arturo Toscanini", Milan, Italy

Mario Botta. Architetture del sacro. Preghiere di pietra
2005.04.30 - 2007.07.30
Gipsoteca Istituto Statale d'Arte, Florence, Italy

2005.11.23 - 2006.01.14
RIBA The Royal Institute of British Architects, London, United Kingdom

Il teatro alla Scala e le architetture del sacro
2005.10.08 - 10.30
Chiesa di San Giuseppe, Alba, Italy

Mostra del libro di architettura
[presentation of the book: Mario Botta, Dario Fertilio, *La lingua degli angeli per princi-pianti*, Skira, Milan 2006].
2007.03.15 - 04.15
Libreria Bernardelli SNC, Centro Einaudi Ragazzi-Galleria Einaudi, Mantova, Italy

Mario Botta. Tredici vasi. Limited Edition Collections
2007.11.17 - 11.25
The Gallery, Brussels, Belgium

Mario Botta. Architetture 1960-2010
2010.09.25 - 2011.01.23
Mart Museo di arte moderna e contemporanea di Trento e Rovereto, Italy

Mario Botta. Architecture et Mémoire / Architektur und Gedächtnis
2011.04.02 - 08.15
Centre Dürrenmatt, Neuchâtel, Switzerland

Mario Botta. 12 oeuvres uniques en marbre de Carrara
2011.05.25 - 07.25
White Moon Gallery, Paris, France

Mario Botta "Tredicivasi"
(Collection of 13 pewter vases produced by NUMA* in a limited, numbered edition of 33)
2011.09.23 - 10.09
The Gallery, Brussels, Belgium

Mario Botta "Vasi"
2012.05.08 - 06.09
Antonia Jannone, Disegni di Architettura, Milan, Italy

Mario Botta. Skizzen Zeichnungen Modelle
2013.01.12 - 03.02
Galerie Kornfeld, Bern, Switzerland

Mario Botta. Architecture and Memory
2014.01.30 - 07.25
Bechtler Museum of Modern Art, Charlotte - North Carolina, USA

Mario Botta. Fra materia e memoria
2014.03.25 - 05.14
Università degli Studi di Torino, Dipartimento di Studi Umanistici, Biblioteca Arturo Graf, Palazzo del Rettorato, Turin, Italy

Mario Botta. Quasi un diario 2003-2013
2014.10.27 - 11.07
Drawings exhibition. Palazzo Bovara, Sale dell'Arte, Milan, Italy

Carte Blanche XII: Mario Botta. Einen sakralen Raum bauen
2014.12.11 - 2015.02.28
Architekturforum Zürich, Switzerland

Mario Botta "13 vasi"
2015.11.20 - 11.21
Foundation Hermann Hesse, Montagnola, Switzerland

马里奥·博塔和门德里西奥建筑学院的学生们（2009年）。

Mario Botta among the students at the Academy of Architecture of Mendrisio (2009).

主要出版物
SELECTED BIBLIOGRAPHY

1979
AA.VV., *Mario Botta. Architettura e progetti negli anni '70 / Architecture and Projects in the '70*, exhibition catalog by Italo Rota, Electa, Milan [Italian/English ed].

1980
Jorge Glusberg, *Mario Botta*, catalog, CAYC-Centro de Arte y Comunicación, Buenos Aires.

1982
AA.VV., *Mario Botta. La casa rotonda*, edited by Robert Trevisiol, L'Erba Voglio, Milan [Italian/English ed.; French ed.: *Mario Botta. La maison ronde*, l'Equerre, Paris 1982; Spanish ed.: *Mario Botta, la casa redonda*, Editorial Gustavo Gili, Barcelona 1983].

Pierluigi Nicolin, François Chaslin, *Mario Botta, 1978-1982. Laboratoire d' architecture*, catalog, Electa Moniteur, Paris [Italian ed.: *Mario Botta 1978-1982. Il laboratorio d' architettura*, Milan].

1984
Mario Botta, Preliminary Studies, exhibition catalog, GA Global Architecture Gallery, Tokyo [English/Japanese ed.].

Yukio Futagawa (edited by), *Mario Botta*, "GA Global Architecture Architect", 3.

Pierluigi Nicolin (edited by), *Mario Botta Bauten und Projekte 1961-1982*, DVA Deutsche Verlags-Anstalt, Stuttgart [English ed.: *Mario Botta Buildings and Projects 1961-1982*, Electa-Rizzoli, New York; Spanish ed.: *Mario Botta Construcciones y Proyectos*, Editorial Gustavo Gili, Barcelona].

1985
AA.VV., *Mario Botta. Architetture 1960-1985*, edited by Francesco Dal Co, Electa, Milan [French ed.: *Mario Botta. Architectures 1960-1985*, Electa-Moniteur, Paris; English ed.: *Mario Botta. Architectures 1960-1985*, Electa-Rizzoli, New York 1986].

1986
Stuart Wrede, *Mario Botta*, exhibition catalog, The Museum of Modern Art, New York.

1987
AA.VV., *Mario Botta. Une architecture trois habitats*, exhibition catalog, École des Arts Décoratifs, Geneva.

1988
AA.VV., *Mario Botta*, "Techniques & Architecture", 377, April-May [monographic issue].

Benedetto Gravagnuolo (edi-ted by), *Mario Botta, Studi preliminari per la Banca del Gottardo a Lugano*, exhibition catalog, Edizioni A. Salvioni, Bellinzona 1988.

1989
Francesco Dal Co (edited by), *Mario Botta. Una casa*, exhibition catalog, Electa, Milan.

Jean-Paul Felley, Olivier Kaeser, *Mario Botta, construire les objets. Oeuvre design 1982-1989*, exhibition catalog, Fondation Louis Moret, Martigny.

1990
AA. VV., *Mario Botta. Watari-um Project in Tokyo 1985-1990*, edited by Etsuko Watari, Watari-um, Tokyo.

Peter Disch (edited by), *Mario Botta. La ricerca negli anni ottanta*, ADV, Lugano.

1991
AA.VV., *La tenda / La Tente / Das Zelt*, Edizioni Casagrande-Verlag für Architektur, Bellinzona [Italian/German/French ed.].

Emilio Pizzi (edited by), *Mario Botta. Architectures 1980-1990*, exhibition catalog, Editorial Gustavo Gili, Barcelona 1991 [German ed.: *Mario Botta 1980-1990*, Verlag für Architektur-Artemis & Winkler Verlag, Zürich-München 1991; Portuguese ed.: *Mario Botta. Arquitecturas 1980-1990*, Editorial Gustavo Gili-Fundaçao Calouste Gulbenkian, Barcelona-Lisboa, 1992].

Emilio Pizzi (edited by), *Mario Botta. Obras y Proyectos/Works and Projects*, Editorial Gustavo Gili, Barcelona 1991 [Spanish/English updated reprint 1998; German/French ed.; *Mario Botta*, Verlag für Architektur/Les Editions d'Architecture-Artemis & Winkler Verlag, Zürich-München, re-edited 1998; Italian ed. *Mario Botta*, Zanichelli, Bologna; Portuguese ed.: *ibidem*, Martins Fontes Editora, Sao Paulo 1994; Chinese ed.: *ibidem*, Lnkj Edition, China 2005].

1992
Rolando Bellini (edited by), Mario Botta Architetture 1980-1990, exhibition catalog, Artificio

© ARCHIVE MARIO BOTTA

© ARCHIVE MARIO BOTTA

© ARCHIVE MARIO BOTTA

© ARCHIVE MARIO BOTTA

Edizioni, Florence.
Jean Petit (edited by), Mario Botta progetto per una chiesa a Mogno, exhibition catalog, Collection Forces Vives-Fidia Edizioni d'Arte, Lugano [Italian/ French ed.; id. English/German ed.].

1993
Emilio Pizzi (edited by), *Mario Botta, Das Gesamtwerk, Band 1, 1960-1985*, Birkhäuser Verlag für Architektur, Basel-Boston-Berlin [Italian ed.: *Mario Botta, Opere complete, Vo-lume 1, 1960-1985*, Federico Motta Editore, Milan; English ed.: *Mario Botta, The complete works, Volume 1 1960-1985*, London].

1994
AA.VV., *Mario Botta, Enzo Cucchi. La cappella del Monte Tamaro*, exhibition catalog, Museo Cantonale di Lugano, Umberto Allemandi, Turin [Italian/English ed., updated reprint 1996].

Jean Petit, *Traces dárchitecture-Botta*, Fidia Edizioni d'Arte/ Bibliothèque des Arts, Lugano-Paris.

Emilio Pizzi (edited by), *Mario Botta. Das Gesamtwerk, Band 2, 1985-1990*, Birkhäuser Verlag für Architektur, Basel-Boston-Berlin [Italian ed. *Mario Botta Opere complete, Vo-lume 2, 1985-1990*, Federico Motta Editore, Milan; English ed., *Mario Botta The complete works, Volume 2, 1985-1990*, London].

1995
AA.VV., *Il museo di Arte Moderna e Contemporanea di Trento e Rovereto*, Skira, Milan.

AA.VV., *Un lugar cuatro arquitectos: Botta, Galfetti, Snozzi, Vacchini en el Ticino*, exhibition catalog, Museo de Bellas Artes, Caracas.

1996
AA.VV., *Mario Botta. Cinque Architetture*, exhibition catalog edited by Mario Gemin, Skira, Milan.

Cristina Bechtler (edited by), *Mario Botta - Mario Merz: Im Gespräch Mit Marlies Grüterich*, Kunsthaus Bregenz, Cantz Verlag, Ostfildern-Ruit, Stuttgart.

Benedetto Gravagnuolo (edi-ted by), *Mario Botta. Etica del costruire*, Laterza, Rome-Bari [German/English ed.: *Mario Botta Ethik des Bauens-Ethics of building*, Birkhäuser Verlag, Basel-Boston-Berlin 1997; Portuguese ed., *ibidem*, Ediçoes 70, Lisboa 1998; Japanese ed., *ibidem*, Kajima Institute-Laterza, Bari 1999; French ed., *ibidem*, Editions Parenthèses, Marseille 2005].

Philip Jodidio (edited by), *Musée Jean Tinguely*, "Connaissance des Arts", 98 [monographic issue].

Mario Botta gesehen von/vu par/ seen by Pino Musi, Daco-Verlag, Stuttgart [French/English/ German ed.].

Nicolas Westphal, Denyse Bertoni, *Mario Botta. La cathédrale d'Évry*, Skira, Milan 1996 [updated reprint 1999].

1997
AA.VV., *Mario Botta. Emozioni di pietra. Un percorso fra le architetture pubbliche*, exhibition catalog edited by Luca Molinari, Skira, Milan [English ed.: *Mario Botta. Public Buildings 1980-1990*, Thames and Hudson, London 1998; Spanish ed.: *Mario Botta. Edificios públicos 1990-1998*, Editorial Gustavo Gili, Barcelona 1998; French ed.: *Mario Botta Bâtiments publics 1990-1998*, Skira/Seuil, Paris 1998].
AA.VV., *Mario Botta Museum Jean Tinguely*, Museum Jean Tinguely, Benteli Verlag, Bern [English/French/German ed.].

1998
AA.VV., *Banque et Architecture. Banque Bruxelles Lambert - Genève, Mario Botta - Architecte*, Electa-Banque Bruxelles Lambert, Milan-Geneva [French/ English ed.; reprint 2003].

Emilio Pizzi (edited by), *Mario Botta. Das Gesamtwerk, Band 3 1990-1997*, Birkhäuser Verlag für Architektur, Basel-Boston-Berlin [Italian ed.: *Mario Botta Opere complete, Volume 3, 1990-1997*, Federico Motta Editore, Milan; English ed.: *Mario Botta. The complete works, Volume 3, 1990-1997*, London].

1999
AA.VV., *Borromini sul Lago. Mario Botta, la rappresentazione lignea del San Carlo alle Quattro Fontane a Lugano*, exhibition catalog edited by Gabriele Cappellato, Accademia di architettura USI-Skira, Mendrisio-Milan.

© ARCHIVE MARIO BOTTA

© ARCHIVE MARIO BOTTA

© ARCHIVE MARIO BOTTA

© ARCHIVE MARIO BOTTA

AA.VV., *La chiesa di San Giovanni Battista a Mogno*, Associazione Ricostruzione Chiesa di Mogno, Skira Geneva-Milan.

Philip Jodidio, *Mario Botta*, Taschen Verlag, Cologne [English/French/German ed.; updated Spanish/Italian/ Portuguese and English/French/ German ed., Taschen, Cologne 2003].

2000

AA.VV., *Mario Botta Centre Dürrenmatt Neuchâtel*, edited by Peter Edwin Erismann/Archivio svizzero di letteratura, Birkhäuser Verlag, Basel-Boston-Berlin [Italian/English ed. and French/ German ed.].

Mario Botta, "PA Pro Architect" [Korea], 20, October [Korean/ English ed.].

Mario Botta Centro Swisscom a Bellinzona, Skira, Geneva-Milan [Italian/English ed.].

Luisella Gelsomino (edited by), *Mario Botta. Modelli di architettura*, exhibition catalog, Centro studi dell'abitare OIKOS-Alinea Editrice, Florence [Italian/ English ed.].

Irena Sakellaridou, *Mario Botta Poetica dell'architettura*, Rizzoli, Milan [English ed.: *Mario Botta Architectural Poetics*, Rizzoli, New York 2000; reprint Rizzoli/ Skira, Milan 2002; Thames & Hudson, London 2001].

2001

AA.VV., *Mario Botta The Cymbalista Synagogue and Jewish Heritage Center*, Skira, Geneva-Milan.

Mario Botta 13 Vasen - Skizzen Holz Keramik, exhibition catalog, Galerie Stuker Zurich, Ostfildern [German/English ed.].

Giovanni Pozzi, *Mario Botta Santa Maria degli Angeli sul Monte Tamaro*, Edizioni Casagrande, Bellinzona [id. German/French ed.].

2002

Mario Botta, "PLUS Korean Architecture+Interior Design" [Seoul], 6, 36-73.

2003

AA.VV., *Mario Botta, Luce e Gravità. Architetture 1993- 2003*, exhibition catalog edited by Gabriele Cappellato, Editrice Compositori, Bologna [English ed.: *Mario Botta Light and Gravity: Architecture 1993 -2003*, Prestel Publishing, Munich-Berlin-London-New York 2004; updated reprint: *Mario Botta, Luce e Gravità: Architetture 1993-2007*, Editrice Compositori, Bologna 2008].

AA.VV., *La chiesa di Sartirana ... perché nulla vada perduto*, edited by Gabriele Cappellato, Editrice Compositori, Bologna 2003.

Mario Botta, Giulio Andreolli, Il Museo di Arte Moderna e Contemporanea di Trento e Rovereto, Skira, Milan [id. French/English ed.].

Gabriele Cappellato (edited by), *Mario Botta Mart Museo di Arte Moderna e Contemporanea di Trento e Rovereto*, "OP/1 - Opera progetto Rivista Internazionale d Architettura Contemporanea", Editrice Compositori, Bologna [monographic issue; Italian/ English ed.].

Stefano Crespi (edited by), *Mario Botta. Quasi un diario: frammenti intorno all' architettura*, Le Lettere, Florence [reprint 2004].

Aurora Cuito (edited by), *Mario Botta*, TeNeues Loft, Düsseldorf-New York-West Byfleet-Paris [Italian/French/English/Germand ed.; Chinese ed. 2008].

Zhi Wenjun, Zhu Guangyu (edited by), *Mario Botta*, Dalian Science and Technology University Press, Dalian [English/ Chinese ed.].

2004

Yoshio Futagawa (edited by), *Leeum, Samsung Museum of Art Seoul*, Korea, "GA Global Architecture Document", 83, December, 8-59.

Luca Molinari (edited by), *Mario Botta Chiesa a Seriate, Centro Pastorale Giovanni XXIII*, Skira, Milan.

2005

AA.VV., *Mario Botta. Architetture del Sacro. Preghiere di Pietra*, exhibition catalog edi-ted by Gabriele Cappellato, Editrice Compositori, Bologna [English ed.: *Mario Botta Architetture del Sacro. Prayers in Stone*, Editrice Compositori, Bologna].

AA.VV., *Il Teatro alla Scala, Restauro e ristrutturazione*, edited by Luca Molinari, Skira,

Milan-Geneva.
Brigitte Labs-Ehlert (edited by), *Mario Botta. Architektur und Gedächtnis*, Wege zur Architektur 2, FSB Franz Schneider, Brakel [German/Italian ed.].

Leeum Samsung museum of art, "Space" [Seoul], 446, January, 48-155 [English/Korean ed.].

Seong Tae Park (edited by), *Leeum Samsung Museum of Modern Art*, Samsung Museum of Art, Seoul, 16-57 [English/Korean ed.].

Timothy Verdon (edited by), *Di fronte all'altissimo. La cappella di Mario Botta e Giuliano Vangi ad Azzano di Seravezza*, Electa, Milan [Italian/English ed.].

2006
Mario Botta e Dario Fertilio. La lingua degli angeli per princi-pianti, Skira, Milan.

2007
Mario Botta (edited by), *La chiesa del Santo Volto a Torino*, Skira, Geneva-Milan.

Architects & Design: Mario Botta, edited by Jeong, Ji-Seong, CA Press Co. Ltd. Seoul, Korea.

Mario Botta, Paolo Crepet, Giu-seppe Zois, *Dove abitano le emozioni. La felicità e i luoghi in cui viviamo*, Einaudi, Turin.

Mario Botta. World Great Architects, Cepp Edition [Chinese ed.; reprint 2008].

Alessandra Coppa (edited by), *Mario Botta*, Motta Architettura, Milan [updated ed. 2009; paperback ed.: *Mario Botta, L'architettura I prota-gonisti*, Motta Architettura, Milan, La Biblioteca di Repubblica-L'Espresso, Milano, Vol. 9; Chinese ed.: Motta Architettura, Milano 2008; French ed.: Actes Sud, Arles 2009].

Yun Sung-Chul (edited by), *Mario Botta*, "CA. Contemporary Architecture" [Seoul], Vol. 67, January [English/Korean ed.].

2008
Krassimira Yavasheva, Nikolina Stoykova (edited by), *Mario Botta*, "WAM World Architecture Masters" [Sophia], International Academy of Architecture, 6, 5-88.

2009
AA.VV., *Mario Botta Riflessioni*, edited by +xm Plusform, Dialoghi di architettura/05, Iiriti Editore Reggio Calabria [reprint 2010]

2010
Mario Botta, I maestri dell' Architettura, edited by Grazia Massone, Hachette Fascicoli, Milan.
Mario Botta. Architetture 1960-2010, exhibition catalog, Museo di Arte Moderna e Contemporanea di Trento e Rovereto, Silvana Editoriale, Cinisello Balsamo-Milan [Parts published as French/German ed.: *Mario Botta, Architecture et mémoire/ Architektur und Gedächtnis*, Centre Dürrenmatt Neuchâtel, Silvana Editoriale, Cinisello Balsamo, Milan 2011; English ed. *Mario Botta. Architecture and Memory*, Bechtler Museum of Modern Art, Silvana Editoriale, Cinisello Balsamo, Milan 2013].

2012
Mario Botta. Architektur leben, Ein Gespräch mit Marco Alloni, Stämpfli Verlag AG, Bern; Italian ed.: *Mario Botta. Vivere l'architettura, Conversazione con Marco Alloni*, Edizioni Casagrande, Bellinzona [reprint June 2012]

2014
Stefano Crespi (edited by), *Mario Botta, Quasi un diario 2003-2013*, Le Lettere, Florence.

2015
Mario Gemin (edited by) *Mario Botta. Querini Stampalia*, Fondazione Querini Stampalia Venezia, Giavedoni Editore, Pordenone [Italian/English ed.]

AA.VV., *Mario Botta 1960-2015*, Tongji University Press, Shanghai [Chinese ed.].

2016
Alessandra Coppa (edited by), *Mario Botta. Luce e gra-vità*, Lezioni di Architettura e Design, Corriere della Sera, RCS Media Group, Milan.

2017
Mario Botta, Abitare, Conversazioni e scritti di architettura, Christian Marinotti Edizioni s.r.l., Milan.

© ARCHIVE MARIO BOTTA

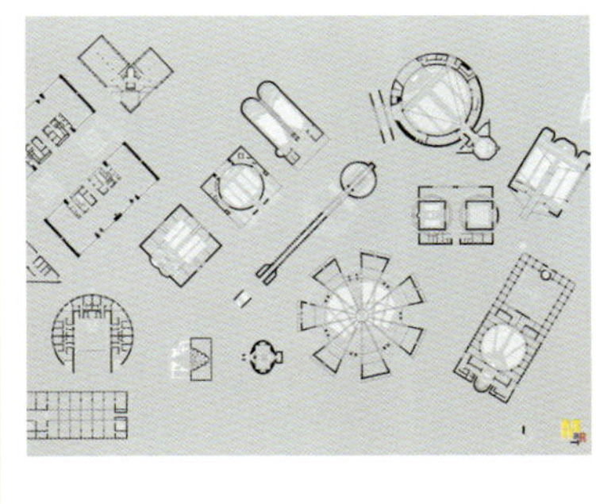

© ARCHIVE MARIO BOTTA

© ARCHIVE MARIO BOTTA

© ARCHIVE MARIO BOTTA

主要建筑项目与设计作品
MAIN ACCOMPLISHED WORKS, DESIGN, WORKS IN PROGRESS

牧师住宅
瑞士，杰内斯特雷里奥
Parish House
Genestrerio, Switzerland
1961-1963

独栋住宅
瑞士，卡代纳佐
Single-Family House
Cadenazzo, Switzerland
1970-1971

独栋住宅
瑞士，圣维塔莱河村
Single-Family House
Riva San Vitale, Switzerland
1971-1973

中学
瑞士，下莫尔比奥
Middle School
Morbio Inferiore, Switzerland
1972-1977

嘉布遣会修道院图书馆
瑞士，卢加诺
Library In The Capuchins Convent
Lugano, Switzerland
1976-1979

独栋住宅
瑞士，利戈尔内托
Single-Family House
Ligornetto, Switzerland
1975-1976

巴勒那公共体育馆
瑞士，巴勒那
Public Gymnasium
Balerna, Switzerland
P 1976, C 1977-1978

巴勒那手工艺中心
瑞士，巴勒那
Craft Centre
Balerna, Switzerland
1977-1979

弗里堡国家银行
瑞士，弗里堡
State Bank
Fribourg, Switzerland
1977-1979

独栋住宅
瑞士，普乐嘉桑那
Single-Family House
Pregassona, Switzerland
1979-1980

独栋住宅
瑞士，马萨尼奥
Single-Family House
Massagno, Switzerland
1979-1981

独栋住宅
瑞士，维嘉内罗
Single-Family House
Viganello, Switzerland
1980-1981

独栋住宅
瑞士，斯塔比奥
Single-Family House
Stabio, Switzerland
1980-1981

独栋住宅
瑞士，波罗尼
Single-Family House
Origlio, Switzerland
1981-1982

兰希拉 1 号楼
瑞士，卢加诺
Building Ransila 1
Lugano, Switzerland
1981-1985

马尔罗文化中心
法国，尚贝里
Espace Malraux
Chambéry, France
1982-1987

"一号"椅和"二号"椅
Chairs "Prima" And "Seconda"
1982

独栋住宅
瑞士，上莫尔比奥
Single-Family House
Morbio Superiore, Switzerland
1982-1983

格塔多银行旧址
瑞士，卢加诺
Formerly Banca Del Gottardo
Lugano, Switzerland
1982-1988

"三号"桌
Table "Terzo"
1983

书籍、影像与声音之家
法国，维勒班
Maison Du Livre, De L' image Et Du Son
Villeurbanne, France
1984-1988

独栋住宅
瑞士，布雷甘佐拉
Single-Family House
Breganzona, Switzerland
1984-1988

"四号"椅
Chair "Quarta"
1984

"壳"家具组合，为 17 届米兰三年展设计
"Guscio" (Shell) Design For The 17Th Triennale Di Milano
1984-1985

"五号"椅
Chair "Quinta"
1985

"六号"扶手椅
Armchair Sesta
1985

"将军"灯具
Lamp "Shogun"
1985

双瓶组合一号、双瓶组合二号
Double Carafe 1 / Double Carafe 2
1985/1989

和多利美术馆
日本，东京
Art Gallery Watari-Um
Tokyo, Japan
1985-1990

西亚尼大街住宅办公综合楼
瑞士，卢加诺
Residential And Office Building

© ALO ZANETTA

© ALO ZANETTA

© ENRICO CANO

Lugano, Switzerland
1985-1990
“菲迪亚”壁灯
Wall Lamp “Fidia”
1986

“Tesi”桌
Table “Tesi”
1986

圣乔瓦尼巴蒂斯教堂
瑞士，蒙哥诺
Church San Giovanni Battista
Mogno, Switzerland
1986-1996

瑞银集团
瑞士，巴塞尔
Ubs Bank
Basel, Switzerland
1986-1995

五大洲中心
瑞士，卢加诺
Centre Cinque Continenti
Lugano, Switzerland
1986-1992

“卡伊马托”建筑
瑞士，卢加诺
Building “Caimato”
Lugano, Switzerland
1986-1993

和平广场
意大利，帕尔玛，皮洛塔花园
Piazzale Della Pace
Giardino Della Pilotta, Parma, Italy
1986/96-2001

独栋住宅
瑞士，瓦卡洛
Single-Family House
Vacallo, Switzerland
1986-1988

奥德利柯小教堂
意大利，波代诺内
Church Beato Odorico
Pordenone, Italy
1987-1992

独栋住宅
瑞士，曼诺
Single-Family House
Manno, Switzerland
1987-1990

圈椅
Chair “Latonda”
1987

独栋住宅
瑞士，洛索内
Single-Family House
Losone, Switzerland
1987-1989

圣彼得使徒教堂
意大利，萨尔迪拉纳
Church San Pietro Apostolo
Sartirana, Italy
1987-1995

布鲁塞尔 - 朗贝银行
瑞士，日内瓦
Banque Bruxelles Lambert
Geneva, Switzerland
1987-1996

“倾斜”单人沙发
Armchair “Obliqua”
1987

“黑色”灯具
Lamp “Melanos”
1986

尼若拉综合大厦
瑞士，贝林佐纳
Residential And Office Building
Bellinzona, Switzerland
1988-1991

住宅区
瑞士，诺瓦扎诺
Residential Settlement
Novazzano, Switzerland
1988-1992

艾维复活大教堂
法国，艾维
Cathedral Of The Resurrection
Évry, France
1988-1995

艾斯兰加购物中心
意大利，佛罗伦萨
Shopping Centre Esselunga
Florence, Italy
1988-1992

瑞士电信大楼
瑞士，贝林佐纳
Swisscom Building
Bellinzona, Switzerland
1988-1998

Mart 现当代艺术博物馆
意大利，罗韦雷托
Mart-Museum Of Modern And Contemporary Art
Rovereto, Italy
1988-2002

“微风”灯具
Lamp “Zefiro”
1988

独栋住宅
瑞士，达罗
Single-Family House
Daro, Switzerland
1989-1992

MoMA 现代艺术博物馆
美国，旧金山
MoMA-Museum Of Modern Art
San Francisco, Usa
1989-1995

独栋住宅
瑞士，科洛尼
Single-Family House
Cologny, Switzerland
1989-1993

瑞士联邦 700 周年庆祝帐幕
瑞士，贝林佐纳
Tent For The 700Th Anniversary Of The Swiss Confederation
Bellinzona, Switzerland
1989-1991

“博塔 91 号”椅子
Chair “Botta ‘91”
1989-1991

独栋住宅及陈列室
瑞士，祖芬根
House And Showroom
Zofingen, Switzerland
1989-1993

“机器人”抽屉柜
Chest Of Drawers “Robot”
1989

© PINO MUSI

© ENRICO CANO

© UELI FRAUCHIGER

独栋住宅
瑞士，蒙塔格诺拉
Single-Family House
Montagnola, Switzerland
1989-1994

教保塔楼
韩国，首尔
Kyobo Tower
Seoul, South Korea
1989-2003

“眼睛”手表
Watch “Eye”
1989

“大教堂”“483 黑色”“483 铜绿”“马伦扎”毯
Carpets “La Cattedrale”, “483Nero”, “483 Verde Rame”, “Marenza”
1990

国家青少年体育中心（阶段二）
瑞士，特内罗
National Youth Sports Centre (Phase 2)
Tenero, Switzerland
1990/98-2001

圣洁天使玛利亚教堂
瑞士，塔玛洛山
Chapel Santa Maria Degli Angeli
Mount Tamaro, Switzerland
1990-1996

普罗温西亚日报总部大厦
意大利，科莫
Headquarters Of The Daily “La Provincia”
Como, Italy
1990-1997

赌场
意大利，意大利金皮庸
Casino
Campione D' italia, Italy
1990-2006

“La Forteza”办公及住宅综合楼
荷兰，马斯垂克
Residential And Office Building “La Forteza”
Maastricht, The Netherlands
1990-2000

枫多托斯工厂
意大利，韦尔巴尼亚
Incineration Plant Thermoselect
Fondotoce-Verbania, Italy
1991-1991

孟德里索办公与住宅综合楼
瑞士，门德里西奥
Quarter Piazzale Alla Valle
Mendrisio, Switzerland
1991-1998

雷达埃利别墅
意大利，贝尔纳雷焦
Villa Redaelli
Bernareggio (Mi), Italy
1991-2001

“尼拉 · 洛萨”屏风
Screen “Nilla Rosa”
1992

维尔纳王宾纬图书馆
瑞士，艾因西德伦
Library Werner Oechslin
Einsiedeln, Switzerland
1992-2004

花瓶
Flower Vase
1992

蒙特卡拉索住宅区
瑞士，蒙特卡拉索
Residential Settlement
Monte Carasso, Switzerland
1992-1996

诺瓦扎诺疗养院
瑞士，诺瓦扎诺
Rest Home
Novazzano, Switzerland
1992-1997

迪伦马特中心
瑞士，纳沙泰尔
Dürrenmatt Centre
Neuchâtel, Switzerland
1992-2000

丁格利博物馆
瑞士，巴塞尔
Museum Tinguely
Basel, Switzerland
1993 – 1996

噪音防护站
瑞士，A2 高速公路
Noise Protection
Highway A2, Switzerland
1993-2004

科学教育中学
意大利，皮耶韦
High School
Città Della Pieve, Italy
1993-2001

奎恩图服务站
瑞士，皮奥塔
Service Area
Quinto, Switzerland
1993-1998

教皇若望二十三世教堂
意大利，塞里亚泰
Church Papa Giovanni XXIII,
Seriate (Bg), Italy
1994-2004

“夏洛特”椅
Chair Charlotte
1994

前阿皮亚尼城市发展区域
意大利，特雷维索
Urban Redevelopment Of The Area Ex-Appiani,
Treviso, Italy
1994-2013

威尼斯斯坦普利亚基金会
意大利，威尼斯
Renovation Of The Fondazione Querini Stampalia
Venice, Italy
1993-2013

提拉波斯奇图书馆
意大利，贝加莫
Library Tiraboschi
Bergamo, Italy
1995-2004

诺亚方舟
以色列，耶路撒冷
Noah' s Ark
Jerusalem, Israel
1995-2001

“布鲁门泽”台钟
Watch “Blumenzeit”
1995

© ARJEN SCHMITZ

© ENRICO CANO

© PINO MUSI

文森佐帆船座博物馆
瑞士，利戈尔内托
Refurbishment Of The Vela Museum
Ligornetto, Switzerland
1995-2001

市政图书馆
德国，多特蒙德
Municipal Library
Dortmund, Germany
1995-1999

塔罗庭院入口
意大利，维奇欧
Entrance Portal To The Tarot Garden
Garavicchio, Italy
1995-2001

三星美术馆
韩国，首尔
Leeum – Samsung Museum Of Art
Seoul, South Korea
1995-2004

辛巴立斯达犹太教堂和犹太遗产中心
以色列，特拉维夫
Cymbalista Synagogue And Jewish Heritage Centre,
Tel Aviv, Israel
1996-1998

“美洲首脑峰会”纪念碑
玻利维亚，圣克鲁斯
Monument For The “Cumbre De Las Americas”
Santa Cruz De La Sierra, Bolivia
1996

塔塔咨询服务公司办公室
印度，新德里
Tcs Offices
New Delhi, India
1996-2002

“马里奥 · 博塔”手表
Watches Mario Botta
1998/2008

奥赛丽娜—卡尔达达
瑞士，洛迦诺
Orselina-Cardada Funicular Stations And Cableway
Locarno, Switzerland
1997-2000

孟提亚 · 丹修道院挂毯
Tapestry For The Monastery
Moutier D' Ahun
1997

希腊国家银行
希腊，雅典
National Bank Of Greece
Athens, Greece
1998-2001

马丁 · 柏德梅基金会图书馆与博物馆
瑞士，科洛尼
Martin Bodmer Foundation, Library And Museum
Cologny, Switzerland
1998-2003

13 只花瓶（梨木和赤陶）
13 Vases (Pear Wood And Terracotta)
1998

莫隆塔
瑞士，马勒赖
Moron Tower
Malleray, Switzerland
1998-2004

国铁手表系列
Mondaine Watches
1995/1998

圣安东尼教堂的正面
瑞士，杰内斯特雷里奥
Façade Of The Church Sant' Antonio Abate,
Genestrerio, Switzerland
1999-2003

新港大楼
荷兰，代芬特尔
De Nieuwe Poort
Deventer, The Netherlands
1998-2009

圣卡尔利诺
瑞士，卢加诺湖
San Carlino,
Lake Lugano, Switzerland
1999-2003

“我的 & 你的”壶具
Jugs “Mia & Tua”
1997

佩特拉酒庄
意大利，苏韦雷托
Petra Winery
Suvereto, Italy
1999-2003

德国浩亭公司总部办公室
德国，明登
Harting Sales Headquarters
Minden, Germany
1999-2001

“塔塔咨询服务”办公楼
印度，海得拉巴
Tcs Offices
Hyderabad, India
1999-2003

洛伊克城堡
瑞士，洛伊克
Renovation Of The Leuk Castle
Leuk, Switzerland
1999-2011

特兰托大学法律系扩建
意大利，特伦托
Law Faculty
Trento, Italy
1999-2006

穆纳里玻璃杯
Munari Glasses
2000

度假别墅
瑞士，卡达达山
Holiday Houses
Cardada, Switzerland
2000-2002

中环巴士总站
瑞士，卢加诺
Shelter For The Central Bus Station
Lugano, Switzerland
2000-2002

国家民族保险大厦
希腊，雅典
Headquarters Of The National Insurance Company Ethniki
Athens, Greece
2000-2006

© ENRICO CANO

© PINO MUSI

贝希特勒现代艺术博物馆
美国，夏洛特
Bechtler Museum
Charlotte, North Carolina, Usa
2000/2005-2009

视野住宅建筑
荷兰，哈勒默梅尔
Residential Building La Vista
Haarlemmermer, The
Netherlands
2001-2008

圣容教堂
意大利，都灵
Church Santo Volto,
Turin, Italy
2001-2006

丧葬礼教堂
意大利，赛拉维扎的阿扎诺
Funerary Chapel,
Azzano Di Seravezza, Italy
1999-2001

斯卡拉剧院修复
意大利，米兰
Restoration Of The Theater Alla
Scala
Milan, Italy
2001-2004

“特隆科”花瓶
Vase “Tronco”
2001

清华大学艺术博物馆
中国，北京
Tsinghua University Art
Museum
Beijing, P.R. China
2002-2016

新圣母玛利亚教堂
意大利，泰拉诺瓦布拉乔利尼
Church Santa Maria Nuova
Terranuova Bracciolini, Italy
2005-2010

Ance 总部
意大利，莱科
Headquarters Of The National
Builders' Association
Lecco, Italy
2003-2008

喷泉和墓地
意大利，蒙塞利切
Fountain And Redesign Of The
Church Parvis
Monselice, Italy
2003-2009

“图亨山地绿洲”健康中心
瑞士，阿罗萨
Spa “Tschuggen Berg Oase”
Arosa, Switzerland
2003-2006

广场与健康中心
瑞士，瑞吉
Square And Spa
Rigi Kaltbad, Switzerland
2004-2012

移动剧院
Travelling Theatre
2004-2007

“马里奥·博塔为凯兰帝设计”钢笔
Pen “Mario Botta For Caran D' ache”
2004

“美丽”桌
Table “Bello”
2004

前坎帕里区域总部与住宅
意大利，塞斯托·圣乔凡尼
Campari Headquarters And
Residences , Area Ex - Campari
Sesto San Giovanni, Italy
2004-2009/2010

蒙库切托酒庄
瑞士，卢加诺
Winery Moncucchetto
Lugano, Switzerland
2005-2010

剧院建筑
瑞士，门德里西奥
Theater Of Architecture
Mendrisio, Switzerland
2005, Under Construction

弗奥利波塔大楼
瑞士，门德里西奥
Building Fuoriporta
Mendrisio, Switzerland
2005-2011

13 只花瓶（白镴）
13 Vases（Pewter）
2005

丧葬礼拜堂
意大利，维琴察
Funerary Chapel Neri Pozza
Longara, Italy
2005-2011

桌 01-04-43
制造商：丽瓦 1920 家具
Table 01-04-43
Manufacturer: Riva 1920
2005/2008

Agorà 俱乐部会所
韩国，济州岛
Club House Agorà
Jeju Island, South Korea
2006-2008

富爵酒庄
法国，圣埃米利翁
Château Faugères
St.emilion, France
2005-2009

可调节的桌子
制造商：丽瓦 1920 家具
Table Variabile
Manufacturer: Riva 1920
2006

国家青少年体育中心（阶段三）
瑞士，特内罗
National Youth Sports Centre
(Phase 3)
Tenero, Switzerland
2006-2013

“圣洛克”教堂
意大利，圣吉奥瓦尼泰阿蒂诺
Church “San Rocco”
San Giovanni Teatino, Italy
2006-In Progress

化石博物馆
瑞士，圣乔治山梅里德
Fossil Museum
Monte San Giorgio, Meride,
Switzerland
2006-2012

“壳”装置，意大利米兰三年展
Guscio, Triennale Di Milano, Italy
2007

© ENRICO CANO

© ENRICO CANO

生物与生物医药系
意大利，帕多瓦大学
Faculty Of Biology And Biomedicine
University Of Padua, Italy
2007-2014

衡山路 12 号酒店
中国，上海
Hotel Twelve
Hengshan, Shanghai, China
2006-2012

清华大学图书馆
中国，北京
Tsinghua University Library
Beijing, China
2008-2011

“桥”桌
Table “Ponte”
2008

马克杯组合
Mugs
2009

安全部队中心
瑞士，门德里西奥
Security Forces Centre
Mendrisio, Switzerland
2008-In Progress

“沙漏”高脚凳
Stool “Clessidra”
2010

新温泉浴场
瑞士，巴登温泉区
Public Thermal Bath And Residences
Baden, Switzerland
2009-In Progress

“安那托利亚”毯
Carpet “Anatolia”
2009

办公楼
比利时，亨克
Office Building
Genk, Belgium
2009-2013

“现成品”
“Bricolages”
2010

“Caterina”居民公寓
瑞士，罗桑那
Residential Settlement “Caterina”
Losone, Switzerland
2009-2015

千禧喷泉居民公寓
瑞士，圣布莱斯
Millennium Fountain
Saint-Blaise, Switzerland
2010-2011

弗朗西斯卡布里尼纪念馆
意大利，米兰中央火车站
Francesca Cabrini Memorial
Milan Central Station, Italy
2010

13 只花瓶（大理石）
13 Vases(Marble)
2012

“石榴石”教堂
奥地利，齐勒，佩恩约克
Garnet” Chapel In Penkenjoch, Zillertal, Austria
2011-2013

圣母玫瑰巴西利卡大教堂
韩国，南阳
Basilica Our Lady Of The Rosary
Namyang, South Korea
2011-In Progress

鲁迅美术学院
中国，沈阳
Shenyang, China
Campus Of The Luxun Academy Of Fine Arts
2011-In Progress

雷内 · 莱俪庄园餐厅
法国，莫代尔河畔温让
Restaurant Villa René Lalique
Wingen-sur-Moder, France
2011-2015

陶器博物馆
中国，南昌
Ceramic Museum
Nanchang, China
2012-In Progress

修复后的木椅
意大利，米兰维波尔多内修道院
Restoration Of A Wooden Chair
Abbey of Viboldone (MI), Italy
2012-2015

“莫雷拉托”椅
Chair “Morelato”
2013

石花餐厅
瑞士，杰内罗索山
Restaurant Fiore Di Pietra
Monte Generoso, Switzerland
2013-2017

溜冰场
瑞士，昂布里
New Ice Hockey Arena
Ambrì, Switzerland
2014-In Progress

“吉欧”花瓶
Vase “Geo”
2014

凯兰帝铅笔
Fixpencil Caran D' ache
2014

“胜利”喷泉，意大利之胜利
意大利，加尔多内 · 里维埃拉
Fontana “Vittoriale”, Vittoriale Degli Italiani,
Gardone Rivera, Italy
2016

© ENRICO CANO

© MARC SOURBRON

© PIERRE MEYSTRE

后记

王晨雅

经过一年的筹备，“理想之境”展览得以成功呈现，这是首个在中国举办的马里奥·博塔建筑艺术展。作为建筑领域的代表性人物，马里奥·博塔因建筑作品的独特厚重感和人文特性为人称道，其建筑生涯始于现代主义建筑发生转向的20世纪60年代，他十分重视历史元素和当地文脉，强调建筑与场地的关系，并以简洁的元素塑造明确的空间。

此次展览呈现了博塔20世纪60年代至今近60年间的重要建筑及设计作品。展出的建筑项目超过80个，分为9种类型，以手绘草图、黑白照片、木质模型、视频等方式展示，博塔的设计主张贯穿始终，地域特点则讲述着每个作品独一无二的存在意义。此外，展览还展示了博塔的设计作品共45件，包括家具、工业产品、实用艺术品、设计手稿等，其设计作品仿佛是建筑的再生，厚重、简洁的形态中蕴含了事物原本的秩序与功能，故被博塔戏称为“微缩版建筑”。无论建筑还是设计，均为表达思想的载体，共同展现了这位建筑大师的创作魅力和人文情怀。

展览策划之初，清华大学艺术博物馆的策划团队曾赴位于瑞士门德里西奥的马里奥·博塔建筑事务所，与其进行当面沟通，这位74岁的建筑师谈及展览时依旧精神矍铄、思路清晰，着实令人佩服。2017年初，经过马里奥·博塔先生挑选的作品基本确定，在与艾莉希亚娜等多位建筑师的合作下，共同完成了逾10万字的文字编写及翻译，以及近千张图片的挑选和编排，并最终促成了这本书籍的出版。

说到展览设计，可谓一汤奇妙的缘分，此次展览的场馆便为马里奥·博塔的建筑作品，他对展览呈现也颇有构想。方案初期，弗朗切斯科建筑师曾到展厅感受空间，并与我们交流想法，最终决定从博塔的建筑中汲取养分，延续简洁明快的设计风格，以统一的语言化“复”为“简”，去除矫饰化元素，直接传递建筑和设计作品的力量。

进入7月以来，展览的实施工作在清华大学艺术博物馆同事们的努力下逐一落定：作品包装与物流、展览视觉形象设计与制作、展厅搭建与布置、各类设备安装与调试……每项工作背后都意味着一个复杂的过程，每个环节都是展览成功的基石。实施过程中的展览呈现出不那么“靓丽”的一面，但想来这与建筑很像，正是“砖瓦”般日积月累的细致工作和专心奉献，才构筑起长久留存的文化遗产。

AFTERWORD

Wang Chenya

After a year of preparations, the exhibition "the Realm of Idealism" was staged with success as the first exhibition of Mario Botta's art of architecture in China. As a representative of the field of architecture, Mario Botta has been widely recognized for the unique profundity and humanistic features in his architectural works. He started his career as an architect in the 1960s, when modernist architecture started to turn. He valued historical elements and local culture inheritance and stressed the relationship between the architecture and the site, trying to create definite space by concise elements.

This exhibition showed the major architectures and design works of Botta since the 1960s, involving over 80 architectural projects lying in 9 categories, displayed in the forms of free-hand sketches, black-and-white photos, wooden models and videos. Botta's design philosophy runs throughout all his work, and the geographical characteristics embodied elaborate the unique meaning of each work. In addition, the exhibition showed 45 design works of Botta, including furniture, industrial products, practical works of art and design manuscripts. His design works are reproduction of his architectures, containing the original orders and functions of matters in heavy yet simple forms, thus nicknamed as "miniature architecture" by Botta. Both architecture and design are vehicles for communicating thoughts, showing the charm and humanistic feelings of the architect's work.

At the beginning of the exhibition's planning, the curation team of Tsinghua University Art Museum visited the architectural firm of Mario Botta located in Mendrisio for face-to-face communication with him. Already 74 years old, the architect was still admirably spirited and clear-minded when talking of his exhibition. In early 2017, Botta's selection of his works for exhibition have been basically confirmed, and in cooperation with architects such as Elisiana etc., we managed to finish the compilation and translation of over 100,000 words and the selection and arrangement of nearly 1,000 pictures, thus making it possible to have the book published.

The exhibition design seemed to be out of some destined connection. The venue of exhibition itself is an architectural work of Mario Botta, so he had some idea about presentation of the show. At the beginning of the scheme making, the architect Francesco visited the exhibition hall to sense the space and exchange his ideas with us, before we finally decided to absorb nutrients from Botta's architecture and follow his design style of simplicity and concision, turning complexity into simplicity by uniform language, removing over-decorative elements and directly delivering the power of architectures and design works.

Since July, the implementation of the exhibition has been fixed with the joint efforts of all staffs in Tsinghua University Art Museum: the packings and logistic works, the design and production of the exhibitionl image, the building and decoration of the exhibition hall, the installation and debugging of types of equipment etc. Each process is complicated and lays a corner stone for the exhibitionto a success. Though the presentation of the exhibition during its implementation seems not so smart to me,it is similar to the practice of architecture: it's just the accumulative work and contributionfunctioned like the "bricks and tiles" that construct long-preserved cultural heritages.